Also Available

CLASSICAL SOCIOLOGICAL THEORY

Steven Loyal & Siniša Malešević

SAGE was founded in 1965 by Sara Miller McCune to support the dissemination of usable knowledge by publishing innovative and high-quality research and teaching content. Today, we publish over 900 journals, including those of more than 400 learned societies, more than 800 new books per year, and a growing range of library products including archives, data, case studies, reports, and video. SAGE remains majority-owned by our founder, and after Sara's lifetime will become owned by a charitable trust that secures our continued independence.

Los Angeles | London | New Delhi | Singapore | Washington DC | Melbourne

CONTEMPORARY SOCIOLOGICAL THEORY

Steven Loyal
I would like to dedicate this book to my family for their support and help and for missing spending invaluable time with them. My mother, Lakbhir Kaur, my partner, Andrea and my sons, Edgar and Theo.

Sinisa Malesevic
I would like to dedicate this book to my parents, Ljubica and Krstan Malešević, who always supported all my life choices.

CONTEMPORARY
SOCIOLOGICAL THEORY

Steven Loyal & Siniša Malešević

$SAGE

Los Angeles | London | New Delhi
Singapore | Washington DC | Melbourne

SAGE

Los Angeles | London | New Delhi
Singapore | Washington DC | Melbourne

SAGE Publications Ltd
1 Oliver's Yard
55 City Road
London EC1Y 1SP

SAGE Publications Inc.
2455 Teller Road
Thousand Oaks, California 91320

SAGE Publications India Pvt Ltd
B 1/I 1 Mohan Cooperative Industrial Area
Mathura Road
New Delhi 110 044

SAGE Publications Asia-Pacific Pte Ltd
3 Church Street
#10-04 Samsung Hub
Singapore 049483

Editor: Natalie Aguilera
Assistant editor: Eve Williams
Production editor: Katherine Haw
Copyeditor: Neville Hankins
Proofreader: Camille Bramall
Indexer: Charmian Parkin
Marketing manager: George Kimble
Cover design: Francis Kenney
Typeset by: Cenveo Publisher Services
Printed in the UK

© Steven Loyal and Siniša Malešević 2021

First published 2021

Apart from any fair dealing for the purposes of research or private study, or criticism or review, as permitted under the Copyright, Designs and Patents Act, 1988, this publication may be reproduced, stored or transmitted in any form, or by any means, only with the prior permission in writing of the publishers, or in the case of reprographic reproduction, in accordance with the terms of licences issued by the Copyright Licensing Agency. Enquiries concerning reproduction outside those terms should be sent to the publishers.

Library of Congress Control Number: 2019956907

British Library Cataloguing in Publication data

A catalogue record for this book is available from the British Library

ISBN 978-1-5297-2574-2
ISBN 978-1-5297-2573-5 (pbk)

At SAGE we take sustainability seriously. Most of our products are printed in the UK using FSC papers and boards. When we print overseas we ensure sustainable papers are used as measured by the PREPS grading system. We undertake an annual audit to monitor our sustainability.

CONTENTS

About the Authors   ix
Acknowledgements   x

Introduction: Sociological Theory in Context   1

1 Parsons and Merton   12

2 Goffman   33

3 Schutz and Garfinkel   54

4 Gramsci   76

5 Lukács   98

6 Althusser   120

7 Marcuse   143

8 Adorno   165

9 Homans, Coleman and Boudon   186

10 Lévi-Strauss, Barthes and Butler   206

11 Foucault   227

12 Elias   248

13 Bourdieu   268

14 Giddens   293

15 Habermas   314

16 Luhmann   336

17 Gellner and Mann	356
18 Collins	376
19 De Beauvoir, Oakley and Smith	397
20 Latour, Hochschild and Hill Collins	417

Index 437

ABOUT THE AUTHORS

Steven Loyal is Associate Professor at the School of Sociology at University College Dublin, Ireland. His areas of interest include sociological theory, migration, the sociology of knowledge, social stratification and historical sociology.

Siniša Malešević is a Full Professor of Sociology at the University College, Dublin. His recent books include *Grounded Nationalisms* (CUP, 2019), The *Rise of Organised Brutality*, (CUP 2017) and *Nation-States and Nationalisms* (Polity 2013). His work has been translated into 12 languages.

ACKNOWLEDGEMENTS

This book together with the accompanying volume *Classical Sociological Theory* were initially commissioned as a single book. However, as the project developed over the years it became clear that the final product was too big for a single volume. Thus, the original manuscript was shortened and split into two books – *Classical Sociological Theory* and *Contemporary Sociological Theory*.

We would like to thank Chris Rojek for commissioning this project and the SAGE editorial team for their continuous support during the writing process. We are especially grateful to Roddy Condon for his work on the boxed pedagogical material and references. We would also like to thank Tim Mooney, Paul Keating and Barry Barnes for help and comments. Most of all we are thankful to our families for their patience and support during the several years that we were working on this project.

Introduction: Sociological Theory in Context

This book, like its companion volume, *Classical Sociological Theory*, follows in the footsteps of Lewis Coser's 1971 classic textbook *Masters of Sociological Thought: Ideas in Historical and Social Context*. Coser's book was rather unusual at the time of its publication: instead of just summarising the key concepts and theories of leading social theorists it attempted to situate each thinker within the broader social, political, cultural and historical context. Whereas most textbooks offered a few general remarks on the author's biography and some would devote a couple of paragraphs to the historical period, Coser's book very successfully integrated a discussion on the key theoretical contributions of each theorist with an extensive treatment of the wider social contexts, biographical and intellectual influences, and the analysis of historical changes that took place during the author's lifetime.

A central approach underpinning Coser's book derives from the sociology of knowledge, which foregrounds the idea that the production of knowledge is context-dependent. The term sociology of knowledge originates with Max Scheler but has its roots in two sociological figures: Marx and his claim that social being determines consciousness; and Durkheim with his analysis of the social nature of the categories and classification systems. There have, however, been attempts to combine both standpoints, specifically in the work of Bourdieu. In his analysis of the work of Heidegger, Bourdieu (1991 [1988]) identifies the existence of socio-political and sociological moments as reflecting two analytically distinct fields. Although both of these fields possess a certain relative autonomy and follow a different 'logic', it is possible for one field to become translated into the other. This forms a central underpinning of our approach.

There is no doubt that sociology, as other social science disciplines, is the brainchild of the Enlightenment. The very idea that one could try to understand and explain the social world without invoking the established religious, mythical or imperial doctrines and the authorities of the Church, monarchy and aristocracy would be anathema to most pre-modern individuals. The rise of Enlightenment ideas and movements in late seventeenth- and early eighteenth-century Europe and North America, was a decisive historical moment that paved the way for the emergence of sociological thought, and also for the establishment of sociology as an academic discipline, at the end of the nineteenth and in the early twentieth century. Nevertheless, sociological theory did not emerge suddenly and out of nowhere in the wake of the Enlightenment. In fact, one can trace the birth and slow rise of sociological thought all the way to the ancient world, including ancient Greece and China with Plato, Aristotle, Confucius and Mozi among many other early thinkers. Although, as we show in the companion volume to this book, *Classical Sociological Theory*, these early social philosophers could not conceive the social world in a secular or methodologically rigorous way, they provided the foundations for the development of social thinking. This is even more the case with Ibn Khaldun, who combined Islamic religious teachings with a powerful social analysis of the world he inhabited. These pre-modern thinkers reflected on the foundations of the social world and have attempted to explain the changing social and historical dynamics of city-states, kingdoms and empires of their time. Although these early social thinkers offered perceptive insights and analyses of their societies, their thinking was still shackled by the traditional understanding of social order, which was largely conceptualised as given and where there was little distinction between society and the state. Some pre-Enlightenment philosophers such as Niccolò Machiavelli (1469–1527), Francis Bacon (1561–1626), Thomas Hobbes (1588–1679) and John Locke (1632–1704) had already made significant breakthroughs in reconceptualising the relationships between the state and society, they nevertheless remained preoccupied with political and normative questions. For example, Machiavelli was arguably the first social and political thinker who clearly separated politics from theology. His key works such as *The Prince* (1532) and the *Discourses on Livy* (1531) differ from the conventional, idealised and religiously infused depictions of social reality that dominated sixteenth-century Europe. Instead Machiavelli provides a nuanced and realist assessment of political actors and events of his time thus providing a stepping stone for empirically grounded analysis of the social world. This gradual shift towards a more secular and empirical understanding of society and politics is even more visible in Hobbes and Locke, both of whom focused on explaining the origins of the state and social order. Although these social philosophers were primarily concerned with the questions of political legitimacy, they also advanced novel theories of social order. Hence in his most influential book *Leviathan* (1651), Hobbes articulates a social contract theory which conceives of human beings as reasonable, but self-interested, creatures who struggle over resources, status and power. He argues that in a State of Nature humans would necessarily be violent to each other, and to prevent this situation of chronic danger and instability, the state emerged as a form of social contract between self-interested individuals. In other words, being rational, yet self-interested, creatures, humans were willing to submit to the authority of a Sovereign in order to avoid the constant threat of violence, and to live in a peaceful society. Locke also subscribed to a version of social contract theory, but his understanding of the State of Nature is very different to that of Hobbes. Unlike Hobbes, who emphasises the incessant war of all against all, Locke sees the State of Nature as one where liberty prevails, and where everybody is free to pursue their interests under peaceful conditions. In contrast to Hobbes, who accentuates individual competition and conflict, Locke argues that the State of Nature is one populated not by individuals but by families (i.e. conjugal societies) involved in voluntary agreements, where they raise children together. Again, unlike Hobbes, who emphasised the political character of early humans, Locke insists on the centrality of their moral relationships. Hence the social contract does not develop in opposition to the State of Nature but as an extension of already existing communal relationships where people unite into 'commonwealths' in order to preserve their resources, lives, liberties and general well-being.

The pre-Enlightenment thinkers had a substantial impact on the development of social and political thought. However, they were still much more concerned with the rise and development of political institutions and the ethics of governance, and less with the dynamics of social change. It is really only with the onset of the Enlightenment that one encounters the birth of modern thinking about society. The Enlightenment movement was composed of a very diverse range of thinkers (often referred to as *philosophes*) with distinct networks of intellectuals based throughout Europe and the key centres in Paris, London, Edinburgh, Glasgow and Königsberg. However, most of these scholars shared a commitment to several key principles: (1) the view that reason and rationality are the only legitimate mode for acquiring and organising knowledge; (2) the idea that empirical analysis is superior to other forms of knowledge acquisition (i.e. the most reliable method for generating knowledge is the accumulation and analysis of empirical facts); (3) rather than following the authority of established political and religious hierarchies, knowledge entails the use of the scientific method; (4) the belief that the rigorous application of scientific principles would improve the human condition and bring about social progress; (5) the view that the traditional social order, rooted in inherited social, political and economic hierarchies, should give way to meritocratic modes of social organisation; (6) belief in the unlimited potential of human beings; (7) propagation of the universalist idea that all human beings are of equal moral worth and that as such all deserve the same rights; (8) the notion that European culture, including its dominant Christian religious tradition, is not superior to those of other civilisations; and (9) belief in the necessity of the separation between the Church and the state. The intellectuals of the Enlightenment offered a radical critique of the traditional world and also articulated new analytical tools for understanding, explaining and enacting social change. The leading lights of the French Enlightenment, namely Voltaire, Montesquieu, Diderot, Rousseau and Condorcet, belonged to different generations, yet were focused on similar issues. They opposed the power of the Church and monarchy even though many of them came from an aristocratic background. They also glorified science and technology, and were firm believers in the possibility of human perfection through education and political, economic and social reforms. In this context Montesquieu's *The Spirit of Laws* (1748) represents one of the first systematic attempts to develop a comparative analysis of different social orders and to explore how societies change through time. It is through his proto-sociology of political orders that Montesquieu articulated his theory of the separation of powers (i.e. legislative, judiciary and executive) which now underpins most state constitutions in the world. He was also one of the first scholars to recognise the significance of causality in explaining social and political processes, arguing that:

> There are general causes, moral and physical, which act in every monarchy, elevating it, maintaining it, or hurling it to the ground. All accidents are controlled by these causes. And if the chance of one battle—that is, a particular cause—has brought a state to ruin, some general cause made it necessary for that state to perish from a single battle. (Montesquieu, 2011)

Rousseau was another central figure of the Enlightenment who shaped the direction of social and political thought for many years. His two key books, *A Discourse on Inequality* (1754) and *The Social Contract* (1762), develop a distinct theory of human nature which directly contradicts the views articulated by Hobbes. Hence, unlike Hobbes who sees the State of Nature as one of ceaseless violence of all against all, Rousseau argues that in fact civilisation corrupts an harmonious natural order so that in a State of Nature, human beings had 'uncorrupted morals'. His key point is that the emergence of private property, states and social hierarchies, destroyed the original innocence of human relations:

> The first man who, having fenced in a piece of land, said 'This is mine', and found people naïve enough to believe him, that man was the true founder of civil society. From how many crimes, wars, and murders, from how many horrors and misfortunes might not any one have saved mankind, by pulling up the stakes, or filling up the ditch, and crying to his fellows: Beware of listening to this impostor; you are undone if you once forget that the fruits of the earth belong to us all, and the earth itself to nobody. (Rousseau, 1754)

The Enlightenment movement was dominated by French intellectuals who initiated the writing of the huge and highly influential *Encyclopédie* edited by Diderot and d'Alembert and aimed at providing a state of the art of all available human knowledge. This huge undertaking took over 20 years to complete (1751–72), and the final version consisted of 29 volumes of text and plates, selling over 25,000 copies throughout the world (Hamilton, 1997: 29). However, the Enlightenment emerged and spread as an international movement with supporters and contributors throughout Europe, the Americas and, sporadically, other parts of the world. In addition to the French intellectual circle, two other centres of enlightenment stood out – the Scottish and the Prussian networks. The leading representatives of the Scottish Enlightenment, David Hume, Adam

Introduction: Sociological Theory in Context

Ferguson and Adam Smith, among many others, were particularly focused on understanding the social and economic dynamics of historical change. While Hume articulated the philosophical foundations of this movement by challenging the established concepts of rationality, and by emphasising the role of 'moral sentiments' in social life, Smith and Ferguson developed proto-sociological models for understanding the nature of human society. In many respects Smith's key book *An Inquiry into the Nature and Causes of the Wealth of Nations* (1776) was a foundational text for the development of political economy and economic sociology, but his interests went much wider with the focus on moral philosophy, and the relationships between political, economic and social life. Ferguson was one of the first scholars to develop the idea of civil society and his key publication *An Essay on the History of Civil Society* (1767) is often identified as the pioneering, historical-sociological analysis of civil society. In this book, Ferguson explores the evolution of social mores and morals over long periods of time, arguing that as societies progress they also tend to abandon many of the communal and civic virtues they previously held. Nevertheless, he was a strong believer in progress, insisting that new commercial societies built on the notion of individual self-interest are likely to generate economic growth and social development. Despite seeing human beings as self-interested creatures, he also emphasised their universal capacity for empathy ('fellow feeling'), which he identified as a unique feature of humankind.

The German lands were also influenced by these ideas with Prussian intellectuals such as Immanuel Kant, Christian Wolff and Wilhelm Abraham Teller advocating and developing ideas associated with *Aufklärung* (the Enlightenment). However, it was Kant more than anybody else who defined the character of the Enlightenment and developed its key philosophical principles. Struggling to reconcile individual freedom with political authority and rationalist thought with religion, Kant found the answer to this in key Enlightenment principles such as reason, toleration and critical thinking. He understood the Enlightenment project as a form of human self-mastery:

> Enlightenment is man's release from his self-incurred tutelage. Tutelage is man's inability to make use of his understanding without direction from another. Self-incurred is this tutelage when its cause lies not in lack of reason but in lack of resolution and courage to use it without direction from another. Sapere aude! 'Have courage to use your own reason!' – that is the motto of enlightenment. (Kant, 1784)

In his view, the Enlightenment entails the understanding that one can use one's own mind to realise one's potential. Rather than just following the established norms and institutions including the monarchy and the Church, one has to reach a substantial degree of intellectual maturity to think for oneself. Hence the project of Enlightenment is the project of self-creation, self-cultivation and liberation.

Although many Prussian scholars were influenced by their French and Scottish counterparts, the German Enlightenment developed in a different direction. While the former was largely a secular project centred on the rights and possibilities of individuals the latter was more tied to collective identity including religion and language. Hence Kant, Wolff and Teller were all preoccupied with the question of how to bring together reason and faith and how to balance individual liberties with collective rights and obligations. In this context *Aufklärung* gradually gave way to the much more influential intellectual movement in the German lands – romanticism.

Romanticism developed in dialogue with and in opposition to the Enlightenment. Whereas the Parisian philosophes were preoccupied with the rights of rational and self-interested individuals, the leading thinkers of romanticism, such as Herder, Goethe and Schiller though acknowledging the uniqueness of individuals, glorified emotional attachments and collective identities. Hence in Herder's view it was shared collective experiences, such as culture and language, that make human life meaningful. In this context he argues that language is the 'organ of thought' which determines the thinking and feeling of language communities. For Herder, nationality represents the ultimate form of collective existence defined by unique tradition, culture, language, climate, education and heredity. The romanticist authors rejected the goal-centred rationality and instrumentality of the Enlightenment by emphasising the spontaneity, irrationality and authenticity of individual and collective experiences. Both Schiller's and Goethe's work venerates heroic suffering, deep emotional commitments and the struggle against conformity.

While the Enlightenment was a central influence on the rise of modern social thought, including sociology, romanticism has also played a significant role in understanding the dynamics of collective relationships. Given the latter, some writers such as Nisbet (1993) have claimed it was the reaction to the Enlightenment which formed the basis of sociological thinking. Nevertheless, since both of these intellectual movements were spearheaded by upper- and middle-class European men, they tended to ignore women, non-European populations and the lower social strata. Although some thinkers of this period, such as Condorcet and Locke, were supportive of equal rights for women and minorities, most objected to this idea. Even though educated upper-class women were involved in intellectual activities during this period, including influential debates in coffeehouses and salons, they were largely marginalised by mainstream society. However, a number of women did publish significant works that influenced the character of the Enlightenment and romanticism: Catherine Macaulay, Mary Astell, Olympe de Gouges, Louise d'Epinay, Mary Chudleigh and Mary Wollstonecraft. In particular Wollstonecraft's and Macaulay's works *The Letters on Education* (1790) and *A Vindication of the Rights of Woman* (1792), respectively, both made compelling arguments for the education of women, which had substantial influence, and in the long term, shaped policy changes.

The intellectual debates initiated by the Enlightenment opened up space for the development of a systematic and rational analysis of social life and ultimately gave birth to sociology. Two French scholars were responsible for the nominal creation of this discipline: Henri de Saint-Simon (1760–1825), who later inspired the rise of utopian socialism; and his disciple and secretary Auguste Comte (1798–1857), who coined the term 'sociology'. In Saint-Simon's view science and technology were crucial means for transforming the social order. He predicted that modernisation would bring about a highly industrialised world where science and technology would replace religious doctrines as the dominant source of authority. Furthermore, Saint-Simon advocated the establishment of meritocratic systems whereby societies would be organised and run by individuals capable of generating sustained and stable economies oriented towards the production of goods and services that would benefit all citizens. In his view, large-scale property owners could maintain political control only as long as they subsidised the educational systems which would advance knowledge and provide opportunity for all to climb the social ladder. In this type of production-centred society there would be no room for war and violence as the unification of European states would eventually halt war activities. He envisaged scientists as the key drivers of social change but also as ethical authorities that would perform a similar role to that priests had during the European Middle Ages.

Drawing on Saint-Simon's ideas, Comte developed his own approach, positivism, which conceptualised social development in evolutionary terms. Just like Saint-Simon he too perceived science, technology and industry as the pillars of modernity. His theory of social change postulated three historical phases in the evolution of the human mind and human societies: (1) the theological stage, dominated by military men and priests; (2) the metaphysical stage, governed by the clergy and lawyers; and (3) the positive stage, ruled by industrial administrators and scientists. This 'law of the three stages' conceptualised human and social development as a gradual and progress-centred transformation: the early humans attempted to explain their world through the acts of gods and spirits (theological stage), their descendants offered interpretations focusing on the final causes and given essences (the metaphysical stage), while the contemporary period is characterised by understanding the limitations of human knowledge and consequently attempting to generalise on the basis of scientific observations of natural and social relations (the positive stage). For Comte social science can only develop if it relies on the use of rigorous scientific methods. His positivist approach was rooted in the idea that all social phenomena could be explained in the same way that natural phenomena are explained. For example, he insisted that social scientists could identify the laws that govern social revolutions and wars in the same way as scientists have identified the laws of gravity or thermodynamics. Once this has been achieved, governments could use such laws for long-term social planning and in this way bring about greater social progress for all their citizens. In Comte's view the fact that social relations are highly complex and very difficult to predict means that they require more advanced forms of science. Hence, in this context, he established a hierarchy of academic disciplines arguing that sciences develop from postulating simple and abstract ideas, towards more complex and concrete experiences: from mathematics, astronomy and physics to chemistry and biology with sociology constituting 'the queen of the sciences'.

Comte and Saint-Simon's ideas have influenced many scholars including Herbert Spencer, the leading late nineteenth-century British social thinker. Spencer drew on Comte's general idea of fixed stages of social development but reframed this approach using evolutionary theory as developed in the biology of his time. Thus, Spencer argues that social development, just like developments in nature, follows an evolutionary logic – from simple to more complex forms of existence. In his view, social evolution involves a gradual transition from undifferentiated homogeneity to differentiated heterogeneity. Much of his work explores how social change and differentiation influence the greater complexity of societies. In this context, he identified two ideal types of societies which have shaped much of human history – militant society and industrial society. He defined militant society as a simple, mostly uniform and undifferentiated order, underpinned by strict hierarchies and the culture of command and obedience. In contrast, industrial society was a complex and highly differentiated, heterogeneous social order that relies on voluntary and contractual social roles and obligations. In Spencer's view, evolutionary development has fostered a gradual shift from the militant to the industrial world. This dichotomy, deeply influenced by the Enlightenment project, has, in one way or another, served as an explanatory cornerstone of classical sociological thought. From Ferdinand Tönnies' distinction between community and society (*Gemeinschaft* and *Gesellschaft*) to Durkheim's mechanical and organic solidarity, to Marx's distinction between feudalism and capitalism or Simmel's idea of differentiation in simple and complex societies, classical sociologies have attempted to make a sense of the how the modern world came into being and to what extent it differs from the traditional orders that dominated human experience for thousands of years.

The Structure of the Book

As emphasised in the accompanying volume, *Classical Sociological Theory*, social thought has largely been dominated by a very narrow social stratum: white, heterosexual, middle- and upper-class European men who were based in powerful imperial states, and who wrote only in English, French or German. The question of a sociological canon is a contested one which cannot be entered in any detail here. While there is greater diversity among scholars working in the second half of the twentieth century and even more so in this century, one still encounters the prevalence of white, middle-class, West European, and now also North American men, among the key sociological theorists. One could also notice that the English-speaking theorists have gained even more dominance over the last few decades. What this indicates is that despite substantial progress being made in terms of gender, 'race' and ethnicity, nationhood, disability, sexuality and other forms of pronounced social divisions, sociologists, as in other professions, are not immune to the hegemonic realities of the world they inhabit. In other words, even though sociologists insightfully theorise the dynamics of social divisions, they themselves remain products of the existing structures and as such are inevitably involved in the reproduction of established

Introduction: Sociological Theory in Context

social relations. Even the basic sociology of sociology would indicate that this is neither unusual nor unexpected as academia, including the sociological profession, reflects the existing social order where the established hierarchies continued to be reproduced. Thus, the existing dominance of white, middle-class, West European and North American men among sociological theorists reflects the long-term historical, geopolitical and structural legacies of the world we have inherited from our predecessors. However, as some of our chapters indicate, this is gradually changing and non-dominant social groups are slowly but surely becoming visible within the canon of contemporary sociological theory. Moreover, even sociological thought produced by individuals who would traditionally represent the establishment has also become much more reflexive of the structurally produced and reproduced group inequalities that affect the unequal representation of many groups among the leading sociological theorists. In this context any attempt to balance artificially the contemporary sociological canon would be a disingenuous attempt to paper over something that still represents a big problem within sociology, and especially within sociological theory, which remains dominated by a very narrow social stratum. The tokenistic approach where a small number of 'minority' theorists are included only because certain groups are not represented would not only be dishonest to those whose work would not be assessed on merit, but also hide the persisting structural inequalities that characterise all aspects of academic life, including sociological theory. Furthermore, elevating some scholars to the canon of contemporary sociological thought only because they belong to a particular group would represent the worst example of what Brubaker calls 'groupism' – 'the tendency to take discrete, sharply differentiated, internally homogeneous and externally bounded groups as basic constituents of social life, chief protagonists of social conflicts, and fundamental units of social analysis' (2002: 164). Most contemporary sociologists would agree that this type of groupism is deeply problematic as it attempts to homogenise diverse individual experiences and also treats individuals as mere representatives of fixed and essentialist group identities. Thus, in this book we treat sociological theorists as individuals who are influenced by their social, political, economic and historical environments and as such are inevitably shaped by their class, gender, ethnicity, sexuality and other identity categories but are never determined by such influences. In addition, our aim was to zoom in on scholars who have moulded sociological thought and who still remain the most influential figures within the discipline. Though the thinkers we have chosen are by no means exhaustive partly reflecting our circumscribed knowledge, academic interests, as well as publisher's and reviewers' comments.

This book focuses on modern and contemporary sociological theorists. We start with the highly influential sociological perspectives that have dominated twentieth-century American sociology: structural functionalism (Parsons and Merton), social interactionism and phenomenology and ethnomethodology (Goffman, Schutz and Garfinkel). The next three chapters examine the key Marxist theorists (Gramsci, Lukács and Althusser), who, together with the Frankfurt School (Marcuse, Adorno and Horkheimer), dominated intellectual debates in twentieth-century Europe. We then zoom in on the sociological approaches that have developed in dialogue with, and in opposition to, structural functionalism, interactionism and Marxism: exchange and rational choice theory (Homans, Coleman and Boudon), structuralism and post-structuralism (Lévi-Strauss, Barthes and Butler). The following chapters explore several theorists who have articulated distinct synthetic approaches to the study of social phenomena and whose work has transformed sociological thought over the last 40 years or so, namely Foucault, Elias, Bourdieu, Giddens, Habermas and Luhmann. The last four chapters discuss the contributions of more recent scholars who have challenged mainstream approaches by opening up new avenues of research and focusing their attention on topics that mainstream sociological theory has mostly neglected – from war, violence, geopolitics, nationalism, emotions and gender, to science, technology and the environment. Hence, we examine the work of Gellner, Mann, Collins, de Beauvoir, Oakley, Smith, Hochschild, Hill Collins and Latour.

As in the companion volume, our intention was to structure the chapters similarly so that they can be read as reflecting the work of specific sociologists through the lens of the time and space they inhabited. Hence, each chapter explores the biographical and intellectual context and then situates respective theorists within the broader social, political and historical contexts. The chapters aims to bring to life the key ideas and arguments of each theoretical approach and then assess the contemporary impact and application of these approaches. Each chapter also contains a critical analysis of each theoretical position.

References

Bourdieu, P. (1991 [1988]) *The Political Ontology of Martin Heidegger*. Oxford: Polity.
Brubaker, R. (2002) Ethnicity Without Groups. *European Journal of Sociology*, 43(2), pp. 163-89.
Coser, L. (1971) *Masters of Sociological Thought: Ideas in Historical and Social Context*. New York: Harcourt Brace Jovanovich.
Ferguson, A. (1966 [1767]) *An Essay on the History of Civil Society*. Edinburgh: Edinburgh University Press.
Hamilton, P. (1987) *Talcott Parsons*. London: Routledge
Hobbes, T. (2016 [1651]) *Leviathan*. London: Penguin Classics.
Kant, I. (2009 [1784]) *An Answer to the Question: 'What is Enlightenment?'* H. B. Nisbet, trans. London: Penguin.
Macaulay, C. (1790) *Letters on Education: With Observations on Religious and Metaphysical Subjects*. London: C. Dilly.
Machiavelli, N. (2008 [1531]) *Discourses on Livy*. Oxford: Oxford World's Classics.
Machiavelli, N. (2003 [1532]) *The Prince*. London: Penguin Classics.

Montesquieu, C.-L. de S. (2011 [1748]) *The Spirit of Laws*. Complete edition. T. Nugent, trans. New York: Cosimo Classics.
Nisbet, R. A. (1993) *The Sociological Tradition*. New Brunswick, NJ: Transaction Books.
Rousseau, J.-J. (2003 [1754]) *A Discourse on Inequality*. M. Cranston, trans. London: Penguin.
Rousseau, J.-J. (1998 [1762]) *The Social Contract, or Principles of Political Right*. H. J. Tozer, trans. Ware: Wordsworth Classics.
Smith, A. (1976 [1776]) *An Inquiry into the Nature and Causes of the Wealth of Nations*. Chicago, IL: University of Chicago Press.
Wollstonecraft, M. (2004 [1792]) *A Vindication of the Rights of Woman*. London: Penguin.

Parsons and Merton

Introduction

'Structural functionalism' is an academic label that has experienced a similar fate to that of 'post-modernism' or 'social Darwinism'. Very few, if any, academics are comfortable with having these labels applied to characterise their approaches. However, while 'social Darwinism' and 'post-modernism' became 'terms of abuse' only after these perspectives lost their influence in the academic world, the label 'structural functionalism' was always contested by the scholars who were deemed to be the key representatives of that perspective – Talcott Parsons and Robert Merton. While this particular label certainly does not cover the wide range of their work, it does capture well what is distinct about this sociological paradigm which centres on the functional interdependency of systems and the role human beings play in the wider social networks. There is no doubt that Parsons and Merton developed distinct and, in some respects, very different sociological theories. Nevertheless, their approaches share the same epistemological foundations.

This chapter explores the key themes of structural functionalism. As in other chapters we start from biographies and the wider intellectual and historical contexts and then move on to the core ideas of Parsons' and Merton's work. The last two sections provide a brief analysis of the recent developments and applications within this tradition or research and zoom in on the key criticisms of structural-functionalist approaches.

Life and Intellectual Context

Talcott Parsons

Parsons was born in 1902 in Colorado Springs, Colorado. He grew up in an affluent and intellectual household. Both of his parents came from well-established patrician families that could trace their origins to colonisation from seventeenth-century England. His father was an ordained Congregationalist minister, who later became a professor of English and the President of Marietta College in Ohio. Parsons' family were well disposed towards the Social Gospel movement, which applied Protestant teachings and Christian ethics to social issues ranging from poverty, crime and racial conflicts to economic inequality, lack of education, alcoholism and war. This religious movement was particularly influential among the clergy and its leadership who tended to be theologically liberal and socially progressive. It seems that young Talcott was influenced by his family's religious ethos.

Following in his father's footsteps, Talcott completed his undergraduate studies at Amherst, a private liberal arts college in Massachusetts, in 1924. At first, he intended to study medicine but changed his mind and pursued biology, sociology and philosophy. At Amherst, he soon became involved in various social activities and established himself as one of the student leaders. He was also a diligent student who early on showed a strong interest in multidisciplinary connections. As an undergraduate, Parsons was exposed to a variety of philosophical and social science traditions of analysis and had shown a marked sympathy for the theory of evolution. After graduation, he moved to the London School of Economics, where he spent a year studying under leading British scholars including L. T. Hobhouse, R. H. Tawney and B. Malinowski. He also befriended a number of fellow students who went on to become world-leading anthropologists, such as Raymond Firth, Meyer Fortes and E. E. Evans-Pritchard.

European Influences

In some ways Parsons was enchanted by European intellectual life and decided to pursue his PhD studies in Germany, at the University of Heidelberg. He studied sociology and economics and had the opportunity to work with and attend lectures of leading German social thinkers including Karl Jaspers, Karl Mannheim, Alfred Weber and Emil Lederer. His PhD project was deeply influenced by Max Weber's work on the Protestant ethic and capitalism and he graduated in 1927 with the thesis entitled '"Capitalism" in Recent German Literature: Sombart and Weber'.

The encounter with Weber's work was a defining moment in Parsons' academic development. In growing up in a religious environment Parsons was always convinced that culture and beliefs play a decisive role in the social world. Hence he found in Weber the conceptual and analytical tools for the study of long-term social change. He also decided to translate Weber's key works. In addition, he established a good working relationship with Weber's widow Marianne Weber.

Parsons started his academic career at Amherst, where he taught briefly from 1926 to 1927. After this he became an instructor at Harvard's economics department where he had the opportunity to work with Joseph Schumpeter and other eminent scholars. However, Parsons had little interest in economic issues and was eager to help establish a sociology department at Harvard.

In 1930 Harvard established a sociology department led by the Russian émigré Pitirim Sorokin and which Parsons joined. However, Sorokin and Parsons never got along partly because Parsons preferred to be active in the numerous informal study groups at Harvard rather than activities organised by the sociology department.

Parsons was also very active in anti-Nazi campaigns. He visited Germany on a few occasions before the Second World War and warned the American public of the dangers that the Nazi movement represented. In 1944 he was promoted to a full professorship and also appointed the chairperson of the department. This was followed by the reorganisation and establishment of the new, multidisciplinary, Department of Social Relations, which aimed to integrate the work of sociologists, psychologists and anthropologists into a unified social science. The new department quickly attracted talented scholars including Allport, Kluckhohn, Stouffer, Murry and Homans among others, and also created a new generation of highly influential social scientists – from Harold Garfinkel, Marian Johnson, Norman Birnbaum, Robert Bellah and Renée Fox to Clifford Geertz, Robert Merton, Neil Smelser and Randall Collins. Parsons was at Harvard until his official retirement in 1973. He had a stroke during a trip to Munich, where he celebrated the 50th anniversary of his Heidelberg degree, and died in 1979.

Robert Merton

Merton was arguably the most influential student of Parsons. He was born in 1910 as Meyer Robert Schkolnick, a son of immigrant Russian Jews. Merton's parents were educated, but impoverished. His father, Aaron, owned a dairy-product shop that burned down and the family subsequently lost their main source of income. To survive [his father] Aaron became a carpenter's assistant and a truck driver. Merton's mother was a free-thinking socialist highly sympathetic to radical and anti-clerical ideas. The young Meyer attended South Philadelphia High School but acquired much of his vast knowledge from recurrent visits to nearby libraries and other cultural institutions. Since he lived in the slums of Philadelphia he was exposed early on to violence and was also involved with juvenile gangs and street fighting. As a teenager Meyer was also fascinated by magic and initially conceived of 'Robert K. Merton' as a stage pseudonym for his magic acts. Eventually his stage name became his real name, as he registered as Robert King Merton at Philadelphia's Temple University where he received a full scholarship to study sociology (between 1927 and 31).

Upon graduation at Temple Merton applied to continue his studies at Harvard and was accepted to work with Sorokin. At Harvard he also studied with Parsons, George Sarton and L. J. Henderson. As a graduate student Merton had already published a number of influential articles ranging from 'Recent French Sociology' to 'Fluctuations in the Rate of Industrial Invention' to (with Sorokin) 'The Course of Arabian Intellectual Development, 700–1300 A.D.'. His first book, *Science, Technology & Society in Seventeenth Century England*, was published in 1938 and was one of the pioneering works in the sociology of science.

Merton's academic career started at Tulane University where he was appointed professor and chair in 1938. After three years he moved to Columbia University where he remained for over 40 years until his retirement, in 1979. In 1963 Merton was appointed Giddings Professor of Sociology, and the university later bestowed on him its highest academic rank, university professor, in 1974. During this period he also attained a degree of public visibility. His brainchild 'focus group research' was used on a mass scale by political associations, marketing agencies and other non-academic institutions, and he was soon recognised as the 'father of the focus group'. Furthermore, he devoted a great deal of energy to making sociology institutionally recognisable and publicly visible. On becoming President of the American Sociological Association in 1957 he oversaw the unprecedented institutional growth of the discipline and its expanding impact on public policy in the United States. He was the first sociologist to win the US National Medal of Science in 1994. Robert Merton died in New York in 2003.

Historical, Social and Political Context

Although Parsons and Merton had already made their intellectual mark before the Second World War, their legacy is firmly linked with the post-war world. The end of the most devastating war ever fought on this planet generated a substantial degree of optimism throughout the world and this was also reflected in the social sciences.

The Rise of the Middle Class

In addition, the late 1940s, 1950s and early 1960s, were periods of intense economic development involving large-scale rebuilding projects in Europe and increased prosperity in the United States. The 1950s were characterised by sustained economic growth and the unparalleled rise of the middle classes. However, it should not be assumed that increased growth rates simply translated into society-wide affluence. Instead, the rise of the middle classes owed a great deal to the legacies of the Second World War. For one thing the development of the war industries stimulated greater spatial and social mobility as it fostered movement from impoverished regions to the 'war-boom communities' (Malešević, 2010: 261). As the US government had to invest heavily in mass-scale military production during the war it offered highly advantageous working conditions for people prepared to move and work in the military factories.

The well-documented case of the Willow Run community in Detroit shows how the government's financial incentives generated new social dynamics. Hence, what before the war was a very small farming community, became home to over 250,000 people who settled in Willow Run to work in the nearby bomber aircraft factory. During the war such new cities provided the opportunity for thousands of Americans to climb the social ladder and become middle class in a very short period of time (Carr and Stermer, 1952). Thus, the new war-related military and civilian industries were crucial in creating the conditions for greater social mobility. After the war, the military industries in part converted to the civilian sector and focused on producing cars, manufacturing goods and other industries which were vital in maintaining full employment.

For another thing, the degree of a society-wide sense of solidarity built during the war was important for preserving stable relationships between the unionised workers and their employers. The United States, in the 1950s, had strong trade unions that boasted huge memberships. The presence of powerful unions provided greater job security and periodic wage increases, both of which contributed towards a decrease in industrial action and wide support for the status quo. This economic prosperity, coupled with a substantial degree of cross-class accord, generated a degree of stability, moderation and conservatism.

Another important feature of this period in US history was the rise of consumerism. The economic growth together with new technological inventions and ever-increasing disposable income allowed ordinary Americans to purchase large houses in new suburbs, big cars and a variety of novel household appliances. The 1950s also witnessed the rise of targeted advertising and marketing and the availability of affordable bank loans, which further stimulated consumerist practices. This combination of cross-class consensus and rampant consumerism fostered the dominance of social conservatism in the United States. Hence it is no accident that structural functionalism emerged and intellectually prospered in this type of social environment focused on consensus. Parsons' and Merton's key ideas reflected well the social realities of their world and also tapped into the widely shared aspirations of the United States in the 1950s and early 1960s – the focus on social stability, a shared normative universe, the functionality of social mores and institutions, and generational social mobility.

Cold War Ideology

However, the United States was not just any economically prosperous society that operated with a high degree of social consensus. It was also a superpower involved in the Cold War with the Soviet Union. Although the United States has already become an important geopolitical factor after the First World War, it was really victory in the Second World War that made both the United States and the Soviet Union global superpowers. As the Cold War (1947–91) unfolded it created a hostile environment between the capitalist liberal democracies and state socialist countries. This protracted ideological conflict intensified political conservatism on both sides. The rulers of Soviet-type societies dealt harshly with any form of dissent, often imprisoning or killing dissenters.

While the US liberal democratic political system did not allow for such extreme measures, the 1950s were characterised by the pervasive intolerance of left-wing ideas and organisations. Not only were many socialist and social democratic groups harassed and delegitimised as traitors and Soviet spies, but the government was also involved in the persecution of individuals deemed to be associated with left-wing politics. This was particularly pronounced during the period of the 'Second Red Scare' (1947–57) when US government officials and the mass media were obsessed with the idea that domestic and foreign communists had infiltrated the federal government, universities, the film industry and civil society. This anti-communist hysteria was spearheaded by the House Committee on Un-American Activities and the Republican Senator Joseph McCarthy.

Much of this campaign, involving the infamous congressional hearings in both houses of Congress and accusations against prominent individuals from academia and politics to Hollywood, was based on hearsay and smear tactics. Furthermore 'McCarthyism' was also associated with organised hostility against homosexuality, which in that period was still criminalised. These political campaigns contributed even further to the social conformity and conservatism that dominated the United States during this period. The onset of the Korean War (1950–3), together with Soviet military and technological triumphs (including successful atomic bomb tests in 1949 and 1951 and the launch of the Sputnik satellite in 1957), generated society-wide fear of the 'Red Menace' and imminent Soviet invasion of the United States.

None of this is to say that Parsons or Merton personally sympathised in any way with McCarthyism or political conservatism. In fact, Parsons was a firm opponent of 'Red Scare' politics and vigorously defended university colleagues accused of having communist views. He argued for the expansion of democracy and saw social and moral integration as a means of achieving this, while simultaneously understanding anomie as denoting the danger of authoritarianism (Gerhardt, 2002: ix–x). He also defended Robert Oppenheimer when he was denounced as a communist supporter in a 1954 security hearing. This prompted McCarthyite officials in the State Department to consider confiscating Parsons' passport (Hamilton, 1983: 45). The point is not that individual scholars, such as Parsons or Merton, were close to specific political positions, but rather that their sociological approaches were deeply influenced by the social and political realities of the post-war United States. Parsons' and Merton's work was generally well received within, and to some extent outside of, academia precisely because it tapped well into the existing zeitgeist. Their evolutionary understanding of social change with the focus on shared normative patterns and the intrinsic functionality of different social roles was largely based on their observations of the 1950s and early 1960s.

Arguments and Ideas

Structural functionalism was never a unified theoretical approach. This was already visible within the works of early functionalist sociologists and anthropologists such as Durkheim, Malinowski, Radcliffe-Brown or Kroeber, all of whom developed a different understanding of social structure, functional patterns or social change. This equally applies to Parsons and Merton, who articulated different theories and who also focused on different sociological questions. However, all structural functionalists share similar epistemological foundations that prioritise societal values and ideas over material and political factors, and look for social structural and functional explanations beyond the motivations and behaviours of individuals.

Talcott Parsons and Social Systems

Although Parsons had already published a number of influential journal articles throughout the late 1920s and 1930s, it was his first book, *The Structure of Social Action* (1937), that established his reputation as a leading American social theorist. Drawing on his extensive intellectual encounters and education in Europe, Parsons aimed to challenge the well-established utilitarian and narrow positivist interpretations of social change that dominated much of American social science. In contrast to the highly individualised, self-interest-based, 'positivistic theory of action', Parsons builds what he terms a 'voluntaristic theory of action'. At the centre of this theory is the 'unit act' composed of an actor, an end, a situation over which the actor has variable control, and the means of action. The voluntaristic theory of action argues that the actions of individuals are not determined by their material conditions, or their social environment, but by the voluntary choices they make. However, this is not to say that human beings are atomised individualists who make random choices. On the contrary, Parsons argues that individual actions are regularly based on, but not determined by, the values that have been attained and developed during one's primary and secondary socialisation. In other words, individual actors always face a variety of alternative modes of action and they tend to make particular choices on the basis of their cultural upbringing and shared value systems.

Building on the classical contributions of Durkheim, Pareto, Marshall and, most of all, Weber, Parsons articulates a synthetic theory of social action that emphasises the centrality of cultural values. According to Parsons the writings of all these thinkers implicitly converge – what was later dubbed a 'the convergence thesis'. A synthesis of the work produced by these four theorists is a step towards formulating a new 'grand theory' of social action. Hence, in contrast to positivist utilitarian accounts that cannot explain the 'Hobbesian problem of order', Parsons insists that social order exists because individuals are socialised into specific systems of cultural values. The presence of these shared value systems contributes towards the establishment and reproduction of the shared social institutions, while the social institutions themselves reinforce a shared normative universe that ultimately helps regulate individual action.

For Parsons, sociology is a study of meaningful action, an attempt to understand how social agents make sense of the world they inhabit. Drawing on the neo-Kantian theory of knowledge, Parsons sees social reality through the prism of what he calls analytical realism: 'an epistemology which stressed that "facts" are statements about experience in terms of specific conceptual scheme which provides a meaningful ordering of that experience' (Hamilton, 1983: 64). In this context, a voluntaristic concept of action stands for the subjective and meaning-oriented views of the world. However, unlike Kant or Whitehead, another major influence, who focus on individual meanings, Parsons shifts attention towards wider social dynamics. Hence, in his approach, voluntaristic action is patterned into specific interactions and social relationships. What make these relationships and interactions hold together, thus also making social order possible, are the shared normative orientations of social actors.

To sum up, the key points of Parsons' voluntaristic theory of action are the following: (1) actors are capable of making choices and engaging in voluntary action; (2) these actions are made in relation to the specific goals, and the available choices, actors aim to achieve; (3) these goals and choices depend upon particular norms, beliefs and values that position such choices and goals; and (4) social action takes place within already existing environmental and biological constraints which limit the choices and the actual realisation of desired ends (Hamilton, 1983: 78).

Social Systems

The Structure of Social Action provided a stepping stone for a more comprehensive structural-functionalist theory that emerges in Parsons' *The Social System* (1951). While the early work was an attempt to make the case for a non-instrumentalist understanding of social action, *The Social System* was a much more ambitious publication that aimed to provide a novel general sociological theory capable of explaining a variety of social phenomena. In this book Parsons establishes the foundations of structural functionalism which he understood not as a particular approach, but as a stage in the development of universal social science. The guiding principle of the structural-functionalist approach is that society is not a conglomerate of self-interested individuals, but a complex system of mutually interdependent parts.

The notion of social systems refers to the patterned interdependence and interrelationships that exist between individuals, groups, institutions, organisations and other social structures and as such operate as a relatively coherent whole. More specifically, Parsons perceives social systems as networks involving interaction processes between two or more actors. In his view they entail the presence of culture and systems of language which allow for the communication and interaction of actors. The aim of *The Social System* was to create a generalised conceptual model which could analyse 'the structure and processes of social systems' by focusing on 'the delineation of the system of institutionalised roles and the motivational processes organised about them' (Parsons, 1951: vii).

Moreover, the task of sociology is to explore social systems through the prism of 'the institutionalisation of patterns of value orientation in roles' (Parsons, 1951: vii). For Parsons, social systems exist independently of any specific individuals as social institutions preserve their forms even when specific actors have been changed. However, this is not to say that individual actions do not matter. Parsons is adamant that social systems exist and operate only in so far as individual actors are motivated by their own personality systems. In this scheme, heavily influenced by Freudian ideas, personality systems involve three different aspects: (1) cognitive, relating to actors understanding of the situation 'in which his [their] needs-dispositions are actuated'; (2) cathectic, involving actors' gratification or deprivation that they receive from the situation; and (3) evaluative, concerning actors' interpretation of the meanings associated with the specific situation (Hamilton, 1983: 100).

In addition to the personality system, which addresses the needs, motivation and orientations of individual actors, and the social system which refers to patterned interdependence of individual actors, institutions and organisations, Parsons also identifies another key component of action theory – the cultural system. The cultural system, often referred to as culture or cultural patterns, binds other aspects of the social world together. The cultural system makes interactions between personality and social systems possible as culture underpins most social action. More specifically, the personality system is imbued with the particular norms and cultural values that shape the behaviour and value orientations of individual actors.

Similarly, social systems entail shared cultural mores that make the operation of everyday actions more functional. In addition to these three-action systems, Parsons later identifies the behavioural organism as another subsystem which provides the source of energy for other subsystems. To explain how these four subsystems operate and interact, he devised a complex model focusing on the four functional imperatives of the system – the AGIL schema.

As we noted above, Parsons' voluntaristic theory of action emphasises that actors make individual choices and also that such choices are shaped by shared cultural norms. To account for the variations in the way choices are made, Parsons introduced the notion of 'pattern variables' – an analytical category that identifies elements present in an individual choice of action and explores whether variables are adaptive or integrative. He distinguishes between four main pattern variables: (1) affectivity vs. affective neutrality; (2) specificity vs. diffuseness; (3) universalism vs. particularism; and (4) ascription vs. achievement. These variables allow for identifying whether particular choices are made in terms of actors' emotional or rational commitments, whether they are more concerned with specific issues or are diffuse, whether they are oriented towards more universalist or particularist goals and whether they involve ascriptive or achieved status.

Nevertheless, since this dichotomous typology proved too restrictive in accommodating the complexity of social action, Parsons developed a more elaborate scheme which zooms in on the four functional problems that every system has to address – adaptation, goal attainment, integration and latent pattern maintenance. He argues that complex societies are characterised by ever-increasing differentiation along functional lines, which leads towards greater specialisation. For example, as societies develop and expand, their economic systems become more complex and more specialised into different organisations, institutions and roles that emerge within different areas of the economy – production, resource allocation, distribution of goods and services, banking, and so on. Hence complexity brings greater differentiation and specialisation and the key issue becomes how large systems maintain a functioning social order.

Parsons explains this through his AGIL schema where the four 'functional imperatives' are related to the specific functional demands they need to face and resolve: (1) Adaptation stands for the system's need to obtain enough resources and to adapt to its environment, as well as to ability of the system to transform its environment so as to fulfil the requirements of the system.

(2) Goal attainment denotes a need of the system to formulate specific goals and to motivate and mobilise energy to achieve such goals. (3) Integration indicates the system's need to co-ordinate the inter-unit rapport between its component parts, in order to preserve coherence and solidarity and avoid any substantive disruptions in the system. (4) Latent pattern maintenance refers to the system's need to generate and maintain cultural patterns that foster, sustain and store the motivational energy of individuals; this functional imperative includes two linked issues: tension management that helps resolve actors' internal tensions and strains; and pattern maintenance involving the provision of ideas, values, symbols, judgements and tastes from the cultural system.

In addition, these four functional imperatives also differ in terms of whether they are external or internal, and whether they are consummatory or instrumental. The first dichotomy refers to the system's inner organisational requirements (internal function) or the system's relationship with its environment (external function). The second dichotomy stands for the system's attainment of desired goals (consummatory function) or the system's acquisition and incorporation of specific means (instrumental function).

These highly abstract categories can be simplified with the use of a specific example – the traditional lifestyle of Hopi Native Americans. In order to survive the tribe needs to interact with the external world by hunting animals, tending livestock, ploughing fields and acquiring other resources (adaptation). The tribe requires a relatively coherent set of short-term and long-term goals (i.e. taking part in tribal conflicts, moving hunting grounds, etc.), which involves a developed mechanism of rule and decision making (goal attainment).

The Hopi possess shared cultural values centred on reverence and respect for all things in nature and their common belief system is built around an idea that one should be at peace with Nature and live in harmony in line with the teachings of Maasaw, the Creator of Earth (integration). The tribe also maintains a system of primary socialisation which teaches key skills and cultural values to the younger members of society and also operates well-established practices and rituals for conflict management and resolution (latent pattern maintenance). Parsons considers these four functional imperatives universal and necessary for the existence of any social system – from the largest, such as the nation-state, to the smallest, such as the face-to-face interaction.

Evolutionary Theory

In his later works including *Societies* (1966), Parsons develops a structural-functionalist evolutionary theory of change. This approach, heavily influenced by Durkheim, analyses social change through the prism of the increasing differentiation of social systems. Parsons (1966: 21–2) identifies three key evolutionary processes: (1) the ever-increasing differentiation of the system's elements into patterns of functional interdependence; (2) the development of new means and structural devices for integration into differentiating systems; and (3) the augmented survival capacity of differentiated systems within their environments.

For Parsons differentiation involves the enhancement of the adaptive capacity of social subsystems, which takes place in an evolutionary fashion. Simply put, in this view social systems resemble organisms as they adapt to ever-changing environments. Hence, as the old subsystems prove inadequate for handling new complexities, evolution fosters the creation of new, more specialised and more differentiated subsystems. In the Parsonian structural-functionalist account social change takes place on four levels: (1) increasing differentiation of social systems from each other; (2) increasing differentiation within the subsystems; (3) the emergence of crises and their resolutions within the differentiated subsystems; and (4) the adaptive upgrading of the survival capacity of subsystems within their environments. Parsons argues that the differentiation process generates new problems including the co-ordination and integration of the new subsystems.

In this context, the evolutionary process entails changes in skills and abilities as well as the presence of a more generalised system of shared values which could accommodate the increased diversity of functions and goals caused by the process of differentiation. In *Societies* (1966), Parsons applies this theoretical model to a variety of social orders through time, arguing that as evolution advances, societies become more differentiated and more functionally interdependent. He explores this evolutionary trajectory starting from what he terms primitive societies of aborigines, to the archaic social orders possessing written language (i.e. Egypt and Mesopotamia), to the 'historic intermediate empires' such as China, India, the Islamic and Roman Empires, to ancient Greece and Israel, which in his view represent the 'seed-bed' societies providing the foundations of the modern social order.

The same evolutionary argument is advanced in *The System of Modern Societies* (1971: 1) where Parsons identifies the West as the cradle of modernity:

> the modern type of society has emerged in a single evolutionary arena, the West, which is essentially the area of Europe that fell heir to the western half of the Roman Empire north of the Mediterranean. The Society of Western Christendom, then, provided the base from which what we shall call the 'system' of modern society 'took off'.

Although Parsons was adamant that societies rise up the evolutionary ladder (from primitive to intermediate to modern), he recognised that evolution was not a unilinear process and that some social orders experience downwards trajectories, collapse or stagnation.

Robert Merton and the Middle-Range Theory

Even though both Parsons and Merton belong to the same theoretical tradition of structural functionalism, their focus, approach and even their writing styles are very different. While Parsons was preoccupied with developing a grand sociological theory that would be applicable to all times and places,

Merton preferred to develop new concepts and ideas that would help explain a more specific sociological phenomena – from crime and deviance to science and ideologies.

The Sociology of Science and Middle-Range Theories

Merton was one of the pioneers of the sociology of science. His first book *Science, Technology & Society in Seventeenth-Century England* (1938), based on his PhD project, focused on the relationship between science and religion. More specifically, drawing on Weber's Protestant thesis, Merton argues that there is a strong historical connection between the rise of Protestant Pietism and Puritanism and the birth of experimental science. The book makes a case that science develops with the gradual accumulation of observations, improvements in methodology and experimental technique. In this context, according to Merton, one could identify striking parallels between the religious backgrounds of the leading scientists and the popularity of science in seventeenth-century England.

Merton attempts to show how the leading inventors and scientists involved with the Royal Society were mostly Puritans and other Protestants. He argues that their Puritan ethos was not necessary for triggering a scientific revolution, but it did contribute towards making scientific and religious values compatible. He finds synergy between Puritan and Pietist ascetic ethics and corresponding lifestyles with the self-discipline, rationality and the long-term ideational commitment that underpins scientific endeavours. Thus, for Merton, Puritan religion gave an impetus to, and justification for, science: science was linked to God's influence on the world, which freed scientific research from previous religious restrictions. However, once science became institutionalised it was gradually decoupled from religion and even became an enemy of religious belief.

Another important contribution in this area was Merton's (1942) analysis of the social norms and social organisation of science. He identified the four key ideals that underpin the actions of scientists and their goals (often referred to as CUDOS): (1) Communism – the shared ownership of scientific discoveries whereby scientists receive esteem and recognition in exchange for giving up their intellectual property. (2) Universalism – the shared principle where truth claims are assessed through the universal and impersonal criteria that have no bearing on issues of group membership (i.e. class, race, ethnicity, gender, religion, etc.). (3) Disinterestedness – the perception that scientists find their fulfilment in scientific activity and as such their rewards are mostly immaterial. (4) Organised scepticism – all ideas and truth claims require testing and are subject to meticulous scrutiny by the scientific community.

Merton also created a number of highly influential concepts to describe and explain a variety of phenomena that often accompany scientific undertakings. For example, together with Harriet Zuckerman (1968) he identified a common practice, which he termed the Matthew effect, whereby well-known scientists often receive substantially more recognition for their work while lesser known scientists receive much less recognition, even for their path-breaking contributions. The persistence of the Matthew effect undermines the universalist and disinterested ambition of science as leading scientists tend to accumulate disproportionally awards, grants and prestigious titles, at the expense of other scientists. Other idioms coined by Merton include 'multiples', referring to independent discoveries of the same phenomena, and 'obliteration by incorporation', when a concept becomes well established in everyday discourse and its creator is forgotten (i.e. charisma, paradigm or self-fulfilling prophecy).

With regard to the latter, Merton begins his justly celebrated paper 'The Self-fulfilling Prophecy' (1968b) by citing the Thomas theorem according to which, 'If men define situations as real, they are real in their consequences'. For Merton this illustrates, that 'men respond not only to the objective features of the situation, but also, and at times primarily, to the meaning this situation has for them' (1957: 475). Merton goes onto to expound a parable concerning the collapse of The Last National Bank. On Black Wednesday 1932, the bank, heretofore a flourishing institution, is beset by a crisis as a result of a false rumour of its insolvency. As a result of this rumour, a belief in its financial viability is replaced with a view that it is insolvent, starting a run on the bank and ultimately its collapse. The introduction of a false or 'unreal definition' for Merton, invariably causes discordant and chaotic conequences: 'The self-fulfilling prophecy is, in the beginning, a false definition of the situation evoking a new behaviour which makes the originally false conception come true' (1968b: 477). Such a process can be extended, he argues, to explain the racism geared towards Jews and African Americans.

Drawing on the examples of classical sociologists, and in particular Durkheim's *Suicide*, Merton argues that any attempt to build an overarching grand sociological theory of everything is largely a futile exercise as such theories become too abstract and too distant from the concrete observations that take place in specific social settings. Hence, instead of theorising about abstract entities such as society, culture or politics in general, Merton suggests developing middle-range theories that zoom in on specific sociological phenomena which allow for the fruitful combination of theoretical analysis with in-depth empirical observation.

Middle-range theory involves a sociological enquiry that utilises a limited range of data in order to provide a generalisable and theoretically informed analysis. As Merton (1967: 39) emphasises middle range theory is positioned 'between the minor but necessary working hypotheses that evolve in abundance during day-to-day research and the all-inclusive systematic efforts to develop a unified theory that will explain all the observed uniformities of social behaviour, social organisation, and social change'. In his view, middle-range theories start from the level of empirical observation which then would lead towards generating more general statements that could be verified by data. However, while Merton was critical of total theoretical systems, he was still committed to the gradual development of a universal theory. He perceived middle-range theories as a stepping stone towards building a more complex and elaborate sociological explanation. For Merton, sociology was not as 'mature' as physics and other sciences and as such it could not generate universal theories. Nevertheless, with the development of more comprehensive middle-range theories sociology would eventually reach the level of other sciences and produce a system of universal laws.

Functional Analysis

Unlike Parsons, who focused on building highly abstract grand systems, Merton's structural functionalism was therefore less systemic, and more amenable to empirical research. For Merton functionalism stood for the analytical attempt to interpret data by identifying the consequences for the larger structures that underpin the data. This type of functional analysis aimed to avoid the inflexibility and static system modelling that characterised traditional functionalism. Hence, Merton agrees with Parsons that functional interdependence is necessary for the existence of the social order and that shared values make such order possible. However, he also argues that not all social action fosters social integration. In this context, he distinguishes between social functions and social dysfunctions. While functions contribute towards social unity, dysfunctions generate tension and conflict. In contrast to Parsons, who understood society as a giant equilibrium, Merton makes clear that disorder and disorganisation are also part of social life. For example, he identified civil wars and the marginalised position of African Americans in the 1950s as examples of dysfunctional social order.

Merton also differentiates between manifest and latent functions. By manifest functions he means the outcomes that one expects to occur, an action that was intended and was perceived exactly as intended. In contrast, latent functions stand for actions that were not intended and often not even perceived to have taken place. For example, traditional societies use the rain dance rituals to generate rain for their crops (manifest function), but these rain dances also foster greater social integration of the tribe engaged in a shared ritual practice (latent function). The strong functional element of latency is also present in Merton's (1936) notion of the unanticipated consequences of social action. This refers to paradoxical situations that are triggered by actions that originally were not intended. For example, the Marxist idea that as capitalism grows and expands it will concentrate wealth in a small number of corporations, and as such would ultimately become its own gravedigger has, according to Merton, generated unanticipated consequences resulting in the development of anti-capitalist movements that reformed ruthless forms of nineteenth-century capitalism into the more humane welfare capitalism of the twentieth century. The unintended consequences of social action can again lead towards a self-defeating prophecy – an announced prediction that ultimately prevents what it predicts from occurring. Typical examples are announcing future price reductions which then hinder current sales. This is the opposite of the self-fulfilling prophecy, which as we noted is achieved because people believe and act according to what they believe is bound to happen.

Theory of Deviance

In addition, Merton made highly influential contributions to the study of crime and deviance. The starting point of his analysis is the functionalist strain theory of deviant behaviour. According to this approach, crime and deviance are by-products of the mismatch between one's expectations and goals on the one hand, and the legitimate opportunities societies provide, on the other. Thus, social progress and reduction in crime levels are achieved in societies where the individual goals match social opportunities. However, when there are no opportunities and individual goals and expectations are blocked, this generates a situation whereby some individuals turn to crime to attain the financial and other material means in order to fulfil socially desirable goals.

For Merton the rising levels of crime and deviance often reflect an anomic social condition. Drawing on Durkheim's idea, Merton (1968) describes anomie as a situation of normlessness that emerges when there is 'an acute disjunction between the cultural norms and goals and the socially structured capacities of members of the group to act in accord with them'. However, Merton recognised that anomie does not automatically lead to crime. Instead, the disconnection between cultural expectations and actual structural conditions often generates a variety of social responses, some of which lead to deviant behaviour. Merton differentiates between five different social responses to anomie: conformity, innovation, ritualism, retreatism and rebellion. The most common social response is conformity with the rules, where individuals aim to attain cultural goals within the system by utilising the socially accepted means.

In contrast, innovation stands for reaching cultural goals in socially unacceptable ways, such as turning to deviant or criminal behaviour. The inventiveness indicates behaviour that goes outside of dominant social norms as individuals invent new ways to achieve specific societal goals. The third response, ritualism, includes acceptance of structural means with the realisation that the stated cultural goals cannot be attained. This ritualist behaviour usually does not lead to crime, but it is likely to generate deviant behaviour such as drug abuse, alcoholism, suicidal behaviour, etc. The individuals who pursue this course of action stay within the acceptable structural means while giving up on the idea of reaching the ever-elusive societal goals. The next social response refers to the rejection of both the cultural goals and structural means – retreatism. This type of social behaviour is also less likely to lead to crime as retreaters focus on finding a way to escape societal goals and the prescribed structural means. The final model of social response is rebellion, which is usually a temporary phenomenon associated with youthful reaction to established norms and structures. This type of behaviour also rejects both the cultural goals and structural means, but in contrast to retreaters who tend to withdraw from action, rebels aim to replace the dominant norms and structures with an alternative system of social order. Thus, for Merton, crime is most likely to emerge among the innovators while ritualism tends to accompany deviant behaviour.

In addition to his substantial conceptual and theoretical contributions Merton also invented a number of methodological techniques which are still used among social science researchers, including the notion of the focus group, role models, status sets and role sets, reference group behaviour and the serendipity pattern in research.

Contemporary Relevance and Applications

Although Parsons was one of the most influential sociologists for decades his influence has largely diminished in significance. Merton's legacy appears stronger in the sense that his methodological and conceptual creations such as the focus group or middle-range theory are still widely referred to and used in empirical contexts, but his functionalist approach has also lost much of its global influence. With the rise of anti-foundational perspectives such as post-structuralism, post-Marxism and post-modernism in the 1980s, 1990s and early 2000s, functionalism found itself under stern critique, or was just ignored. Nevertheless, a number of influential sociologists from Jeffrey Alexander and Neil Smelser in the United States, Piotr Sztompka in Poland, to Niklas Luhmann in Germany have revitalised the structural-functionalist tradition of analysis.

THE RENEWAL OF PARSONS

The standing of Parsonian social theory within sociology has been subject to great fluctuation. Having dominated the discipline during the 1950s, it came under increasing attack during the 1960s, before being virtually dismissed in the 1970s. Yet, despite this rejection, the shadow of Parsons continued to loom large in the plurality of emerging, largely micro-sociological approaches. It was not long, therefore, before Parsons made a return in the 1980s, notably in German sociology. This renewal of Parsons continues today, with an identifiable revisionist interpretation of the theory and theorist at present. Whether Parsons may yet again come to be rejected remains open. What is certain, however, is his central role in consolidating the sociological frame of reference.

However, the most influential and innovative reworking of structural functionalism has taken place in the works of Jeffrey Alexander. Initially Alexander (1985) developed a neo-functionalist theory which attempted to address some shortcomings of the classical functionalist approach. Hence, Alexander argued that neo-functionalism can address the micro as well as the macro level of analysis; that social systems are not rigid and fixed but involve historical contingencies and interactional creativity; that social conflict is also part of social order; and that functionalism can calibrate its analytical tools to understand historical change as dynamic and unpredictable. In contrast to Parsons, who devotes little attention to actors, Alexander emphasises individual actions and argues that social action depends on the will of concrete individuals who operate in complex social networks. This neo-functionalist refinement of Parsons developed further into what Alexander (2004) termed 'a strong programme in cultural sociology'.

The main ambition of the strong programme was to uncouple culture from social structure and emphasise the cultural autonomy of the social. In this view, values, ideas and symbols are not dependent variables but autonomous forces that shape social institutions, politics and the economy. As Alexander's closest collaborator Philip Smith (2005: 4) puts it in his analysis of war narratives: 'war is not just about culture, but it is all about culture'. Alexander and his collaborators draw on the functionalist tradition, including the works of later Durkheim, Weber, Geertz and Parsons and combine these insights with structuralism and hermeneutics, in order to develop a culture-centred explanatory model. In this context, Parsons is criticised as lacking a 'hermeneutic dimension' and therefore could not explain the dynamics of social values. To illustrate the analytical value of the strong programme, Alexander explores a variety of social phenomena – from cultural traumas and social performance to iconic consciousness and further afield. For example, in his studies of collective traumas, Alexander argues that catastrophic events do not create social traumas by themselves but have to undergo a relatively protracted period of narration and signification to be popularly understood as shared traumas.

He deploys the examples of the Holocaust and Watergate, among others, to argue that 'only if the patterned meanings of the collectivity are abruptly dislodged is traumatic status attributed to an event. It is meanings that provide the sense of shock and fear, not the events in themselves' (Alexander, 2004: 10). Hence, the strong programme in culture maintains the structural-functionalist emphasis on ideas, values and symbolic action, but unlike Parsons, it sees culture as a fully autonomous and historically dynamic force.

Robert Merton's work has also been developed further by several contemporary scholars. Thus, Piotr Sztompka (1986, 1993, 2007) has explored Merton's ethos of science in the contemporary context pointing to difficulties in maintaining trust in the scientific enterprise which characterised the world after the Second World War. While Merton identified the trustworthiness of scholarship as the key principle of science, Sztompka demonstrates that with the privatisation of science, commodification of research results and ever-increasing bureaucratisation of scientific institutions, one can identify a decrease of trust in science. Robert Agnew (2006) has also revised and expanded Merton's strain theory to explain different types of deviance and crime. Agnew argues that the focus on social class or specific cultural attributes cannot capture the variety of deviant behaviours.

Instead, he pushes structural functionalism further and insists that individual norms shape social behaviour. In his general strain theory, the emphasis is on one's immediate social environment, and in particular, on one's emotional responses. Hence, Agnew insists that one's anticipated or actual failure to attain positively valued goals is likely to generate an emotional strain. In addition, the strain can also result from the anticipated or actual presentation of negative stimuli or anticipated removal of positively valued stimuli. In this context, the recurrent episodes of frustration and anger are likely to foster negative self-perceptions which foster one's alienation from society. The continuous experiences of rejection are likely to develop and feed into the further development of negative emotions, which ultimately may push individuals towards deviance and crime.

Criticisms

Parsons' and Merton's work remained highly influential throughout the 1960s and early 1970s. However, the rise of civil rights movements and the protracted Vietnam War had profound impacts on undermining the consensus-oriented social science of the period, which was reflected in increased criticism of the structural-functionalist paradigm. Early critics such as C. Wright Mills and Alvin Gouldner focused on the verbose, jargon-filled, Parsonian terminology, the functionalist inability to explain social conflicts and class polarisation. Mills was also highly critical of Parsons' positivist ambition to build a grand theory, arguing that much of Parsons theory building was not grounded in any actual analysis of data, while his positivism could not account for the contingent character of social life. Moreover, within the changed social environment of the post-1960s, the new criticisms challenged the entire epistemological and political foundations of structural functionalism. Hence Parsons, Merton and other representatives of this approach have been criticised for their epistemological idealism. Structural-functionalist accounts of social order overemphasise the role that ideas, values and norms play in social life. In this approach individuals and groups are rarely understood as autonomous creatures defined by their diverse free wills, emotions and rationality and much more as the by-products of the cultural worlds they inhabit – a form of normative determinism.

Furthermore, the overemphasis on the cultural patterns and internalisation of social values prevents one from seeing how central the coercive, political and economic factors are in the formation and maintenance of specific social orders. For example, Parsons' analysis of family relationships indicates the limits of culture-centred analysis. For Parsons, the nuclear family is conducive to the social and emotional stability of individuals and as such it is a cornerstone of primary socialisation. In this view the division of gender roles with men undertaking 'instrumental roles' (going to work and providing financial support) and women assuming 'expressive roles' (taking care of children and the home) helps maintain the social stability of the family and the wider social system (Parsons and Bales, 1956).

However, this approach remains utterly blind to the power dynamics that operate within patriarchal families and wider patriarchal societies. Hence, this culture-centred view cannot account for the economic and political inequalities within the household or for the presence of domestic violence and other power-related aspects of everyday social life in patriarchy. This criticism also applies to the neo-functionalists' approaches including Alexander's strong programme in cultural studies and Luhmann's system theory, both of which overemphasise cultural factors.

Other criticisms of structural functionalism focus on its present-centric and teleological understanding of social change. For one thing, most structural-functionalist accounts shy away from analysis of large-scale processes, yet when they do undertake them, the emphasis is more on recent historical transformations. In his later publications, Parsons attempted to address this problem by developing an evolutionary theory of system differentiation. However, this evolutionary modernisation theory of change is very static, and rather teleological, in its organisation. Even when he makes clear that his model is not unilinear, the central assumption that underpins this theory – the notion of ever-increasing functional interdependence and complexity – is highly problematic as it leaves little room for historical contingencies and multidirectional change.

For example, Parsons' (1975) explanation of the 'ethnic revival' that took place in the 1960s and early 1970s in the United States, emphasises its temporary and unexpected character. Thus for Parsons, the resurgence of ethnic politics is a historical aberration reflected in the transitory de-differentiation which itself was caused by the intensity of dramatic social changes. In this view such temporary processes cannot stop the evolutionary path towards the greater differentiation of social systems. This type of analysis wrongly assumes that the salience of ethnic identification represents a return to 'the atavistic past' rather than what it actually is – the product of inter-group competition in a modernising social environment. For another thing, Parsons' modernisation theory is deeply Eurocentric as it assumes that all social orders develop according to a similar historical logic.

Thus, his system determinism establishes rigid hierarchies between societies with the West at the helm of this social pyramid. However, as much of recent scholarship has documented well, rather than representing a historically continuous entity that has experienced uninterrupted rise and development, 'the West' is a modern ideological construction that has no historical reality, as the centres of political power have shifted through time and space (GoGwilt, 1995).

Merton's functionalist analysis has also faced similar criticisms, pointing to its overemphasis on culture over economic and political power, its static understanding of the social order and its one-dimensional evolutionary understanding of modernity. Furthermore his early work linking Puritanism and Pietism with the rise of science has been empirically challenged by several scholars, who argue that many major scientific breakthroughs took place outside of Protestant Europe (i.e. Galileo, Descartes, Copernicus, da Vinci, etc.) and that many Protestant leaders were hostile to science (Becker, 1992; Ferngren, 2002). Some scholars have also criticised Merton for ignoring the role philosophy and mathematics have played in the birth of experimental science. Merton's work on crime and deviance has also been put under the spotlight and contemporary criminologists find some of his ideas inadequate to explain the variety of motivations involved in crime. For example, Brym and Lie (2007) argue that the strain theory developed by Merton focuses mostly on the street crime traditionally associated with the working classes that have no resources, while ignoring the white-collar crime prominent among middle- and upper-class individuals.

Conclusion

Structural functionalism has lost much of the appeal and influence it had in the twentieth century. Once a dominant sociological paradigm throughout the world, the classical structural-functionalist theories have now either become relatively marginal or evolved into much more complex system theories. However, Parsons' and Merton's intellectual legacies have been much wider than their original functionalist theories. For one thing, Parsons initiated the ongoing debate on the role that structure and agency play in the organisation of social order. His ideas have also contributed to recent links between cybernetics and social theory, and his studies of cultural systems have influenced a variety of new approaches within and beyond sociology. Merton's work has also left a lasting legacy. The idea of the middle-range theory has become a norm in much of social science. His methodological inventions including the focus group, the reference group, role models and role sets, have become a staple of contemporary research techniques across different disciplines. Even his strain theory of deviance is still influencing new generations of criminologists. Thus structural functionalism is not dead; its intellectual legacies are still shaping much of the contemporary world.

References

Agnew, R. (2006) General Strain Theory: Current Status and Directions for Further Research. In: F. T. Cullen, J. P. Wright and K. R. Blevins (eds). *Advances in Criminological Theory: Vol. 15: Taking Stock: The Status of Criminological Theory*. Piscataway, NJ: Transaction Books, pp. 101-23.

Alexander, J. C. (1985) *Neo-Functionalism*. London: Sage.

Alexander, J. C. (2004) *Cultural Trauma and Collective Identity*. Berkeley, CA: University of California Press.

Becker, G. (1992) The Merton Thesis: Oetinger and German Pietism, a Significant Negative Case. *Sociological Forum*, 7(4), pp. 641-60.

Brym, R. and Lie, J. (2007) *Sociology: Your Compass for a New World*, 3rd edition. Belmont, CA: Thomson Wadsworth.

Carr, L. J. and Stermer, J. E. (1952) *Willow Run: A Study of Industrialization and Cultural Inadequacy*. New York: Harper.

Ferngren, G. B. (2002) *Science and Religion: A Historical Introduction*. Baltimore, MD: Johns Hopkins University Press.

Gerhardt, U. (2002) *Talcott Parsons: An Intellectual Biography*. Cambridge: Cambridge University Press.

GoGwilt, C. (1995) *The Invention of the West: Joseph Conrad and the Double Mapping of Europe and Empire*. Stanford, CA: Stanford University Press.

Hamilton, P. (1983) *Talcott Parsons*. Chichester: Horwood.

Malešević, S (2010) *The Sociology of War and Violence*. Cambridge: Cambridge University Press.

Merton, R. K. (1936) The Unanticipated Consequences of Purposive Social Action. *American Sociological Review*, 1(6), pp. 894-904.

Merton, R. K. (1938) *Science, Technology and Society in Seventeenth Century England*. New York: Howard Fertig.
Merton, R. K. (1942) Science and Technology in a Democratic Order. *Journal of Legal and Political Sociology*, 1, pp. 115-26.
Merton, R. K. (1967) *On Theoretical Sociology*. New York: Free Press.
Merton, R. K. (1968a) *Social Theory and Social Structure*. New York: Free Press.
Merton, R. (1968b) The Self-fulfilling Prophecy. In: *Social Theory and Social Structure*. New York: Free Press, pp. 475-90.
Parsons, T. (1951) *The Social System*. London: Routledge & Kegan Paul.
Parsons, T. (1966) *Societies: Evolutionary and Comparative Perspectives*. Eaglewood Cliffs, NJ: Prentice Hall.
Parsons, T. (1968 [1937]) *The Structure of Social Action, 2 vols*. New York: Free Press.
Parsons, T. (1971) *The System of Modern Societies*. Hemel Hempstead: Prentice Hall.
Parsons, T. (1975) Some Theoretical Considerations on the Nature and Trends of Change of Ethnicity. In: N. Glazer and D. P. Moynihan (eds). *Ethnicity: Theory and Experience*. Cambridge, MA: Harvard University Press.
Parsons, T. and Bales, R. F. (1956) *Family Socialization and Interaction Process*. London: Routledge & Kegan Paul.
Sztompka, P. (1986) *Robert K. Merton: An Intellectual Profile*. New York: St. Martin's Press.
Sztompka, P. (1993) *The Sociology of Social Change*. Oxford: Blackwell.
Sztompka, P. (2007) Trust in Science: Robert K. Merton's Inspirations. *Journal of Classical Sociology*, 7(2), pp. 211-20.

Goffman

Introduction

Erving Goffman is considered as one of the most important sociologists of the second half of the twentieth century (Collins, 1988: 41). He is one of the few theorists to be read widely outside of the social sciences and his key concepts have become very familiar to sociologists: selves, roles, norms, institutions, interactions. Yet his interest in social interactions to understand aspects of the self, social order and the organisation of social structure is discussed in a profoundly unique and penetrating way. Although Goffman is described as a 'social theorist' some commentators believe his work lacks the systematic ambition of other writers, with ideas developed and expanded in various case studies; that is, in use. Nevertheless, these case studies transcend their exemplifications and can be systematically ordered to reveal the operation of general social processes (Giddens, 1987). In addition to his profound illumination of the structured nature of interactions, he made important contributions to the study of mental illness and deviance, social stigma and gender patriarchy.

Life and Intellectual Context

Scant details are known about Goffman's biography since, as Shalin (2014: 2) notes, he was averse to self-revelation and secretive about his life: he forbid the taping of his lectures, of pictures being taken of him, and the publication of his unpublished manuscripts. Nevertheless, some facts are known (Winkin, 1999; Fine and Manning, 2000; Shalin, 2010). He was born in Manville, Alberta, on 11 June 1922, and his parents Max Goffman and Ann Auerbach were Ukrainian Jews who escaped from a Russian pogrom and arrived in Winnipeg in 1917 (Winkin, 1999). They ran a department store in Dauphin, Manitoba, and had two children, Frances and Erving Manual. Although Jewish, and speaking Yiddish at home, the family were not particularly religious and grew up experiencing relatively little anti-Semitism. As a boy, drama fascinated Goffman and he often attended the theatre, while his sister went onto become an actor and broadcaster. After attending St John's Technical High School, he studied chemistry at the University of Manitoba in 1939 before dropping out to begin work at the National Film Board in Ottawa between 1943 and 1944. There he met the sociologist Dennis Wrong, who persuaded him to study sociology. He began his sociological career under C. W. M. Hart and Ray Birdwhistell while at the University of Toronto, where he also met the anthropologist Elizabeth Bott. Under Hart he became influenced by Durkheim, Radcliffe-Brown and Parsons (Fine and Manning, 2000: 458).

The Move to Chicago

After graduating in 1945, Goffman moved to the University of Chicago, one of the leading US sociology departments at the time. Although he found the transition to graduate studies difficult, he met other students including Howard Becker, Joseph Gusfield and Gregory Stone. He also became interested in the work of Freud, Proust and Sartre. His teachers included Kenneth Burke, C. W. Mills, Robert Burgess, Everett Hughes, Daniel Bell and David Reisman. For his Master's thesis, supervised by Lloyd Warner, he undertook research on audience responses to a radio soap, collecting data from over 50 upper-class women. After questioning its methodological basis, he developed his own research scheme examining direct and indirect responses, which he completed in 1949. The next two years were spent on the island of Unst, part of the Shetland Isles, undertaking fieldwork for his doctoral dissertation. During this period he was also affiliated with the Department of Anthropology at the University of Edinburgh run by Ralph Piddington. Goffman returned to Chicago in 1952, and in July of that year married Angelica Schuyler Choate, a psychology graduate, with whom he had a son, Tom. The next year he defended his thesis, entitled 'Communication Conduct in an Island Community'. In the thesis he pointedly remarks 'This is not the study of a community: it is a study that occurred *in* a community' (Winkin, 1999: 26). Thus, rather than analysing the social structure of the community, as had been suggested by his supervisors, his focus switched to patterns of interaction and communication. As a result, the thesis was severely criticised by Warner and Everett Hughes. He moved to Bethesda near Washington in 1954 as a 'visiting scientist' in the National Institute of Mental Health. One year of this was spent undertaking observations at the St. Elizabeth's Hospital, under the guise of assistant to the athletic director. This research was subsequently developed and published as *Asylums* (1961). In 1957 he was invited by Herbert Blumer to take a position as visiting assistant professor in the Department of Sociology at Berkeley, California. Parts of his doctoral thesis became the basis for his first major book, *The Presentation of Self in Everyday Life* (1959). In the same year, he published an important paper on status degradation and impression management, 'On Cooling the Mark Out' (1952). Although *Presentation* received good reviews, his fellow faculty members were not impressed: 'The work is thought to be too soft, too literary, while the person appears too abrasive, too difficult' (Winkin, 1999: 28). Nevertheless, Goffman was promoted to full professor in 1962, a year after the publication of both *Asylums* (1961) and *Encounters* (1961). These works were followed two years later by *Stigma* (1963) and *Behavior in Public Places* (1963), which continued his focus on self-presentation strategies and communicative gestures.

Anecdotes appear to suggest that Goffman was ambivalent about his teaching and university life (Winkin, 1999). He was also a keen gambler, often attending casinos in Las Vegas, counting cards in blackjack, and betting both for pleasure and ethnographic purposes. He trained to become a blackjack dealer, and some of these experiences were later discussed in his book, *Interaction Ritual* (1967). In 1964 his wife, who had mental health issues, sadly committed suicide. During a sabbatical year at the Harvard Center for International Relations in 1966 Goffman came into contact and under the influence of Thomas Schelling, whose game-theoretic accounts of human action featured in Goffman's book *Strategic Interaction* (1969). In 1968 he took up the Benjamin Franklin Chair in Sociology and Anthropology at the University of Pennsylvania. There he developed his notion of human interaction as an extension of animal interaction or ethology, later elaborated in his book *Relations in Public* (1971), while simultaneously working on what he considered his most important book, *Frame Analysis*. The latter, which took a decade in the making, was eventually published in 1974. In 1979 Goffman published *Gender Advertisements* (1979) and, a couple of years later, a highly original analysis of the structure of conversations, *Forms of Talk* (1981). In the same year he married his second wife, Gillian Sankoff, a linguist, with whom he had a daughter, Alice. After contracting stomach cancer he died on 20 November 1982. His planned paper to the American Sociological Association, which had intended to bring his work full circle with his doctoral dissertation, was posthumously published a year later as 'The Interaction Order' (1983).

Intellectual Influences

Numerous prominent sociologists including Albion Small, G. H. Mead, Robert Park, W. I. Thomas and Herbert Blumer taught at Chicago, which became the leading department of sociology in the United States from the early 1900s until the arrival of Talcott Parsons at Harvard. Although Goffman never referred to Mead, Thomas or Blumer in his work, it is clear that aspects of the symbolic interactionist perspective influenced his work. His eschewal of a grand overarching theory and the development instead of relatively concrete concepts and ideas through case studies demonstrate this. The importance of the social self, a core focus of Mead in his distinction between the 'I' and the 'Me', also appears evident in Goffman's work. However, Goffman questioned the utility of the label 'interactionist' as applied to him, arguing that such labelling was both unnecessary and misleading – 'I don't believe the label covers anything' (Verhoeven, 1993: 317). He also criticised the approach for its restricted focus on the definition of the situation and social meanings, while ignoring actors' motives, moves and strategies (*Strategic Interaction* (1969)). Other influences on his work include Simmel, a thinker many of the Chicago School were sympathetic towards following his introduction into the United States by Albion Small. Simmel not only provided idiosyncratic and quirky analyses of everyday life such as flirting, for example, but more generally focused on society as a web of patterned interactions. Simmel attempted to study these latter sociations in diverse settings, by examining small-scale aspects of behaviour through his formal method of sociology as well as developing various typologies and classifications (Smith, 2006: 31).

The other classical sociologist who had an immense influence on Goffman's approach was Durkheim as well as the anthropologist influenced by his work, Radcliffe Brown (Collins 1986; 1988). It was Durkheim's *Elementary Forms of Religious Life* (1912), with its focus on rituals in which individuals in face-to-face situations develop a mutually aware focus of attention on objects and symbols, including religious symbols, and through a process of social effervescence develop a shared emotional mood and moral sentiments, that deeply impressed Goffman. As Collins notes:

> Goffman spent much time following up Durkheim's remark that the individual had become the principle 'sacred object' in modern secular society. Thus, unlike Mead, Thomas, and Blumer, the self in Goffman is not something that individuals negotiate out of social interactions: it is, rather, the archetypal modern myth. We are compelled to have an individual self, not because we actually have one but because social interaction requires us to act as if we do. (2000 [1986]: 74)

Other more specialised influences include: Sartre (Goffman had spent a year in Paris at the Sorbonne writing his thesis); Thomas Schelling, whose strategy of conflict examined strategic and bargaining or conflictual behaviour and influenced Goffman's view of strategic interaction; Ray Birdwhistell, who analysed body motion and the symbolic significance of behaviour; Gregory Bateson, who undertook animal behavioural studies and whose ethological approach had a strong influence on Goffman; and finally the work of linguistic philosophers such as Austin and Wittgenstein, who influenced his later work on language and conversation analysis as did Schutz and Garfinkel.

Historical, Social and Political Context

At the end of the Second World War, the United States' fear of communism spreading to the West saw the emergence of a protracted global Cold War manifesting a deep political antagonism based on the threat of nuclear war and destruction. This constituted the political framework within which all nation-states developed for the next 40 years. Economically speaking, the post-war United States experienced a huge explosion of economic demand for goods and services following an intense period of war-directed production, creating an acute demand for workers, which would continue for the next few decades.

Burgeoning production and consumption during the 1950s paradoxically saw both the emergence of a broad social conservatism and simultaneously the emergence of rebellious youth cultures focused on music, especially rock and roll, and, over time, the development during the 1960s of anti-establishment forms of counter-culture challenging the values of the American social system. The 1960s were marked simultaneously by continuing economic expansion and growth, and by deep political and social crises including the Civil Rights movement, increasing class conflict and peace protests against war. In 1960 J. F. Kennedy, a liberally inclined Democrat, became President, and a confident and optimistic mood swept the country. Unemployment remained low and with increasing investment in higher education, few doctoral students remained without work. When Kennedy was assassinated in November 1963, his Vice President Johnston took over, announcing a 'War on Poverty' in the United States – later part of a 'Great Society' programme of Medicaid for the needy. The investment in welfare and education measures also entailed the growth of a massively expanding and imposing state bureaucracy and credential sector.

Development of Discourses of Self-expression and Freedom

With the simultaneous growth of the media during the 1960s new forms of self-expression especially for a small, but already burgeoning oppositional youth, also began to develop. Traditional relations of authority, gender relations, war, sexuality (with the emergence of birth control), racial segregation and censorship became increasingly challenged through popular music, literature and fashion. Often espousing alternative anti-establishment values centred on a liberation of the self as a free actor, this younger oppositional generation also promoted the use of psychotic drugs to enhance free expression, and established a focus on peace and love as manifested by hippies. In the context of the development of the free self, the 1960s also saw the emergence of an anti-psychiatry movement stimulated by the work of Thomas Szasz, David Cooper, R. D. Laing, as well as Michel Foucault, who regarded psychiatry as part of the problem rather than solution for mental illness. This socio-cultural context facilitated the reception of Goffman's work, especially *Asylum* and *Stigma*, which were two of his most popular books, read widely outside of academic circles. *Asylum* alone sold over a million copies and helped to establish Goffman as a 'hero-anthropologist' (Collins, 1980: 171). But the same socio-political context foregrounding free individuals and self-expression also ensured his work was read in a certain way – a reading emphasising agency, and the social construction of reality by individuals in the context of the oppressiveness of organisations. In examining Goffman's popular reception Collins notes:

> Goffman resonates with the public moods over the years. He treated games and strategies, con men and international espionage amid the nuclear shadows of the CIA-infested 1960s. He conveyed a sense of

why people are wary of each other on the public street that went far beyond the violence of crime, protest, and ghetto uprising. And he leapfrogged to a deeper level of reflexivity upon the mind-blowing happenings of the psychedelic era. (1980: 171)

There was, however, a major shift in the socio-political milieu characterising the United States in the 1970s. The early to mid-1970s saw the emergence of stagflation following an oil crisis and a period of protracted recession in the American economy. In the wake of the ongoing disastrous war in Vietnam, Nixon began an invasion of Cambodia in 1970. His impeachment in 1974 following the Watergate affair publicly demonstrated the high level of corruption in politics, and the widespread deception practised by politicians. More corruption was made evident during the Carter administration, which replaced Ford as President in 1977, as FBI investigations discovered that congressmen were taking bribes. The year of 1981 saw the swearing in of Ronald Reagan on a platform of increasing defence spending and lowering of taxes through a reduction of domestic programmes.

According to Berman, Goffman's writing in the late 1960s and early 1970s and especially his book *Relations in Public* depict the major changes underway in American society following Nixon's inauguration. Everyday life now became menacingly 'ominous, fraught with hidden dangers' (Berman, 2000: 273–4).

Ambivalence Towards Politics

Goffman spent a considerable part of his academic years at both Chicago and Berkeley, both politically progressive academic institutions. However, his own political position remained ambiguous and he tended to remain aloof from politics and political processes. His reluctance to speak about himself and provide a biographical context for his writings, and the cool detachment with which he wrote on moral and emotional issues, exacerbated this issue. As Gamson notes:

> Someone once asked Goffman, 'What are your politics?' He seemed momentarily taken aback by the question. 'My "politics?" (pause) I don't think I have any "politics". (Another pause.) If anything, anarchist.' But his politics were certainly not anarchist in the anarcho-syndicalist tradition. (1985: 605)

Some writers, namely Mary Rogers (1980: 102–3), Marshall Berman (2000) and Tom Burns (1992: 60), have seen Goffman's work, and especially his moral stance, as implicitly progressive and aimed at freeing or valuing the individual against the constraints of hierarchy, power and status and their effects on the social self. This, they argue, is especially evident in his support for the underdog in *Asylum* and *Stigma*, which examine the humiliations and curtailments individuals conceived as different or damaged face through categorisation and marginalisation. Berman refers to him as the 'Kafka of our time' (2000: 267), who communicates the horror, anguish and absurdity of modern everyday life developing a politics of authenticity in referring to the individual's quest for selfhood and identity, a central feature of 1960s life. However, others have pointed to the more conservative political aspect of his thinking and writing, and his obsession with social order and its reproduction. According to Gouldner, Goffman's sociology with its focus on the construction of the self was a symptom and manifestation of the new bourgeois welfare state social order that existed in the United States after the Second World War:

> The dramaturgical model reflects the new world, in which a stratum of the middle class no longer believes that hard work is useful or that success depends upon diligent application. In this new world there is a keen sense of the irrationality of the relationship between individual achievement and the magnitude of reward, between actual contribution and social reputation... Dramaturgy marks the transition from an older economy centred on production to a new one centred on mass marketing and promotion, including the marketing of the self. (Gouldner, 1972: 381)

Equally Collins argues that Goffman's focus on how the social structure was ritually stratified, and how individuals enact rituals to maintain the normative order of society, made him a defender of the status quo: 'Goffman was always much more conservative than most of his public thought him ... *Asylums* itself, like Goffman's other writings on mental illness, explicitly says that mental hospitals and the social pressures towards conformity are functionally necessary for the protection of society's roles as a whole' (2000 [1986]: 74).

Ideas and Arguments

Goffman's work may be usefully divided into three phases (Collins, 2000 [1986]: 79). An early phase from the 1950s to mid-1960s examined interaction rituals and the self; a second phase covering the mid-1960s to the mid-1970s analysed strategic interactions, moves and counter-moves by actors based on a Machiavellian model; a final phase from the mid-1970s was increasingly preoccupied with human thought, language and social epistemology.

Traversing these phases and constituting a central theme underpinning and running through the 11 major books he published is the notion of an 'interaction order'. This involved two or more individuals in face-to-face interaction within a social situation (Goffman, 1983: 1). Such a narrow focus on physical co-presence or 'body to body' social interactions (Goffman, 1983: 1) as a substantive domain in its own right differentiates his analysis from sociological approaches that centre on the contrast between, for example, village and city life, or domestic and public settings. It constitutes a form of micro-sociological analysis that diverges from more large-scale macro approaches characteristic of thinkers such as Marx, Durkheim and Parsons.

For Goffman, society is composed of series of encounters in which two or more individuals take account of each other's behaviour. This meant the sociologist had to reveal the taken-for-granted, insignificant, almost trivial, aspects of human behaviour as manifested in social encounters of 'co-presence'. He designated these as forms of 'impression management' or 'face-work'. In explaining social interactions Goffman often utilises a series of metaphors, the most central one of which is the dramaturgical analogy. Social life is akin to a stage or theatre performance in which individuals all wear masks and play roles – analogous to Shakespeare's claim that 'all the world is a stage'. Connected to this metaphor are two dialectically interpenetrating and sometimes conflicting images of actors as on the one hand, highly moral and concerned with maintaining and (re)producing the social order through everyday rituals and routines, and on the other of social agents undertaking self-interested and strategic actions in order to improve the impressions others have of them and in order to maintain their face.

Early Writings

The ideas and arguments presented in Goffman's early work up to, and including, *The Presentation of Self* (1959) often reappear and provide the groundwork for his later analyses. His Master's thesis explored the connection between socio-economic status and personality, challenging the appropriateness of quantitative and positivistic forms of methodology in interpreting Thematic Apperception Test (TAT) responses. More explicit and refined discussions of impression management and performance with reference to class status reappear in his first published essay, 'Symbols of Class Status' (1951). According to Goffman, 'specialised' status symbols for displaying one's social position can be used in a 'fraudulent' way 'to signify a status which the claimant does not in fact possess' (1951: 296). That is, they can be employed to give the impression of a person possessing a higher social status than they actually have. Goffman then outlines the existence of a number of mechanisms in the social world restricting the opportunities for this deception to take place.

Cooling the Mark

In a subsequent paper, 'On Cooling the Mark Out' (1952), Goffman discusses how individuals adapt to failure or loss 'with defences, strategies, consolation, mitigations, compensations and the like' (Goffman, 1952: 463). As Fine et al. note: 'with its explicit use of metaphor and its open concern with the self this paper marks the point at which Goffman discovered he was Goffman' (2000: xviii). Fraudulent practices centred on misrepresentation again reappear but this time through the case study of confidence tricksters, 'cons' who defraud victims, 'marks', so that the 'victims find they must suddenly adapt themselves to the loss of sources of security and status which they had taken for granted' (Goffman, 1952: 451). After the mark loses his or her total investment as a competent, shrewd member of society, they are expected to go on their way 'a little wiser but poorer' (1952: 452). However, some may report the matter to the police or chase the perpetrators. To avoid such an awkward scenario the con artists may leave one of their members behind with the mark to act as a 'cooler', to keep 'the anger of the mark within manageable or sensible proportions' (1952: 452). Such acts show that following the 'self-destruction of the self', the self has to adapt through repair work, and such a process can be generalised to examine the operation of the self and its 'involvements' in statuses and roles operating and functioning throughout society.

Goffman's analysis provides insights into the nature of the self in society, especially its profoundly social nature. Persons who become involved in roles and statuses make public claims to possess a value or property in question. The sense of self tied to a status requires validation by social organisations and other persons.

The Importance of Face

Goffman develops this idea of the self in another important essay, 'On Face Work' (1967 [1955]), in which he draws heavily on Durkheim's emphasis on the moral dimension of society, in which emotional sentiments and feelings of right and wrong are central. There are a number of key concepts running throughout Goffamn's work including: the individual, the self, stigma and interaction order, but perhaps the most important, is face. In social encounters individuals act out what can be called a *line* – a 'pattern of verbal and non-verbal acts by which he expresses his view of the situation and through this his evaluation of the participants, especially himself [sic]' (1967: 5). This self-image is necessarily connected with possessing a *face* – a positive social value that an individual claims for him- or herself based on social attributes (1967: 5). In this scenario individuals continually monitor not only themselves, but also the responses of others with whom they interact, modifying their actions in accord with presenting a line and performance that is deemed adequate by others. Such lines, maintained during contact with others, 'tend to be of a legitimate institutionalised kind'. They are pregiven supplied by society rather than inhering or created by the individual. This equally applies to face:

> The person's face clearly is something that is not lodged in or on his body, but rather something that is diffusely located in the flow of events in the encounter and becomes manifest only when these events are read and interpreted for the appraisals expressed in them. (1967: 7)

Lines and face are analogous to the existence of a limited number of different masks supplied by society that individuals wear on different socially determined occasions, in order to ensure a particular *expressive order* is sustained. Social actors aim to save their own face not only by maintaining or being in face in order to maintain self-respect and pride, but also through considerateness, tact, and duty, towards sustaining the face of others. They monitor and evaluate the responses of others on an ongoing basis, attempting to avoid loss of face, which entails emotional feelings of embarrassment, and instead seeking pride. Goffman refers to this as 'face-work'.

According to Goffman, the self then is not an enclosed private attribute of individuals but a public, institutionalised reality, penetrated and created by society and constructed in public interactions: 'while his social face can be his most personal possession and the centre of his security and pleasure, it is only on loan to him from society' (1967: 10). Although face-saving practices vary across cultures, all societies, by and large, require them in order to exist as social orders.

The Presentation of Self

In *The Presentation of Self in Everyday Life* (1959) Goffman provides his most systematic outline of his sociological approach to social life understood as a staged performance. According to Goffman, interactions entail performances: 'the activity of a given participant on a given occasion which serves to influence in any way any of the other participants' (1984: 26) and are undertaken to depict a sense of 'realness'. In these performances individuals give off signals in their expressive conduct not only through what they say and their appearance – *the impression that he or she gives* – but also and more importantly through involuntary expressive behaviour, such as body language – *the impression that he or she gives off*. This information combined with the individuals' past experiences of interactions in similar situations and with similar types of people, help to shape the individuals' definition of the situation and determine how they will undertake a performance corresponding with that definition. Individuals simultaneously attempt to shape the definition of the situation in accord with their interests. Goffman gives the example of a girl who, because her dormitory mates will adduce evidence of her popularity by the number of phone calls she receives, will arrange to have calls made in order to influence the definition of the situation, to convey a desired self-image. However, behaviour should not be understood solely as intentionally self-interested and calculated.

Given that individuals are likely to present themselves in a way that is favourable to them, others may consciously focus on the impression they unintentionally give off, rather than the controllable impression they provide. Thus, one crofter's wife on the Shetland Isles would not only listen for the compliments she received for the meal she had cooked for a guest, but also observe the eagerness with which the guest ate the food. However, an individual in turn, in knowing he or she is being observed, may exploit this possibility by deliberately eating fast. This manipulation of what are ordinarily deemed spontaneous aspects of behaviour produces an 'information game, a potentially infinite cycle of concealment, discovery, false revelation and rediscovery' (1984: 20).

Front and Backstage

Goffman extends the dramaturgical metaphor by distinguishing between regions of behaviour, more specifically between a front and a backstage, which constitute a physical and socio-spatial division. The 'front' is 'the expressive equipment of a standard kind intentionally or unwittingly employed by the individual during his performance' (1984: 32). This may entail 'a setting', usually fixed, including furniture, physical layout, as well as background items which as 'stage props' provide scenery for the performance, for example a living room. It may also include a 'personal front' – expressive equipment or sign vehicles such as insignia of rank, clothing, sex, gender and ethnic characteristics, size and looks, posture, speech patterns, bodily and facial gestures. The personal front can be divided according to 'appearance', which tells us the performer's social status, as well as the temporary 'ritual state' – whether the performer is engaging in formal or recreational activity, and 'manner', which tells us of the interaction role that the performer will play in the oncoming situation, for example by deploying an aggressive or apologetic manner. Audiences usually expect some consistency between appearance, manner and setting, for example a doctor wearing a white coat, talking to patients in a detached manner.

A discrepancy between these may lead to concern. Moreover, fronts tend to become institutionalised with stereotyped expectations tied to them – they become in Durkheim's words 'collective representations'. As a result: 'when an actor takes on an established role, usually [s]he finds that a particular front has already been established for it.' Thus: 'fronts tend to be selected not created' (1984: 37, 38). Again, repeating claims from his analysis of face, he argues actors choose a front from those which are socially available which they deem fits the situation. Sometimes fronts required to fit a situation may not exist, leading to strained and questioned performances and a failure to impose a definition of the situation. For an individual's activity to become significant for others, it needs to be *dramatically realised* – he or she must mobilise his or her activity 'so that it will express during the interaction what [s]he wishes to convey' (1984: 40). The front region of a performance to a public can be contrasted with the backstage or back region, a more private realm, where suppressed, or unrevealed aspects of the self reside. As he notes:

> A back region or backstage may be defined as a place, relative to a given performance, where the impression fostered by the performance is knowingly contradicted as a matter of course... Here the performer can relax; he can drop his front, forgo speaking his lines, and step out of character. (1984: 114–15)

Since the vital secrets of a show are usually kept backstage, away from the public gaze, it is important that this remains invisible to the audience. Regions are bounded to some degree by barriers to perception. Goffman gives many examples of the divide between front and backstage outside of the theatre context, for example between the kitchen space and dining space in the hotel in the Shetlands where he worked, or between bathrooms and bedrooms on the one hand and living rooms and front rooms on the other, where guests are met: 'Bodies that are cleansed and clothed and made up in these rooms can be presented to friends in others' (1984: 124–15). As individuals move from backstage to the front they reveal a putting on and off of character.

Goffman's concern about the structure of self remains a central feature of the book. His position challenges the view of a self-directing, coherent, autonomous, sovereign self that brings about or creates the social world. Instead, like Mead, he attempts to discern what the self is externally, and from the outside so to speak, by examining the conduct of social individuals. However, Goffman appears to have a fractured image of the self: a human self, a performing self, and the self as a character.

As he notes:

> The expressive coherence that is required in performances points out a crucial discrepancy between our all-too-human selves and our socialized selves. As human beings we are presumably creatures of variable impulse with moods and energies that change from one moment to the next. As characters put on for an audience, however, we must not be subject to ups and downs. (1984: 63)

However, his understanding of the self tends to alter in his other writings (Goffman, 1974: 573–4; Manning, 1992: 44–6; Branaman, 1997: li; Smith, 2006: 101). There is, for example, a shift in discussion from the self as a rational, calculative, manipulator which is in thrall to its emotions, and therefore lacking individuality, on the one hand, and a view of the self as a sacred individual who needs to be venerated in the Durkheimian sense, on the other.

Damaged and Confined Selves: Asylum, Stigma and Gender

Asylum

According to Goffman not all selves in modern societies have acquired the sacred attribution of personhood – there also exist 'non-persons', 'problematic' or non-normal individuals who do not fit so easily into the interaction order. These are the focus of three major works: *Asylums* (1961), *Stigma* (1963) and *Gender Advertisements* (1979). *Asylums* was based on a year's fieldwork at St. Elizabeth's Hospital in Washington, DC, between 1955 and 1956. Subtitled *Essays on the Social Situation of Mental Patients and Other Inmates*, the book underpins the concept of the total institution:

> A total institution may be defined as a place of residence and work where a large number of like-situated individuals, cut off from the wider society for an appreciable period of time, together lead an enclosed, formally administered round of life. (1991: 11)

Such institutions possess 'encompassing tendencies' or a 'total character' and are spatially and physically divided off from an outside world, for example architecturally, including locked doors, high walls, barbed wire, cliffs, etc. Moreover, many provide different functions:

- care for persons incapable or harmless – the elderly and sick, aged, orphans;
- care of those incapable of looking after themselves and who may represent a threat to the community – TB sanitaria and mental hospitals;
- those designed to protect the community from intentional dangers – prisons, POW camps;
- those designed to pursue a work-like task – boarding schools, work camps;
- those designed as retreats from the world – monasteries and convents (1991: 16).

Despite their differences, they share certain characteristics or family resemblances. A taken-for-granted attribute of modern societies is that the individual tends to sleep, play and work in different places, mingling with individuals under diverse regimes of authority, without an overarching plan determining this. However, total institutions dissolve these barriers:

> First, all aspects of life are conducted in the same place and under the same single authority. Second, each phase of the member's daily activity is carried on in the immediate company of a large batch of others, all of whom are treated alike and required to do the same thing together. Third, all phases of the day's activities are tightly scheduled, with one activity leading at a prearranged time into the next, the whole sequence of activities being imposed from above by a system of explicit formal rulings and a body of officials. Finally, the various enforced activities are brought together into a single rational plan purportedly designed to fulfill the official aims of the institution. (1991: 17)

A central feature of total institutions is the handling of a diversity of needs of a large group of people, split off and held at a considerable social and communicative distance, by a small supervisory staff. This takes place within a bureaucratic type of organisation geared towards a surveillance of their activities.

When examining the induction of patients into the mental asylum Goffman notes that the inmates arrive with a 'presenting culture' derived from their home world and entailing taken-for-granted expectations and norms about societal living, coping strategies, and stable social arrangements and supports. On entry into the institution, however, these supports are stripped from them through a series of 'abasements, degradations, humiliations, and profanations of self' (1991: 24). As a result, the self becomes 'mortified' causing a shift in the individual's moral career as his or her earlier role schedule becomes disrupted, creating role dispossession and following a loss of contact with the outside world. Such processes of initiation and 'welcome' aimed at securing deference may involve an 'obedience' or 'will breaking test' with the inmate to assess and shape his or her future compliance. Not only is personal clothing taken away, but so are intimate possessions such as cosmetics, which normally supply individuals with an 'identity kit' needed for the management of their personal fronts. The loss of equipment prevents individuals from presenting their usual image of themselves to others. The territories of the self thereby become violated through contaminative exposure, as things, persons and feeling, which in the outside world could be held at a distance, now invade the self through enforced interpersonal contacts and practices.

Moreover, the staff at the asylum as 'people workers', who retain contact with the outside world, remain trapped between the dictates of providing humane treatment to inmates as ends in themselves and meeting the requirements for institutional efficiency, which they rationalise in various ways. They also avoid developing sympathetic identification with patients in order to prevent being emotionally 'burned'.

Stigma

In *Stigma* (1963), subtitled *Notes on the Management of Spoiled Identity*, Goffman analyses individuals disqualified from full social acceptance. Categorising persons and the attributes that are deemed to be ordinary and natural is, he argues, a social process. Stigma refers to an attribute that is 'deeply discrediting' and Goffman makes an important distinction between the plight of the discredited and the discreditable. The former refers to visible stigmas that are known or evident on the spot, while the latter designates those that are invisible and are yet unknown by others. He identifies three different discredited forms of stigma that identify their holders as different from 'normals' within situations of 'mixed contact':

> First there are abominations of the body – the various physical deformities. Next there are blemishes of individual character perceived as weak will, domineering or unnatural passions, treacherous and rigid beliefs, and dishonesty, these being inferred from a known record of, for example, mental disorder, imprisonment, addiction, alcoholism, homosexuality, unemployment, suicidal attempts, and radical political behaviour. Finally there are the tribal stigma of race, nation, and religion, these being stigma that can be transmitted through lineages and equally contaminate all members of a family. (1990: 14)

It can be the case that those deemed to have a stigma also view the world in the same terms as normals do, of perceiving themselves as flawed, of having a stigma, of possessing a damaged or spoiled social identity.

Nevertheless, discredited individuals respond to their situation in different ways. They may try to correct the physical failing, or feel that they are constantly 'on' and immersed in impression management and the continuing regulation of tensions generated in social interactions. Many stigmatised individuals therefore have similar moral careers in terms of their plight and changes in their self conception. By contrast, the central focus of those individuals who are deemed discreditable is on managing information about their failing: 'To display or not to display; to tell or not to tell; to let on or not to let on; to lie or not to lie; and in each case, to whom, how, when, and where' (1990: 57). In this context Goffman refers to 'passing'. Passing involves concealing a stigma possibly through dissimulation, on a day-to-day basis.

The Framing of Gender

Goffman continues his analysis of disadvantaged categories of persons in his work on gender. In *Gender Advertisements* (1979 [1976]) he examines how gender relations enacted in social situations are reproduced through ritualised gestures and ceremonies which both affirm basic social arrangements through solemnisation, and simultaneously present benchmark doctrines about humans and the world. As part of expressive behaviour, gender displays are assumed to derive from an individual's biological nature. However, rather than using the 'doctrine of natural expression' to attempt to account for gender expressions, Goffman emphasises the portrayal of gender as a social accomplishment:

> What the human nature of males and females really consists of, then, is a capacity to learn to provide and read depictions of masculinity and femininity and a willingness to adhere to a schedule for presenting these pictures, and this capacity they have by virtue of being persons, not females or males. One might just as well say there is no gender identity. There is only a schedule for the portrayal of gender. (1979: 8)

Such scheduled portrayals operate through rituals which affirm individuals' place in the social order and entail ideal conceptions of the two sexes and their structural relationship. It is through social interactions in social situations, through gender displays – which offer 'evidence of the actor's alignment in a gathering' and which draw on stereotyped cultural differences – that a hierarchical gendered social structure is reproduced. These ritualistic aspects are subsequently adopted, reproduced and amplified by commercial advertisements:

> By and large, advertisers do not create the ritualized expressions they employ; they seem to draw upon the same corpus of displays, the same ritual idiom, that is the resource of all of us who participate in social situations, and to the same end: the rendering of glimpsed action readable. If anything, advertisers conventionalize our conventions, stylize what is already a stylization, make frivolous use of what is already something considerably cut off from contextual controls. Their hype is hyper-ritualization. (1979: 84)

Framing and Forms of Talk

Although he continues to examine the relation between self and society throughout his writings, there is a marked shift in Goffman's later sociological vision, which is evident in *Gender Advertisements* but rooted in his work *Frame Analysis* (1974), subtitled *An Essay on the Organization of Experience*. Not only is this Goffman's longest book, but it is also more abstract and generalised than earlier work. Drawing on a phenomenological, hermeneutical and cognitive approach he aims to understand the principles that shape our everyday experience, how we perceive the world around us and how these perceptions are organised.

By analysing 'strips' from the ongoing stream of social activity Goffman argues that people subjectively understand social situations and events by imposing frames upon them, a term borrowed from Gregory Bateson. Frames help to shape the definition of the situation and the goings on around individuals, providing a shared 'footing'. Frames shape both the meaning of a situation and the normative expectations required within it. In the social world there exists multiple frames, with frames imposed upon frames. When undertaking social analysis, sociologists add a further frame of understanding upon the multiple frames that everyday actors use.

The last chapter of the book, 'Frames of Talk', examines interactants' conversations and statements. The themes initially discussed here are developed and elaborated in Goffman's last book, *Forms of Talk*, especially by examining three themes characterising talk: ritualisation, participation frameworks and embedding (1981: 3). Much talk, he argues, takes place in social interactions aimed at aligning a person with another in that interaction. Even 'self-talk', talking to oneself, for example exclaiming expletives or saying 'oops', are used in social interactions as a part of impression management, through curse words or 'response cries'. Such cries do not so much express an emotion as indicate a social stance towards a situation and the impression one is aiming to make in that situation, of saving one's face. Hence for example, by exclaiming 'oops', an individual is attempting to convey they are for the most part a competent member of society who ordinarily does not drop things or make mistakes.

Contemporary Relevance and Applications

A Goffmanian school of sociology has failed to emerge, partly given the difficulty of reproducing his eclectic methodological style of approach. But it is also partly a result of the difficulty of reproducing Goffman's profound insights into the minutia of social life. Bourdieu (1980), for example, refers to him as the 'discoverer of the infinitely small'. His work has nevertheless been influential. His writings on social interactions have been taken up and used by amongst others Anthony Giddens, Jeffrey Alexander and Pierre Bourdieu. His writings also have strong parallels with the work of Norbert Elias (Kuzmics, 1991) and Foucault (Burns, 1992). More explicitly, his theorising has featured markedly in the work of Randall Collins, Thomas Scheff, and in the gender analysis of Candace West and Don Zimmerman.

THE PRESENTATION OF THE ONLINE SELF

Goffman's theory provides an especially suitable explanatory framework for considering self-presentation in the online world. It has informed analyses of digital identities on social networking sites as well as self-presentation in online dating. Though there are important substantive differences between online and offline sociation affecting aspects of Goffman's theory, such as the absence of face-to-face interaction and the abstraction of the audience from direct observation, the central concerns of the dramaturgical approach are essentially enhanced in computer-mediated interaction. Social media intensify the strategic negotiation between actor and audience, shaping attempts to stage a character. A curated digital self occupies the online front stage. With successful self-presentation dependent upon communicating a favourable self-image, the concept of impression management becomes central for considering the selectivity and editing behind such digital selves. Of critical concern today is to what extent authentic self-presentation is possible online, and how the dominance of selective self-presentation affects the self more generally.

In his book *Microsociology* (1990), Scheff draws on Goffman's different analyses of interaction situations, especially his focus on face, deference and embarrassment, to develop a general micro-oriented sociology connecting emotions with human action. Rather than focusing on motives in isolated individuals, as has traditionally been the case, Scheff focuses on the importance of social bonds in shaping motives. Central to this is a communication system, involving language which enables speakers to make known each other's thoughts, and a deference–emotion system that enables the evaluation of others' status, which for the most part is non-verbal. Such processes permit 'reciprocal ratification'. Here the deference individuals receive from others is crucial in guiding their actions as their emotions lead them to seek a sense of pride in interactions while avoiding a sense of shame, or loss of face. For Scheff, drawing on the work of Helen Lewis and Goffman, individuals can become caught in feeling traps based on shame or embarrassment:

> Goffman suggests that embarrassment is especially contagious between interactants; and Lewis, within them. Lewis suggests that the original stimulus for shame, say a comment that one takes to be critical of self, may be only the first step in a long shame sequence. Once ashamed, one can be ashamed of being ashamed, each shame state serving as stimulus for further shame. For this reason, she implies, it is possible for shame-prone persons to be in a more or less chronic shame state. (Scheff, 1990: 18)

Goffman's work has also made an important contribution to gender studies where it shares similarities with the work of Judith Butler. In their article 'Doing Gender', West and Zimmerman (1987) critically extend Goffman's notion of gender display while also drawing on the work of Harold Garfinkel. The authors make a marked distinction between sex, sex category and gender. Sex entails the assignment of a newborn on the basis of socially agreed upon biological criteria to one of two sexes on the basis of genitalia or sometimes chromosomal typing before birth. Although placement in a sex category is achieved through the application of sex criteria, in everyday life it is sustained by socially required identificatory displays that proclaims one's membership, external insignia of sex including dress, deportment and bearing. It therefore become possible to claim membership in a sex category even when sex criteria are missing. Finally, gender is the activity of managing situated conduct in light of normative expectations and attitudes, being accountable to cultural conceptions of conduct. Gender is not something rooted in biologically given differences, nor an characteristic of individuals, but a routine, a methodological accomplishment embedded in everyday interactions. It is not a given attribute, something ascribed, but something routinely achieved in social situations in which individuals 'do' gender – that is they enact a performance:

> In one sense, of course, it is individuals who 'do' gender. But it is a situated doing, carried out in the virtual or real presence of others who are presumed to be oriented to its production. Rather than as a property of individuals, we conceive of gender as an emergent feature of social situations: both as an outcome of and a rationale for various social arrangements and as a means of legitimating one of the most fundamental divisions of society. (West and Zimmerman, 1987: 126)

The authors also draw on Garfinkel's (1967) study of Agnes to illustrate their argument. The accomplishment of gender is simultaneously interactional and institutional. Gender hegemony is a social product which is amenable to social change (West and Zimmerman, 2009: 114). This analysis was further extended to examine the intersections between gender, ethnicity and class in 'Doing Difference' (West and Fenstermaker, 1995).

Criticisms

Although many have seen Goffman's work as illuminating the everydayness of encounters that humans take for granted, he has often been read as someone whose writings are hugely entertaining but who fails to engage in deep sociological problems. The most sustained criticism of Goffman comes from Alvin Gouldner (1972). For Gouldner, Goffman's dramaturgical approach focuses on appearances rather than underlying essences, and is ahistorical and non-institutional:

> It is a social theory that dwells upon the episodic and sees life only as it is lived in a narrow interpersonal circumference, ahistorical and noninstitutional, an existence beyond history and society. (1972: 379)

Goffman's approach, Gouldner argues, avoids examining social stratification and the importance of power differences in society. With its focus on episodic encounters of face-to-face interaction the important influence of the social structure 'drifts away into the background' (1972: 280). Thus, rather than examining how individuals seek to change the social structures, Goffman examines how they adapt to them – it is a theory of secondary adjustments. Moreover, Goffman fails to explain why some selves rather than others are selected and projected by persons or why others reject or accept such proffered selves. His approach simply reflects middle-class values. However, many of these abrasive criticisms have been refuted by Mary Rogers (1980), who argues that Goffman does acknowledge the role of power, hierarchy, institutions, class and status in his work.

Others have also criticised the superficiality of his work, arguing that it consists of a proliferation of taxonomies of interacting actors, a descriptive but not explanatory exercise wherein 'a confused or inchoate epistemic rationale struggling for expression meets a synoptic compulsion and is overwhelmed by it' (Cioffi, 2000: 102; 1971).

Other criticisms refer to Goffman's treatment of rules. Barnes argues that although Goffman moves beyond Parsons with regards to seeing norms and rules as open to examination and calculative manipulation by the actors, he has no clear account of norms, and therefore lacks a rigorous sociological account of social order: 'he is clear that we make norms interactively, but on the making he is silent' (1995: 74). In this regard, Barnes sees Garfinkel's work as superior (see also Manning, 1992: 156–65). Still other writers have found ambiguities in Goffman's discussion of the self. Macintyre, for example, has argued that Goffman is unsystematic in defining the self and when he does so, he does not apply those definitions consistently throughout his *oeuvre* (MacIntyre, 2000: 332). This may partly stem from the differing metaphors he employs with their different emphases on social interaction, the dramaturgical metaphor which emphasises impression management, the game metaphor which emphasises strategies, and the ritual metaphor which emphasises maintaining the social order. Finally, with regard to his last paper on the interaction order (Goffman, 1983), it remains unclear how the two spheres of an interactional order and a social structure are robustly connected.

Conclusion

Although often interpreted as providing a frivolous analysis of human foibles and quirks, Goffman's analysis provides a deep and fruitful account of the persistence and reproduction of the social order on an ongoing basis and its achievement by social actors. In some ways, through the multiplicity of his case studies, he also attempts to provide a substantive account of the importance of the moral individualism adumbrated in the philosophy of Rousseau and Kant, and the sociology of Durkheim. We can therefore understand his work in Durkheimian terms, as concerned with the increasing use of social rituals that treat the self or the other as a sacred object in society – the cult of the individual.

References

Barnes, B. (1995) *The Elements of Social Theory.* Princeton, NJ: Princeton University Press.
Berman, M. (2000) Weird But Brilliant Light on the Way We Live Now: Review of *Relations in Public*. In: G. A. Fine and G. W. H. Smith (eds) *Erving Goffman: A Four Volume Set.* London: Sage, pp. 266–277.
Bourdieu, P. (1980) 'Erving Goffman: Discoverer of the Infinitely Small'. In: G. A. Fine, P. Manning and G. W. H. Smith (eds) *Erving Goffman, Vol. 1.* London: Sage. pp. 1–2.
Branaman, A. (1997) Goffman's Social Theory. In: C. Lemert and A. Branaman (eds) *The Goffman Reader.* Malden, MA: Blackwell, pp. xlv–lxxxii.
Burns, T. (1992) *Erving Goffman.* London: Routledge.
Cioffi, F. (1971) Information, Contemplation and Social Life. In: G. N. A. Vesey (ed.) *The Proper Study: Royal Institute of Philosophy Lectures, Vol. 4.* London: Macmillan.
Cioffi, F. (2000) Stating the Obvious: What does Goffman Really Tell Us? In: G.A. Fine, P. Manning and G. W. H. Smith (eds) *Erving Goffman: Sage Masters of Modern Thought, Vol. 11.* London: Sage, pp. 97–104.
Collins, R. (2000 [1986]) The Passing of Intellectual Generations: Reflections on the Death of Erving Goffman. In: G. A. Fine, P. Manning and G. W. H. Smith (eds) *Erving Goffman: Sage Masters of Modern Thought Vol. 1.* London: Sage, pp. 71–83.
Collins, R. (1988) *Theoretical Sociology.* London: Harcourt Brace Jovanovich.
Fine, G. and Manning, P. (2000) Erving Goffman: Shifting Impressions and Tight Frames. In: G. Ritzer (ed.). *The Blackwell Companion to Major Social Theorists.* Oxford: Blackwell, pp. 457–485.
Fine, G. A., Manning, P. and Smith, G. W. H. (2000) Introduction. In: G. A. Fine, P. Manning and G. W. H. Smith (eds). *Erving Goffman, Vol. 1.* London: Sage, pp. ix–xliv.
Gamson, W. A. (1985) Goffman's Legacy to Political Sociology. *Theory and Society,* 14(5), pp. 605–22.
Garfinkel, H. (1967) *Studies in Ethnomethodology.* Englewood Cliffs, NJ: Prentice Hall.
Giddens, A. (1987) *Social Theory and Modern Sociology.* Cambridge: Polity.
Goffman, E. (1951) Symbols of Class Status. *British Journal of Sociology,* 2(4), pp. 294–304.
Goffman, E. (1952) On Cooling the Mark Out: Some Aspects of Adaptation to Failure. *Psychiatry,* 15(4), pp. 451–63.
Goffman, E. (1984 [1959]) *The Presentation of Self in Everyday Life.* Harmondsworth: Pelican.
Goffman, E. (1991 [1961]) *Asylums: Essays on the Social Situation of Mental Patients and Other Inmates.* London: Penguin.
Goffman, E. (1990 [1963]) *Stigma: Notes on the Management of Spoiled Identity.* London: Penguin.

Goffman, E. (1961) *Encounters: Two Studies in the Sociology of Interaction.* London: Allen Lane.
Goffman, E. (1963) *Behavior in Public Places: Notes on the Social Organization of Gatherings.* New York: Free Press.
Goffman, E. (1967) *Interaction Ritual: Essays on Face-to-face Behavior.* New York: Pantheon Books.
Goffman, E. (1969) *Strategic Interaction.* Oxford: Basil Blackwell.
Goffman, E. (1971) *Relations in Public: Microstudies of the Public Order.* New York: Basic Books.
Goffman, E. (1974) *Frame Analysis: An Essay on the Organization of Experience.* New York: Harper & Row.
Goffman, E. (1979) *Gender Advertisements.* Cambridge, MA: Harvard University Press.
Goffman, E. (1981) *Forms of Talk.* Oxford: Blackwell.
Goffman, E. (1983) The Interaction Order: American Sociological Association, 1982 Presidential Address. *American Sociological Review,* 48(1), pp. 1–17.
Gouldner, A. (1972) *The Coming Crisis of Western Sociology.* London: Heinemann Educational Books.
Kuzmics, H. (1991) Embarrassment and Civilization: On Some Similarities and Differences in the Work of Goffman and Elias. *Theory, Culture & Society,* 8(2), pp. 1–30.
Manning, P. (1992) *Erving Goffman and Modern Sociology.* Cambridge: Polity.
Rawls, A. (2000) The Interaction Order Sui Generis: Goffman's Contribution to Social Theory. In: G. Fine and G. Smith (eds) *Erving Goffman, Vol. 2.* Thousand Oaks, CA: Sage. pp. 252–74.
Rogers, M. F. (1980) Goffman on Power, Hierarchy, and Status. In: J. Ditton (ed.). *The View from Goffman.* London: Palgrave Macmillan, pp. 100–33.
Scheff, T. J. (1990) *Microsociology: Discourse, Emotion, and Social Structure.* Chicago, IL: University of Chicago Press.
Shalin, D. (2014) Interfacing Biography, Theory and History: The Case of Erving Goffman. *Symbolic Interactionism,* 37 (1), pp. 2–40.
Smith, G. (2006) *Erving Goffman.* London: Routledge.
Verhoeven, J. C. (1993) An Interview with Erving Goffman, 1980. *Research on Language and Social Interaction,* 26(3), pp. 317–48.
West, C. and Fenstermaker, S. (1995) Doing Difference. *Gender & Society,* 9(1), pp. 8–37.
West, C. and Zimmerman, D. H. (1987) Doing Gender. *Gender & Society,* 1(2), pp. 125–51.
West, C. and Zimmerman, D. H. (2009) Accounting for Doing Gender. *Gender & Society,* 23(1), pp. 112–22.
Winkin, Y. (1999) Erving Goffman: What is a Life? The Uneasy Making of Intellectual Biography. In: G. Smith (ed.) *Goffman and Social Organization Studies in Sociological Legacy.* London: Routledge, pp. 19–41.

3

Schutz and Garfinkel

Introduction

Much conventional sociology has historically been associated with the study of large-scale structural processes that generate social asymmetries in power, class and status among different groups. In this context the emphasis has been on identifying the political, economic or ideological sources of social differences. Phenomenology and ethnomethodology have shifted this research focus towards understanding how social meanings and social order are created and reproduced on an ongoing basis by knowledgeable social actors. In this chapter we explore the key ideas of these two interpretative sociological traditions of analysis. As in previous chapters we zoom in on the life and intellectual context of the two key representatives of these theories – Alfred Schutz and Harold Garfinkel – and then look at the wider social, historical and political developments that have shaped these two approaches. The chapter also provides an analysis of the key ideas of phenomenology and ethnomethodology as well as the recent applications and criticisms of these theoretical positions.

Life and Intellectual Context

Alfred Schutz

Schutz (1899–1959) was a major thinker who transposed phenomenology from its philosophical context into the social sciences to understand the social world. He was born in Vienna in 1899 as the only child of Johanna Schutz (née Fialla) and Alfred Schutz. His father died a few months before Alfred was born and his mother remarried his uncle, Otto. Johanna never disclosed to young Alfred that his father died before he was born, and he lived under the assumption that Otto was his biological father for much of his youth. He only discovered the truth when he applied to join the military in 1916. However, he was not subsequently bitter towards his mother about this. On the contrary, it seems that this revelation strengthened his emotional commitment towards his parents that lasted until their respective deaths.

Alfred grew up in an upper middle-class Jewish family. Otto was a bank executive who ran the well-regarded Viennese banking firm Ephrussi and Col. Alfred's mother was responsible for his early education and she played a crucial role in initiating his lifelong appreciation of music. Young Alfred became well versed at playing the piano. She was also instrumental in preparing him for the Esterhazy Gymnasium, which he attended until graduation in 1918. Schutz was an excellent student who graduated summa cum laude. Although he was only 17 at the time of graduation, he soon volunteered to join the artillery division in the Austro-Hungarian military and fight in the First World War.

It seems he experienced a major crisis during this period and expected to die on the frontline. He was soon promoted to the rank of second lieutenant and took part in several dangerous military actions on the Italian front. He was awarded silver and bronze medals for bravery on the battlefield. After spending 10 months on the frontline, Schutz returned home and soon after the Austro-Hungary military was defeated and the empire collapsed.

After the war Schutz continued his education at the University of Vienna where he studied law and social sciences. In 1921 he attained a law degree and then enrolled into a graduate programme that focused on economics, philosophy, sociology and international law. His professors were world-leading scholars including Ludwig von Mises, Friedrich von Wieser and Hans Kelsen, among others. During his graduate studies Schutz regularly attended well-established intellectual circles including the Mises Circle and the later famous 'Vienna Circle' led by Moritz Schlick that also included leading philosophers such as Rudolf Carnap, Otto Nuerath and Ludwig Wittgenstein. It is in the Mises Circle that Schutz encountered the work of Max Weber, Max Scheler and Werner Sombart. During his studies in Vienna Schutz had the opportunity to attend Max Weber's lectures, which spurred a lifelong interest in the question of meaning. While working on his PhD under Hans Kelsen, Schutz was employed as a bank clerk. He completed his PhD project in less than three years. Just before finishing his thesis Schutz was appointed as an executive secretary in the Association of Austrian Middle Banks. In this role he consulted for the government of Austria on banking legislation. In 1926 he married his long-time girlfriend Ilse Heim, who sacrificed a promising academic career to devote herself to raising their children and also helping Alfred with his publications. As Barber (2004: 23) documents: 'She discontinued work on her own dissertation to help him with his work, and she took the dictation of all his papers, at least until the invention of tape recorders, one of the first of which she gave him as a birthday present.'

In 1927 Schutz became an executive office of Reitler and Company, the leading private banking company in Vienna. During this period he combined his banking career with sociological and philosophical research. His first book, *The Phenomenology of the Social World*, heavily influenced by Edmund Husserl's work, was published in 1932. He sent a copy of this work to Husserl, who was highly impressed by it and invited Schutz to work with him at Freiburg.

However, Schutz had to support his family and decided to continue with his banking career while pursuing philosophy and sociology in his spare time. This highly unusual situation prompted Husserl to call Schutz a banker by day and a phenomenologist by night.

After the annexation of Austria in 1938, Schutz and his family moved to Paris, where he was employed as an international lawyer for Reitler and Company. In 1939 he and his family then settled in the United States where he continued his banking and law career but was also appointed as a part-time faculty member at the New School of Social Research, in New York. At the New School he was elected Chair of the Philosophy Department and taught sociology and philosophy. Schutz also helped many other European scholars to emigrate to the United States. He published a number of influential essays and also engaged in a powerful dialogue with Talcott Parsons, whose *Structure of Social Action* he admired, but remained highly critical of. Schutz saw his work as complementing both the marginalist Austrian school of economics and Parsons' work. Schutz died on 20 May 1959 in New York City while still working on his second book.

Harold Garfinkel

Garfinkel (1917–2011) established ethnomethodology both as a distinct approach within the phenomenological tradition, and as a field of empirical study within sociology. He was born in Newark, New Jersey, on 29 October 1917 and was raised in a middle-class Jewish family. His father, Abraham, ran a small furniture business and expected Harold to work with him in the company. Initially Harold devoted a lot of his time to company business but soon decided to become a full-time student at the University of Newark, where he enrolled to study accounting.

However, he soon realised that his academic interests lay elsewhere as he was highly impressed by the theoretical questions raised by the Columbia sociology graduate teaching assistants, who did most of the teaching at Newark. After graduation, Garfinkel travelled to Georgia, where he worked as a volunteer at the Quaker camp. This experience of working with young people from very different social, political and cultural backgrounds, together with his theory lessons at Newark University, led Garfinkel towards developing a strong interest in micro sociology.

Consequently, he decided to enrol in the Master's sociology programme at the University of North Carolina, which specialised in public work projects, such as the one he was involved in at the Quaker camp in Georgia. He graduated from the university in 1942 with a Master's thesis on inter-racial homicide. During this period, he also wrote a short story 'Color Trouble', centred on the experience of an African American woman who refused to sit at the back of a bus when it crossed the North–South line on the way from New Jersey to North Carolina, thus anticipating Rosa Parks's actions in 1955. The story was originally published in the journal *Opportunity* in 1940 and in 1941 was included in a collection of the best short stories. Soon after his graduation Garfinkel was drafted into the Army Air Corps and spent much of the war as a trainer at an air base in Florida, instructing soldiers how to attack tanks. At the end of the war he was transferred to Mississippi, where he met Arlene Steinback, who remained his lifelong partner for 65 years. They soon married and had two children – Leah and Mark.

After his discharge from the military Garfinkel decided to continue his studies in sociology and was soon accepted at Harvard, where he had the opportunity to work with Talcott Parsons at the recently created Department of Social Relations. Garfinkel was initially deeply influenced by Parsons, and wrote highly theoretical and jargon-filled academic papers. Nevertheless, he soon realised that, unlike Parsons, he was much more interested in empirical questions and field research. In the late 1940s he was invited to work with Wilbert E. Moore at Princeton University, where he spent two years as a research and teaching assistant on a project focusing on organisational behaviour.

At Princeton he attended lectures by leading social scientists including Gregory Bateson, Paul Lazarsfeld, Philip Selznick and Kenneth Burke, among others. In 1952 he completed his PhD thesis, 'The Perception of the Other: A Study in Social Order', at Harvard. In 1954 he was appointed assistant professor in the sociology department at the University of California, Los Angeles where he remained until retirement in 1987. In the same year he attained his academic job at UCLA, he coined the term 'ethnomethodology', in a paper on the behaviour of jury members that he presented at the American Sociological Association in Urbana at the University of Illinois. In the 1970s, he was a visiting professor at the Centre for Advanced Study in Behavioural Sciences at Stanford University (1975–6) and Oxford University (1979–8). In the 1990s, his work received wider international claim and he was awarded the ASA 'Cooley–Mead Award' and an honorary doctorate from the University of Nottingham. Harold Garfinkel had a long life and died aged 93 on 21 April 2011.

Historical, Social and Political Context

The sociological approaches of Schutz and Garfinkel have their intellectual and historical roots in European phenomenological philosophy and particularly in the work of Edmund Husserl (1859–1938). The phenomenological tradition grew out of various scholars' dissatisfaction with the positivist turn that dominated late nineteenth-century and early twentieth-century philosophy and the social sciences. *Fin de siècle* Vienna was an intellectual centre of both positivism and various anti-positivist traditions. Moreover, some philosophers such as Ludwig Wittgenstein started off as staunch positivists and gradually transformed into radical anti-positivists.

Viennese Enlightenment

Although Austro-Hungary was an authoritarian empire which generally did not allow political dissent, it offered unprecedented social and institutional space for the development of social science, philosophy and the arts. The empire was also a rather wealthy entity sporting a large middle class interested in new ideas and new intellectual developments. By 1914 the empire boasted a very large population of 52.8 million people. Despite pronounced corruption and mismanagement, the economy of the empire was nevertheless in a very healthy state. For example, from 1895 to 1913 Austro-Hungary's gross national product quadrupled when compared with the previous 20 years, while the industrial production rate grew by 6.3% from 1903 to 1907 (Barber, 2004: 7). The main cities of the empire experienced substantial population expansion as industrialisation and urbanisation fostered movement from the countryside to urban areas.

The empire was ruled through an enormous bureaucracy which was conservative, corrupt and inefficient, yet also strongly lenient, and even accommodating, of various new developments including novel philosophical traditions and the rise of science and technology. Although the rulers were hostile towards any substantive initiatives towards democratisation, they showed less hostility towards the liberalisation of economic and cultural space. In fact, by the end of the nineteenth century, Austro-Hungarian rulers advocated a version of enlightenment absolutism which was open to new ideas focusing on the rationalisation of state organisation, the economy, education and scientific development.

In this context Vienna soon became a centre of European scientific and artistic developments. Its famous cafés, clubs and restaurants often served as the epicentres of intellectual life that gave birth to unprecedented creativity in the arts, sciences and philosophy, including such names as Freud, Klimt, Loos, Mahler, Schoenberg, Wittgenstein, Popper, Buber, Bauer, Löwenstein, Pauli, Perutz, Strauss, Zweig, Voegelin and many others. A number of these upper-middle-class intellectuals, through art and aesthetics, and philosophy, fused, to varying degrees, a liberal culture-based reason and law, with an aristocratic culture based on feeling and grace (Schorske, 1981: 7). Many scholars, philosophers and artists were members of leading intellectual circles such as the positivist 'Vienna Circle', the Mises Circle and the Mind Circle (Geistkreis) among many others. While the Vienna Circle led by Moritz Schlick was the centre for scholars developing the philosophy of logical positivism, the Mises Circle included mostly liberal intellectuals interested in a variety of academic positions. Ludwig von Mises, a classical liberal, and anti-socialist, economist, established his circle in 1922 to provide a forum for scientists, economists and other academics to present their research and new ideas.

The Mind Circle founded by Friedrich Hayek and Herbert Furth was more focused on the social sciences and humanities, and was also open to a variety of intellectual approaches. Schutz was an active member of the Mises Circle and the Mind Circle, where he presented his initial phenomenological ideas but also engaged with the work of Max Weber. Like Weber, Schutz for the most part foregrounded the notion of value neutrality and portrayed himself as a detached or impartial observer of social life. However, he did pursue certain normative commitments centred on recognizing the plurality of values in societies and valorising the subjective viewpoints of actors. As Barber argues he:

affirmed a kind of epistemic normativity insofar he affirmed that the opinion of the well informed citizen ought to take precedence over that of experts and the uninformed ... he asserted that democracy needs to be assessed in ethical terms of how well it allows the point of view of its individual citizens to be heard or recognized, particularly in small public forums. (2004: xii)

In this respect, Schutz displayed a strong sympathy to the Austrian liberal economists with whom he studied:

by basing democracy more on the active participation of individual citizens than on the anonymous votes of majorities, Schutz developed in the political sphere the Austrian insight that the economy needed to be understood in terms of the activities of individual entrepreneurs and consumers rather than of anonymous economic laws. (Barber, 2004: xii)

In addition to Austrian economics, Schutz also developed a strong interest in Bergson's philosophy of intuitionism and vitality, which pushed him closer to phenomenology. However, it was the work of Edmund Husserl which had the most significant impact on his work.

Husserl's Legacy

Husserl, a difficult and relatively inaccessible thinker, attempted to establish a new way of handling philosophical problems through what he termed 'phenomenology' – the science of things as they appear to consciousness. Unlike a number of earlier predecessors, Husserl focused on the mundane world of everyday actors and what was given or 'indubitable in the perception of consciousness'. His descriptive psychology, later termed 'essential analysis' or 'transcendental phenomenology', set out to present a careful non-reductive description of what appears to consciousness as a basis to refound the sciences. As Smith (2003: 3) notes, 'transcendental phenomenology involves a switch of interest – away from the world, towards our own conscious life in which such a world presents itself to us'. As part of this approach, Husserl examined the intentional nature of mental acts – that they were intended or 'directed' towards something, an object or idea; this notion of intentionality reaching beyond itself was a fundamental quality of consciousness. Intentionality was directed to what he termed 'the lifeworld'. This made him highly suspicious of positivistic approaches, for example those in sociology such as functionalism, which miss the important 'sense' of phenomena of consciousness, by employing unsuitable methods to understand the social world. For Husserl the extension of the methods of mathematical logic to the social and philosophical or life-world by positivism was highly problematic, since they stripped the latter of broader metaphysical questions of meaning: 'Positivism, in a manner of speaking, decapitates philosophy' (1970: 9). Science was in fact rooted in the everyday world. As Bauman notes:

> To the smug self-restraint of positivism, reducing its vision to the observable, sentient and contingent, Husserl opposed the search for necessary, essential knowledge—the Platonic invariant—which no contingent evidence is potent enough to undermine. Against the feeble foundation of empirical evidence, for which positivism was prepared to settle, Husserl set the quest after objective essences—those that no subjective project of an empirical individual is capable of challenging. (1973: 5)

Husserl endeavoured to examine the stream of consciousness and what was immediately given to it, without relying on any presuppositions; it was an attempt to 'get back to the things themselves', including objects, categories and ideas.

Though beginning with a focus on the individual ego, in his later work, especially, Husserl attempted to analyse the individual's encounter with the 'other' through empathy and the construction of an intersubjective reality (Steinbock, 1995). Subjectivity, intersubjectivity and world, he argued, come to presence together (Husserl, 1989). The objective world was experienced as an intersubjective reality, a life-world. There were two attitudes towards the world: a 'natural attitude', which took the world naively for granted as something given to individuals; and a 'philosophical' or 'transcendental attitude' where through the application of a methodological *epoché* philosophers refrain from judgement, and bracket and treat the objects and contents of experience simply as phenomena, and not in terms of how they exist for individuals. The *epoché* puts in relief not just the object experienced but the whole experience of the object in order to challenge our everyday acceptance of it. This reduction, which 'follows the nature of the things to be investigated', therefore entailed a three-stage method of going back to what is bracketed: a descriptive stage which describes the totality of experience; an eidetic stage which examines the essential or invariant features of the phenomena; and a transcendental stage that examines the conditions of possibility of having any such experience.

Such a procedure of reduction allowed philosophers to escape from relativism and to understand the ultimate ground of being. In the natural world individuals take the world as given, an experiential world consisting of a 'horizon of horizons'. There were many intersecting and overlapping life-worlds in which individuals as conscious agents live, from the proximate 'home world' to those they experience as distant or foreign, such as foreign cultures.

In addition to Husserl, Schutz developed his approach by drawing on and developing Weber's 'interpretive sociology'. Like Weber, Schutz aimed to understand the social world in terms of the meanings that actions had for the social actors who undertook them, through interpretation. He discussed this in his first book *The Meaningful Constitution of the Social World* published originally in 1932 and only translated into English in 1967 as *The Phenomenology of the Social World* (1967).

For Weber, understanding action and the meaning it had for actors was achieved through a process of *Verstehen* – putting oneself in the position of the actor in order to understand the subjective meaning of the act. Schutz followed Weber by taking actors' subjective understandings, their knowledge and how they thought about the world as the basis for interpreting the actors' objective social world. As well as Weber's notion of Verstehen and his methodological individualism, Schutz also remained sympathetic to Weber's notion of ideal types, which enabled the social scientist to interpret the meaning of social behaviour and how social actors created the social world, as a meaningful reality. However, Schutz found Weber's work failed to account fully, in a deep and generalisable way, for human action, its meaning and significance, and the important role that knowledge played in underpinning action.

The Californian Liberation

Harold Garfinkel was also influenced by the work of Husserl and Weber. However, his encounter with their ideas was mostly mediated through the work of Schutz. Garfinkel's interest in phenomenology developed out of his critique of Parsons' ambition to create a grand, or general theory of society. After reading and engaging with Schutz's work, Garfinkel came to understand that one could not develop a top-down general theory of society but instead should focus on the micro-sociological world of everyday life. Although Garfinkel was explicit that ethnomethodology was not a form of phenomenology, but a separate intellectual enterprise, he acknowledged similarities and the impact of phenomenological thinking on his ideas. Nevertheless, phenomenological thinking developed in a very different social, political and economic context: whereas Schutz's ideas were articulated in the imperial world of *fin de siècle* Vienna, Garfinkel created an ethnomethodological research programme in California in the 1950s and 1960s. In some respects, the development of ethnomethodology reflected the social, cultural and political changes taking place in US society in this period. The structural transformations initiated by the legacy of the Second World War, Cold War paranoia, and the gender, race and class emancipation movements of the 1960s, all undermined the traditional understandings of one's social role in society. Although ethnomethodology focuses on the minute details of everyday interaction, its epistemological foundations are rooted in the ever-present questioning of existing norms. In contrast to Parsons' structural functionalist models, which in many respects exalted the status quo and its dominant value system, Garfinkel's research method indirectly subverted the very foundations of any social order. The popularity of ethnomethodology and its breaching experiments grew on the back of the new social movements which, from the 1960s onwards, questioned all authorities and all modes of social interaction. As Gouldner (1972: 394–5) notes behind ethnomethodological demonstrations and breaching experiments there is an impulse to bring routines to a halt, to demonstrate the vulnerability of the everyday world to disruption, what Gouldner terms a 'genteel anarchism'.

This anarchism appealed to the activistic youth of the 1960s and the politically rebellious campuses, as well as other individuals alienated from the status quo, conferring on them a potency and power. As a micro-confrontation ethnomethodology: 'is a substitute and symbolic rebellion against a larger structure which the youth cannot, and often does not wish to, change. It substitutes the available rebellion for the inaccessible revolution' (Gouldner, 1972: 394). Although Garfinkel's approach was grounded in Schutz's philosophy and sociology, the social and political context of 1960s California proved crucial in radicalising phenomenology and taking it to its logical conclusion.

Ideas and Arguments

Alfred Schutz and Phenomenology

A central concern for Schutz was the essential aspects of the meaningful structure of our everyday world, a world in which we were born, and within which our life develops, until we pass away. Social reality consists of:

> The sum total of objects and occurrences within the social cultural world as experienced by common-sense thinking of men living their daily lives among their fellow-men, connected with them in manifold relations of interaction. (1962: 53)

Schutz sought to understand the principles according to which daily life became ordered and organised in the natural attitude. Human behaviour was already meaningful and intelligible in daily life through common-sense understandings of actors, so that when social scientists wished to understand it, they needed to understand the subjective meaning that it had for those actors in their day-to-day lives. In addition, the everyday social world composed of animate beings and objects was experienced by actors in a taken-for-granted way, where all doubt in its existence as socially and contingently created was suspended:

> Phenomenology has taught us the concept of phenomenological *epoche*, the suspension of our belief in the reality of the world as a device to overcome the natural attitude by radicalizing the Cartesian method of philosophical doubt. The suggestion may be ventured that man within the natural attitude also uses a specific *epoche* of course quite another one than the phenomenologist. He does not suspend belief in the outer world and its objects, but on the contrary, he suspends doubt in its existence. What he puts in brackets is the doubt that the world and its objects might be otherwise than it appears to him. We propose to call this epoché the *epoché of the natural attitude*. (Schutz, 1967: xliii)

> [Republished with permission of Northwestern University Press from *The Phenomenology of the Social World*, A. Schutz, 1967]

Social actors share taken-for-granted 'stocks of knowledge' – typifications of the common-sense world ('naive standpoints' in Husserl's language) – as idealisations with which they make sense of their everyday world. Everyday actors also ordinarily assume the world has a past – it pre-existed them – a present and a future, and that it currently exists for them. Moreover, the common-sense social world that these actors found meaningful, which may be meaningful in a vague and confused way, was incomplete, sometimes contradictory and often based on their limited experience. This constituted their 'life-world' which remained within the frame of the natural attitude. The knowledge individuals held was effectively akin to cookery book knowledge: 'efficient recipes for the use of typical means for bringing about typical ends in typical situations' (Schutz, 1964: 14).

Throughout their lives, actors accumulate more and more typifications and 'recipes' with which they interpret their experiences. These stocks of knowledge became the basis for future actions – they allow individuals to improvise in new situations, in ways circumscribed by their knowledge and imagination. Drawing on Husserl's distinction between the philosophical and the natural attitude, Schutz distinguishes between the world of the social scientist and everyday actors. Social scientists generate different kinds of concepts and develop them in a way at odds with everyday actors. They investigate the essential, taken-for-granted structure of the social world, its a priori conditions of possibility, which allows the common-sense world to exist. Thus, they examine the multiplicity of typifications that constitute the world – the typical forms of action and belief held by social actors and how the world is typically interpreted by them – their typical projections and anticipations. This contrasts with everyday actors who organise their world and common sense on the basis of 'here and now' where they are at a certain time and place.

The world is also meaningful for social scientists but, for the latter, the context of meaning within which they interpret this world is different: it is that of 'systematizing scrutiny rather than that of living experience'. Unlike the *epoche* of the natural attitude, the phenomenological *epoche* suspends disbelief in the taken-for-granted-ness of the world. Not only do everyday actors use acts of typification in their ordinary day-to-day conscious awareness of the world in order to make sense of it, give it meaning and make it a world of first-order constructs, but so too do social scientists. To that extent social scientists also remain partially embedded in the natural attitude. However, they also adopt a position of social scientific doubt towards common-sense attitudes entailed in the practical reasoning of everyday actors. Moreover, their typifications and scientific concepts are 'second-order constructs' aimed at grasping the meaning which the actor bestows upon his or her act, and which need to be interpreted through *Verstehen*. Second-order constructs derive from first-order constructs, they are logically tied to them; it is only by understanding the meanings of everyday actors, their intentionalities, that sociology can progress to provide a scientific understanding of the social world using technical concepts:

> It is to these already meaningful data that his scientific concepts must ultimately refer: to the meaningful acts of individual men and women, to their everyday experience of one another, to their understanding of one another's meanings, and to their initiation of new meaningful behavior of their own. (Schutz, 1967: 10)

Schutz refers to three criteria to assess the validity of second-order constructs (Filmer et al., 1973): the postulate of logical consistency – that concepts follow a logical order; the postulate of subjective interpretation – what the subjective meaning of the act holds for the actor; and the postulate of adequacy – that the constructs could be understandable for the actor him- or herself with reference to common-sense schemas.

Thus, like Weber, Schutz places meaningful action at the centre of his interpretive sociology as well as acts of consciousness and interaction. Actions which take place within the horizon of social reality and are related to other actions can either be covert, that is refraining from an action, or overt projected and purposive forms of action. In these actions, the actor uses motives both geared towards a future end to be achieved, 'in order to motives', and past motives explicable by the actor's background, 'because motives'. These actions are often undertaken on the basis of 'relevance' to the actor's desires, convictions and interests. The most important of these is the fear of death, which for Schutz constitutes the fundamental anxiety humans face.

Although Schutz begins his analysis by examining how meaning is constituted in the individual experience of the solitary Ego, especially through 'internal time consciousness', as it lives through its experience, he also analyses the understanding and experiences of others and knowledge of other persons. He recognises that our daily world is intersubjectively experienced: 'The world of daily life into which we are born is from the outset an intersubjective world' (Schutz, cited in Natanson, 1962: xxx). It is an intersubjective, taken-for-granted world which develops through communication and language: the latter constitutes a sedimented stock of knowledge. Through face-to-face situations, 'we relations' unfold in which there exists an ego and alter ego, possessing a mutually learned 'reciprocity of perspectives' and entailing a community of others – consociates, contemporaries, predecessors and successors. Moreover, like Husserl, Schutz believes that social actors live within many different social spheres, a multiplicity of realities or 'provinces of meaning' which constitute their life-world, and that they are 'geared' into each of these worlds.

Harold Garfinkel and Ethnomethodology

Garfinkel developed a related field of sociology, namely ethnomethodology, which expanded on Husserl's and Schutz's phenomenological focus on the taken-for-granted nature of everyday knowledge, by applying it to research. Ethnomethodology examines the methods human use to construct, account for and give meaning to the social world. Like Schutz, it examined how the social world was not something given but instead actively created by social actors, who attempt to make sense of their surroundings and circumstances and act on the basis of these on an ongoing moment-to-moment basis. And again, like Schutz, ethnomethodology views common-sense of actors and for the most part, tacit and unutterable knowledge and rules, as incomplete phenomena.

Ethnomethodology does not attempt to make 'humanistic arguments' or correctives to people's knowledge and practical actions. Rather it focuses on the shared tacit understandings and cultural assumptions including of the most trivial, routine and mundane aspects of social life, held by social actors. Social order is not given but produced. One of Garfinkel's central theoretical targets was the work of Talcott Parsons, under whom he studied, and especially Parsons's understanding of social order as in effect a stable normative order held together by shared norms and values internalised into the superego of individuals. For Parsons, drawing on Durkheim's view of the social world as a reality *sui generis*, the 'social system' was composed of institutions, themselves consisting of status and roles composed of norms, expectations and values. These norms and values were enacted by individuals according to the needs of the social system and not in relation to their own self-interests, which individuals struggled against. Norm-conforming behaviour was also reciprocally sanctioned by others. It was this internalisation of norms and their reciprocal sanctioning for Parsons, that ensured the stability of the social system and helped to reproduce a stable social order.

Rather than give cultural norms and individual internal motivations and promtings causal explanatory weight, and thereby conceive individuals as unreflexive 'cultural dopes', Garfinkel empowers reflexive individuals, their shared albeit tacit knowledge and common-sense understanding of the social world, and their practical actions in creating the social order on an ongoing basis. This involves moving from the large, reified, abstractions and focus on general rules characterising Parsonian theory, to concrete, situated, everyday practices, in order to reveal how social life is made 'to happen' through knowledgeable human conduct in determinate, yet, fluctuating social contexts. Garfinkel argues that society cannot simply be seen as something given, something external constraining individuals, that is as a social fact in Durkheim's sense. Rather the 'real world' refers to 'the organised activities of everyday life' created and sustained in the mundane activities of social actors (Garfinkel, 1967: ii).

Ethnomethodology is:

> Directed to the tasks of learning how members' actual, ordinary activities consist of methods to make practical actions, practical circumstances, common-sense knowledge of social structures, and practical sociological reasoning analysable; and of discovering the formal properties of commonplace, practical common-sense actions, 'from within' actual settings, as ongoing accomplishments of those settings. (1967: vii–viii)

These organised activities presuppose norms that are interpreted, applied and reapplied by actors on a situation-to-situation basis by artful, creative social actors as a practical accomplishment:

> In contrast to certain versions of Durkheim that teach that the objective reality of social facts is sociology's fundamental principle, the lesson is taken instead and used as a study policy, that the objective reality of social facts as an ongoing accomplishment of the concerted activities of daily life, with the ordinary, artful ways of that accomplishment being by members known, used and taken for granted is, for members doing sociology, a fundamental phenomenon. (1967: vii)

According to Garfinkel, ordinary individuals creatively and methodologically make sense of the world jointly. As members of society their reasoning and understanding demonstrate shared methods – ethno-methods – through which they act and which the sociologist can study, but which also apply to sociologists themselves, in their sense-making activities. Sociologists too, presuppose common sense, arbitrary rules and procedures. As Mennell notes:

> Many of the 'facts' which sociologists tend to accept as data have been created in everyday situations for practical purposes. They are not facts but 'accomplishments'... To this extent, it is argued, 'conventional' sociology is merely on a par with any person's understanding of his everyday situation – a 'first degree' corpus of knowledge 'competitive' with everyday practical knowledge. (1975: 289–90)

According to Garfinkel, the shared methods that everyday actors use demonstrate members' common-sense reasoning which facilitates them in jointly creating the social world. This includes a societal members' grasp of 'What Anyone Like Us Necessarily Knows' (Garfinkel, 1967: 54) – what people know and know others know. Although he accepts that actors exhibit rationality or reason in their actions, this is not the same as a logical form of rationality, but rather a practical rationality, applying and recreating context specific rules and understandings which may vary from context to context, in the classroom, in courts and in work settings, for example. Rather than 'cultural dopes' actors are competent, conscious, self-reflexive, knowledgeable and accountable to one another; that is, their actions are 'observable and reportable' (1967: 1). Accounts help individuals make sense of the world to one another and each other. Actor's primarily tacit reasoning activities, by drawing on common-sense knowledge and implicit rules of roles and statuses, help them to define situations and act in them, thereby reproducing those very institutions and social structures. Such practical actions and reasoning require context-dependent knowledge and the use of indexical expressions to accomplish reality. The latter are:

> Expressions whose sense cannot be decided by an auditor without his necessarily knowing or assuming something about the biography and the purposes of the user of the expression, the circumstances of the utterance, the previous course of the conversation, or the particular relationship of actual or potential interaction that exists between the expressor and the auditor. (1967: 4)

In his most important book, *Studies in Ethnomethodology* (1967), Garfinkel reveals the practical implementation of these methods and forms of common-sense reasoning in a series of essays and case studies. The attempt to reveal the background assumptions and the creative nature of human actions, through a series of breaching experiments. By disrupting the rules of a game of noughts and crosses, for example, a sociologist can see the anger generated when joint sense-making routines with assumed background expectations are violated and ordinary sense-making thwarted. In contradistinction to a view of social reality as composed of hardened, rigid, social facts, breaching demonstrates the immense vulnerability of the social world to disruption by challenging its tacit assumptions.

Such breaching demonstrates that individuals hold one another mutually accountable in social encounters, both with reference to making such encounters intelligible and on a moral basis of demonstrating respect and playing the game 'fairly'. Rules not only provided guides to action but informed reasoning about that action: 'Activities whereby members produce and manage settings of organised everyday affairs are identical with members' procedures for making those settings accountable' (1967: 1). Further 'breaching experiments' demonstrating background common understandings, reciprocal expectations and moral propriety, included students who were asked to act for 15 minutes to an hour as boarders or tenants in their parents' homes, and refraining from speaking until spoken to. According to Garfinkel, some students refused to undertake the activity; in others the family made sense of the situation either as a 'joke' or because their daughter was trying to acquire something by being nice. However, in four-fifths of the 49 cases the family was:

> Stupefied. They vigorously sought to make the strange actions intelligible and to restore the situation to normal appearances. Reports were filled with accounts of astonishment, bewilderment, shock, anxiety, embarrassments, and anger, and with charges by various family members that the student was mean, inconsiderate, selfish, nasty, or impolite. Family member's demanded explanations: What's the matter? What's gotten into you? Did you get fired? Are you sick? What are you being so superior about? Why are you mad? Are you out of your mind or are you just stupid? (1967: 48)

As Heritage notes:

> The study highlights the extent to which we all use background knowledge to 'typify' or 'normalize' our view of everyday events. The students suspended their use of these assumptions for just a few minutes and found they were 'seeing' in a dramatically different way that they found uncomfortable and not quite 'real'. (1998: 181)

Still other breaching experiments included repeatedly asking 'what do you mean?' to someone, expressing physical ailments, or researchers posing as counsellors randomly answering yes and no to those seeking guidance in their life. These also demonstrated the importance of making sense activities, establishing situational meaning, and the importance of background knowledge, not only in filling in and framing what people do to achieve a mutual understanding of a situation and social reality, but also the moral anger induced by failing to employ such knowledge and the breach of trust involved.

This 'filling in' of background knowledge revealed the operation of what Garfinkel, following Mannheim, calls a 'documentary method of interpretation', which provides a framework or a *gestalt* through and in which actions are interpreted. The documentary method involves a circular self-validating process entailing:

> Treating an actual appearance as 'the document of', as 'pointing to', as 'standing on behalf of' a presupposed underlying pattern. Not only is the underlying pattern derived from its individual documentary evidences, but the individual documentary evidences in their turn are interpreted on the basis of 'what is known' about the underlying pattern. Each is used to elaborate the other. (Garfinkel, 1967: 78)

Garfinkel sees sociologists as on par with everyday actors – as 'practical theorists' – in the sense that they also draw upon a common-sense, taken-for-granted, world. Social facts have to be understood and interpreted by sense-making sociologists; this includes quantitative studies that describe how persons are selected for treatment in outpatient clinics' medical records. For Garfinkel, social facts are not given but reproduced through individuals holding one another to account and drawing on background knowledge and expectations, and interpreting their social reality through a documentary method. Social actors sustain the coherence of day-to-day life through processes of *ad hoc-ing* where general descriptions and representations that actors possess are made to fit localised settings in order to interpret and act within them. However, sociologists often mistakenly and unreflectively use statistical or quantitative data such as official statistics without critically examining their production (Cicourel, 1967). In his analysis of suicide for example, Douglas (1967) argues that suicide rates reflect categorisations and everyday judgements applied by coroners to certain forms of death, but that they interpret these deaths, and what constitutes 'suicide', in inconsistent ways. Garfinkel therefore urges sociologists to become conscious and more reflexive of their approach and assumptions with regard to employing common sense assumptions in 'doing sociology'.

Garfinkel highlights the importance of *ad-hoc-ing*, indexicality and background assumptions in his discussion of Agnes, an intersexed person, who was 'born a boy with normal appearing male genitals' (1967: 120) but who wished to undertake a sex change operation and whose appearance was 'convincingly female' (1967: 119). Rather than sex and gender being naturally given, Agnes, as a practical methodologist, demonstrated how a social status, that has become reified, as a gender role, was in fact achieved by social actors through 'doing gender'. This was not only through dressing in an appropriate manner, but also through acting like a woman, 'passing' as a female. Agnes demonstrated that she was 'really' a natural female needing a sex change operation, through her performance of playing a female and hiding her 'male' features. As Garfinkel notes:

> Her studies armed her with knowledge of how the organised features of ordinary settings are used by members as procedures for making appearances-of-sexuality-as-usual decidable as a matter of course. The scrutiny that she paid to appearances; her concerns for adequate motivation, relevance, evidence, and demonstration; her sensitivity, to devices of talk; her skill in detecting and managing 'tests' were attained as part of her mastery of trivial but necessary social tasks, to secure ordinary rights to live. Agnes was self-consciously equipped to teach normals how normals make sexuality happen in commonplace settings as an obvious, familiar, recognizable, natural and serious matter of fact. Her speciality consisted of treating the 'natural facts of life' of socially recognized, socially managed sexuality as a managed production so as to be making these facts of life true, relevant, demonstrable, testable, countable, and available to inventory, cursory representation, anecdote, enumeration, or professional psychological assessment; in short, so as unavoidably in concert with others to be making these facts of life visible and reportable-accountable for all practical purposes. (1967: 180)

[Republished with permission of Polity from *Studies in Ethnomethodology*, H. Garfinkel, 1967]

In other work, Garfinkel (Garfinkel et al., 1981) also extends his analysis of how the social world is made by examining how the natural sciences operate and rationalise their findings.

Contemporary Relevance and Applications

Although Schutz retained a marginal position in sociology during his lifetime, his work came to prominence during the mid-1960s and early 1970s, especially through its use in the writings of Berger and Luckman and Harold Garfinkel.

THE SCHUTZ–PARSONS CORRESPONDENCE

Invited to review *The Structure of Social Action*, Schutz was so stimulated by the work as to produce a long and detailed paper that he then sent to Parsons for comment. This initiated an intense debate through mail correspondence that, through failure to establish productive common ground, concluded in a somewhat embittered impasse. It was Schutz's open conviction that Parsons' theory was an important and valuable contribution but lacked philosophical grounding. Here, he saw his own work, *Der sinnhafte Aufbau der sozialen Welt* [The Phenomenology of the Social World], as providing a suitable foundation. Though Parsons had read Schutz's book, he failed to see the relevance for his purportedly scientific programme in social theory, which he preferred to separate entirely from philosophical considerations. Ultimately, opposing perspectives on the relationship between philosophy and social science was at issue. This disagreement even filtered down into terminological confusions, further impeding the dialogue. Despite sharing several important concerns, in the end neither alluded to the debate in subsequent writings.

In their book *The Social Construction of Reality* (1966) Berger and Luckmann extend many of Schutz's arguments. The book is subtitled *A Treatise in the Sociology of Knowledge* and their major contention is not only that reality is socially constructed, but also that the sociology of knowledge examines how this process takes place. The book is often seen as a foundation of the social constructionist perspective. As well as drawing on Marx's work and his dialectical perspective, the authors draw heavily on Durkheim's injunction about society's objective facticity and Weber's emphasis on the subjective meaning of action within an overarching Schutzian framework. A central question they confront is how it is possible that subjective meanings become objective facticities? Divided into three parts, the book examines the foundations of knowledge in everyday life, society as an objective reality and society as a subjective reality. The construction of social reality, they argue, entails three steps: externalisation, objectivation and internalisation.

Berger and Luckmann define social reality as a quality-appertaining to phenomena that we recognise as having become independent of our volition, while knowledge is 'the certainty that phenomena are real and that they possess specific characteristics' (1966: 13). The man in the street takes knowledge for granted, while a philosopher questions its validity. However, the sociologist, deploying a sociology of knowledge framework, assumes a mid-way position by concerning him or herself with knowledge whether it is valid or invalid, that is with the social construction of reality.

Berger and Luckmann take Schutz's analysis of the taken-for-granted-ness of everyday life as their starting point, but they also draw upon the phenomenological foregrounding of: the intentionality and temporality of consciousness, the existence of multiple social realities, that reality is shared with others, and the importance of language as sedimented stocks of knowledge. They argue that humans do not have a fixed relationship with their environment, rather their relationship to the world, is characterised by 'world openness' because of their unspecialised and undirected instinct or drive structure. Despite this plasticity and openness to social processes, social order is nevertheless recurringly produced on an ongoing basis, as a product of human activity. To understand why this happens, they turn to the notion of habituation. All human activity is subject to habituation. Repeated actions become 'cast into a pattern, which can then be reproduced with an economy of effort' (1966: 70–1). Habituation means action can be performed again in the same manner and with the same effort.

In addition, the repetition of actions by actors that are based on socially shared knowledge, including typifications, over time, leads to the creation social institutions: 'Institutionalization occurs whenever there is a reciprocal typification of habitualized actions by types of actors' (1991: 72). These institutions become solidified over history in the form of roles. They appear as reified, thing-like entities. It is only on this basis of an institutional world experienced as an objective reality that we can talk of the existence of a social world, confronting the individual in a manner akin to the natural world. Nevertheless, it is a socially created world often pre-existing the individual who is born into it.

According to Berger and Luckmann, the process by which the externalised products of human activity attain the character of objectivity is objectivation. This is part of a dialectical process containing three moments entailing externalisation, objectivation and internalisation. Humans externalise their actions to create a world: this world becomes an objective reality; this objective reality is in turn internalised by humans through primary socialisation – emotional learning and secondary forms of socialisation – acquiring role-specific knowledge which turns them into a member of society. These three moments which constitute social reality can be summarised as: 'Society is a human product. Society is an objective reality. Man is a social product' (1991: 79).

Moreover, for Berger and Luckmann, the institutional world requires a form of legitimation which entails not only power and authority, but 'second order objectivations of meaning' that concern knowledge and behavioural values. These are acquired as we learn the institutional order. Throughout the book the authors highlight the role of not only everyday knowledge but also of language and religion in creating and legitimating the social world in which everyday actors live.

Garfinkel's work has also left a strong legacy and has been applied and developed further by many contemporary scholars. For example, Harvey Sacks, Emanuel Schegloff, Gail Jefferson and Andrei Korbut utilised Garfinkel's contributions to develop conversation analysis which focuses on the mutual accountability of actors and the structure of conversational interaction (Sacks et al., 2015). These authors analysed the organisation of talk-in-interaction in order to identify the internal, sequentially ordered characteristics of conversation, including the use of specific vocabulary, silences, pauses, restarts, turn-taking and occasional laughter.

Other scholars such as Maynard and Clayman (2003) have explored institutional settings and how they shape interactional structures that are relatively unique to particular settings. Contemporary ethnomethodologists have also used breaching experiments to study how different social activities (i.e. work) are achieved and how specific meanings are generated in lived contexts.

Criticisms

Both phenomenology and ethnomethodology have been criticised for their epistemological idealism which leaves little explanatory room for the role of material, historical and structural factors in social life. For example, both Gellner (1979) and Bauman (1976) argue that all interpretivist approaches including phenomenology and ethnomethodology fail to grasp the significance of structural and historical contexts in shaping human action. Hence Schutz insists that state, economy, class, politics or race are all typifications of a second order and as such exist only hypothetically in our heads, not in reality. For Schutz the phenomena are nothing more than mental abstractions. However, Gellner and Bauman profoundly disagree.

As Bauman (1976: 63) states, the social reality of concepts such as the state, society or class is determined by their historical influence on large groups of people: 'for all practical purposes, concepts like society or class enter the lifeworld of the human individual as myths, sedimented from a long and tortuous process of abstraction of which the member himself lost control at a relatively early stage'. By stripping these concepts from their material and historical realities one loses the analytical tools to study their long-term impact. Moreover, Bauman argues that phenomenology does not offer the possibility of a critique of society, since the entirety of the social order is de-contextualised and reduced to mental concepts.

Bourdieu (1990) and Habermas (1987) have also criticised aspects of Schutz's approach. Thus, Bourdieu is critical of what he terms the 'subjectivism' that underpins both phenomenology and ethnomethodology. He sees these two positions as 'the purest expression of the subjectivist vision', which contrast with Durkheim and Marx, who developed an 'objectivist' social science. For Bourdieu, sociology has to reconcile this subjectivist vs. objectivist division, by developing more integrated models of social analysis. To avoid the pitfalls of both subjectivism and objectivism, he argues, it is crucial to recognise that objective structures and subjective perceptions are deeply interconnected, as is the case with the notion of the habitus. This is a 'system of models of perception and appreciation' but is also created and sustained by wider, objective, social structures (Bourdieu, 1990: 131). Gouldner (1972) expresses similar criticisms, pointing to phenomenology's and ethnomethodology's inability to examine the connections between the macro and micro worlds, and more specifically how macro processes shape and are shaped by micro realities. By contrast, Habermas criticises what he terms an overly culturalist understanding of social life and especially Schutz's concept of the life-world. For Habermas (1987: 135), the life-world is not just a cultural phenomenon that is disconnected from structural contexts. Instead, personality structures and normative orders have to be fully integrated into the notion of the life-world.

The phenomenological and ethnomethodological perspectives have also been scrutinised for what critics see as their inherent relativism. For Hindess (1972), Schutz distorts Husserl's phenomenology by sociologising the domain of transcendental intersubjectivity. In this interpretation there is no room left for scientific objectivity since all social behaviours are devolved to the actions of individuals. According to Hindess such an approach leads towards an extreme form of relativism where social science is nothing more than 'special kinds of story-telling'. Hindess finds this relativist approach troubling as it leaves no space for rational politics and it also undermines the development of social science.

A further failing of ethnomethodology is its inability to deal with, or even contemplate, the importance of the unintended consequences of human actions (Mennell, 1975: 299). By dissecting the minute details of everyday human interactions, ethnomethodologists often do not see the wood for the trees since a great deal of human action generates unintended consequences which ultimately influence the direction of social action and the social world. Focusing only on the 'common sense world' one cannot, Mennell argues, fully comprehend the larger social processes nor the historical dynamics of social change.

The two interpretative perspectives have also been criticised on methodological grounds. Positivist-oriented scholars have questioned phenomenology's ability to provide a reliable and replicable methodological tool to study everyday life. This particularly concerns Schutz's approach, which has for the most part developed as a theoretical enterprise. Cuff and Payne (1979) point out that although Schutz has laid the theoretical framework for the phenomenology of social life, he has never operationalised this approach for empirical purposes. In other words, it is not clear how phenomenology can operate as a comprehensive empirical programme to study the social world. By contrast although ethnomethodology has been conceptualised as a practical and empirical undertaking with a variety of novel methodological techniques including the breaching experiments, indexicality, conversation analysis, and so on, critics believe it is not conventionally empiricist, since it lacks the methodological rigour of other empiricist forms of social science.

Conclusion

Both phenomenology and ethnomethodology have influenced significantly the development of social thought in the twentieth century, and have continued to attract intellectual attention in the twenty-first century. These approaches have contributed substantially towards a better understanding of how social order is created, maintained and reproduced, but also how human beings creatively generate meanings in everyday life. Drawing on the phenomenological tradition in philosophy, these interpretative perspectives have generated novel insights about the social world and have also contributed towards advancing innovative research techniques for exploring the social dynamic of everyday encounters and the production of the social order. The pioneering ideas of Schutz and Garfinkel have had a profound impact on the development of contemporary interpretivist sociological approaches. Nevertheless, the focus on human actions and consciousness comes at the expense of a more rounded analysis of the social world in terms of understanding the explanatory role of power and structural forces in shaping social life.

References

Barber, M. D. (2004) *The Participating Citizen: A Biography of Alfred Schutz*. New York: SUNY Press.
Bauman, Z. (1973) On the Philosophical Status of Ethnomethodology. *Sociological Review*, 21(1), pp. 5–23.
Bauman, Z. (1976) *Towards a Critical Sociology: An Essay on Commonsense and Emancipation*. London: Routledge & Kegan Paul.
Berger, P. L. and Luckmann, T. (1966) *The Social Construction of Reality: A Treatise in the Sociology of Knowledge*. Garden City, NY: Doubleday.
Berger, P. L. and Luckmann, T. (1991) *The Social Construction of Reality: A Treatise in the Sociology of Knowledge*. London: Penguin.
Bourdieu, P. (1990) *In Other Words: Essays Towards a Reflexive Sociology*. M. Adamson, trans. Stanford, CA: Stanford University Press.
Cicourel, A. V. (1967) *The Social Organization of Juvenile Justice*. New York: Wiley.
Cuff, E. C. and Payne, G. C. F. (1979) *Perspectives in Sociology*. London: George Allen & Unwin.
Douglas, J. D. (1967) *The Social Meanings of Suicide*. Princeton, NJ: Princeton University Press.
Filmer, P., Phillipson, M., Silverman, D. and Walsh, D. (1973) *New Directions in Sociological Theory*. Cambridge, MA: MIT Press.
Garfinkel, H. (1967) *Studies in Ethnomethodology*. Englewood Cliffs, NJ: Prentice Hall.
Garfinkel, H., Lynch, M. and Livingstone, E. (1981) The Work of a Discovering Science Construed with Materials from the Optically Discovered Pulsar. *Philosophy of the Social Sciences*, 11(2), pp. 131–158.
Gellner, E. (1979) *Words and Things: An Examination of, and an Attack on, Linguistic Philosophy*. London: Routledge & Kegan Paul.
Gouldner, A. W. (1972) *The Coming Crisis of Western Sociology*. London: Heinemann.

Habermas, J. (1987) *The Theory of Communicative Action, Vol. 2: Lifeworld and System: A Critique of Functionalist Reason.* T. McCarthy, trans. Cambridge: Polity.

Heritage, J. (1998) *Garfinkel and Ethnomethodology.* Cambridge: Polity.

Hindess, B. (1972) The 'Phenomenological' Sociology of Alfred Schutz. *Economy and Society,* 1(1), pp. 1-27.

Husserl, E. (1970) *The Crisis of European Sciences and Transcendental Phenomenology.* Evanston, IL: Northwestern University Press.

Husserl, E (1989) *Ideas Pertaining to a Pure Phenomenology and to a Phenomenological Philosophy – Second Book: Studies in the Phenomenology of Constitution* R. Rojcewicz and A. Schuwer, trans. Dordrecht: Kluwer.

Maynard, D. W. and Clayman, S. E. (2003) Ethnomethodology and Conversation Analysis. In: L. Reynolds and N. Herman-Kinney (eds) *Handbook of Symbolic Interactionism.* Walnut Creek, CA: Altamira Press, pp. 173-202.

Mennell, S. (1975) Ethnomethodology and the New 'Methodenstreit'. *Acta Sociologica,* 18(4), pp. 287-302.

Natanson, M. (1962) Introduction. In: A. Schutz, *Collected Papers, Vol. 1: The Problem of Social Reality.* The Hague: Nijhoff.

Sacks, H., Schegloff, E., Jefferson, G. and Korbut, A. (2015) A Simplest Systematics for the Organization of Turn-Taking in Conversation. *Russian Sociological Review,* 14(1), pp. 142-202.

Schorske, C. (1981) *Fin-de-siècle Vienna.* New York: Vintage.

Schutz, A. (1962) *Collected Papers, Vol. 1: The Problem of Social Reality.* The Hague: Nijhoff.

Schutz, A. (1964) *Collected Papers, Vol. 2: Studies in Social Theory.* The Hague: Nijhoff.

Schutz, A. (1967) *The Phenomenology of the Social World.* Evanston, IL: Northwestern University Press.

Smith, A. (2003) *Husserl and the Cartesian Meditations.* London: Routledge.

Steinbock, A. (1995) *Home and Beyond: Generative Phenomenology after Husserl.* Evanston, IL: Northwestern University Press.

Gramsci

Antonio Gramsci has been described as the most original Marxist thinker produced in the West since 1917 (Hobsbawm, 1977: 206). He was, however, hardly known during his lifetime and only recognised in Italy at the end of the Second World War. His work began to be more widely read in Europe following de-Stalinisation and translations of his books in the 1970s. Gramsci's fame rests on one major work, his *Prison Notebooks*, a collection of his writings composed while he was in prison, and never intended for publication. The central concept he deals with and has become renowned for, is hegemony, which breaks down the binary contrast between domination by force, or through consent. Hegemony refers to the dominance of one social bloc over another largely through cultural and moral processes. Part of Gramsci's appeal rests on the way he engages with an array of non-economic topics often sidelined by Marxists: the role of intellectuals, the structure of the ruling classes, how relations of authority are sustained, leadership, morality, the function of literature and folklore culture, philology and linguistics, the relation between state and civil society, and the consciousness of the peasantry. But his popularity also partly arises from the fact that the *Prison Notebooks* are textually ambiguous, allowing for a diversity of interpretations.

Life and Intellectual Context

Gramsci was born on 22 January 1891 in Ales in Sardinia into a family of six siblings. His father, Francesco Gramsci, a clerk in the local registrar's office, was imprisoned between 1898 and 1904 for embezzlement and extortion, perhaps as a vendetta for supporting an opposition political candidate. As a result Antonio grew up in deep poverty. In order to provide for her children, his mother, Guiseppina Marcias, sold their small plot of land and became a seamstress. At the age of three Gramsci suffered from Pott's disease, leading to a deformation of the spine and rendering him a hunchback, frequently suffering bouts of illness. In 1898 he began to attend school but his schooling remained unfinished since the family's financial situation necessitated his finding work.

He took up a job at the age of 11 at a local municipality office where he carried heavy registers, further exacerbating his physical ailments. Following his father's release from prison, Gramsci, in 1905, resumed his education at Santa Lussurgiu, moving in with his brother, who was an active campaigning member of the Italian Socialist Party (PSI). Antonio won a scholarship in 1911 to Turin University, where he specialised in linguistics, Latin, Italian literature, geography, Greek literature, moral philosophy and modern history.

However, he left university to join the Italian Socialist Party in 1912. The PSI, which retained strong ties with the Second International, also contained Benito Mussolini (1883–1945), who would later become the leader of Italian fascism. Between 1915 and 1916 Gramsci became a journalist for two socialist newspapers, the weekly *Il Grido del Popolo* (*The City of the People*) and *Avanti*! (*Forward*), for which he worked as a theatre critic. Following the 1917 Russian Revolution, which had a profound impact on his thinking, he published the *Revolution against Capital* which, *pace* Marx, recognised the possibility of socialism taking place in less economically developed countries, including his native Italy. In May 1919, along with Palmiro Togliatti, he founded the journal *L'Ordine Nuovo* (*The New Order*). Subtitled 'Review of socialist culture', the journal supported the Turin Workers' factory councils and workers' control and, among other things, examined workers' culture, education and consciousness, as well as Taylorist forms of production, serving as an organ for proletarian culture. Following the quashing of a general strike held by the factory councils in 1920, Gramsci left the PSI and became elected to the central committee of the newly founded Italian Communist Party (PCI) led by Amadeo Bordiga, an elitist and dogmatic figure. In 1922 Gramsci moved to Moscow as a delegate representing the PCI in the Comintern (Communist International), where he met and later married Julia Schuct in 1923. Following his return to Italy via Vienna, in 1924, he replaced Bordiga as leader of the PCI. In 1925 he began his unfinished essay 'Some Aspects of the Southern Question'.

Following an assassination attempt on his life, Mussolini introduced a wave of repressive policies directed at socialists, as well as reducing parliamentary power as a whole. Before Gramsci could challenge the introduction of such emergency measures, he was arrested on 8 November 1926. After a trial in 1928 in which the prosecutor is reputed to have stated 'we have to stop this brain for working for 20 years', he was sentenced to 20 years' imprisonment. Initially incarcerated in Turin until 1933, he was subsequently moved to a clinic in Formia between 1933 and 1935, and finally to the Quisisana Clinic in Rome. While in prison he began writing what became known as his *Prison Notebooks*. Initially only permitted to write to his sister in Italy, Tatiana, and his wife, he later gained a general permission to write in 1929. Without access to the works of Marx or Engels, Gramsci often quoted their work from memory and used elliptical phrases and pseudonyms to evade the prison censor. With a rapid deterioration of his health brought on by his life in prison, he suffered a major stroke, and a few days after his release, he died on 27 April 1937. After his death, his sister-in-law smuggled 33 notebooks containing 2,848 pages of text from the prison with the aid of the Italian economist Pierro Sraffa (1898–1983). The *Prison Notebooks* were published in Italy between 1948 and 1951 and translated into English in 1971.

Intellectual Influences

By contrast to the Marxists of the Second International, such as Kautsky and Bernstein, as well as widespread technologically deterministic and economically reductionist understandings of Marx, Gramsci sought to provide a more nuanced and plausible interpretation of how a workers' revolution could come about, both in the West generally, and in Italy specifically, given the latter's predominant rural or economically semi-developed nature. In this regard he drew on a number of traditional Marxist sources including Marx and Lenin, but also non-Marxist thinkers such as Machiavelli, and the Hegelian philosopher, Croce.

In his famous work, *The Prince*, Niccolò Machiavelli (1469–1527) had sanctioned the use of both brute force and deceit as necessary tools for a 'new prince' to establish and maintain his rule. Taken as a central tract of *realpolitik* of means justifying ends: his work has been read as a justification for instrumental policies that enable governments to maintain their rule. Gramsci, however, was less impressed with Machiavelli's notion of instrumentality than his notion of dual struggle – 'there are two methods of fighting, the one by law and the other by force', Machiavelli's scientific detachment, and his belief in bringing the mass of peasants into political life by, for example, including them in the militia. In this sense Gramsci saw Machiavelli as akin to Marx, a precursor of the 'modern Jacobins' – those political radicals who had brought about the revolution in France.

The Hegelian philosopher Benedetto Croce (1866–1952) also exercised a deep influence on Gramsci's thinking. A member of the Italian Senate, becoming Minister of Education between 1921 and 1922, Croce used much of his work to criticise positivism, which had taken on a widespread influence, especially in universities, as well as in Marxist thinking, and to replace it with a Hegelian form of historical idealism. Croce believed individuals did not adopt ideas because of their truth values, or because they were the best ones available, but rather because they found them more amenable, hiding the reality of existence. In his journal *La Critica*, Croce attempted to institute a form of cultural renewal in Italy. According to Gramsci:

> Credit must therefore be given to Croce's thought for its instrumental value and in this respect it may be said that it has forcefully drawn attention to the study of factors of culture and ideas as elements of political domination, to the function of great intellectuals in state life, to the moment of hegemony and consent as the necessary form of the concrete historical bloc. (1995: 332)

A central concept that Gramsci took from Croce was his notion of 'ethico-political history', a history of moral or civil life which Gramsci saw as 'the real crowning achievement of Croce's whole philosophical work' (1995: 367).

Historical, Social and Political Context

Like Lukács, Gramsci responded to what he perceived as the fatalism and mechanical determinism inherent in Second International Marxism, as well as in the PSI. By emphasising the political and active dimension of Marxism, the importance of the state and the subjective outlook of the proletariat, like Lenin, he sought to foreground the 'primacy of politics' (Simon, 1991: 15). Gramsci's work was deeply shaped both by the ongoing polemic in the European workers' movement, and by the Italian national context within which it developed. As Hobsbawm (1977) notes, Italy contained a number of peculiarities and contradictions that were reflected not only its national political thought – ranging from Machiavelli's work in the sixteenth century to Pareto and Mosca in the twentieth century – but also its literary and artistic output.

Italian Unification

In Italy, an elite national Italian culture developed before nation-state formation took place. The unification of the country through the *Risorgamento* was a slow and uneven process, taking over 100 years, beginning in 1815. Moreover, though formally declaring itself a state in 1861, Italy and its unification remained, in some ways, unfinished. Hobsbawm summarises these Italian socio-political peculiarities concerning the advent of a bourgeois revolution and national unification:

a. That Italy pioneered modern civilization and capitalism several centuries before other countries, but was unable to maintain its achievement and drifted into a sort of backwater between Renaissance and Riorgimento.

b. That unlike France the bourgeoisie did not establish its society by a triumphant revolution, and unlike Germany it did not accept a compromise solution offered it by an old ruling class from above. Instead it effected it a 'partial' revolution: achieved from above – by Cavour – and from below Garibaldi.

c. The Italian bourgeoisie failed – or partly failed – to achieve its historic mission to create the Italian nation. Its revolution remained incomplete. (1977: 207)

Italy itself represented a microcosm of the broader world economy. It contained both advanced and developed regions, such as Turin, driven forward by the Fiat industry and a powerful proletarian labour movement, and a profoundly undeveloped and almost semi-colonial region, including Sardinia, with a predominantly rural peasant population. Gramsci grew up in the latter, but lived a large part of his adult life, and based himself in the former. This contrast between an industrialised capitalism in the north of the country and a rural feudalism in the south, was expressed in what we would now consider as proto-racist northern views of the south as backward and uncivilised. Politically, it was the north that dominated rule in the country while the south followed. Even the major figures of national unification reflected this division with Cavour deriving from the north, while Mazzini and Garibaldi represented the south.

The pronounced national, socio-economic schism played a key role in Gramsci's work. Not only did it allow him to view both regions and contrast their diverging capitalist and semi-feudal socio-economic development, but also, politically, he sought to complete the unfinished process of national unification by the proletariat, under a socialist state. Italy was also sharply divided ideologically between a left and right, often holding each other in check and the country in stasis. In terms of religion, the Catholic Church remained a powerful force supporting the Italian ruling classes independently of the state. In the latter part of the nineteenth century, aping other successful European powers, Italy also began a policy of colonialism, colonising parts of Africa including Eritrea. Its position of neutrality as a member of the Triple Alliance soon ended as it entered the war in the spring of 1915. The need for increased war-time production led to huge strikes throughout the country. Nevertheless, war fuelled industrial production grew – the workforce at Fiat, for example, grew 10-fold from a base of 4,000 workers. In addition, at the beginning of the war in 1914, the labour movement, reflecting the deep national divide, was characterised by a unique configuration, compared with other European states, containing both industrial workers and a rural peasantry.

The First World War and Russian Revolution

Much of the Italian population, but especially the left, was opposed to the war, which they perceived had no clear benefits for them. The war was also to have profound consequences for a country characterised by a poorly trained and ill-equipped army, a fragmented political and governmental regime, and highly strained finances. Its aftermath engendered a profound economic crisis. Many peasants had been drafted, depleting agricultural production, while state financing of the war resulted in huge debt and sky-rocketing inflation. Living standards had also fallen for the majority, though some capitalists gained through war-time production. In such a catastrophic context, trade unions, to which workers turned, were perceived by many as bureaucratic, elitist and unconnected to the life they lived. In their stead Factory Councils of workers began to emerge and express their interests. Gramsci believed that these Councils could replace both trade unions and capitalists by increasing the technical capacity of workers and facilitating their control over the workplace: 'they must be the organs of proletarian power, replacing the capitalist in all his useful functions of management and administration' (Gramsci, 1977: 65).

In the context of a war-torn world, facing a huge economic crisis, and following the Russian Revolution, the 'mechanical determinism' of the Second International and the Comintern became highly influential. Their ideological stance engendered a passive attitude in the proletariat of waiting for the inevitable economic collapse of capitalism engendered by its contradictions – induced by technology or overproduction. Such contradictions in the economic base of society would, it was posited, automatically lead to socio-political changes in the political superstructure. Such a political, tactical and organisational stance thwarted the exercise of political initiatives by the labour movement. Moreover, Italy in 1917 was a place where both the objective and subjective conditions for a revolution existed – more so than the UK, France and Germany (Hobsbawm, 1977: 207). Instead of socialism, however, in October 1922, and following his 'March to Rome', Mussolini became President of the Council of Ministers and heralded the beginnings of fascism in Europe.

Notwithstanding the Russian Revolution, Gramsci's work, like that of other Marxists and the Frankfurt School, needs to be understood as developing during a period in which the worker's movement had suffered many defeats (Jones, 2006: 42). This included the failure of the German, Austrian and Hungarian Revolutions; the losses suffered by the Italian factory workers' movement in 1920; and significantly, the victory of Mussolini's fascism. Such losses focused Gramsci on the necessary theoretical and tactical choices facing the working class if it were to succeed in establishing a socialist future, especially in a context where the bourgeoisie had reorganised and fortified themselves following various workers' revolutions.

The failure of the spontaneous uprisings instigated by the Communist Party in Germany (the KPD) in 1921 which had challenged Prussian power – often referred to as the March Action – and the development of an ultraleftist line by the Communist International in 1928 in which revolution was seen to be immanent and inevitable and social democracy reductively identified with fascism, led Gramsci to conceptualise his notion of revolutionary strategy in terms of a long-term strategy of attrition dubbed a 'war of position'. This was absolutely necessary he believed in advanced, developed capitalist states and contrasted with the policy of immediate overthrow or 'war of manoeuvre' characterising the disastrous March Action and policies of the Comintern of the Third Period. The war of position foregrounded the importance of gradually and patiently winning over the masses to revolutionary Marxism before acquiring power through the development of a United Front (Anderson, 2017: 115). Gramsci, like many other Marxists including Lukács, therefore attempted to rework old Marxist concepts in the precarious and rapidly changing historical and geographic context of his time, often by using the language of Machiavelli or Croce. But the structure of capitalist production and its correlative production techniques had dramatically changed since Marx's day. In his work, Gramsci therefore discusses the rise of Americanism and Fordism, of the development of assembly line production, especially by Henry Ford in his factories, as well as the 'scientific management' techniques of 'Taylorism'.

Arguments and Ideas

The *Prison Notebooks*

Written between 1929 and 1936, the *Prison Notebooks* undoubtedly constitute Gramsci's major contribution to sociological theory. There are, however, a number of difficulties with the book. As ongoing notes they were not intended for publication, and are instead opaque, fragmented, contradictory and disjointed. Gramsci also infuses old Marxist concepts with new meanings and discusses novel ideas and concepts in, for example, the language of Croce. Gramsci is also deliberately vague in his writings in order to escape the prison censor, for example, Marxism is referred to as 'the philosophy of practice', or Lenin is referred to by his Christian name, Illich. The unknown order of the articles, as well as the separate books, therefore made it difficult to compile them into a coherent overall work. Paradoxically, however, it was precisely their open and tentative character that permitted the development of an undogmatic Marxism, and gave the book its broad appeal.

Hegemony

The central idea underpinning Gramsci's concept of hegemony is that social classes, and their representatives, dominate subordinate or 'subaltern' groups, through a combination of coercion and consent, force and persuasion. Hegemony is a relation which focuses primarily on the latter: domination through consent, by means of rational political, cultural and moral leadership. The key terms involved in hegemony are 'directing', 'leadership' and 'consent'. The concept of hegemony has its origins in Greek thought (*egemonia*) and dates as far back as Homer where it meant to guide or to lead (Anderson, 2017: 2). The concept was then used by Russian Marxists such as Plekanov in the 1880s to denote the need for the working class to lead an alliance with other oppressed groups, including the peasantry, for the overthrow of tsarism in the context of a weak ruling bourgeoisie. It was subsequently used by Lenin who argued that revolution did not arise automatically from economic crises and that the working class, in alliance with the peasantry, should act as the leading hegemonic force in a bourgeois democratic revolution geared to the overthrow of the tsarist autocracy. For Lenin, hegemony was a strategy of leadership which a minority working class deployed in order to gain the support of other dominated groups – including the peasantry, but also various national minorities – which together constituted the majority of the population.

Although Gramsci explicitly credits Lenin with the concept (Gramsci, 1971: 381), and he may have picked it up while in Moscow as a member of the Comintern, it was also often used in Italian thought in the late nineteenth century (Boothman, 2008). Moreover, Gramsci modifies and extends the use of the term. With Gramsci it now included strategies used by other classes, principally bourgeois classes, in acquiring state power, but also in maintaining power following its attainment, and it was now also to be understood and applied to the West rather than only in the East. Hegemony is then a relationship of both domination and leadership based on cultural and moral direction of one class by another, an alliance that primarily suits the dominant hegemonic strata though the subordinate grouping may also partly benefit from this direction. A class can only achieve hegemony by acknowledging and taking on board the values, aspirations and outlooks of the other social classes and movements and including them with its own interests. By acquiring the consent of other classes and various social movements, through cultural, moral, political and ideological struggle, the hegemonic class achieves hegemonic leadership. It is only with the existence and development of rational forms of leadership that a class can acquire state power in the first place:

> The supremacy of a social group manifests itself in two ways, as 'domination' and as 'intellectual and moral leadership'. A social group can, indeed must, already exercise 'leadership' before winning governmental power (this is indeed one of the principal conditions for the winning of such power); it subsequently becomes dominant when it exercises power, but even if it holds it firmly in its grasp, it must continue to 'lead' as well. (Gramsci, 1971: 57–8)

Force and Consent

Hobsbawm has argued that 'Gramsci's major contribution to Marxism is to have pioneered a Marxist theory of politics' (1977: 207). This entails seeing politics as an autonomous activity, irreducible to economics, as in a crude Marxist base/superstructure understanding, though nonetheless structured by class and historical forces. Gramsci is centrally concerned with *both* the strategic means of socialists winning state power *and* what socialism will look like after power has been acquired. As Hobsbawm notes: 'for Gramsci (as for Marx) the struggle to overthrow capitalism and build socialism is essentially a continuum, in which the actual transfer of power is only one moment' (1982: 28). Politics is the core means for arriving at socialism and of socialism as an end itself. Both of these processes of politics as a means, and as an end, include economic criteria relating to the socialisation and regulation of production geared to need rather than profit. But they additionally require political and ideological socialisation and education. The working class then needs to achieve hegemony before attaining power, during the seizure of power and also after acquiring power.

The dialectical balance between force and consent in ruling and in national life, generally, is for Gramsci, fundamental. Drawing on Machiavelli's notion of a minotaur, half-human, half-animal, as signifying what he refers to as a 'dual perspective' of force and consent, Gramsci argues that the working class can only:

> become the leading and the dominant class to the extent that it succeeds in creating a system of class alliances which allows it to mobilize the majority of the working population against capitalism and the bourgeois state. (1994: 320)

A hegemonic class for Gramsci needs to transcend its own limited 'economic–corporate' struggles by introducing compromises with other groups into its policy formation and intellectual and moral outlook. Corporate classes remain trapped in their narrow economic interests, while hegemonic classes expansively impose their own ends and vision onto society as a whole. A hegemonic class needs to recalibrate its formulation of policy in the light of other sectional and often non-economic interests. These interests be based, for example, on popular, nationally focused or democratic demands that remain irreducible to the struggle between capital and labour. They include the right to vote, women's rights, the peace movement or environmental issues. Both the bourgeoisie and the proletariat therefore take part in a struggle to make robust alliances with other economic and non-economic groupings and to win the 'hearts and minds' of the population. By incorporating these alternative subaltern progressive interests and worldviews or values into its own agenda, a hegemonic class simultaneously transforms and renews itself. Such an understanding militates against a simplistic use of Marx's base–superstructure metaphor, which would deem 'superstructural' conflicts in politics, culture, law, etc. as peripheral struggles, compared with those within the process of production. Instead of referring to the base–superstructure as an explanatory concept Gramsci instead talks of what he calls a 'historic bloc'. When a hegemonic revolutionary class is able politically, morally and intellectually to lead its subaltern allies composed of a broad alliance of social classes and groups, it becomes a power or historical bloc. Such a bloc exercises leadership not only in the process of production but also in civil society, with a long-term and broad-based popular appeal. It possesses, a *'national–popular dimension'*. Unlike many Marxist writers, Gramsci places significant emphasis both on the uniqueness of different national histories and trajectories, and on the national popular dimension of social formations, especially given the context of the national division of Italy:

> In reality, the internal relations of any nation are the result of a combination which is 'original' and (in a certain sense) unique: these relations must be understood and conceived in their originality and uniqueness if one wishes to dominate them and direct them. To be sure, the line of development is towards internationalism, but the point of departure is 'national' – and it is from this point of departure that one must begin. (1971: 240)

Traditions of national struggle for liberation, according to Gramsci, entail patriotism and nationalism which help mobilise powerful emotional responses akin to religious fervour. A hegemonic class therefore gains national leadership by successfully including patriotic struggles and values within its own corporate class interests. These are important not only because hegemony needs to delve deeply into emotional forms of identification, in addition to rational adherence, but also because national forms of patriotism possess almost universal appeal. In addition, in his discussion of the *Risorgimento* Gramsci argues that the bourgeois strategy for building alliances entailed a *passive revolution*: that is, it was often imposed from above by the state. Gramsci saw fascism in such terms. By contrast, the working class relies on an anti-passive revolution involving popular participation and struggles from below.

The Organic and the Conjunctural

Gramsci also distinguishes between what he calls 'organic' long-term socio-economic and political processes and movements from more short-term, superficial, 'conjunctural' analyses:

> In studying a structure, it is necessary to distinguish organic movements (relatively permanent) from movements which may be termed 'conjunctural' (and which appear as occasional, immediate, almost accidental). Conjunctural phenomena too depend upon organic movements to be sure, but they do not have any far-reaching historical significance; they give rise to political criticism of a minor day-to-day character, which has as its subject top political leaders and personalities with direct governmental responsibilities. Organic phenomena on the other hand give rise to socio-historical criticism, whose subject is wider social groupings—beyond the public figures and beyond top leaders. (1971: 178)

[Republished with permission of International Publishers from *Selections from the Prison Notebooks* (Q. Hoare & G. Nowell-Smith, trans. & ed.), A. Gramsci, 1971]

According to Gramsci, historical and political analyses often confuse what is conjunctural with what is organic, thereby 'presenting causes as immediately operative which in fact only operate indirectly, or to asserting the immediate causes are the only effective ones' (1971: 178). The first standpoint indicates an excess of economism or mechanical causes; the second of 'ideologism' or an overemphasis on the voluntarist and individual element of classes.

Given that a hegemonic class maintains hegemony on a day-to-day basis in the context of shifting socio-political and economic conditions, new and fresh compromises with other classes or social forces need to be continually effected in order adapt within the ever-unfolding political conjuncture. With changing circumstances the hegemonic position that a ruling or leading class holds can disappear. In certain exceptional conditions, characterised by deep, long-term socio-economic and political crises and profound instability – 'organic crises' – new struggles over hegemony can emerge:

> A crisis occurs, sometimes lasting for decades. This exceptional duration means that incurable contradictions have revealed themselves (reached maturity) and that, despite this, the political forces which are struggling to conserve and defend the existing structure itself are making every effort to cure them, within certain limits, and to overcome them. These incessant and persistent efforts … form the terrain of the 'conjunctural' and it upon this terrain that the forces of opposition organize. (1971: 178)

[Republished with permission of International Publishers from *Selections from the Prison Notebooks* (Q. Hoare & G. Nowell-Smith, trans. & ed.), A. Gramsci, 1971]

In such a context, the hegemonic class may need to undertake major transformations in its political alliances, values, moral orientation, practices and mode of rule in order to maintain its dominant position.

Strategies for Gaining Power in the East and West

According to Gramsci, the Bolsheviks' acquisition of power in Russia could not be straightforwardly emulated by working-class parties in Western Europe where the balance of class forces and the relationship between civil society and stated differed. Drawing on a military metaphor, he makes a distinction between what he calls a 'war of manoeuver' operative in the East, and a 'war of position' which would be required to gain power in the West. In the East, civil society was comparatively undeveloped with power concentrated largely in the state. Power could therefore be 'captured' through a frontal attack on the state. In the West, however, power has become diffused throughout civil society and its various institutions including the parliament, the media and schools, which now stands behind the state. In the West, there exists 'a powerful system of fortresses and earthworks', thwarting an abrupt revolution against the state. Given such a scenario, and in opposition to sections of the PCI, Gramsci believed a short, sharp, frontal or direct attack on the state was therefore impossible. Instead, a long-term process of 'siege warfare' in which the working class made alliances to gain hegemony was necessary. The complex array of institutions and practices within civil society in the West were made evident to Gramsci following the defeat of the Factory Councils and of various socialist uprisings between 1918 and 1919 in Germany and Hungary.

State and Civil Society

Gramsci operates with a richer and broader understanding of the concept of civil society compared with both Hegel and Marx. It not only entails the family as for the former, but also includes other 'private' organisations. Nevertheless, like Hegel and Marx, civil society takes its substantive meaning in relation to the concept of the state:

> What we can do, for the moment, is to fix two major superstructural 'levels': the one that can be called 'civil society', that is, the ensemble of organisms commonly called 'private', and that of 'political society' or 'the state'. These two levels correspond on the one hand to the functions of 'hegemony' which the dominant group exercises throughout society and on the other to that of 'direct domination' or command exercised through the state and 'juridical' government. (Gramsci, 1971: 12)

However, like many of his key concepts in the *Prison Notebooks*, his understanding of civil society contains many ambiguities. It appears to include 'private' and consensual organisations such as the trade unions, churches, schools, families, political parties, sports and cultural associations, and the media, which are distinguished from the 'public' and coercive organisation of the state, as well as the process of production. It is the sphere in which a plethora of class and social struggles occurs. However, in addition 'secondary' conflicts that remain irreducible to economic criteria based on nation, sex, region, etc. can also take place in this sphere. In addition, civil society also includes banal or 'quotidian' struggles over values and beliefs, everyday practices, and activities. As Jones notes:

> Civil society certainly includes the legal apparatus, but it also includes children's parties, shopping trips and going on holiday. As it becomes more and more a matter of 'everyday life', so it becomes increasingly difficult to recognize that civil society has some connection with the operations of power... Gardening, for instance, is certainly bound up with issues of, among other things, home ownership, family life, nationality and consumerism, and therefore contains within it certain wisdoms about the world which are functional to modern capitalism. But it cannot be reduced to those things, and nor is it likely to be articulated in these terms. Rather than being expressed in terms of class, it may be expressed in terms of other social divisions such as gender or age, or in terms of other categories entirely, such as pleasure. Yet it is precisely in this private realm that ruling values seem most natural and therefore unchangeable. A corollary to this is that a transformative politics which could thoroughly penetrate this realm would be both successful and durable. (2006: 32)
>
> [Copyright 2006 from *Antonio Gramsci* by S. Jones. Reproduced by permission of Taylor and Francis, a division of Informa plc]

Indicating a further shift away from Marx's base–superstructure metaphor, civil society then takes on an importance not just in class terms, as Marxists ordinarily view it, but also in everyday cultural terms, of how people live their lives and confer meaning on their activities, and the power relations that underlie these. Gramsci attempts to balance the two factors of economics and culture by conceptualising them as dialectically shaping one another.

As we noted above, the term 'civil society' derives its meaning in relation to the concept of the state or what Gramsci also terms 'political society'. Like Weber, who refers to the state's monopolisation of coercion and violence, political society refers primarily to coercive relationships which find expression in the military, courts, police force and state security, or 'which depend in the last resort for their effectiveness on the state's monopoly of coercion' (Simon, 1991: 71). According to Gramsci, when consent cannot be achieved in civil society, the state as a coercive body steps in:

the apparatus of state coercive power which 'legally' enforces discipline on those groups who do not consent either actively or passively. This apparatus is, however, constituted for the whole of society in anticipation of moments of crisis of command and direction when spontaneous consent has failed. (1971: 12)

Though primarily an institution of coercion, the state is also involved in securing consent. When it operates in such a way, it constitutes an 'integral state', a term used to indicate that the hegemonic class effects and wields power within the state both through its coercive institutions and through civil society, that is, through its voluntary organisations. Gramsci therefore understands state power in a more diffuse way than Lenin's discussion of power as concentrated in the state through bodies of armed men, etc. Moreover, the state, he argues, cannot be reduced to an instrument of the ruling class, but possesses a relative independence as an outcome of the contestation of class forces:

the dominant group is coordinated concretely with the general interests of the subordinate groups, and the life of the State is conceived of as a continuous process of formation and superseding of unstable equilibria (on the juridical plane) between the interests of the fundamental group and those of the subordinate groups – equilibria in which the interests of the dominant group prevail, but only up to a certain point, i.e. stopping short of narrowly corporate economic interest. (Gramsci, 1971: 182)

[Republished with permission of International Publishers from *Selections from the Prison Notebooks* (Q. Hoare & G. Nowell-Smith, trans. & ed.), A. Gramsci, 1971]

As in Bourdieu, the state is both the body through which rules and laws are effected, and which through its socialisation and educative function, shapes individuals and their thinking – it regulates social life:

If every State tends to create and maintain a certain type of civilisation and of citizen (and hence of collective life and of individual relations), and to eliminate certain customs and attitudes and to disseminate others, then the Law will be its instrument for this purpose (together with the school system, and other institutions and activities) ... the State must be conceived of as an 'educator', in as much as it tends precisely to create a new type or level of civilisation ... the State is an instrument of 'rationalisation', of acceleration and of Taylorisation. It operates according to a plan, urges, incites, solicits, and 'punishes'... The Law is the repressive and negative aspect of this entire positive civilising activity undertaken by the State. (Gramsci, 1971: 246–7)

[Republished with permission of International Publishers from *Selections from the Prison Notebooks* (Q. Hoare & G. Nowell-Smith, trans. & ed.), A. Gramsci, 1971]

For Gramsci the school has a 'positive educative function' while the courts possess a 'repressive and negative educative function' (1971: 258). The state retains an ethical function raising the mass of the population to a particular cultural and moral level, a level that corresponds to the needs of the productive forces for development and the interests of the ruling class. Rather than peripheral elements of the superstructure, both culture and politics are therefore relatively autonomous spheres with their own rules and logic, but nevertheless still connected to economic processes. For Gramsci, the working class needed to struggle against the state and the bourgeois class simultaneously.

Ideology, Intellectuals and Culture

Since Gramsci gives culture, beliefs and politics a central role in his theorising, his therefore also gives prominence to ideology, the role of consciousness and intellectuals. Intellectual and moral reform entails transforming the way in which the mass of the population conceives itself. Intellectuals play a significant role in this process through organising hegemony in civil society by shaping the consciousness of various strata and by giving this consciousness some kind of coherence. Intellectuals operate as 'organisers of masses of men'. They must have the 'capacity to be an organiser of society in general, including all its complex organism of services, right up to the state organism because of the need to create the conditions most favourable to the expansion of their own class' (Gramsci, 1971: 5–6). It is not the role of the intellectual simply to be eloquent, but 'in active participation in practical life, as constructor, organiser, "permanent persuader" and not just a simple orator' (1971: 10). Furthermore, Gramsci eschews the view that intellectuals are a specialised strata of individuals characterised by the practice of thinking. In fact, all men, including workers and proletarians are characterised by 'a minimum of creative intellectual activity' (1971: 8). Everyone therefore thinks, or has a worldview:

> Each man, finally, outside his professional activity, carries on some form of intellectual activity, that is, he is a 'philosopher', an artist, a man of taste, he participates in a particular conception of the world, has a conscious line of moral conduct, and therefore contributes to sustain a conception of the world or to modify it. (1971: 9)

Although all individuals have a conception of the world which guides them, only some function to help organise, lead, educate in the sphere of production, culture and politics: 'all men are intellectuals one could say: but not all men have in society the function of intellectuals' (1971: 9).

Every class, Gramsci argues, creates its own representative group of intellectuals who speak for it, and rationalise its actions and value systems into a coherent whole. Distinguishing between 'organic intellectuals' and 'traditional intellectuals', he argues that organic intellectuals represent rising classes such as the bourgeoisie or workers. For the bourgeoisie, they include for example, managers, teachers, technicians, civil servants, writers and journalists. By contrast, traditional intellectuals tend to refer to intellectuals from former social formations, or 'out of the preceding economic structure' (1971: 6), deriving especially from classes who are no longer central to the modern capitalist system, such as the aristocracy, petty bourgeoisie and peasantry. These intellectuals include, for example, ecclesiastics, priests, lawyers and doctors. Intellectuals are also conceived to be part of the revolutionary party, understood in Leninist terms as a vanguard organisation of the proletariat, but with a greater degree of interaction between members and leaders deriving from a democratic centralism. By creating a collective will, instituting a process of 'intellectual and moral reform', instilling discipline and innovation, the Party constitutes what, alluding to Machiavelli, Gramsci calls the 'modern prince'.

It is also the role of intellectuals to examine and reconfigure the extant common sense of individuals. Common sense refers to the tacit, unsystematic, spontaneous and taken-for-granted belief system shared by members of capitalist society, through which they organise their daily living experiences and make sense of them. It was on this historical and unstable ground on which a nation's thinking rested. Common sense plays a central role in hegemony, by protecting the ruling class from the critical scrutiny of opponents, and by rationalising and justifying a social order and its values and thinking. Being sourced from a number of contradictory elements, the composite personality and consciousness of an individual can be incoherent:

> When one's conception of the world is not critical and coherent but disjointed and episodic, one belongs simultaneously to a mass of human groups. The personality is strangely composite: 'it includes Stone Age elements and principles of a more advanced science, prejudices from all past phases of history and intuitions of a future philosophy which will be that of a human race united the world over.' (Gramsci, 1971: 324)

As a result:

> each individual is the synthesis not only of existing relations, but of the history of these relations. He [sic] is a precis of all the past. (1971: 353)

People's consciousness is not only a summation of the historical past but continually re-negotiated in a complex process of hierarchical class struggle: between the differentiated and competing worldviews of various class strata, the bourgeoisie and proletariat, or struggles between the Church and class strata. It is by effectively harnessing these worldviews, based on both emotional and rational forms of identification, to their own class conception of society that the bourgeoisie or Catholic Church maintains hegemonic domination, preventing the proletariat or other subaltern groups from challenging an unjust social order.

It is the task of working-class organic intellectuals to disentangle the progressive aspects of such contradictory common sense from the reactionary bourgeois elements, in order to heighten the socialist standpoint and transform the contradictory consciousness into a more coherent 'good sense', a broad and encompassing, critical socialist worldview – a positive common sense.

Discussions of popular culture, linguistics, national literature, theatre and opera play a significant explanatory role in Gramsci's account of how classes acquire and maintain state power or how they communicate their power and reproduce it. Gramsci remained concerned throughout his life with developing ideas rooted in the everyday life of the masses. In some cases, he argued, forms of popular culture, folklore or regional dialects offer resistance to officially sanctioned national language and culture. As Jones argues:

> while most intellectuals view folklore as 'picturesque' and old-fashioned, his [Gramsci's] own conception treats it as a living 'conception of the world and life' which stands in implicit opposition to 'official' conceptions of the world. Because subjugated people, and particularly semi-literate or illiterate people, lacking the centralizing institutions (such as printing) which could standardize their conceptions of the world, folklore is unelaborated, deeply traditional, unsystematic and many-sided. Yet it is neither dead nor limited, for new scientific and social understandings will be incorporated into it, in however haphazard a fashion, and it is 'tenacious', providing people with a rich cultural and emotional orientation towards the world which is extremely difficult to change. Gramsci's purpose is not to simply endorse folklore, for he acknowledges that much of the culture of subordinate people is conservative and fatalistic. Instead he proposes that such 'fossilized' conceptions be disaggregated from those 'which are in the process of developing and which are in contradiction to or simply different from the morality of the governing strata' (1971: 190). Only by doing this could peasants and intellectuals be organized into part of the coalition in which communication could take place. (2006: 37)

[Copyright 2006 from *Antonio Gramsci* by S. Jones. Reproduced by permission of Taylor and Francis, a division of Informa plc]

Gramsci believed it was possible to study, within a country, all the forms of cultural organisation including schools, churches, universities and newspapers that kept the ideological world in movement and to assess the gaps and gulf between the ideas of the intellectuals and the masses.

Influence and Application

Gramsci's work has been used widely in many empirical studies in political theory, sociology, literary studies, cultural studies, post-colonial theory and international relations. In literary theory Raymond Williams in *Marxism and Literature* (1977) drew on Gramsci's discussion of hegemony to outline two oppositional forms of culture, the residual and the emergent. In international relations the work of Giovanni Arrighi has studied forms of imperialism as part of the dominant–subordinate relations between states in *The Geometry of Imperialism* (1977) and *The Long Twentieth Century* (1994). In post-colonial theory his work has been central to the development of subaltern studies, and the study of subaltern classes including the peasantry and urban poor, especially in the work of Ranajit Guha in books such as *Elementary Aspects of Peasant Insurgency in Colonial India* (1983) and *Dominance Without Hegemony* (1997). In political/historical/sociological terms Gramsci's work had a strong influence on the development of the British New Left, including the work of Perry Anderson and Tom Nairn, who were largely responsible for his introduction into the English-speaking world.

WESTERN MARXISM

After the deaths of Marx and Engels, a dogmatic version of Marxism became dominant, presenting it as a scientific theory of society and history focused on economics and politics. This orthodox determinism prompted a subsequent generation of theorists in Europe to advance a critical version of Marxism following the Russian Revolution. In addition to the work of Antonio Gramsci, Georg Lukács's *History and Class Consciousness* (1971 [1923]) and Karl Korsch's *Marxism and Philosophy* (2013 [1923]) inaugurated this heterodox tradition, which also encompasses the Frankfurt School. As opposed to the orthodox emphasis on scientific and economic aspects of Marxian theory, Western Marxism emphasises critical, Hegelian, humanist and dialectical aspects, seeing Marxism as primarily a critical theory concerned with the self-conscious transformation of society. Drawing from sociological and philosophical moments in Marx, Western Marxism is characterised by a focus on culture, ascribing it much more importance and autonomy than the orthodox reduction to the economic base.

In his essay 'Origins of the Present Crisis' (1964), Anderson undertakes an analysis of British history using Gramsci's ideas to argue that England in the 1960s, is in a state of crisis, including a long-term industrial decline. This organic crisis was to be explained by a series of historical developments specific to English class society from the civil war onwards: that it had the first and 'least pure' bourgeois revolution of any major European country; it produced the first Industrial Revolution and proletariat while socialist doctrines were still forming; it had the largest empire in history; and it remained undefeated in two world wars. These historical developments, especially the early industrial revolution, meant that for the most part England did not experience a 'proper' bourgeois revolution comparable with France in which the monarch was removed. Instead of emerging under an urban bourgeoisie, capitalism and culture developed under the yoke of a powerful *ancien régime*, an aristocracy which subsequently shaped its path of incomplete modernisation, a pre-modern state anchored in 1688, primitive and uninnovative forms of industrial development, and a highly stratified and stifling aristocratic culture. The aristocracy constituted the hegemonic class determining the character and customs that diffused throughout society. Such hegemony resulted in a traditionalism in outlook, empiricism in philosophy, and an absence of a revolutionary labour movement. Like Gramsci, Anderson attempted to trace the development of national society from the bourgeois revolution, which shaped the need for a specific socialist strategy in the West.

Gramsci's work was also taken up by Ernesto Laclau and Chantal Mouffe in their book, *Hegemony and Socialist Strategy* (1985). In a context of a number of newly emerging plural social struggles and multiplicity of subjects in flux – including those of gender, ethnicity and sexuality – which escape the singular reductive focus on class struggle of classical Marxism, Laclau and Mouffe argue that Marxism needs to be deconstructed and transformed. By focusing on a universal homogeneous working class that automatically and inevitably becomes conscious of its exploitation as a result of its position in the sphere of production, Marxism provides an 'essentialist' conceptualisation of politics which needs to be replaced, they argue, by a post-Marxist approach.

The authors attempt to develop a new understanding of hegemony within the framework of a post-structuralist notion of discourse, in which there are no fixed identities or interests, and subject positions in society are discursively constructed and politically negotiated. This forms the basis for the possible development of a radical democratic political programme. Although drawing on Gramsci's arsenal of concepts including the war of position, hegemony, historical bloc, intellectual and moral leadership, their analysis 'deconstructs' these concepts to develop a different approach from Gramsci, whom they believe remained too wedded to Lenin's class reductionism. For Laclau and Mouffe, hegemony is less about domination, and more about a strategy for creating a national–popular, politically constructed, collective will. Moreover, rather than framing Gramsci's concepts within a cultural materialism they embed them within what they conceive of as free-floating discursive sign systems. The aim of their political project is not to usher in a revolutionary socialism, through an alliance of classes, as Gramsci envisaged, but of a radical, libertarian, plural democracy in which socialism remains but one element. The subjects of this strategy are not social classes but subordinated groups whose identities and subject positions, created through discourse, remain irreducible to the sphere of production, and who participate in popular struggles operating on an indeterminate and open basis, that is in the 'moment of politics'. Such groups unify their diverse demands, through processes of 'articulation', developing a collective will on a contingent basis, with shared symbols and a common attempt to realise democratic demands. More recently their work has had a major impact on the development of hegemonic left populism, for example of Podemos in Spain. Prior to that their writings were widely influential in the development of Eurocommunism.

Gramsci's influence on culture and cultural studies came primarily through the work of Stuart Hall. Originally from Kingston, Jamaica, Hall became a Rhodes Scholar studying English literature at Oxford in 1951. A pioneering figure in the British New Left, he became editor of the *New Left Review* in 1960. As head of the Birmingham School of Cultural Studies, a position he acquired in 1964, he took up a detailed examination of popular culture drawing initially on Gramsci, but later Louis Althusser and post-structuralism. In *Resistance Through Rituals* with Tony Jefferson (1975) Hall examined the formation of oppositional subcultures in working-class youth, which challenged the hegemony of the dominant culture. These analyses were extended in his *Policing the Crisis* (1978) in which Hall analysed the emergence of various reactionary 'moral panics' around mugging, especially as articulated by the police, media and judiciary. Black youth represented 'folk devils' within the context of a major organic crises within the British state that began in the 1960s. Anticipating the rise of Margaret Thatcher to power in 1979, Hall argued that Thatcherism attempted to offer a solution to this crisis – welding together two distinct conservative tendencies, one focusing on tradition, authority, law and order, and the other on freedom and the market. Their combination resulted in an original hegemonic national–popular political vision and an understanding of common sense, that challenged the idea of a Keynesian welfare state and reversed the historic compromise between labour and capital, in place from 1945 onwards. The arguments concerning Thatcher's retention of power and hegemonic ability to mobilise social forces, to consolidate a 'swing to the right', were further developed in his article 'The Great Moving Right Show' (1979). The swing to the right from a labour centrist position was not, he argued, simply a symptom of the economic crisis, for such an argument:

> takes for granted what needs to be explained: how a capitalist economic recession is presided over by a social democratic party in power (politically) with mass working class support and organized depth in the trade unions; and 'lived' for increasing numbers of people through the themes and representations (ideologically) of a virulent, emergent 'petty-bourgeois' ideology. (1979: 14)

Instead, Hall argues, sociologists need to examine the attempt by the right to respond to the crisis by creating a new 'historic bloc', entailing a profound restructuring of the state, and the creation of ideological discourses through which these processes are understood and lived. The ideas of law and order, anti-collectivism, social discipline and authority emerged in the context of what the right saw as a conspiracy by enemies of the state. This included the dilution of British stock by immigrants, poor education creating illiteracy, and falling social standards, constituting part of an ideology of 'authoritarian populism'. This ideology been able to insert itself into the vacuum created by the inherent contradictions of social democracy, created in turn from attempting to regulate and intervene in a crisis-ridden capitalism:

> What makes these representations popular is that they have a purchase on practice, they shape it, they are written into its materiality. What constitutes them as a danger is that they change the nature of the terrain itself on which struggles of different kinds are taking place; and they have pertinent effects on these struggles. Currently, they are gaining ground in defining the 'conjunctural'. (1979: 20)

Although Hall's later work, drawing on Foucault and Derrida, increasingly focused on the politics of difference and identity, Hall considered Gramsci 'as the theorist of the political *par excellence*' (Hall, 1991: 8) and his analysis remained a central aspect of his approach.

Criticisms

Gramsci has been criticised on a number of fronts. These criticisms partly reflect the cryptic and provisional nature of *Prison Notebooks*. In his *Antimonies of Antonio Gramsci*, Anderson (2017) indicated a number of elisions and antinomies running through Gramsci's book, including his inconsistent use of state, civil society and hegemony, questioning their 'internal coherence as a unified discourse' (2017: 32). As Anderson argues with regard to the relationship between the state and civil society:

> there is thus an oscillation between at least three different 'positions' of the state in the West in these initial texts alone. It is a 'balanced relationship' with civil society, it is only an 'outer surface' of civil society, it is the 'massive structure' which cancels the autonomy of civil society. These oscillations, moreover, concern only the relationship between these terms. The terms themselves, however, are subject to the same sudden shifts of boundary and position. (2017: 41)

For Anderson, Gramsci also exaggerates the role of consent at the expense of the use of force in processes of socio-political domination. Roger Simon has criticised Gramsci's notion of organic and traditional intellectuals, arguing that they are both too undeveloped, and that his view that 'all men are intellectuals' is too 'all-embracing' (1991: 96). Hobsbawm also suggests that the role of intellectuals in some countries is 'less significant than he suggests' (1977: 210). Gramsci's concept of nationalism and its unreflective use by later Gramscians has also been criticised for being too narrow and for ignoring how race often articulates with nation. As Gilroy notes: 'Its enthusiasm for the language of nation and a national focus leads to contemporary association between British racism and British nationalism being overlooked' (1987: 26). It has also been argued that Gramsci's work does not go in enough detail or with sufficient clarity into the mechanisms through which hegemony is won, and maintained, on an ongoing basis (Anderson, 2017). Others, though lauding his attempt to move away from economic reductionism, have seen Gramsci's conferral of a high degree of autonomy to culture vis-à-vis economic processes, as resulting in an excessively idealist position (Bobbio, 1979). However, as Jones, referring to *Marx's Critique of Political Economy*, points out:

> Gramsci continues to believe that it is the contradictions in the economic sphere which create new organisational and ideological consciousness (2006: 33). The two processes operate on each other dialectically, as his concept of historic bloc tries to demonstrate.

Conclusion

Gramsci's writings are difficult and allow for a multiplicity of readings. His analysis of hegemony and cultural and moral leadership provides a useful counterpoint to economically reductionist readings of Marxism. However, issues of an excessive idealism and voluntarism are consequently seen to haunt his work. Yet, its optimistic nature in the context of socialist defeat and rising authoritarianism, is also of note. As he famously quipped: 'pessimism of the intellect, optimism of the will' (1977: 188).

References

Althusser, L. (2018) An Afternoon with Althusser. *New Left Review*, 113, September–October, pp. 59–66.
Anderson, P. (2017) *The Antinomies of Antonio Gramsci*. London: Verso.
Anderson, P. and Nairn, T. (1964) Origins of the Present Crisis. Reprinted in: P. Anderson (1992) *English Questions*. London: Verso, pp. 15–47.
Arrighi, G. (1977) *The Geometry of Imperialism: The Limits of Hobson's Paradigm*. London: New Left Books.
Arrighi, G. (1994) *The Long Twentieth Century: Money, Power, and the Origins of Our Times*. London: Verso.
Bobbio, N. (1979) Gramsci and the Conception of Civil Society. In: C. Mouffe (ed.). *Gramsci and Marxist Theory*. London: Routledge & Kegan Paul, pp. 21–47.
Boothman, D. (2008) The Sources of Gramsci's Concept of Hegemony. *Rethinking Marxism*, 20(2), pp. 201–15.
Gilroy, P. (1987) *There Ain't No Black in the Union Jack*. London: Unwin Hyman.

Gramsci, A. (1971) *Selections from the Prison Notebooks*. Q. Hoare and G. Nowell-Smith, trans. and ed. New York: International Publishers.
Gramsci, (1977) *Selections from Political Works*. London: Lawrence and Wishart.
Gramsci, A. (1994) *Pre-Prison Writings*. R. Bellamy (ed.). Cambridge: Cambridge University Press.
Gramsci, A. (1995) *Further Selections from Prison Notebooks*. D. Boothman, trans. and ed. London: Lawrence & Wishart.
Guha, R. (1983) *Elementary Aspects of Peasant Insurgency in Colonial India*. Oxford: Oxford University Press.
Guha, R. (1997) *Dominance Without Hegemony: History and Power in Colonial India*. Cambridge, MA: Harvard University Press.
Hall, S. (1978) *Policing the Crisis*. London: Macmillan.
Hall, S. (1979) The Great Moving Right Show. *Marxism Today*, January, pp. 14–20 [online]. Available at: http://banmarchive.org.uk/collections/mt/pdf/79_01_hall.pdf (accessed 10 July 2019).
Hall, S. (1991) Introductory Essay: Reading Gramsci. In: R. Simon, *Gramci's Political Thought*. London: Lawrence and Wishart, pp. 1–7.
Hall, S. and Jefferson, T. (1975) *Resistance Through Rituals: Youth Subcultures in Postwar Britain*. Birmingham: Centre for Contemporary Cultural Studies.
Hobsbawm, E. J. (1977) Gramsci and Political Theory. *Marxism Today*, July, pp. 205–13 [online]. Available at: http://banmarchive.org.uk/collections/mt/pdf/07_77_205.pdf (accessed 10 July 2019).
Hobsbawm, E. J. (1982) Gramsci and Marxist Political Theory. In: A. Showstack-Sassoon (ed.) *Approaches to Gramsci*. London: Writers and Readers, pp. 19–36.
Jones, S. (2006) *Antonio Gramsci*. London: Routledge.
Korsch, K. (2013 [1923]) *Marxism and Philosophy*. London: Verso.
Laclau, E. and Mouffe, C. (1985) *Hegemony and Socialist Strategy: Towards a Radical Democratic Politics*. London: Verso.
Lukács, G. (1971 [1923]) *History and Class Consciousness: Studies in Marxist Dialectics*. R. Livingstone, trans. London: Merlin.
Simon, R. (1991) *Gramsci's Political Thought: An Introduction*. London: Lawrence & Wishart.
Williams, R. (1977) *Marxism and Literature*. Oxford: Oxford University Press.

LUKÁCS

Introduction

Although rarely discussed nowadays, Georg Lukács was arguably one of the most important Marxist theorists of the twentieth century. His work covers over 50 years of writing, encompassing an enormous variety of topics including sociology, philosophy and literary theory, and runs into thousands of pages. His most important book is undoubtedly *History and Class Consciousness* (*HCC*) (1922) written in the aftermath of profound revolutionary and social changes that took place from 1914 onwards, including the First World War and the Russian Revolution. Kolakowski describes *History and Class Consciousness* as 'the most important theoretical work of twentieth century Marxism' (1972: 85) and the book added a new depth and complexity to what was at the time a very orthodox and simplistic understanding of Marx's *oeuvre* after he died. This 'mechanical-materialist' interpretation of Marxism was led by Engels and taken up by the German Social Democratic Party (SPD), and various Soviet Marxist thinkers including Plekanov.

Though always a fervent admirer of Lenin, Lukács argued against cruder and more deterministic–materialistic understandings of Marxism by asserting the central role of human consciousness and agency in social life, as well as the philosophical dimension of Marx's thought deriving from Hegel. *History and Class Consciousness* also became famous for eliciting a version of Marx's theory of alienation and Marxist humanism from within a highly economistic interpretation of *Capital* (1867) that was dominant at the time. This was significant because Marx's (1961 [1844]) *Economic and Philosophic Manuscripts* of 1844 were only subsequently published in 1932. Central to Lukács's work, and constituting a major contribution to sociological theory, is his theory of reification, which has parallels with Marx's theory of alienation, and refers to society as possessing a thing-like facticity which coercively imposes itself upon individuals and increasingly shapes their everyday behaviour, and the concept of totality, drawn from Hegel, foregrounding the importance of understanding the whole of society as prior to its parts.

Life and Intellectual Context

Georg Lukács was born on 13 April 1885 in Budapest into a wealthy Jewish family. His father Josef Lowinger, an investment banker, was knighted as a baron by the Austro-Hungarian Empire, which effectively made Lukács a baron through inheritance. Rejecting both a career in banking and his noble title, he joined the Revolutionary Socialist Students of Budapest led by Ervin Szabo in 1902. Through Szabo, an important socialist thinker at the time, he was introduced to the syndicalism of George Sorel. In 1904 Lukács helped found a dramatic society, the *Thalia*, which aimed to bring theatre to the working classes of Budapest. Having read Marx while still at school, he made a study of Marx in 1908, which together with the work of Simmel and Weber, formed the basis of a book on modern drama, *The Sociology of Modern Drama* (1965 [1909]).

He continued his readings of the work of Marx and Engels while studying at the Royal Hungarian University, and the University of Berlin, eventually acquiring a doctorate in philosophy at the University of Budapest in 1908. In Berlin he came into contact with the sociologist Georg Simmel with whom he studied between 1909 and 1910. After publishing *The Soul and Forms* (1991 [1911]) he later resumed his studies of Marx, which had initially been developed 'through spectacles tinged by Simmel and Weber' (Lukács, 1971b: ix) but were now increasingly interpreted through Hegel. In 1913, while in Heidelberg, he studied under the neo-Kantian philosophers Wilhelm Windleband and Heinrich Rickert. He also met Emil Lask, Max Weber and Ernst Bloch, and became a leading member in 1915, of the Sunday Circle, a group of predominantly Hungarian intellectuals, which included Karl Mannheim, Arnold Hauser, and Karl Polanyi. He was also a member of Weber's Heidelberg Circle. Deemed unfit for military service during the First World War, a war he vehemently opposed, he was jolted out of his deep depression by the Russian Revolution. It had, he noted, 'opened a window to the future ... we saw at last! At last! – a way for mankind to escape from war and capitalism' (1971: xi). His *Theory of the Novel* (1972 [1920]) saw him move away from the philosophical influence of Kant and the neo-Kantians, increasingly towards Hegel. In the book he proposed both a historicisation of aesthetic categories, and a view in which the novel emerged within a specific historical bourgeois context of secularisation. But the theme of an individual severed from their community and unable to lead an aesthetically fulfilling life, remained a central concern.

The Communist Party

On joining the Hungarian Communist Party in December 1918, Lukács became a committed Marxist political activist. During the short-lived Hungarian revolutionary government of 1919 led by Bela Kun, and consisting of a Republic of Councils, he held a ministerial post as 'People's Commissar' for Culture and Education. He fought with the revolutionary army on the Tisza front, subsequently fleeing when the persecution of former Communist Party members began following the collapse of the government on 1 August 1919.

After a period of hiding he moved to Vienna, where he met communists from Poland and the Balkans, and became a member of the underground movement. Here he began editing an ultra-leftist review which supported the Third International – an organisation advocating world communism, entitled *Kommunismus*. As well as befriending Victor Serge and Antonio Gramsci, during this time in Vienna he composed some of the essays which later became part of *History and Class Consciousness* (1922), which, as Kilminster (1979: 25) notes, 'marked a watershed in Marxist thinking'. Seen as a 'heretical' Marxist analysis, the book angered many orthodox adherents to Marxism, including Grigory Zinoviev, a central member of the Soviet politburo.

Following a short work on Lenin in 1924, he immersed himself in practical politics, briefly becoming General Secretary of the Hungarian Communist Party in 1928. In the same year he published his 'Blum Theses' in which he argued that conditions in Hungary did not facilitate a direct transition to a Soviet Republic, and that a democratic dictatorship of workers and peasants was needed. In order to prevent his expulsion from the Communist Party for writing a 'half-social democratic liquidationist theory', he penned an open letter of self-criticism in 1929. He also ceased being a political activist, devoting himself instead singularly to intellectual activity between 1930 and 1955. After a 10-year stay in Vienna he moved to Berlin between 1929 and 1933 with an intermittent one-year period in Moscow, where he spent time at the Marx–Engels Institute working on Marx's Paris Manuscripts under the direction of David Ryazanov. His reading of the manuscripts and Lenin's posthumously published *Philosophical Notebooks* made him reconsider his earlier theoretical views. In 1933 he undertook his first self-criticism of *History and Class Consciousness* for its 'messianic utopianism', remaining critical of the book throughout his life. Following the rise of the Nazis to power, he returned to Moscow, producing *The Young Hegel* (1938) before going back to Hungary in 1945 to become a professor of aesthetics and philosophy of culture at the University of Budapest. Here he published *The Destruction of Reason* (1954) and *The Historical Novel* (1955). In 1956, he became involved in the Hungarian uprising serving as a minister of culture. He was arrested for a short period and sent to Romania following the revolt, but returned to Hungary in 1957 and again devoted himself to writing and study. His later work tended not to deviate too much from a Soviet Marxist orthodoxy, though he remained committed to Hegel. His last incomplete work, *The Ontology of Social Being* (1978 [1918]), aimed to furnish a basis for the study of ethics by engaging with, among others, Hartmann, Heidegger, Hegel and Marx. He died on 4 June 1971 aged 86.

The Teutonic Influence

As Anderson notes, although born in Hungary: 'Lukács himself was largely formed in Heidelberg, and always remained more German than Hungarian in culture' (1977: 25). At the end of the nineteenth century and the beginning of the twentieth, neo-Kantianism was the dominant intellectual philosophy in the

German-speaking world. Of the two constituent camps, the Marburg School represented by Herman Cohen (1842–1918) and Paul Natorp (1854–1924) focused on issues of philosophy of science, epistemology and logic, and emphasised the scientific or conceptual aspects of Kant's works. By contrast the South West or Heidelberg School included Wilhelm Windleband and Heinrich Rickert, who were more concerned with issues tied to history, culture and values. Lukács drew on both schools, but more emphatically on the South West School for its anti-naturalism. As Parkinson notes:

> He takes over from Rickert the distinction between the sensible world of science on the one hand, and on the other hand the non-sensuous objects of experience, such as art, which are known by 'understanding' and he argues that such understanding can be achieved only through flashes of intuition. (1970: 4)

Both Simmel and Weber – the former discussing reified social forms, especially money, the latter rationality, dehumanisation and cultural degeneration – were to influence Lukács strongly and were also themselves markedly influenced by neo-Kantian thinking. Lukács was, however, later to regard neo-Kantianism as insufficiently historical and shifted towards a Hegelian form of Marxism. As well as the early neo-Kantian influence he was also sympathetic to the existentialist writings of Kierkegaard, Dostoyevsky and the *Lebensphilosophie* of Wilhelm Dilthey. These thinkers, when combined with the ideas and arguments of Hegel and Marx, made a strange and somewhat contradictory synthesis of neo-Kantian ethics, Hegelian dialectics and Marxist political activism. As Lukács reflected in his 1967 Preface to *History and Class Consciousness* (HCC):

> All this produced a highly contradictory amalgam of theories that was decisive for my thought during the war and the first few years after it... If Faust could have two souls within one breast, why should not a normal person unite conflicting intellectual trends within himself ... my ideas hovered between the acquisition of Marxism and political activism on the one hand, and the constant intensification of my purely idealistic ethical preoccupations on the other. (1971: x)

That Hegel profoundly influenced Lukács is evident and it is through a Hegelian lens that he interprets Marx. For Lukács, central to the materialist dialectic in Marxism was its emphasis on the whole or *totality*, or more precisely, the 'concrete totality'.

Marx and Commodity Fetishism

Lukács's discussion of reification and fetishistic illusions in *HCC* draws heavily on Marx's discussion of commodity fetishism in *Capital*. For Marx, a central factor for understanding fetishism was the separation of workers from the means of production. With the proliferation of generalised commodity exchange, the market became the only way through which society could organise the distribution of what it produced. However, capitalism disguised this mechanism of production and exchange as a result of the separation of the producers from one another:

> the producers do not come into contact until they exchange the products of their labour… In other words, the labour of private individuals manifests itself … only through the relations which the act of exchange establishes between products, and through their mediation between the producers. (Marx, 1994: 233)

Marx then adds:

> A commodity is therefore a mysterious thing, simply because in it the social character of men's labour appears to them as an objective character stamped upon the product of that labour; because the relation of the producers to the sum total of their own labour is presented to them as a social relation, existing not between themselves, but between the products of their labour. This is the reason why the products of labour become commodities, social things whose qualities are at the same time perceptible and imperceptible by the senses… It is only a definite social relation between men that assumes, in their eyes, the fantastic form of a relation between things. (2007: 83)

As well as drawing on Marx's discussion of commodity fetishism Lukács's concept of reification also leans on Weber's claim that the world is becoming increasingly rationalised, so that instrumental, calculative rationality was driving the world into a standardised, machine-like, rule-bound, social order where actors acted on the basis of self-interest rather than higher values. For Weber, this process was widespread and manifested itself in a multiplicity of domains from the structure of music, to the organisation of impersonal bureaucracies, to the reshaping of economic practices, and was based on cost–benefit principles of accounting.

Historical, Social and Political Context

HCC was written in the context of widespread global social and political turmoil and unrest with the spontaneous emergence of many workers' movements and strikes. As part of the dual monarchy in the Austro-Hungarian Empire, Hungary was seen, and saw itself, as socially and historically undeveloped. Capitalism in Hungary had developed comparatively late with feudal and bureaucratic state interests retarding its progression. Characterised by numerous political and ideological divisions and standpoints including a reactionary conservatism, liberalism, Marxism, anarcho-syndicalism, nationalism and bourgeois radicalism, the complex concatenation of contradictory forces effectively cancelled each other out, rendering Hungarian society inert. The Austro-Hungarian Empire was also divided in terms of its two monarchies which came under the common rule of Emperor Franz Joseph. When the empire sent 9 million individuals to fight in the First World War, over 4 million were conscripted from Hungary, and it suffered the heaviest losses. The war exacerbated an already deteriorating economic situation, leading to numerous factory strikes and even insurrections within the army.

In this volatile context, Jewish emancipation and minority emancipation against Hungarian dominance also came increasingly to the fore. Although the Hungarian Jewish bourgeoisie was gaining social and economic independence from the Austrian ruling classes, it was simultaneously confronted by the rise of the industrial working class. In his early work, Lukács undertook an ongoing ethical polemic against the rising bourgeoisie. Along with poets such as Endre Ady, a major influence on Lukács, he saw society in global and messianic terms of 'either salvation or total disaster' – revolution for him existed as a desire, a hope or dream (Mészáros, 1972: 42).

By contrast to Hungary, Germany underwent rapid development between 1871 and 1914. However, in the midst of this economic growth, intellectuals lost their previously held privileged social positions, and many came to adopt an anti-capitalist romanticism or a tragic world view including Simmel and Weber.

The First World War and Russian Revolution

The First World War also had profoundly destructive effects on the German and Hungarian populations. More specifically, the war plunged progressive intellectuals into a deep despair in the wake of mass killing and relentless fighting on behalf of the interests of capital. The onset of the Russian Revolution, however, offered the hope of a solution to a profoundly war-ravaged world. Many strategists of the left believed that the overthrow of imperialist governments was possible and an epoch of socialist revolutions underway. As Lukács argued:

> This means that the actuality of the revolution is no longer only a world-historical horizon arching over the self-liberating working class, but that revolution is already on its agenda… The actuality of the revolution provides the key-note of the whole epoch. (Cited in Anderson, 2017: 166)

The short-lived November Revolution in Germany in 1918, led by Rosa Luxemburg (1871–1919) and Karl Liebkneckt (1871–1919), was matched by the Aster Revolution in Hungary in 1918. Mihály Károlyi initially came to power, leading a social democratic government intent on disarmament. Following various military incursions annexing part of the country, the communists led by Béla Kun then seized power in 1919. However, even after the Hungarian Revolution, and in contrast to Russia, there was no powerful social agency that could undertake the revolutionary social changes Lukács sought and desired. As had been the case in the November German Revolution, the communist accession to power was short-lived, partly as a result of the unstable nature of the enterprise: the communists had taken power prior to acquiring widespread ideological support from the workers' councils; and partly as a result of its lack of preparedness for assuming political power with a reformist SPD party (Nineham, 2010: 6). Following a defeat to Romania, a counter-revolution led by Miklos Hórthy effectively saw right-wing forces take power, initiating a White Terror in which as many as 5,000 communists, as well as Jews, were murdered. It is difficult to understand Lukács's work, as both an intellectual and a political/practical intervention, without making reference to the profound social and political turmoil in which he was embedded, and the attendant political polarisation between the left and right. As his former student István Mészáros argued:

> whatever the limits of adaptability of the individual philosopher might be, the point is that he does not learn from books the important issues of his time, but lives them … in this situation the historical situation itself has primacy over the intellectual influences. (1972: 20–21)

In addition to Lukács's participation in the Hungarian Revolution, the Russian Revolution and its aftermath was to profoundly shape his intellectual outlook. It is in relation to the political writings of those involved in the Marxist Second International (1889–1916) – an organisation of socialist and labour parties which included such diverse figures as Otto Bauer, Eduard Bernstein, Nikolai Bukarin, Rudolf Hilferding, Vladimir Lenin, Karl Kautsky, Rosa Luxemburg and Dimitri Plekanov – that Lukács responded. The works of the authors were characterised by a multiplicity of political positions within a broadly left standpoint ranging from a reformist Marxism – for example, Bernstein's view that socialism would come about progressively through the democratic parliamentary system without a need for proletarian revolution – to a more a deterministic/fatalistic explanation for socialism, derived from Kautsky or Plekanov which argued that socialism was inevitable and evolved or arose automatically and teleologically.

Moreover, many of the discussions in the Second International centred on the role of various parties including the SPD, and their narrowly nationalistic support of the war. Writers such as Lenin and Luxemburg – on the far left of the SPD, by contrast, saw the war as furthering imperial interests and a betrayal of working-class solidarity. Although they held a great deal in common, Luxemburg and Lenin, however, disagreed on various issues including agrarian policies, national self-determination and the role of the party. While foregrounding the role of the proletariat, Lenin advocated that it should be led by a vanguard party to challenge reformist inclinations, while Luxemburg tended to sympathise with the more 'spontaneous' initiative and self-activity of the workers. Luxemburg also saw Lenin as holding an over-centralised view of party organisation.

In his early work, Lukács had criticised capitalist or bourgeois society largely from an ethical mystical or 'messianic' standpoint, often deriving from a neo-Kantian understanding of the social world. Following his admission into the Communist Party, it became one based on revolutionary principles taking a stance somewhere, as Rockmore notes, 'between the disparate positions of Lenin and Rosa Luxemburg' (1988: 2). More specifically, Löwy refers to this shift as one from romanticism to bolshevism (Löwy, 1979). If, as many Second International thinkers believed, socialism would inevitably arise from the unfolding contradictions in capitalism, especially those located in the economic sphere, this then, Lukács asserted, led to a position justifying a reformist stance in politics in which working-class passivity could be accepted. What took place in the economic base, it was argued by these thinkers, would immediately be reflected in the political and cultural superstructure. Lukács, by contrast, aimed like Lenin in his *What is to Be Done?* to foreground the importance of the consciousness and action of the proletariat. However, Lukács went further than Lenin in adopting an ultra-leftist line, promoting what has been referred to as *teilaktion*, a partial armed revolt against the capitalist state to awaken workers' consciousness based on the belief of the immediate revolutionary character of the time, rather than in determinate and extant concrete political preconditions.

A central concern for Lukács was how working-class consciousness and liberation could arise within a dehumanising capitalist system. Nevertheless, Lukács felt he was defending Marx against the revisionist interpretations of his thought that offered an 'economic fatalist' view of the world. *HCC* therefore reflects partly his experience of the defeat of the short-lived Hungarian Soviet of 1919 and the victory of the Russian Revolution and partly his attempt to develop a more agency and subjective understanding of Marxism.

Ideas and Arguments

History and Class Consciousness

HCC is a difficult and complex work composed of a collection of eight separate essays which constitute and attempt to 'clarify the theoretical problems of the revolutionary movement in the mind of the author and his readers' (1971: xli). Nevertheless, the book's unity of vision is captured by its subtitle: *Studies in Marxist Dialectics*. For Lukács, the fundamental task of the book is to 'understand the essence of Marx's method and to apply it correctly' (1971: xlii). This concern is not simply underpinned by a theoretical rationale, but also one pregnant with urgent practical and political implications:

> The war, the crisis and the Revolution, not excluding the slower tempo in the development of the Revolution and the new economic policy of Soviet Russia have not thrown up a single problem that cannot be solved by the dialectical method – and that method *alone*. (Lukács, 1971: xliii)

In focusing on Marx's dialectic method Lukács intends to bring back the influence of Hegel. For Lukács, in the context of numerous debates concerning what is the 'true' interpretation of Marxism and various 'vulgar' forms of Marxism, 'orthodox Marxism' refers exclusively to method rather than to any of Marx's central theses. Even if all the arguments adumbrated in historical materialism or *Capital* were found wanting or were disproved, a Marxist orthodoxy centred on dialectics remained:

> Orthodox Marxism, therefore, does not imply the uncritical acceptance of the results of Marx's investigations. It is not the 'belief' in this or that thesis, nor the 'exegesis' of a 'sacred' book. On the contrary, orthodoxy refers exclusively to *method*. (Lukács, 1971: 1)

According to Lukács Marx's method emphasised the dynamic relation between the subject and object of knowledge and sharply contrasted with Engels' interpretation of dialectics especially in his *Anti-Duhring* ([1972] 1878) as well as his *The Dialectics of Nature* (1940 [1883]). For Lukács, Engels' understanding of dialectics led to a contemplative view of thought and reality, one in which dialectics referred to the laws of all reality, not just *social* reality. This prevented the development of an activist viewpoint in which thought aims to change the *social* world. Lukács saw the relation between human subjects and society (or the object) dialectically – they reciprocally affected one another. The subject did not simply reflect the social world, or object, that is the proletariat was not a passive reflection of the material world, but acted upon it shaping it and altering it, changing itself simultaneously. The proletariat transformed the world through its activity and practice or *praxis* (the German equivalent). Theory and practice became *united* within the proletariat. For Lukács, Marxist reformists, 'revisionists' or 'opportunists' had purged Marx of this important Hegelian dialectical legacy. They adhered, as did bourgeois economists, to a form of positivism, which saw facts as isolated phenomena:

> they seek refuge in the methods of natural sciences, in the way in which science distils 'pure' facts and places them in the relevant contexts by means of observation, abstraction and experiment. They then oppose this ideal model of knowledge to the forced constructions of the dialectical method. (Lukács, 1971: 5)

Positivism was an expression of capitalist logic to the extent that facts were reduced to their quantitative essence, and expressed through numbers: 'If such methods seem plausible at first this is because capitalism tends to produce a social structure that in great measure encourages such views' (1971: 5).

Reification

A society in which commodity production had become universalised presupposed a process of *reification* which may be defined as 'thingification' (Craib, 1984: 176) – that is, *dynamic social* processes become transformed into *static* relations between *things*. As Lukács notes, for Marx capital is: 'not a thing but a social relation between persons mediated through things' (1971: 49). Thus, in the context of an increasing division of labour, the capitalist market interposes itself between the individual producers. The reification of the workplace, entailing division of labour and the breakdown of tasks, is re-expressed in the creation knowledge, including the valorisation of positivism, which, like production, emphasises quantitative exactness. The increasing mechanisation and reification of the world are also reflected in various other social forms of thinking including mainstream economics. They are further reflected in the emergence of disciplinary divisions in knowledge, for example between philosophy, law and art, or in the division between theory and practice. Positivism, neo-Kantianism and 'vulgar Marxism' as a result, all remain trapped within appearances (1971: 9). In distinguishing his dialectical approach from these three other standpoints, Lukács reformulates the distinction made by Hegel, between *understanding* focused on isolated objects and *dialectics*. The other approaches are either deployed as part of the ideological weapons of the bourgeoisie or, in the case of vulgar Marxism, have come under its influence.

In contrast to positivism, the dialectical method punctures through the empirical illusions generated by capitalism and the commodity form, the phenomenal appearances of the social world, and understands the reality underlying them. By challenging 'the unscientific nature of this seemingly so scientific method' dialectics proposes that facts can only be interpreted historically and within the framework of a totalistic system. This framework is the concrete unity of the whole, or *totality*. Capitalism, for Lukács, is a structured totality in which the parts are mediated by the whole. The internal structures of social facts are historical and interconnected within a whole – they are integrated within a totality, which alone provides us knowledge of reality. These interconnected aspects 'mediate' or interact with one another. According to Lukács, the emphasis on totality means that the whole has explanatory primacy over the parts. Such an interaction between the parts and whole is not akin to billiard balls colliding with one another, but one that results in a change in form of the objects framed within a social process:

> the interaction we have in mind must be more than the interaction of otherwise unchanging objects. It must go further in its relation to the whole: for this relation determines the objective form of every form of cognition. Every substantial change that is of concern to knowledge

manifests itself as a change in relation to the whole and through this as a change in the form of objectivity itself... Thus the objective forms of all social phenomena change constantly in the course of their ceaseless dialectical interactions with each other. The intelligibility of objects develops in proportion as we grasp their function in the totality to which they belong. This is why only the dialectical conception of totality can enable us to understand *reality as a social process*. (1971: 13)

[Republished with permission of Merlin Press from *Selections from History and Class Consciousness: Studies in Marxist Dialectics* (R. Livingstone, trans.), G. Lukács, 1971]

What distinguishes Marxism from 'bourgeois scientific approaches' is precisely the emphasis on totality and not, for example, the primacy of economic motives, or any of substantive Marxist theses, as many Second International thinkers claim.

Through a process of reification what are social and historical forms in process are reduced to a natural, eternal and thing-like qualities. The dialectical method, by contrast, understands the appearance of these isolated facts as products of a definite historical epoch, capitalism. They are historical products which through the fetishistic forms of objectivity created by commodity capitalism appear as supra-historical essences.

The increasing universality of the commodity form in modern societies means that all needs are now satisfied through commodity exchange. For Lukács his entails the breakdown of human community and the dissolution of social bonds between people. In this transformation, quantitative principles replace qualitative ones. Rationalisation means specialisation: that labour is broken down, as Adam Smith had noted in his discussion of division of labour, into rational, abstract specialised operations. Work is reduced to monotonous repetition and the worker loses contact with his or her finished product – a process exemplified most fully in Taylorist forms of production. According to Lukács, people's own activities, their own labour, become something objective and independent of them: 'something that controls him [sic], by virtue of an autonomy alien to man' (1971: 87).

Such a process of alienation contains both an objective and a subjective dimension. Objectively a world of objects and relations between things emerges, including commodities, and their movements confront humans as invisible forces, with their own power which the individual is unable to modify. Subjectively people's activity becomes estranged from themselves, and transformed into a commodity, subordinate to the non-human objectivity of natural laws of society. Social institutions, which are in reality produced by humans, appear as objective relations hostile to them. Of most significance here is the market, which exists as an alien power standing over and above the producers and controlling them. The market transforms human social relations into a network of exchange relations between things while controlling them. Through reification human qualities come to be regarded as things, and take on a non-human mysterious life of their own.

The Spread of Reification

The division of labour in which substantive processes are increasingly broken down into specialisms, the domination of the worker by the capitalist, and the authority relations it entails, all become generalised from the workplace and factory to the broader society, which becomes increasingly fragmented and rationalised. Commodity fetishism 'permeates every expression of life', it 'penetrates society in all its aspects and to remould it in its own image' (Lukács, 1971: 84, 85). Now drawing on Weber, Lukács argues that rational mechanisation and calculability 'embrace every aspect of life' (1971: 91).

As capitalism reproduces itself at increasingly higher levels, so it sinks in more deeply in men's consciousness and their reified temporal understanding of the world. For example, 'time sheds its qualitative, variable, flowing nature; it freezes into an exactly delimited, quantifiable continuum filled with quantifiable "things" ... in short, it becomes space' (1971: 90).

Weber, he argues, captures a fundamental truth about society when he foregrounds the modern capitalist concern with calculability, rational organisation of work and rational technology, and their diffusion throughout society. In the sphere of justice, for example, a judge's behaviour is no longer based on his or her sense of fair play, instead:

> the judge is more or less an automatic statute dispensing machine in which you insert the files together with the necessary costs and dues at the top, whereupon he will eject the judgement together with more or less cogent reasons for it at the bottom: that is, to say, where the judge's behaviour is on the whole *predictable*. (Weber, cited in Lukács, 1971: 96)

And it is evident in the whole consciousness of individuals including their physical and psychic nature:

> His [sic] qualities and abilities are no longer an organic part of his personality, they are things which he can 'own' or 'dispose of' like the various objects of the external world. And there is no natural form in which human relations can be cast, no way in which man can bring his physical and psychic 'qualities' into play without their being subjected increasingly to this reifying process. We only need think of marriage ... of the way in which Kant, for example, described the situation with the naively cynical frankness peculiar to great thinkers: 'Sexual community', he says, 'is the use made by one person of the sexual organs and faculties of another ... marriage is the union of two people with a view to the mutual possession of each other's sexual attributes for the duration of their lives.' (Lukács, 1971: 100)

[Republished with permission of Merlin Press from *Selections from History and Class Consciousness: Studies in Marxist Dialectics* (R. Livingstone, trans.), G. Lukács, 1971]

The Proletariat as the Subject–Object Identical

In *HCC* Lukács foregrounds the standpoint of the proletarian class as a class that expresses the totality, privileging the latter's understanding of reality and its ability to transform it. It is only the proletariat that can combine theory with practice:

> Reality can only be understood and penetrated as a totality, and only a subject which is itself a totality is capable of this penetration … The scientific superiority of the standpoint of class (as against that of the individual) has become clear from the foregoing. Now we see the reason for this superiority: only the class can actively penetrate the reality of society and transform it in its entirety. (1971: 39)

For Lukács, in contrast to feudal times when relations between humans appeared as natural relations, it is only in capitalism that individuals can become conscious of themselves as social beings who are 'simultaneously the subject and object of the historical process' (1971: 19). As a totalising phenomenon capitalism destroys the spatio-temporal barriers between different lands and territories, and the legal partitions between estates, making it possible for individuals to envisage themselves as social beings. However, social life under capitalism also continues to remain opaque and impenetrable under the commodity nature of capitalism, which makes society appear as a 'second nature' (1971: 19). Only the proletariat, given its majority position in society, the fact that it has become a commodity like any other, and with its ability to 'make' society through its labour, can understand and see capitalist society dialectically. In attempting to understand its own position within capitalist society, the proletariat is forced to understand the totality of society.

By contrast, the fragmented bourgeoisie, with its partial relation to the social world, is incapable of obtaining self-knowledge because of its preoccupation with its self-interest. Capitalists remain concerned with expanding their capital and wealth, and the competition between them means they remain blind to the overall effects, irrationalities and consequences of a system of production driven by profit. Only the proletariat can succeed in breaking through the reified, fractured, image of the world; it is simultaneously the subject – that which makes knowledge – and the object – that to which knowledge refers. In this sense the proletariat, like Hegel's notion of the absolute spirit, constituted the *subject and object identical*.

Class Consciousness

Lukács accepts the widely held Marxist view that class is determined by position in the process of production, but he attempts to provide a dialectical understanding of class consciousness emphasising it as an 'objective possibility'. This entails examining collective class consciousness and not reified forms of individual class consciousness; that is, imputing what members of the class should believe if they had grasped their situation adequately and rationally:

> By relating consciousness to the whole of society it becomes possible to infer the thoughts and feelings which men would have in a particular situation if they were able to assess both it and the interests arising from it in their impact on action and the whole structure of society... This consciousness is, therefore, neither the sum nor the average of what is thought or felt by the single individuals who make up the class. And yet the historically significant actions of the class as a whole are determined in the last resort by this consciousness and not by the thought of the individual – and these actions can be understood only by reference to this consciousness. (1971: 51)

[Republished with permission of Merlin Press from *Selections from History and Class Consciousness: Studies in Marxist Dialectics* (R. Livingstone, trans.), G. Lukács, 1971]

This imputed class consciousness may diverge widely from empirical or actual consciousness or the real psychological thoughts men and women have about their life and existence. It may differ for different classes depending how they themselves are related to society as a whole and whether the differences are so great that they constitute qualitative distinctions.

Lukács was concerned about the degree to which a class performs actions that history has imposed on it either consciously or unconsciously. Only the bourgeoisie and the proletariat are 'pure classes' in capitalism because their existence depends on the development of production. Other classes, such as the petty bourgeoisie or peasantry, have an ambiguous or sterile existence, and are linked to earlier feudal social formations: they consequently constitute transitional classes. It is through their changing consciousness developed through class struggle and their agency that the proletariat can transform society, but this is not inevitable:

> The objective economic evolution could do no more than create the position of the proletariat in the production process. It was this position that determined its point of view. But the objective position could only give the proletariat the opportunity and necessity to change society. Any transformation can only come about as the product of the – free – action of the proletariat itself. (1971: 208)

The obstacles which prevent a class realising its imputed consciousness, in practice, are greater in the proletariat than in the bourgeoisie. This is because, in a context where reified relations of capitalism appear as natural, 'this consciousness is divided "within itself"', especially between the economic struggle and the political struggle and between its short-term and long-term interests. By modifying a view of the political party found in Luxemburg and Lenin, Lukács argues that in aiming to achieve its imputed consciousness the proletariat needs to be aided by a party, a disciplined moral and ethical organisation, supporting the spontaneous revolutionary masses, both within and outside a period of economic crisis. Given that workers' consciousness often lagged behind what it should ideally be, the Party remedies this gulf. The Party acts as the mediator between the proletariat and history bringing dielactical theory into contact with the proletariat, whose experience and the knowledge it is based upon, yet nevertheless, supersedes.

Contemporary Applications and Influence

Lukács's foregrounding of the concept of praxis was highly influential in leading to a reinterpretation of Marx that focused on classes composed of creative actors who shape the historical world and who as a collective constitute the motor of historical change. Following a lull in its reception after the Second World War, Lukács's work was taken up again during the 1960s, when many political revolutionaries and radical students again saw the possibility of a socialist revolution arising.

REIFICATION AND THE FRANKFURT SCHOOL

The Frankfurt School appropriated Lukács's theory of reification and its particular combination of Marx and Weber to advance their programme of an interdisciplinary critical theory of society. With each successive generation advancing a specific version of the theory, reification is a central concept shaping critical theory's distinctive critique of capitalism. The first-generation theorists used 'reified consciousness' as an explanatory device to consider the integration and pacification of the proletariat, the severance of the utopian aspect of modern culture and the ever-present threat of totalitarianism in advanced capitalist societies. Habermas superseded Lukács's theory on altered normative and sociological foundations to diagnose the colonisation of the life-world by economic and bureaucratic–administrative systems in late capitalist welfare state societies. Most recently, Axel Honneth has reconsidered the theory within the framework of his recognition paradigm, interpreting reification as a structurally induced subjective forgetting of an antecedent form of intersubjectivity.

Lukács's work has had a major impact on Marxist thinking generally, and on the Frankfurt School in particular – including Benjamin, Marcuse, Adorno, Habermas and Honneth – especially his concept of reification and his attempt to marry Weber's notion of rationalisation with Marx's discussion of the commodity form in capitalism. We shall discuss some of their work in the following chapters. His ideas were also taken up by Agnes Heller and her student, István Mészáros. Lukács's analysis of reification also influenced thinkers outside of Marxism, including Maurice Merleau-Ponty, Martin Heidegger and Peter Berger. His work has also provided the basis of a profound sociology of knowledge perspective: knowledge of the social world depends on where you are located within it. Two figures who drew heavily on this notion are Karl Mannheim and Lucien Goldmann.

Karl Mannheim

Karl Mannheim (1893–1947), a fellow Hungarian and member of Lukács's 'Sunday Circle' taught first in Frankfurt, Germany and then, following Hitler's rise to power, at the University of London, drew heavily on Lukács's notion of class consciousness and the perspectival nature of knowledge in developing his sociology of knowledge approach. Also writing against the backdrop of Weimar politics, he interrogated the relationship between society and knowledge, arguing that all knowledge is socially constructed. Rival political ideologies, he argued, had proliferated in Weimar society engendering acute ethical, existential and philosophical problems. Mannheim identifies the production of knowledge, that knowledge is bounded to existence, by referring it to its sociological context using the concept of 'existential determination' or *Seinsverbundenheit*:

> The central problem for all sociology of knowledge and research into ideology is the linkage between thinking and knowing on the one hand, and existence on the other (*Seinsgebendenheit allen Denkens und Erkennens*). (Mannheim, 1986: 31)

According to Mannheim, facts make sense within the contexts of frameworks within which they are generated, that is through a worldview (*Weltanschaung*). Recognising that competing groups have different and antagonistic conceptions and perspectives on the world which often talk past each other, Mannheim distinguishes between various types of ideology: the particular, representing segments of an opponent's thought entailing deceptions and disguises used to mask interests; the total, representing all of an opponent's thought, its basic presuppositions and thought categories; and the general concepts of ideology representing all thought, including the sociologist's own, and which formed the basis for the sociology of knowledge proper, as he understood it. All thought, he argued, with the exception of mathematics, is shaped by socio-historical context and group struggles. Group competition was at the core of cultural change. Such thought carried forward by groups rather than individuals was shaped not only by class but also by generational divides, status grouping and professional occupation, such as bureaucrats, since the relation between thought and existence could be variable. However, in order to escape from the relativistic implications of such a historicist standpoint in which belief systems were socially and historically determined and therefore each had as much value as any other, as well as from the absolutist position of neo-Kantians, Mannheim introduced the term 'relationism'. All thought derives from a certain social position that structures it, so that relationism refers to the location within the social system that beliefs and thoughts derive from. Even though ideas and thoughts are socially structured, and represent a 'perspective' or 'standpoint', that does not mean they do not contain a truth value. The partial viewpoints of each of these groups can only be understood when placed in a more encompassing holistic perspective, a totality or 'total vision'. According to Mannheim, rival thought structures entailing various political positions could be synthesised into a complementary whole, by an ideologically 'free', relatively detached strata of intellectuals, able to provide a provisional, dynamic, totality of thought, albeit containing certain limitations. This allows them to produce a new form of '"objectivity" … in a roundabout fashion' (Mannheim, 1960 [1929]: 270). Sociology as a foremost social science could achieve such a synthesis. Lukács's proletariat with their privileged vantage point on the world thereby becomes replaced by Mannheim, by a strata of free-floating intellectuals.

Rather than regarding ideology as a concern with distorted beliefs, Mannheim therefore sought to uncover worldviews enmeshed in a group's mental structure. In *Ideology and Utopia* ([1929] 1960) he reinterpreted his earlier understandings of ideology, envisioning ideology as representing socially useful beliefs that signified the existing order or status quo, but were out of sync with the real world – outmoded, antiquated ideas which could not be realised, such as the idea of heaven in medieval society:

> As long as the clerically and feudally organized medieval order was able to locate its paradise outside of society, in some other-worldly sphere which transcended history and dulled its revolutionary edge, the idea of paradise was still an integral part of medieval society. (1960 [1929]: 174)

As Kumar notes:

> 'ideology' is a form of thinking which aspires to objects which the existing social order cannot possibly offer or allow but which it finds convenient to incorporate in its own official, socially approved beliefs. (2007: 173)

By contrast, utopia referred to the beliefs of hope of revolutionary or messianic movements that were also out of kilter with existing reality but ahead of their time, representing an alternative future to the present which can be practically realised:

> Utopias express 'those ideas and values in which are contained in condensed form the unrealized and the unfulfilled tendencies which represent the needs of each age'. (Mannheim, 1960 [1929]: 179)

For Mannheim the primary ideologies that existed, which constitute a function or are imputable to a specific social location, were political ideologies including socialism, liberalism and conservatism. In his essay on conservatism, Mannheim (1986) identifies specific thought styles, a notion which he takes from the history of art. Here he aims to describe two styles of thought in the specific context of early nineteenth-century Europe and to identify their social carriers – the rising bourgeoisie and the conservative reaction to the Enlightenment. The two starkly opposed styles of thought he identifies are the natural-law or bourgeois thought-style, which originated in France and held sway up to and just after the Revolution, and the conservative thought-style, which originated in Germany between 1800 and 1850 (Barnes, 1994). The philosophical and political reaction to both liberalism and to the Enlightenment and its embodiment in the French Revolution, as Mannheim points out, was overwhelming. Its two fundamental representatives were conservatism and, to a lesser extent, romanticism. The conservative style of thought arose explicitly in diametric opposition to all the central characteristics of natural-law thinking. For Mannheim, the core of conservatism was that it was 'traditionalism become reflective'. In contrast to the codified and reflective natural-law style of thought, it was external to the conservative form of life and opposed the former on all fronts. It was empirical as opposed to rationalistic, cautious as opposed to optimistic, concrete as opposed to abstract, holistic as opposed to atomistic (Barnes, 1994). In many circumstances, it sought to preserve the status quo rather than transform institutions wholesale. In addition to a pessimistic view of human nature based on egoism, power and mutual suspicion, it normatively postulated a stratified social order where 'communal' property explicitly carried differential privileges, rather than expressing the relationship of an individual to an alienable commodity. Conservatism sought to valorise the actions and thoughts of everyday life rather than criticise them. For conservatism, experiencing and thinking are connected to what is immediate and concrete in a practical way; it is against progressive action that is animated by a consciousness of what is abstractly possible or speculative. The emphasis is in life over reason, practice over norms and being over thought (Bloor, 1983: 162). In addition to a generalised conservative attack upon the Enlightenment and its liberal preoccupations, there arose a romantic response to its rationalism. Many romantic writers questioned the emphasis placed by the Enlightenment on the rational basis of human action. As a result, there were some overlapping tendencies between conservatives and romantics. Romanticism also emphasised the concrete over the abstract, variety over uniformity, nature over culture, the organic over the mechanical, freedom over constraint, the emotional over the logical. In contrast to conservatism, however, the unique individual was paramount for romanticism. It emphasised the organic and whole nature of the world as a spiritual unity which had been shattered by the modern capitalist world in which individuals had become divorced from themselves and, more importantly, from nature.

Mannheim, in contrast to Lukács, attacked Marxism as a doctrine, regarding it as another ideology with a partial insight into the world. His own political position was as a radical social democrat arguing for a form of democratic social planning tied to education as discussed in his book *Man and Society in an Age of Reconstruction* (1940). It was this book that prompted a major ideological rebuttal by Hayek, in his *Roads to Serfdom* (2001 [1944]).

Lucien Goldmann

In his adaptation of Lukács's approach, which he dubs 'genetic structuralism', the Romanian Marxist Lucian Goldmann (1913–70) contributes towards what Fowler terms 'a historical sociology of cultural production' (2015: 105). Goldmann sought to reconstruct the collective mental structures of various groups that underlie modes of thought as they were expressed in literature and philosophy – world visions including rationalism, empiricism, romanticism, the tragic and the dialectical (Mayrl, 1978: 26). Using a dialectical approach focused on the concept of totality derived from Lukács and a developmental model from Piaget, he sought to provide an analysis of human society in general by examining the functions of consciousness. The acting subject for Goldmann is a trans-individual collective subject. In contrast to the 'real' everyday consciousness of actors, which remained vague, contradictory and uneven, certain individuals, including artists and philosophers, represented a more coherent form of the social class consciousness, or a group's worldview containing a maximum possible form of consciousness. This was a distinction akin to Lukács's division between ascribed and imputed consciousness.

In his study of the seventeenth-century writers Pascal and Racine, Goldmann (1964) examines 'the form of the content' of their work and points to the 'tragic vision' at the heart of their literary production, outlining their affiliation to an extremist form of Jansenism and a tragic disposition to the world in which they sought salvation through grace. This consciousness reflected the existential and material crises afflicting their social position as part of the *noblesse de robe* – disempowered and increasingly marginalised by the monarch's move towards a more centralised absolutism.

Criticisms

Lukács's work has been criticised both by sympathetic Marxists and by non-Marxists alike. Following criticisms from within the Communist Third International, Lukács himself criticised his earlier work as being characterised by a 'messianic utopianism'. He also argued that in *HCC* he had tried to 'out Hegel Hegel'. For Lukács the explanation of ideological phenomena in terms of economic processes was problematic since 'labour as the mediator of the metabolic interaction between society and nature, is missing' (1971: xvii). The dynamic process whereby humans transform nature and themselves through their labour remains absent, resulting in a limited conceptualisation of praxis.

In addition, Lukács, following Hegel, had seen alienation and objectification as interwoven processes. However, following his reading of Marx's *Economic and Philosophical Manuscripts* he now argued that the two concepts had to be distinguished. Objectification for Marx was a universal process of humans as they interacted and mediated with nature. However, in specific social orders, especially following the development of private property and division of labour (which Marx sees as two sides of the same coin), objectification becomes alienated. Critics have argued that Lukács's work is idealistic (Steadman Jones, 1977) while others such as Gillian Rose (1978) have argued that it exaggerates the role played by commodity fetishism in Marx's work. Lukács's discussion of the proletariat as a universal class also fails to account for the divisions and fractions within the class, envisaging it in almost metaphysical terms as an homogeneous grouping. Moreover, his idea that the proletariat has a privileged access to the truth of society as a whole has been questioned since it presupposes what the truth is (Parekh, 1982: 171–2). Moreover, this is contrary to what Marx argues:

> Marx does not think that the proletarian experiences represent the whole of social reality or that capitalism is only about the exploitation of the proletariat. There are areas such as the international trade, colonisation and the intra-bourgeois competition in which the proletariat is not the principal subject and which are not reducible to its experiences. Further, although the relations between the bourgeoisie and the proletariat are, for Marx, the basis of capitalism, such important forms of relation as those between the bourgeois 'fractions' and between the landed classes and the agricultural workers are not fully 'visible' from the proletarian point of view. Although more comprehensive than the bourgeois point of view, the latter is still partial and cannot be considered the 'standpoint of the whole'. (Parekh, 1982: 182)

[Republished with permission of The John Hopkins University Press from *Marx's Theory of Ideology*, B. Parekh, 1982. Permission conveyed through Copyright Clearance Center, Inc]

Other critics have noted that his analysis fails to account for the division of imputed and real consciousness and how these are to be bridged (Callinicos, 1999: 208). However, Lukács sometimes refers to the proletariat as moving to imputed consciousness through their struggle, while at other times he suggests the role of the Party. But the latter neglects the disastrous authoritarianism characterising the Bolshevik Party, following the Russian Revolution, albeit in the context of international isolation. Similarly, his understanding effectively makes the Party appear as an elite stratum, arguably against his own intentions. As Parkinson notes:

> The purpose of the party is to assist and accelerate the development of class consciousness in the proletariat… Lukács notes that the party

sometimes has ... to show them the right way through the negation of their present will. It must be supposed, however, that Lukács views the party as a kind of priestly caste, bringing wisdom to the proletariat, who have merely to receive passively what they are given... No doubt there is a possibility of elitism in all this, but it does not seem that this is what Lukács intended. (1970: 14–15).

Conclusion

Lukács made several contributions to different fields. In the field of aesthetics and literature he developed an anti-modernist Marxist theory of realism, in philosophy he foregrounded the idea of dialectics, while in sociology and politics he offered a profound critique of capitalism and commodification. Pointing presciently to the unrelenting unfolding of division of labour, he noted how the market affected and seeped into all spheres of society, including education, knowledge and people's psychic lives, creating a commodification of identity. However, though undeniably important in reemphasising the role of agency in Marx's work in the context of a reductive economism and the pervasive nature of reification in the modern world, there remain a number of lacunae in his overall analysis.

References

Anderson, P. (1977) *Considerations on Western Marxism*. London: New Left Books.
Barnes, B. (1994) Cultural Change – the Thought-Styles of Mannheim and Kuhn. *Common Knowledge*, 3, pp. 65–78.
Bloor, D. (1983) *Wittgenstein: A Social Theory of Knowledge*. London: Macmillan.
Callinicos, A. (1999) *Social Theory: A Historical Introduction*. Cambridge: Polity.
Craib, I. (1984) *Modern Social Theory: From Parsons to Habermas*. New York: Harvester Wheatsheaf.
Engels, F. (1972 [1878]) *Anti-Duhring*. Moscow: International Publishers.
Engels, F. (1940 [1883]) *Dialectics of Nature*. New York: International Publishers.
Fowler, B. (2015) Lucien Goldmann's Key Sociological Problems and his Critical Heritage: From the Hidden God to the Hidden Class. In: A. Law and E. Royal Lybeck (eds) *Sociological Amnesia: Cross-Currents in Disciplinary History*. London: Routledge, pp. 105–24.
Goldmann, L. (1964) *The Hidden God: A Study of Tragic Vision in the Pensées of Pascal and the Tragedies of Racine*. London: Routledge & Kegan Paul.
Hayek, F. (2001 [1944]) *The Road to Serfdom*. London: Routledge.
Kilminster, R. (1979) *Praxis and Method: A Sociological Dialogue with Lukács, Gramsci, and the Early Frankfurt School*. London: Routledge & Kegan Paul.
Kolakowski, L. (1972) Lukács's Other Marx. *Cambridge Review*, 28, pp. 85–90.

Kumar, K. (2007) Ideology and Sociology: Reflections on Karl Mannheim's *Ideology and Utopia*. *Journal of Political Ideologies*, 11(2), pp. 169-81.
Löwy, M (1979). *From Romanticism to Bolshevism*. London: Verso.
Lukács, G. (1965 [1909]) *The Sociology of Modern Drama*. Oshkosh, WI: Green Mountain Editions.
Lukács, G. (1991 [1911]) *The Soul and the Forms*. London: Merlin Press
Lukács, G (1972 [1920]) *The Theory of the Novel*. London: Merlin Press
Lukács, G. (1975 [1938]) *The Young Hegel*. R. Livingstone, trans. London: Merlin.
Lukács, G. (1980 [1954]) *The Destruction of Reason*. London: Merlin.
Lukács, G. (1989 [1955]) *The Historical Novel*. London: Merlin.
Lukács, G. (1971) *History and Class Consciousness: Studies in Marxist Dialectics*. R. Livingstone, trans. London: Merlin.
Lukács, G. (1978) *The Ontology of Social Being*, 3 vols. D. Fernbach, trans. London: Merlin.
Mannheim, K. (1940) *Man and Society in an Age of Reconstruction*. London: Routledge & Kegan Paul.
Mannheim, K. (1960 [1929]) *Ideology and Utopia: An Introduction to the Sociology of Knowledge*. London: Routledge & Kegan Paul.
Mannheim, K. (1986) *Conservatism: A Contribution to the Sociology of Knowledge*. London: Routledge.
Marx, K. (1961 [1844]) *The Economic and Philosophical Manuscripts*. Moscow: Foreign Languages Publishing House.
Marx, K. (2007 [1867]) *Capital: A Critique of Political Economy*. New York: Cosimo Classics.
Marx, K. (1994) *Selected Writings*. L. H. Simon, trans. Indianapolis, IN: Hackett.
Mayrl, W. W. (1978) Genetic Structuralism and the Analysis of Social Consciousness. *Theory and Society*, 5(1), pp. 19-44.
Mészáros, I. (1972) *Lukács Concept of Dialectic*, London: Merlin
Mészáros, I (1979) *The Work of Sartre: the Search for Freedom*, vol 1. Brighton: Harvester Press.
Nineham, C (2010) *Capitalism and Class Consciousness*, London: Counterfire.
Parekh, B. (1982) *Marx's Theory of Ideology*. London: Johns Hopkins University Press.
Parkinson, G. H. R. (1970) *Georg Lukács: The Man, His Work, and His Ideas*. London: Weidenfeld & Nicolson.
Rockmore, T. (ed.) (1988) *Lukács Today: Essays in Marxist Philosophy*. Dordrecht: D. Reidel.
Rose, G. (1978) *The Melancholy Science: An Introduction to the Thought of Theodor W. Adorno*. New York: Columbia University Press.
Steadman Jones, G. (1977) *Western Marxism: A Critical Reader*. London: New Left Books.

Althusser

Introduction

Louis Althusser was a French communist philosopher and social theorist who has been described as one of the last great thinkers of Marxism (Roudinesco, 2008: 103). He became recognised as a major thinker following the publication of two books in 1965, a collection of his essays in *For Marx* (1965) and, a book written with his student, *Reading Capital* (Althusser and Balibar, 1965). In these books, he developed a form of 'structural Marxism' that challenged heretofore dominant humanist, historicist, Hegelian and moralising interpretations of Marxism. The latter had become increasingly influential in France following the work of Sartre, Merleau-Ponty and Roger Garaudy, and especially following a period of de-Stalinisation by the French Communist Party (PCF). Althusser sought to defend Marxism as a science rather than morality. Like all Marxists, his work had an explicitly political as well as a theoretical underpinning. By reconstructing Marxism, Althusser sought to revert to a more traditional Marxist–Leninist understanding of Marx, following what he considered its deformation by Stalinism, the Communist Party of the Soviet Union (CPSU) and the PCF. Throughout his life, he remained a critical and outspoken member of the PCF. Drawing on an emerging structuralist theoretical current, he also offered a radically new understanding of ideology. His work is seen as bringing a new level of sophistication and complexity to Marxism but also as generating a number of theoretical problems.

Life and Intellectual Context

Althusser was born in Birmandreis in Algeria on 16 October 1918, where his father, Charles-Joseph Althusser, was a *pied-noirs* (French people who had settled in Algeria, which was then a colony), and worked as a banker after serving as a lieutenant in the French Army. His mother, Lucienne Marthe Berger, was an ardent Catholic employed as a schoolteacher. Although Althusser paints a rather bleak picture of their emotionally suffocating life in his autobiography (Althusser, 1992), the family led a materially comfortable life. After attending Lycée Saint-Charles, he studied at the Lycée du Parc in Lyon, where he became profoundly influenced by Catholicism, joining the Jeunesse Étudiante Chrétienne, a Catholic youth movement. Catholicism was to exert a marked impact throughout his life. Having excelled in his studies, and undertaken a two-year preparatory course – the *Khâgne* – at the age of 20, Althusser gained a place at the highly prestigious École Normale Supérieure (ENS) based in Paris in August 1939. However, in September of the same year, he was drafted into the army, serving as a student officer in Issoire. Captured by the Germans in Vannes in 1940, he was to spend the rest of the war in a prisoner-of-war camp, Stalag XA, near Schleswig-Holstein. Here he was introduced to Marxist ideas by Pierre Courreges, a Parisian lawyer.

After his release at the end of the war, Althusser resumed his studies at the ENS to prepare for the *agrégation*, an examination that would allow him to teach philosophy. Struggling to return to academic life, he began to suffer from severe depression, diagnosed as manic-depression psychosis in 1947, exacerbated following the removal of a hernia that had caused him acute digestive problems. These intense periods of depression followed by 'normality' were reflected in his work, which was often composed of short essays and written during periods of respite. In 1946 he met Helene Rytmann, a former member of the resistance, a communist and a sociologist, who was eight years his senior and who later became his wife. In 1947 he passed his *diplôme d'études supèrieures* under the supervision of Gaston Bachelard, 'On Content in the Thought of G.W.F. Hegel' (1947). In 1948 he passed the *agrégation* and was made a tutor at the ENS offering courses on specialised philosophical topics to *agrégation* students. Located at the rue d'Ulm, Althusser spent the next 35 years teaching at the ENS, France's most prestigious and elite teaching university. In October 1948, he also joined the PCF, which had gained a strong political presence and high level of membership after the war. Though a committed party member whose aims he promoted, he was always to remain a heterodox voice within it.

From the 1950s Althusser began teaching on the history of philosophy including courses on Plato, Descartes, Machiavelli, Hobbes, Montesquieu and Rousseau. He also started to distance himself from his earlier admiration of Hegel, whose work he now saw as intrinsically representing a bourgeois worldview. In the late 1950s and early 1960s, Althusser published several important works. Beginning with a collection of Feuerbach's writings, he also began to interrogate the complex relation between Hegel, Feuerbach and Marx, discussed in his articles on Feuerbach's 'Philosophical Manifestoes' written in 1960; 'On the Young Marx: Theoretical Questions' written in 1961; 'The 1844 Manuscripts of Karl Marx' written in 1962; 'On the Materialist Dialectic' written in 1963; and 'Marxism and Humanism' written in 1965. Together with his important essay 'Contradiction and Overdetermination' these essays were collected in his first book, *For Marx* (2005 [1965]). The book was followed in the same year by another based on a course that he gave at the ENS with his students Etienne Balibar, Roger Establet, Pierre Macherey and Jacques Ranciere, and entitled *Reading Capital* (Althusser et al., 2015 [1965]). *Reading Capital* drew heavily on Spinoza, Freud and Lacan to propose a 'symptomatic reading' of Marx's *Capital*. Together the books, although causing widespread controversy and criticism, established Althusser as a leading philosopher of Marxism and a central thinker of the PCF.

Following a period of stringent criticism of his work, Althusser began a period of self-criticism after 1967 and made substantial, though by no means wholesale, changes to his perspective published later as *Essays in Self-Criticism* (1976). In addition to organising a 'Philosophy Course for Scientists' at the end of the 1960s – later published as *Philosophy and the Spontaneous Philosophy of the Scientists* (1974) – he published a notable article on Lenin and Philosophy in 1968 (1971). In 1969 he wrote a ground-breaking essay on ideology, entitled 'Ideology and Ideological State Apparatuses', first published in English in 1971, and an essay entitled 'Marxism and Class Struggle'. These works both consolidated his reputation and saw him rise to become a central intellectual figure in Latin America. From the early 1970s, Althusser became even more critical of the PCF's political position, especially during the rise of Eurocommunism, and its failure for him, to think 'scientifically', publishing a serious of articles in *Le Monde* entitled 'What Must Change in the Party'. He also wrote several articles for the Italian communist newspaper, *Il Manifesto*, as well as a work on Machiavelli in the mid-1970s. During this time, his already acute depression began to increase, his treatment with high doses of medication and shock therapy, resulted in memory loss and hallucination. These delusions culminated in him tragically killing his wife, Helene Rytmann, on 17 November 1980.

Following her death, Althusser withdrew from public life and published very little. However, there were some exceptions: a manuscript he began entitled 'The Underground Current of the Materialism of the Encounter' was later published as *Philosophy of the Encounter* (2006) and formed the basis for an 'aleatory materialism'. In addition, he published an autobiography written to clarify what he would have said concerning the death of his wife, had he been allowed to speak before a court (Althusser, 1992; Elliott, 1994). He spent his last years at a psychiatric hospital in La Verrière, in Paris, where he died of a heart attack on 22 October 1990, a few days after his 72nd birthday.

Intellectual Influences

Althusser wrote in an intellectual context in which structuralism, especially as espoused in the work of Lévi-Strauss, was emerging and challenging the heretofore dominant ideas of existentialism and phenomenology. The latter foregrounded the individual, and his or her subjectivity and their choices. While the structuralist approach had roots in Durkheim's injunction to treat social facts as things, as forces above individuals that shaped them (Bourdieu and Passeron, 1967). A structuralist standpoint was also central to the work of the Freudian psychoanalyst Lacan, and Althusser's student, the historian of ideas, Michel Foucault. These writings proposed 'decentring' actors and agents, as well as human consciousness, principally through language. Although he shared many structuralist preoccupations, it is of note that Althusser never regarded himself as a structuralist (Althusser and Balibar, 1990: 7).

Other significant influences on Althusser's work include Baruch Spinoza (1632–77) and Gaston Bachelard (1884–1962). In his philosophical writings Spinoza had transformed religious and ethical thinking by focusing on the operation of determinism, rationalism and necessity in the natural and social world. He also highlighted the problematic nature of reading texts. Althusser drew on all of these ideas including the operation of determinism and necessity in social life and of a 'symptomatic' reading (though the term is Freud's) of texts. By contrast, Gaston Bachelard, a French philosopher of science who taught Althusser, challenged the view that science and knowledge developed cumulatively. Instead, he argued, the history of science was characterised by 'epistemological breaks' between different ways of understanding the world. This was especially true of the pre-scientific or aconceptual or common-sense knowledge given in everyday life, and the 'constructed' scientific or conceptual understandings of the world. Moreover, Bachelard argued, concepts acquired their meaning only within the context of a network of other concepts. These arguments played a central role in Althusser's epistemological writings.

Historical, Social and Political Context

Catholicism and Marxism

Althusser's intellectual formation took place in the 1950s, as he merged his initial Catholicism with Marxism while a prisoner of war. The major international and national upheavals characterising the 1950s and 1960s markedly shaped the configuration of his thought, especially as they were filtered and interpreted through the lens of the PCF. The post-war period not only saw the development of a Cold War rift between the United States and the Soviet Union but also the Chinese Communist Revolution. Beginning in 1946, after the Second Sino-Japanese War, the Communist Party of China led by Mao Zedong established the People's Republic of China by 1949. The first five-year plan between 1950 and 1956, which doubled output in industry with the help of Soviet aid, was followed by the Great Leap Forward in 1958 advancing small-scale decentralised industry and agriculture, and extending the commune system in agriculture (McLellan, 1998: 239). This took place within a hierarchical Leninist party structure dividing the mass of workers from the decision making of a rigid politburo.

Moreover, in 1959, a Sino-Soviet split emerged following Russia's policy of détente – of peaceful co-existence with the United States – at a time when the latter was extending its foreign policy into the Pacific. With the divergent paths of development, a Chinese sense of isolation, and a feeling of economic inferiority to Russia, tensions between the socialist countries became inflamed. Within Europe and France the 1960s were also a period of tremendous social and political upheaval. Taking place within the context of heightening Cold War rivalries, numerous dramatic socio-political events unfolded. This included: the student protests against Vietnam; a major student revolt in Paris; the Czech uprising against the Soviet invasion or 'Prague Spring'; revolution in Cuba and Marxist revolutions in the developing world; and the rise of Maoism and the Cultural Revolution in China between 1966 and 1969. The Cultural Revolution sought to re-vivify the importance of Mao's teachings with its emphasis on moral, ideological factors, and consciousness in shaping society, of attaining a balance between industrial and agricultural production, and support for Third World revolutions. It placed a greater emphasis on the explanatory role of culture within society as than was ordinarily permitted by crude Soviet interpretations of the Marxist base–superstructure model.

The Renewal of Marxism and the PCF

Althusser, like many other Marxists, was preoccupied with the unfolding of specific social, political and economic issues which he tried to understand through a renewal of Marxist theory. These issues centred principally on socialist transformation. How and in what context or through which means could a new socialist society emerge from a capitalist one? This raised some ancillary questions. Why had socialism arisen predominantly in rural 'backward' countries rather than in the industrially advanced West – initially Russia, but later China and Cuba? And secondly, how and under what conditions would a socialist revolution arise in the West?

All of Althusser's work needs to be understood in these political terms, but also, as a consequence of his adherence to the Marxist–Leninism of the PCF; in the context of the crisis of post-war Stalinism; and of the continuing social and political defeats that the progressive left faced, including the retreat of working class militancy and the collapse of French communism. From the 1930s onwards the PCF's leaders had consistently followed an orthodox Stalinist line, including adhering to a rigid interpretation of Marxism centred on the linear development of the modes of production in which society's productive forces continually expanded. However, in terms of practice, during the occupation of France in the Second World War, the PCF played a leading progressive role in organising the Resistance. It also participated in the provisional government of liberation between 1944 and 1947, augmenting its popular support and ensuring it gained a high level of the electorate's vote. Post-war France under Auriol had been characterised not only by a strong anti-German feeling, but also simultaneously, by fear of a Soviet-communist takeover. Unlike many other powers France therefore expanded, rather than reduced her army, taking an intransigent line with regards to holding on to its colonial possessions, including Indo-China, then seen as a bulwark against communism. This led to an unpopular war in Indo-China (1946–54) immediately followed by a war with Algeria (1954–62) led by Guy Mollet's government. The end of 1956 also saw the unfolding of the 'Suez crisis' further illustrating the enduring nature of Anglo-French Western imperialism as France attempted to regain control over the Suez Canal from the Egyptian President, Gamal Nasser. In this context of a polarised, fractious and unstable atmosphere, a powerful left opposition emerged with Sartre acting as the spokesperson for a left humanism through his existentialist philosophy. Politically, however, de Gaulle, as a representative of the centre right, became president again in 1959, flanked further on the right by the militant OAS. The PCF's allegiance to Moscow and rejection of any criticism aimed at the Soviet Union, including supporting its quelling of the Hungarian uprising in 1956, the 'pacification' of Algeria initiated two years prior, and later the Czech uprising, meant that although the PCF half-heartedly supported the workers' strikes in 1968, for the most part it condemned the student movement and uprising and its support dwindled. Moreover, the PCF became increasingly tied to a reformist or a non-revolutionary approach to acquiring power. Unlike intellectuals such as Sartre and Merleau-Ponty, who through their journal *Les Temps Modernes* chose to remain outside of the party, Althusser decided to remain in the PCF, not as a blind adherent, but as a 'fellow traveller' or dissident voice trying to change it from within. As he noted:

> There was no way out for a philosopher. If he spoke and wrote the philosophy the Party wanted he was restricted to commentary and slight idiosyncrasies in his own way of using the Famous Quotations. We had no audience among our peers. Our enemies flung in our faces the charge that we were merely politicians. (Althusser, 2005 [1965]: 27)

Though irreducible to it, it is difficult to understand Althusser's work without acknowledging the development and direction of the PCF. This, obediently followed, for the most part, the direction of the Communist Party of the Soviet Union, which dictated tactical and strategic political policy, as well as dogmatically determining the 'true' or 'correct' theoretical interpretation of what constituted Marxism. Althusser therefore sought to adapt and develop Marx's thinking in a party context where it had become rigidified, in order to make it more attuned to the political problems facing communists in a deepening Cold War context. For him, this entailed accepting neither Stalinist dogmatism nor Hegelian humanist philosophy, which had become the party line following Khrushchev's 'secret speech' at the Twentieth Party Congress. For Althusser, the reaction to Stalin's crimes unveiled by Khrushchev in his speech had resulted in an upsurge in discussions of 'morality', 'liberation', 'man', ethics, 'the human person' and 'alienation'. The new 'official' interpretation of Marxism became inflected by a moral underpinning, that humans overcame their alienation through a teleological process of the negation of the negation. It was a theme developed by the official philosopher of the PCF, Roger Garaudy. For Althusser, however, such an emphasis on the philosophy of man, morality, on voluntarism and idealism, belonged to a bourgeois mode of thought. Marx's early works which emphasised such a humanist approach had 'been a war-horse for petty bourgeois intellectuals in their struggle against Marxism' (Althusser, 2005 [1965]: 10). According to Althusser, the process of theoretical renewal involved challenging Stalinist economism dominant both in Second and Third International interpretations of Marxism. Such reductive understandings included a fatalist schema wherein the economy was perceived as the central explanatory principle determining and explaining all other social relations, including politics and ideology, as found for example in the base–superstructure metaphor. But later, it also included rallying against what he perceived as the voluntarism, idealism, empiricism and historicism of the new party line that drew heavily on Hegel and shared an affinity with the early Marx.

For Althusser, a well-developed Marxist account of dialectical materialism was missing from Marxism, notwithstanding Engel's own efforts. A philosophy 'that is capable of accounting for the nature of theoretical formations and their history, and therefore *capable of accounting for itself*, by taking itself as its own object' (2005 [1965]: 39). Althusser sought to develop such a scientifically grounded Marxist philosophy by ensuring that it respected the autonomy of the natural sciences yet also underwrote the scientific nature of historical materialism. As Elliott (2006: 125) notes:

> Althusser sought to reconstruct historical materialism in such a way that it provided a viable basis for the investigation and illumination of the complexities of real history and concrete societies, thereby furnishing guidance to revolutionary politics. The obstacles to its scientific vocation were to be found not only outside but inside it. In the final analysis, these could be tracked down to a single culprit: Hegelianism. Althusser sought to secure the total novelty of Marx's theory by attempting to demonstrate: (i) the irreducibility of the Marxist dialectic to the Hegelian; (ii) the irreducibility of the Marxist conception of the social whole (and the causality governing it) to the Hegelian; and, as a consequence, (iii) the difference between the Marxist science of history and every philosophy of history (Hegel's being the most rigorous of the genre). Behind Stalin, paradoxically, stood Hegel. So any critique of Hegelianism and Second-International orthodoxy was simultaneously – albeit cautiously – directed against theoretical Stalinism and its spectres. Althusser was going against official and underground currents – against 'right' and 'left' Hegelianism, past and present, alike.
>
> [Republished with permission of Pluto Press from *Althusser: The Detour of a Theory*, J. K. Elliott, 1987]

Although the events in May 1968 played a profound role in shaping the development and reception of Marx's writings, they appear to be negligible in shaping Althusser's work – he missed them as a result of being hospitalised for severe depression. Moreover, his position on the uprising remained ambivalent, seeing it as both a major event, yet also maintaining the PCF line that it represented anarchistic elements in the student movement. As a result, he received sharp criticism from many progressive students who stood to the left of the PCF, or who were sympathetic to Maoism. This condemnation later fed into his various ongoing auto-critiques.

Ideas and Arguments
The Two Marxisms

In *For Marx*, Althusser argues that Marx's early writings, though they shared similarities with his later work, were in fact distinct from them. They were divided by a what he called an 'epistemological break', a term borrowed from Bachelard. Marx's early and later writings, Althusser argues, were embedded in different and distinct 'problematics'. The latter constituted a broad framework akin to Kuhn's notion of a paradigm, in which certain problems were posed and resolved, while other problems remained invisible, absent or undiscussed. Hence, although Marx uses the term 'political economy', 'alienation' or 'class struggle' in both problematics, their meaning differs in each, being shaped by the broader framework of words and concepts used in the respective problematic. Marx's early work was developed in an *ideological* problematic which drew liberally on the ideas of the Young Hegelians, and especially Feuerbach. Preoccupied by alienation and subjective and ethical criticisms of the capitalist world, this standpoint argued that these phenomena would be overcome by a proletariat that became conscious of its centrality in producing or 'making' the world, and discovered its 'duty' or mission to recover its alienated freedom in a revolutionary transition to socialism. Inhering or immanent in such a teleological vision with a predetermined end, was a Hegelian logic, in which humans are firstly alienated or negated, but subsequently overcome or supersede this alienation through a process of recuperation or recovery, the negation of the negation. This view was also underpinned by a moral view of individuals recapturing a freedom stolen by capitalism. This ideological problematic, however, was followed by a second *scientific* anti-humanist problematic which emerged from around 1845 with the German ideology (what Althusser refers to as the work of the break, i.e. epistemological break), which rather than foregrounding humans, subjectivity, anthropology and alienation, developed a scientific theory of historical materialism, a science of history – focused on structural explanations centred on the contradictions between the forces and relations of production.

According to Althusser, this division between two problematics divided by an epistemological break was not apparent to Marx himself, but required a 'symptomatic reading'. Drawing on Spinoza, Althusser argued that no reading was 'innocent', rather every interpretation involved theoretical and political presuppositions which usually remained unstated.

The idea of a symptomatic reading not only drew on Spinoza, but also on Freud via Lacan. Just as Freud examined a patient's dreams which, though complex and contradictory, and containing gaps, silences and absences, nevertheless revealed underlying symptoms of the patient contained in their unconscious, so a theorist reading a text looked to the 'unconscious' underpinnings of the text as it appeared partially, or in refracted form, in the visibly written words of the text itself. This opened the 'way to an understanding of the determination of the visible as visible, and conjointly, of the invisible as invisible, and of the organic link binding the invisible to the visible' (Althusser and Balibar, 1990: 25). Such a structuralist view where what was absent from or unstated in a text, as well as its structure, was important, more so than the conscious intentions of the author, differed markedly from naive empiricist readings of a text where the meaning of a text was immediately accessible, or could be directly seen in the text. The latter stance correlated with bourgeois philosophy. Such forms of empirical understanding remained a central target throughout Althusser's writings.

Moreover, according to Althusser, an ideological problematic remained closed, in that it did not allow for the development or a deepening of knowledge to take place, instead confirming its own presuppositions. A science, by contrast, was open, allowing a continual transformation and development of concepts and ideas.

Rather than a singular break Althusser refers to Marx's 'works of the break'. The works between 1845 and between 1857 constitute 'transitional theoretical works'. It is only really Marx's works written between 1857 and his death that constitute his mature scientific works. By founding the science of historical materialism Marx simultaneously broke with his old ideological philosophical understanding and found a new philosophy – dialectical materialism. By undertaking an epistemological break with his earlier writings Marx opened up a:

> new 'continent' that of history, just as Thales opened up the 'continent' of mathematics for scientific knowledge, and Galileo opened up the 'continent' of physical nature of scientific knowledge. As a result 'we can claim that Marx established a new science: the science of the history of "social formations"' (Althusser, 2005 [1965]: 14, 13). Just as Thales 'induced' a Platonic philosophy and Galileo a Cartesian philosophy, so the development of the science of history has 'induced' the birth of a Marxist philosophy or dialectical materialism, though this currently 'lags behind' historical materialism. Such an enquiry requires 'a new and rigorous method of investigation'. (2005 [1965]: 156)

Anti-humanism

Moreover, descriptions of Marx as someone who remained a Hegelian, but superseded him by distinguishing Hegel's method from his content, or in another metaphor standing Hegel's system back on its feet through an 'inversion', were deeply misleading.

For Althusser, history was a process without a subject. Here, Althusser not only railed against historicism – the belief that ideas or events need to be placed in their historical context to be understood, for its relativism – but also humanism. Humanism consisted of two parts: firstly, 'that there is a universal essence of man'; and secondly, 'that this essence is the attribute of "each single individual"' (Althusser, 1971: 228). Humanism, or the philosophical idea of man, constituted a central bourgeois ideological myth taking us away from proper scientific analysis. As Althusser states in his essays on self-criticism:

> One thing is certain: one cannot *begin* with man, because that would be to begin with a bourgeois idea of 'man', and because the idea of *beginning with* man, in other words the idea of an absolute point of departure (= of an 'essence') belongs to bourgeois philosophy. This idea of 'man' as a starting-point, an absolute point of departure, is the basis of all bourgeois ideology; it is the soul of the great Classical Political Economy itself. 'Man' is a myth of bourgeois ideology: Marxism-Leninism cannot *start* from 'man'. It starts 'from the economically given social period'; and at the end of its analysis, when it 'arrives', *it may find real men*. These men are thus the *point of arrival* of an analysis which starts from the social relations of the existing mode of production, from class relations, and from the class struggle. These men are quite different men from the 'man' of bourgeois ideology. (Althusser, 1976: 52–3)

Rather than focusing on humans, Althusser argues that we need to instead hone in firstly on social structures, and secondly on the fact that people are not conscious of what they do but irretrievably remain trapped in ideology. In *Reading Capital*, Althusser and Balibar argue:

> The fact that the structure of the relations of production determines the places and functions occupied and adopted by the agents of production, who are never anything more than the occupants of these places, in so far as they are the 'supports' (Träger) of these functions. The true 'subjects' (in the sense of constitutive subjects of the process) are therefore not these occupants or functionaries, are not, despite all appearances, the 'obviousness' of the 'given' of naïve anthropology, 'concrete individuals', 'real men' – but the definition and distribution of these places and functions. The true 'subjects' are these definers and distributors the relations of production (and political and ideological social relations). But since these are relations they cannot be thought within the category of 'subject'. (1990: 180)

Human individuals were a product of the distribution of social relations within a mode of production, or social formation. They accepted this role as subjects through ideology. Rather than focusing on individuals, Althusser believed Marxist science needs to focus on class struggle.

A Theory of Knowledge

According to Althusser, Marx's theoretical and scientific revolution broke with all previous 'theoretical ideologies' and contained two components: historical materialism, as the science of social formations; and dialectical materialism, the science of theoretical practice. It was dialectical materialism, Marx's philosophy, which remained undeveloped but rather implicit in 'working form' in *Capital*. This not only moved away from a residual idealism but also provided a theory of the production of knowledge. Althusser's contention that knowledge was autonomous from ideological interests, including those of the state and party, ran against Zhdanov's claim that they could not be separated.

Through a symptomatic reading of Marx's later work, it would become clear that Marx was not an empiricist, that is someone who understood the real world by seeing it and breaking it down through a process of abstraction – a knowing subject confronting an object to be known. In such an empiricist epistemology, concepts directly captured reality and through observation allowed the investigator to ascertain their truth.

Instead Marx sought to resolve various epistemological problems by highlighting the role of *practice*:

> By *practice* in general I shall mean any process of *transformation* of determinate given raw material into a determinate *product*, a transformation effected by a determinate human labour, using determinate means (of 'production'). In any practice thus conceived, the *determinant* moment (or element) is neither the raw material nor the product, but the practice in the narrow sense: the moment of the *labour of transformation* itself, which sets to work, in a specific structure, men, means and a technical method of utilizing the means. (Althusser, 2005 [1965]: 166–7)

Drawing on Marx's 1857 *Introduction*, Althusser argues that knowledge was not out there ready to be enveloped in concepts, but an act of production, a *theoretical practice*, an object to be appropriated. It was theoretical practice which produced objective knowledge. Althusser made a sharp break between the real object, or social reality, and the thought-object, the theoretical system constituting science. The development of theory and science took place on the 'thought-object', which ultimately provided us with knowledge of reality:

> Knowledge, never as empiricism desperately demands it should, confronts a *pure object*, which is then identical to the real object, of which knowledge aimed to produce precisely ... the knowledge. Knowledge working on its 'object', then, does not work on the *real* object but on the peculiar raw material, which constitutes, in the strict sense of the term, its '*object*' (of knowledge), and which, even in its most rudimentary forms of knowledge, is distinct from the *real object*. (Althusser and Balibar, 1990: 43)

Theoretical practice, like other social practices, entailed three moments or aspects: a raw material which he called Generality I or an object or ideology; this is worked on by a theory or problematic (Generality II); to produce a transformed object, knowledge – Generality III. The whole process of a theoretical practice took place wholly in thought: thought operates only on a theoretical object, it does not confront the real world, which remains separate from it. Through such a rational process the ideological or common-sense understanding of the world was transformed into scientific knowledge of it. According to Althusser, rather than an empirical criterion of truth, each science had its own rigorous internal mode of validation free of external, ideological or social influences. Dialectical materialism equally contained its own validity.

Theoretical practice, which produced objective knowledge, was, moreover, relatively autonomous from other practices in the social formation, of which, Althusser argues, there are many, but of which he only lists three others – economic, political and ideological. All social practices are based on the model of economic practice or production – a raw material that is worked on by labour power, tools and a means of production, to produce a specific resulting product. Political practice involves political parties or organisations transforming social relations to create new social relations (a revolution, for example); ideological practice transforms ideas and people's consciousness of the world.

The social world was then seen as composed of a number of heterogeneous practices which include economic, political and ideological practices, and which are structured in terms of relatively stable social relationships. Herein, the economic, ideological and political constituted the central instances or levels of society.

Overdetermination

In his important essay 'Contradiction and Overdetermination' drawing on Marx, Lenin and Mao, Althusser extends his idea that Marx makes a fundamental break with Hegelian and humanist anthropology in his later works. According to Althusser, the form of the Hegelian dialectic cannot be extracted from the substance and content of Hegelian philosophy. Rather, in Hegel, the most important levels of any social order – the economy, polity and ideological – are seen as expressions of a single, self-manifesting and unfolding, spiritual essence, the Idea. Hegelian philosophy therefore remains reductionist, speculative and idealist. Hegel's notion of contradiction is a simple, expressive one, wherein an internal principle, the development of Spirit or consciousness, at a certain stage in history, is reflected within the totality of social processes.

By contrast, Althusser claims that Marx's notion of dialectic presupposes a different object – material history. Marx had a more complex view of social totality than the expressive one deployed by Hegel. This entailed a hierarchy of reciprocal multi-level processes of causation, or what Althusser dubs 'overdetermination', entailing reciprocal causation of the economic, political, ideological and theoretical levels. In such a scenario the economy remains determinant, but only in the last instance.

In actual societies, or 'social formations', any of these superstructural moments – politics, ideology, etc. – can also be dominant. Nevertheless, the contradiction between the relations and forces of production determines the overall character of the social totality by determining which level or instance is to become the dominant instance or level in a social formation. Each social formation – an actual social order usually containing or combining more than one mode of production – not only has a dominant mode of production, feudal or capitalist, but also has a structure in dominance – namely, the economy, polity or ideology – and it is this that usually shapes historical development. Different societies can be differentiated according to which structure or level is in dominance. In feudalism, for example, politics and ideological structures had a more significant role; in early capitalism, it was the economic sphere, whereas in more developed capitalist formations it has become the political (Benton, 1984). Each social formation has a structure in dominance which unifies it. Although Althusser follows Engels by arguing that the economy was dominant 'in the last instance' this may not be the case in reality:

> the economic dialectic is never active *in the pure state*; in History, these instances, the superstructures, etc. – are never seen to step respectfully aside when their work is done or, when the Time comes, as his pure phenomena, to scatter before His Majesty the Economy as he strides along the royal road of the Dialectic. From the first moment to the last, the lonely hour of the 'last instance' never comes. (2005 [1965]: 113)

Althusser therefore develops the concept of overdetermination in order to challenge reductive base–superstructure models employed by crude orthodox understandings of Marxism, including those deriving from Stalin and the PCF. It may be that the political and ideological sit above the economic base as this geological metaphor insists, but they are not determined by it, they merely depend upon it: superstructures possess a 'relative autonomy' and significant 'indices of effectivity', in relation to the economic base. Moreover, the distinct levels exist at uneven stages of development and in the real historical world, 'articulate' with each other according to their own distinct temporalities, and relations of subordination and domination. As Benton notes:

> Since there is no single 'essential' contradiction leading of necessity to a higher-level revolutionary synthesis and supersession, it follows that fundamental transformations in the forms of social life are to be thought of as contingent outcomes of a 'fusion' or 'condensation' of multiple contradictions and struggles. There is no place here

for history as a linear sequence of stages leading inexorably to some pre-defined end-state, a doctrine often masquerading as the Marxian view. (1992: 6)

Ideology and Ideological State Apparatuses

Althusser's theory of ideology draws in part on Gramsci, in order to acknowledge cultural or ideological forms in securing capitalist compliance in the working class. Ideology's function has, moreover, to be understood in relation to the state. To understand the state, Althusser argues, we need to distinguish not only between state power and the state apparatus, but also between the repressive apparatuses of the state, and its ideological apparatuses. The Repressive State Apparatus (RSA) includes the government, the administration, the army, the police, the courts, the prisons, etc., which ultimately rest on the function of violence (repression in the case of administration). By contrast, the Ideological State Apparatuses (ISAs) include the religious ISA (churches), the educational ISA (public and private schools), the family ISA (which also intervenes in the production of labour power), the legal ISA (which also belongs to the RSA), the political ISA (the political system including parties), the trade union ISA, the communications ISA (press, radio and television, etc.) and the cultural ISA (literature and the arts, sports, etc.).

According to Althusser, the reproduction of the relations of production is secured by the exercise of state power in both the RSAs and ISAs. The former use repression or brutal physical force to secure relations of exploitation to renew themselves, whereas the latter secure reproduction 'behind the shield' of repression through adumbrating the ruling ideology. In earlier social formations such as feudalism the number of ISAs was not just smaller – religious, familial and political (Estates General and Parliament, the Communes, *Villes* and guilds) – but the dominant ISA was the religious ISA, and most ideological struggle from the sixteenth to the eighteenth century was concentrated in anti-religious struggle. In modern, mature, capitalist social formations, however, it is the educational ISA that holds the dominant position, despite political ISAs through parliamentary democracy, parties and universal suffrage appearing to do so. Thus the school–family couplet has replaced the Church–family couplet:

> It takes children from every class at infant school age, and then for years, the years in which the child is most 'vulnerable', squeezed between the family-State apparatus and the educational State apparatus, it drums into them, whether it uses new or old methods, a certain amount of 'know-how' wrapped in the ruling ideology (French, arithmetic, natural history, the sciences, literature) or simply the ruling ideology in its pure state (ethics, civic instruction, philosophy). Somewhere around the age of sixteen, a huge mass of children are ejected 'into production': these are the workers or small peasants. (2008: 29)

In capitalist society, although the school is seen as neutral and objective, providing a liberating and empowering environment where teachers are respectful of the 'free conscience' of children and facilitating them on a path of freedom, morality and responsibility, in fact readies them for a life of labour.

In addition to discussing ISAs, Althusser also attempts to provide 'a schematic outline' of a *general* theory of ideology rather than of specific or *particular* ideologies which express class positions. Ideology in the general sense has no history, like the Feudian unconscious, it is eternal:

> the peculiarity of ideology is that it is endowed with a structure and a functioning such as to make it a non-historical reality, i.e. an omni-historical reality, in the sense in which that structure and functioning are immutable, present in the same form throughout what we can call history ... the history of class societies. (2008: 35)

He qualifies this by proposing two theses. Firstly, ideology represents the imaginary relationship of individuals to their real conditions of existence:

> it is not their real conditions of existence, their real world that 'men' [*sic*] 'represent to themselves' in ideology but above all it is their relation to those conditions of existence which is represented to them there... It is this relation which contains the 'cause' which has to explain the imaginary distortion of the ideological representation of the real world. (2008: 38)

Ideology therefore constitutes an imaginary relation to real relations. In his second thesis, Althusser proposes that ideology has a material existence and not a 'spiritual' or 'ideal' existence. By this he means that: 'an ideology always exists in an apparatus, and its practice or practices. The existence is material' (2008: 40). Matter here is understood not akin to a rifle or a stone, but, as Aristotle argued, as retaining various modalities all rooted in the last instance in 'physical matter'. Individuals do not live in a free-floating world of spiritual ideas which they choose to adhere to. Rather, individuals are subjects embedded in existing determinate practices, which shape them. It is by engaging in rituals and practices that humans take up ideas. This, for Althusser, is akin to Pascal's view that if you physically kneel and move your lips you will, as a result, become religious:

> I shall talk of actions inserted into practices. And I shall point out that these practices are governed by the *rituals* in which these practices are inscribed, within the *material existence of an ideological apparatus*, be it only a small part of that apparatus: a small mass in a small church, a funeral, a minor match at a sports' club, a school day, a political party meeting, etc.... Besides, we are indebted to Pascal's defensive 'dialectic' for the wonderful formula which will enable us to invert the order of the notional schema of ideology. Pascal says more or less:

'Kneel down, move your lips in prayer, and you will believe.' He thus scandalously inverts the order of things. (Althusser, 2008: 43)

Althusser thus removes the normal correlation of ideology with ideas. The terms 'subject', 'consciousness', 'belief', 'action' remain, but these are conjoined with practices, rituals and ideological apparatuses. In this understanding the subject acts in so far as he is 'acted by the system'.

The concept of 'subject' or 'subjectivication' remains central to Althusser's theory of ideology. The category of the subject is constitutive of all ideology in so far as all ideology has the function of 'constituting' concrete subjects. Ideology contains both a recognition and a misrecognition function that makes arbitrary processes 'obvious'. It transforms 'concrete individuals' into 'concrete subjects'. All ideology:

> hails or interpellates concrete individuals as concrete subjects ... ideology 'acts' or 'functions' in such a way that it 'recruits' subjects among the individuals (it recruits them all), or 'transforms' the individuals into subjects (it transforms them all) by that very precise operation which I have called *interpellation* or hailing, and which can be imagined along the lines of the most commonplace everyday police (or other) hailing: 'Hey, you there!'... Assuming that the theoretical scene I have imagined takes place in the street, the hailed individual will turn round. By this mere one-hundred-and-eighty-degree physical conversion, he becomes a *subject*. Why? Because he has recognized that the hail was 'really' addressed to him, and that 'it was *really him* who was hailed' (and not someone else) ... the existence of ideology and the hailing or interpellation of individuals as subjects are one and the same thing. (2008: 48)

Given its important function in creating subjects, rather than disappearing in a future communist society as Marxists ordinarily maintain, ideology, Althusser believes, will always remain, albeit in a modified form in socialism, though and in a manner that does not contribute towards social domination.

Aleatory Materialism

In his last writings between 1978 and 1987, posthumously published as *Philosophy of the Encounter* (2006), Althusser continued his quest for an anti-Hegelian Marxism focusing on the problem of history, inevitability and revolution. In this context Althusser argues that Marxist philosophy is part of a materialist tradition deriving from Epicurus to Spinoza, which includes Machiavelli, Hobbes, Rousseau, Marx, Heidegger and Derrida. Rather than being idealists foregrounding freedom, as they have been misleadingly interpreted, the latter thinkers developed a non-teleological, or contingent, materialism, a materialism of the encounter. The term 'aleatory' derives from the Latin, *alea*, referring to dice or games of contingency or chance. Here necessity comes about from the contingent or chance encounters of social forces and not as inhering within a teleological Hegelian approach. Extending arguments from his discussion of overdetermination, Althusser argues that history is the outcome of a conjuncture, a concatenation of processes:

> that is, the aleatory encounter of elements in part already in existence, but also in part unforeseeable. Every conjuncture is a singular case like all historical individualities, like all that exists. (2006: 45–6)

Contemporary Relevance and Applications

Althusser taught and influenced an important new generation of French thinkers including Michel Serres, Etienne Balibar, Pierre Macherey, Pierre Bourdieu, Jacques Derrida, Alan Badiou and Michel Foucault. And his work had an enormous influence on sociology and especially in literary theory from the mid-1980s to the mid-1990s, before being supplanted by post-structuralism.

THE MURDER OF HÉLÈNE RYTMANN

The murder of his wife, Hélène Rytmann not only tarnished Althusser's reputation as a renowned intellectual in France at the time, but also continues to affect the reception of his work today. Beyond the murder itself, the additional issue is that Althusser was never criminally charged. After reporting it himself, Althusser was immediately hospitalised and a psychiatric assessment carried out. He was deemed to have murdered Rytmann without conscious awareness during a hallucinatory episode and was found incapable of understanding the associated charges. The court then ruled Althusser mentally irresponsible and, according to a French law since changed, beyond prosecution. Stripped of his legal personhood, a non-being, he was also denied the possibility of pleading guilty in court and taking responsibility for his symptoms and for commiting the act. Public criticism suggested status privileges and highlighted how little consideration was given to the victim. Althusser later attempted to account for the murder in his autobiography, which was only published posthumously. This last phase in his life raises moral and political questions regarding a theorist's intellectual work and whether or not this can be easily separated from his or her biography as well as highlighting the complex nature of legal and ethical responsibility.

Althusser's ideas became highly influential in Britain during the 1970s, when they were feverishly taken up not only by the New Left, in the work of Perry Anderson, Terry Eagleton, Goran Therborn, Stuart Hall and Gareth Steadman Jones. His reworking of Marxism and his clarification of the central concepts in historical materialism also led to the to development of Analytical

Marxism, which included Gerry Cohen, Erik Olin Wright and Andrew Levine. But his arguments were also taken up by writers attempting to extend but also criticise his theoretical analysis including Barry Hindess and Paul Hirst in their books: *Pre-Capitalist Modes of Production* (1975) and *Mode of Production and Social Formation* (1977), and, with Anthony Cutler and Athar Hussain, the two-volume *Marx's Capital and Capitalism Today* (1977). As Resch (1992) argues, Hindess and Hirst sought to develop a post-Althusserian, post-Marxism which foregrounded theoretical practice and regarded discourses as 'autonomous' from the material sphere and from historical conditions. Advocating an 'anti-epistemology' they questioned realist claims of the reality of objects, and rejected all forms of history and historical analysis taking Althusser's anti-historicism and anti-humanism to its logical conclusion.

The view that knowledge was a theoretical practice was also influential on the work of critical realism led by Roy Bhaskar in his *A Realist Theory of Science* (1975) and *The Possibility of Naturalism* (1979). In these books, Bhaskar develops what he terms a 'qualified anti-positivist naturalism' or realism. The aim of his approach is both to 'specify the (ontological) conditions that make, and the (epistemological) conditions that must be satisfied, for this naturalist project top be possible' (1979: 2). Scientific laws have to be conceived as 'the tendencies of transfactually active structures' existing within a stratified reality with 'ontological depth'. Such a reality necessitates a distinction between observable processes and the unobservable structures and mechanisms that generate them, or between 'the real', 'the actual' and the 'empirical'. Bhaskar, nevertheless, acknowledges important differences in accounting for processes in the social and the natural world:

> Social structures, unlike natural structures, do not exist independently of the activities they govern.
>
> Social structures, unlike natural structures, do not exist independently of the agents' conceptions of what they are doing in their activity.
>
> Social Structures, unlike natural structures, may be only relatively enduring. (1979: 38)

Although social processes take place for the most part in 'open systems' as compared to the 'closed systems' of experimental laboratories, they can still be understood scientifically. Upon this basis, Bhaskar also develops what he calls the Transformational Model of Social Activity, which examines the connection between persons and society, which are ontologically distinct but connected and in which society is:

> both the ever-present *condition* (material cause) and the continually reproduced outcome of human agency... Hence the model of the society/person connection I am proposing could be summarized as follows: people do not create society. For it always pre-exists them and is a necessary condition for their activity. (1979: 36)

Bhaskar regards society as an ensemble of structures and practices which individuals either reproduce through their actions or transform. In this regard society does not have an existence above individuals, as a reified structure, nor is it simply derivative from their action, an error often made by voluntarist approaches.

In addition, Althusser's theory of ideology was influential on the work of Judith Butler and Slavoj Žižek. However, the somewhat inflated estimation of his importance as part of a new intellectual fad was followed by an equally stringent overreaction to it from the late 1970s and 1980s, especially expressed in E. P. Thompson's *The Poverty of Theory* (1978). It was of significance that the sharp criticism of his anti-humanist approach emerged in a context of growing individualism in both the UK and the United States, a period seeing the emergence of individualism and rational choice theory, even in Marxism (Montag, 2003: 4).

Althusser's attempt to challenge economic reductionist approaches to the state through the concepts of overdetermination was taken further in the work of the Greek-French Marxist, Nicos Poulantzas, who, drawing on both Gramsci and Althusser, discussed the relative autonomy of the state which, he argued, remained institutionally separated from the capitalist economy. His conceptualisation of the state as a social relation rather than a thing, and as something that reflected a condensation of class forces and struggles was forcefully expressed in his books *Political Power and Social Classes* (1973) and *State, Power, Socialism* (1978). As Jessop (1985: 4) notes, in addition to his interest in superstructural phenomena, Poulantzas was also centrally preoccupied with the nature of political forms and revolutionary strategy, including bourgeois democracy and fascism. Although relatively autonomous from capitalism, which no longer required extra-economic coercion to extract profits, the state was nevertheless imbued with class interests and served as a modality of class domination. The liberal ideals of sovereignty and individual rights foregrounding an idea of popular representation, in reality allowed the state to serve dominant class interests. Not only did the state manage tensions within the dominant class – especially responding to those capitalists who only pursued short-term profits at the expense of the system as a whole – it also manged tensions between the dominant and the dominated classes, often through hegemonic or nationalistic discourses. As an institution the state recognised members of the working class as isolated individuals, as they existed solely in the political sphere, abstracting them from the economic relations which in actuality shaped their life trajectory. His structural understanding of the state led to a prolonged debate with Ralph Milliband concerning the nature of the state, the importance of those personnel occupying central roles within it, and the state's relationship to the capitalist economy and members of the bourgeois class.

Criticisms

In some ways Althusser, who saw his work as provisional and open to refutation, was his own most stringent critic. As he noted on several occasions, including in his introduction to *For Marx*, the essays were provisional – they were the 'first stages of a long-term investigation, preliminary results which obviously demand correction' (2005 [1965]: 9). After 1967, Althusser criticised his own earlier approach and developed new ideas which were subsequently published as *Essays in Self-Criticism*. In both his book *Self-Criticisms* and the English edition of *For Marx* he criticises himself on two grounds. Firstly, on the theoretical criterion of not entering 'into the question of the unity of theory and practice within political practice'; and, secondly, for inviting a positivist reading of his work by not clearly distinguishing between 'philosophy and science'. Althusser now argued that philosophy did not provide science with validity, but was rather 'in the last instance, the class struggle in theory' (1976: 11).

There have also been a number of criticisms of his work from other writers. These can be grouped into five broad areas: (1) his claim that Marx broke substantively with Hegel in his later work; (2) his rationalist epistemology; (3) his denigration of human agency; (4) his discussion of ideology; and (5) his politics.

Althusser's claim that Marx broke decisively with Hegel in terms of instituting a new problematic, a repudiation of his past, though emphatically asserted, is not supported by textual evidence. In fact, Marx continued to use Hegelian ideas and concepts, including that of alienation, even in his later works, including the *Grundrisse*, his blueprint for *Capital*. As Elliott notes:

> if the developments in Marx's thought c. 1845 did indeed set him on the road which led to *Capital*, they did not amount to a break as conceived by Althusser: one involving the repudiation – and interdiction – of everything that preceded them. If Althusser's treatment of the 'works of the break' is unsustainable, his reading of the so-called 'transitional works' is, in all conscience, at best tendentious. (2007: 113)

Although Althusser's work had the merit of bringing a more modern non-Marxist philosophy of science to Marxism as opposed to Stalinist *diamat*, it also created many problems. In drawing on French conventionalism Althusser ends up arguing that knowledge is an intra-theoretical process of production (Geras, 1977; Thompson, 1978). But this leads to a major dilemma. If the concrete-in-thought differs from the real concrete, how do we assess its validity without recourse to the latter? Or how are we to determine whether knowledge remains ideological – that is, governed by interests outside of knowledge? Althusser's solution is a strong form of rationalism in which he argues that it is according to rational criteria that science produces its own facts. But how are these 'scientific criteria' to be judged? Althusser's theoretical arguments therefore remain disassociated from any controls of evidence, leading to a 'self-generating conceptual universe' (Thompson, 1978: 205). As Callinicos argues:

> If Althusser has argued very effectively in favour of the relative autonomy of the sciences, he has failed completely to show wherein lies the relative character of this autonomy. On the one hand, theoretical practice is assimilated to those familiar constituents of the superstructure, politics and ideology, as one of the practices that, together with, and

under the determination in the last instance of, the economy, form the social totality. On the other hand, any suggestion that the sciences are part of the superstructure is firmly rejected. (1976: 72)

[Republished with permission of Pluto Press from *Althusser's Marxism*, A. Callinicos, 1976. Reproduced with permission of the Licensor through PLSclear]

As Benton adds, Althusser was unable to resolve his attempt to provide a historicist understanding of the production of knowledge with his view of the scienticity of historical materialism (1992: 7).

A further set of criticisms concerns Althusser's view of history as 'a process without a subject', which denigrates the role of human agency. According to Thompson (1978), in his stringent polemic against Althusser, history is not a process without a subject but should rather be seen as containing 'ever-baffled, ever resurgent human agents' undertaking 'unmastered human practice' in which humans convert objective determinations into subjective initiatives through their experience, including forming social classes because of different interests. Humans make choices, choose values and pursue various ends 'but not necessarily in conditions of their own choosing', as Marx had argued.

In addition, Althusser's belief that ideology will continue to exist in communist societies is one not shared either by Marx or by Marxists. As Callinicos argues:

There remains, therefore, a contradiction in Althusser's work. It derives from the juxtaposition of his altered theory of ideology, which sees ideologies as the site of class struggles and the reflections of class interest, rather than as the illusions that precede the Truth of Science, and his rejection of any form of epistemology, on the one hand, and the assertion that ideology is necessary to any society on the other. This results form a survival from his previous position, an epistemological conception of ideology. (1976: 100–1)

Finally, other critics have questioned Althusser's political position. It has been argued that his work remains Stalinist (Thompson, 1978) or at least remains ambiguous in relation to Stalinism (Callinicos, 1976). Though mounting an attack from the 'left', critics argue he is not sufficiently critical of Stalin's position, and by remaining in the PCF he effectively endorses it. Geras, as well as questioning Althusser's residual idealism, challenges his reading of the connection between theory and practice, arguing that 'Marxist theory was not produced outside of the working-class movement' as Althusser contends, but was rather internal to that very movement (1977: 268).

Conclusion

Althusser provided a sophisticated theory that moved Marxism away from an economic or class reductionism through the notion of theoretical practice, overdetermination and his new conceptualisation of ideology. He also undertook a rigorous clarification of many of Marx's key concepts, as well as interrogating the idea that Hegel could simply be 'inverted' and inserted into a Marxist framework. Such conceptual innovations were driven by an attempt to rethink Marxist politics away from their dogmatic Stalinist encasement. However, his attempt to postulate an epistemological break and draw on a rationalist philosophy of science created as many problems as solutions. Yet the idea of history as a process without a subject, with a focus on social relationships, is a radical one, which is difficult to assess in today's world with its preoccupation with the individual and responsible action.

References

Althusser, L. (2005 [1965]) *For Marx*. B. Brewster, trans. London: Verso.
Althusser, L. (1968) Lenin and Philosophy. In: L. Althusser (1971) *Lenin and Philosophy and Other Essays*. New York: Monthly Review Press, pp. 23–67.
Althusser, L. (1971) Ideology and Ideological State Apparatuses. In: L. Althusser (2008) *On Ideology*. London: Verso, pp. 1–60.
Althusser, L. (1990 [1974]) *Philosophy and the Spontaneous Philosophy of the Scientists*. London: Verso.
Althusser, L. (1976) *Essays in Self-Criticism*. London: New Left Books.
Althusser, L. (1992) *The Future Lasts Forever: A Memoir*. New York: The New Press.
Althusser, L. (2006) *Philosophy of the Encounter: Later Writings, 1978–87*. London: Verso.
Althusser, L. (2008) *On Ideology*. London: Verso.
Althusser, L. and Balibar, E. (1990 [1965]) *Reading Capital*. London: New Left Books.
Althusser, L., Balibar, E., Establet, R., Macherey, P. and Ranciere, J. (2015 [1965]) *Reading Capital: The Complete Edition*. London: Verso.
Benton, T. (1984) *The Rise and Fall of Structural Marxism: Althusser and his Influence*. London: Macmillan.
Benton, T. (1992) Louis Althusser. In: R. Benewick and P. Green (eds) *The Routledge Dictionary of Twentieth Century Political Thinkers*. London: Routledge, pp. 5–7.
Bhaskar, R. (1979) *The Possibility of Naturalism: A Philosophical Critique of the Contemporary Human Sciences*. Brighton: Harvester Press.
Bourdieu, P. and Passeron, P. (1967) Sociology and Philosophy in France: Death and Resurrection of a Philosophy Without a Subject. *Social Research*, XXXVI(1), pp. 162–212.
Callinicos, A. (1976) *Althusser's Marxism*. London: Pluto Press.
Elliott, G. (2007) *Althusser: The Detour of a Theory*. London: Verso.
Geras, N. (1977) Althusser's Marxism: An Assessment. In: *New left Review* (eds) *Western Marxism a Critical Reader*. London: New Left Books, pp. 232–72.

Hindess, B. and Hirst, P. (1977) *Mode of Production and Social Formation: An Auto-Critique of Pre-Capitalist Modes of Production*. London: Macmillan.

Hindess, B., Hirst, P., Hussein, A. and Cutler, A. (1977) *Marx's Capital and Capitalism Today*, 2 vols. London: Routledge & Kegan Paul.

Jessop, B. (1985) *Nicos Poulantzas: Marxist Theory and Political Strategy*. London: MacMillan.

McLellan, D. (1998) *Marxism After Marx: An Introduction*, 3rd edition. Basingstoke: Macmillan.

Montag, W. (2003) *Louis Althusser*. New York: Palgrave Macmillan.

Poulantzas, N. (1973) *Political Power and Social Classes*. London: New Left Books.

Poulantzas, N. (1978) *State, Power, Socialism*. London: New Left Books.

Resch, R. P. (1992) *Althusser and the Renewal of Marxist Social Theory*. Berkeley, CA: University of California Press.

Roudinesco, E. (2008) *Philosophy in Turbulent Times: Canguilhem, Sartre, Foucault, Althusser, Deleuze, Derrida*. New York: Columbia University Press.

Thompson, E. P. (1978) *The Poverty of Theory*. London: Merlin Press.

Marcuse

Introduction

As one of the core members of the Frankfurt School, Herbert Marcuse was a philosopher and social theorist who was arguably the most widely discussed philosopher of the 1960s (Kellner, 1984: 1), with work discussed in both academic contexts and the popular press. *Fortune* magazine referred to him as the 'improbable guru of surrealist politics' and his later work was written at a time of a rising counter-culture, student activism, the civil rights movement and the Vietnam War. His discussions of freedom, liberation, sexuality, civil rights issues and Third World politics captured the zeitgeist. Dubbed the 'father of the new left' Marcuse's work emphasised the possibility for liberation from an oppressive, stultifying 'one dimensional society' in which profit, greed, instrumental/technical rationality and mass consumerism were the central maxims defining the age. His work combined a synthesis of three major movements of modern Continental thought: phenomenology; Hegelian Marxism; and psychoanalytical theory. Marcuse was prepared to revise Marx in what he perceived was now a fundamentally different socio-economic context, though he retained Marx's philosophical anthropology, developed in *The Economic and Philosophic Manuscripts*. Unlike many of the other writers in the Frankfurt School, Marcuse remained partly optimistic regarding the possibility of a new society organised in a fundamentally alternative way.

Critical Theory

Critical theory, often dubbed the Frankfurt School, contains a diverse range of thinkers, sometimes sharing little in common save the fact that many from the first generation were from wealthy Jewish backgrounds (Jeffries, 2016). The Institute for Social Research, which still survives today, is often seen as containing two or three generations: a first generation containing Adorno, Marcuse, Horkheimer, Fromm, Pollack; a second generation containing

Habermas and Karl-Otto Apel; and a third generation led by Honneth and, more recently, Hartmuth Rosa. Many of these thinkers attempted to critically appropriate the ideas of Marxism, while rejecting Marx's restrictive emphasis on economic processes, and instead foregrounded the important roles of the cultural and ideological spheres in shaping society.

The Origins of Critical Theory

The origins of critical theory are to be found in the Institute for Social Research (*Institut für Socialforschung*) founded in 1923 in Frankfurt. Ironically, given its Marxist sympathies – it was informally referred to as 'Café Marx' – the funding for the Institute came from the son of a wealthy millionaire grain merchant, Felix Weil. Though connected to the University of Frankfurt, Weil's endowment allowed the Institute to pursue independent research. Its first director, Carl Grunberg, was replaced by Max Horkheimer, whose background in philosophy profoundly shaped the Institute's increasingly philosophical direction. Following the rise of the Nazis to power in 1933, the Institute moved first to Geneva, then in 1935 to Columbia University in New York. However, some of its key members, including Horkheimer and Adorno, moved to Los Angeles. Following the war both returned to Germany where the Institute was re-established in 1953, though operating in a new direction and context following the experiences of American social and cultural life of the founders. Marcuse, however, decided to remain in the United States.

Reacting equally to the development of fascism and Soviet state socialism, the members of the Institute attempted to provide a more refined and updated understanding of Marxism for the mid- to late twentieth century. They saw Marxism as containing a number of lacunae. Firstly, it was deemed that Marx, especially in his later writings, had imported a positivist method into his understanding of the social world, one based on the assumptions and methodology of the natural sciences where causal invariant laws dominated. For the members of the Institute this was a wholly inappropriate way to study the human sciences. Secondly, Marx's base–superstructure metaphor was deemed highly reductionist and problematical: consciousness, politics, culture and ideology (or superstructural phenomenon), they argued, should not be given a peripheral role in social explanation. Thirdly, Marxism contained a Judaeo-Christian standpoint shared with the Enlightenment of progress in history. Such a view was, however, wholly inadequate in a world where fascism, bureaucratic state socialism and authoritarianism had become pervasive. Fourthly, Marx had an unequivocal view of the proletariat as an emancipatory agency, but this again had been undermined by history. Instead, with the development of the culture industry, symbolic forms had to be given greater explanatory weight.

Although they were critical of Marxism, or at least Soviet or vulgar orthodox interpretations of it, critical theorists nevertheless continued to see the importance of political economy, though to a less significant degree than Marx. They also continued to recognise the importance of the material world in shaping, rather than determining, ideas and culture. In addition, these theorists also highlighted the dehumanising effects of technology and techniques of mass production, of a machine age imbued with reified social relations.

Traditional and Critical Theory

Horkheimer's distinction between traditional and critical theory in his essay 'Traditional and Critical Theory' (1937) is often regarded as a defining manifesto of the movement. Traditional theory, which has as its paradigmatic example the mathematico-deductive method deriving from Descartes's *Discourse on Method*, refers to a methodology or form of explanation that had become accepted as the norm since the eighteenth century. Here a theory was characterised by a few central principles or propositions, from which everything else was seen as deriving. Moreover, the parts of the theory or system elegantly formed a coherent and cohesive whole. Such a standpoint did not follow subjective whims but was neutral and objective, and through experimentation allowed intellectuals to develop what were envisaged as objective scientific causal laws that facilitate the control and prediction of the natural and social world. Such an explanatory model, which was later brought under the label 'positivism' or 'scientism' by critical theory, was, they believed, highly problematical.

Firstly, it assumed everything could be understood under general principles allowing for no exceptions, which in sociology meant that society was seen as a system excluding free will. Secondly, traditional theory was regarded as independent from society, stripping scientists from their social context and ignoring the impact of funding regimes – effectively reproducing the ideology of capitalism. Moreover, traditional theory understood interpretations of the natural and social world passively, when in fact humans actively structured the world through their concepts and frameworks of understanding. Human sense organs were a product of human history and had been shaped by it and through culture. Finally, the idea of an objective nature of facts was misleading since much of what was deemed as 'nature' has been transformed by humans gradually and over centuries.

Drawing on Kant's and Hegel's notion of critique, Horkheimer strove to examine the irrationality of modern life. Critical theory, he argued, aims to move beyond the tension between the individual's rationality and his or her actual social relations. It highlights the fact that society is not simply unchanging and given, but to a limited extent capable of human control or influence. Critical theory aims to highlight the injustice and social domination characterising the world, to show these are human products. As with Aristotle and Hegel, it believes that it is beneficial when a thing realises its potentialities, but this is only possible in a rationally ordered social world. Critical theory therefore draws both on the Greek ideal, and on German idealism, to advocate the goal of freedom and rationality. By unveiling existing ideology as constituting a form of false-consciousness, it adopts a form of 'immanent criticism' or negative or non-identity thinking, exposing the untruth or deception inherent in capitalism's values that derive from within the framework of capitalism itself. By closely examining the central capitalist values of 'free exchange', 'economic individualism' and 'free competition', critical theory can examine just how well such concepts actually correspond to society, the referent or object of the concept.

In addition, a full understanding of the social world requires not only a dialectical standpoint as opposed to a positivist one, but also an interdisciplinary approach. Just as Hegel saw history as the gradual unfolding and self-understanding of spirit's movement through time, and as conceptualisations of reality moved into their opposites, demonstrating their one-sided nature, so too does the dialectic in critical theory. However, in contrast to Hegel's closed or teleological dialectic, critical theory operates with a dialectic that is open-ended.

Life and Intellectual Context

Herbert Marcuse was born in Berlin on 19 July 1898 into an upper-middle-class Jewish family, integrated into German society. His father, Carl Marcuse, was a businessman, who married Gertrud Kreslawsky. Attending first the Mommsen Gymnasium in 1911, followed by the Kaiserin-Augustin, Herbert was conscripted into the military during the First World War but remained in the homeland because of his poor eyesight. In 1918 he began attending the university in Berlin. Immersing himself in a deep study of Marx's work, Marcuse returned to his studies at the Humboldt before moving to Freiburg to study German literature, philosophy and political economy.

He completed his dissertation, 'The German-Artist Novel', which drew heavily on the work of Hegel, Dilthey and Lukács, in 1922. Returning to Berlin, he worked in an antiquarian book and publishing firm and married his first wife, Sophie. After reading Heidegger's *Being and Time* in 1927, Marcuse just returned to Freiburg to work with the latter, remaining there until 1932, before the ascent of the Nazis. Heidegger, the leading German philosopher of the time, had a profound influence on Marcuse's development, though he became an ardent supporter of the Nazi Party notoriously claiming as University Rector: 'Let not doctrines and "ideas" be the rules of your being. Today and in the future, only the *Fuhrer* himself is German reality and its law' (cited in Marcuse, 1970: 9).

From Heidegger to Hegel

Having completed his habilitation under Heidegger on *Hegel's Ontology and the Theory of Historicity* (later published in 1987) Marcuse left to join the Institute for Social Research based in Frankfurt in 1933. When the Institute, then under the Directorship of Max Horkheimer, moved to Columbia University in 1934, following Hitler's accession to power, Marcuse moved with it and continued in its project of developing an interdisciplinary critical theory of society that foregrounded philosophy and social theory. On joining the Institute, he began to replace Heidegger's thought with Hegel. His initial research at the Institute examined the causes and consequences of fascism, especially as an outgrowth of capitalism. One of his first essays, 'The Struggle against Liberalism in the Totalitarian View of the State' (1968 [1934]), was written as a response to Hitler's speech in Dusseldorf, and highlighted the continuity between capitalist liberalism and fascism. Similar ideas were expressed in his essay 'Authority and Family in German Sociology to 1933' (1936) written two years later, and partly influenced by Wilhelm Reich.

While working at Columbia during the 1930s and 1940s Marcuse also wrote and published his first major work, *Reason and Revolution* (1955 [1941]), introducing the importance of the radical, political and ethical dimension of Hegel's thinking. In 1942 he, together with Franz Neumann and Otto Kirchheimer, joined the Office of War Information, part of the US Office for Strategic Services (OSS) dealing with information and propaganda. Marcuse worked as a political analyst developing intelligence reports on central Western Europe, before being transferred to the State Department, where he became Head of the Central European Bureau in 1945. Given his political outlook his position in the State Department became untenable with the onset of the Cold War. However, his wife Sophie had been diagnosed with cancer, which prevented him from leaving Washington. Now without work, Marcuse found it difficult to acquire a university teaching post as a Marxist. After his wife died in 1951, he eventually took up a post in political theory at Columbia University in the Russian Institute. In 1954 he moved to a new post in Brandeis University, where he remained until 1965. While there, in 1955 he published his next major work, which attempted a synthesis of Marx and Freud, *Eros and Civilisation* (1966 [1955]). After the death of his colleague, Franz Neumann, in a car crash, Marcuse married his widow, Inge Neumann, in 1956. His next book was a detailed critical analysis of Soviet society, *Soviet Marxism* (1958). The work, which partly drew on his empirical research carried out while working in the State Department, ran against Marxist currents at the time of the Cold War with regard to its critical tone.

While at Brandeis, he also published probably his best-known work, *One-Dimensional Man* (1964). The work became a bestseller, catapulting him into fame and as the spokesperson for a generation of radical youth, including students. *One-Dimensional Man* was followed in 1965 by an essay 'Repressive Tolerance' that characterised capitalist democracies as partly totalitarian. With Brandeis refusing to renew his employment given his radical politics, Marcuse moved to the University of California San Diego. Increasingly sought by the New Left and radical activists, he vocalised their demands for revolutionary upheaval in works such as *An Essay on Liberation* (1969b), *Five Lectures* (1970) and *Counterrevolution and Revolt* (1972). Following the death of his second wife, Inge, he married Erica Sherover in 1974. His last major work, *The Aesthetic Dimension* (1978), returned to his earlier analysis of aesthetics and focused on the qualitative change in aesthetic and moral values necessary to bring about a socialist society in the context of the material abundance provided by capitalism. Marcuse died of a stroke on 29 July 1979 at the age of 81 and was buried in the Dorotheenstadt Cemetry in Berlin.

Intellectual Influences

Heidegger's early work had a huge impact on Marcuse's early work. In his *Being and Time* (2010 [1927]) Heidegger contended that human existence differs radically from animal life because every human being (as *a Dasein* or 'being-there') exists ahead of itself in a projected future and because its way of existing futurally is always an issue for it. Drawing on Husserl amongst others, Heidegger sought to describe our immediate experience of 'Being-in-the-world' as a being-involved or being-engaged in trivial or significant projects. Humans, Heidegger argued, could choose to live authentically towards a self-transformative future or be carried along inauthentically in the world in relation to the received norms and the values of the 'they'. Marcuse's first published article, 'Contributions to a Phenomenology of Historical Materialism', was one of the earliest attempts to marry phenomenology and Marxism in order to revitalise both approaches. This included an attempt to remedy Marxism's neglect of the individual, and phenomenology's inability to deal with actual, concrete history:

> [Marxism's] central concern is with the historical possibility of the radical act—of an act that should clear the way for a new and necessary reality as it brings about the actualization of the whole person. Its standard-bearer is the self-consciously historical human being; its sole field of action is history, revealed as the fundamental category of human *Dasein*. Thereby, the radical act proves itself to be the revolutionary and historical action of 'class' as the historical unit. (Marcuse, 2005: 4)

A second major influence on Marcuse's work was Freud, especially his later work in *Civilization and its Discontents* (2002 [1929]). According to Marcuse the central argument running through Freud's *Civilization and its Discontents* was that civilisation required repression, that it could only be built 'on the permanent subjugation of the human instincts' (1966: 4) so that 'free gratification of man's instinctual needs is incompatible with civilized society' (1966: 4). For Marcuse, although Marx's work was important it lacked a psychology underpinning it and, more specifically, a psycho-dynamic understanding of the theory of revolution where the hidden forces of the unconscious played a decisive role. As well as explaining the failure of socialist revolutions, Freud, he believed, could also help to uncover the subjective motivations underpinning fascism and Nazism, consumerism and Cold War rivalries. The central text in which Marcuse developed Freud's thinking was *Eros and Civilization* (1966 [1955]).

The third major influence on Marcuse's work derived from Hegel. Marcuse examined Hegel's work both in his habilitation with Heidegger and later in *Reason and Revolution* (1941). Hegel would remain an enduring influence on his work, who initially is interpreted through the work of Heidegger, Dilthey, Lukács and Karl Korsch.

Historical, Social and Political Context

The major political and economic convulsions that characterised the world economy after the turn of the century had a profound influence on the work of Marcuse. As a soldier conscripted to fight, Marcuse saw at first hand the geopolitical conflict between major superpowers unfold. In political terms the Bolshevik revolution in 1917 entailing the overthrow of the tsarist regime, defeat of the Whites by the Bolsheviks, and the failed German Revolution of 1919 led by Liebknecht and Luxemburg were all significant in shaping the contours of his work. The formation of workers' councils, socialist organisations, strikes, struggles and protests against the war in Germany provided the immediate context in which he joined the German Social Democratic Party (SPD) in 1917. Marcuse witnessed first hand a series of general strikes and military uprisings in Germany including by the shop stewards of the metal workers' union, and most likely read about the insurrection by soldiers in Kiel and the Soviet in Munich. In the aftermath of defeat in the war and as a member of a soldier's council, Marcuse also attended the heated debates between Friedrich Ebert of the SPD and Karl Liebknecht of the Sparticist League, which constituted a prelude to the German Revolution. In November 1918, and as part of the civilian security force Kellner notes:

> Marcuse found himself standing in Berlin Alexanderplatz under orders to fire at snipers who shot periodically at demonstrators and at those involved in the revolutionary movement. (1984: 16)

After leaving the army in December 1918, Marcuse also left the SPD, in response to its 'alliance with reactionary, destructive, and repressive forces' (Marcuse, 1970: 103), essentially because of its supporting role in the murder of Liebknecht and Luxemburg by far-right Freikorps in 1919. This betrayal, for him, marked the end of the German Revolution. The massive economic turmoil including the Great Depression and rise of hyperinflation in Germany during the interwar period were initially read by most Marxists as indicative of the breakdown of capitalism and augurs of a socialist revolution. However, in nearly all cases, there emerged instead forms of fascism. For those who had not abandoned the theory, this forced many Marxists to fundamentally rethink their politics and into a period of despair.

The theories of the Frankfurt School therefore have to be understood in the context of the succession of defeats that the far left suffered historically and what they perceived as the impotence of the working class. Marcuse's early work can be seen as an attempt to grapple with the failure of socialism and the rise of fascism as an ideology and practice. As a Jew and a communist, Marcuse was forced to leave Germany with Hitler's accession to power in March 1933 and specifically his passing of the Nuremburg Laws in 1935 depriving all Jews of citizenship. Moreover, the consolidation of Stalinist rule in the Soviet Union containing show trials and labour camps, as well as Hitler's pact with Stalin, further disillusioned many on the left. This was exacerbated by the carnage engendered by the Second World War. As Kellner notes:

> The outbreak of the Second World war further displaced 'class struggle' and the 'construction of socialism' from the contemporary Marxian agenda, and the efforts of many Marxian militants – including the Institute members – were directed towards the war effort and the defeat of fascism. As a result of this historical situation, some members of the Institute recoiled from their previous Marxian stances and commitments and around 1940, critical theory began to distance itself from Marxism. (1984: 126)

In moving from Germany to the United States, Marcuse experienced not only a national–cultural displacement but also a shift in socio-political context from a war-ravaged country in the midst of economic collapse – characterised for example, by Cabaret during the Weimar period, to a country undergoing huge economic growth and wealth accumulation partly expressed through Hollywood and consumerism.

Industrialisation in the United States

Ordinarily it is the First World War which is taken as the beginning of the century for understanding European history, but in the United States and in socio-economic terms, the electrification of the nation, and the introduction of the model T car in 1908 by Henry Ford, instituted the beginnings of Fordist forms of mass production. Taking off in the 1920s, almost 4 million workers were employed in that industry by the end of that decade (Remini, 2009: 208). In 1910 the first film studio was established in Hollywood inaugurating what would become the entertainment industry. Industries that were big prior to the war had become enormous and with this wealth, partly based on a revolution in technology and the rich resources including land, the United States became the world's leading economic and political power. Although playing an active role in aiding the US fight against Germany, the post-war fallout for many of the left was generally very negative.

Truman's first address as president to the joint session of Congress just before the end of the war had already identified communism and its spread to the free world as the greatest danger facing the world. In a post-war context, the Soviet Union had controlled and occupied much of Eastern Europe and part of Berlin. Here a Marxist–Leninist orthodoxy prevailed, proposing a rigid and dogmatic interpretation of dialectical materialism or *Diamat*. Over the following decades, communism and its westward spread, 'the red scare', became the principal issue shaping US foreign and domestic policy, including military intervention abroad and economic aid through the Marshall Plan. The seizure of Czechoslovakia in 1948 by communists confirmed the fear of a communist spread. The war between North Korean communists and the South of the country, in October 1949, the institution of communism in China with rebels led by Mao Zedong and the Cuban Revolution of 1959 only exacerbated these worries. In the United States the formation of the Committee on Un-American Activities in 1945, and anti-communist witch-hunts led by McCarthyism, initially pursuing communist infiltration in the State Department, ushered in the beginnings of an entrenched Cold War, consolidated with the development of an alarming nuclear rivalry. As an illustration of this, the US defence budget rose from $13 billion in 1950 to $40 billion by 1960 (Remini, 2009: 260). The postwar economic demand for goods in the United States grew immense and, with unions claiming almost 15 million members, so did demands for higher wages. This was conjoined with Truman's 'Fair Deal' extending the New Deal, a policy then further extended by Eisenhower, and entailing increased social spending on housing, education and social security, precipitating a further economic boom. The emergence of youth culture centred on rock and roll, developing into hippie counter-culture by the end of the 1960s, was predicated on both a capitalist consumer culture, and on a zeitgeist valorising the individual, self-realisation and freedom. In the context of such a massive economic boom, it was believed by many intellectuals that Western capitalism had succeeded in overcoming the recurrent crises and depressions affecting it by consolidating sustained economic growth through regular state intervention. The increasing centralisation of national economies had also produced and institutionalised processes of economic bargaining engendering a form of organised capitalism. It was widely articulated that there had now emerged in the United States a general consensus upon goals of economic advance and political liberation, replacing the old marked polarisation of social classes. The tremendous growth in US capitalism as a way of life was recognised by a number of intellectuals such as Galbraith, referring to the *Affluent Society* (1999 [1958]), and Daniel Bell, referring to *The End of Ideology* (2000 [1960]), as well as Seymour Lipset's *Political Man* (1981 [1960]), indicating a shift from discussing capitalism to industrialism, and the incorporation of the working class into capitalist society. The social sciences in the United States also became increasingly dominated by positivistic forms of thinking focusing on the study of facts, at the expense of values. As a result, a stable, consumer-oriented, affluent capitalist culture, reinforced through television advertising, and the media, became the norm. Correspondingly, the prospect of a socialist revolution in the United States seemed more remote than ever. It was in light of this changed context that Marcuse responded by reinterpreting and reshaping Marxism as a theory of liberation.

Despite the growth of the economy and consumerism in absolute terms, deep divisions nevertheless endured within the United States. The civil rights movement initially led by Martin Luther King in 1955, following the Rosa Park bus incident, but continuing well into the 1960s and increasingly radicalised with Malcolm X and the Black Panthers, was one important manifestation of the ethno-racial contradiction at the heart of American society. In 1964, the Cold War continued with President Lyndon Johnson sending in troops to South Vietnam to prevent communists in the North gaining victory. In the mid-1960s such a policy cost almost $2 billion a month to effect (Remini, 2009: 274). With over 700,000 troops drafted and stationed in Vietnam, huge military spending and frequently reported carnage led to wide-scale protests, especially by counter-cultural students standing up against the invasion. Demonstrations attended by millions continued following Nixon's bombing of Cambodia and the invasion of Laos. The burgeoning and oppositional counter-culture, often centred on values of love, the celebration of the individual, human liberation and self-realisation, provided a huge audience for Marcuse's emerging work. He retained his revolutionary fervour throughout his life, appealing to a libertarian form of socialism conjoined with theories of self-realisation and sexual self-fulfilment.

Arguments and Ideas

Marcuse's Work

Fascism and Totalitarianism

Marcuse's understanding of totalitarianism, fascism and Nazism is evident in his early essays including 'The Struggle against Liberalism in the Totalitarian View of the State' written in 1934 (Kellner, 1984: 96). The totalitarian state represents the development and response to the crises inherent in monopoly capitalism and working-class resistance. Fascism is conceived as an extension of liberalism and its defence of the capitalist mode of production: 'we can say it is liberalism that "produces" the total authoritarian state out of itself, as its own consummation at a more advanced stage of development' (Marcuse, 1968 [1934]: 19).

Marcuse expands on such a view in *Reason and Revolution*, where he roots fascism in the antagonism between growing industrial monopolisation and the democratic system:

> In Europe after the first World War, the highly rationalized and rapidly expanding industrial apparatus met increasing difficulties of utilization, especially because of the disruption of the world market and because of the vast network of social legislation ardently defended by the labour movement. In this situation the most powerful groups tended to assume direct political power in order to organize monopolistic production, to destroy the socialist opposition, and to resume imperialist expansionism. The emerging political system cannot develop the productive forces without constant pressure on the satisfaction of human needs. This requires totalitarian control over all social and individual relations, the abolition of social and individual liberties, the incorporation of the masses by means of terror... The fascist organization of society requires a change in the entire setting of culture. (1955: 410)

> [Republished with permission of Routledge & Kegan Paul from *Reason and Revolution: Hegel and the Rise of Social Theory* 2e, H. Marcuse, 1955. Reproduced with permission of the Licensor through PLSclear]

Given this correlation, Marcuse refers to contemporary Western liberal democracies also as totalitarian, although he remains conscious of the differences between them, and fascist totalitarianism. This was in fact at the heart of his decision to join the US war effort: 'Bourgeois democracy is still infinitely better than fascism' (cited in Giddens, 1982: 160). Totalitarianism reflects the transmutation of early liberal forms of capitalism based on bourgeois rights including freedom of speech, formal equality, etc., into modern monopoly or organised forms of capitalism, which draw on the state to politicise the totality of life in order to quell criticism, and adverse reaction against the free market.

Hegel and Marx

In addition to demonstrating the relation between Hegel and Marx, *Reason and Revolution* sets out to defend Hegel against charges of fascism, but also to demonstrate the virtues of his radical thinking, which Marcuse believes challenges capitalist social arrangements and institutions and provides the basis for envisaging an alternative, non-repressive society. The first part of the book situates Hegel in the context of the French Revolution, arguing that Hegel wrote his philosophy largely as a response to the 'challenge from France to reorganize the state and society on a rational basis' (1955: 3). Marcuse describes Hegel's system as a 'negative philosophy', in which the central role is played by reason and critical rationalism: 'The core of Hegel's philosophy is a structure the concepts of which – freedom, subject, mind, notion – are derived from the idea of reason' (1955: 5). Reality now had to meet the standards of reason 'which can be antagonistic to the existing state of affairs'. Hegel differentiates between actual existence and unrealised essences, between actually existing, irrational states of affairs, and the possibility and potential of realising a rational ordering of life, as things and societies move to higher levels through a process of contradiction and *aufhebung*. Rather than left and right Hegelians being the heir to Hegel, it is Marx who takes over his philosophical insights centred on reason:

> Hegel was the last to interpret the world as reason, subjecting nature and history alike to the standards of thought and freedom. At the same time, he recognized the social and political order men had achieved as the basis on which reason had been realized. His system brought philosophy to the threshold of its negation and thus constituted the sole link between the old and the new form of critical theory, between philosophy and social theory. (Marcuse, 1955: 252–3)

Marx takes Hegel's concepts and transforms them into a social theory centred on political economy and social practice and in which the universal suffering of the proletariat transforms it into a revolutionary subject:

> the transition from Hegel to Marx is, in all respects, a transition to an essentially different order of truth, not to be interpreted in terms of philosophy ... all the philosophical concepts of Marxian theory are social and economic categories, whereas Hegel's social and economic categories are all philosophical concepts... Every single concept in the Marxian theory has a materially different foundation. (Marcuse, 1955: 258)

Freud and Marx

It was *Eros and Civilisation* (1966 [1955]) that actually established Marcuse's reputation as an intellectual, selling in excess of 350,000 copies. Written in a post-war American context of increasing sexual repression, McCarthyism, rigid social laws, consumerism, and the petrification and bureaucratisation of the Soviet Union, its broad context of production was one of defeat for the libertarian left. Nevertheless, it contains a utopian moment missing from the work of other critical theorists. Rather than focusing on the subversive nature of the proletariat, who had been co-opted into capitalism, the book focuses on the subversive nature of human sexual desires and drives. Marcuse attempts to historicise what he considers is for the most part an unhistorical biologism, a psychologism, running through Freud's work; that is, he aims to use Freud against himself. For Marcuse, Freud's theory is 'in its substance, "sociological"'.

Moreover, despite discussing alienation and anxiety, Marcuse argues that Freud is generally not taken as a political thinker, but instead one who took capitalism as a given. However, Marcuse attempts to reinterpret him as an eminently political writer by arguing that 'all of Freud's "psychological categories" have become political categories' (1966: xi). According to Marcuse the sociopolitical context and the development of the individual are integrally interconnected, especially in the development of capitalism, which now saturates and dominates individuals and their experiences in a totalised world.

Eros is more than the sex drive, it is also the instinct which joins us to others. The repression of instincts is the precondition not only of culture, but also of work; it is required to meet human survival needs, especially in a world characterised by scarcity. Hard work, discipline and delayed gratification become necessities in 'the primordial struggle for existence'. To exist, society therefore requires a fundamental transformation in man's nature and unconscious drives, from the *pleasure principle* to the *reality principle*. This in turn entails a shift in values from: immediate satisfaction to delayed satisfaction; pleasure to the restraint of pleasure; joy (play) to toil (work); receptiveness to productiveness; and absence of repression to security.

However, Freud's de-historicised view of scarcity and economic processes, for Marcuse, ignores their existence as a by-product of capitalist-organised dominance, and of distribution as an outcome of this particular hierarchical social order. The distribution of scarcity is not a given but something that has been artificially created and imposed upon individuals initially by violence, and subsequently through more rational means of control, by groups who wish to sustain their power and maintain domination. Moreover, capitalism creates a '*surplus repression*' – repression over and above the basic repression needed to create and reproduce society.

Under capitalist relations of domination, the reality principle takes on a specifically intensive configuration, taking the form of what Marcuse calls the 'performance principle' in which individuals become compelled to compete economically with one another. Humans become shaped or regulated, and their libidinal drives structured, in terms of their function to meet the capitalist system's needs. A polymorphous perversity and pre-genital stage of development that characterised early childhood is now replaced by a narrowed focus on genitals as organs of pleasure. In the prevalent social organisation of labour, unfulfilled, unhappy, alienated individuals work under the pressures of capitalist competition which underlies their repression:

> labour time, which is the largest part of the individuals' life time, is painful time, for alienated labour is absence of gratification, negation of the pleasure principle. Libido is diverted for socially useful performances in which the individual works for himself only insofar as he works for the apparatus, engaged in activities that mostly do not coincide with his own faculties and desires. (Marcuse, 1966: 51)

Alienated labour divides the day between meaningless work and restricted leisure time. The latter, in turn, becomes dominated by the culture and advertising industry championing a consumerist ideology, repressed or commodified sexuality, instrumental rationality, as rational repression erodes *Eros*. The result is that *Thanatos*, in the form of violence and aggression, becomes normalised.

Yet for Marcuse, Freud's meta-psychology also provides an alternative vision. Given their mutability, human instinctual drives can be formed in an alternative way – they contain elements that break through this rationalisation of repression, to offer a more nuanced balance between the pleasure and reality principles: 'they shatter the predominant tradition of Western thought and even suggest its reversal', denying the 'equation of reason with repression' (1966: 33). Capitalism creates the preconditions of its own transcendence, despite the barbarities it produces: 'There is, however, the possibility of a non-repressive civilization free from tensions based on a fundamentally different experience of being, a fundamentally different relation between man and nature, and fundamentally different existential relations' (1966: 5). Freedom expressed in a radically different form of life means not only moving past the Marxist notion of toil – in the sense of production beyond scarcity – but also sexual repression.

Increased material productivity, technology and mechanisation has meant that more people can work for less time, and thereby acquire more free time to pursue activities that bring them happiness. Instead, however, in modern industrial rationalised society these technological leaps have been used to enforce more control and consolidate domination:

> Throughout the world of industrial civilization, the domination of man by man is growing in scope and efficiency. Nor does this trend appear as an incidental, transitory regression on the road to progress. Concentration camps, mass exterminations, world wars, and atom bombs are no 'relapse into barbarism,' but the unrepressed implementation of the achievements of modern science, technology, and domination. And the most effective subjugation and destruction of man by

man takes place at the height of civilization, when the material and intellectual attainments of mankind seem to allow the creation of a truly free world. (1966: 5)

Drawing on the imagery of Orpheus, Narcissus and Freud's own conception of the Nirvana principle, Marcuse argues that the increase in the capacity of production and correlative reduction in the labour time needed for work should be deployed for the promotion of leisure, play and the expression of a non-repressed sexuality. Moreover, past aspirations towards freedom and happiness from the womb or childhood remain in the unconscious of the individual as subversive alternative visions of happiness. Although repelled by consciousness, they 'continue to haunt the mind' and remain in the liberating potential of memory: 'the psychoanalytical liberation of memory explodes the rationality of the repressed individual' (1966: 34). Expressed in phantasy, daydreaming, art and fiction they entail a 'return of the repressed'. By bursting through repressively imposed social relations the liberation of these energies could 'break the fatal unity of productivity and destruction, liberty and repression' (1966: 11) by creating a more holistic, erotic form of happiness and fulfilment, with libidinal energies providing the basis for new modes of cultural creativity, a 'Gay science' in Nietzsche's terms.

One-Dimensional Man

The cautious optimism Marcuse expressed in the mid-1950s had, however, disappeared by the time he wrote his next major work, *One-Dimensional Man* (1964). Again he reiterates how modern advanced industrial societies thwart the human possibility of a better life, especially in the context of the greater productive capabilities that now exist to meet human material needs. The critique of technological domination, technical rationality and progress, evident from his earlier works also resurfaces here. *One-Dimensional Man* opens by asserting that: 'A comfortable, smooth, reasonable, democratic unfreedom prevails in advanced industrial civilization, a token of technical progress' (1964: 1). In such a context, liberal democracy has effectively become totalitarian containing a 'non-terroristic economic-technical coordination which operates through the manipulation of needs by vested interests' (1964: 3).

According to Marcuse, advanced industrial society has become one-dimensional pervaded by a one-dimensional form of thinking or thought, as opposed to a bi-dimensional dialectical or critical form of thinking, which offered alternative visions of how the world could be. A pervasive technological rationality ideologically masks social forms of domination and alienation. Such developments indicate the emergence of new insidious forms of social control that prevent the possibility of radical change taking place. These controls reflect the fundamental changes in the structure of capitalist society since Marx's heyday: a monopoly form of consumer capitalism has replaced nineteenth-century competitive capitalism, which permits the control, management and regulation of the capitalist economy and its attendant crises and depressions. In addition, a welfare state has become married to a warfare state, both operating under the aegis of a technical instrumental rationality: 'Today, domination perpetuates and extends itself not only through technology but as technology, and the latter provides the great legitimation of the expanding political power, which absorbs all spheres of culture' (Marcuse, 1964: 158).

The idea of technological rationality, embedded in science and rational administration, has strong affinities with Weber's notion of instrumental rationality, and points to the operation of abstract forces shaping society beyond human control. It constitutes the basis of power in modern advanced industrial societies, limiting bourgeois rights and liberties. For Marcuse, the contradictions of capitalism have effectively been surpassed by this technological rationality that stimulates the proliferation of organisational hierarchies. The increasing concentration of capital, powerful developments in science and technology, mechanisation and automation have facilitated, and fed back off, growing administrative bureaucracies. In this corporatist context, the state, large corporations and unions combine to augment productive growth in an economy bureaucratically regulated through state intervention. With a ratcheting up of the Cold War, the state and corporations have invested heavily in the armaments race, using Soviet socialism and communism as a dangerous foil 'within and without'. The threat of communist infiltration and nuclear war has helped to unify otherwise divergent political parties–capital and labour in the West.

In addition, management and labour are united in their common consumption strategies. Exploitation and oppression become masked under what appears as neutral administration. The proliferation of mass media, culture, advertising and consumerism effectively lock in and integrate the working class. Opposition, critique and the power of negativity in relation to capitalism have all but disappeared via incorporation and co-optation. Although the working class and bourgeoisie are still 'the basic classes':

> the capitalist development has altered the structure and function of these two classes in such a way that they no longer appear to be agents of historical transformation. An overriding interest in the preservation and improvement of the institutional status quo unites the former antagonists in the most advanced areas of contemporary society. (Marcuse, 1964: xii)

The consumer economy creates a 'second nature' that ties humans 'libidinally to the commodity form, instilling false needs and desires'. The oppositional and critical aspects of 'high' culture have also been absorbed through a process of 'repressive sublimation'. The appropriation of culture by the media and communication industries has washed any vestiges of radicalism from it, and made everything easily and readily consumable. Thus, for example, the powerful liberatory potential of eroticism becomes reduced to permissive sexuality. In such a society notions of autonomy become reduced to a form of pseudo-autonomy. Humans are enslaved to a capitalist system and its technological instrumental ethos. Governed through a repression which controls their actions and which they misrecognise through their superficial understanding of sexual and other pleasures, they become tied to productivity.

Like Adorno and Horkheimer's *Dialectic of Enlightenment* (1997 [1944]) Marcuse believes that as science takes up an instrumental and exploitative relation to nature and the environment, it ultimately serves to reinforce human domination:

> The scientific method which led to the ever more effective domination of nature thus came to provide the pure concepts as well as the instrumentalities for the ever more effective domination of man by man through the domination of nature. Theoretical reason, remaining pure and neutral, entered into the service of practical reason. The merger proved beneficial to both. (1964: 158)

In the third section of the book Marcuse posits an alternative social scenario based on a transcendent project that moves beyond the limitations of technical rationality. Such a one-dimensional system, he argues, cannot be altered through piecemeal reform but only through a fundamental transformation of social relations. Thus, despite revising Marx's work in dramatic respects, Marcuse always remained a revolutionary. If the revolutionary potential of the working class has been bought off through consumption, then it is only forces that have not been sufficiently integrated into advanced industrial society that offer hope for initiating any radical change. This includes the lowest substratum of society and the world: 'the outcasts, the outsiders, the exploited and the persecuted of other races and of other colours, the unemployed and the unemployable'. In slightly more optimistic works of the late 1960s these groups were joined by the peasant masses of the Third World, The National Liberation Front in Vietnam, exploited ethnic minorities, but also intellectuals and radical students, all taking part in the 'Great Refusal'.

Contemporary Relevance and Applications

Marcuse's influence reached its peak in the 1960s and was integrally tied to the politics of the time with his writings contributing to structuring the zeitgeist. As Kellner notes:

> Marcuse's ideas fit remarkably well into the cultural and political milieu of the 1960s. His uncompromising critique of advanced industrial society articulated the anger and disgust felt by a generation of young people outraged by the Vietnam war, the oppression of blacks and other minorities, and the continued existence of poverty alongside the wealth of the consumer society. Widespread revolt erupted against the oppressive conformity of complacent middle-class life, fuelled by the belief that the price of entry into the affluent society involved 'selling out' to corporate society and submission to alienated labour. Rebellion against bureaucracy and the socio-economic apparatus spread as individuals

recoiled from becoming cogs in the machine, or faceless members of an impersonal, technocratic society. Many perceived the university to be a factory for processing servants of the corporation and the bureaucratic machine, with professors as purveyors of the kind of 'one-dimensional', conformist thinking that Marcuse so sharply criticized. (1984: 2)

[Republished with permission of Macmillan from *Herbert Marcuse and the Crisis of Marxism*, D. Kellner, 1984. Reproduced with permission of the Licensor through PLSclear]

For Kellner, the ambiguity of whether this widespread alienation, libidinal repression and social dislocation was a result of a machine-like technological rationality or capitalism paradoxically ensured that his work was appreciated by those not identifying themselves singularly as Marxists. Marcuse's arguments tapped into the ethos of the 1960s. His powerful critique of advanced capitalist society resonated with all radicals, including those fighting for civil rights, free love and flower power, or against Vietnam, as well the sense of anger generally felt by the younger generation. His influence in shaping the New Left was also significantly facilitated by his critique of actually existing dogmatic forms of Soviet socialism from a libertarian socialist position, as well his desire to make Marxism relevant for the contemporary malaise through a rejuvenated language, and his unflinching commitment towards revolutionary rather than piecemeal change – a Great Refusal. However, as the counter-cultural zeitgeist dissipated during the 1970s, so his popularity waned. His work influenced subsequent generations of the Frankfurt School including Habermas and Honneth. Yet his reputation and influence did not endure in the same way as his more pessimistic colleague, Adorno. Nevertheless, it had a large impact on some of the New Left, even though this movement also began to fracture, especially in the work of his students including Abbie Hoffman, Andrew Fenberg, Russell Jacoby and Angela Davis.

MARCUSE AND THE NEW LEFT

Marcuse's label 'father of the New Left' was furthered by the student slogan 'Mao, Marx and Marcuse'. He himself rejected this role, however, rejecting also the idea that the New Left needed an ideological leader or father figure in order to act. Instead, Marcuse saw his role as one of modest influence through the coincidental timing of his writings. Though critical of aspects, Marcuse admired the libertarian and anti-authoritarian moments that originally defined the movement. He also admired the diffuse, flexible and autonomous form of political organisation enacted, seeing this as foreshadowing the basic organisation of libertarian socialism. Considering whether the New Left ultimately failed, Marcuse argued that the elaboration of a new dimension of radical social change was historically significant; the lasting achievement of the movement was in redefining the idea of revolution to a radicalisation of cultural values, and the articulation of a qualitatively different form of life.

Angela Davis emerged as a prominent counter-cultural activist during the 1960s. She was a member of the Communist Party, connected to the Black Panthers and the civil rights movement, who, coming under the influence of Marcuse at Brandeis University, followed him to the University of California, San Diego. Marcuse influenced her in terms of his radical political stance, which envisaged a connection between theory and practice (James, 1998: 319), his notion of utopia, which retained an important role for the liberatory potential of art (Davis, 2004), his critique of American culture and his anti-fascist standpoint. As Jeffries notes:

> One could interpret some of Davis's later writing and campaigning as a continuation of her one time teacher's analysis of fascist tendencies. Davis would go onto argue that what she called the 'prison-industrial complex' militated against the civil rights for which African-Americans fought during the civil war struggles. But the over-incarceration of people of colour, she argued, was a result of a shift of capital from human services, from housing, jobs, education, to profitable arenas. (2016: 320)

According to Davis, prisons have become the primary and punitive response to deal with issues of poverty, homelessness and drugs all categorised under the label 'crime' and correlated with people of colour – constituting more than 70% of the prison population. Black women comprised the fastest growing group of prisoners, and Native Americans are the largest interned group per capita. Shifting away from government, these prisons themselves have become part of big business and private corporations, or the punishment industry which has affinities with the military industrial complex:

> Prisons thus perform a feat of magic. Or rather the people who continually vote in new prison bonds and tacitly assent to a proliferating network of prisons and jails have been tricked into believing in the magic of imprisonment. But prisons do not disappear problems, they disappear human beings. And the practice of disappearing vast numbers of people from poor, immigrant, and racially marginalized communities has literally become big business. (Davis, 1998: 1)

On the list of the FBI's 10 most wanted, Davis was incarcerated for a period in the early 1970s. She wrote on a diverse range of important social issues including feminism and its intersection with class and race, racism and racial segregation, Marxism, prisoner's rights, critical theory and revolutionary consciousness.

Criticisms

Anderson (1976) situates Marcuse as part of a tradition of Western Marxists including Adorno, Horkheimer, Lukács, Althusser, Gramsci, Korsch and Sartre. By contrast to an earlier generation situated in the East of the globe and including

Kautsky, Lenin and Trotsky, who were shaped by the First World War and the Russian Revolution, and who were connected to and often led Marxist parties, Western Marxists were shaped during a period of stark failure for socialism including the abortive German and Hungarian revolutions. Moreover, given the Stalinisation and bureaucratisation of the Soviet Union, many Western Marxists remained aloof or retained a weaker relation to far-left political parties (with the exception of Gramsci), and with the consolidation of a crude base–superstructure understanding of Marxism, instead focused on issues of aesthetics, philosophy ontology and epistemology in their writings. The divorce of theory from working-class practice meant that such analysis came at the expense of understanding concrete economic and political issues. Their seclusion into universities not only fostered the development of a difficult and abstruse linguistic style but also a pessimistic standpoint towards the world. As he notes with regard to Marcuse: 'Marcuse evoked the utopian potentiality of the liberation of nature in man, only to deny it more emphatically as an objective tendency in reality, and to conclude that the industrial working classwas itself perhaps absorbed past recall within capitalism' (1976: 89).

Marcuse's work has garnered a good deal of criticism. Perhaps the most vociferous and caustic has come from Alistair Macintyre, who claims that: 'all of Marcuse's key positions are false' (1970: 7). According to MacIntyre, rather than making arguments, Marcuse simply provides unsubstantiated assertions: 'Above all there is entirely absent from his writing any attempt on his own part to suggest or consider the difficulties that arise for his positions and hence also no attempt to meet them' (1970: 17). Not only does Marcuse work with an undeveloped notion of what counts as truth if and when empiricism is rejected as an ideology, but he also fails to specify why he selectively includes only certain positivist philosophers in his account. This 'makes him exaggerate "the homogeneity of the philosophical thought of a given age"' (1970: 19). Positivism, which he regards as reactionary and conservative, had radical and socialist adherents including the Vienna Circle. For MacIntyre, Marcuse's relation to classical Marxism is also questionable since he deploys abstractions and concepts in his work that would be foreign to Marxism; these include an abstract notion of 'man' rather than 'real historical men', but also the connection between freedom and happiness, rather than the Marxist notion of self-realisation. Finally, he questions Marcuse's use of Freud in *Eros and Civilization*, both as a complement to Marxism, given its inherent conservatism, and by asking 'what will we actually do in this sexually liberated state?' (1970: 47).

Not only does the question of what a non-repressive sublimation and private pursuit of happiness look like remain unanswered in Marcuse's work, but there is also an ambivalence running through his account of *Eros and Civilization*. Critics such as O'Connor (2019: 11) note:

> Marcuse seems at times to be committed to the notion that surplus repression is a secondary repression which is subsequent to the biologically explained basic repression. Basic repression as a non-normative event, so to speak, is of no concern to critical theory. But

Marcuse also maintains that all repression is antagonistic to our biological being – our hedonistic orientation – and that genuine emancipation would amount to a comprehensive transformation of our sensory being. That emancipatory ideal expands, in other words, to include a concern with all repression.

In a more sympathetic critique Anthony Giddens argues that there are other ambivalences pervading Marcuse's later work, especially as a result of his terminological shift between a Marxist and Weberian understanding of modern society – organised capitalist or advanced industrial dominated by instrumental rationality (Giddens, 1982). Marcuse, he argues, also underplays the conflict that exists in the United States, by painting a picture of stultifying homogeneity in contrast to other more pro-capitalist writers, who argued that the United States was a plural and diverse society:

> Both 'internally', and in the context of international economic and political relations, the USA and other capitalist societies were much more divided and conflictual than Marcuse's analysis suggest… Marcuse sought to stand pluralism on its head… For him, the picture was one of increasing 'totalitarian conformity': the others argued that the western societies were becoming more internally differentiated, although they also supposed that a balance of 'cross-cutting conflicts' dissolved the likelihood of radical social change. (Giddens, 1982: 154)

Marcuse's singular focus on the United States, which he takes as the model of how capitalist societies will become in the future, also means his work has a limited plausibility. Martin Jay sees his analysis, and that of the Frankfurt School generally, as embodying an elitist understanding of high culture as a goal, and end of human practice. He sees Marcuse's understanding of culture as compatible with the conservative and reactionary views of leading members of German mandarins depicted by Fritz Ringer: 'they wrote works permeated more with a sense of loss and decline than with expectations and hope. They also shared the mandarins' distaste for mass society and the utilitarian, positivistic attitudes it fostered' (Jay, 1973: 294).

Finally, Whitfield (2014) has argued that Marcuse was too harsh a critic of liberal democracy, seeing it simply as a correlate of totalitarianism. Writers, he believes, should be seeking to strengthen democracy rather than simply impugn it. This was connected with the little faith Marcuse had in the working class, especially following the rise of fascism. It led him to focus instead on those who no longer had a stake in advanced capitalism – composing a motley of outcasts including the unemployed, student activists and peasants in the developing nations. Such a shift away from class, and a focus on repression and total administration, meant that Marcuse failed to see the rise of the New Right or the growing divisions in inequality in Europe and North America. This neo-liberal, New Right emerged just a couple of years after his death.

Conclusion

Although undoubtedly a imaginative thinker who combined very diverse strands of thinking including Heideggarian Phenomenology, Freud, Hegelianism and Marxism together to argue for the importance of sexual and human liberation, Marcuse's work contains numerous tensions and ambiguities which tend to render it rooted and only apposite for the period in which it was elaborated. It bears the cleaved and unresolved imprints of both the pessimism pervasive in Germany during the 1930s and the optimism which emerged in America during the late 1960s.

References

Adorno, T. and Horkheimer, M. (1997 [1944]) *Dialectic of Enlightenment*. London: Verso.

Anderson, P. (1976) *Considerations on Western Marxism*. London: Verso

Bell, D. (2000 [1960]) *The End of Ideology*. Cambridge, MA: Harvard University Press

Davis, A. (1998) *Masked Racism. Reflections on the Prison Industrial Complex*. Available at: https://www.historyisaweapon.com/defcon1/davisprison.html (accessed 19 March 2019).

Davis, A. (2004) Marcuse's Legacies. In: J. Abromeit and M. Cobb (eds) *Herbert Marcuse: A Critical Reader*. London: Routledge, pp. 43–50.

Freud, S. (2002 [1929]) *Civilisation and its Discontents*. London: Penguin.

Galbraith, J. (1999 [1958]) *The Affluent Society*. London: Penguin

Giddens, A. (1982) *Profiles and Critiques in Social Theory*. London: Macmillan.

Heidegger, M (2010 [1927]) *Being and Time*. Albany, NY: State University of New York Press.

Horkheimer, M. (1937) Traditional and Critical Theory. In: M. Horkheimer (2002) *Critical Theory: Selected Essays*. M. J. O'Connell, trans. New York: Continuum, pp. 188–243.

James, J., (1998) (ed.) *The Angela Y. Davis Reader*. Oxford: Blackwell.

Jay, M. (1973) *The Dialectical Imagination: A History of the Frankfurt School and the Institute of Social Research 1923–1950*. London: Heinemann.

Jeffries, S. (2016) *Grand Hotel Abyss: The Lives of the Frankfurt School*. London: Verso.

Kellner, D. (1984) *Herbert Marcuse and the Crisis of Marxism*. London: Macmillan.

Lipset, S.M. (1981 [1960]) *Political Man*. Baltimore, MD: John Hopkins University Press.

MacIntyre, A. (1970) *Marcuse*. London: Fontana.

Marcuse, H. (1968 [1934]) The Struggle against Liberalism in the Totalitarian View of the State. In: *Negations: Essays in Critical Theory*. Boston, MA: Beacon Press. pp. 3–42.

Marcuse, H. (1936) Authority and Family in German Sociology to 1933. In: M. Horkheimer, *Autorität und Familie*. Paris: Alcan, pp. 737–752.

Marcuse, H. (1955 [1941]) *Reason and Revolution: Hegel and the Rise of Social Theory*, 2nd edition. London: Routledge & Kegan Paul. First edition, 1941.

Marcuse, H. (1966 [1955]) *Eros and Civilization: A Philosophical Inquiry into Freud*. Boston, MA: Beacon Press.

Marcuse, H. (1958) *Soviet Marxism: A Critical Analysis*. New York: Random House.

Marcuse, H. (1964) *One-Dimensional Man: Studies in the Ideology of Advanced Industrial Society*. Boston, MA: Beacon Press.

Marcuse, H. (1965) Repressive Tolerance. In: R. P. Wolff, B. Moore and H. Marcuse, *A Critique of Pure Tolerance*. Boston, MA: Beacon Press, pp. 95-137

Marcuse, H. (1969a) Repressive Tolerance. In: R. P. Wolff, B. Moore, Jr, and H. Marcuse, *A Critique of Pure Tolerance*. Boston, MA: Beacon Press, pp. 95–137.

Marcuse, H. (1969b) *An Essay on Liberation*. Boston, MA: Beacon Press.

Marcuse, H. (1970) *Five Lectures*. J. Shapiro and S. Weber, trans. Boston, MA: Beacon Press.

Marcuse, H. (1972) *Counterrevolution and Revolt*. Boston, MA: Beacon Press.

Marcuse, H. (1978) *The Aesthetic Dimension: Toward a Critique of Marxist Aesthetics*. Boston, MA: Beacon Press.

Marcuse, H. (1987) *Hegel's Ontology and the Theory of Historicity*. S. Benhabib, trans. Cambridge, MA: MIT Press.

Marcuse, H. (2005) *Heideggerian Marxism*. R. Wolin and J. Abromeit, trans. Lincoln: University of Nebraska Press.

Marcuse, H. (2009) *Negations: Essays in Critical Theory*. J. J. Shapiro, trans. London: MayFly Books.

O'Connor, B. (2019) Marcuse and the Problem of Repression. In: P. Gordon, E. Hammer and A. Honneth (eds) *The Routledge Companion to the Frankfurt School*. Abingdon: Routledge, pp. 311-22.

Remini, R. V. (2009) *A Short History of the United States*. New York: Harper Perennial.

Whitfield, S. (2014) Refusing Marcuse: 50 Years After *One-Dimensional Man*. *Dissent*, Fall 2014 [online]. Available at: https://www.dissentmagazine.org/article/refusing-marcuse-fifty-years-after-one-dimensional-man (accessed 12 July 2019).

Adorno

Theodore Adorno was one of the leading post-war philosophers and radical social theorists, and, with Max Horkheimer and Herbert Marcuse, a central figure in the Frankfurt School. His writings were self-consciously difficult, and his writing style contorted and abstruse to militate against passive or consumerist forms of reading. For Adorno, the critique of capitalism also entailed a critique of the ideologies that helped to reproduce capitalism. As well as providing powerful critiques of the Enlightenment, technology, philosophy – including German idealism, positivism, scepticism, phenomenology, existentialism – and literature and art, he provided one of the earliest introductions to the sociology of music and developed an acerbic critique of mass culture and consumption. Equally critical of capitalism and state socialism, he saw the differences between fascism and liberal democracy in terms of differences in degree rather than in kind. A central focus of all his work was the 'obliteration' of the individual and his or her freedom in a bureaucratic-technocratic, reified capitalist society characterised by instrumental rationality, mass culture and consumption. Moreover, cohesive and systematic theoretical frameworks could never capture a split, fractured and antagonistic social world without distorting, masking and doing violence to that social reality.

Life and Intellectual Context

Born Theodor Ludwig Wiesengrund in Frankfurt am Main on 11 September 1903, Adorno was the child of a wealthy assimilated Jewish wine merchant, Oskar Wiesengrund, and his Catholic wife, Maria Calvelli Adorno della Piana, a professional opera singer. Initially taking his father's surname he later adopted his mother's. Adorno's upbringing was within the context of a highly cultured, upper bourgeois family. Precocious both musically and intellectually, he studied music at the local conservatory and later as an undergraduate, becoming an accomplished pianist. As he noted later in a letter to Thomas Mann: 'I studied philosophy and music. Instead of deciding exclusively for one subject or the other, I have always had the feeling that my real vocation was to pursue one and the same thing in both of these different domains' (Adorno and Mann, 2006: Letter 11, 5 July 1948). Adorno often used his atonal view of music to criticise philosophy, and vice versa, and it is of some significance that about half of his Collected Works are devoted to music (Rose, 1978: x).

At the age of 15, he was introduced to German classical philosophy by the Austrian cultural theorist, Siegfried Kracauer, who strongly influenced his subsequent understanding of philosophy. In 1921 he graduated from Kaiser Wilhelm Gymnasium in Frankfurt and enrolled at the Johann Wolfgang Goethe University. At the precocious age of 21, he received a doctorate in philosophy in which he examined the work of Husserl and entitled 'The Transcendence of the Material and Noematic in Husserl's Phenomenology'. In 1925 he moved to Vienna to become a student of Alban Berg and Eduard Stuermann and became heavily influenced by the Second Viennese School, and particularly Schoenberg's atonal music. Following his return to Frankfurt from Vienna in 1927, he undertook a *Habilitationsschrift* – a prerequisite for accessing an academic post – entitled: 'The Concept of the Unconsciousness in the Transcendental Theory of Mind'. During this period Adorno became part of the Institute of Social Research under the directorship of Carlo Grunberg. The intellectual circle in which he participated included a number of unorthodox Marxists: Ernst Bloch, Bertolt Brecht, Kurt Weil and, most significantly, Walter Benjamin; the latter exercised an immense influence on Adorno's subsequent thinking. In order to secure a post in Frankfurt, Adorno undertook a second *Habilitationsschrift*, this time on Kierkegaard: 'Kierkegaard's Construction of the Aesthetic', published in 1933, the day Hitler came to power.

Adorno in Exile

Following the rise to power of the Nazis, Adorno's Marxist sympathies and his Jewishness meant he was forced into exile, moving first to London and then taking a position as an advanced student at Merton College, Oxford. Here he was to be supervised by the analytical philosopher Gilbert Ryle and undertook a critique of Husserl, later partially published as *Against Epistemology* (2015 [1956]). Intellectually and socially isolated, Adorno's four-year exile in the UK was for the most part an unhappy one. However, with the help of Horkheimer, in 1938 he secured a position as a senior researcher on Princeton University's Radio Research Project directed by Paul Lazarsfeld. The experience in New York was again not a positive one, given his inexperience and theoretical hostility towards quantitatively-oriented empirical research. In 1941 he moved to Los Angeles to join Horkheimer, where he became ensconced in a circle of intellectuals including the composers Arnold Schoenberg and Hans Eisler, as well as the novelist Thomas Mann.

Despite his profound hostility towards Hollywood, Adorno also met various film stars including Charlie Chaplin. It was during this period that, with Horkheimer, he composed one of his most famous works, *Dialectic of Enlightenment* (1997 [1944]). After the war and along with Horkheimer and Pollack, he decided to return to Frankfurt in 1949, to take up a position at the now reinstituted Institute for Social Research. However, he returned with ideas and themes formulated in the United States and intermittently returned there. It was primarily in West Germany (as opposed to East Germany where other Marxist-inclined thinkers including Ernst Bloch and Bertolt Brecht returned after the war) that he published some of his most important and widely read books, *Minima Moralia* (2006 [1951]), his jointly edited *Aspects of Sociology* (1973 [1956]) and his important essay, 'The Essay as Form'. He also contributed to a much discussed debate with Karl Popper about positivism in 1961, subsequently published as *The Positivist Dispute in German Sociology*. One of his most important books, and perhaps his magnum opus, *Negative Dialectics*, was published in 1964 (1973 [1964]). During the student upheavals and protests in the 1960s Adorno took a rather conservative stance. In 1969, for example, he refused to take a radical or activist political position and on one occasion even called the police during a student occupation of the Institute. Confronted by protesters during his lectures, some of whom bared their breasts and threw flowers at him, Adorno abandoned the lecture course and took a break from the Institute to travel with his wife, Gertrud, to the Swiss Alps. However, after a strenuous trip to the Matterhorn, he died of a heart attack on 6 August 1969. A massive book on aesthetics and art, *Aesthetic Theory*, remained unfinished and was published posthumously in 1970.

Intellectual Influences

The multiplicity of thinkers who influenced Adorno's work remains contested. Kowlakowski (1978: 368) notes a number including Karl Marx, George Hegel, Friedrich Nietzsche, George Lukács, Henri Bergson and Ernst Bloch. However, he omits to mention the fundamental importance of Benjamin and Freud. Others, such as Martin Jay (1984: 14), highlight five major influences. These include Western Hegelian Marxism deriving from George Lukács and Karl Korsch; aesthetic modernism and its preoccupation with form, as exemplified in the work of Schoenberg and Picasso; a mandarin cultural conservatism entailing a profound distaste of mass culture and aversion to political practice; Jewish thought drawing from his own background but also gleaned from the work of Walter Benjamin; and finally Nietzschean forms of deconstruction that emphasise the particular at the expense of the universal.

Although Adorno accepted Marx's materialist analysis and his critique of the commodity form, he remained highly critical of it, and especially of the Soviet-inflected orthodox interpretations of Marx's thinking. Adorno believed that Marxism suffered from a form of economic reductionism as displayed in his base–superstructure metaphor, and that it was too optimistic in its adherence to Enlightenment ideas of progress. From Nietzsche, Adorno derived the latter's attack on anti-systemic thinking and his stylistic attempt to provide a non-systemic philosophy that questioned the Enlightenment and regarded knowledge as a mode of domination connected to a will to power. From Lukács Adorno took the idea of the pervasiveness of reification in the modern world, and its spread from the workplace to all spheres of life, especially in modern forms of culture. A commodified life in which unlike things become alike, just as diverse, qualitative use values become reduced to a singular, quantitative exchange value. Finally, from Ernst Bloch he took the idea of a utopia that existed outside of the current modern context, but which remained content-less.

Historical, Social and Political Context

The development of critical theory, and Adorno's work in particular, was shaped in the context of the profound global turbulence, crises and developments in European capitalism. The Bolshevik Revolution, which took place in Russia – a markedly undeveloped country, and therefore contrary to Marx's predictions, was followed by unsympathetic international foreign blockades of the country and a civil war in which more than 7 million individuals died. The interwar Weimar period in Germany was also one of great national instability. The reactionary German imperial Junker-led system of Kaiser Wilhelm II, which was seen as responsible for leading the country into a disastrous war, had been replaced by the installation of the Social Democratic Party that pursued a parliamentary form of government centred on universal suffrage based on the ideas of a 'republic, democracy and peace' (Held, 1980: 17).

However, the German socio-economic situation after the war remained precarious. The Allies' naval blockade continued until 1919 and led, according to some estimates, to almost 750,000 deaths through disease and starvation. Moreover, a peace settlement signed in Versailles meant that Germany was humiliatingly forced to accept full responsibility for the war and made to pay huge war reparations. The European socialist movement had also become characterised by a major split between deterministic thinkers such as Eduard Bernstein, who argued that socialism was inevitable given the inexorable historical laws of capitalism that Marx had identified, and a more voluntaristic model to socialism proposed by Lenin that argued for the need for violent revolution spearheaded by a revolutionary party. In such an ideological context Social Democrats were sandwiched between a far left and the right. Revolutionary forces from the left included soldiers and workers' councils calling for socialism, which highlighted the political division between their views and those of the Social Democrats – a political divide that was mirrored in the German working class. The German Revolution of 1919 led by Luxemburg and Liebknecht was soon crushed by reactionary, counter-revolutionary forces, including far-right *Freikorps* supported by the SPD, leading to the further fragmentation and repression of the socialist movement.

Socialist Defeat

Such processes were mirrored elsewhere in Europe: the singular success of the socialist revolution in Russia contrasted with its suppression and failure in other Western European countries, including Italy, Austria, Hungary, Bulgaria and Germany. More than anyone else in the Frankfurt School, Adorno's work is marked by the effects of socialist defeat and the rise of fascism. As Adorno remarked at the beginning of *Negative Dialectics* with implicit reference to Marx's Eleventh Thesis on Feuerbach, 'Philosophy, which once seemed outmoded, remains alive because the moment of its realization was missed' (1973a: 3). Instead, between 1922 and 1940 highly organised and determined Nazi and fascist political movements garnered the support of large sections of the working class: Mussolini came to power in 1922, Hitler in 1933 and Franco in Spain in 1939. In 1939 the Nazis had begun systematically murdering handicapped Germans through the T4 action, with around 70,000 men, women and children gassed en masse by 1941 (Hawes, 2017: 180). By 1942 they began planning and enacting the murder of European Jews through the *Endlosung* – or 'Final solution' – in purpose-built extermination camps. As well as Jews, those murdered included Romanies, Poles, Russian POWs and communists, many gassed and killed in camps in the conquered territories of Poland and Russia including Auschwitz, Belzec, Sobibór, Treblinka and Majdenek. Treated as a sub-human grouping and seen as close to vermin, up to 11 million people were annihilated, constituting a major challenge to the idea of Enlightenment civilisation and progress. The Holocaust, along with the rise of fascism, was to shape profoundly Adorno's Jewish inflected thinking. He famously remarked: 'To write poetry after Auschwitz is barbaric' (1967: 34). His deep despair also carried over into all his writings. His book of aphorisms, *Minima Moralia* (2006), written while in America, is subtitled: *Reflections From a Damaged Life* and begins with a quote from Ferdinand Kürnberger 'Life does not live' (2006: 19). Even the dedication to Horkheimer conveys his despondency:

> To speak immediately of the immediate is to behave much as those novelists who drape their marionettes in imitated bygone passions like cheap jewellery, and make people who are no more than component parts of machinery act as if they still had the capacity to act as subjects, and as if something depended on their actions. Our perspective of life has passed into an ideology which conceals the fact that there is life no longer. (2006: 15)

In the context of international isolation, and a war-torn economy, the Russian Revolution began to move away from its original socialist idealisation. Such a process was consolidated by the rise to power of Stalin in 1927, who instilled a repressive and, authoritarian form of rule. It is estimated that approximately 30 million Soviet citizens died or were murdered by Stalin alone. Moreover, under the careful watch of a stringent Communist International, deviation from Stalin's dogmatic orthodoxy became impossible for European socialist parties, including the German Communist Party, and many socialist thinkers. Adding to the sense of despair and resignation that many German intellectuals faced was a triumphant capitalism, a burgeoning fascism and a failure of working-class revolutions to emerge or succeed as envisaged by Marx. Things came to a head when the bureaucratic, repressive and dogmatic form of socialism that emerged in the Soviet Union merged with fascist forces following Stalin's pact with Hitler in August 1939. The prospect of a horrendous Second World War also brought further misery.

Exile in the United States

Such historical events forced writers sympathetic to the Marxist project, such as Adorno, to re-evaluate not only the inevitability of socialism, but also the relationship between theory and practice, the party and the working class. Yet in addition to the failure of socialism, the rise of fascism and the Holocaust, Adorno's writing was also profoundly shaped by his exile in the United States, particularly in California. Here capitalism had come into its own, having moved away from its earlier nineteenth-century liberal forms based on small businesses and enterprises to a form of 'monopoly capitalism' characterised by huge concentrations of capital and wealth, representing what Fredrick Pollack referred to as a form of 'state capitalism'. In this conceptualisation, the state was now seen to intervene actively in the economy to prevent or alleviate the worst excesses of economic crises in order to prevent revolutionary ferment, a process facilitated by the move of capitalist organisations of production from private ownership to professional managers who ruled through a technocratic managerial ideology.

Here, as Weber had predicted, efficiency underpinned by an instrumental rationality became key to consolidating a centralised, bureaucratic state. The pessimism evident throughout Adorno's writings, especially following the rise of fascism, is reflected in *The Dialectic of Enlightenment*. Towards the end of the Second World War, but also before that period, the United States had become the most advanced capitalist society in the world, generating huge economic output and growth. Not only had the motor car and mass production industries become pervasive features of society, but so too had the development of mass media – including films, radio and newspapers – what Adorno would refer to as the 'Culture Industry'. The *Dialectic of the Enlightenment* therefore constitutes an expression of the political and social disenchantment the authors experienced as exiles, documenting the unfolding dynamics of American monopoly capitalism. The proletariat, Adorno believed, had become integrated into capitalism both materially and subjectively. Moreover, consumption and commodification had become pervasive features of Western societies. Signs and symbols through which humans made sense of their lives became commodified and mechanised, paving the way for totalitarian control of people's minds through the growth of mass media including novels, magazines, films, television and radio.

For Adorno not only had the working-class revolution failed, but so too had Marx's thesis concerning the immerisation and homogenisation of the proletariat. The socio-economic conditions of the working class had instead improved both in Germany and in the United States as part of capitalism's attempt to preserve itself. Traditional or vulgar forms of Marxism espoused by the Second and Third International, which often drew on a positivistic or scientistic understanding of the social world, failed to capture the real movement of history and its complexities. Moreover, changes in the Soviet Union followed a similar instrumentally rational path, with less formal freedom and even greater technocratic management.

Post-war Germany

The Germany to which Adorno returned following the war had been reset to Ground Zero, and divided between the Western Allies – the Bundesrepublik and a communist East – the German Democratic Republic (GDR). Konrad Adenauer, the first Chancellor of West Germany, who remained in power until 1963, was determined to face the country towards the free West through a policy of Western integration. West Germany became a member of NATO in 1955 and of the EEC in 1957. As part of his policy of restoration, he also allowed the return into power of former Nazi officials, as well as banning the Communist Party and its members from joining the civil service. In the context of the Cold War geopolitical divide, increasing numbers of educated Germans moved from the East to the West averaging 200,000 a year (Hawes, 2017: 199). As a result, a wall was erected in 1961 to curb further migration between East and West, an *ostflucht*.

While the Frankfurt–Auschwitz trials between 1963 and 1965 saw numerous individuals charged for their roles in Auschwitz and served as a further reminder of Germany's Nazi past, the Spiegel Affair, in which the editor of a weekly political magazine was imprisoned for publishing a story concerning NATO, demonstrated the ongoing fragility of a newly emerging state as well as its ability to sustain the rule of law and free speech. It was within the space created between a Nazi past and a valorisation of a wholesale US capitalist consumerism that many of Germany's student protests emerged, questioning both as well as the war in Vietnam. In the face of such protests the German state sometimes replied with repressive measures, in turn radicalising students even further to the left, for example through the emergence of a Red Army Faction aiming to retaliate against state violence with violence. But the emerging student left was also offset by the rise of a racist, far-right party – the NPD – taking almost 5% of the national vote.

Although Adorno shared a number of affinities with Marxism, it would be misleading to see his work simply as Marxist. Its divorce of theory from practice, the negligible role he allots to the working class that is largely seen as co-opted by capitalism and the high degree of scepticism towards a revolution render it, as Bottomore argues, 'quite incompatible with Marxism' (1984: 31). Adorno's politics, however, remain complex and contradictory given his overall theoretical position. On the one hand, he railed against totalising intellectual and economic systems – Hegel and capitalism, for example – in the name of the individual, thereby providing an anarchic–libertarian focus in his work. Yet, on the other hand, he remained sympathetic to the social and universal nature of humans and humanity. He believes that is is possible to create a reasonable or rational organisation of society in which individuals could develop their potentialities, albeit as a utopian negativity. His work should therefore probably be seen as vacillating between a radical social democratic tradition that aims to defend and strengthen liberal democracy, which constituted for him the least bad alternative available, when compared with the capitalist West and the Soviet East and a possible utopian ideal of socialism that required a fundamental transformation in social relationships.

For Adorno 'right living' was not possible given the structures of the modern world and this could not be solved by revolutionary theory since this itself was problematic (Freyenhagen, 2014: 874). Instead, given the present social conditions, with a working class already effectively incorporated into consumer capitalism, the role of the intellectuals was to theorise and interpret the world, not intervene to change it. The combination of his pervasive pessimism, with his refusal to support any extant radical political movement, led Lukács to argue that Adorno had taken up residence in the 'Grand Hotel Abyss':

> it is a hotel provided with every modern comfort, but resting on the edge of the abyss, of nothingness, of the absurd. The daily contemplation of this abyss, in between the excellent meals and artistic entertainments, can only enhance the residents' enjoyment of this superlative comfort. (1962: 22)

Ideas and Arguments
Negative Dialectics and Identity Thinking

In many ways Adorno remained highly reflexive and self-conscious about the role of philosophical and sociological thinking and especially about the use and application of concepts to understand the social world. He often refers to the relation between subject and object. The subject included the person doing the thinking or acting, while the object included an inanimate object, a person, nature or social phenomena generally. For Adorno, concepts as they were applied by actors in everyday life, and especially by intellectuals, distorted and masked social reality. Concepts never quite captured the objects to which they referred – there was always a remainder, facet or aspect of the object, which the concept missed or excluded. The erroneous belief that concepts captured the object constituted for Adorno a form of 'identity thinking'. Identity thinking covered a broad range of phenomena: it implied not only that concepts were inadequate to capturing their objects but also that the attempt to do so had an instrumental rationale underpinning it. It was based on the subject's anthropological or survival needs of controlling or predicting what the object would do in the future, what Nietzsche referred to as the 'will to power'. As Rose notes:

> identity thinking, which is our normal mode of thinking, implies that the concept is rationally identical with its object. However, given the present state of society (the capitalist mode of production), the concept cannot identify its true object. The consciousness which perceives this is non-identity thinking or negative dialectic. Adorno claims that the possibility of thinking differently from our paradigmatic mode of thinking is inherent in that very mode of thinking. (1978: 44)

Identity thinking is especially manifest both in the pervasive forms of instrumental reason which are concerned with looking at the world and the logic underpinning most theoretical knowledge processes in modern society. Knowledge becomes an instrument, a means to realise practical ends. Here ends can be abstracted and the most efficient 'scientific', i.e. value free means established to achieve them. Knowledge is effectively an expression and an instrument of domination, of repression and unequal power relations. The major exemplar of this is positivism, which we will discuss later.

Identity thinking is also manifest in the current way humans treated nature, as a pliable mass or substance, something to be exploited and used according to instrumental needs, rather than something that was autonomous, complex, organic and developmental, as the German romanticists conceived it. Identity thinking characterises the majority of sociological and philosophical approaches to understanding the social world. These judged the latter in terms of how it appeared rather than by its underlying essence, trying to force the world to fit into its closed models or systems of categories and concepts. Like Hegel, whom he otherwise criticised as producing another grandiose 'system' of thought, Adorno believed that social reality was a process, a becoming, something developing and changing. Things were in flux moving from their actuality to their inherent and possible potentiality. However, as well as missing this important processual aspect of the social world, philosophical and sociological approaches also overlook the particularities of objects. Concepts did 'violence' to their objects. It is also on this basis that Adorno undertakes an immanent critique which 'remains inside' what it criticises, rather than a transcendental critique, coming from outside, so to speak (Jarvis, 1998: 6). Thus, for example, the bourgeois concept of freedom contained ideas and images which were both less and more than was expressed through the concept. It contained a definition 'which the object itself might fail to fulfil' (Held, 1980: 216). As Adorno notes:

> The judgement that a man is free refers to the concept of freedom; but this concept in turn is more than is predicated of the man, and by other definitions the man is more than the concept of his freedom. The concept says not only that it can be applied to all men defined as free; it feeds on the idea of a condition in which individuals would have qualities not to be ascribed to anyone here and now. (1973 [1956]: 150)

The concept or notion of freedom, when looked at in terms of what Adorno refers to as its 'rational identity', contained properties and conditions that could be fulfilled. Yet in capitalist, inegalitarian societies, this correspondence between the concept of freedom and freedom in the real world did not pertain. Freedom was instead restricted by class relations, and therefore could be actualised only by some groups who exploited and dominated. There existed a 'non-identity', a gap or disjuncture, between the concept of freedom, and its object – actually existing society. As Rose notes:

> To believe that a concept really covers its object, when it does not, is to believe falsely that the object is the equal of its concept. According to Marx, emancipation, for example, is not real, human emancipation, if it is merely political emancipation. Adorno reaffirms this. To claim that the concept 'emancipation' correctly describes a state of affairs, when it is not real emancipation, is to make unequal things equal. Adorno construes the process of commodity exchange as involving an analogous mechanism. (1978: 46)

Against Systems and Systemic Thinking

For Adorno, capturing the 'whole' of society through the application of reason and categories and concepts was impossible and mythical. Like the modern, commodified world where social experience was reified and abstract, so too sociological thinking was reified and abstract. Adorno was highly critical of sociological systems which proposed a one-size-fits-all methodology, such as functionalism or positivism, and that applied this methodology to all and every piece of the social world. Everything that existed was interdependent with everything else. In a sense philosophy and sociology as ordinarily conceived in their positive, explanatory sense were impossible – all they could do was to negate or challenge what existed and reveal the pitfalls of identity thinking, as well as to demonstrate how such thinking contributed towards social domination. As he and Horkheimer noted in justifying a critical sociology:

> only a critical spirit can make science more than a duplication of reality by means of thought, and to explain reality means, at all times, to break the spell of this duplication. Such a critique, however, does not imply subjectivism, but rather the confrontation of the objects with its own concept. The given will only offer itself up to the view which regards it from a perspective of true interests – the perspective of free society, a just state, and the full development of the human being. Whoever does not measure human beings by what they themselves are supposed to signify will not merely see superficially but falsely. (Adorno and Horkheimer, 1973 [1956]: 11)

[Republished with permission of Verso from *Aspects of Sociology*, T. Adorno & M. Horkheimer, 1997. London: Heinemann]

Adorno aimed to demonstrate how existing society was oppressive with regard to the human potential for freedom, self-realisation, rational reflection and decision making. The alienated and reified world humans have produced limited their freedom and constrained and oppressed individuals. Like Lukács, Adorno believed we live in a world pervaded by reification. However, his conceptualisation of reification differed marginally from Lukács's which he regarded as too idealist in its focus on the subject's consciousness. Instead, Adorno argued that 'all reification is a forgetting' and focused on how a relation between men appears in the form of a natural property of a thing (Rose, 1978: 31). Moreover, by contrast to Lukács, who emphasised the Hegelian notion of totality as a central methodological tool for understanding the social world, Adorno conceived totality both factually and normatively.

Like Lukács he believed that all social facts were 'mediated' within a social whole or totality and could not be explained as isolated units, as positivists thought. Yet societies were, or attempted to become, totalistic, or in capitalism, totalitarian: oppressive forces aiming at total domination and control. Inverting Hegel's famous dictum that 'the whole is true', Adorno argued that 'the whole is false'. The concept of totality was therefore double edged in his work.

By attempting to acquire a total knowledge of social reality, intellectual systems or frameworks ended up dominating and oppressing individuals living in that world. In the modern 'administered' world including both Western democratic and Eastern socialist societies, freedom for Adorno could only mean the capacity to escape from the totality and totalising thinking.

Thus, as well as totalising societies, such as monopoly capitalism or state socialism, there also existed totalistic thinking and experience, imposing a broad general system of categories and knowledge on the world through which it was to be understood and acted upon. For Adorno, by contrast, an autonomous theory and non-identity thinking contained an 'interpretive' moment that was always necessary, as was the role of autonomous intellectuals operating independent of any political practice, especially in monopoly capitalism.

In discussing the logic that underpins identity theory Adorno draws heavily on Marx's discussion of commodity fetishism. Through a process of commodity fetishism, the qualitative differences between commodities with regard to their usefulness, and the different types and quantities of labour needed to produce them, were overlooked in favour of the abstract universal measurement of their worth; that is what they had in common – their exchange value. Central to Adorno's approach was the view that unequal or different things were treated or transformed into equal or similar things. Such a process also underlay identity thinking, which masks the non-identical.

By contrast, Adorno attempted to develop his anti-systemic approach by revealing contradictions which may appear peripheral to the thought system, or which do not readily fit into it; that is, by highlighting the manner by which the particular could not be made to fit into the universal. His emphasis on the peripheral, or marginal to highlight broader social processes, could be seen, for example, in his essay on the *Los Angeles Times* astrology column, a column that is ordinarily perceived to hold a marginal position within a serious newspaper. Non-identical thought and experience were open and responsive to objects in their own right. As O'Connor notes:

> Non-identical experience – experience that is not distorted or reduced to manipulation – involves, by contrast, openness to the objects – people, the things of nature – that we encounter. Experience in this sense does not seek to confirm to us what we already think reality is… In non-identical experience the individual thinks and conceptualizes in a way that is responsive to the objects with which the individual is engaging. The individual does not attempt to constitute the world. But nor is experience passive: it is the active process of interaction in which the articulations of the subject are challenged and refined. (2013: 16)

[Republished with permission of Routledge from *Adorno*, B. O'Connor, 2013. Permission conveyed through Copyright Clearance Center, Inc]

Adorno was averse both to the separation of the subject and object, and especially to the former's domination of the latter. But he remained equally antipathetic to their primeval unity as expressed in Hegelian Marxism or Heideggerian philosophy, in which humans were in unity with their world. Instead of an idealist identity of subject and object, Adorno gave priority to the object.

Such an approach, which aimed at understanding object and social phenomena in terms of constellations and approximations, and which recognised the problematic nature of language as 'congealed history' and concepts as masking social experience as a form of damaged life, required its own style and stylistic modes, in order to interrogate the relation between ideas and the world. Adorno describes *Negative Dialectics* as advocating 'an anti-system' (1973: xx). As an anti-system *Negative Dialectics* was deliberately composed in order to be difficult to summarise. Nevertheless, a central concern of the book was the philosophical preoccupation with searching for an absolute starting point, a ground, bedrock or first principles on which everything could subsequently can be reduced and explained – a form of 'identity thinking'. Adorno's use of diverse styles included 'constellations', a term derived from Benjamin that referred to the juxtaposition of various elements rather than their integrated hierarchical ordering. This facilitated 'unregimented' forms of thinking, eschewing first principles, yet remaining open to discovering the social world 'as it was' or letting the sociological object 'speak for itself' – without preconceptions – that is, dialectically. Adorno characterised his own approach as 'interpretive' and at other times as dialectical. However, and in reaction to Hegel, Adorno did not offer a positive developmental dialectic in which oppositions were raised to a higher level. Instead, he provided 'determinate negations' through which those aspects of the object which thought misidentified received an indirect, conceptual articulation.

The *Dialectic of Enlightenment*

Initially published in 1944 before being reprinted in Amsterdam in 1947, *Dialectic of Enlightenment* (1997) lacked a coherent set of thematic chapters, continuing Adorno's use of a disjointed and fragmented method: the book was originally entitled *Philosophical Fragments*. Nevertheless, there were central themes running throughout anchored in the ideas of reason and progress. Continuing their view of identity thinking as a form of domination, Adorno and Horkheimer began their analysis of the Enlightenment by arguing that it had turned from engendering a form of progress into its opposite. Enlightenment thinking, as postulated by Kant, had promised to liberate people from ignorance, disease and toil, creating free, autonomous, self-directing subjects.

Instead, it trapped individuals within a bureaucratic world of domination, expressed in liberal democracy, fascism, Stalinism and mass destruction: 'In the most general sense of progressive thought, the Enlightenment has always aimed at liberating men from fear and establishing their sovereignty. Yet the fully enlightened earth radiates disaster triumphant' (Adorno and Horkheimer, 1997: 3). Rather than standing for freedom and progress, the Enlightenment has operated as an ideology, masking its oppressive and domineering nature in modern capitalism. Moreover, in place of the seventeenth century, the roots of Enlightenment thinking stretched back as far as the Jewish scriptures and Homeric Greece.

Drawing on Nietzsche's view of knowledge as an instrument of domination or will to power, they argue that 'technology is the essence of this knowledge' (1997: 4). With the wide-scale adoption of scientific, instrumental thinking, which saw nature as something to be known in order to be controlled, a broad synthesising and open conception of reason as *Vernuft*, rooted in German idealism, became progressively and irretrievably displaced by what Weber termed 'instrumental reason', *Verstand*. The latter expressed the principle of exchange and fostered the domination of nature, creating an 'administered world'. The Enlightenment thereby contains a duality or dialectic, moving between freedom and subjugation. Progress through science and technology is pursued at whatever cost, and nature simply becomes a means to this progress. Such progress aims towards the extirpation of myth and mystery, including animism. From a situation in which Enlightenment and myth had relationally defined one another, and in which myth had some rational aspects, we arrive at a point where Enlightenment attempts to exclude all myth from social life, but this itself is a mythical undertaking. Important philosophical concepts and enquiries into the nature of 'substance and quality, activity and suffering, being and existence' (1997: 5) became replaced by narrow scientific models preoccupied with mathematics and calculation: 'For the Enlightenment, whatever does not conform to the rule of computation and utility is suspect, and to the Enlightenment, that which does not reduce to numbers, and ultimately to the one, becomes illusion: modern positivism writes it off as literature' (1997: 6, 7). Only that which repeats itself and recurs in a cycle is measurable or of interest to Enlightenment thinking, so that everything that is knowable is known in advance:

> there is nothing new under the sun because all the pieces in the meaningless game have already been played, and all the great thoughts have already been thought ... what was different is equalised. (1997: 12)

However, the treatment of nature as a mere object to be manipulated and used instrumentally, largely as a survival mechanism for material beings, comes back to haunt humans as demonstrated, for example, in fascism, as part of a process of what Freud referred to as 'the return of the repressed'. Power and domination over the physical world was extended to domination over the social world. Human subjects become the objects of science, treated as isolated units, until they too can be technologically controlled and dominated like nature. As a result, Adorno and Horkheimer argue that: 'enlightenment is as totalitarian as any system' (1997: 24).

Capitalist, instrumental rationality, technology and science drive the system forward, ensnaring humanity further into domination and destruction. National socialism and genocide are therefore not historical aberrations or anomalies, but the logical and necessary outcomes of an unfolding instrumental Enlightenment logic of domination.

The Culture Industry

Throughout his work Adorno remained hostile to popular culture. His views on culture developed as part of his own experience of the technology-pervaded mass culture of the Weimar era, Nazi folk culture and American popular culture from the 1940s (Huyssen, 1975: 4). In *Dialectic of the Enlightenment* Adorno and Horkheimer refer to culture as part of a 'culture industry' which functions as a form of mass deception. In a later essay (Adorno, 1991a), Adorno clarifies the use of the term, arguing that he and Horkheimer replaced the term 'mass culture' with 'culture industry' in order to highlight that culture was not democratic, nor did it arise 'spontaneously from the masses themselves' (1991a: 85). Moreover, the term 'culture industry' should not be taken too literally, he argued, it referred to the standardisation of culture, to the rationalisation of distribution techniques, industrial forms of organisation, its machine-like control promulgated for the most part by cinema and radio, rather than specifically to the production process itself:

> The culture industry fuses the old and familiar into a new quality. In all its branches, products which are tailored for consumption by masses, and which to a great extent determine the nature of that consumption, are manufactured more or less according to a plan... This is made possible by contemporary technical capabilities as well as by economic and administrative concentration. The culture industry intentionally integrates its consumers from above. To the detriment of both it fuses together the sphere of high and low art, separated for thousands of years. (1991a: 85)

In his analysis of music, art and aesthetics, Adorno tends to associate legitimate culture with high culture. 'Good' true art has the ability to transcend reality by capturing and refracting societal contradictions, expressing suffering and pointing to the 'good life'. However, in the modern administered world, in which totalitarian harmony was a central ideology, and art increasingly commodified and shorn of its critical impetus, the distinction between high and low art became increasingly blurred. Classical music or opera accompanied films, and classical painting features in adverts. In such a context, the notion of harmony itself needed to be challenged. Genuine art contained non-identity thinking, pointing to the disjuncture between concept and reality. It was in the work of certain modernists preoccupied with form or style, such as Picasso, Schoenberg and Becket, that art reached its true potential as both autonomous from society, embodying a 'truth-content', and critical. It meets 'true' needs, seen in terms of expressing the real freedom and rational powers of human beings, rather than the perverted false needs of consumerism and advertising. By contrast, the culture industry contained a dual function: to finds new markets and products and to control people's minds. Consumption did not follow the needs of consumers as autonomous subjects, rather they are objects worked upon through advertising and manipulation. Equally, films, art, stories were all formulaic, repetitious and predictable, embodying a changing content, but static form:

> As soon as the film begins, it is quite clear how it will end... In light music, once the trained ear has heard the first notes of the hit song, it can guess what is coming and feel flattered when it does come. (1997: 125)

The emphasis of the culture industry is on the packaging, 'the effect' rather than the work itself. The whole and the parts are in harmony, there is no antithesis or contradiction which constituted the basis of great bourgeois works of art.

The culture industry requires a specific personality structure, a personality not just receptive to passive consumption, but one that actively seeks to be passive. The individual, in effect masochistically, yearns to be dominated. The culture industry combines, through the medium of entertainment and fantasy combined, what are usually deemed irreconcilable elements – culture, art and distraction – into a unity. Although the world of leisure is ordinarily seen as constituting a radical break with the alienating world of work and the pressures of capitalist life, for Adorno the two remain dialectically intertwined: leisure time bears the imprint of work constituting a form of escapism, but one which is detrimental in the sense that it inculcates a passivity and stultifying conformism. The industry provides a form of escapism, diverting minds from the realities of the contradictions in capitalism they face, helping them escape from everyday drudgery:

> In spite of the films which are intended to complete her integration, the housewife finds in the darkness of the movie theatre a place of refuge where she can sit for a few hours with nobody watching, just as she used to look out of the window when there were still homes and rest in the evening. The unemployed in the great cities find coolness in summer and warmth in winter in these temperature-controlled locations. (1997: 139)

A central logic underpinning the culture industry was the promise of happiness, and, paradoxically, its denial at one and the same time: the culture industry perpetually cheats its consumers of what it perpetually promises – emotional or sexual satisfaction: 'all it actually confirms is that the real point will never be reached, that the diner must be satisfied with the menu' (1997: 139). Yet, this world of distraction engendered by the cuture industry, allowed people's irrational tendencies to be exploited. A contempt for oneself and others was expressed in laughter and the eagerness of individuals to laugh at anything, especially and derisorily at the expense of others, a collectivism which Adorno and Horkheimer regarded as barbaric. The only resistance individuals have is the resistance that the industry has inculcated in them. In such a context even consumers who see through the products are left with a Hobson's choice of joining in or being left behind and shunted by others.

The Adorno–Benjamin Debate

In addition to the essays on the culture industry, Adorno's response to popular cultural forms was expressed in two highly negative essays, 'On the Fetish Character of Music and the Regression of Listening' and 'Perennial Fashion – Jazz' (1991b: 119–32), Written in response to Benjamin's 'The Work of Art in the Age of Mechanical Reproduction' (2008 [1935]) and under the pseudonym

Hector Rottweiler, the pen name gives an indication of his animosity to these cultural products. In the essay on Jazz he states: 'jazz has in its essence remained static, nor does it explain the resulting enigma that millions of people seem never to tire of its monotonous attraction' (1991b: 121). In another essay, Adorno was to become involved in a long correspondence with Walter Benjamin concerning the liberating or dominating aspects of popular culture, the role of mass art and autonomous art, and the role of technology, which was to become known as the 'Adorno–Benjamin Debate'. Although they shared dialectical perspective that interrogated myth and history in their correspondence, Adorno, often dubbed by critics as a 'Cultural Mandarin' (Jay, 1984), remained more sympathetic to bourgeois high culture, including certain forms of classical music, painting and literature as well as more contemporary modernist forms than Benjamin, who tended to dismiss these as 'counter-revolutionary' (Ross, 2014) and detached from the masses. As Benjamin argued:

> At no point in time, no matter how utopian, will it be possible to win the masses for a higher form of art. It will only be possible to win them for one which is closer to them. And the difficulty consists precisely in creating this form of art in such a way that it would be possible, with a clear conscience, to assert that it was a higher form of art. (cited in Wiggershaus, 2007: 212)

Nevertheless, and despite his acknowledgment of avant-garde modernism and high culture as closer to autonomous art, Adorno believed that both high and low culture 'bear the stigmata of capitalism, both contain elements of change… Both are torn halves of an integral freedom to which, however, they do not add up' (Adorno et al., 1977: 109).

Studies in Fascism, Prejudice and Authoritarian Personality

A central preoccupation running throughout Adorno's work was his attempt to understand and explain his first-hand experience of the rise of fascism, authoritarianism and anti-Semitism from the 1930s onwards. After the war, as the deleterious effects of the Holocaust became evident, he increasingly began to acknowledge his Jewish ancestry and as Jay notes (1984: 19) the implications of Auschwitz became 'an obsession'. The rise of anti-Semitism and authoritarianism also constituted a core concern of the Frankfurt School generally, including Marcuse, Pollack and Horkheimer. Like Adorno, they emphasised what they perceived to be as a continuity between a liberal democratic order and a totalitarian order given that both were underpinned by the development of a monopolistic 'post-competitive' form of 'state capitalism'. As Horkheimer noted: 'he who does not wish to speak of capitalism should be silent about fascism' (1989 [1939]: 77). An unstable monopolistic system required the intervention of a totalitarian and authoritarian state to secure economic growth and expansion through maximising and underpinning efficient production.

Fascism was built into modern forms of capitalism and its tendencies were displayed both in the American culture industry and in Nazi Germany. As part of a research team including Else Frenkel-Brunswick, Daniel Levinson and R. Nevitt Sandford, Adorno wrote *The Authoritarian Personality* (Adorno et al., 1969 [1950]) based on a large-scale study of Americans using survey data. The book's central hypothesis was:

> that the political, economic, and social convictions of an individual often form a broad and coherent pattern, as if bound together by a 'mentality' or 'spirit', and that this pattern is an expression of deep lying trends in his personality. The major concern was with the potentially fascistic individual, one whose structure is such as to render him particularly susceptible to anti-democratic propaganda. (1969 [1950]: 1)

Adorno and his colleagues sought to reveal a socio-psychological personality structure or 'syndrome', including various sub-syndromes, that indicated pre-fascist tendencies in individuals, including prejudiced, rigid and dogmatic forms of thinking. These were to be quantitatively measured on a personality scale – the F-Scale (F for fascism) – which included several variables: conventionalism, authoritarian submission, authoritarian aggression, superstition and stereotype, power and toughness, destructiveness and cynicism, projectivity, and sex. This subjective and overtly psychological understanding of the rise of prejudice, aggression and fascist conformism was complemented with a more 'objective' analysis of socio-economic forces and philosophical thinking as elaborated in the 'Research Project on Anti-Semitism' (1941), 'Anti-Semitism and Fascist Propaganda' (1946) and *Dialectic of Enlightenment*. In the latter Adorno and Horkheimer situate anti-Semitism in the context of the rise of instrumental reason, the domination of nature and capitalist production: 'bourgeois anti-Semitism has a specific economic reason: the concealment of domination in production' (1997: 173). Jews operated as scapegoats for anti-capitalism. Such a view, developed further in *Negative Dialectics* with regard to philosophy, understood Jews as emblematic of the non-identical. In an age of totalistic, domineering thinking, with regard to their refusal to integrate into the administered world, and in the face of the paranoid projections of Western culture and thinking, Jews constituted the absolute unassimilable Other.

Contemporary Relevance and Applications

Adorno's work pre-dated and was in some ways offered as a precursor to postmodern thinking, especially in the work of Derrida (Eagleton, 1981: 141), but also in the post-structuralist analysis of Foucault (Jay, 1984: 22). Adorno's critique of technology and bureaucratic rationalisation also appealed to certain sections of the middle class in the 1960s. Yet Adorno did not share the practical implications that students derived from his critical perspective.

THE CULTURE INDUSTRY TODAY

The appeal of Adorno's critique of mass culture lies in its polemical thrust. The theory of the culture industry emphasises the power of mass-mediated products in shaping perceptions of reality, presenting a compelling account of the ideological function of mass culture in advanced capitalist societies. Rather than enabling the reflexivity, critique and autonomy required for individuation and social change, the culture industry promotes self-deception, affirmation and manipulation, such that inherent contradictions of capitalist society are effectively contained. But, with mass culture having changed considerably since Adorno's time, today we should consider whether present cultural forms vindicate or contradict this thesis. Is current mass culture entirely ideological? Contemporary radical theorists, such as Slavoj Žižek, or cultural theorists, such as Douglas Kellner, tend to take a more nuanced view, akin to Walter Benjamin or Ernst Bloch, finding aspects of both affirmation and critique, or ideology and utopia, within popular culture today.

Adorno's critique of culture and the culture industry has found resonance in a number of texts including Stuart Ewan's (2001) work *Captains of Consciousness: Advertising and the Social Roots of the Consumer Culture*, which sees consumer culture as the growth of the corporate control of everyone's lives, the transformation of 'social class' into a 'mass' and the creation of individuals who gain their satisfactions from consuming. The relevance of Adorno's writings has also been defended by Albrecht Wellmer (1998) as well as by the Marxist Frederick Jameson. In his book *Late Marxism: Adorno, or, the Persistence of the Dialectic* (2007) Jameson attempts to demonstrate Adorno's relevance, especially through his notion of nominalist immanence, for the currently existing 'postmodern world':

> Here at length, in this decade which has just ended but is still ours, Adorno's prophecies of the 'total system' finally came true, in wholly unexpected forms. Adorno was surely not the philosopher of the thirties (who has to be identified in retrospect, I'm afraid, as Heidegger); nor the philosopher of the forties and fifties; nor even the thinker of the sixties... But there is some chance that he may turn out to have been the analyst of our own period, which he did not live to see, and in which late capitalism has all but succeeded in eliminating the final loopholes of nature and the Unconscious, of subversion and the aesthetic, of individual and collective praxis alike, and, with a final fillip, in eliminating any memory trace of what thereby no longer existed in the henceforth postmodern landscape. (2007 [1989]: 5)

[Republished with permission of Verso from *Late Marxism: Adorno, or, The Persistence of the Dialectic*, F. Jameson, 2007]

In *Postmodernism or the Cultural Logic of Late Capitalism?* (1991), Jameson argues that we live in a postmodern, post-monopoly capitalism. This late capitalist world is characterised by multinationals, financial markets, and an international division of labour. Here the distinction between the cultural and economic sphere has dissolved, space dominates time, culture foregrounds surface and appearances, while a new affect and emotional structure in individuals pertains.

However, the most influential heir of Adorno's work, and for a time his assistant, was Jürgen Habermas, who takes a much more positive attitude towards the social world, and the role of Enlightenment reason within it, as well as the possibility of establishing a emancipatory position of critique founded on communication through discourse ethics. His work is discussed in a later chapter.

Criticisms

There have been a number of criticisms of Adorno's work, some sympathetic, others less so. Kowlakowski (1985) has questioned Adorno's use of an abstruse style: 'The pretentious obscurity of style and the contempt that it shows the reader might be endurable if the book were not also devoid of literary form' (1985: 357). He also criticises Adorno's view that negative dialectics cannot be criticised either from a logical or factual point of view since Adorno does not accept these criteria of judgement. The result is that negative dialectic is wholly speculative, 'simply a blank cheque, signed and endorsed by history' which 'requires little empirical or theoretical corroboration' (1985: 364–5). This applies equally to Adorno's use of the concept of totality, as a something that is pervasive and shapes, mediates and structures all social processes, yet is not itself a fact among others. As Hans Albert notes: 'the untestability of Adorno's assertion is basically linked to the fact that neither the concept of totality used, nor the nature of the dependence asserted, is clarified to any degree' (1976 [1961]: 175n).

Although often invoking the evil of reification, Adorno fails to tell us how a non-reified world in which humans would be free would look like, nor how it would come about. This partly follows from his understanding of utopia drawn from Bloch. Other writers such as Perry Anderson (1976) have also picked up on the profound pessimism underpinning his work. His work though critical of society ultimately, since it recoils from practice, remains apolitical.

Others critics such as Held have argued that Adorno exaggerates the degree of cohesion in modern administered society and postulates an 'overharmonious relation between state, administrative apparatuses and the economy' (Held, 1980: 365), which is probably an artefact of his experience of fascism and Nazism (1980: 365). Moreover, as Jay notes, if reification is all pervasive then how does Adorno as a critic see past it to maintain a critical position? As Jay argues:

> Adorno, however, never justified his privileged status beyond talking vaguely of 'a stroke of undeserved luck' that 'has kept the mental composition of some individuals not quite adjusted to the prevailing norms'. (1984: 117)

Jay also notes Adorno's 'relentless animus towards mass culture' (1984: 119) and it is this area which has borne the brunt of the criticism directed towards his work. Various critics have argued not only that Adorno is unjustified in his belief that North American liberalism can simply be equated with German fascism, but also have asked whether it is justified to see consumer culture as of one piece and bereft of all critical dimension. For example, is the work of Charlie Chaplin the same as that of the Three Stooges? Or is the work of Bob Dylan equivalent to that of Abba in terms of its critical component? Others such as Robins (1994) and Hall (1981) have tried to demonstrate the need to understand audiences as 'active' rather than 'passive'. The belief that the masses in the United States are being duped and misled has led to a broader question of how integrated the masses really are. As Craib notes:

> The failure in the USA to integrate different national communities into a common 'melting pot', despite the use of all the instruments of the culture industry, is strong evidence that process of domination is not quite as complete as much Frankfurt theory would lead us to think. (1984: 199)

Craib also notes that there is also a lack of proper structural analysis in Adorno's arguments that could allow for a more nuanced understanding of contemporary capitalism.

Conclusion

Adorno provides a powerful and penetrating criticism of expansive philosophical and sociological systems of thought. Although his work is dense and complex, it offers a challenging contrast to the assumptions of isolated and atomised thinking characteristic of positivistic approaches which he challenged in the 'Positivist Dispute'. However, his work is deeply pessimistic looking only to individual rebellion, and despite postulating a dialectical approach, often one-sided in its negative assessment of the world. It is also highly elitist, and many of his arguments concerning the culture industry, though provactive and demonstrating the intrinsic politics of mass culture, can be said to lack empirical validity on occasions and to minimise the role of conscious social agency.

References

Adorno, T. (2006 [1951]) *Minima Moralia: Reflections from a Broken Life*. London: Verso.
Adorno, T. (2015 [1956]) *Against Epistemology*. Cambridge: Polity.
Adorno, T. (1973 [1964]) *Negative Dialectics*. London: Routledge & Kegan Paul.
Adorno, T. (1967) *Prisms*. London: N. Spearman.
Adorno, T. (1991a) The Culture Industry Reconsidered. In: *The Culture Industry: Selected Essays on Mass Culture*. London: Routledge.
Adorno, T. (1991b) *Prisms*. Cambridge, MA: MIT Press.
Adorno, T. and Horkheimer, M. (1997 [1944]) *Dialectic of Enlightenment*. London: Verso.
Adorno, T. and Horkheimer, M. (1973 [1956]) *Aspects of Sociology*. London: Heinemann.
Adorno, T. W. and Mann, T. (2006) *Correspondence 1943–1955*. Cambridge: Polity.
Adorno, T., Frenkel-Brunswik, E., Levinson, D. J. and Nevitt Sanford, R. (1969 [1950]) *The Authoritarian Personality*. New York: Norton.
Adorno, T., Benjamin, W., Bloch, E., Brecht, B. and Lukács, G. (1977) *Aesthetics and Politics*. London: Verso.

Adorno, T. (1997 [1970]) *Aesthetic Theory*. R. Hullot-Kentor, trans. London: Bloomsbury.
Albert, H. (1976 [1961]) The Myth of Total Reason. In T. Adorno, H. Albert, R. Dahrendorf, J. Habermas, H. Pilot and K. Popper (eds) *The Positivist Dispute in German Sociology*. London: Heinemann, pp. 163-197
Anderson, P. (1976) *Considerations on Western Marxism*. London: New Left Books.
Bottomore, T. (1984) *The Frankfurt School*. Chichester: Horwood.
Craib, I. (1984) *Modern Social Theory, From Parsons to Habermas*. Brighton: Wheatsheaf.
Eagleton, T. (1981) *Walter Benjamin or Towards a Revolutionary Criticism*. London: Verso.
Ewan, S. (2001) *Captains of Consciousness: Advertising and the Social Roots of the Consumer Culture*. New York: Basic Books.
Freyenhagen, F. (2014) Adorno's Politics: Theory and Praxis in Germany's 1960s. *Philosophy & Social Criticism*, 40(9), pp. 867-93.
Hall, S. (1991) Encoding, Decoding. In Duhring, S. (ed) *The Cultural Studies Reader*. London: Routledge, pp. 90-103.
Hawes, J. (2017) *The Shortest History of Germany*. London: Old Street Publishing.
Held, D. (1980) *Introduction to Critical Theory: Horkheimer to Habermas*. Cambridge: Polity.
Horkheimer, M. (1989 [1939]) The Jews and Europe (1939). In: S. Bronner and D. Kellner (eds), *Critical Theory and Society. A Reader*. New York, London: Routledge, pp. 77-94.
Huyssen, A. (1975) Introduction to Adorno. *New German Critique*, 6, pp. 3-11.
Jameson, F. (2007 [1989]) *Late Marxism: Adorno, or, the Persistence of the Dialectic* London: Verso.
Jameson, F. (1991) *Postmodernism or the Cultural Logic of Late Capitalism?* London: Verso.
Jay, M. (1984) *Adorno*. Cambridge, MA: Harvard University Press.
Jarvis, S. (1998) *Adorno*. Cambridge: Polity.
Kolakowski, L. (1978) *Main Currents of Marxism: Its Origins, Growth and Dissolution, Vol. 3: The Breakdown*. Oxford: Oxford University Press.
Kolakowski, L. (1985) *Main Currents of Marxism: Its Origins, Growth and Dissolution, Vol. 2: The Golden Age*. Oxford: Oxford University Press.
Lukács, G. (1962) *The Theory of the Novel: A Historico-Philosophical Essay on the Forms of Great Epic Literature*. London: Merlin.
O'Connor, B. (2013) *Adorno*. New York: Routledge.
Robins, K. (1994) Forces of Consumption. *Media, Culture and Society*, 16, pp. 449-68.
Rose, G. (1978) *The Melancholy Science: An Introduction to the Thought of Theodor W. Adorno*. New York: Columbia University Press.
Ross, A. (2014) The Naysayers: Walter Benjamin, Theodor Adorno, and the Critique of Pop Culture. *The New Yorker*, 8 September [online]. Available at: https://www.newyorker.com/magazine/2014/09/15/naysayers (accessed 1 July 2019).
Wellmer, A. (1998) *The Persistence of Modernity: Essays on Aesthetics, Ethics and Postmodernism*. Cambridge: Polity.
Wiggershaus, R. (2007) *The Frankfurt School: Its History, Theories and Political Significance*. Cambridge: Polity.

Homans, Coleman and Boudon

Introduction

Utilitarian sociological approaches such as social exchange theory and rational choice theory are riddled by a paradox: they advocate methodological individualism and emphasise that no proper explanation is possible unless it is 'couched wholly in terms of facts about individuals' (Lukes, 1973: 110), yet their primary ambition is not to trace actions of single individuals, but to explain the behaviour of thousands or millions of human beings. The utilitarian tradition deploys economic and psychological models of analysis to understand the large-scale collective action. In this chapter we explore the key contributions of the three leading representatives of sociological utilitarianism: George Homans, the founder of social exchange theory, and James Coleman and Raymond Boudon, the two influential social theorists who developed distinct rational choice explanatory models. The chapter opens with the broader intellectual, social and political context where these utilitarian ideas emerged and developed and then zooms in on the key sociological contributions by Homans, Coleman and Boudon. The last two sections look at the contemporary applications and advancements within this theoretical perspective and then offer a brief critique of utilitarian sociology.

Life and Intellectual Context

George Casper Homans

Homans was born in Boston, Massachusetts, in 1910. He grew up in a wealthy and highly privileged family which, on his mother's side, could trace its roots directly to the 'founding fathers' of the United States: George was a great-great-great grandson of John Adams, the second US president, and was also a great-great grandson of the sixth US president, John Quincy Adams (Homas, 1984). His family also included a plethora of influential doctors and lawyers and George's father was also a lawyer and a fellow of Harvard Corporation. Between 1923 and 1928 young George attended a highly prestigious preparatory school – St. Pauls in Concord, New Hampshire. In 1928 he enrolled to study English and American literature at Harvard where he graduated in 1932.

His parents expected George to continue the family tradition and become a lawyer, but he was eager to pursue a career as a journalist. He was offered a job at the *Gazette* in Kansas but as the Depression decimated that newspaper, he soon lost his job. In this new environment he decided to continue with his studies and, under the influence of one of his lecturers, Lawrence Henderson, opted for sociology. Homans attended Henderson's seminar at Harvard and was mesmerised by his lectures on the unity of all sciences. Homans also joined the Pareto Circle, a Harvard discussion group which was inspired by the theories of Vilfredo Pareto and was led by Henderson.

This early influence of Pareto and Henderson was clearly visible in Homans's first publications including his co-authored maiden book *An Introduction to Pareto*, published in 1934. In the same year Homans was awarded a junior fellowship in sociology and remained in this position until 1939 when he was appointed an instructor in Harvard's sociology department. During his fellowship he undertook an extensive project that focused on thirteenth-century rural England. This study was later published as *English Villagers of the Thirteenth Century* (1941) and was central to Homans' later receiving tenure at Harvard. Soon after, the United States entered the war and Homans was drafted into the Naval Reserve. He served for over four years and fought in the war mostly on anti-submarine military operations. After the war, he settled on a teaching and research life at Harvard, where he taught sociology and medieval history and was also involved in the poetry circles that were active at Harvard. In 1946 he received tenure and was appointed associate professor. In 1953 he become a full professor. He also had several visiting professorships in Europe in the 1950s and 1960s including Cambridge, Kent and Manchester. In 1964 he was elected president of the American Sociological Association. George Homans died in 1989 in Cambridge, Massachusetts.

James Samuel Coleman

Coleman was born in 1926 in Bedford, Indiana. His parents were upper-middle-class professionals who moved to Ohio and then to Louisville, Kentucky, where young Coleman completed his education at Dupont Manual High School. Initially, he was not academically oriented and was mostly interested in sports. In 1944 he enrolled in a small college in Virginia but soon decided to enlist in the US Navy. In this capacity he was involved in military operations during the war. Afterwards, he enrolled in the chemical engineering programme at Purdue University where he graduated in 1949.

Soon after graduation he was employed at Eastman Kodak Company, but he found that job, and the profession as a whole, unsatisfactory and decided to change career. He took several evening courses in social psychology and eventually enrolled in the Columbia graduate sociology programme in 1951. He received a PhD from Columbia in 1955 where he was deeply influenced by the leading empirical sociologist at that time, the Austrian-American Paul Lazarsfeld. While completing his PhD he worked as a research associate in Lazarsfeld's Bureau of Applied Social Research. Soon after graduation he was employed as a fellow at the Center for Advanced Study of Behavioral Science at Stanford University and then joined the faculty at the University of Chicago as an assistant professor. After a few years he moved to Johns Hopkins University. There he founded the Department of Sociology and was also involved with Project Camelot, a military research operation centred on counter-insurgency training funded by the US military's Special Operations Research Office.

In 1973, he returned to Chicago's sociology department as a professor and a director of the National Opinion Research Center. In addition to his pioneering work on mathematical sociology, the problem of collective action, social theory and the sociology of education, Coleman was also involved in public policy. He became a well-known figure after the publication of the Coleman Report, a large case study dealing with the equality of educational opportunities in the United States. In this context his work had a significant impact on the US government's education policy. The Coleman Report was presented to the US Congress in 1966 and as such influenced education policies throughout the late 1960s and early 1970s. The central conclusion of the report was that children from impoverished minority backgrounds were academically more successful in integrated middle-class schools. This finding contributed significantly to the change of government policy, including the newly initiated and later prevalent practice of busing students to achieve ethnic and class balance in public schools. This policy created controversy with many parents opposing the practice of busing. In the mid-1970s Coleman changed his view on this policy and concluded that its ambition was not achieved as many middle-class white parents avoided integration by opting for private schools and this led to a further declining of public schools. In 1991 Coleman became president of the American Sociological Association and was often listed as one of the most influential American sociologists. He died in 1995 in Chicago.

Raymond Boudon

Boudon was born in 1934 in Paris. His upper-middle-class family lived comfortably but, as all French citizens, experienced difficulties during the Nazi occupation from 1940 to 1944. However, the family recovered after the war and had the financial means to send young Raymond to the best secondary schools in Paris: Condorcet and Louis le Grand. As a bright pupil he was successful in primary and secondary education and as such enrolled into the École Normale Supérieure in 1954. In 1955, he received a scholarship to spend a year at the University of Freiburg im Breisgau (Baden-Württemberg) and completed his undergraduate studies in 1958. In the late 1950s he was drafted to serve in the Algerian War (1954–62) but much of his military service was focused on working for CERPA (the French Army's psychological research unit) where he was active between 1958 and 1960.

In 1961 Boudon won a scholarship from the Ford Foundation to spend a study year at Columbia University in New York where he had the opportunity to work with Paul Lazarsfeld and Robert Merton. In 1962 he started working at CNRS (the National Centre for Scientific Research). Soon after that he was accepted to work on a PhD project with Jean Stoetzel and later undertook another PhD, with Raymond Aron, at the Sorbonne where he graduated in 1967. While working on his PhD he also taught at the University of Bordeaux from 1964 until 1967, and was also a member of CNRS. Initially, he was interested in quantitative research and mathematical sociology, fully reflected in his thesis 'The Mathematical Analysis of Social Facts', which was successfully defended and then published in 1967. However, under the influence of Raymond Aron he became more interested in social theory and his later works tended to focus on theoretical issues. The thesis 'What is the Notion of Structure for?' challenged the dominant structuralist theories of its time and laid a foundation for Boudon's methodological individualism. The thesis was published by the leading French publisher, Gallimard, in 1968. As a PhD student, he had another opportunity to study abroad and spent the 1964–5 school year at Harvard. Upon completion of his PhD projects he was appointed professor at the University of Paris-Sorbonne (Paris IV) in 1967 where he worked until retirement in 2002. At the Sorbonne, he also directed a research laboratory, the Study Group on Methods of Sociological Analysis (GEMAS). Raymond Boudon died in 2013.

Historical, Social and Political Context

The social thought of Homans, Coleman and Boudon was influenced by the social changes that were taking place in the United States and France in the second half of the twentieth century. Nevertheless, living in the two countries with a rather different historical and political legacies meant that they had a very different position in their societies and have also left different legacies.

The Sources of Economic Rise and Decline in the United States

US society in the 1970s, 1980s and 1990s experienced a substantial degree of economic development. Although the oil crisis in the 1970s generated a deep recession which was still felt in the 1980s, much of this period was characterised by substantial levels of economic prosperity. For example, US GDP growth rates in the 1970s were rather high (i.e. 1972, 5.2%; 1973, 5.6%; 1976, 5.4%; 1978, 5.5%). The 1980s and 1990s also experienced several years of low growth but the two decades were characterised by quite high levels of economic development, with some years experiencing a substantial GDP increase. For example, in 1984 the GDP growth rate was a staggering 7.2% while in much of the 1990s it ranged from 3 to 4.8% (Amadeo, 2019). The leading economists provided very different explanations for this rise in economic prosperity: while Keynesian scholars emphasised the long-term benefits of the managed market economy, neo-classical economists touted the significance of private initiative.

Keynesian economics, which insists on the structural advantages of joint co-ordination between the public and the private sectors, dominated much of post-war economic policy. The Keynesians argued that economic recessions and inflation are integral parts of the capitalist economies: as aggregate demand is unpredictable and changeable it will inevitably create inflation (when demand is high) or recessions or even depressions (when demand is low). To alleviate these periodic crises, it is necessary for governments to intervene in the business cycle. These interventions are most useful when centred on fiscal policy actions (i.e. raising taxes) or when adjusting the monetary policy (i.e. raising or lowering interest rates by the central bank). Since the Keynesian approach focuses on co-operation and stability it proved highly popular in the post-war period.

However, the series of economic and political crises in the 1970s undermined the global consensus on economic growth. This started with the US government's unilateral decision to pull out of the Bretton Woods Accord in 1971. This agreement pegged the US dollar to the price of gold and other currencies were pegged to the dollar. Hence by leaving the Gold Exchange Standard the United States undermined economic stability and fostered a mass exodus from the Gold Exchange Standard, thus leading to a greater printing of money in the United States, UK, France and other states. This overproduction of money led to higher inflation and also to depreciation of the dollar and other Western currencies. Since oil was priced in dollars the real income of oil producers plummeted. In this context the OPEC countries agreed to increase oil prices and peg them to the price of gold. The consequences of these political decisions were two major oil crises in 1973 and 1979 that had direct knock-on effects on the global economy, leading to oil shortages, increased prices of various goods and services and to recession and economic stagnation. This new global instability and economic volatility undercut Keynesianism as a principal government policy and presented opportunities for other economic approaches.

The leading alternative to Keynesianism was neo-classical economics and particularly the Chicago School, the representatives of which challenged the traditional Keynesian arguments and emphasised the value of monetarism and self-interest. Leading Chicago School economists such as Milton Friedman and Gary Becker argued that private actors, and not the state, are the main generators of economic growth. For the neo-classicists, sound economic policy involves enabling unconstrained market conditions where the rules of supply and demand would determine the economic outcomes. Unlike Keynesians who argue that the market economy has to be managed by the government in order to mitigate against deep recessions and high inflation, neo-classicists see the market alone as the principal generator of economic prosperity. Neo-classical economics became highly influential in the late 1970s, 1980s and 1990s. The new conservative governments in the United States under Reagan, and in the UK, under Thatcher, embraced the recommendations inspired by neo-classical economics and embarked on new economic policies centred on tax cuts, monetarisation, privatisation of public assets and reduction of some state apparatuses. These policies were gradually developed into a relatively coherent economic, political and ideological project now often referred to as neoliberalism. The end of the Cold War created a much larger space for the proliferation of neo-classical economic models, while the globalisation of the world economy allowed big private corporations to move their base in the search for a cheaper labour force. Further, conventional economies grounded in cycles of production and consumption were gradually supplemented and in some instances even replaced by speculative financial activities. Hence between 1980 and 2008 financial services accounted for a substantial part of the national income for many countries. In this environment debt-to-equity ratios experienced an unprecedented increase, thus changing the character of the world economy. In this social context Coleman's key ideas about instrumental rationality, self-interest and utility maximisation all reflected the dominant zeitgeist. It is no accident that Coleman worked in the same university that was the cradle of neo-classical economics – Chicago.

Utilitarianism in France

In direct contrast to Coleman and Homans, who worked in a society that has always been sympathetic towards utilitarian and individualist epistemologies, Boudon developed his theories in a very different social milieu. The French public in the 1970s and 1980s was anything but supportive of neoliberal individualism. The French political establishment was always much more statist and centralists as such inclined towards Keynesian economic policies: while the political left was always deeply hostile to *laissez-faire* economics the political right was also protective of the French state apparatus and its role in governing the country. Hence advocating a neo-classicist economic policy in France was not popular in the late twentieth century. The civil society and the strong and vibrant trade unions were also averse to introducing what they would often refer to as 'the Anglo-Saxon economic models' and 'Anglo-Saxon educational philosophies' (Chabal, 2013). It is only more recently that the French political establishment has become open to neoliberal drives in the economy. Furthermore, French intellectuals were even more ill-disposed towards instrumentalist understandings of social life. From the classics of social thought including Rousseau, Comte and Durkheim to the more contemporary thinkers such as Althusser, Bourdieu and Wacquant, French sociology was much more in tune with the collectivist/holist epistemologies where the focus was not on self-interest of individual agents, but on structural and cultural explanations of social reality. Thus, Boudon's methodological individualism emerged as a minority position within French academia. In contrast to the United States where many academics embraced ideas of neo-classical economics, French intellectuals largely showed hostility or a lack of enthusiasm for this position. In addition, while in the United States and UK the governments under Reagan and Thatcher wholeheartedly embraced the neo-classical economic recommendations, the French government under socialist president François Mitterrand, who ruled between 1981 and 1995, showed a more ambivalent inclination towards the neoliberal agenda. Hence Boudon's ideas received much less attention than those of his American utilitarian contemporaries. Nevertheless, Boudon was still involved in public debates and attempted to articulate an alternative political and sociological interpretation that resonated with some audiences within French society and the academic community.

Arguments and Ideas

There is no doubt that social exchange theory and rational choice theory share some central epistemological propositions. For one thing they both subscribe to methodological individualism – the view that the causal relationships between social phenomena require the analysis of actions of individual agents. In other words, for methodological individualists accurate explanations are only possible if 'couched wholly in terms of facts about individuals' (Lukes, 1973: 110). For another thing, the rational choice approach within sociology has largely developed out of social exchange theory and as such it maintained many of its key tenets. Nevertheless, there are also some pronounced differences between the two perspectives. Let us explore these similarities and differences in more detail.

Social Exchange Theory

From very early on in his career George Homans was preoccupied with the idea of making social science methodologically and theoretically compatible with the natural sciences. Even his first substantive publication, *English Villagers of the Thirteenth Century* (1941), which nominally provides a historical analysis of the population in the English medieval countryside, was in fact a quantitative study focused on establishing statistical correlations between different settlement patterns and field systems among the villagers. His study indicated that the open field system was strongly linked with specific village settlement patterns including the inheritance structure privileging the eldest sons. This early work fostered further interest in group dynamics and in 1950 Homans published *The Human Group*, which provides the contours of what will later become social exchange theory. This book represented an attempt to move away from the dominant macro-structural-functionalist interpretations towards more micro-level explanations of social phenomena. More specifically, Homans argued that the social system is not to be equated with a specific group but instead a variety of different groups. Hence, rather than assuming that the entire society shares certain social attributes, it is paramount to explore small-scale group dynamics. Focusing on micro-level interaction, Homans found that the frequency of interaction between individuals strengthened their attachment to each other.

Furthermore, the study also indicated that equality in social rank fosters greater interaction between individuals, whereas unequal social ranking does the opposite. The book was deeply influenced by Lawrence Joseph Henderson's idea of a conceptual scheme which distinguishes between different concepts (i.e. variables) and establishes relationships between these concepts. In this context Homans differentiates between three levels of analysis: (1) the level of social events; (2) the level of customs; and (3) the relationships and processes through which customs are changed or preserved. The book also introduces concepts such as exchange and reinforcement which would be developed later in his other works and would loom large in the social exchange approach.

The foundations of Homas's social exchange theory were laid down in several influential articles and books including *Social Behavior as Exchange* (1958) and *Social Behavior: Its Elementary Forms* (1961). The guiding idea in these publications was the notion that human beings are self-interested creatures who seek to maximise their personal rewards. Since these personal benefits and gratifications are often attained in social interactions the tendency is to seek gratifications through interactions with other individuals. In *Social Behavior* (1961) Homans draws on B. F. Skinner's behaviourism and articulates a psychologistic understanding of social action. In this book Homans articulates a methodologically individualist position which is grounded in the idea that all collective activity can be explained in reference to the behaviour of individual actors. In this sense sociology was conceptualised as a social science that is closer to economics and psychology than to anthropology, political science or history. He conceived sociology as a discipline applying principles of behavioural psychology and micro economics to specific social situations. For Homans any sociological theory entails a deductive system of reasoning where explanations are based on the empirical testing of hypotheses framed in terms of individual behaviour. This positivist epistemology was rooted in the idea that sociologists operate in the same explanatory realm as economists and psychologists.

Social exchange theory is grounded in the simple idea that most social relations are based on instrumental motives involving exchange and reciprocity. Human relations involve the process of negotiated exchange of tangible or intangible entities and activities that result in rewards and costs. In Homas's (1958: 606) own words:

> Social behavior is an exchange of goods, material goods, but also non-material ones, such as the symbols of approval or prestige. Persons that give much to others try to get much from them, and persons that get much from others are under pressure to give much to them. This process of influence tends to work out at equilibrium to a balance in the exchanges.

Hence, for Homans, social behaviour is a form of exchange involving multiple modes of social interaction where individual agents tend to behave according to their instrumental preferences and in this process generate complex networks of interaction. Nevertheless, Homans emphasises that instrumental behaviour does not necessarily relate to material advantages, but in fact is more oriented towards symbolic attainments where social approval and status enhancement are seen as the ultimate social rewards. For Homans most social relationships involve interdependence, where individuals exchange goods, services, support and social approval between each other.

There are five central propositions that underpin social exchange theory: (1) when individuals find that their previous actions have been rewarded they aim to repeat such behaviour (the success proposition); (2) the stimulus which has been rewarded in the past is likely to trigger a similar response and will be repeated in the present (the stimulus proposition); (3) the actions which are regarded as valuable to the actor are likely to be repeated by that actor (the value proposition); (4) the rewards received in the past determine present-day actions in the sense that the more often one receives a specific reward, the more the value of any further such reward diminishes (the deprivation–satiation proposition); and (5) the actors that receive more than they expect, or do not experience anticipated penalties or punishments, are likely to be satisfied and behave in an approving way (Homans, 1961).

Although Homans developed an approach that emphasises individual behaviour, much of his work focuses on understanding and explaining the dynamics of macro-structural realities. In other words, his principal aim was to identify the micro foundations of social exchange as it operates in large formal institutions. In this context, he argues that profit maximisation is an insufficient motive for explaining the full complexity of social relations. Rather than focusing on one's private gain at the expense of others, most human beings seek a normative balance between awards and costs. For if this were not the case people would not limit their quest for social acceptance by high normative costs that affect their personal integrity. To explain this wider social dynamic of group behaviour Homans articulates a theory of distributive justice. The key notion underpinning distributive justice is reciprocity: 'a man in an exchange relation with another will expect that the rewards of each man will be proportional to his investments – the greater the investments, the greater the profit' (Homans, 1961: 75). By this Homans means that the participants in the relationships of social exchange operate according the shared normative universe where individuals evaluate the equity of human interactions. Hence, although individuals are utility maximisers their actions are also determined by the wider world of shared norms, conformity with the rules, the group produced and upheld status networks and other structural variables. This shared moral universe allows for public acceptance of the hierarchical distribution of material resources and social esteem. For example, bricklayers generally accept lower financial renumeration and lower social status than brain surgeons as they understand their relationships in terms of distributive justice – the latter group is associated with bearing higher responsibility costs than that of the former group.

Homans also finds that the formal institutions generate new layers of complexity where the patterns of exchange and reciprocity become blurred and multifaceted. For one thing, large social organisations involve the indirect allocation of rewards and punishments. For example, factory workers do not receive their salaries from their direct supervisors but from the company's financial officials, the bank clerks or the individuals responsible for the computerised transactions of salaries. For another thing, formal organisations include what Homans calls 'generalised reinforcements' which also foster indirect relationships. For example, the companies offer standardised systems of rewards and punishments – money and pay increases vs. pay deductions, suspensions and loss of job. These standardised reinforcements are also applicable for use in a variety of other contexts which further impact on the complexity of social relationships.

Social exchange theory recognises the significance and complexity of social structures, but it ultimately postulates that all such complexities can be explained through the analysis of individual behaviours. In this context Homans accepts that he is a psychological reductionist who sees sociology as a 'derivate of psychology at least in the sense that social phenomena require for their explanation psychological propositions' (Homans, 1974: 81). This methodologically individualist mode of analysis is also applied by Homans to the study of key sociological processes including power and social stratification. For Homans, power stands for the mismatch in individual rewards:

> when the total reward of a person A, associated with taking action which rewards the person B is lower – at least in B's perception – than the total reward of B linked to the performance of action, which rewards A, and as a result B alters his/her behaviour in a way advantageous to A, then A exercises power over B. (1974: 83)

In a similar vein he understands social stratification through the prism of subjective perceptions of individuals. Rather than exploring the structural causes of status hierarchies and group inequalities, Homans argues that stratification is rooted in perceptual differentiations (1974: 307). He is highly critical of Marxist theories of class conflict, arguing that the idea of expropriation of surplus value is just a speculation based on one's perception: 'when someone says that one group exploits another', this means only that one does not accept 'the way in which the rewards are distributed between these two groups' (1974: 251).

Rational Choice Theory

Rational choice theory (RCT) developed in part from the social exchange model. While exchange theory was still influenced by some traditional understandings of social structure, RCT emerged as an attempt to break from all aspects of what theorists of RCT termed 'methodological collectivism'. In other words, while Homans was still hopeful of developing a synthetic approach which combines methodological individualism with some conventional sociological explanations, the rational choice theorists such as James Colman, Raymond Boudon, Jon Elster or John Goldthorpe were adamant that such a synthesis is neither possible nor productive in explanatory terms. Instead, they advanced an approach which is deliberately reductionist and as such understood as the most promising model to explain human behaviour.

One of the foundational propositions of the rational choice approach is that human beings are primarily rational and self-interested creatures who are motivated by a similar and fairly consistent set of preferences. As Hechter (1995: 296) argues: 'it can be expected that everyone will prefer more wealth, power and honour to less, because attaining these goods often makes it easier for individuals to attain other (perhaps more idiosyncratic) goals'. RCT scholars insist that the behaviour of most individuals can be explained by reference to their attempt to maximise their advantages in order to gain more material and symbolic resources. There is some recognition that when individuals make their rational and instrumental choices, they are restricted by their previous experiences, dominant social norms and the availability of adequate information necessary to make the most rational choices. In other words, this approach conceives of human beings as *homo economici*, utility maximisers who engage in collective action only when it is profitable to do so. Hence, for RCT sociologists successful social action is only possible when and if individual agents perceive such a joint enterprise as mutually beneficial for all involved.

James Coleman (1990) argues that all social behaviour has individualist underpinnings. He sees human beings as individuals who possess stable and rational preferences which can be recognised and linked to specific values and who as such act independently on the basis of available and relevant information. In his view this applies equally to individual action and collective behaviour: while individuals are motivated by utility maximisation, collective agents such as private corporations or states aim to maximise profits or revenue. Although individual agents can sometimes work against their own self-interest (i.e. when the poor and unemployed vote for political parties that cut welfare provisions and reduce taxes for the wealthy), this too can be explained through the well-established RCT categories. For Coleman this situation involves an individual's conscious and initially instrumentally driven 'transfer of control'.

This transfer, where an individual grants authority to another individual, can ultimately lead towards a hierarchical relationship or a subordination of some individuals by others. This new situation, which other sociologists would refer to as 'social structure', is for Coleman still a product of individual rational decisions, although the complexity of choices made might result in a social reality which does not necessarily reflect the original choices made by the subordinated individuals. Hence, for Coleman social structures are still generated through the actions of individuals who originally were motivated by what they perceived to be rational decisions. In Coleman's (1990: 292) view, even social norms have an instrumentalist basis as they represent an individual's decision to give up some 'rights of control over one's own action and the receiving of partial rights of control over the actions of others'. In this context norms stem from one's self-interest as they are 'initiated and maintained by some people who see benefits resulting from the observation of norms and harm stemming from the violation of these norms'.

This utilitarian model of social action is fully developed in Coleman's most ambitious book, *Foundations of Social Theory* (1990). One of the main aims of this work was to recast sociological theory through the prism of a rational choice approach. Hence, in contrast to functionalism and other structural perspectives, which explain social action through shared normative universes or structural inequalities, Coleman frames sociology as a discipline centred on individual behaviour. Hence the book utilises RCT to explain a variety of structural and collective phenomena – from trade unions and private corporations to revolutions and state formation. This work also explores tensions between different social institutions and family networks and offers a set of causal mechanisms that are open for the quantitative testing of his general theory.

One of the most influential ideas from this book, also developed in several previously published articles, is Coleman's theory of social capital. Although this idea was articulated by other theorists, including Pierre Bourdieu and Robert D. Putnam, Coleman's notion of social capital differs substantially from the more structuralist theories of Bourdieu and Putnam. For Coleman social capital stands for resources that one can acquire within family networks or in specific social organisations. He differentiates between three principal forms of capital: (1) human capital – involving one's knowledge, skills and experience, which determine one's value in a specific society; (2) physical capital – including tangible private goods and resources that originate from the creation of tools necessary for production; and (3) social capital, which relates to anything that can foster individual and collective action, including extended networks of relationships built around an enhanced sense of trust, shared social norms and the established mechanisms of reciprocity (Coleman, 1988: 98).

Coleman finds social and human capital as often operating synchronically – the possession of requisite knowledge, skills and experiences makes it possible for individuals to attain higher social status and also to receive more social capital. However, this is not an automatic process and many highly skilled individuals never attain substantial social and physical capital. Hence, the key question here is how one's capital can be successfully translated into other capitals. In particular Coleman was interested in explaining when and how individual skills, knowledge and embeddedness in social networks can be utilised to achieve 'micro–macro transitions'; that is, to expand one's influence beyond family networks to wider social organisations.

The theory of social capital emphasises the rational choices of individuals. Since he conceives of social relations as being predominantly instrumental, they are grounded in reciprocity. This is most visible in the exchange of favours, which Coleman calls 'credit slips'. By agreeing to do a favour one gives a credit slip to that person, expecting that a favour will be returned in service or goods. However, the credit slip system can only exist in relatively stable social environments with high levels of trust and under conditions where one's favour can be fully reciprocated.

Coleman (1990) argues that the investment in physical and human capital is less risky than investing in social capital – buying a property or acquiring a university degree brings more certainty of potential success, while investing in social capital may not materialise in any concrete instrumental benefit. Nevertheless, such investments might also bring a greater payoff in the long term, as social capital could offer a prolonged benefit. For example, the well-established networks of college friends might eventually dominate the economic, political and cultural life of a particular city, which would open many doors and provide many economic and social opportunities for the members of the network.

While Coleman's approach is firmly grounded in the utilitarian tradition of American social science, Raymond Boudon offers a broader theoretical model that is influenced by a variety of classical European social thinkers – from Simmel, Durkheim and Tocqueville, to Scheler and Aron. Nevertheless, much of Boudon's work was inspired by a distinct, materialist interpretation of Weber's work. Boudon challenges the traditional, mostly Parsonian, interpretations that cast Weber as an idealist, a neo-Kantian, a sociologist who prioritises values, beliefs and ideas over the materiality of social relations. For Boudon, Weber is first and foremost a methodological individualist whose most influential explanations centre on identifying the rational choices made by individual agents. In this context, Boudon develops a distinct, neo-Weberian model of RCT that aims to explain social phenomena through the prism of individual actions and beliefs. Although Boudon shares with Coleman and Homans the view that sound sociological analysis can only start from individual rationality, he nevertheless operates with a wider concept of rationality than the one employed by Coleman and Homans. For Boudon instrumental rationality associated with one's self-interest is not enough to capture analytically the complexity of human motivation and behaviour. Hence Boudon (1989) identifies two other types of rational action: axiological rationality and cognitive rationality.

Axiological rationality resembles in part Weber's idea of value rational action where individual action is less motivated by utilitarian goals (i.e. more wealth, power or honour) but by specific values. Simply put, axiological rationality stands for one's own 'good reasons' for pursuing a particular course of action which might be driven by religious belief, strong ideological commitment or sense of responsibility towards others. However, Boudon does not subscribe to the view that ideological beliefs are driven by non-economic or irrational motives such as 'fanaticism'. Instead, he argues that all such beliefs have strong rational and material underpinnings. For him, such beliefs are rational, but mostly based on false claims. Moreover, he argues that in the modern world all such belief systems utilise the discourse and power of science: 'all ideologies, major and minor, right-wing and left-wing, Marxism, Third Worldism, Liberalism and development theory, are based on the authority of science' (Boudon, 1989: 67). He recognises that ideological doctrines often make emotional appeals, and as such, can influence the behaviour of those who are susceptible to such appeals. Nevertheless, it is the individuals who make conscious decisions to follow a particular doctrine, and the key prescriptive and descriptive propositions of such doctrines remain open to rational analysis. A good example of axiological rationality is the paradox of voting in democratic systems: narrow instrumental logic cannot explain why anyone should take part in elections as a single vote makes no difference, yet most people take part in the election process because they share a belief in the democratic process.

In addition to instrumental and axiological rationality, individuals can also be motivated by cognitive rationality. This concept stands for the situational causes of action which for uninformed outsiders might seem to involve an irrational course of action. For example, believing that a shaman's chants can heal individuals or that ritualistic dances can bring rain are typical examples of situational, cognitive rationality. The individuals involved in these actions do not act irrationally but rely on the best available information to make rational decisions. The same applies to a change of beliefs: people gradually accept different belief systems once they find new interpretations situationally plausible and capable of explaining more events. Boudon (2010: 18) uses the example of the flat earth theory to make this point. It becomes:

> cognitively rational to endorse a given explanation of a phenomenon, if the explanation is made of acceptable and mutually compatible statements and if the competing available theories are weaker in one way or another ... [in this context] the theory that the earth is round explains more convincingly a number of phenomena than the theory that the earth is flat.

Boudon's much wider theory of rationality provides a challenge to conventional rational choice approaches. However, he understood his contribution not as a critique of utilitarian tradition, but as an analytical extension of this tradition. His approach is still firmly committed to methodological individualism and the view that collective action is never irrational, but driven by complex networks of individual rationalities.

Contemporary Relevance and Applications

Both social exchange theory and RCT have evolved substantially since the early works of Homans, Coleman and Boudon. The contemporary versions of these approaches have become more formalised and positivist, including stronger grounding in mathematics, logic and game theory modelling. More recently, these approaches have influenced the development of analytical sociology that relies extensively on the use of social simulations, modelling and computational science.

THE PECULIARITY OF NEO-UTILITARIAN SOCIOLOGY

If understanding classical sociology is understood as emerging through various critiques of utilitarianism, then the exchange and rational choice theories are particularly peculiar. Sociology is generally characteriszed by giving society ontological primacy. Yet, these theories are strongly individualistic, showing little concern for actors' preferences or the social sources of such preferences. Although derived from neo-classical economics, these theories curiously emerged within sociology itself. This surprising movement is best understood as a specific rejection of Parsonian structural functionalism. In opposing Parsons's abstract and macro-structural focus, neo-utilitarianism favours an empiricist and micro-individualist paradigm aimed at explaining specified phenomena with predictive and formal rigour. This approach theoretically elaborates defined sociological problems for the purpose of explanatory social research. The result is a seemingly ahistorical and de-political social theory that especially suited the governmental order and policy programmes of the 1990s and early 2000s.

In the works of Peter Blau and Richard Emerson social exchange theory has shifted towards more structured, formal and logic-driven systems. Hence for Blau (1995, 1986), sociology advances through logical deduction: the explanatory power of a theory is determined by its predictive capacity, which is rooted in the quality of its logic. In this context, Blau interprets social life as consisting of self-interested interactions where individuals seek something from interaction and also give something in return. Unlike Homans who focused on immediate psychological motivations, Blau understands exchange as a sociological process that often involves behaviour centred on socially mediated goals.

Hence, human beings not only are focused on the attainment of material or symbolic resources, but also on value-laden social interactions. Nevertheless, according to Blau (1986: 17) such interactions do not have an intrinsic value in themselves but offer a long-term benefit for those involved: 'The tendency to help others is frequently motivated by the expectation that doing so will bring social rewards... A basic reward people seek in their associations is social approval, and selfish disregard for others makes it impossible to obtain this important reward.' Thus, the complex power dynamics that often seem irrational to outsiders can be explained in reference to the long-term interactions of presumed and expected reciprocity.

Just like Blau, Emerson (1976) was interested in articulating a formal explanatory model. He viewed the social exchange model not as a fully fledged sociological theory, but as a simple framework for analysis that offers an economic explanation of non-economic social relations. He also shared Blau's interest in the relationship between social exchange and power but, unlike Blau he conceptualised social exchange through the prism of the reinforcement of rules. He formulated a power–dependence theory which identifies social exchange as pivotal in all power relations. For Emerson, power and dependence were inversely correlated, with the weaker individuals and groups being more dependent on existing relationships, while more powerful individuals were able to detach themselves from such relations. This approach understands power as a dynamic balancing mechanism that continuously shapes exchange relations. Thus, acquiring more power provides an advantage, but using power may lead to its loss, thus shifting the balance between those involved in the social exchange network.

RCT has undergone a similar transformation with the development of highly formalised models of analysis, many of which have lost a visible connection to mainstream sociological theory. Nevertheless, some contemporary rational choice scholars have attempted to bring the key postulates of this approach closer towards the sociological cannon. Hence Jon Elster (2009, 1990, 1986) develops a broader theoretical model that draws on classical Marxism. Although many rational choice models are highly sympathetic to neo-classical economics and public choice theory, Elster is highly critical of such approaches, arguing that their explanatory power is weak. Instead, he articulates a methodologically individualist neo-Marxist approach that centres on the unintended consequences of human action.

This rational-choice Marxism contests the conventional, structuralist, theories that focus on the historical changes in the 'modes of production', 'social formations' and other traditional Marxist concepts, and shifts the emphasis towards the micro economics of social action. More specifically, Elster argues that Marx's work offers a good foundation for explaining the instrumental foundations of individual action. Elster's aim is to dispense with the 'metaphysical' aspects of Marx's work such as his theory of ideology and zoom in on his 'micro-foundations for collective action'. In Elster's (1986: 363) reading, Marx's ideas are highly compatible with game theory models. Marx explores the motives and strategies of individuals as they make choices to join class-based associations: 'workers no less than capitalists might engage in collective action because they find it selfishly rational'.

Other contemporary rational choice theorists have focused more on applying this utilitarian epistemology to specific sociological phenomena ranging from religion, education and the environment, to gender and sexuality. For example, Michael Hechter (1995) and Michael Banton (1997, 2015) question the conventional understandings of ethnicity and race as intrinsically group-centred experiences. Instead, they argue, ethnic identities are no different than other social categories such as class, status, profession or religion, all of which operate according to similar sociological principles. Hence, when individuals compete over resources, power, prestige or any other material or symbolic benefits, they will maximise any advantage they can including their ethnic identities and racial markers. In other words, an individual will enhance his or her cultural or physiological markers to demarcate the boundaries of group membership if such action will lead towards increased benefits for the individual.

For example, a Malay shop owner might discriminate against Chinese customers by refusing to sell them high-quality goods if this will result in an increased number of Malay customers willing to pay more for such goods. The logic of this behaviour is summarised well in Banton's point that 'when people compete as individuals, this tends to dissolve the boundaries that define the groups; when they compete as groups, this reinforces those boundaries' (1997: 208). Other rational choice sociologists have developed sophisticated research techniques that rely on social simulations, modelling and computational science to predict individual and collective behaviour in complex social networks. One of the leading analytical sociologists, Peter Hedström (2005), has developed a social contagion and social mechanisms analysis which maps the spatial diffusion of different collectivities including trade unions, political parties and social movements.

Criticisms

The utilitarian analytical tradition has long historical roots in social and political theory – from Machiavelli and Hobbes, to Mill and Bentham, among many others. This approach has received a great deal of criticism for its reductionist understanding of human action and for its overemphasis of self-interest. Although social exchange and rational choice theories attempt to develop a more grounded theoretical and empirical analysis, they too have experienced a great deal of criticism. Among various criticisms three pronounced weaknesses of this approach stand out: (1) its tautological character; (2) its unidimensional understanding of rationality; and (3) its neglect of culture and politics.

Firstly, the two approaches often offer circular arguments that are guilty of post hoc reasoning. The overemphasis on the rationality of individuals prevents rational choice and social exchange scholars from focusing on other sources of action as they 'conceive of their task as demonstrating the fact that social practices which are prima facie irrational are actually rational after all' (Baert, 1998: 166). The focus shifts from explanation towards persuading others that the majority of individual and social behaviour is rational even when it seems not to be so. These tautologically framed arguments are for the most part not falsifiable, and as such, do not offer much explanatory power (Malešević, 2004: 104).

Secondly, the concept of rationality deployed by this research tradition is often defined in very vague and wide terms whereby any type of activity is deemed ultimately to be rational and intentional. Boudon goes even further and broadens the concept of rationality to include almost any form of social activity such as cultural values or political motives. However, as Hindess (1988) and Dex (1985) argue, the assumption of an individual's rationality is not the same as rational motivation for action. Assuming that people have consistent preferences and behaviour does not tell us much about the substance of their beliefs. Furthermore, rationality is not a fixed trait but something that changes, with some individuals shifting their motivations from rational to emotional, habitual or inertial. The attempt to stretch the notion of rationality to account for most forms of action makes this concept too wide and thus reduces further its explanatory potential. If everything is ultimately rational then what is the point of any sociological analysis?

Thirdly, the two approaches overemphasise the economic factors, thus leaving little room for the autonomy of politics and culture. The choices individuals make and the social exchanges they are part of are never culture-free. There is a wealth of empirical studies pointing out that the different cultural milieus impact profoundly on human preferences and as such not all individuals are driven by the same motives. In some cultural contexts self-interest maximisation is shunned or even despised, while in other societies the emphasis is given to co-operation over competition and self-fulfilment is attained through non-instrumental goals (Lehtinen and Kuorikoski, 2007). For example, anthropologists have identified numerous traditional societies where European competitive sports such as soccer or cricket were introduced but adjusted to accommodate the existing, non-competitive, values.

It is no historical accident that social exchange and rational choice theories have proliferated and gained in popularity in the late 1970s, 1980s and 1990s when the Keynesian economic models were gradually overtaken by the neoclassical economic policies in the United States, UK and then in many other parts of the world. James Coleman taught at the University of Chicago where the architects of neoliberal economics, the Chicago School of Economics, were the dominant thinkers: Milton Friedman, George Stigler, Gary Becker, Robert Fogel, Thomas Sowell and Robert Lucas among others. These neoliberal economists became highly influential advocates of free market economies, reducing public expenditure and the role of the state in economy, deregulation, privatisation of public assets and properties, and promotion of entrepreneurial ethics in social life. There is no doubt that their ideas have influenced Coleman and other rational choice and social exchange sociologists. This is particularly visible in Coleman's public activities, where he gradually embraced the neoliberal model of education.

In the 1960s James Coleman and his collaborators were commissioned by the US Office of Education to undertake a study on educational inequalities in US schools. In 1966 'the Coleman report' was published, concluding that the pronounced differences in the exam scores across ethnic and racial groups were largely determined by the economic and educational attainment of their parents. This report influenced government policies on school education in the late 1960s and early 1970s, leading to the introduction of integrated school busing systems. The aim here was to bring together the pupils from different socio-economic and cultural backgrounds in order to reduce social divides.

However, while initially focusing on the socio-economic status as a cause of inequalities, Coleman changed his views over the years to focus more on individual and collective self-interest. Hence, in 1975, he produced another policy report dealing with the integrated school busing systems. This report offered a very different conclusion, arguing that integrated busing and other such policies contributed to the deterioration of public schools because the more prosperous, mostly white, students avoided integration by moving to other neighbourhoods (i.e. 'white flight'). In 1981 Coleman published another research report on education policy where he made the case that private and

Catholic schools that emphasise discipline and centre on individual performance provide superior educational environments to public schools. This gradual shift from a public-centred educational policy towards the advocacy of private education reflects Coleman's theoretical transformation over the years towards a more rational choice understanding of social life. Hence just as his theoretical contributions received a great deal of criticism so did his education policy recommendations. Throughout the late 1970s and early 1980s many members of the American Sociological Association expressed strong criticism of the various Coleman reports and recommendations. Some ASA members even started initiatives to revoke his membership of this professional association.

Conclusion

Although the utilitarian tradition of social thought goes all the way back to Niccolò Machiavelli, Thomas Hobbes, Adam Smith and Jeremy Bentham, among many others, it is only in the twentieth century that sociologists have articulated the distinct and sophisticated explanatory models that centre on the individual rationality of human beings. George Homans, James Coleman and Raymond Boudon developed highly influential sociological theories that prioritise the instrumentality of individual action and understand social behaviour through the prism of co-ordinated self-interests. This chapter outlined the main ideas of this utilitarian analytical approach, traced its intellectual and historical development, and identified the key criticisms of this perspective.

References

Amadeo, K. (2019) US GDP by Year Compared to Recessions and Events: The Strange Ups and Downs of the US Economy Since 1929. *The Balance*, 8 June [online]. Available at: https://www.thebalance.com/us-gdp-by-year-3305543 (accessed 16 June 2019).
Baert, P. (1998) *Social Theory in the Twentieth Century*. Cambridge: Polity.
Banton, M. (1997) *Ethnic and Racial Consciousness*, 2nd edition. London: Longman.
Banton, M. (2015) *What We Now Know About Race and Ethnicity*. New York: Berghahn Books.
Blau, P. (1986) *Exchange and Power in Social Life*, 2nd edition. New York: Routledge.
Blau, P. (1995) A Circuitous Path to Macrostructural Theory. *Annual Review of Sociology*, 21, pp. 1–19.
Boudon, R. (1989) *The Analysis of Ideology*. Cambridge: Polity.
Boudon, R. (2010) The cognitive approach to morality. In: S. Hitlin and S. Vaisey (eds) *Handbook of the Sociology of Morality*. New York: Springer, pp. 15–34.

Chabal, E. (2013) The Rise of the Anglo-Saxon: French Perceptions of the Anglo-American World in the Long Twentieth Century. *French Politics, Culture & Society*, 31(1), pp. 24-46.

Coleman, J. (1988) Social Capital in the Creation of Human Capital. *American Journal of Sociology*, 94, pp. 95-120.

Coleman, J. (1990) *Foundations of Social Theory*. Cambridge, MA: Belknap Press of Harvard University Press.

Dex, S. (1985) The Use of Economists' Models in Sociology. *Ethnic and Racial Studies*, 8(4), pp. 516-33.

Elster, J. (1986) *Rational Choice*. Washington Square, NY: New York University Press.

Elster, J. (1990) *Nuts and Bolts for the Social Sciences*. Cambridge: Cambridge University Press.

Elster, J. (2009) *Reason and Rationality*. Princeton, NJ: Princeton University Press.

Emerson, R.M. (1976) Social Exchange Theory. *Annual Review of Sociology*, 2, pp. 335-362.

Hechter, M. (1995) Explaining Nationalist Violence. *Nations and Nationalism*, 1(1), pp. 53-68.

Hedström, P. (2005) *Dissecting the Social: On the Principles of Analytical Sociology*. Cambridge: Cambridge University Press.

Hindess, B. (1988) *Choice, Rationality and Social Theory*. London: Unwin Hyman.

Homans, G. C. (1960 [1941]) *English Villagers of the Thirteenth Century*. New York: Russell & Russell.

Homans, G. C. (1988 [1950]) *The Human Group*. London: Routledge.

Homans, G. C. (1958) Social Behavior as Exchange. *American Journal of Sociology*, 63(6), pp. 597-606.

Homans, G. C. (1961) *Social Behavior: Its Elementary Forms*. New York: Harcourt, Brace & World.

Homans, G. C. (1974) *Social Behavior: Its Elementary Forms*. Revised edition. New York: Harcourt Brace Jovanovich.

Homans, G. C. (1984) *Coming to My Senses: The Autobiography of a Sociologist*. New Brunswick, NJ: Transaction Books.

Homans, G. C. and Curtis, C. P. (1970 [1934]) *An Introduction to Pareto: His Sociology*. New York: Howard Fertig.

Lehtinen, A. and Kuorikoski, J. (2007) Unrealistic Assumptions in Rational Choice Theory. *Philosophy of the Social Sciences*, 37(2), pp. 115-38.

Lukes, S. (1973) *Individualism*. New York: Harper & Row.

Malešević, S. (2004) *The Sociology of Ethnicity*. London: Sage.

Lévi-Strauss, Barthes and Butler

Introduction

Structuralism and post-structuralism are not just analytical approaches but have also been associated with the specific intellectual movements that originated in France and then spread throughout the world. The two schools are also deeply linked in a sense that post-structuralism grew out of the structuralist movement and gradually developed as the antithesis of structuralism. In many instances this metamorphosis took place within the work of the same authors. Hence the early work of Roland Barthes and Michel Foucault was characterised by structuralist interpretations while their later contributions shifted towards a pronounced post-structuralism. Although both structuralism and post-structuralism developed mostly outside sociology, the two approaches had significant impact on sociological thought, and many structuralist and post-structuralist ideas and concepts are discernible in the work of leading sociologists – from Bourdieu and Giddens, to Bauman, Laclau, Mouffe and Hall, among others.

In this chapter we review the main representatives of structuralism and post-structuralism. We first explore their intellectual development and the wider historical context and then elaborate their main contributions. The last two sections explore briefly the contemporary relevance of their work and the main criticisms of the structuralist and post-structuralist positions.

Life and Intellectual Context

Claude Lévi-Strauss

Lévi-Strauss was born in in 1908 in Brussels. He grew up in Paris in a family of artists and he regularly attended exhibitions, opera, museums and other artistic events. Lévi-Strauss received good primary and secondary education in Paris where he attended the Lycée Janson de Sailly and the Lycée Condorcet. In 1927, he enrolled to study law and philosophy at the Sorbonne but soon decided to drop law and focus only on philosophy, which he graduated from in 1931. Upon graduation Lévi-Strauss worked briefly as a secondary school teacher together with Jean-Paul Sartre and Simone de Beauvoir in the Lycée Janson de Sailly. During this period Lévi-Strauss became interested in ethnology, a discipline he discovered by reading Robert Lowie's *Primitive Society* (1920).

In 1934, he took up an offer to join the French cultural mission to Brazil where he also applied for the visiting sociology professorship at the University of São Paulo. From 1935 to 1939 he conducted ethnographic studies in the Amazon rainforest and Mato Grosso. He undertook two expeditions with the indigenous populations including the Guaycuru, Bororo, Nambikwara and Tupi-Kawahib societies. This Brazilian experience was a defining moment in Lévi-Strauss's intellectual development as it shaped his long-term preoccupation with key anthropological themes such as the structure of kinship, incest, taboo and myths. With the start of the war Lévi-Strauss returned to France and was drafted as a liaison agent to the Maginot Line. With the capitulation of France in 1940 he worked briefly at the *lycée* in Montpellier but was soon dismissed, and as a Jew, was also stripped of his French citizenship.

He escaped from France by taking a boat to Martinique, and from there he travelled to the United States where he was offered a post, together with other émigré Jewish intellectuals, at the newly created New School for Social Research in New York. From 1946 to 1947 Lévi-Strauss worked as a cultural attaché at the French Embassy in Washington, DC. He returned to Paris in 1948 where he completed his PhD thesis and his habilitation on the basis of his ethnographic work in Brazil. In the 1950s, he published a number of influential studies and was appointed professor at the École Pratique des Hautes Études. With the publication of his Brazilian trip memoir *Tristes Tropiques* in 1955, which instantly became a bestseller, he was soon regarded as France's leading public intellectual. In 1959 Lévi-Strauss was appointed to the prestigious chair in social anthropology at the Collège de France, and in 1973 he was elected to the Academie française. Lévi-Strauss lived a very long life and died in 2009, aged 100.

Roland Barthes

Roland Barthes was born in Cherbourg, France, in 1915. His navel lieutenant father died during the First World War and Roland was raised by his mother. They moved to Paris in 1926 where he attended the Lyceée Montaigne and Lyceée Louis-le-Grand. His mother worked as a bookbinder to put young Roland through school. As an exemplary student Barthes was accepted to the Sorbonne where he earned a degree in classical literature and philology in 1939. He also studied French literature and Greek tragedy. He soon embarked on his PhD studies at the Sorbonne but due to his pulmonary tuberculosis had to spend a substantial time isolated in a sanatorium. His ill health interrupted his studies on several occasions, including periods between 1934–5 and 1942–6.

Due to his illness he was exempt from the military service during the war. During the occupation of France, Barthes produced his first publications, received an MA in 1941 and established a theatrical group, Groupe de Theatre Antique. After the war he struggled to obtain a proper academic position and held short-term teaching contracts at various institutions in France, Egypt and Romania. During this period, he wrote numerous newspaper articles for the leftist Parisian magazine *Combat*. These articles were later collected in his first book *Writing Degree Zero* (1984 [1953]). Through the 1950s he worked for two state institutions – from 1950 to 1952 as Direction Générale des Affaires Culturelles, and from 1952 to 1959 as a researcher at the Centre National de la Recherche Scientifique. At this latter institution, he had the opportunity to engage in extensive sociological research and wrote extensively about popular culture.

His short contributions were initially published in the magazine *Les Lettres Nouvelles* and were later collected in the book *Mythologies* (1993 [1957]). In the same year he briefly taught at Middlebury College in Vermont. In 1960 he was appointed a director of studies at the École Pratique des Hautes Études and occupied this post until 1976. He was also Directeur d'études in the Sociology of Signs, Symbols and Representations until 1976 when he was elected to a Chair of Literary Semiology at the College de France. He was very close to his mother with whom he lived for 60 years until her death in 1977. Roland Barthes died only three years later, in 1980 after being running over by a van.

Judith Pamela Butler

Butler was born in Cleveland, Ohio, in 1956. Her parents, a dentist father and a fair housing advocate mother, were practising religious Jews of Hungarian and Russian ancestry. Her childhood in Cleveland was shaped in part by regular attendance at the local synagogue and Hebrew school, where she enjoyed classes in Jewish ethics. In these ethics tutorials, she was exposed to the works of Immanuel Kant, Baruch Spinoza, Georg W. F. Hegel and Martin Buber. It seems that this early exposure to ethical questions in theology led her towards a strong interest in philosophy. She started her undergraduate studies at Bennington College, a private liberal arts college in Vermont, United States, and then moved on to Yale University, where she received a BA degree in 1978, and then proceeded towards an MA (1982) and PhD (1984). Her PhD thesis was later published as *Subjects of Desire: Hegelian Reflections in Twentieth-Century France* (1987). She also held a Fulbright scholarship at Heidelberg University in Germany (1979).

Much of her graduate and postgraduate work was focused on philosophical themes including phenomenology, German idealism and Frankfurt School sociology. She taught at several universities including Wesleyan University, George Washington University and Johns Hopkins University. In 1993 she joined the University of California, Berkeley where she was appointed Maxine

Elliot Professor of Rhetoric and Comparative Literature in 1998. In 2002, she held the Spinoza Chair of Philosophy at the University of Amsterdam. Since 2006, she has held a Hannah Arendt Professorship of Philosophy at the European Graduate School in Saas-Fee, Switzerland. In addition to being a highly prolific academic, Butler is also a public intellectual who regularly comments on various political and social issues – from feminism, gay and lesbian rights to anti-war movements, affirmative action and social inequalities. She has also been a vocal critic of Israel's treatment of the Palestinian population and has supported the sanction campaigns against Israel. She also served as chair of the International Gay and Lesbian Human Rights Commission board.

Historical, Social and Political Context

Post-war France

Both structuralism and post-structuralism are intellectual approaches that initially developed in France and then spread throughout the world. In the aftermath of the most devastating war ever fought on this planet, World War Two, many intellectuals started to question the Enlightenment paradigm that was rooted in the assumption of humanity's linear progress from a barbaric and violent past towards a reasoned and peaceful future. The mass slaughter of civilians, the deliberate policies of extermination of entire populations, culminating in the Holocaust and genocides of other groups, the use of atomic bombs and carpet bombing to destroy whole cities – all shattered traditional understandings of social change.

In addition, France's early capitulation in 1940, together with the liberation largely undertaken by US and UK forces, generated a sense of national humiliation that affected the public mood. Although there was relief and happiness that the war ended, the manner in which it ended on French soil raised some profound soul searching among French intellectuals and the wider social strata. France in the late 1940s and early 1950s was a society struggling with the issues of war defeat, the Vichy regime's collaboration with the Nazis, the pronounced political and social divides, and the loss of the French overseas empire. In this environment, when much of the traditional political and military establishment was discredited either through the defeat to Nazi Germany, or even more so, through the Vichy government's collaboration, only two political forces retained a degree of popular support – Charles de Gaulle's republican movement, and the communists.

Both of these political groupings spearheaded French resistance against Nazi rule and as such were supported by various sections of French society. De Gaulle's sovereignist movement attracted centrist and right-wing groups while the communists attracted support from left-wing intellectuals, workers and the poorer sectors of society. The French Fourth Republic (1946–58) experienced rapid industrial development and an economic boom, helped in great part by the Marshall Plan (1948–51), through which France received around

$4.9 billion in financial aid from the United States, including $2.3 billion with no repayment. The post-war era saw the rebuilding of infrastructure, agriculture and industry. Nevertheless, the Fourth Republic was beset by political instability with very frequent changes in government – between 1946 and 1958 France had no less than 21 different governments. One of the key unresolved issues that affected this permanent political instability was the legacy of colonialism that led towards two protracted wars: the First Indo-China War (1946–54) and the Algerian War (1954–62), both of which brought about the collapse of the Fourth Republic and the establishment of the Fifth Republic under de Gaulle.

These two wars polarised public opinion, with the traditional conservative forces supporting the war, and the leftist movements spearheaded by communists, opposing the overseas fighting. Although the Communist Party of France (PCF) was initially involved in the governing coalitions between 1944 and 1947, it was politically isolated until 1956, and with the establishment of the Fifth Republic, it split among different factions including the Stalinists, the Maoists and the reformists. However, the Stalinist faction remained dominant and largely sided with the 1956 Soviet invasion of Hungary, and never condemned the 1968 Soviet crushing of the Prague Spring. This hard-line approach caused a great deal of disillusionment among left-wing intellectuals, many of whom left the PCF in this period.

However, the political instability, coupled with deep social polarisation, gave birth to vibrant intellectual debates. The disastrous legacy of the Second World War, together with the ongoing wars in Algeria and Indo-China, contributed towards rather pessimistic philosophies. Hence, the dominant intellectual approaches were sceptical about the human potential for creating a better world. Among these, French existentialism, as articulated by Sartre, de Beauvoir and Camus, gained influence and shaped many early debates. These rather pessimist interpretations of social reality, focusing on the inherent paradoxes that underpin human existence and the permanent fear of inevitable death, emphasised the absurd character of human life.

The existentialists interpreted human existence through the ideas of never-ending existential angst and despair within the individual that follow in the wake of one's realisation that life has no ultimate meaning. Although existentialism was largely a philosophical movement, it lacked an explanatory dimension that would help make sense of the wider social changes. Hence, structuralist ideas emerged as an explanatory challenge to existentialism. In other words, while the generation of the 1940s and 1950s was preoccupied with the meaninglessness of life in the wake of the destruction during the war, the new intellectual movements of the 1960s, shifted the focus towards universalist explanations of social relations.

Furthermore, while existentialism emphasised individual autonomy, authenticity and free will, structuralism downplayed these features and centred its analytical gaze on identifying the structural determinants of human behaviour. While some structuralists combined Marxist ideas with structural analysis, others understood the structuralist method as being at odds with Marxist revolutionary politics. The immediate intellectual origins of structuralism can be traced to two different traditions of linguistics scholarship – the early work of Swiss semiotician Ferdinand de Saussure and the Prague School of structural linguistics led by Roman Jakobson. De Saussure introduced an influential distinction between language and speech that he referred to as *langue* (an idealised abstraction of language) and *parole* (language as actually used in everyday life through speech). This distinction allowed him to argue that a 'sign' consists of a 'signifier' (the sound and/or visual image) and a 'signified' (an abstract idea). Roman Jakobson built on de Saussure's work and created a field of linguistic typology that classifies languages on the basis of their structural and functional features in order to identify their common properties. In particular, Jakobson focused on specifying linguistic universals that occur systematically across different languages throughout the world (i.e. nouns and verbs, consonants and vowels, etc.). Both Lévi-Straus and Barthes were deeply influenced by these ideas and have developed them further in order to understand the wider social dynamics.

Student Uprisings

The 1960s were a turbulent period in French history, culminating in the May 1968 massive general strikes, and student uprisings, and ending with the death of de Gaulle in 1970. The failure of May 1968 was also a period when disillusioned intellectuals started questioning the established ideological paradigms and moved gradually away from the dominant explanatory models of social change including existentialism, Marxism and structuralism. France in the 1970s and 1980s also experienced economic decline. Initially, France was deeply affected by the 1973 world oil crisis and in 1979 had experienced another national oil crisis, both of which contributed towards the erosion of living standards and increased the unemployment rate. The election of a socialist leader François Mitterrand in 1981 raised hopes for substantive social change. The new government was initially successful in introducing some social reforms, including liberalisation of the media, reform of the inheritance tax and establishing a solidarity tax on wealth, the abolition of the death penalty and the liberalisation of laws dealing with sexuality.

However, as France soon encountered another economic recession coupled with high inflation, much of the government's economic programme remained unfulfilled. Instead of tackling social inequalities the government soon shifted its focus to more neoliberally inclined fiscal and spending restraints. This environment of instability fostered further social polarisation and gave birth to new social movements bent on dismantling the hegemony of the Gaullist and Communist Parties. These new social movements drew on the novel intellectual ideas that challenged the established approaches as articulated by Marxism, existentialism and structuralism among others. The new paradigms were hostile towards the universalist ambitions of the traditional approaches. Hence instead of privileging the proletariat as in Marxism or deep social structures as in structuralism, the new approaches centred on the deconstruction of existing explanatory narratives. So post-Marxists challenged conventional Marxism, post-modernists attacked the modernist visions of social order and the post-structuralists objected to the determinist understandings of social reality that they associated with structuralist explanations. In some instances the same authors, such as Foucault and Barthes, questioned their own youthful ambitions and moved away from structuralism to post-structuralism.

The new post-structuralist ideas also resonated outside of France, and most of all, in the United States. In the 1970s and early 1980s the United States experienced some of the same social problems that affected France – rising social inequalities, deep recessions, runaway inflation, the long-term effects of the 1970s oil crisis, and a rising financial deficit and unemployment. The election of Ronald Reagan led to fiscal restraint in many areas, except for the military and police funding, and also adversely affected the more impoverished strata. However, unlike France, the United States was the world's leading superpower and had invested heavily in the arms race with the Soviet Union, which intensified during the early 1980s. Reagan's administration also focused on the privatisation of the economy and set the foundations for the neoliberal policies that were to dominate the world economy for the next several decades. This new environment undermined the traditional ways of life and also gave birth to new social movements, and new intellectual developments, including identity politics and post-structuralist feminism associated with the work of Judith Butler and others.

Arguments and Ideas

None of the main representatives of structuralism and post-structuralism is nominally a sociologist: Lévi-Strauss was an anthropologist; Barthes was a literary scholar and semiologist; while Butler is a philosopher. However, all three of them, together with Foucault, have had an enormous influence on sociological theory and their ideas still shape the contemporary debates within sociology.

Kinship Structures

Several of Lévi-Strauss's key ideas had a profound impact on sociological theory. His first major book *The Elementary Structures of Kinship* (1949) was conceived as a response to Durkheim's *The Elementary Forms of the Religious Life* and both books were focused on identifying the pristine forms of social organisation. More specifically, in his book Lévi-Strauss questions the conventional understandings which tie kinship to shared belief in common ancestors. Instead, for Lévi-Strauss, kinship was first and foremost an expression of an alliance between two families forged through the exchange of women through marriage.

He conceptualised kinship as a system that is not connected to the conscious acts of specific individuals but was continuously reproduced through existing structural frameworks. In this context, Lévi-Strauss attempted to explain the nearly universal incest taboo not as a biological or psychological phenomenon, but as a structural regularity rooted in the rules of social exchange. In his view, the incest taboo makes culture possible as it replaces natural inclinations with social regulations: 'The first logical end of the incest prohibition is "to freeze" women within the family, so that their distribution, or the competition for them, is within the group, and under group and not private control' (Lévi-Strauss, 1977 [1949]: 45). This interpretation of incest taboo leads Lévi-Strauss to the conclusion that both Émile Durkheim and Marcel Mauss were mistaken in their belief that symbols are products of the social order and as such can be explained through the analysis of social relations.

Instead, Lévi-Strauss insists that social order rests on symbols and what is required is not the analysis of the social origin of symbols, but the analysis of the symbolic origin of society. Simply put, Lévi-Strauss argues that all social actions are symbolic as social order and human societies cannot exist without symbolism: 'No social phenomenon may be explained, and the existence of culture itself is unintelligible, if symbolism is not set up as an a priori requirement of sociological thought' (1963: 517–18). In this understanding symbolism stands for the rule-governed social order that makes up a system. For Lévi-Strauss culture is nothing more than a combination of different symbolic systems that individuals live and reproduce unconsciously. The key guiding principle of structuralism is that meaning is generated and reproduced within a culture through systems of signification. Social order does not exist independently from the symbolic realm, but emerges and operates through foundational beliefs and symbolic practices. For example, both the presence of a particular religious belief and one's geographical location shape the social life of a particular group. However, a religion differs from a mountain range as the former is a thing and the latter is an artefact, a social institution. Hence, while the mountain range does not require human signification to exist, religion entails shared beliefs and practices that make it real and meaningful.

Mythologies

Throughout 1950s, 1960s and 1970s Lévi-Strauss published several influential studies that fully articulated his structuralist model of analysis. The most important among these publications was his four-volume masterpiece *Mythologiques* (*The Raw and the Cooked*, 1964; *From Honey to Ashes*, 1966; *The Origin of Table Manners*, 1968; and *The Naked Man*, 1971). In *Mythologiques* Lévi-Strauss explores the structure of myths and narratives of Native Americans from Alaska to Patagonia. Although there is a wide repertoire of stories and characters that appear in these myths, what Lévi-Strauss finds remarkable is how homologous these narratives are. Despite the nominal diversity, most myths share a very similar, if not identical, narrative structure.

For Lévi-Strauss, this indicates that the human mind operates in a very similar way, and that all societies have to rely on the same categorical apparatus to make sense of the world they live in. In his view, myths express a pristine form of the human mind – they contain the mental building blocks which appear before a human becomes a conceptual being. He argues that mythical structures develop and operate outside of human consciousness. The myths are transmitted from generation to generation and no individual is aware of how they are constructed and reproduced. In his view, myths represent a fundamental category of the human mind. They utilise fixed dichotomies and oppositions, such as raw vs. cooked, fresh vs. rotten, moist vs. parched, in order to generate conceptual tools for abstract thinking that combines these dichotomies into specific propositions.

Mythologiques explores over 800 particular myths taken from different Native American tribes across North and South America. Drawing on de Saussure's structural linguistics, Lévi-Strauss emphasises the centrality of binary oppositions and also how they help structure everyday social life. For example, the raw vs. cooked dichotomy represents a distinction between nature and culture, and as such is central to many foundational myths among the Native Americans. The function of mythic thought is to reduce complex and unpredictable reality to a set of mutually exclusive binary codes that help build meaningful narratives which make sense of the existing social order. Hence, despite their nominal diversity, most myths contain similar structural properties which are rooted in structural logic and as such are independent of specific historical conditions. His analysis focuses on the elementary units of myth – mytheme. To identify these mythemes, he dissected different versions of a specific myth and analysed the micro-structure of each sentence that composes the myth narrative. It is here that he noticed that the myth structure is rooted in binary oppositions.

However, Lévi-Strauss is adamant that myths and universal binary logic do not override the materiality of human life. Instead, since myths originate in the human brain they can also evaporate as specific human cultures disappear: 'myths signify the mind that evolves them by making use of the world which it is itself a part' (Lévi-Strauss, 1986: 341). Furthermore, he sees language structures as resembling myth structures in the sense that they both operate outside of human consciousness and survive independently of individual human will. Echoing Wittgenstein's point that there is no such thing as a private language, Lévi-Strauss emphasises how we are all born into a world that already contains a well-elaborated language and mythical structures which we reproduce during our lives and leave to other generations on our deaths.

In 1962, Lévi-Strauss published *La Pensée Sauvage (The Savage Mind)* which became a major success. The book offered a new, structuralist theory of culture and also opened a wider debate on the relevance of cultural diversity in the modern world. The notion of 'savage mind' stands for Lévi-Strauss's idea that the human mind is untamed thought which continuously develops and deploys structures to make sense of the wider world. To illustrate this power of 'savage thought' he differentiates between the engineer and the bricoleur: while the engineer deploys specific tools and materials to create a predesigned product, the bricoleur has many skills and constructs things from whatever is available.

Hence, for Lévi-Strauss the human mind operates as a bricoleur by putting together what is at hand in new ways, and thus generating new things. This book also gives an initial insight into Lévi-Strauss's understanding of cultural difference, another theme that appears in many of his later works. In his view diversity is a precondition for social development, since cultures emerge and advance through interaction and conflict with other worlds. For Lévi-Strauss, progress entails mutual exchanges with other cultures and isolated societies cannot make major cultural advancements. In a series of later essays and books, he emphasises the centrality of cultural diversity. In this context, he invoked the notion of the 'technique of estrangement' which allows a scholar to distance him- or herself from their own time and space by 'putting their own culture in perspective' and 'by confronting contemporary concepts with those of other times and other places' (Lévi-Strauss, 1977: 272).

Nevertheless, this is not to say that cultural interactions are easy, smooth or tolerant. On the contrary, Lévi-Strauss was well aware that genuine cultural difference involves disagreements and conflicts as complete understanding is likely to undermine cultural difference eventually. Thus, for Lévi-Strauss cultural diversity is a precondition for human creativity and even though the human mind is capable, like a bricoleur, of building from what is at hand, the abundance of cultural resources makes for a better bricolage.

Signs and Images

Just like Lévi-Strauss, Roland Barthes was influenced by Durkheim, Jakobson and de Saussure. Barthes's early ideas were also shaped by his reading of Lévi-Strauss's work and especially his theory of myth. By the late 1950s Barthes, Lévi-Strauss, Foucault and Lacan were considered the leading representatives of the French structuralist tradition. However, by the mid- to late 1960s only Lévi-Strauss remained a structuralist, while the other three scholars developed distinct post-structuralist perspectives. The early Barthes, heavily influenced by de Saussure, utilised linguistic theories to analyse how signs and symbols contribute to the reproduction of social order. One of his early books, *Writing Degree Zero* (1984 [1953]), provided a critique of the established canons of literary criticism and conventional understandings of the author's role in the writing process. He argues that all writing has a strong structural logic involving conventions that shape style and language.

What makes writing creative is the writer's use of form, that is the individual choices made to manipulate conventions of style. However, the form can also become conventional once it enters the public domain. For Barthes, this indicates that creativity entails continuous change and reaction that would navigate away from the ever-present structural determinism that is inherent in the language. Much of Barthes' early work focused on what he called myths, that is second-order cultural representations, that were reproduced in the everyday signs, images and objects. His essays collected in *Mythologies* (1993 [1957]) dissect a variety of cultural products such as advertising messages, political imagery, food products and magazine photographs in order to show the latent massages that such images impart.

For example, his analysis of the *Paris Match* front cover with the young black soldier saluting and wearing a French uniform represented a colonial myth. For Barthes this photograph conveyed the ideological message that France was a great colonial power capable of assimilating culturally diverse worlds: 'France is a great empire, that all her sons, without any colour discrimination, faithfully serve under her flag' (Barthes, 1993 [1957]: 116). In his view, these myths help reproduce the status quo and also manipulate the public into believing that the French imperial project is not experiencing a deep crisis of legitimacy.

In the early 1960s, Barthes published several books which elaborated and illustrated the key ideas behind his distinct structuralist approach. In *Elements of Semiology* (1963) he linked Durkheim's notion of collective conscience with language and speech. In the book, he differentiates between 'denotation' as a primary form of signification, and 'connotation' as secondary signification, which is the focus of his analysis: the signs, signifiers and signified that all compose the denoted system. For Barthes, it is this level of secondary signification that really matters as it produces myths that help sustain and reproduce the existing power structures. He argues that myths operate effectively through the unconscious meanings that images and texts convey.

Barthes was also influenced by the Marxist notion of ideology as a form of manipulation and this is particularly visible in his other early book – *The Fashion System* (1985 [1967]). This book focuses on how fashion reflects and reproduces the dominant bourgeois ideals of beauty, elegance and success. More specifically Barthes shows how particular and arbitrary ideas of attractiveness are naturalised and accepted as universal truths. For example, if the fashion establishment declares a particular item of clothing to be valuable and suitable for particular occasions, the mass media reinforce this message to a wider audience, who then turn this arbitrary bourgeois choice into an unquestioned reality of the latest fashion, which is then manufactured on a mass scale and sold to that audience.

Post-structuralism and Text

In 1970s Barthes published several books which marked his post-structuralist phase: *S/Z* (1970), *Empire of Signs* (1983 [1970]), *Sade, Fourier, Loyola* (1971), *The Pleasure of the Text* (1975), *A Lover's Discourse* (1978) and *Camera Lucida: Reflections on Photography* (1980). These books shift the focus from people towards texts. While the previous structuralist works were preoccupied with identifying the latent truths behind the manifest images and representations, the new publications centre on interpreting texts in their own terms. In this view, historical reality is not to be understood as a set of fixed events but as an ever-changing narrative – history itself is the word that has no ultimate meaning. For Barthes, writing history represents an attempt to codify in a system something that is utterly contingent and rich with multiple meanings in order to generate a uniform 'truth'.

However, the conventional writing of history imposes order and 'truth' on what is a disorderly world of different signs, meanings and symbols. Thus, his new books focus less on what is represented in the texts or why some representations dominate others, but rather on how the texts can be read and interpreted in so many different ways. For example, in *Sade, Fourier, Loyola* (1971) he explores three different texts and treats them as three distinct languages that allow for different interpretations. He also analyses the different modes of reception and evaluation of these texts.

More specifically, Barthes makes a distinction between a 'writerly' (scriptable) text that the reader can rewrite or wishes to write, and a 'readerly' (lisible) text that can only be read. This focus on textuality is further developed in *The Pleasure of the Text* where he draws on Lacanian psychoanalysis to explore the relationship between desire, pleasure and texts. The book deploys the Lacanian idea of *jouissance* and links the experience of reading and writing with enjoyment and lack of enjoyment. Barthes' frequent travels to Japan resulted in another post-structuralist work, *Empire of Signs*, in which he questioned the structuralist premise that one can write a history from a singular, scientific and objective point of view. By deploying his semiotic method Barthes attempted to dissect and deconstruct the established narratives of Japanese cultural history. He argues that the authority of history in the West rests on the specific logic that in ancient Greece stood for the metaphysical logos. In his view it is this logos that predetermines a particular historical narrative, and by relying on scientific discourses, it in fact reproduces yet another mystical interpretation of the past.

Hence, the aim of post-structuralist analysis is not to explain the world but to deconstruct its universalist ambitions by pinpointing the particularist origins and ambitions of different interpretations. This attack on the singularity of truth and meaning is fully articulated in Barthes' highly influential 'The Death of the Author' (1977). In this essay he questions the authority of an author and the view that literary products should be judged and defined by ultimate meanings and explanations imparted by an author. Instead, Barthes argues that meanings are never fixed, and that the author's will always remains unknown, which suggests that there are no 'knowable texts'. Hence by attributing to a literary creation an ultimate set of meanings, one makes it only consumable and as such an object of specific market value.

Performing Gender

The post-structuralist approach, as developed by Barthes, Foucault and Lacan among others, had a lasting influence in the United States. However, while the French post-structuralists were preoccupied with critiquing the legacies of structuralism and other universalist approaches, American post-structuralists, such as Judith Butler, focused their attention on more specific issues such as gender and sexuality, religion, race and ethnicity, war and capitalism. Much of Butler's early work deals with the constitution of gender. In 1988 she published an influential essay 'Performative Act and Gender Constitution', which provides the contours of her theory of gender performativity. This essay, together with the 1990 book *Gender Trouble: Feminism and the Subversion of Identity*, questioned the established views of gender and provided a new interpretation that emphasised the plasticity and performativity of gender identities.

Drawing on de Beauvoir and Merleau-Ponty, Mead and Husserl, she argues that gender has a strong theatrical quality in the sense that it is a lived experience which has to be performed. Unlike sex, which is a biological fact, gender involves a cultural interpretation or signification of that biological experience: 'gender is in no way a stable identity or locus of agency from which various acts proceed; rather it is an identity tenuously constituted in time – an identity instituted through the stylised repetition of acts' (Butler, 1988: 519). In this sense, gender requires a particular scripting and an audience which will engage with the gender performance. The conventional inability to distinguish between sex and gender stems from the fact that particular gender scripts have been transmitted from generation to generation, and as such have become internalised as established truths.

Hence what seems to be a natural gender binary is in fact something that is rooted in the performative repetition of individual and collective acts that one identifies with female or male. For Butler one's body acquires specific gender attributes through 'a series of acts which are renewed, revised and consolidated through time' (1988: 520). In this interpretation gender is not a given quality but something that is created and sustained through the performance of gender. The theory of gender performativity is further developed in *Gender Trouble* (1990), a book deeply influenced by Foucault, Lacan, Kristeva and other French post-structuralists. The book's key argument is that both sex and gender are culturally constructed through the repetition of stylised body acts in time. Although the categories of sex and gender seem natural, stable and fixed, they are in fact sustained by performative acts. Drawing on Foucault, Butler argues that such performative acts are rarely voluntary and should be analysed through the existing disciplinary regimes that normalise particular forms of sexuality and proscribe other modes of gender performance as deviant. Butler insists that these 'frameworks of intelligibility' coerce individuals to embrace particular stylised body acts in order to sustain the established gender binary, although it is these coercive disciplinary discourses that create these 'core' performative gender roles in the first place. In this context, Butler contends that feminist critique, which does not recognise that gender roles are coercively created through disciplinary discourses where heterosexuality is posited as the naturalised norm, is unlikely to succeed in challenging patriarchy. Furthermore, she is critical of traditional feminist ideas that were centred on protecting 'women' as a separate and disadvantageous group. In her view such a perspective reinforces the traditional gender binary. Instead, her ambition is to dissect traditional gender narratives and deconstruct and de-centre gender roles so that sex, gender and sexuality are presented not as given essences but as free, malleable and plastic forms of one's experience.

In the 1990s Butler published several books that developed her performative theory further, while applying the key insights to different set of issues, including the free speech and censorship debate, the formation of the subject, and the body. In *Bodies that Matter: On the Discursive Limits of 'Sex'* (1993), she links performativity to the continuous repetition of regularised norms. She points out that performing gender and other social roles stems in part from the iterability which she attributes not to individual agents but to structural contexts:

> this repetition is not performed by a subject; this repetition is what enables a subject and constitutes the temporal condition for the subject. This iterability implies that 'performance' is not a singular 'act' or event, but a ritualized production, a ritual reiterated under and through constraint, under and through the force of prohibition and taboo, with the threat of ostracism and even death controlling and compelling the shape of the production. (Butler, 1993: 95)

In *Excitable Speech: A Politics of the Performative* (1997) she questions the dominant liberal and conservative understandings of free speech. Drawing on Foucault, Derrida and Lacan she argues that hate speech cannot be removed from social life through simple censorship campaigns. For Butler hate speech is a product of state power – a particular discourse becomes 'hate speech' only when the state authorities declare it to be such. This implies that the state maintains power to limit acceptable discourses. Nevertheless, the attempt to censor speech ultimately propagates that very speech as it inevitably reproduces the language it seeks to ban and police. For example, the government in Victorian England was obsessed with controlling the sexual discourse and in that respect introduced a variety of policing and censorship measures. However, these measures had the opposite effect as they intensified the presence of sexual discourses in everyday life. For Butler, censorship is integral to language as linguistic competence developed through the control of speech.

Butler's more recent work focuses on contemporary political issues including war and violence, grief and mourning, ethnicity, religion and inequalities. In *Precarious Life: The Powers of Mourning and Violence* (2004) she criticises US military adventures in Afghanistan and Iraq and explores how a sense of post-9/11 vulnerability and lack of control has generated a violent conflict where the world's most powerful military chases an invisible enemy and where symbolic attack is answered with never-ending wars on terror. For Butler this situation of insecurity and vulnerability was also a 'dislocation from the first world privilege', which as such 'offers a chance to start to imagine a world in which that violence might be minimised, in which an inevitable interdependence becomes acknowledged as the basis for the global political community' (Butler, 2004: xii). The notion of inherent vulnerability is also tackled in her *Frames of War: When is Life Grievable?* (2009) where she analyses the mass media's depiction of Western armed conflicts. The central issue is the asymmetrical representation of human suffering where certain lives are implicitly or explicitly seen as more or less worthy of grief. The American mass media tend to focus on the relevance of troop deployments and questions of military security and as such frame the lives of Afghani or Iraqi civilians as less valuable. This raises the question of how precarious human lives are in general. Butler argues that all human lives involve mutual precarity and as such require recognition of their precariousness. The role of the media is highlighted in framing precariousness as they differentiate 'the cries we can hear from those we cannot, the sights we can see from those we cannot, and likewise at the level of touch and even smell' (Butler, 2009: 51).

Contemporary Relevance and Applications

Lévi-Strauss's work on kinship has shaped the ongoing debates within social sciences and given birth to the British neo-structuralist school of anthropology, including Edmund Leach and Rodney Needham. These scholars drew on Lévi-Strauss's research to challenge the dominance of structural functionalism within British anthropology and sociology. They focused on complex kinship systems and developed the structuralist idea further by demonstrating how generalised exchange systems involve not only symbolic but also economic and political dimensions.

For example, in his studies of Kachin kinship systems Leach (1970) shows that the marriage rules vary across societies and that they tend to be shaped by specific political and economic contexts. However, these rules also showed the relevance of structuralism in understanding and explaining wider exchange networks. Lévi-Strauss has also influenced the cognitive sciences, including cognitive psychology and anthropology. He is often referred to as a pioneer of true cognitive anthropology and sociology, as his work provided foundations for the study of mental mechanisms that underpin the structure of the human mind. His work on myths and semiotics has also been utilised within singularity theory. These mathematical models drew in part on Lévi-Strauss's structuralist ideas.

Furthermore, some researchers have developed software that analyses the myth structure of oral history accounts throughout the world to demonstrate the validity of Lévi-Strauss's approach. More recently, computational science scholars have developed simulation models that use Levi-Strauss's structuralist methodology in order to gauge how mythical thought operates (Doja, 2010: 21).

WHAT'S STRUCTURAL ABOUT STRUCTURALISM?

Structuralism is best understood in the context of French sociology, which was largely shaped by the dominance of Émile Durkheim. Describing society as a reality of itself, one that operates over the heads of social actors, Durkheim's theory left little room for individual agency. Structuralism takes this concern for social structures but shifts it to more sharply defined linguistic structures. These reflect fundamental structures of the human mind, which unconsciously shape social action and latently determine the developmental path of society as a whole. By decoding linguistic structures, structuralism hoped to chart the objective system behind human society with the precision of natural science. Post-structuralism came to reject this search for universalistic foundations, but nonetheless carried forward the concern for language and cultural forms.

Roland Barthes' work has also influenced different fields of research and especially cultural studies, social theory, literature, the sociology of culture and advertising, communication studies, photography, semiotics and anthropology. For example, his short and memorable analyses of modern cultural phenomena provided the foundation for cultural studies and anticipated the emergence of the critical cultural theory of Stuart Hall and the Birmingham School.

His short essays from *Mythologies* (1993 [1957]) such as 'The World of Wrestling', 'The Face of Garbo' or 'Soap-powders and Detergents' offer a sociologically informed critical analysis of everyday social life. For example, in his analyses he shows that professional wrestling is not about winning or losing but represents a staged spectacle where actors/wrestlers stereotypically portray human weaknesses (i.e. the cheater, the traitor, the greedy weakling) and are theatrically punished with a view of enhancing the belief in the myth of justice. This path-breaking model of analysis has influenced the sociology of everyday life from Henri Lefebvre to the ethnomethodology of Harold Garfinkel.

Barthes' post-structuralist ideas had a profound impact on the rise of postmodern philosophy and literary criticism. In particular his essay 'Death of the Author' (1977), which challenged traditional understandings and argued that the authors and their written products are not necessarily connected, contributed towards the deconstructionist turn in social science and humanities. His post-structuralist ideas influenced the French and American deconstructivists including Jacques Derrida, Julia Kristeva, Paul de Man and Barbara Johnston. Derrida even wrote an ironic essay as a homage to Barthes' famous essay – 'The Deaths of Roland Barthes'. Kristeva developed the post-structural deconstructivism further and introduced the notion of 'intertextuality', which stands for the idea that texts are related and share similar meanings in the sense that meanings are context dependent and both the readers and authors create their own meanings from the existing texts.

Unlike Lévi-Strauss and Barthes, whose influence was mostly confined to academia, Butler's work has reached much wider audiences and had an impact not only on political philosophy, sociology, literary and cultural studies, and queer theory, but also on third-wave feminist and anti-capitalist movements as well as gay, lesbian and transgender activism. Butler does not shy away from everyday politics and has been involved in a variety of protests and movements ranging from gay and lesbian rights, anti-war activism, Occupy Wall Street events, to the struggle for Palestinian rights and anti-racist movements, including more recently support for Black Lives Matter.

Butler's theory of performativity and her work on gender and sexuality have shaped the ongoing debates within academia but have also entered public discourse throughout the world. In particular her work has informed public discussions about gender relations, gay parenting and the rights of transgender individuals. Her academic contributions together with her activism have inspired many marginalised groups to contest the status quo and the unequal treatment of minorities of all kinds. For example, the Russian feminist and anti-capitalist punk rock and performance art collective 'Pussy Riot' have been influenced by Butler's work. As the leading member of the collective, Nadya Tolokonnikova, emphasises:

> Judith Butler was my intellectual mentor when I was studying in the university and exploring different genders. I wasn't in contact with her at that time, but I would catch every moment to get her book while I was in New York, and then I would bring those books to Russia and translate it to my fellow students. (Cauterucci, 2018)

Butler's non-essentialist view of gender, and her post-structuralist insistence that power constitutes subjectivity, have also influenced recent feminist and queer debates within and outside of academia.

Criticisms

Both structuralism and post-structuralism have received a great deal of criticism from different quarters. Lévi-Strauss and the early Barthes have been accused of neglecting the historical specificities of social phenomena and developing rigid, deterministic, interpretations that offer little room for contingency. Many critics, including Habermas (1987) and Giddens (1993), have challenged the ahistorical positivism of the structuralist approach. For Giddens, structuralism offers an overly mechanical understanding which privileges structures and social systems over individual and collective agency and as such cannot explain the historical complexities and arbitrary choices made by powerful individuals.

In a similar vein, Habermas (1987) and Castoriadis (1987) accuse structuralists of ignoring the complex relationships between language, symbolism and the social. Castoriadis insists that Lévi-Strauss reduces all language and symbolic mediation to the simple logic of binary oppositions. Other critics have questioned the epistemological idealism which underpins Lévi-Strauss's structuralist explanations that leave little or no room for power politics or socio-economic factors. For example, Ricoeur deems Lévi-Strauss to be a Kantian 'without a transcendental subject', while Andreski criticised his scholarship that relies more on the metaphorical use of algebraic equations, while making sweeping generalisations that are not corroborated by empirical evidence. More recently feminism and post-colonial scholarship have challenged what they argue to be patriarchal and Eurocentric views that are reflected in some of Lévi-Strauss's work.

For example, Bouchet (2015: 909) argues that Lévi-Strauss's theory of kinship, where men reinforce social arrangements through the exchange of women is overly naturalist: 'It is most likely that there were social reasons for this: women, had to cope with the fact that men had the monopoly of violence.' Although Lévi-Strauss was often seen as the pioneering scholar who defended cultural diversity, some critics believe that he did not go far enough as he provided no critique of the colonial state.

Barthes' structuralism was subjected to a similar type of criticism: as a positivist, ahistorical analysis that lacks interest in the agency and contingency of human action; the formulaic and structurally determinist understanding of social processes; the simplified binary logic of analysis; and so on. However, since Barthes also integrated some Marxist ideas into his analyses, he was criticised less about the lack of economic and political variables in his work. The same applies to issues of gender, as Barthes was much more sensitive to the questions of sexuality and the hegemony of patriarchal images of masculinity and femininity. Nevertheless, some critics identified a similar pattern of Eurocentric views that also characterise some of Lévi-Strauss's works.

For example, Leys (2013) questions Barthes's indifference towards ordinary people during the Cultural Revolution in China. He wrote, and later published, a diary of his trip to China where there is little if any reference to the suffering of individuals under Mao's regime. Some critics also identify strong Eurocentric attitudes in his work on Japan. However, once Barthes moved to his post-structuralist phase, he was critical of his own early contributions: while before the focus was on structural regularities, now his studies emphasised discursive irregularities and contingencies.

Nevertheless, post-structuralism has attracted even more criticism than structuralist analyses. Whereas structuralism was still accepted as offering a legitimate explanatory position, the post-structuralist hostility towards scientific methodology, and science, has been fiercely criticised by many scholars. For example, Taylor (1984), Habermas (1987) and Gellner (1992) see post-structuralism as an approach that is grounded in a deeply relativist epistemology and as such it lacks a firm analytical and normative basis. In other words, if one recognises that all truth claims are provisional and arbitrary, and that all social realities are discursive and epistemologically equivalent, then one cuts the ground from under one's feet. If all truth claims are to be deconstructed why should one value more Barthes' and Butler's analyses over those developed by a person on the street?

Furthermore, post-structuralism has been challenged for its overemphasis on discursive narratives and the downplaying of material realities. For example, Nussbaum (2000) has criticised Butler for neglecting the material aspects of social life. In Nussbaum's view, post-structuralists such as Butler ignore the physical realities of sex and gender and see culture as dominating nature in all forms. In contrast, Nussbaum argues that one cannot ignore biology and the empirical evidence about the complex interplay between nature and nurture. Instead of completely rejecting biology, more comprehensive analyses are bound to integrate the material and cultural aspects of social life. Other critics question Barthes' and Butler's obsession with textual analysis and discursive frames. Bordo (1992) claims that some post-structuralists reduce gender to language and discourse which ultimately leads to the conclusion that gender and other forms of group divisions are completely arbitrary. In other words, in arguing that gender (and other identities) are just an act of performance one loses the sight of the structural inequalities that shape gender and other identities. Fraser has particularly been vocal on these issues, insisting that post-structuralists overemphasise cultural issues and are largely deaf to social and economic inequalities in the world. For Fraser (1998: 149) Butler's culturalism leaves little room for political economy and capitalism, which still structure most social relations. According to Fraser (1998: 144) gender issues and the oppression of homosexuals are forms of status injury rooted in 'misrecognition'; that is, 'the material construction through the institutionalisation of cultural norms of a class of devalued persons who are impeded from participatory parity'. Namaste (2009) has also scrutinised Butler's neglect of issues such as intersectionality and transgender realities.

Finally, post-structuralists have also been criticised for their almost incomprehensible and difficult jargon, a very loose use of key concepts, and for their overreliance on metaphors, wordplay and elitist expressions.

Conclusion

Structuralism and post-structuralism have been highly influential approaches that have shaped intellectual debates over the past 50 years. Although these traditions of thought are firmly identified with French academia, both approaches have had much wider impact and as such have affected intellectual developments throughout the world. While structuralism has lost much of the influence it had in the 1950s, 1960s and 1970s, post-structuralism is still vibrant and influential today. More recently, post-structuralism (and post-modernism) have even appeared in public forums with some right-wing commenters identifying these movements as being responsible for what they see to be a contemporary malaise and the proliferation of identity politics. On the other hand, left-wing groups have also recognised the impact of post-structuralism on social change as it successfully articulated the voices of the marginalised: women, sexual minorities, and the groups affected by ethnic and racial discrimination. These ongoing public debates remain important and continue to shape sociological thought and research.

References

Barthes, R. (1984 [1953]) *Writing Degree Zero: Elements of Semiology*. London: Cape.
Barthes, R. (1993 [1957]) *Mythologies*. London: Vintage.
Barthes, R. (1963) *Elements of Semiology*. New York: Hill and Wang.
Barthes, R. (1974 [1970]) *S/Z: An Essay*. R. Miller, trans. Oxford: Blackwell.
Barthes, R. (1971) *Sade, Fourier, Loyola*. Paris: Éditions du Seuil.
Barthes, R. (1975) *The Pleasure of the Text*. New York: Hill and Wang.
Barthes, R. (1977) The Death of the Author. In: *Image Music Text: Essays*. S. Heath, trans. London: Fontana, pp. 142-8.
Barthes, R. (1978) *A Lover's Discourse: Fragments*. New York: Hill and Wang.
Barthes, R. (1980) *Camera Lucida: Reflections on Photography*. New York: Hill and Wang.
Barthes, R. (1983) *Empire of Signs*. London: Cape.

Barthes, R. (1985) *The Fashion System*. London: Cape.
Bouchet, D. (2015) Levi-Strauss, Claude (1908-2009). In: J. D. Wright (ed.) *International Encyclopædia of the Social & Behavioral Sciences*. New York: Elsevier, pp. 904-10.
Bordo, S. (1992) Postmodern Subjects, Postmodern Bodies. *Feminist Studies*, 18(1), pp. 159-175.
Butler, J. (1987) *Subjects of Desire: Hegelian Reflections in Twentieth-Century France*. New York: Columbia University Press.
Butler, J. (1988) Performative Acts and Gender Constitution: An Essay in Phenomenology and Feminist Theory. *Theatre Journal*, 40(4), pp. 519-31.
Butler, J. (1990) *Gender Trouble: Feminism and the Subversion of Identity*. London: Routledge.
Butler, J. (1993) *Bodies that Matter: On Discursive Limits of 'Sex'*. London: Routledge.
Butler, J. (1997) *Excitable Speech: A Politics of the Performative*. London: Routledge.
Butler, J. (2004) *Precarious Life: The Powers of Mourning and Violence*. London: Verso.
Butler, J. (2009) *Frames of War: When is Life Grievable?* London: Verso.
Cauterucci, C. (2018) "I think Trump could be useful": Pussy Riot's Nadya Tolokonnikova on transgender inclusion, finding hope in dark times, and what Vladimir Putin has in common with Donald Trump. Slate, [online] 25 May. Available at: https://slate.com/news-and-politics/2018/05/pussy-riots-nadezhda-tolokonnikova-on-trans-rights-trump-and-the-activist-messiah-complex.html (accessed 13 June 2019).
Castoriadis, C. (1987 [1975]) *The Imaginary Institution of Society*. Cambridge: Polity.
Doja, A. (2010) Claude Lévi-Strauss (1908-2009): The Apotheosis of Heroic Anthropology. *Anthropology Today*, 26(5), pp. 18-23.
Fraser, N. (1998) Heterosexism, Misrecognition and Capitalism: A Response to Judith Butler. *New Left Review*, 228, pp. 140-9.
Gellner, E. (1992) *Postmodernism, Reason and Religion*. London: Routledge.
Giddens, A. (1993) *New Rules of Sociological Method: A Positive Critique of Interpretative Sociologies*. Stanford, CA: Stanford University Press.
Habermas, J. (1987 [1985]) *The Philosophical Discourse of Modernity: Twelve Lectures*. Cambridge, MA: MIT Press.
Leach, E. (1970) *Claude Lévi-Strauss*. New York. Viking Press.
Lévi-Strauss, C. (1977 [1949]) *The Elementary Structures of Kinship*, 2nd edition. London: Eyre & Spottiswoode.
Lévi-Strauss, C. (1955) *Tristes Tropiques*. Paris: Plon.
Lévi-Strauss, C. (1966 [1962]) *The Savage Mind*. London: Weidenfeld & Nicolson.
Lévi-Strauss, C. (1964) *Mythologiques: Le Cru et le Cuit*. Paris: Plon.
Lévi-Strauss, C. (1966) *Mythologiques: Du Miel Aux Cadres*. Paris: Plon.

Lévi-Strauss, C. (1967) *Structural Anthropology*. New York: Doubleday.
Lévi-Strauss, C. (1968) *Mythologiques: L'Origine des Manières de Table*. Paris: Plon.
Lévi-Strauss, C. (1971) *Mythologiques: L'Homme Nu*. Paris: Plon.
Lévi-Strauss, C. (1986) *The Raw and the Cooked*. Harmondsworth: Penguin.
Leys, S. (2013) *The Hall of Uselessness: Collected Essays*. New York: New York Review of Books.
Lowie, R. (1920) *Primitive Society: Boni and Liveright*. New York.
Namaste, V. (2009) Undoing Theory: The 'Transgender Question' and the Epistemic Violence of Anglo-American Feminist Theory. *Hypatia*, 24(3), pp. 11–32.
Nussbaum, M. (2000) *The Professor of Parody: The Hip Defeatism of Judith Butler. The New Republic*, [online]. Available at: https://newrepublic.com/article/150687/professor-parody (accessed 13 June 2019).
Taylor, C. (1984) Foucault on Freedom and Truth. *Political Theory*, 12(2), pp. 152–83.

Foucault

Foucault entered the French intellectual scene following the publication of *Madness and Civilization* in the 1960s, and since then has become one of the most influential thinkers of the twentieth and twenty-first centuries. He is currently the most cited thinker in the social sciences. Though not strictly speaking a sociologist – the name of the position that he designated himself at the Collège de France was 'Professor in History of Systems of Thought' – his work, nevertheless, has strong sociological themes and resonances. He pioneered an original and penetrating historical method for studying human beings and explaining the ills of modern society which has become used in a diversity of disciplines including psychiatry, cultural studies, anthropology, history, the sociology of knowledge, philosophy, geography and literary studies.

His early work uses a structuralist 'archaeological' method, while his later, more explicitly Nietzschean writings, examine the 'genealogy of power', though there is also a strong continuity in his examination of the strategies, practices and structures of knowledge (*epistemes*) which are imposed upon the social world to know and to control it, especially through scientific establishments and later the state. As he himself argued, his central aim was to 'create a history of the different modes by which, in our culture, human beings are made subjects. My work has dealt with ... modes of objectification which transform human beings into subjects' (Foucault, 1982: 77).

Life and Intellectual Context

Born Paul Michel Foucault on 25th October 1926, in Poitiers, a beautiful but provincial city in France, he was raised in an upper bourgeois family. Both his father and grandfather were named Paul Foucault, but he later changed his name to Michel, stating to friends that he did not want the same name as his father with whom he had a distant relationship. The second of three siblings, Foucault's father was a highly regarded surgeon. A gifted student, Michel's secondary education from 1940 took place in Saint Stanislas, where he was taught by a gifted history teacher, Father de Montsabert, engendering a love of history in him. During this time Poitiers had been occupied by Germans for several weeks, and the city, despite containing members of the resistance, was sympathetic to the pro-German Vichy government of Petain.

In 1945, on leaving what he considered the stifling atmosphere of Poitiers, Foucault moved to Paris for two years to the prestigious Lycée Henri-IV, to prepare for the entrance exams necessary to enter the prestigious École Normale Supérieure (ENS) on the Rue d'Ulm. In his biography, Eribon describes him not only as a young 'provincial' but as 'an unsociable, enigmatic, and withdrawn boy' (1991: 16). It was at the Lycée Henri-IV that Foucault came under the influence of Jean Hyppolite, who taught on Hegel's phenomenology. At the ENS Foucault studied philosophy, graduating with a *licence* in 1948. As a homosexual in France during this period, life was difficult, and, exacerbating this, Foucault was unable to adapt to communal life, constantly arguing with his cohabitants, and even attempting suicide in 1948. It is of some note that both madness and sexuality feature prominently throughout his work, as well as issues concerning death. His unique biography may also partly account for Foucault's fascination not only with groups who were excluded and marginalised in society, but also with writers who discussed transgressing accepted societal norms and values, for example by promoting excess, including Bataille, Blanchot and Klossowski, all of whom he wrote about.

As well as attending lectures at the ENS by Lacan and Althusser, Foucault visited patients at the Hopital Sainte Anne (the institution which he would later refer to in his book *Madness and Civilization*) as part of a course on the introduction to psychopathology. Here, he became acquainted with reformist and progressive currents in psychology and gained a *licence* in that subject in 1949. After passing his *agrégation* exam, Foucault began teaching psychology at the ENS between 1951 and 1955. During this period, he also secured a position as an assistant in psychology at the University of Lille in 1952, where he taught psychology and history. He published his first work, *Mental Illness and Psychology* in 1954 (1987 [1954]), criticising the work of psychoanalysis and the communist-backed psychiatrist Pavlov from a Heideggerian/Marxist perspective. This was followed by an essay 'Dream, Imagination and Existence', which featured as a preface to the book by the existentialist phenomenological psychiatrist and analyst, Ludwig Binswanger, entitled *Dream and Existence* (1985 [1954]). In August 1955 Foucault left France to become director of the Maison de France in Uppsala in Sweden, a position he secured for three years. Here he taught and carried out various administrative, managerial and official functions tied to promoting French culture and thought. He also began writing *Madness and Civilization*. Following an increased teaching workload and a feeling of dissatisfaction with the country, he left the post in 1958.

Working Abroad

In 1958 Foucault moved to Warsaw as director for the Centre for French Civilisation, with the aid of Georges Dumezil. Responsible for organising cultural events, he taught on contemporary French theatre and philosophy. However, he was forced to leave the country, possibly because of homosexual relations with a young man who may have been an informant for the police (Eribon, 1991: 89). He then became director of the French Institute in Hamburg in Germany, with similar duties to those he had in Poland. Here he completed his doctorate in 1961 on madness, supervised by Jean Hyppolite (an enormous thesis over 800 pages long), and began his secondary thesis on Kant's anthropology. The doctorate, subsequently published as *Madness and Civilization* (1961), earned him a major reputation and secured a professorship in philosophy at the University of Clermont-Ferand in 1962. It was here that he met his partner Daniel Defert, with whom he lived until his death. He followed *Madness and Civilization* with a new book, *The Birth of the Clinic* (1963), and a work on the literary theorist and novelist Raymond Roussel, an obscure and marginalised literary figure, which he considered as his most personal work. In 1966 he published his next major book, which drew heavily on structuralist thinking, *The Order of Things*. Criticising both Marxism and humanism the book, although a dense tome, became a bestseller. In the same year, with the help of Georges Canguillem, Foucault moved to Tunis to take up a post as Chair of Philosophy, living in Sidi Bou Said. Here he began, but abandoned, a book on Manet and wrote *The Archaeology of Knowledge* (1972 [1969]).

Foucault returned to France and helped establish the Department of Philosophy at the newly founded University of Vincennes. His experience during these turbulent political times was not a pleasant one, though he left Vincennes after two years as an engaged and militant academic. In 1970 at the age of 43, and with a reputation as a major public intellectual, he gained a chair in the most prestigious academic institution in France, the *Collège de France*. He remained there until his death. His inaugural lecture, signalling a break and a new political underpinning to his work, was entitled 'The order of discourse', subsequently published as 'The Language of Discourse'. At the College his tasks included giving regular public lectures. He lectured on various topics including: 'The will to know' (1970–1), 'The punitive society' (1971–2), 'Society must be defended' (1975–6), 'Security, territory, and population' (1977–8), 'The birth of biopolitics' (1978–9), 'On the government of the living' (1979–80) and 'The hermeneutics of the self' (1981–2).

Political Engagements

During the early 1970s Foucault became a public intellectual and began to participate in various demonstrations and campaigns aiding immigrants and prisoners. He also contributed to the founding of a left newspaper *Liberation*. In the spring of 1975, he was invited to Berkeley where he became a regular speaker and a visiting professor in 1981. Fond of the freedom he experienced in New York and San Francisco, he later stated that he felt 'at home' in the homosexual scene and neighbourhoods in the United States. In 1975 he published what is arguably his most important if not best-known work, *Discipline and Punish* (1977 [1975]). This was followed by the first volume of *The History of Sexuality* (1990 [1976]), another popular book but one generally given a cool reception by critics.

After agreeing to write journalistic pieces for the newspaper *Corriere della sera* Foucault travelled to Iran in 1978–7, amid a volatile political situation. His articles, which were generally in favour of the religious opposition leader, Ayatollah Ruhollah Khomeini, meant he was heavily criticised following Khomeini's accession to power in February 1979 and the bloody acts of repression that Khomeini effected. In 1980, Foucault joined the struggle of the banned Polish trade union Solidarity, supporting Lech Walesa. In 1984 what are labelled volumes 2 and 3 of the *History of Sexuality* – *The Uses of Pleasure* (2006 [1984]) and *The Care of the Self* (1988 [1984]) – were published. After fainting in his apartment, he was admitted to the Salpetriere Hospital on 9 June 1984. Following several months of complaints of flu-like symptoms and major headaches, he passed away shortly afterwards on 25 June 1984, at the age of 57 from what was diagnosed as AIDS.

In France, philosophy has held a pre-eminent place in the nation's intellectual culture since at least the nineteenth century, but especially after the Second World War. Both preceding and following the war, the philosophy of three major thinkers became highly influential: Hegel, Husserl and Heidegger (Descombes, 1980). Hegelianism was established as a dominant philosophy by Alexander Kojève who came to teach at the École Pratique des Hautes Études. But an interest in Hegel's work was also expressed in the writings of Henri Lefebvre, Jean Wahl and Jean Hyppolite, who later came to supervise Foucault, and was a major influence on his thinking. This Hegelianism became combined with an increasing interest in France in Husserl and his phenomenological approach, and its extension in the work of Heidegger. These thinkers formed the platform from which the work of the most influential post-war philosopher, Jean-Paul Sartre, and his existentialist phenomenology derived. Foucault was initially heavily influenced by phenomenology and especially the work of Heidegger and Freudian psychoanalysis, manifest in his writings on the German existential analyst Ludwig Binswanger. However, there were also counter-currents to this phenomenological way of thinking. The work of the historian of science Georges Canguilhem, and Georges Dumezil, a specialist in Indo-European mythology, focused respectively on the importance of philosophical concepts for thinking in science and on recurring structures which underlay myths. The structuralism of Lévi-Strauss also became increasingly influential in the 1950s. By the mid-1960s nearly all the cultural, philosophical and social scientific journals and intellectual reviews were referring to structuralism which came increasingly into vogue, with the work of Althusser and Lacan. Structuralism sought to replace the primacy of lived or reflected consciousness with the primacy of the concept, system or structure and talked about 'the death of man'. It had a huge impact on Foucault's thinking, though he later refused the label. As well as phenomenology and structuralism his work also became heavily imbued by the writings of Nietzsche in which the pursuit of truth was seen as an human expression of the will to power.

Historical, Social and Political Context

Since at least the Dreyfus affair – in which both Zola and Durkheim intervened – there has been an ongoing and integral connection between French intellectuals and political processes (Gutting, 2005). Following the Second World War a huge resurgence of Marxism took place. The French Communist Party (PCF) had played a major role in the French resistance and subsequently acquired a high moral and symbolic standing, supported by about 25% of the electorate at the time. The major intellectual force to emerge in France following the war was Jean-Paul Sartre. Though Sartre was on the left, he never joined the PCF, preferring to remain outside its repressive party structure, which was seen as intimately linked to Stalinist dogmatism and a mechanical and orthodox form of Marxism. It was in reaction to the Sartrean intellectual landscape that Foucault's thought and political position developed. Sartre's philosophy had been attacked not only from the right – by Heidegger for example – but also from the left in the work of structuralists such as Lévi-Strauss and Louis Althusser.

Marx and Nietzsche

At the ENS and under the influence of Althusser, Foucault joined the Communist Party in 1950, but his relation to Marxism remained ambiguous throughout his life. During the early 1950s and following the war in Indo-China, Foucault was to describe himself as a 'Nietzschean communist'. But he left the PCF following Stalin's arrest of a number of Jewish doctors in 1953. Such antipathy to Marxism increased following the publication of the Khrushchev Report in 1956, which condemned the 'personality cult of Stalin' and, further, following the suppression of the Hungarian uprising by Soviet troops in the same year. Two years previously, the French had begun a violent war in Algeria, and in 1958 the French government voted to implement special powers to facilitate pacification of Algeria. The PCF broadly supported this policy, leading to large numbers of intellectuals leaving the party. Such political turmoil was in turn exacerbated by the election in 1958 of a centre–right government under General de Gaulle, heavily supported by French Algerians, advocating an increasingly bellicose imperial policy. Foucault, then living in Tunis, missed much of the upheaval surrounding the war in Algeria and the developments in politically left organisations that followed. Instead of Marx, Nietzsche's work became increasingly influential on him during the mid-1960s. Foucault's politics were never easy to classify. Though he was generally a man of the left, he maintained a distance from militant political activity until May 1968. It has also been argued that he became 'violently anti-communist' following his stay in Poland (Eribon, 1991: 136). In addition to a Marxist and a Nietzschean, he has also been described as a technocrat and Gaullist, because of his contribution to a commission towards the development of Gaullist university reforms initiated by the education minister Christian Foucet, between 1965 and 1966. Still others, such as Habermas (1981), have referred to him as a 'young conservative' because of his total critique of modernity and sympathy to anti-modernist, reactionary philosophers including Nietzsche and Heidegger. Fraser (1994), however, has questioned such a political designation but has noted that his anti-humanist position allows for a multiplicity of political readings. Nevertheless, by the time Foucault wrote *The Order of Things* he saw Marxism as a philosophy limited to the nineteenth century: 'Marxism exists in nineteenth century thought like a fish in water: that is, it is unable to breathe anywhere else' (1994: 262). By the mid-1970s, Paris had become the centre of intellectual reaction against Marxism (Anderson, 1983). Like many other French intellectuals including Phillipe Sollers, André Glucksman and Bernard Henri-Levy, who began to associate Marxism with a form of authoritarianism or totalitarianism, especially following the publication in France of Solzenisyn's book, *The Gulag Archipelago* (2003), Foucault shared in their mistrust of Marxism and the foregrounding of the working class, especially at the expense of other social movements and their identity politics. Yet, though not explicitly acknowledging Marx, Foucault focuses on issues such as political economy and neoliberalism in a number of his works including *Discipline and Punish* and in his later writings on biopolitics and governmentality.

A Specific Intellectual

Although he missed most of the intense political activism in France during May 1968, similar political protests had begun at the University in Tunis in 1966. A wave of unrest and violent riots lasting for a year had been spearheaded by left-wing Maoist students opposing President Bourguiba's regime. Foucault aided many of these students when they faced arrest and detention, often lobbying on their behalf. When he returned to France in Autumn 1968, he often joined protests with Sartre on various issues. By contrast to Sartre, whom he saw as a universal or total intellectual, someone who spoke on all matters with authority, Foucault saw himself as a 'specific intellectual' focusing on limited issues and local problems of which he had specialised knowledge. As a militant he also began to participate in various demonstrations and campaigns, for example as part of the Committee for the Defence of the Rights of Immigrants. In addition, he founded the Group d'informations sur les prisoners (GIP), which included prisoners and intellectuals working together to improve prison conditions. Foucault also supported various workers' struggles including groups fighting to improve the social and economic situations of health workers.

Ideas and Arguments

Madness and Civilization

Foucault's first major work, *Madness and Civilization* (1961), is an abridged version of his doctorate (later published in full in 2006 as *History of Madness*) and is many ways the work which established his reputation as a major thinker. The book examines how madness was socially and historically constructed and shifted along with alterations in political, economic, social and institutional life, but also with developing forms of knowledge and classification. Drawing on philosophical, literary, institutional, medical and artistic expressions of madness, he attempts to outline the historical conditions for the emergence and changing conceptualisation of reason and madness, especially following the rise of science. In order to explore this process, Foucault argues that researchers must shed not only their preconceptions of madness, but also the medical or scientific concepts of psychopathology with which they think. This is especially by interrogating the development of scientific approaches that aimed to standardise and 'know' insanity in order to control those deemed insane.

The book, subtitled *A History of Insanity in the Age of Reason*, starts from the Middle Ages moving through the Renaissance to the Age of Enlightenment and Reason, and then, finally, into the nineteenth century. According to Foucault each period's view of madness tended to shift in relation to a prevailing 'code of knowledge', so that each period was marked by a rupture or discontinuity with the other. However, the themes of spatial exclusion and spiritual reintegration traverse these periods, providing an underlying continuity beneath the discontinuous cultural understandings of madness and reason.

Although opposed to reason, madness during the Middle Ages was also in dialogue with it, providing a different vision of the world. The mad were variously seen as expressing a 'tragic experience', of indicating the existence of animality, or an inaccessible truth of the world, but were nevertheless given a place in society, so that unreason and reason 'speak to each other' – they communicated. However, the Renaissance marked the beginnings of an absolute division between reason and unreason. Madness gradually became disentangled from reason and then subjugated and dominated by the latter.

The Great Confinement

According to Foucault, two events were of major importance in shifting the understanding of madness: the creation of the Hôpital général in 1697, which saw the beginning of the 'great confinement' of the poor and mad, now deemed dangerous; and, a century later, in 1794, the freeing of chained inmates in Bicêtre by the reformer Phillipe Pinel. Not only did these events create a conceptual exclusion between madness and reason, a 'breach in their communication', but this was also mirrored by practical or physical exclusion of those designated as mad. Leperoriums in which lepers were originally housed, and divided off from mainstream society, now became used as houses of confinement for a mix of marginalised categories – the unemployed, the poor, criminals and madmen:

> Poor vagabonds, criminals, and 'deranged minds' would take the part played by the leper, and we shall see what salvation was expected from this exclusion, for them and for those who excluded them as well. With an altogether new meaning and in a very different culture, the forms would remain essentially that major form of a rigorous division which is social exclusion but spiritual reintegration. (Foucault, 2001: 7)

According to Foucault, 'a monologue of reason about madness' was established on the basis of a muteness about the latter. Madness was reduced to silence. Nevertheless, the voices of the mad still emerged in the literature of the nineteenth century, for example in the writings of Holderin, Nietzsche and Artaud, whose arational, transgressive thoughts revealed truths about the world that went beyond the normal constricts of reason, uprooting prevailing norms.

In his later work, Foucault would more explicitly discuss the relation between power and discourse, how discourses could provide or name the truth about people, and thereby define them and control them as 'subjects', as 'mad', as 'insane', as 'psychopaths' or 'deranged'. Discourses produced the truth about people, events and things – they had truth effects. Nevertheless, many of the themes and preoccupations he addresses in *Madness and Civilization* re-emerge in his later works, including the discontinuous codes of knowledge and classification through which people are categorised, defined, confined and excluded, and the division and regulation of populations into semi-enclosed domains to be cured, corrected or reformed.

In *The Birth of the Clinic* (1963), published two years after, Foucault examined the origins of modern medicine in France, following the French Revolution. In a new intellectual context where structuralism was increasingly coming into vogue in France, he aimed to uncover the establishment of a medical 'gaze' on death and disease, which looked beyond surface phenomena or experience, to the hidden structures underlying it. Foucault investigated the socio-historical conditions for the formation of certain subjects, such as criminals, the mad or insane, and how they were made into objects of knowledge up to and including the present (Smart, 2002: 17). Unveiling the historical conditions of possibility of medical concepts, he interrogated what it was possible to see and say according to various concepts and discourses in a specific historical period. In mapping the change in language used between 1794 and 1820, Foucault discusses how the individual's body became an object of scientific and medical knowledge: that is, an object of 'positive knowledge'.

The Archaeology of Knowledge and *The Order of Things*

In his next two works, Foucault shifted his focus from the examination of the historical conditions of possibility of substantive social processes, including madness and medical perception, to epistemological questions which had underpinned his earlier work, but which only remained vaguely developed. *The Order of Things* (1966) was concerned with examining how human beings came to understand themselves – that is, how they become objects of knowledge. The structure of language, he argued, determined what it was possible to know. In such a counter-intuitive conception, it was not the actor who spoke and used language, but the reverse: language, as an autonomous structure, spoke though us. It was therefore the unconscious structure of language that needed to be uncovered. Following a popular strain of modernist literature, he focused on how people became lost in language or, as structuralists had termed it, the 'death of the author'. This, for example, was one of the central questions in his famous essay 'What is an Author?'.

The Order of Things was subtitled *An Archaeology of the Human Sciences*, and Foucault used a geological metaphor of archaeology to outline the emergence and the variable structures of the human sciences, specifically biology, economics and linguistics. These sciences, he argued, were rooted in universal human conditions of life, labour and language. A central theme of the book was the point in history when man became an object of knowledge in Western culture. Eschewing an analysis of singular social objects and the events, the focus was on discursive and conceptual frameworks in which the sciences appeared. These discourses constituted autonomous and independent frameworks. As Hall notes by discourse he meant:

> A group of statements which provide a language for talking about – a way of representing the knowledge about – a particular topic at a particular historical moment. Discourse is about the production of knowledge through language. But since all social practices entail meaning, and meanings shape and influence what we do – our conduct – all practices have a discursive aspect. (Hall, 1992: 291)

> Discourse concerned both language and practice, it was through discourse that a topic was constructed, by producing the objects of our knowledge and how it could be discussed and interpreted or, when looking at people, which actions were deemed as acceptable. (Hall, 2003: 22)

The human sciences, according to Foucault, were organised on a different basis and according to different principles at different stages in history. They constitute distinct, but internally coherent, discourses or codes of knowledge – *epistemes*. Such *epistemes* could be compared with what Kuhn calls 'paradigms', or broad theoretical frameworks. In the *Archaeology of Knowledge* (1972) Foucault defines an *episteme* thus:

> A total set of relations that unite, at a given period, the discursive practices that give rise to epistemological figures, sciences and possibly

> formalized systems... The episteme is not a form of knowledge ... it is the totality of relations that can be discovered, for a given period, between the sciences when one analyses them at the level of discursive regularities. (1972: 191)

Epistemes constituted implicit conceptual structures allowing a certain form of thought to be possible and ruling out other forms as impermissible: they allowed certain forms of thinking while wholly disqualifying others. Contra the Enlightenment, rather than progressing, knowledge and the discourses it appeared within, or *epistemes*, merely supplanted one another – their movement was discontinuous. Western thought could be divided into three major epochs each with its own *episteme*: the Renaissance, the Classical Age (halfway through the seventeenth century) and the Modern Age (from the beginning of the nineteenth century).

From Discourse to Power

According to Foucault, nothing meaningful exists outside of discourse; that is not to say there was no reality outside of it in terms of material things or actions, but rather these things could not be understood outside of discourse. From the 1970s, Foucault's work began to move away from a structuralist analysis of autonomous discourses to a focus on power. Rather than an absolute shift, however, there is a partial recalibration of his work, whereby the archaeological method becomes reconnected to social and institutional practices and, more specifically, to power relations. This movement was initially expressed in two articles 'Discourse on language', his inaugural lecture at the College de France (1971) and reprinted in the *Archaeology of Knowledge*, and his essay 'Nietzsche, Genealogy, History' (1971). As he noted in the former: 'I am supposing that in every society the production of discourse is at once controlled, selected, organized, and redistributed according to a certain number of procedures, whose role is to avert its powers and its dangers, to cope with chance events, to evade its ponderous, awesome materiality' (1972: 216). Knowledge was now intrinsically connected to power, or constituted part of a 'power/knowledge' configuration. Such power operated through institutions and techniques or 'technologies'. The loci of power were only not institutions, practices, and techniques but also the human body. Power was inextricably tied to knowledge not just in terms of repression, as ordinarily understood, but also as a productive force, a force that attempted to produce a truth about the world. According to Foucault, social analysts should not study something to ascertain whether it constructs the truth, but instead to examine 'truth effects' or various 'regimes of truth'.

Power, he argues, does not flow in a single direction or derive from a single origin, but circulates across the whole social body: all individuals become caught up in the net of power; it exists at all levels of society pervading knowledge, discourses, institutions, practices, mechanisms, techniques and individual bodies. Power is everywhere and, yet, localised. This microphysics of power operates through the capillaries of society, through the production of knowledge and meaning, and via discourses concerning the body. The operation of power, moreover, also leads to resistance, which is much more localised and contingent than the Marxist focus on social classes.

Foucault aims to provide a 'history of the present'. This entails an analysis that demonstrates how the past brought us to where we are now, the power relations involved and the knowledge forms tied to this, in order to denaturalise what we take for granted. Individuals do not become liberated or freed with knowledge, as Enlightenment thinking suggests, but instead become constituted through discourses which define what they are, what they can do and their position within the social world. Such discourses come from a variety of sources and institutions including religion, education, the state, the family, the economy, all proposing their version of a discourse tied to truth but ultimately connected to power.

The Body Inscribed by Power: *Discipline and Punish* and *The History of Sexuality*

This novel analysis of power is operationalised in two of Foucault's most important books, *Discipline and Punish* (1977 [1975]) and *The History of Sexuality*, Volume 1 (1990 [1976]). *Discipline and Punish* is subtitled *The Birth of the Prison* and begins with a graphic depiction of the public execution in France, in 1757, of Robert Damiens, an ex-soldier who had threatened the king with a knife, but eventually gave himself up after only inflicting a minor wound. Damiens was arrested, tried and convicted for the crime of regicide and subsequently hung, drawn and quartered. Foucault's graphic description of power as a spectacle is vivid and disconcerting:

> On 2 March 1757 Damiens the regicide was condemned 'to make the *amende honorable* before the main door of the Church of Paris', where he was to be 'taken and conveyed in a cart, wearing nothing but a shirt, holding a torch of burning wax weighing two pounds'; then, 'in the said cart, to the Place de Grève, where, on a scaffold that will be erected there, the flesh will be torn from his breasts, arms, thighs and calves with red-hot pincers, his right hand, holding the knife with which he committed the said parricide, burnt with sulphur, and, on those places where the flesh will be torn away, poured molten lead, boiling oil, burning resin, wax and sulphur melted together and then his body drawn and quartered by four horses and his limbs and body consumed by fire, reduced to ashes and his ashes thrown to the winds' (Pièces originales: 372–4). 'Finally, he was quartered,' recounts the Gazette d'Amsterdam of 1 April 1757. 'This last operation was very long, because the horses used were not accustomed to drawing; consequently, instead of four, six were needed; and when that did not suffice, they were forced, in order to cut off the wretch's thighs, to sever the sinews and hack at the joints.' (1977: 3)

[Excerpt(s) from *Discipline and Punish: The Birth of the Prison* by Michel Foucault, translated by Alan Sheridan, translation copyright © 1977 by Alan Sheridan. Used by permission of Pantheon Books, an imprint of the Knopf Doubleday Publishing Group, a division]

Foucault juxtaposes this harrowing and brutal description with a bland and banal list of house rules for the House of Young Prisoners in Paris, drawn up by Leon Faucher some 80 years later in 1838. The timetable enumerates in detail the activities offenders must follow, including when they will wake up, how long they will work, where they will enunciate prayers, how they will walk to work and when they will go to bed. Although separated by less than a century the two examples demonstrate a major alteration in the economy of punishment, especially with the removal of torture as a public spectacle. According to Foucault:

> The spectacle is replaced by the discreet application of constraint, aimed at protecting the social order. Punishment which was earlier deemed to exceed or be in excess of the crime is now replaced by punishment aimed at governing and converting of 'the soul' or 'psyche'. (1977: 7).

This shift is not underpinned by a more enlightened philosophy based on less punishment, but by an ethos of more effective punishment. The body is still punished in the later description in terms of internment and deprivation of various desires and freedom, but punishment now enters 'abstract consciousness' and is seen in terms of its inevitability, not its 'visible intensity'. Moreover, it is no longer the crime, but the criminal that becomes the focus. The apportioning of blame is also redistributed so that 'it is the conviction itself that marks the offender with the unequivocally negative sign' wherein execution just becomes an 'additional shame' (1977: 9). This modification in the 'punishment-body relation' entails a broadening of the techniques of power. Herein bodies, the individual psyche and subjectivity can be better controlled, regulated and supervised. Such a process entailed the increasing use of 'scientific knowledges' which facilitated tailor-made, individualised punishments.

In this 'age of sobriety in punishment' (1977: 14) disciplinary control is primarily exercised and expressed upon the body, through training, supervision and control of individual bodies. Three major processes are involved in this new technique of power: hierarchical observation, normalising judgement and examination. Hierarchical observation, initially rooted in military camps, facilitates continuous and precise observation – a disciplinary gaze – allowing bodies to be controlled and regulated. Normalising judgement ensures that correct behaviours conforming to strict rules and dictates are followed, and that not only punishment, but rewards are applied, thereby effecting a process of 'normalization'. Through a process of examination, individuals are not only made visible but documented, made into 'cases', to be controlled, organised and recorded in files and reports, and individualised; cases were enclosed in 'a network of writing' (1977: 189).

Focused initially on problem populations, such a disciplinary gaze became generalised in the workings of other parallel disciplinary institutions and organisations that proliferated roughly at the same time as prisons: schools, hospitals, barracks and factories, which share family resemblances. They were all underpinned by a method of social surveillance and regulation of the individual's use of space and time through disciplinary measures, time restrictions, timetables, etc., constituting the emergence of a *disciplinary society*.

Paradigmatic of such surveillance in modern society was Bentham's model of a prison – the Panopticon. This highlighted the connection between visibility and power, and operates on the basis of maximum efficiency, by controlling large numbers with minimal staff, but also an institution generating knowledge about prisoners. As Smart notes, the Panopticon:

> Constituted a programme for the efficient exercise of power through the spatial arrangement of subjects according to a diagram of visibility so as to ensure that at each and every moment any subject might be exposed to 'invisible' observation. The Panopticon was to function as an apparatus of power by virtue of the field of visibility in which individuals were to be located, each in their respective places (e.g. cells, positions, rooms, beds, etc.), for a centralized and unseen observer. In this schema subjects were to be individualized in their own spaces, to be visible, and to be conscious of their potentially constant and continuous visibility. Given that those illuminated by power were unable to see their observer(s) the latter condition, a consciousness of being in a visible space, of being watched, effectively ensured an automatic functioning of power. As a result individuals became entangled in an impersonal power relation, one which automatized and dis-individualized power as it individualized those subject to it. (2002: 82–3)

[Republished with permission of Routledge from *Michel Foucault. Revised Edition*, B. Smart, 2002. Permission conveyed through Copyright Clearance Center, Inc]

The gaze of the institution became internalised by the internee, so that rather than force or constraint creating good behaviour, the prisoner's actions became self-directed and self-censured. Prisons sought not only to deprive liberty from individuals, but also to change them, to normalise delinquents, to re-inscribe and individualise their bodies as objects of knowledge by acquiring biographical information about them.

The History of Sexuality

Foucault extends his elaboration of a genealogy of power discussed in *Discipline and Punish* to examine sex and sexuality and the process through which disciplinary techniques, knowledge and power transform humans into subjects. His aim is not to write a history of sexual behaviour, nor its representation, but rather a history of sexuality as a notion. The term 'sexuality' did not appear until the nineteenth century and its development is, he argues, connected to a number of other processes including biological knowledge centred on reproduction; the establishment of rules and norms supported by religious, judicial, pedagogical and medical institutions; and the ways in which individuals experienced themselves and interpreted their actions. A core concern of his analysis is to challenge what he dubs the 'repressive hypothesis'. This avers that during the early seventeenth century there were few prohibitions, taboos and restrictions concerning the sexuality of individuals: sex for the most part was discussed in an open and frank manner. However, a fundamental change took place during the latter part of the seventeenth century, reaching its apogee in the Victorian era wherein sexuality then became taboo and moved into the private realm of the home.

By contrast, for Foucault, rather than a repressive censorship there developed a 'veritable discursive explosion' (1990: 17) about sexuality during this period, as discussions of sex multiplied and proliferated under modern power conditions, especially with the growth of Catholic confession. Part of the failure to adequately comprehend the problem concerning the 'repressive hypothesis', Foucault argues, stems from an intellectual entrapment in a certain juridical image of power, a restrictive negative view of power that saw it merely as repression, as prohibition, as censorship, rather than as productive. Power is not exerted over unwilling bodies but with their compliance – what he refers to as the rule of immanence.

The key questions correspondingly become an examination of how sexual knowledge emerges, to whom it refers and how it is applied? A new relationship between the state and individual concerning sex and sexual practices emerged entailing 'a new regime of discourses' (1990: 27). These authorised knowledges included those developed through medical, legal, demographic, psychological, ethical, pedagogical, psychiatric and religious knowledges and discourses, but also pervading various institutions, including schools.

Governmentality

In his later work Foucault began discussing another original theoretical concept, *bio-power* concerned with the diversity of modern forms of power shaping human beings or 'administering life' in terms of normality. According to Foucault, for a long period one of the characteristic privileges of sovereign power was the right over life and death, or more specifically the right to take life and let live. However, since the seventeenth century, in the West at least, there has been a transformation in the mechanisms of power away from such a deductive view of power to a 'power that exerts a positive influence on life, that endeavors to administer, optimize and multiply it, subjecting it to precise controls and comprehensive regulations' (1990: 137). This shift in power took two basic interdependent forms. The first was an *anatomy-politics of the body*. this was:

Centred on the body as a machine: its disciplining, the optimization of its capabilities, the extortion of its forces, the parallel increase of its usefulness and its docility, its integration into systems of efficient and economic controls. (1990: 139)

Whereas the second, a *biopolitics of population*, was formed later. This:

focused on the species of the body, the body imbued with the mechanisms of life and serving as the basis of biological processes; propagation, births and mortality, the level of health, life expectancy and longevity, with all the conditions that can cause these to vary. Their supervision was effected through an entire series of interventions and regulatory controls. (1990: 139)

The discipline, subjugation and administration of the body, and the calculated management, control and regulation of the population constitute two poles across which the organisation of power over life became manifested, no longer primed to kill individuals but instead to invest in life. According to Foucault, bio-power, by focusing on the population as a resource to be improved and optimised, was a condition of possibility for the development of capitalism. But it also operated as a force in the hierarchisation and segregation of populations. It was against this background that sex became politicised.

Foucault develops these arguments concerning biopolitics and governmentality or government rationality in his lectures at the Collège de France, especially 'Security, territory and population' (1979) and 'The birth of biopolitics' (1978), as well as in an essay derived from these lectures, 'On Governmentality' (1980). By the term 'governmentality' he meant three things:

1. The ensemble formed by the institutions, procedures, analyses and reflections, the calculations and tactics that allow the exercise of this very specific albeit complex form of power, which has as its target population, as its principal form of knowledge political economy, and as its essential technical means apparatuses of security.

2. The tendency which, over a long period and throughout the West, has steadily led towards the pre-eminence over all other forms (sovereignty, discipline, etc.) of this type of power which may be termed government, resulting, on the one hand, in the formation of a whole series of specific governmental apparatuses, and, on the other, in the development of a whole complex of knowledges (saviors).

3. The process, or rather the result of the process, through which the state of justice of the Middle Ages, transformed into the administrative state during the fifteenth and sixteenth centuries, gradually becomes 'governmentalized'. (1980: 102–3)

Contemporary Relevance and Applications

Foucault's work has been highly influential not only in sociology, but also in psychology, organisation studies, history, philosophy and geography. It has also exerted a strong influence on feminist studies, for example the work of Lois McNay, Judith Butler and Dorothy Smith, and in ethno-racial studies of power in the work of, for example, Laura Stoler and Edward Said, the latter, a key figure in the development of post-colonial studies.

THE FOUCAULT–CHOMSKY DEBATE

In 1971, Michel Foucault and Noam Chomsky, two of the most prominent public intellectual activists of the era, engaged in a televised debate for a Dutch series. While the exchange covered a range of topics, the salient point of contestation concerned whether we may propose some defined human nature, providing a normative foundation for societal critique. From his rationalist perspective, Chomsky suggested an innate human nature could be identified in creativity, which is only realised to varying degrees in different societies. One task of social theory then, as an intellectual domain of political action, is to envisage social structures in which this essence may be more fully realised. Foucault countered, from his anti-modernist and anti-essentialist perspective, that because such ideas of human nature have been developed within capitalist modernity, they remain intrinsically tied to its structures of discourse and power. For this reason, not only should such ideas be treated with deep suspicion, but also they cannot form part of the struggles to fundamentally transform society.

In *Orientalism: Western Conceptions of the Orient* (1995 [1978]), the Palestinian intellectual Edward Said draws on Foucault's notion of discourse as a form of power to examine the West European construction of the notion of the Orient as a fixed object of knowledge that could be defined, known and controlled. For Said 'Orientalism' refers to a 'way of coming to terms with Orient that is based on the Orient's special place in European western experience' (1995: 1). It refers to several interdependent processes: from the academic discourse within which intellectuals teach, wrote, researched and defined the Orient, including historians, sociologists and anthropologists; to a style of thought based on an ontological and epistemological distinction between the 'Orient' and the 'Occident' developed by novelists, writers, philosophers, political theorists and imperial administrators to develop theories and accounts concerning the Orient from Aeschylus to Marx; and on a more material basis it can be seen as a corporate institution for dealing with the Orient, by making statements about it, ruling it. As Said argues:

> My contention is that without examining Orientalism as a discourse one cannot possibly understand the enormously systematic discipline by which European culture was able to manage—and even

produce—the Orient politically, sociologically, militarily, ideologically, scientifically, and imaginatively during the post-Enlightenment period. Moreover, so authoritative a position did Orientalism have that I believe no one writing, thinking, or acting on the Orient could do so without taking account of the limitations on thought and action imposed by Orientalism. In brief, because of Orientalism the Orient was not (and is not) a free subject of thought or action. This is not to say that Orientalism unilaterally determines what can be said about the Orient, but that it is the whole network of interests inevitably brought to bear on (and therefore always involved in) any occasion when that peculiar entity 'the Orient' is in question. How this happens is what this book tries to demonstrate. It also tries to show that European culture gained in strength and identity by setting itself off against the Orient as a sort of surrogate and even underground self. (1995: 3)

[Excerpt(s) from *Orientalism* by Edward W. Said, copyright © 1978 by Edward W. Said. Used by permission of Pantheon Books, an imprint of the Knopf Doubleday Publishing Group, a division of Penguin Random House LLC. All rights reserved]

Such discursive practices, including both ideological and material aspects, have had the effect not only of producing a stereotypical image of a static, passive and non-democratic 'Other' against which a dynamic and progressive West has defined itself, but also of essentialising the Orient as an homogeneous entity. The Orient has also been represented in such a way as to produce a racialised knowledge of the Other as constituting deracinated individuals which become used as a means to rationalise and justify processes of colonialism and imperialism. The construction of the 'Orient', which Said examines from antiquity onwards through the seventeenth and eighteenth centuries, was not merely the development of an idea which did not correspond to a reality, but a material investment of power.

Foucault's thought has also been used and reinterpreted in the work of Nikolas Rose. In his book *Governing the Soul* (1989), Rose attempts to understand the subjective existence of people and their relations with reference to scientific experts and power within liberal democratic societies, especially by examining Foucault's notion of governmentality as the calculated supervision and maximisation of the forces of society. Questioning the view that our subjectivities, feelings and desires are a personal matter, Rose examines them as objects of new forms of knowledge, governmentality and power, especially as these have developed in the UK and United States from the 1930s. Fundamental shifts have taken place in the governance of the human soul from the past, he argues. Governments have become more concerned to regulate the conduct of individuals, for example through the school or welfare system, by acting upon their mental capacities and propensities. The management of subjectivity has also become a central task for modern organisations including offices, factories, hospitals and prisons. And a new expertise has emerged, the expertise of subjectivity. Here the scientific status of psychology has played a major role in attempting to maximise human resources in institutional life as well as providing the impetus for the study of the group as a new field of analysis. As Rose notes:

> With the development of new languages for speaking about subjectivity, and new techniques for inscribing it, measuring it, and acting upon it, the self became calculable and manageable in new ways. Psychological expertise staked its claim to play a key role within any practice for management of individuals in institutional life. (1989: x)

Such 'psychological' preoccupations were especially evident within post-war industry in discussions concerning labour productivity, industrial unrest and in maximising the commitment of the worker. They also interpreted work as essential for psychological well-being, as well as enhancing profits and leading to individual self-actualisation. Rose also examines how the objectives of government have intervened in family life in terms of regulating behaviour through the use of psychological discourses concerned with the rearing of healthy and well-adjusted children, discourses often diffused by social workers and health visitors. This has, he argues, been achieved less by coercive imposition than by acting upon the wishes and desires of adults. Such processes connected to psychological expertise are also tied to the emergence of a 'therapeutic culture of the self' manifesting new conceptions and techniques of the self that aim to reshape subjectivities.

Criticisms

Given its breadth, Foucault's work has unsurprisingly suffered from a number of criticisms. Historians have questioned his historical findings in *Madness and Civilization*, questioning, for example, how pervasive the Great Confinement was in the West. In his analysis of madness in the UK, Porter has argued that Foucault exaggerates the numbers of people interned deemed mad during the seventeenth century and that many 'lunatics typically remained at large, the responsibility of their family under the eye of the parish' until at least the nineteenth century (Porter, 1990: 48).

Although Sartre had borne the brunt of many of Foucault's criticisms, in his response to Foucault's early work, he indicates Foucault's failure to discuss the mechanisms responsible for the shift in *epistemes*, or how and why they succeeded one another:

> what Foucault presents us with is – and Kanters saw this very well – a geology, a series of successive layers that make up our 'ground'. Each of these layers defines the conditions of possibility of a certain type of thought prevailing throughout a certain period. But Foucault does not tell us the thing that would be the most interesting, that is, how each

thought is constructed on the basis of these conditions, or how mankind passes from one thought to another. To do so he would have to bring in praxis, and therefore history, which is precisely what he refuses to do. Of course his perspective remains historical. He distinguishes between periods, a before and after. But he replaces cinema with the magic lantern, motion with the succession of motionless moments. (Cited in Eribon, 1991: 163)

Moreover, Marxists have heavily criticised Foucault's notion of discourse for being too expansive and for ignoring what they consider as more important material: that is, structural and economic factors that shape both the social world and power relations. Although Foucault may be correct in challenging economically reductionist views, his own position, they argue, gives too much autonomy to what they designate as 'superstructural factors'. Foucault also fails to examine more macro forms of power, especially in his early work. For Marxists, this is connected with an inflated and contradictory analysis of power generally. In addition, Lukes (2005) also criticises the ultra-radicalism of Foucault's account of power, in which domination is everywhere so that there is no escaping from it, or reasoning independently of it. Moreover, he argues, that much of Foucault's style and subversive discussion though rhetorically impressive, lacks methodological rigour. There is also an unacknowledged shift in Foucault's work from conceiving of individuals as products of discourses in his earlier work, to conceptualising them as creating themselves as subjects, for example in his last two volumes of *The History of Sexuality*:

In sum, Foucault's first way of interpreting the key idea central to his view of power that power is 'productive' through the social construction of subjects, rendering the governed governable made no sense. Taking this to mean that those subject to power are 'constituted' by it is best read as a striking overstatement deployed in his purely ideal-typical depictions of disciplinary and bio-power, not as an analysis of the extent to which the various modern forms of power he identified actually succeed, or fail, in securing the compliance of those subject to it. Indeed, for all his talk of 'micro-physics', 'analytics' and 'mechanisms', Foucault was a genealogist, concerned with the historical recovery of the formation of norms (such as the mad, the sick, the criminal and the abnormal) and as such he had no interest in analysing such mechanisms by examining variation, outcomes and effects: he just asserted that there were such effects. And yet Foucault's writings have had an extraordinarily wide impact, encouraging scholars in many fields and disciplines to engage in just such an analysis analysing fields of practices that he identified, by putting, so to speak, his dramatically exaggerated ideal types to empirical work, by asking, precisely, just how and to what extent the governed are rendered governable. I do not think it altogether fanciful to suggest that

Foucault's writings thereby themselves exhibit an interesting kind of power: the power of seduction. (Lukes, 2005: 98)

[Republished with permission of Palgrave Macmillan from *Power: A Radical View*, 2nd edition, S. Lukes, 2005]

Foucault has also been challenged for his rejection of a notion of truth or scientific knowledge. His position, it is argued, leads to a form of relativism in which all knowledge is inflected by power, and therefore lacks the emancipatory potential foregrounded by Enlightenment understandings of knowledge (Habermas, 1990). He has also been described as working with a Eurocentric approach, taking France as the centre of his analysis without looking at the role of the French Empire in effecting forms of international domination (Said, 1995).

Conclusion

Though often encased in a dense conceptual vocabulary Foucault provides an immensely original and powerful account of the constitution of social relations and their reproduction. His questioning of Enlightenment views of knowledge as liberating and of humanism as a tool of social analysis is heterodox and provokes arguments that prompt social theorists to question their complacent presuppositions. His concept of power/knowledge, although developed at a high level of abstraction, nevertheless makes itself amenable to use in empirical analyses and is used to powerful effect in *Discipline and Punish*. Nevertheless, there are tensions and ambiguities in his work centring on his lack of empirical rigour, his notion of power and the image of what an alternative form of society to the one he criticises for its pervasive forms of domination would look like.

References

Anderson, P. (1983) *In the Tracks of Historical Materialism*. London: Verso.
Descombes, V. (1980) *Modern French Philosophy*. Cambridge: Cambridge University Press.
Eribon, D. (1991) *Michel Foucault*. Cambridge, MA: Harvard University Press.
Foucault, M. (1985 [1954]) *Dream and Existence*. Atlantic Highlands, NJ: Humanities Press.
Foucault, M. (1987 [1954]) *Mental Illness and Psychology*. Berkeley, CA: University of California Press.
Foucault, M. (2001 [1961]) *Madness and Civilization: A History of Insanity in the Age of Reason*. London: Routledge.
Foucault, M. (1989 [1963]) *The Birth of the Clinic*. London: Routledge.
Foucault, M. (1994 [1966]) *The Order of Things: An Archaeology of the Human Sciences*. London: Routledge.

Foucault, M. (1972) *The Archaeology of Knowledge and The Discourse on Language*. A. M. Sheridan Smith, trans. New York: Pantheon Books.
Foucault, M. (1990 [1976]) *The History of Sexuality, Vol. 1: The Will to Knowledge*. Harmondsworth: Penguin.
Foucault, M. (1977) *Discipline and Punish: The Birth of the Prison*. London: Allen Lane.
Foucault, M. (1980) *Power/Knowledge: Selected Interviews and Other Writings 1972-1977*. C. Gordon (ed.). New York: Pantheon Books.
Foucault, M. (1982) The Subject and Power. *Critical Inquiry*, 8(4), pp. 777-95.
Foucault, M. (1988 [1984]). *The Care of the Self. Volume 3 of the History of Sexuality*. New York: Random House.
Foucault, M. (2006 [1984]) *The Uses of Pleasure: Volume 2 of the History of Sexuality*. London: Penguin.
Foucault, M. (2006) *History of Madness*. London: Routledge.
Foucault, M. (2008) *The Birth of Biopolitics: Lectures at the Collège de France, 1978-79*. M. Senellart (ed.) and G. Burchell (trans.) Basingstoke: Palgrave Macmillan.
Foucault, M. (2009) *Security, Territory, Population: Lectures at the Collège De France, 1977-78*. M. Senellart (ed.) and G. Burchell, trans. Basingstoke: Palgrave Macmillan.
Fraser, N. (1994) Michel Foucault: A 'Young Conservative'? In: M. Kelly (ed.) *Critique and Power: Recasting the Foucault/Habermas Debate*. Cambridge, MA: MIT Press, pp. 185-210.
Gutting, G. (2005) *Foucault: A Very Short Introduction*. Oxford: Oxford University Press.
Habermas, J. (1981) Modernity versus Postmodernity. *New German Critique*, 22, pp. 3-14.
Habermas, J. (1990) *The Philosophical Discourse of Modernity*. Boston, MA: MIT Press.
Hall, S. (1992) The West and the Rest. In: S. Hall and B. Gieben (eds.) *Formations of Modernity*. Cambridge: Polity, pp. 275-331.
Hall, S. (2003) *Representation: Cultural Representations and Signifying Practices*. London: Sage.
Lukes, S. (2005) *Power: A Radical View*. London: MacMillan.
Porter, R. (1990) Foucault's Great Confinement. *History of the Human Sciences*, 3(1), pp. 47-54.
Rose, N. (1989) *Governing the Soul: The Shaping of the Private Self*. London: Routledge.
Said, E. W. (1995 [1978]) *Orientalism: Western Conceptions of the Orient*. London: Penguin Books.
Smart, B. (2002) *Michel Foucault*. Revised edition. London: Routledge.
Solzenitsyn, A. (2003). *The Gulag Archipelago*. London: Vintage.

12

Elias

Norbert Elias was one of the last of the classical sociologists. In scope and depth, his work sits comfortably alongside that of predecessors such as Karl Marx, Max Weber and Émile Durkheim, as well as contemporary sociologists such as Pierre Bourdieu. His sociology examined the long-term changes in individual behaviour and connected these with gradual shifts in power balances between social groups. All of the elements of what has come to be known as 'figurational' sociology (he himself preferred the term 'process sociology') are woven into his magnus opus published in 1939, *Uber den Process der Zivilization*, later translated as *On the Process of Civilisation* (2012) or *The Civilizing Process* (2000) in the first English translations. These diverse themes – including a processual theory of knowledge, a historical sociology of the Holocaust, the relationship between personality and culture, the role of language in human development, the triad of social, psychological and ecological controls which characterise all phases of human development, the relation between the market and the state, a process sociology of knowledge, sociology and the unconscious mind – are elaborated in the 18 volumes of his *Collected Works*. Strictly speaking Elias never saw himself as only a sociologist but as a '*Menschenwissenschatftler*' – a scientific analyst of human beings (Hackeschimdt, 2004: 59). Fame came late to Elias; even though he lived to the age of 93 his work only became recognised when he was in his mid-50s.

Life and Intellectual Context

Like most other sociologists Elias's life-story is relevant to understanding his sociological work in general. He was born on 22 June 1897 to Hermann and Sophie Elias into a Jewish, but German-oriented family. His father was a businessman in the textile industry and they resided in Breslau, which was then in German Silesia, now the Polish city of Wrocław. He was educated there in the humanities and sciences at the Johannes-Gymnasium. Although he denied experiencing any anti-Semitism it is likely it constituted a formative experience for many Jewish families in Germany at that time. And it is of note that one of his first articles is on anti-Semitism in Germany (Elias, 2006) and that he was a member of a Zionist youth movement, *Blau-Weiss* (Blue-White), which foregrounded the idea of a Jewish renaissance and which he joined in 1913. As a Jew and a homosexual, he tended to remain a relative outsider throughout his life. During the First World War Elias fought on both the Eastern and Western fronts as part of a signals regiment. He ended his conscription as a medical orderly.

This experience brought him into direct contact and experience with the harsh brutalities of war and violence, having witnessed the death of many colleagues. He then attended the University of Breslau where he studied both philosophy and medicine, eventually dropping the latter in favour of philosophy. He went on to undertake a doctoral degree with Richard Honigswald, a leading philosopher in Germany at the time, who trained him in terms of Kantian philosophy, which Elias was to reject, resulting in a major disagreement with his supervisor. His doctorate was entitled 'The Idea and Individual', submitted in 1924. His rejection of philosophy and its a priori and individualistic assumptions led to Elias continuing his education in sociology in Heidelberg where Alfred Weber (Max's brother) and Marianne Weber were active in promoting Max Weber's work. Here he undertook his *habilitation* (post-doctoral qualification required in Germany for teaching) under Alfred Weber but also came under the influence of Karl Mannheim. When the latter moved to the University of Frankfurt, housed in the *Institut für Sozialforschung* (also known as the Frankfurt School where Adorno and Horkheimer among others were based), Elias joined him as an academic assistant. It was here that Elias completed his *Habilitationschrift* in 1933, which later was published in English as *The Court Society* (1983) just as Hitler came to power. Like many other German intellectuals, Elias sought exile in Paris where he invested what little money he had in making wooden toys.

He then moved to England in 1935 where he lived hand to mouth. Here, while spending considerable time in the British Library, he completed *On the Process of Civilisation*, which he had begun in Paris and which was published in 1939 in Switzerland. Elias's father died in Breslau in 1940 and his mother was murdered by the Nazis in Treblinka in 1942. Her death constituted a traumatic experience that he felt throughout his life. After gaining a senior research fellowship at the London School of Economics, along with many other Jews Elias was interned on the Isle of Man during the war in 1940, where he met Asik Radomysler, an intimate friend, who committed suicide in 1952. Elias consequently published very little for the next few years. In 1950, together with S. H. Foukes, he founded the Group Analytic School of Psychotherapy. In 1954, aged 57, he secured his first academic job at the University of Leicester, retiring just eight years later in 1962. After teaching in the University of Ghana for two years he returned to teach part-time in Leicester, which at the time contained one of the foremost departments of sociology in the country with Illya Neustadt, Percy Cohen, John Goldthorpe and Anthony

Giddens. Here he published important work such as *The Established and the Outsiders* with John Scotson (1965) and on the sociology of sport including *Quest for Excitement* (1986) with Eric Dunning. Following the republication of *The Civilizing Process* in 1969, which gained him an intellectual reputation in Germany and the Netherlands, he moved to Amsterdam, and for a short time acted as a visiting professor at Bielefeld. During this period, he published numerous essays and books such as *Time* (2007a [1992]) and *Involvement and Detachment* (2007b). He died in 1990 aged 93.

Elias did not discuss his intellectual debts in any great detail. However, his works were constituted during a period when a number of important thinkers had been writing. These include Max Weber, Émile Durkheim, George Simmel, Sigmund Freud, Karl Mannheim, in addition to Kant, Hegel and Marx. Thus, for example, from Hegel he takes the idea of society as a process rather than a reified thing and the importance of developing concepts which are attuned to this fact. From Durkheim, he derives the idea of individuals in society becoming increasingly interdependent with one another, while from Weber he draws on the idea of the state as holding a monopoly of violence. Finally, from Marx he takes the centrality of class analysis (Loyal, 2004) while from Freud he derives the importance of the structuring and curtailment of human drives.

Historical, Social and Political Context

Germany came late to unification in 1871 but it remained divided between an industrially productive Catholic South-West Germany and an agriculturally focused East Elbian Junker class. The latter maintained hegemony over this formally united country through control over parliament by its leader, Bismarck. His policy of forming a Dual Alliance with Austria–Hungary in 1879 in an attempt to thwart Russia and Slav nationalism, led to a strong Protestant reaction including the rise of anti-Semitism, articulated forcefully in the work of the German historians such as Heinrich von Treitschke, in articles including 'A Word About Our Jews' (1880). Anti-Semitism constituted a powerful and radical movement centred on the ideology of an aristocratic German race, and by the 1890s it became a pervasive and accepted ideology. By this time Germany was also going through rapid industrialisation, a low-wage, export-driven economy with many exports going to the UK led by the self-interested, martial, Junker class. Low wages coupled with a relatively well-educated workforce facilitated the growth of socialism and Marxism within the Social Democratic Party (SPD). In 1897, the year Elias was born, Kaiser Wilhelm II was both King of Prussia and German Emperor. The First World War between Prussia–Germany and Austria–Hungary against the UK, France and Russia was a complex affair, with Prussia seeking to reconfigure German–Slav power relations under General Ludendorff and Field Marshall Hindenburg. Following the Russian Revolution in 1917, when the Bolsheviks seized power, Lenin sought peace with Germany, but Ludendorff refused, aiming to restore the Romanov dynasty. With the United States coming into the war and Germany fighting on both the Eastern and Western fronts it had by September 1918 lost the war.

The Crisis of Post-war German Society

As a teenager and young man Elias was therefore caught in the middle of profound and unstable social, economic and political changes underway in Germany. In addition to the tremendous loss of life following the Great War, the installation of the Weimar Republic in August 1919 saw the beginning of a number of turbulent and watershed years in German history. Humiliating terms imposed by the Treaty of Versailles in 1919 psychologically compounded the four years of war and famine. Among the treaty's clauses were that Germany had to claim responsibility for starting the war, pay the Allies large reparations, surrender its colonies within Europe, drastically reduce the size of its army to 100,000 and surrender various territories to its European neighbours, including Posen, bringing into existence Poland. The post-war period of acute destabilisation characterised by widespread hunger and unemployment also saw the emergence of extremist far-right and far-left factions. These included the Sparticists led by Rosa Luxemburg and Karl Liebknecht, the Freikorps to which Hitler was attached, as well as the Prussian–German pro-monarchist and anti-Semitic National People's Party (DNVP), which became the second largest party by 1924. The battles between the Freikorps and the left are discussed in some detail in his book *The Germans* (1996). These two extremist groupings effectively sandwiched the SDP and Catholic Party, who were situated in the centre of the political spectrum.

An already destabilised society was further exacerbated by the emergence of hyperinflation in 1922 following the promissory notes Germany had issued and huge debts it had accumulated during and after the war, including reparations bills. The exchange rate for the Reichsmark increased from 4.2 to a dollar in 1914 to 4.2 trillion to a dollar nine years later (Hawes, 2017: 155) wiping out the savings of the middle classes. Despite a flowering of Weimar culture and a marked shift from Prussian absolutism reflected in support for the SPD in 1928, the 1929 crash in the United States, which was supplying Germany with credit, saw the re-emergence of mass unemployment, reaching 6 million in 1933. The protracted struggles and coalition with the DNVP, as well as Protestant support, eventually led to the Nazis acquiring total power in 1933, ending the period of a provisional Weimar government. Hitler's entry into the Rhineland in 1936, union with Austria in 1938 (*Anschluss*), acquisition of the Sudetenland in the same year, as well as the *Kristallnacht* pogrom in which Jewish shops and synagogues were looted and burned down, constituted important preludes to the Second World War. The rise of the Nazis also forced a requestioning of the concept of civilization. These events frame Elias's magnum opus, *On the Process of Civilisation*, which ruminates on violence, the state and the conflict between what Elias calls 'survival groups' to demonstrate that civilisation although accepted as 'second nature', in fact has a thin and fragile veneer.

The Question of Civilisation

On the Process of Civilisation, often translated as *The Civilising Process* (2000), is a long-term investigation of the development of civilised behaviour through behavioural codes and how they became generalised and normalised for most people in Western societies and beyond, despite or in the face of the rise of National Socialism. Important discussions of civilisation had featured in the work of, among others, Thomas Mann in his *Reflections of a Non-Political Man* (1987 [1918]) and Sigmund Freud in his *Civilisation and its Discontents* (2002 [1930]). Elias attempts to interrogate the long-term development of civilised behaviour. As Mennell notes:

> To be civilized is to be polite and good mannered and considerate towards others; clean and decent and hygienic in personal habits; humane and gentle and kind, restrained and self-controlled and even-tempered; reluctant to use violence against others save in exceptional circumstances… Above all, though, to be civilized is to live with others in an orderly, well organized, just, predictable and calculable society. (1998: 29)

Elias investigates how individuals develop more rounded self-restraints in the context of increasingly pacified societies from the Middle Ages onwards, and how this is connected with the state's monopolisation of violence. This for Elias is an ongoing process with no end and no beginning. A central moral–political concern underpinning his work is how people can live peaceably with one another without injuring or killing one another. Elias remained acutely aware of the possibility for for what he called 'decivilization' processes (Dunning and Mennell, 1998; Elias, 1996; de Swaan, 2001).

Nevertheless, Elias tended to remain aloof from direct political statements and comments, often referring to the need for the relative detachment of social scientists who examine social configurations of humans and the unplanned consequences of their interdependent actions (Elias, 2007). They could be compared to the fantasy-driven, relatively involved, political and sociological accounts which focus on individual actions. There is nevertheless a political underpinning to his work. As societies become increasingly complex, opaque and relatively more equal, and individuals more interdependent, no one group can control society's direction. This can result in disastrous consequences. Elias therefore argues that social scientists should aim to produce reality congruent knowledge to help equip humans to control the deleterious and unplanned consequences of interdependent human actions for the overall good of humanity; that is, to improve the 'human means of orientation'. His theoretical framework has some affinities with social democratic ideology. As Mennell notes:

> Figurational or process sociology, with its strong emphasis on the ubiquity of chains of social interdependence and the consequential ubiquity of power ratios in the relations between people and groups

of people, tends to be associated with the left of centre socialist or (more usually) moderate social democratic traditions, with their concern for collective welfare and greater equality – not to mention their sympathy for less powerful *outsiders*. (2018)

Arguments and Ideas

Towards a Figurational or Process Sociology

A figurational approach holds that human beings are born into relations of interdependency and that the social structures that they form with each other have emergent dynamics that cannot be reduced to individual actions or motivations. These emergent dynamics shape the growth, development and trajectory of individuals' lives. Figurations are in a constant state of flux and transformation, and long-term transformations in human social figurations are largely unplanned and unforeseen. Elias sees the development of knowledge taking place within such figurations.

The Court Society

His first work, written in 1933 but not published until 1969, was *The Court Society*, which examined the social pressures facing the 'court nobility' under the reign of Louis XIV. Elias saw the court rationality of the nobility, in which rank and prestige determined expenditure, contrasting with the economic rationality of the bourgeoisie, where consumption was subordinated to income. For Elias these courts instituted a decisive social transition by transforming a warrior nobility into a court nobility, through a process of *courtisation*. This 'taming of the warriors' occurred during the reign of Louis XIV (1643–1715).

As a two-front stratum – a term derived from Simmel – the court nobility found themselves squeezed between the king above them and a rising mercantile bourgeoisie pushing up from below. In such a context social rank became all-important. Rank determined how large an individual's house was to be compared with those of higher and lower rank, as well as an individual's level of required spending. The nobility were forced to spend large amounts of money towards maintaining a display to maintain their rank, even if this often led to financial ruin. For Elias, the nobility's precarious social position, prestige and situation meant that they became finely tuned to variations and fine distinctions in terms of etiquette, speech, behaviour and manners. They also developed greater self-control in terms of their drives and emotions so that short-term desires or affects were replaced by longer term goals and aims. This ethos of self-control, in which the image of the self-enclosed individual and a peculiar understanding of self-experience takes centre stage, is captured in the literature and philosophy of the period, for example in the work of Descartes. The analysis of court society, Elias believed, provided a crucial corrective both to Max Weber's discussions of instrumental and value rationality, as well as qualifying Marx's simple binary contrast between feudalism and capitalism by emphasising the distinctive impact of the absolutist social order.

The Civilising Process

This same group of courtiers formed the focus of *On the Processes of Civilisation*, which drew on Marx, Mannheim, Weber, Simmel and Freud to offer an investigation of psychological and behavioural transformations among the secular upper classes in the West. One of the fundamental sociological problems that Elias wanted to help solve in the book, while researching manners and state formation, was how human personality and behaviour – Elias uses the term 'habitus' – changes over many generations. In this case he tracks these shifts over a 500-year period in Europe. For Elias, habitus is simply defined as a 'second nature', the learned social standards of behaviour and feeling we all embody; to that extent his work can be seen as a 'historical social psychology'. The book was originally divided into two volumes, which, though integrally and reciprocally connected, were misleadingly published separately. Volume 1 examines changes in the behaviour of the secular upper classes in the West and contains two parts: On the sociogenesis of the concepts of 'civilisation' and 'culture'; and Civilisation as a specific transformation of human behaviour. Volume 2 interrogates state formation and civilisation. This volume can be further sub-divided into two parts: Feudalisation and state formation; and Synopsis: towards a theory of civilising processes.

Volume 1: *Changes in the Behaviour of the Secular Upper Classes in the West*

The subtitle of volume 1 of *The Civilising Process* is *Changes in the Behaviour of the Secular Upper Classes in the West* and in this volume Elias asks how it was that certain classes in the developing nation-states of Western Europe came to think of themselves as 'civilised' and how this became generalised as a badge of Western superiority over non-Western cultures. He then goes on to discuss the concept of civilisation. Civilisation is a controversial word which is shot through with 'value judgements' and moral connotations. According to Elias, by the nineteenth century European people had come to describe themselves as civilised, and to see themselves as 'superior' to other people, whom they described as 'primitive' or 'savage' or 'barbaric'. They also came to think of themselves as inherently, or innately 'civilised'. In fact, he argues there was nothing inherent about their ways of behaving and feeling (and nothing inherently superior either), these were changing products of history and socialisation.

Though the term civilisation did not play an important role in the French Revolution (1789–99), it was subsequently used to justify the colonial expansion of the French and other Europeans. Whole nations began henceforth to consider the process of civilisation as completed within their own societies – while forgetting the social conditions of its emergence – and came to see themselves as superior standard bearers of an expanding civilisation and architects of colonial conquest. Elias argued that civilisation came to express the self-consciousness of the West: it summed up everything in which Western society of the last two or three centuries believed itself superior to earlier societies or 'more primitive' contemporary ones. This pride could be related to its level of technology, its type of manners, its development of scientific knowledge or to its religious ideas and customs. These ways of behaving and feeling had become so deeply habituated, and so taken for granted, that they felt innate even to European people themselves. Such individuals had become unconscious of the fact that they had learned these ways of behaving, and that their standards were the product of a long inter-generational learning process. For Elias, then, the term civilisation was more fully formed in the second half of the eighteenth century, replacing the concepts of 'courtesy', 'civilite' and 'politesse', which, before its arrival, had performed the same function – that of expressing the self-image and sense of superiority of the European upper classes by comparison with others whom they considered simpler, more primitive or more barbaric.

However, the term did not mean the same thing in different societies. The French and English use of the concept contrasted with that of the Germans, who used it to refer to things that are useful but only of secondary value. It was the concept of *Kultur* (culture) which came to express the self-image of the Germans and their pride in their own achievements. While the French and English use of 'civilisation' was expansionary, outward-looking and emphasised what was common to all human beings, the German concept of *Kultur* accentuated national differences, group identity and was inward-looking. The conceptual antithesis between *Culture* and *Civilisation* reflected the two different worldviews and the marked social division between a relatively powerless middle-class German intelligentsia, which emphasised genuineness, personality, sincerity, intellectual development, on the one hand, and a French-speaking, politically powerful, court nobility, which championed outward appearance and manners, on the other. This conceptual and social contraposition in turn reflected the political fragmentation of Germany as compared with the more unified and centralised 'good society' found in both France and England, in which the rising middle classes more readily adopted aristocratic traditions and behavioural models, and only showed a moderate reformist opposition to its worldview. Despite its variegated and contested interpretation, Elias sought to continue to use the term in a technical sense, to examine the change in human habitus over a long-term period of 500 years or so. That is, he sought to examine people's changing behavioural codes, the shifts in their standards of feeling and thinking and in the regulation of their biogical drives and instincts.

Volume 2: State Formation

In part 2 of volume 1 of the book, Elias deals with the way manners have changed over the centuries, as they were depicted in 'manners books' from the thirteenth to the nineteenth century, in Germany, France, Italy and England. These changes also meant changes in feelings and emotions. Manners books, as for example Erasmus of Rotterdam's *De civilitate morum puerilium*, were addressed specifically to the upper classes – to courtiers and would-be courtiers – and then later to bourgeois groups rather than to the mass of the population. Erasmus is not the first; in fact for Elias similar questions occupied the men of the Middle Ages and Graeco-Roman antiquity, and he adds: 'This process that has no beginning cannot here be traced back indefinitely' (2000: 48). It is therefore surprising then that they discuss, and had to discuss, things that we now take for granted. These include table manners, using a knife or spoon, for instance, as well as the regulation of our 'natural functions' such as blowing one's nose, defecation and urinating, spitting and behaviour in the bedroom. According to Elias the medieval books set out some basic rules but did so briefly, and there are not many changes in these rules. In the medieval world in the case of eating, for example, 'everything is simpler, impulses and inclinations are less restrained' (2000: 50). Again, Tannhäuser, in his book *Hofzucht* addresses 'the upper class, the knights who lived at court'. In these books courteous behaviour is constantly contrasted to 'coarse manners', which are identified with the peasantry.

For example, by the end of the Middle Ages in about the sixteenth century, the fork appears by way of Italy, then France, England and Germany, in the upper classes as an instrument for taking food from the common dish. It remains a luxury item until at least the seventeenth century, being usually made of gold or silver. However, from the Renaissance onwards rules regarding manners and conduct become increasingly elaborate, and more is said. Once these rules become accepted and generalised much later, less needs to be said, and some things cannot be said.

Elias studies 'outward bodily propriety' because all human societies have some rules or standards about how biological needs are handled. Since all human infants are born in the same emotional condition, the lifetime point of departure is always the same. Therefore, when the social standards for dealing with these matters change over time, the changes are easy to track. According to Elias the overall trend, despite oscillation, and a to-ing and fro-ing, exhibits a sequential order of development. People also became aware of more things being forbidden. For Elias this indicates 'An invisible wall of affects [emotions] growing up between people's bodies' (2000: 56). There is therefore an 'advance of the threshold of shame and embarrassment [or repugnance]', as 'the frontiers of sensibility and the reserve which they expected of each other were increasing' (2000: 56). Within this context more and more activities are moved behind the scenes of social life and for Elias, in a sense, behind the scenes of mental life too, as activities become repressed into the unconscious.

These changes in 'the affect structure' of humans is also seen in terms of aggressive impulses. For Elias, retaining a holistic analysis throughout his approach, we should not separate different instincts into separate compartments, rather 'they complement and in part superseded each other' (2000: 157). The level of aggressive impulses in modern societies is much lower than that of earlier societies even when we recognise there are variations between modern nations.

For Elias, the major impetus that explains this trend are not what we ordinarily take them to be, 'material' or economic reasons, nor do they reflect increasing concerns relating to health and hygiene. Instead, he argues, we need to examine the significance of 'reasons of respect'. It is only quite late in the process that standards come to apply to everyone and in all circumstances. Moreover, for Elias, it is not simply a question of more self-control. Elias acknowledges that earlier societies often had areas of extreme self-control, such as Native Americans, ascetic monks, etc. Rather, Elias highlights how standards gradually come to be more even, more automatic, more all-embracing for everyone. He continually points to the connection between the social structure of a society and its personality structure, or habitus.

Though Elias was not concerned simply with a history of manners, the transformation of manners constitutes the primary subject of volume 1 of *The Civilising Process*. He charts the long-term transformations in manners, behavioural codes and thresholds of repugnance concerning bodily functions, all of which involved an internalisation of social restraints. His work traces the establishment of a characteristic habitus, involving increasing superego restraints over affective impulses and drives (including violent behaviour), as a compelling aspect of court society. Upper-class manners and affective sensibility, through processes of distinction and imitation, became generalised as examples of polite behaviour and gradually diffused through other strata. This blind and unplanned process is nevertheless structured and directional.

In volume 2 of *The Civilising Process*, Elias firmly links these changes in manners, affects and personality structure to state formation, the 'sociogenesis' of the absolutist states, and shows how the internalisation of restraints and the resulting transformation in behavioural codes were intimately connected with transformations in the division of labour, demographic shifts, societal pacification, urbanisation, and the growth of trade and a money economy. His discussion of state formation begins with the onset of the Middle Ages and the end of the Western Roman Empire. Elias demarcates two expansive periods during the Middle Ages. In the first period from around 850 to 1050, he argues that centrifugal forces predominated wherein rule was fragmented between various lords, each ruling over a small circumscribed territory – what Perry Anderson refers to as 'parcellized sovereignty' (1974) – and therefore characterised by a process of feudalisation containing ties of fealty between a lord and a vassal. A lord provided land to subordinates in order to gain their obedience and extract duties. Here, society is characterised by a cellular structure of self-contained units in which social ties and territorial connections, and therefore forms of interdependence, are relatively undeveloped.

However, this *centripetal* period was followed by a second *centrifugal* period from around the twelfth century onwards in which there was an increasing growth in the centralised power of kings in relation to local magnates. With the possibility of acquiring more and more land becoming increasingly difficult (land rather than money was the central resource during this period and unlike the latter was finite), and following several interlocking factors including a sharp rise in population, competition between lords intensified. The conflict between warring lords eventually led to a single dominant ruler or king in much the same way as competition between a number of small firms leads to a single firm possessing monopoly – an idea taken from Marx. In this case it leads to an absolutist ruler possessing an administration itself equipped with members whose habitus contains a relatively high degree of foresight and rational calculation.

The State as a Monopolisation of Violence and Taxation

In *Economy and Society* Max Weber had defined a state as: 'an organisation which successfully upholds a claim to successful rule-making over a territory, by virtue of commanding a monopoly of the legitimate use of violence' (1978: 54). Elias extends this analysis in two ways: firstly, by demonstrating the process in which this monopolisation takes place; and secondly, by referring to the state's monopoly of physical violence *and* taxation. Here a spiralling and virtuous process operates: growth in the urban money economy facilitated, but also critically depended upon, the power and the monopoly of violence achieved by the central state authority. Greater access to these economic circuits gave access to greater military resources relative to the landed warlord–nobility, whose principal source of economic and military power was control over finite and depreciating land assets.

This shifting power ratio transformed a formerly independent warrior class into an increasingly dependent upper class of courtiers. Greater pacification facilitated trade and economic growth, which in turn underwrote the economic and military power of the central authority and led to growing power for the middle classes. When declining aristocratic power and increasing middle-class power were approximately equal, monarchs were able to lay claim to 'absolute power'. In their newly pacified domains, and particularly within the court, these developments systematically rewarded more restrained patterns of behaviour. External restraints, associated with the authority relations of state formation, were gradually and increasingly internalised as self-restraints, resulting in a characteristic shift in habitus and personality structure.

The Established and the Outsiders

Elias extends many of the arguments developed in both *The Court Society* and *The Civilising Process* into his other works. *The Established and the Outsiders* (2008 [1965]), written with John Scotson, is a study of a small suburban community in Leicester (fictitiously) named Winston Parva. The book examines the dynamics between three distinct neighbourhoods or 'zones': zone 1 inhabited by a middle-class population; zone 2 characterised by an 'old' established working-class population; and zone 3 characterised by a newly arrived population which was working class. The old communities refused to have dealings with the new community other than those imposed by occupational ties. Elias and Scotson show that, even without any visible ethnic markers, tension could arise between groups within a community simply on the basis of differences in their length of local residence. Elias and Scotson point to four major tendencies shared by established–outsider relationships. A tendency: to see outsiders as anomic; for the established to judge outsiders according to the 'minority of the worst'; for outsiders to internalise their stigmatisation and group disgrace; and for established groups to perceive outsiders as 'unclean' or polluting (Dunning, 2004: 82).

Although often mistakenly interpreted as separate from *The Civilising Process*, the discussion of established–outsider relations in fact also forms a central part of that work, albeit in this case abstracted from a longer term historical framework. Issues concerning the length of chains of interdependency, social cohesion, the self-restraint of drives and affects, adherence to behavioural codes and claims of status superiority as more 'civilised' are all present in the study of Winston Parva. Elias's central point in this work is that it is the configuration of their social relationships, and not their characteristics per se, that explains the relationship of domination between groups. Central to established–outsider relations, therefore, are not the characteristics of the groups themselves. A singular emphasis on race, racialisation, nationality, religion or ethnicity – whether the focus is on differences in skin colour or cultural values – draws attention away from what Elias considers a broader and more pertinent causal factor that explains the process of domination and discrimination: a differential in the power ratio between groups. *The Established and the Outsiders* thus constitutes a small-scale investigation into the sociology of power underwritten by an analysis of the structure of social figurations. The discussion of power is prioritised over other conventional sociological taxonomies invoking class, race, religion, nationality, etc. The latter are second-order categories that 'take on force' or explanatory significance when seen in relation to the former. When established groups feel exposed to an attack against their monopolised power resources, they use stigmatisation and exclusion as weapons to maintain their distinct identity, assert their superiority and keep outsiders in their place. In Winston Parva, processes of group charisma and group disgrace involved maintaining a positive 'we-image' by the established residents and a negative 'they-image' through the stigmatisation of outsiders and the propagation of collective fantasies (Elias and Scotson 2008 [1965]: 73–81). This, in turn, involved generalising the worst characteristics from the 'anomic minority' of a group to the whole group – attributing to all those living in zone 3 negative characteristics that only pertain to a small 'minority of the worst', while simultaneously attributing the best 'most nomic' behaviour onto the established group – modelling the self-image of the dominant group in terms of characteristics held by the 'minority of the best'.

The established–outsider framework, according to Elias, serves as an empirical paradigm of a universal human theme involving power, exclusion and inequality. For Elias the material and socio-psychological dynamics underpinning discrimination are ultimately manifestations of a long-term conflict rooted in the struggles between survival units and the different levels of power that exist between them.

What is Sociology?

In other works, such as *What is Sociology?* (1978 [1970]), Elias reiterates his claim that sociologists must avoid treating single individuals or whole societies as static givens – a reflection of inappropriate language and conceptualisation that reduces processes to states. It is for this reason his work is sometimes labelled 'process sociology'. A *scientific* sociology also requires that the *Homo clausus* ('closed person') view underlying methodological individualism be replaced with an orientation towards pluralities of 'open people' – *homines aperti*. This is the basis of a relational view of power as linked to the functions individuals have for one another. Here drawing on Simmel, Elias outlines his game models.

In these game models, Elias imagines the simplest hypothetical social processes in relation to games involving two or more players. In the first model – the primal contest – he discusses the functional interdependence, unequal strength and uneven reciprocal imposition of constraints of two competing groups, both chasing shrinking food resources. For Elias the primal contest is important because it demonstrates that, even in the absence of any active, ongoing relationship, groups and individuals provide functions for each other by the simple fact of co-presence – necessitating reciprocal anticipation, foresight and planning. A central question which follows from this, and in many ways one of the key problems of any civilising process, is how people are able to regulate their interdependencies and meet their animalic needs in such a way that they need not resort to violence:

> If one wanted to reduce the key problem of any civilizing process to its simplest formula, then it could be said to be the problem of how people can manage to satisfy their elementary animalic needs in their life together, without reciprocally destroying, frustrating, demeaning or in other ways harming each other time and time again in their search for this satisfaction – in other words, without fulfillment of the elementary needs of one person or group of people being achieved at the cost of those of another person or group. (Elias, 1996: 31)

The main purpose of these models was to demonstrate the way in which social processes generate emergent dynamics which cannot be reduced to or derived from a simple aggregation of many component individual actions or decisions, and constrain and mould both the habitus and behaviour of individuals.

Involvement and Detachment

A further aspect, and one of the most important aspects of Elias's work, relates to problems that philosophically minded sociologists refer to as epistemology but which Elias himself preferred to conceptualise as a sociological theory of knowledge. In *Involvement and Detachment* (2007a), *Time: An Essay* (2007b) and *The Symbol Theory* (2011), Elias sought to combine a Comtean theory of knowledge with a sociology of knowledge processes. A historical sociology of the knowledge process shows that earlier stages of human development were characterised by animistic, magico-mythical ideas and feelings with high degrees of fantasy and 'involvement'. Over many millennia, a steady shift in the balance from emotional involvement towards 'detachment' has made possible a steadily increasing reality-congruent understanding (Elias avoids using the word 'truth') of 'natural forces', and a correspondingly greater degree of control over and reduced danger from these forces. Knowledge of social processes. however, has remained relatively less autonomous and people are still very much at the mercy of 'social forces'. Sociologists, Elias concludes, need to create professional procedures and conventions like those at work in the natural sciences that will, to a degree, insulate the knowledge process from wider social processes and allow researchers to build up stocks of knowledge that can be of practical use.

The Germans

In *The Germans* (1996) Elias extends his arguments from *The Civilising Process* to provide an account of German social development from the seventeenth century to the late twentieth century focusing on the development of a German national habitus. While recognising the discontinuities in its development he also demonstrates the absence of courtier manners and a taming of warriors process that characterised French development, and therefore, instead, the presence of a marked military inheritance in the German habitus. This phenomenon for Elias is illustrated in the continuance of duelling fraternities which demonstrated the transference of military values, including the code of honour, from aristocratic officers to the middle classes in universities; for example, both Marx and Weber were involved in duelling. Elias also investigates what he calls the shift in a 'formality-informality span' of German society and its underpinning of the spread of nationalism, to argue: 'If one asks how Hitler was possible, then with the benefit of hindsight the spread of these socially sanctioned models of violent action and of social inequality belong among the prerequisites' (1996: 27).

Contemporary Relevance and Applications

As we noted above, Elias's later writings develop and also expand upon his theory of civilising processes. His contribution to the sociology of sport in *Quest for Excitement* (with Eric Dunning, 1986), applies the idea of Western civilising processes to the links between the 'parliamentarisation' of English politics and the codification of sports such as boxing, foxhunting and cricket. Elias and Dunning argue that civilising processes involve, as one of their aspects, processes of routinisation which lead to feelings of emotional staleness in people. As a result, institutions have developed which perform a de-routinising function through movement, sociability, excitement and identification. This brings about the common features of 'highbrow' activities, such as the arts, and 'lowbrow' activities, such as sports.

NORBERT ELIAS AND TALCOTT PARSONS

There are many interesting parallels between Elias and Parsons that allow us to consider the alternative fates bestowed upon these different theorists and how these affect the development of social theory itself. Both theorists were of the same generation and quite close in age. Both were deeply influenced by the work of Max Weber, albeit in their own ways. They both published their first major works in the late 1930s, both of which were ambitious and large volumes, and both of which were also consigned to relative obscurity for significant periods of time. However, whereas Parsons's career accelerated and his reputation rose to prominence in the 1950s, Elias remained relatively marginalised. Nonetheless, Elias regarded *The Civilising Process* as a contribution competing with that of Parsons, offering a more dynamic and processual framework compared with Parsons' rather static analyses focused on systems. Though rising in popularity in recent years, Elias's contrasting approach in some sense remains a road not taken by mid-century sociology.

Two peculiarities of Elias's reputation should be mentioned. Firstly, recognition of his work came right at the end of his life – so he is in a sense a 'more recent' figure than his dates imply. Moreover, although his work has been well received in Europe – especially the UK, France, Italy and the Netherlands – it has largely been ignored in the United States possibly because a stronger focus on short-term sociological analysis based in the individual is a predominant framework within the sociological community. Though he called himself a sociologist, his work is much wider than conventional sociology today, and he often seems to attract more interest from scholars outside his own discipline.

Elias's work, rather than being Eurocentric, was applied largely to Europe and Elias himself envisaged others extending his accounts to other countries outside of Western Europe. These include Castro (2006), who applies the civilising process framework to Mexico; Ikegami (1995), who applies it to Japan and specifically to the Samurai. Stauth (1997) examines such processes in Singapore; Volkov (2000) attempts to understand Russia and Stalinism with such an Eliasian framework, while Young (1997) applies it to South-East Asia.

Mennell (2007) examines *The American Civilizing Process*, and attempts to explain 'why America is as it is' (Mennell, 2007: x). Consciously following Elias's framework the book analyses, *inter alia*, popular usages of civilization, American we-images, the development of manners, state formation, territorial expansion and monopolization of the means of violence. The book aims to provide insights into the paradoxes characterising contemporary North American social relationships but from a longer-term and processual point of view: between an agreeable day-to-day civility and capital punishment; from banning to allowing an unfettered possession of deadly weapons; between a spirit of classlessness to staggering levels of income and wealth inequality; as the foremost centre of scientific and technological development but with a level of religious adherence topping nearly all comparative survey charts in the developed world. Mennell attempts to reveal, in fine-tuned detail, the historical development of social character in America, based unusually not on one single model-setting elite, but several competing 'good societies'; and to interrogate the long-standing and overwrought question concerning 'American exceptionalism'.

Elias's work has also been used to reinterpret world history, especially in the important work of Johan Goudsblom in *Fire and Civilization* (1992). Drawing on archaelogy, ethology and anthropology, Goudsblom attempts to account for the long-term and gradual human mastery and control of fire beginning with the origin of the species up to and including its regulation in modern life. Rather than focusing on the importance of the agricultural revolution, associated with the domestication of plants and animals, or the industrial revolution associated with the use of inanimate energy, he aims to examine the role of fire in shaping civilisation. Unlike other human attributes such as language and the use of tools, which some animals share in a limited sense, the use of fire is uniquely human.

In the course of this long-term process, what was initially a wild, incalculable and dangerous natural force was tamed to a certain degree, and incorporated into human society. Goudsblom dealt here with a development extending over many hundreds of millennia, long before the emergence of *Homo sapiens*, which is closely connected with the entire process of humanisation or the formation of humanity in its present shape (Goudsblom, 1987: 457).

According to Goudsblom fire became possible only when a certain level of socio-cultural development and social interdependence has been reached by humans, including a level of social and self-control and foresight necessary in the handling of fire. As he notes:

> In dealing with fire it is of vital importance that people can command an appropriate balance of daring and caution, that they neither immediately panic nor grow reckless and forget how dangeropus fire is. A certain measure of self-control is part and parcel of technical control – this applied to tending a fire just as much as to any other skill. (1987: 469–70)

Elias's work has also been applied to analyse gender and sexuality. Extending Elias's essay on the long-term shift in gender roles, Wouters (2004) has attempted to examine these changes by looking at manners books in four different countries. In addition, Elias's writings have also been used in criminology (Garland, 1990; Wood, 2004, 2007) as well as the field of international relations in the work of Linklater (2003, 2007) and the study of organisations (Dopson, 1997; Van Wree, 1999). Others have used his sociological framework in a more delimited way. Hughes (2003) has applied it to examine tobacco and smoking while Gerritsen (2000) has focused on alcohol and opiates. The field of the sociology of sport has been strongly shaped by an Eliasian tradition following the arguments laid out in *Quest for Excitement* (Elias and Dunning, 1986; Dunning et al., 2004; Maguire, 1999). Still others have employed his work to examine and compare national characteristics as in Austria and the UK (Kuzmics and Axtmann, 2007) as well as to understand decivilisation, violence, war and genocide (Zwaan, 2001; Watson, 2007; Haring and Kuzmics, 2008).

Criticisms

Elias's work has often been criticised for its circumspect use of the term 'civilisation', which carries ethnocentric echoes of imperialism and Victorian progress theory. However, this is usually a misunderstanding of his intention. Elias attempts to distinguish his own approach from everyday morally and politically loaded accounts by using the term in a technical sense; that is, he does not use it as an *emic* term used by everyday actors, but as an *etic* term used by social scientists. Nevertheless, the use of the term has caused confusion and sometimes led to a pre-emptory criticism. Moreover, from being a universal theory of development or of moral and cultural progress, as some commentators have implied, *The Civilising Process* offers a delimited account of the different trajectories of development in the UK, France and Germany, and the genesis and subject matter of the book cannot be understood without reference to Elias's experience of the social and political crisis of German society and the global impact of the rise of Nazism.

As a sociologist trespassing into the field of history, Elias's work has often been received with some scepticism among medieval historians (Rosenwein, 2002; Roth, 2012). In part this was a function of the staggered process of translation referred to above, but also because his work often fails to conform to modern scholarly conventions in relation to citation and referencing. In this sense there is a similarity with a work such as Huizinga's *Homo Ludens* (1938) – much criticised but invariably remaining a central point of reference.

Elias's view that violence has decreased in modern societies has also been criticised. On the one hand, although it may be argued that everyday forms of violence have been diminishing since the Middle Ages, the implications of Elias's arguments are of an increased prevalence of violence that can be traced further back. However, archaeological evidence for violence in pre-settled societies is unclear. Writers such as Sahlins (1974) portray a very different pacified picture of hunter–gatherer societies. On the other hand, it has been argued that rather than violence diminishing it has increased in modern societies. In his book *The Age of Extremes*, Eric Hobsbawm points out that:

> Local, regional or global, the wars of the twentieth century were to be on an altogether vaster scale than anything previously experienced. Among seventy four international wars between 1816 and 1965, which American specialists, who like to do that kind of thing, have ranked by the number of people they killed, the top four occurred in the 20th century: the two world wars, the Japanese war against China in 1937–9, and the Korean war. (1994: 24)

Thus, rather than increasing pacification in everyday life we see increasing violence and slaughter as the state as an organisational entity expands (Malešević and Ryan, 2013; Malešević, 2017; Mann, 2018). Here a distinction perhaps needs to be drawn between the increasing intensity of wars and violence which operate simultaneously, with a generally increasing pacification in other spheres of life – war is moved behind the scenes so to speak.

Conclusion

Elias's ability to combine micro and macro accounts of social processes to transcend the individual–society dichotomy, to combine theoretical insight with a breadth of empirical evidence, and to provide a consistently rigorous social and historical account of the world is amply demonstrated in *On the Process of Civilisation*. However, whether his elegant theoretical analysis stands up to close empirical scrutiny, especially in accounting for violence, remains an open matter requiring further investigation.

References

Anderson, P. (1974) *Lineages of the Absolutist State*. London: Verso.

Castro, J. E. (2006) *Water, Power, and Citizenship: Social Struggle in the Basin of Mexico*. Basingstoke: Palgrave Macmillan.

De Swaan, A. (2015) *The Killing Compartments: The Mentality of Mass Murder*. New Haven, CT: Yale University Press.

Dopson, S. (1997) *Managing Ambiguity and Change: The Case of the NHS*. London: Macmillan.

Dunning, E. (2004) Aspects of the Figurational Dynamics of Racial Stratification: A Conceptual Discussion and Developmental Analysis of Black-White Relations in the United States. In: S. Loyal and S. Quilley (eds) *The Sociology of Norbert Elias*. Cambridge: Cambridge University Press, pp. 75–94.

Dunning, E. and Mennell, S. (1998) Elias on Germany, Nazism and the Holocaust: On the Balance Between 'Civilizing' and 'Decivilizing' Trends in the Social Development of Western Europe. *British Journal of Sociology*, 49(3), pp. 339–57.

Dunning, E., Malcolm, D. and Waddington, I. (2004) *Sport Histories: Figurational Studies of the Development of Modern Sports*. London: Routledge.

Elias, N. (1978 [1970]) *What is Sociology?* New York: Columbia University Press.

Elias, N. (1983) *The Court Society*. Oxford: Blackwell.

Elias, N. (1996) *The Germans: Studies of Power Struggles and the Development of Habitus in the Nineteenth and Twentieth Centuries*. Cambridge: Polity.

Elias, N. (2000) *The Civilizing Process: Sociogenetic and Psychogenetic Investigations*. Revised edition. Oxford: Blackwell.

Elias, N. (2006) *The Court Society. Collected Works of Norbert Elias*, Vol. 2. Dublin: University College Dublin Press.
Elias, N. (2007a) *Involvement and Detachment. Collected Works of Norbert Elias*, Vol. 8. Dublin: University College Dublin Press.
Elias, N. (2007b) *Time and Essay, Collected Works of Norbert Elias*, Vol. 9. Dublin: University College Dublin Press.
Elias, N. (2011) *The Symbol Theory, Collected Works of Norbert Elias*, Vol. 13. Dublin: University College Dublin Press.
Elias, N. (2012) *On the Process of Civilisation: Sociogenetic and Psychogenetic Investigations. Collected Works of Norbert Elias*, Vol. 3. Dublin: University College Dublin Press.
Elias, N. and Dunning, E. (1986) *Quest for Excitement: Sport and Leisure in the Civilizing Process*. Oxford: Basil Blackwell.
Elias, N. and Scotson, J. L. (2008 [1965]) *The Established and the Outsiders. Collected Works of Norbert Elias*, Vol. 4. Dublin: University College Dublin Press.
Freud, S. (2002 [1929]) *Civilisation and its Discontents*. London: Penguin.
Garland, D. (1990) *Punishment and Modern Society: A Study in Social Theory*. Oxford: Clarendon Press.
Gerritsen, J. W. (2000) *The Control of Fuddle and Flash: A Sociological History of the Regulation of Alcohol and Opiates*. Boston, MA: Brill.
Goudsblom, J. (1987) The Domestication of Fire as a Civilising Process. *Theory, Culture & Society*, 4(2–3), pp. 457–76.
Goudsblom, J. (1992) *Fire and Civilization*. London: Penguin.
Hackeschimdt, J. (2004) The Torch Bearer: Norbert Elias as a Young Zionist. *The Leo Baeck Institute Year Book*, 49(1), pp. 59–74.
Haring, S. A. and Kuzmics, H. (eds) (2008) *Das Gesicht des Krieges: Militär aus emotionssoziologischer Perspektive* (The Face of War: The Military Seen from a Sociology-of-Emotions Perspective). Vienna: Sicht.
Hawes, J. (2017) *The Shortest History of Germany*. London: Old Street Publishing.
Hobsbawm, E. J. (1994) *The Age of Extremes: The Short Twentieth Century, 1914–1991*. London: Michael Joseph.
Hughes, J. (2003) *Learning to Smoke: Tobacco Use in the West*. Chicago, IL: University of Chicago Press.
Huizinga, J. (1938) *Homo Ludens*. London: Penguin
Ikegami, E. (1995) *The Taming of the Samurai: Honorific Individualism and the Making of Modern Japan*. Cambridge, MA: Harvard University Press.
Kuzmics, H. and Axtmann, R. (2007) *Authority, State and National Character: The Civilizing Process in Austria and England, 1700–1900*. Aldershot: Ashgate.
Linklater, A. (2003) Norbert Elias and International Relations: Figurations. *Newsletter of the Norbert Elias Foundation*, 19, pp. 4–5.
Linklater, A. (2007) *Critical Theory and World Politics: Citizenship, Sovereignty and Humanity*. London: Routledge.

Loyal, S. (2004) Elias on Class and Stratification. In: S. Loyal and S. Quilley (eds) *The Sociology of Norbert Elias*. Cambridge: Cambridge University Press. pp. 122-41.

Maguire, J. A. (1999) *Global Sport: Identities, Societies, Civilizations*. Cambridge: Polity.

Malešević, S. (2017) *The Rise of Organised Brutality: A Historical Sociology of Violence*. Cambridge: Cambridge University Press.

Malešević, S. and Ryan, K. (2013) The Disfigured Ontology of Figurational Sociology: Norbert Elias and the Question of Violence. *Critical Sociology*, 39(2), pp. 165-81.

Mann, M. (2018) Have Wars and Violence Declined? *Theory and Society*, 47(1), pp. 37-60.

Mann, T. (1987 [1918]) *Reflections of a Non-Political Man*. New York: Ungar.

Mennell, S. (1998) *Norbert Elias: An Introduction*. Dublin: University College Dublin Press.

Mennell, S. (2007) *The American Civilizing Process*. Cambridge: Polity.

Mennell, S. (2018) The Political Implications of Figurational Sociology. Global Interdependencies: What's New in the Human Society of Individuals? *The Political and Academic Relevance of Norbert Elias's Work Today*. Université Saint-Louis, Brussels, pp. 5-8. Unpublished.

Rosenwein, B. H. (2002) Worrying about Emotions in History. *American Historical Review*, 107(3), pp. 821-45.

Roth, R. (2012) *American Homicide*. Cambridge, MA: Harvard University Press.

Sahlins, M. (1974) *Stone Age Economics*. New York: Aldine De Gruyter.

Stauth, G. (1997) Elias in Singapore: Civilizing Processes in a Tropical City. *Thesis Eleven*, 50(1), pp. 51-70.

Swaan, A. de (2001) Dyscivilization, Mass Extermination and the State. *Theory, Culture & Society*, 18(2-3), pp. 265-76.

Van Wree, W. (1999) *Meetings, Manners and Civilisation*. Leicester: University of Leicester Press.

Volkov, V. (2000) The Concept of Kul'turnost': Notes on the Stalinist Civilizing Process. In: S. Fitzpatrick (ed.) *Stalinism: New Directions*. London: Routledge, pp. 210-30.

Watson, K. D. (ed.) (2007) *Assaulting the Past: Violence and Civilization in Historical Context*. Newcastle upon Tyne: Cambridge Scholars.

Weber, M. (1978) *Economy and Society: An Outline of Interpretative Sociology*. In: G. Roth and C. Wittich (eds) Berkeley, CA: University of California Press.

Wood, J. C. (2004) *Violence and Crime in Nineteenth-Century England: The Shadow of Our Refinement*. London: Routledge.

Wood, J. C. (2007) Recent Work on Elias and Violence: History, Evolutionary Psychology and Literature. *Figurations: Newsletter of the Norbert Elias Foundation*, No. 28, pp. 6-8.

Wouters, C. (2004) *Sex and Manners: Female Emancipation in the West, 1890-2000*. London: Sage.

Young, K. (1997) State Formation in Southeast Asia. *Thesis Eleven*, 50(1), pp. 71-97.

Bourdieu

Introduction

Pierre Bourdieu is one of the leading sociological theorists whose work is extensively used today. At the time of his death in 2002, he was one of France's most high-profile intellectuals. His writing style and dense vocabulary, however, makes his writings challenging to access and understand. Nevertheless, his approach remains very popular, after Foucault, he is currently the second most cited social theorist. Although he was initially trained as a philosopher, his work from the late 1950s on Algeria was primarily based on empirical enquiry and fieldwork, and the concepts that he developed were forged within these substantive contexts and designed to explain them.

He has also undertaken sociological enquiries into a broad variety of areas within sociology including the operation of a gift economy, marriage strategies, education and schooling, rituals and social practice, class and consumption, language and power, the state and state bureaucracy, masculine domination, the housing market, role of art and artists, religion, law, the family, journalism and television, sport, and neoliberalism and politics. Given his orientation to theoretically informed empirical work, his influence has been enormous and many of his key concepts have become used or part of the sociological lexicon, such as habitus and field, cultural, social and symbolic capital. A central concern throughout his work has been to reveal the hidden mechanisms through which social reproduction and social domination take place in modern societies.

Life and Intellectual Context

Born 1 August 1930 in Lasseube, a small village in the South-Western Pyrenees, the son of a peasant who subsequently became a postal worker, Bourdieu was raised speaking Béarnese (a Gascon dialect) at home. His working-class roots played an important part in his subsequent sociological trajectory, and throughout his life, he felt himself an outsider in the academic establishment, generating a highly conscious and critical attitude towards it. In his semi-auto biographical work, he refers to possessing a 'cleft-habitus' (Bourdieu, 2008). A highly gifted and diligent student, after studying at the lycée in Pau followed by the Lycée Louis le Grand in Paris, he gained entrance to the prestigious École Normale Supérior, where he studied philosophy. Following his *agrégation* in 1954, he began work as a teacher in a provincial lycée in Moulin.

In 1954, he started, but later abandoned, a thesis under the supervision of George Canguilhem on 'Temporal Structures of Affective Life', before being reluctantly conscripted into the army in October 1955 and sent to Algeria during the Algerian War of Independence (1954–62) at the age of 25. Posted to an air force unit of the military staff in the Chelif Valley, he was later transferred to the Service de Documentation et d'Information of the Gouvernement General (Yacine, 2013: 18). Collecting information on the rural and urban context of Algerian life and society, he eventually secured a position teaching sociology and philosophy at the University of Algiers in 1957. He returned to France in 1960, in order to work as an assistant to Raymond Aron at the Sorbonne. In 1961, he joined the faculty of letters in Lille as a lecturer in sociology, becoming director of a research group, the Centre de sociologie européenne (CSE). In 1964, he became Directeur d'études at the École Pratique des Hautess Études en Sciences Sociales, in Paris. However, it was several years later in 1972 that he published his ground-breaking work on kinship, ritual and social exchange based on his Algerian fieldwork, *Outline of a Theory of Practice* ([1972] 1977). In 1975 he founded a hugely influential French social scientific journal *Actes de la recherche en sciences sociales* to promote the cause of a scientific sociology. In 1979 Bourdieu published another significant work making a major impact on the social sciences, *Distinction: A Social Critique of the Judgement of Taste*. On the recommendation of Michel Foucault, he was appointed professor of sociology at the College de France in 1981.

The 1980s also saw the publication of several important works, including *Homo Academicus*, *Language and Symbolic Power*, *The State Nobility*. After remaining out of the spotlight or being 'neutral' with regard to public politics in France, he increasingly intervened in various political campaigns and social movements, defending marginalised groups including irregular immigrants, the homeless, the unemployed and striking workers during this period. Between January 1990 and January 1991, Bourdieu gave a number of lectures at the Collége de France on various topics including Manet, Habitus and field, classification struggles and the state. He died on 23 January 2002, from cancer.

Intellectual Influences

Bourdieu's intellectual development draws heavily on the *sociological* work of Marx, Weber and Durkheim, using each to criticise and complement the insights of the other. But his overall theory is grounded in a critical appropriation of the phenomenology of Husserl and Merleau-Ponty which then became modified by the *anthropological* work of structuralism, and based on the philosophical work of phenomenology, and later from the late 1970s, the ordinary language philosophy of John Austin.

The post-war French intellectual field included within it both sociological and philosophical writers such as the phenomenologists and existentialists Husserl, Heiddegger, Merleau-Ponty and Sartre, as well the structuralists Lévi-Strauss, Dumezil, Braudel and Althusser. All of them were to play an important role in shaping Bourdieu's work. His early education was as a philosopher and, as Descombes (1980) notes, the generation of philosophers in France between 1930 and 1960 were preoccupied with three dominant Hs – Hegel, Husserl and Heidegger – while an older generation from the 1960s were more concerned with the three masters of suspicion – Marx, Nietzsche and Freud. Hegel became especially prominent following Kojève's (1980) anthropological reading of the master–slave dialectic, which foregrounded the notion of desire and the 'fight for recognition'. Although Sartre was intellectually the dominant figure in French phenomenology, it was Husserl, Heidegger and Merleau-Ponty who played a more direct and significant role in the development of Bourdieu's thinking (Bourdieu, 1990: 5). Husserl, who saw phenomenology as the descriptive, non-reductive science of what appears, especially through and in the subjective and intersubjective medium of consciousness, attempted to provide a grounding for the conditions of possibility of objective knowledge, especially in opposition to empiricism and positivism. His philosophical account of conscious cognition, which also discussed the environments, horizons or world (as the 'horizon of horizons') within which consciousness functioned, centred on the role of intentionality and the taken-for-granted, unproblematic, natural attitude in which the world existed for us. Husserl argued that it was the philosopher's role to place this natural attitude under suspension (*epoché*) to get back to 'the things themselves'. Silhouetting the natural attitude allowed us to uncover its implicit meaning (Mooney, forthcoming). According to Husserl, theoretical analysis developed on the basis of our practical knowledge, which was itself rooted in the natural attitude and everyday life-world (Husserl, 1973). Although he occasionally refers to a singular life-world, Husserl also talks of a number of intersecting and overlapping life-worlds including the 'home world' (*Heimwelt*) and 'alien worlds' of other cultures. We inhabit such life-worlds, which are given in advance, but which are 'on hand' (*vorhanden*) and experienced as a unity (Moran, 2005: 9), in a pre-theoretical, pre-predicative manner. The natural attitude is characterised by *doxa*, or mere opinion. This focus on the intentionality of consciousness required a form of phenomenological reflection turning consciousness back on itself, to explore the essence of conscious acts as part of a transcendental phenomenology. According to Husserl, the most fundamental form of conscious life was temporality (Smith, 2003: 116), and he distinguishes between protention as the anticipatory and pre-flexive (if practically coloured) aiming at what is to come, and which pervaded the present, and that practical, yet, reflective positing of a future project that was possible, but relatively undetermined. Bourdieu draws sparingly upon this distinction, especially in his early work on Algeria. As Lane argues:

> Husserl argues that time is not experienced as so many discrete moments in a linear causal series, but rather as a 'field' or 'network of intentionalities', of past experiences, 'retentions', which are incorporated into a structure of 'intuitive expectations', or 'practical anticipations' as so many protentions', a 'practical sense' of what does or does not constitute an 'objective potentiality'. He terms this structure of dispositions a 'habitus'. (2000: 24)

Heidegger took phenomenology further by opening Husserl's phenomenological brackets and distinguishing between objects that were ready-at-hand (*Vorhanden*) to be used immediately in an unthinking way, and present-at-hand (*Zuhanden*), of a theorist or scientist looking at or observing something. In addition, Merleau-Ponty made a sharp distinction between the intentional or cognitive relation to objects, activity and space, and a somatically projective or 'motor intentional' understanding, which involved a bodily 'know-how'. Hence, beneath our conscious directness or intentionality, Merleau-Ponty discerns a deeper bodily intentionality (an 'operative intentionality') that humans count on, but which they are rarely aware of. Here, the body was not seen as an object in the world: 'but as our means of communication with it, to the world not conceived as a collection of determinate objects, but as the horizon latent in all our experience and itself ever-present and anterior to every thought' (Merleau-Ponty, 1962: 92). Humans depend on a vast repertoire of immediately available skills, a 'habitual body' or practical bodily memory continually at our disposal. The unreflexive bodily understanding of space and activity could be counterposed to reflexive, cognitive, intentional acts in terms of a spatiality of situation, rather than position. Understanding was not achieved through representations or articulations but contained in bodily memory as a pre-reflexive understanding; that is, as beneath consciousness.

Phenomenology was to be later challenged by structuralism, especially following the work of Lévi-Strauss in the *Elementary Structures of Kinship* (1949) and *Tristes Tropiques* ([1955] 2012). For Lévi-Strauss, examining both kinship and myth, the way to move beyond positivism and humanism was by identifying an autonomous order of reality, the symbolic order where cultural meanings inhere and which exists prior to and independently both of the material world and the individuals who undertake symbolisation. This objective meaning of the symbolic order resided in the unconscious, which mediates between people and the world, and can be understood scientifically. Going back to Durkheim's injunction of treating social facts as things, such an approach priorised the importance of society and objective social relations over and above individuals and their consciousness.

Historical, Social and Political Context

Many of the arguments of the post-war philosophers and social analysts have to be situated in relation to the optimistic standpoint of the Third Republic in which philosophy was seen as part of the mission of the state to foster

Republican institutions (Clarke, 1970). Debates centred on the issue of the role of reason and the predicament of man and pointed to the close relationship between academic and political life in France. Immediately following the Second World War, France was a society riven with enormous contradictions: on the one hand, following the Second World War, a peasant class consisting of up to 45% of the population, and, on the other, a country with an urban liberal consumer society, where cultural and literary production, and intellectual journals boomed, especially in the philosophical, literary and human sciences (Anderson, 2009: 140). It was a land where economic growth took off but at the expense of class inequality; a country whose national ideological stance centred on *Liberté, égalité, fraternité*, but was simultaneously riven by status distinctions and the colonial subjugations of the people of Indo-China and Algeria. Finally, it was a country espousing the importance of freedom in relation to other international powers, including the United States, but stifled internally by its own bureaucratic centralism.

With regard to economic development, post-war France was characterised by a period of rapid economic boom with growth rates comparable with Germany and Britain. This was coupled with an uneven process of modernisation, initially under the watch of de Gaulle, that lasted until the oil crisis of the 1970s. Although French economic policy was comparable with other countries that formed a Keynsian corporatist compact between capital, state and labour to ensure full employment, it also contained its own specific trajectory. The existence of a powerful PCF (French Communist Party) and a strong regulatory and interventionist state, played a central role in shaping economic policy and promoting high levels of investment in infrastructure and construction projects that dramatically increased the number of people entering the labour market. State intervention also underpinned the rapid growth of the welfare state and a higher education sector promising greater equality of opportunity to French citizens irrespective of class. Other contradictory aspects of the economy, a sector based on luxury goods – *foie gras* and champagne – small-scale market produce, a large public economic sector and high-technology modernisation, also reflected this regulation. But the 30 years of growth that ended in the mid-1970s – *les trente glorieuses* – saw a reversal in economic and social regulation and the opening up of the French economy to the global economic order. This national deregulation was partly evidenced in the growth of multinational corporations and the increasing entry of women into a burgeoning tertiary, services-oriented, labour market. In tandem with the entry of new services and commodities into the market, was an expanding middle and petty-bourgeois class, which Bourdieu discusses at some length in *Distinction*.

The shifts in production from two-thirds working in agriculture and industry after the war to two-thirds working in the services sector by the mid-1990s, reflected these dramatic changes. Various economic crises in the 1970s, 1980s and 1990s not only produced long-terms mass unemployment – since 1982, unemployment had never fallen below 9% (Forbes and Hewlett, 1994: 177) – but these disproportionately affected young workers and members of immigrant families. Economically neither state intervention nor market forces could cure these widespread socio-economic problems. Instead, market forces, in particular, produced socially profound inequalities: poverty, conflict around issues of immigration, ethnicity, the Muslim religion and urban unrest, especially among the second-generation children of immigrants. Increasing family reunification by Moroccan, Tunisian and Algerian migrants, predominantly Muslim, also saw a rapid cross-class increase in support for Le Pen's National Front anti-immigrant party, especially after 1984.

The Long Durée of Political Instability

France has a long history of radicalism, political instability, revolt and conflict. As one commentator notes: 'Between the revolution of 1789 and the end of the Second World War, all political regimes without exception had been brought to an end by revolution, *coup d'état* or war' (Forbes and Hewlett, 1994: 3). Entry into and leadership of the European Community in 1972, following a path laid deeply by Monnet and Schuman, were significant events in shaping later French politics. After the war, the internecine conflict between the hard right of the Vichy government led by Pétain, which co-operated with the Nazis, and a large resistance movement, including both de Gaulle, holding a centre-right position, and the French Communist Party, spilled over into the post-war context. This meant that, by contrast to most other West European post-war states, France did not see the emergence of a compact or a form of politics where political parties were broadly in agreement and consent.

Instead, the presence of overt conflict, extreme ideologies, including a strong communist party (the PCF holding about 25% of the vote shortly after the war) and a formidable trade union movement (including the Confédération générale du travail), characterised the country. However, in a Cold War context, the Communist Party, with an adherence with the Soviet Union, was shunned by other liberal democratic parties. This binary political opposition was to find further expression in events in May 1968 and the emergence of a radical student movement where protestors took to the streets, fought police, and were supported by mass strikes and the occupation of factories. Many believed a revolution was possible. Their combined effects were to change French politics firstly by the introduction of liberal social and economic reforms introduced under Pompidou, and then, from 1974, under Giscard d'Estaing. Such reforms lasted until the beginning of the 1980s, and the arrival of François Mitterrand, a socialist president taking an increasingly neo-liberal turn by eschewing earlier promises of state intervention geared towards social justice. During this period, political radicalism also gradually waned and became replaced by a more moderate political consensus. Nevertheless, Mitterrand's earlier radical rhetoric did introduce some changes, including a trio of structural reforms: the nationalisation of five industrial groups increasing the number of state employees from 11% to 25%; the legitimation of trade unions within firms; and a programme of decentralisation to mediate the relationship between the individual and the state. However, economic crises also saw the imposition of pragmatic policies and profusion of technocratic discourses by the Socialists (PS), including pay freezes and increases in tax. By 1983, high unemployment rates and increasing income differentials began to characterise the country. Support for the PCF had also been in long-term decline as evidence for its support of Stalinism became more evident, and the work of dissident Soviet writers such as Solzhenitsyn on the Soviet Gulags became well known during the mid-1970s. By the time of his re-election in 1988, Mitterrand, after a period of co-habitation with a prime minister from the right, was socialist only in name. The election of Chirac sealed the resurgence of the centre right. It was in this economic malaise characterised by neoliberal and managerial discourses that the far-right Front Nationale led by Le Pen began to gain working-class support.

War in Algeria

In terms of international policy it was the war in Algeria between 1954 and 1962 in which as many as 400,000 died, and as many as 2 million Algerians underwent profound social upheaval and displacement, that significantly shaped the work of a number of French intellectuals, including Bourdieu (Le Seuer, 1998). The war not only refracted a divided politics between a far-left supported by the PCF which retained an ambiguous position with regard to it, and an extreme fascist right represented by the *Organisation de l'armée secrète* (OAS), but also tore into the heart of French cultural and social life with prominent intellectuals such as Camus and Sartre supporting opposing sides. The subordination of the Algerian economy to France's economic needs and interests was established through the introduction of a new form of capitalist agriculture, transforming its landowning structures. This was complemented by an attempt at a wholesale ideological conversion of Algerian 'bodies and souls' through the imposition of European social relations and values and through forced resettlement projects or *regroupments* aimed at pacification (Bourdieu and Sayad, 1964). Following the war 900,000 *pied-noirs* (European Algerians) fled to France in fear of repercussions, adding to an already volatile and divisive context. It also led to the emergence of a Fifth Republic with increased powers conferred on the president following an attempted *coup d'état* by the army in May 1958.

A Committed Intellectual

Although Bourdieu eschewed the idea of direct political involvement in politics in his early work, from the mid- to late 1980s, in a context where neoliberalism as a doctrine became increasingly dominant in Western Europe and France, his work became *explicitly* political (Lane, 2006). Rather than seeing himself as a 'total intellectual' in the style of Sartre, who like Foucault, he criticised for commenting on the political implications issuing from all aspects of social life, Bourdieu regarded himself as an intellectual committed to discussing the political implications of topics on which he had researched, often as part of a group; that is, as part of a collective intellectual (Lenoir, 2006). Moreover, within an increasing neoliberal context, Bourdieu sometimes became less concerned with providing an immanent and acerbic critique of republicanism in terms of its theory and practice, than in defending its attributes of universalism and social equality in the face of this ideological onslaught (Yair, 2009). Despite this overt shift from implicit interventions mediated through the scientific status of sociology to more explicit forms of political engagement, all his work from the late 1950s onwards bears the mark of a political intervention of some sort, with the reproduction of inequality and domination as its central concern. For Bourdieu politics entailed the power to impose a legitimate vision of the social world, and developing a scientific sociology was inescapably caught up in this.

Indeed, Bourdieu himself has often been a key protagonist in the intellectual and political debates such changes generated (2000: 5). This includes analysing the effects and implications of French decolonisation in his early writings on Algeria during the 1950s and 1960s; or understanding the role of anthropology and its colonial and political implications in *Outline of a Theory of Practice* and *The Logic of Practice*. It is also evident in his interrogation of the expansion of the French system of education based on the idea of meritocracy in books such as *The Inheritors* and *Reproduction*, and the implications of class renewal following May 1968 in *Homo Academicus*, *Distinction*. His analysis of the development of a new power elite in *The State Nobility* and its implementation of a neoliberal ideology in *The Social Structures of the Economy* (Lane, 2000) also express his political interventions.

In many of his later political discussions concerning neoliberalism and the market, Bourdieu began to contrast the struggles between a minor state nobility, with moderate to high levels of cultural capital and who often represent welfare institutions or see the traditional role of government as public service, with a senior state nobility, with high levels of economic capital. The latter represented the sphere of finance and promotes market-oriented neoliberal reforms. This division between a minor and senior nobility constituted a conflict what he termed between the 'left hand' and the 'right hand' of the state.

Although shifting by degrees, his political worldview remained that of a left republican/socialist. Many of his analyses of Algeria, education and class as noted, express a critical engagement with the ideas and ideals of republicanism, their instantiation and their deformation in actual practice. In that regard, his political project bears striking parallels with the slightly intellectually elitist, scientifically grounded socialism of Durkheim, which itself was a reformist and revisionist type of French socialism led by Jaures, and diverged strongly from orthodox Marxism. In such a selective perspective, the *doxa* or common sense understanding of the social world which characterises the outlook of the majority of everyday social actors, and in which social and political relations are endemically misrecognised, can only be challenged and replaced by a more by scientific interpretation of the world provided through the *episteme* of social scientists.

Arguments and Ideas

Given Bourdieu's substantial output, including almost 40 books and over 200 articles covering nearly half a century, his *oeuvre* is not of one piece. It may be useful to distinguish five major phases in his *oeuvre*: (1) An early phase on Algeria and Béarn peasantry; (2) a phase looking at education and class reproduction; (3) a phase analysing practice and domination; (4) a phase foregrounding symbolic power; and (5) a final phase, discussed above, in which his work becomes increasingly an overt political intervention. Although divergent in many respects, all five phases focus on modes of domination, their dissimulation and reproduction within specific empirical domains.

Algeria and the Béarn Peasantry

Although not generally discussed – partly because his key concepts of habitus, field and capital were absent (Lane, 2000: 9) – his writings on Algeria had a profound impact on his subsequent work. Bourdieu's decision to carry out systematic fieldwork into the harsh realities and brutal policy of 'pacification' and 'resettlement' introduced by the French colonial authorities set him apart from other intellectuals writing on the war – both those who supported it and those opposed to it. It also precipitated his shift from philosophy to anthropology and finally to sociology. Amongst other things, the work on Algeria attempted to analyse how Algerians, fashioned by rural economic dispositions acquired in a pre-capitalist world, tried to adjust to a new colonially imposed world of capitalist values.

In his first book, *The Algerians*, written in 1958 (though reprinted and expanded in 1961 and 1962), together with his work *Travail et travailleurs en Algérie* (Bourdieu et al., 1963), and *Le Déracinement* (1964) with Abdelmalek Sayad, Bourdieu focused primarily on revealing the universal laws tied to issues of acculturation, deculturation and cultural interpenetration in Algerian society characterised by widescale upheaval. He noted how structural and cultural similarities led various ethnically diverse groupings to employ strategies aimed at constructing differences. What he would later refer to as 'group making' (Bourdieu, 1987) involved agents actively pursuing a logic of distinction and differentiation. The pursuit of recognition and distinction would form the foundation of his subsequent philosophical anthropology centred upon recognition and misrecognition. Bourdieu saw cultural interpenetration and contagion in terms of a 'clash of civilizations', between a traditional Algerian society 'that has always looked to the past for its ideal way of life' (Bourdieu, 1961: 94) and a dynamic forward-looking European civilisation. The overall result of such a clash was 'social, economic and psychological disaggregation' (2013: 40). The extreme differences in power between the groups influenced the self-perception, or what he would later call the 'habitus', of all the actors concerned, as dominated groups came to see themselves through the eyes of the dominant. Stereotypes of Algerians as uneducated and feckless, and of Europeans as holding positions of prestige and power, become generalised frameworks for interpreting one another's behaviour.

Studies on the Béarn peasantry

Equally crucial to Bourdieu's intellectual development was research he carried out on his native Béarn on the fundamental changes affecting the peasantry during France's post-war boom, analysed through the prism of bachelorhood. In parallel with his studies on Algeria, Bourdieu's focus was on the erosion of a rural way of life or ethos by capitalist modernisation and urbanisation, and the social, moral and psychological effects engendered by such a process.

For Bourdieu, the ball held at Christmas – like French cultural imposition in Algeria – represented 'the scene of a real clash of civilizations' through which 'the whole urban world, with its cultural models, its music, its dances, its techniques for the use of the body, bursts into peasant life' (2008: 83). Specifically, old-style dances marked and bearing the peasant way of life in terms of their rhythms and names give way to urban dances from the towns. Following Merleau-Ponty, the body, rather than individual consciousness, becomes the locus of this shift, and it is this that bears the stamp of the old peasant way of life. As Bourdieu notes: 'it is clear that the truly *empaysanit* ("empeasanted") peasant is not in his element at the ball'. Instead, like the uprooted peasantry of Algeria, they experience 'the wretchedness of the peasant condition' in terms of an 'existence that has no present and no future' (2008: 93).

Education and Social Reproduction

Bourdieu's work on schooling and education remained a consistent theme throughout his work, featuring in numerous books: *Reproduction in Education, Society, and Culture* (Bourdieu and Passeron, 1990), *Academic Discourse* (Bourdieu et al., 1996), *Homo Academicus* (Bourdieu, 1988 [1984]) and *The State Nobility* (Bourdieu, 1998 [1996]). The central arguments concerning education and social reproduction are, however, most cogently expressed in his earliest work exploring these themes, *The Inheritors*, jointly written in 1964 with Jean-Claude Passeron while at the CES (Bourdieu and Passeron, 1979). The core concern of the book was the relation of French university students to culture and how this contributes to social inequality. Social classes, Bourdieu argued, were unequally represented in higher education where the children of workers make up only 6% of the student population and where a senior executive's son is 80 times more likely to enter a university than a farm worker's son (Bourdieu and Passeron, 1979: 1, 2).

Not only were there hierarchies between universities, but there are also class differences within them. Students from working-class and lower-middle-class backgrounds were relegated into specific disciplines – primarily the arts and science, being simultaneously excluded from the more prestigious subjects of medicine, law and pharmacy, where the children from the higher classes predominated. Higher education was expensive, requiring financial resources supplied by the family. However, economic factors could not singularly account for such 'educational death rates' (Bourdieu and Passeron, 1979: 8). Rather cultural processes, which follow a similar logic to economic factors, were foremost. There was, according to Bourdieu, a strong elective affinity between the culture of school and higher education, and the 'general culture' of the elite classes. Hence, educational culture was a class culture. Schools and universities presupposed previously acquired cultural habits and social values themselves acquired through family background – the structure of language spoken, familiarity with culture in the home, the theatre, galleries and concerts. He termed this extra-curricular culture, together with educational certificates as 'cultural capital'. The dominant classes, and especially those coming from Paris, acquired this cultural capital for the most part, implicitly, through osmosis, rather than explicit instruction.

Through this affinity, the school and higher education served as social mechanisms of class reproduction while masking that reproduction beneath the ideological veneer of individual talent or giftedness. The elective affinity between school and family culture allows the children of the middle classes to:

> feel at home in educational institutions which is expressed in a confident self-belief in their giftedness and abilities and manifest in the diversity and breadth of subjects they study and cultural interests they adopt, as well as their manner of elegance, and assuredness. Their family background has provided them not only with 'habits, skills and attitudes which served them directly in scholastic tasks', but they 'also inherit from it knowledge and know-how, tastes and a "good-taste" whose scholastic profitability is no less certain for being indirect'. (Bourdieu and Passeron, 1979: 17)

By contrast, those from the working class and lower middle class, who did not share the same cultural past, feel out of place in the school or university. Lacking the 'cultural hereditary' of the elite, the latter's cultural habits and past serve as a handicap expressed in terms of early ill-informed decisions and forced choices. As was the case in his previous writings, broad social processes, and their effects, are perceived by those who experience them in terms of personal failings.

Habitus

It was on the basis of this early fieldwork that Bourdieu developed his subsequent theoretical and empirical work on education, his studies of the Kabylia and social practice in *Outline of Theory of Practice* (1977) and the *Logic of Practice* (1992 [1990]) and his analysis of class and consumption in *Distinction* (1984). In addition, he developed his fundamental concepts of capital, strategies, reflexivity, recognition, the economy of practices and, most importantly, of habitus and field. The rationale underpinning the concepts of habitus and field, which constitute the lynchpin for all his work, was to overcome a number of oppositions that Bourdieu argued had plagued the social sciences, principally between subjectivism – how the constructed social world appeared to individuals as in phenomenology – and objectivism – how the objective structures of the social world over and beyond individuals' perceptions structured and determined their actions as expressed in structuralist thinking.

The concept of 'habitus' has a long intellectual tradition going back to Aristotle, the scholastics, was also used in the work of Durkheim, Mauss, Husserl, Elias and Panofsky. According to Bourdieu, it was introduced in order to 'get out from under the philosophy of consciousness without doing away with the agent' (1977: 14). He defines habitus as: 'durable, transposable dispositions, structured structures predisposed to function as structuring structures, that is, as principles which generate and organize practices' (1992: 50). Habitus refers to dispositions derived from pre-existing socially structured environments, which inclined social agents to act in determinate ways, without fully determining them.

Moreover, the concept could usefully be contrasted with Parsons' theory of socialisation. Rather than referring to explicitly taught values or rules that were consciously acquired or implanted in people's heads, dispositions were unconscious or, at least, semi-conscious. They produced a social order without actors consciously following rules, and they were not restrictively associated with the mind, but implicated the whole body, or bodily *hexis* in terms of internalised body movements, gestures and postures. However, like Parsonian processes of socialisation, these structured dispositions were acquired primarily in early childhood and formed the basis upon which future experience and practices were shaped. Crucially, such dispositions reflected the social conditions of existence or particular social context in which they had been acquired, becoming internalised within the body through 'osmosis', as within determinate environments. Hence, individuals from similar social, material or class conditions, though unique in some respects, shared similar dispositions; they tended to think, act and judge the social world in similar ways, as well as acquiring a similar practical sense of social situations or a homogeneous 'feel for the game'. This 'regulated improvisation' included semi-consciously inculcating chances of success or failure in terms of future actions, *anticipations*, gained through past experience which were internalised and transformed into individual aspirations and expectations.

The similar material conditions of existence of a group or social class, especially in terms of their early upbringing, led to the internalisation of these objective necessities and structures, and produced a homogeneous group whose practices were harmonised without any conscious intention, reference to a norm or explicit co-ordination. It was the homogeneity of habitus, which in terms of similarity in dispositions, ethos and taste, causes practices to be intelligible, foreseeable and taken for granted. As a pre-reflexive embodiment of social structures and material environment, habitus was in a sense history transformed into nature.

Social Fields

According to Bourdieu, the concept of habitus could only be understood *relationally* in terms of what he called social *fields*, the various social spheres and contexts within which agents act. The term 'field' allows Bourdieu to move beyond the visible interactions discussed by symbolic interactionism to the concealed objective social positions that agents occupied in the social world or, in his terms, 'social space'. Fields referred to the structure and patterning of social relationships:

> In analytic terms, a field may be defined as a network, or a configuration, of objective relations between positions. These positions are objectively defined, in their existence and in the determinations they have upon their occupants, agents or institutions, by their present or potential situation (*situs*) in the structure of the distribution of species of power (capital) whose possession demands access to the specific profits that are at stake in the field, as well as by their objective relation to other positions (domination, subordination, homology, etc.). (Bourdieu and Wacquant, 1992: 97)

Fields develop historically: as societies diversify, so more fields arise: 'the historic process is one of differentiation of the world into spheres' (Bourdieu, 2014: 75). For example, over time, the economic field becomes increasingly separated from the political field. Fields take a variety of forms such as the educational field, the economic field, the cultural field, the political field, the scientific field, the religious field, etc., and could be further divided into subfields, such as the field of higher education. As well as shaping and structuring the actions of agents who enter into them, fields elicited and triggered specific responses from agents with a particular habitus.

Although each field had distinctive characteristics and a unique logic or procedural rules, all fields contained or express certain universal properties. Firstly, they were semi-autonomous from each other, and thereby *relatively* impervious to the external influences and determinations of different fields – art was followed for art's sake, politics for power, action on the stock market for wealth, etc. Secondly, fields were 'fields of force': like magnetic fields that attracted and repelled, they were characterised by tension and struggle, power and conflict, wherein agents compete with one another to preserve or alter the constellation of positions, and their place within them, that exists within the field.

Cultural, Social and Symbolic Capital

Bourdieu's third key and interrelated concept was capital. Capital referred to any resource which enabled people to appropriate profits from participating within specific fields. Although outlining a variety of forms of capital, he tended to focus on four main types: economic capital referring to money (including very high salaries), material and financial assets and private property; cultural capital referring to scarce symbolic goods, educational credentials and titles; social capital referring to social connections and profits accruing from group membership; and symbolic capital, which referred to recognition and prestige or the effects of any form of capital when they were not perceived for what they are, but misrecognised (Bourdieu, 1986). These capitals could also appear in various states. Economic capital was generally *objectified* in goods or things, whereas cultural capital could be objectified in books, but could also take on an *embodied* state as dispositions of the mind/body, and an *institutional* state as rare educational qualifications.

For Bourdieu, a person's position in social space was determined by both the amount of capital they possess – the overall *volume* – and the type of capital they own – the *composition* of their capital:

> The structure of the distribution of the different types of capital at a given moment in time represents the immanent structure of the social world, i.e., the set of constraints, inscribed in the very reality of the world, which govern its functioning in a durable way, determining the chances of success for practices. (1986: 242)

This determines agents' power and play or how they act within fields or different markets or games:

> We can picture each player as having in front of her a pile of tokens of different colours, each corresponding to a given species of capital she holds, so that her relative force in the game ... depend[s] both on the total number of tokens and of the composition of the piles of tokens she retains, that is on the volume and structure of her capital. (Bourdieu and Wacquant, 1992: 99)

The analogy of the game was central to Bourdieu's whole approach. People who played or participated in games within fields did so because they agreed to do so, because they believed they had stakes, or vested interests in the game, that is an *illusio* that the game was worth playing.

Modifying Durkheim and Mauss's (2009) discussion of the social nature of the categories, Bourdieu argues that the forms of categories and classifications were not only social, *pace* Kant, but also embodied hierarchical power relations. Moreover, because of the direct and spontaneous correlation between social categories and social structures, they have the political effect of naturalising the social world, or producing a form of *doxa*.

In *Outline* Bourdieu developed his arguments concerning habitus, field and capital both in determinate empirical contexts, especially in analysing the logic of a gift and honour economy in Algeria, and in terms of a general science of the 'economy of practices'. With regard to the former, and restating the importance of temporality, Bourdieu argued that the structuralist approach, which sees gift exchange solely in terms of mechanical necessity, ignores the temporal structure of gift exchange, which in fact 'defines the full truth of the gift' (1977: 5). Gifts may not be returned either because of ingratitude or as an insult. It was the lapse of time interposed between receiving and giving a gift that 'enables the gift or counter-gift to be seen and experienced as an inaugural act of generosity, without any past or future, i.e. without calculation' (1977: 171). This time lag, which consisted of manipulating time or the tempo of the action, also allows sociologists to introduce agents, strategies and improvisation into social understanding.

In addition to his discussion of temporality, Bourdieu also discusses his theory of an economy of practices. Through this concept he hopes to be:

> capable of re-appropriating the totality of practices which, although objectively economic, are not and cannot be socially recognized as economic, and which can perform only at the cost of a whole labour of dissimulation or, more precisely, *euphemization*, must endeavour to grasp capital and profit in all their forms and to establish the laws whereby the different forms of capital (or power, which amounts to the same thing) change into one another. (1986: 243)

Using the concept of economic in a wide sense, his framework implies that all practices – including economic, cultural, political, scientific practices – aim at increasing or augmenting one's capital holding. All practices are economic and cultural practices directed towards the maximising of material, or *symbolic profits*, which follow an 'economic logic' in the broad sense.

Within the contexts of fields and struggles, and according to their position in social space, actors employ 'strategies' either to maintain or to improve their social position. These strategies are not necessarily consciously chosen strategies, as in rational choice theory, but embodied strategies incorporated in the body as dispositions.

Distinction

This, together with themes of culture and recognition, consumption, lifestyle, taste and class, are central themes of *Distinction* (1984) published in 1979. In the book, Bourdieu reconsiders Weber's distinction between a class and a status group, arguing that the hierarchy of lifestyle is the misrecognised retranslation of the hierarchy of classes. Secondly, subtitled *A Social Critique of the Judgement of Taste*, *Distinction* is conceived as a response to Kant's *Critique of Judgment*. According to Bourdieu, a detached aesthetic sense of taste and judgement are commonly assumed to be qualities inherent in gifted individuals, but are in fact, the product of social and historical processes entailing power. He aims to explain how aesthetic outlook, taste, sensibility and consumption not only contribute to class identity, but also to argue that the legitimation of certain lifestyles consolidates the dominant class's power. Taste, he argues, is a relational phenomenon.

A person's taste is always a distaste of other people's taste; it is defined negatively in terms of distaste: 'Aesthetic intolerance can be terribly violent. Aversion to different lifestyles is perhaps one of the strongest barriers between classes' (1984: 56). The dominant classes always distinguish their lifestyles from the dominated classes, who serve as the negative frame of reference for their choices. Processes of distinction entail endemic struggles over classification, as he notes: 'taste classifies, and it classifies the classifier' (1984: 6). Taste is above all a manifestation of distinction:

> It is found in all the properties – and property – with which individuals and groups surround themselves, houses, furniture, paintings, books, cars, spirits, cigarettes, perfume, clothes and the practices in which they manifest their distinction, sports, games and entertainments. (1984: 173)

According to Bourdieu, there are three major social classes – the bourgeoisie, the petty bourgeoisie and the working class – with the first two classes containing class fractions within them. These can be analysed in terms of the opposition between two forms of taste: the taste of freedom of the dominant class; and the tastes of necessity of the dominated. But he qualifies this argument by pointing to a three-fold division within the dominant taste based on the volume and composition of the capital they possess.

Reflexivity

A central methodological feature underpinning all of Bourdieu's broad sociological approach, is an emphasis on epistemological reflexivity. Epistemological reflexivity enables sociologists scientifically to ground the sociological standpoint given the importance of unthinking social practices and practical knowledge in the constitution of social life. According to Bourdieu, it is not only the particular power relation between a Western anthropologist and the tribe or people which he or she is studying that needs to be consciously acknowledged by the anthropologist in terms of ethnocentric bias, but also *all* intellectual/academic forms of projection involving the study of human behaviour. Unreflexive intellectuals, writing from a standpoint characterised by *skolé*, leisure or the 'scholastic point of view', invariably project their passive, theoretical and academic relation onto the social world, onto the subjects they are studying. They therefore understand what for these subjects are unthinking, immediate practices, involving bodily activity, or an operative intentionality, in terms of a spectacle that needs to be decoded or hermeneutically interpreted. A rigorous social scientific analysis, by contrast, crucially entails a break with this 'scholastic reason' and involves a reflexive analysis of the effects of the relation of the social separation between the intellectual and the object of study which must be included in the social analysis. It is only by instituting this reflexivity that one can bring to light the 'practical mode of knowledge in all practice'.

Bourdieu attempts to provide a broader epistemological grounding for the social sciences in the *Craft of Sociology* (1991) written with Jean-Claude Chamboredon and Jean-Claude Passeron. Drawing heavily on the historians of science Bachelard, Koyré and Canguilhem, Bourdieu et al. argue that the scientific act has to be won, constructed and confirmed. Epistemological facts contain a logical order involving first a break with ordinary concepts and phenomenal appearances; second the construction of a hypotheses using a coherent theoretical model; and finally, the testing of these hypotheses against this model. Such a process of winning, constructing and confirming facts takes place within the historical emergence of a semi-autonomous scientific field that is continually under threat from the impinging interests of other fields, including the economic and political field.

Symbolic Power

An essay on symbolic power, written in 1977, marks a significant development in Bourdieu's work (Bourdieu, 1992: 164). Synthesising a neo-Kantian and idealist position that emphasises the productive and constitutive activity of consciousness, Bourdieu argues that symbolic power functions as a power of constructing social reality that establishes a *gnoseological* order (philosophical order of cognition). This provides the immediate shared meaning individuals have of the social world. In a second synthesis, this argument is conjoined with approaches such as those of Marx and Weber, that examine the political function of symbolic and ideological processes as instruments of domination and power that are presented as universal interests but in fact serve particular interests. Consequently, all relations of meaning and communication are seen inseparably as power relations that depend on the material or symbolic power that agents possess.

The essay on symbolic power was Bourdieu's attempt to provide a less class reductionist account of ideological production without giving the latter an absolute autonomy. Symbolic power then is a power of making people see the social world in a specific way, of creating a vision of divisions that affirms or transforms how social agents perceive the world. Symbolic capital:

> is any property (any form of capital whether physical, economic, cultural or social) when it is perceived by social agents endowed with categories of perception which cause them to know it and to recognize it, to give it value. (1993: 9)

Symbolic power and what he terms symbolic violence are exercised in an invisible way so that those beholden to them remain unaware of their very existence. Symbolic violence and domination: 'really begins when the misrecognition implied by recognition, leads those who are dominated to apply the dominant criteria of evaluation to their own practice' (Bourdieu and Boltanski, 1976: 8).

Language, speech and social categories do not simply describe the social world but simultaneously constitute the very reality they describe. Words, dictums and ritualised forms of expression are part of the symbolic struggles of everyday life which imply claims to symbolic authority as a socially recognised power to impose a particular vision and division of the social world. For Bourdieu, the power of words is not to be located in the words themselves, but comes from 'outside', from the institution that mandates and gives the individual the authority to speak (Bourdieu, 1991).

The Centrality of Recognition and Misrecognition

Rather than his concept of cultural capital, for which Bourdieu has become renowned, it is the concepts of symbolic power and symbolic capital that constitute the core of his later approach. Connected to this the concepts of recognition and misrecognition underpin his entire *oeuvre*. Given the direct correspondence between the objective social order and the subjective categories internalised as a product of that social structure, the social world appears to individuals in a *doxic* manner. The concept of *doxa* refers to the everyday common-sense understanding in which social and arbitrary processes imbued with power appear as natural and necessary, as given and self-evident. Social processes and social practices are therefore misrecognised. However, misrecognition is also used in another sense in his work, referring to individuals and groups who are not 'properly' recognised in terms of conferring upon them a dignity or prestige, but instead seen in a demeaning or distorting manner sometimes through processes of 'class racism'. The notion of recognition in which humans require recognition from others in order to justify their otherwise meaningless, contingent and finite existence is central to Bourdieu's philosophical anthropology. This existentialist vision of humans, and the desire to emerge from their absurd, indifferent existence and give meaning to life and death by participating in society, is discussed in one of his last major works, *Pascalian Meditations* (2000: 237–45). It is on the basis of acquiring greater symbolic capital or prestige that agents act and struggle.

The State

Though explicitly discussed in one of his last works, the theme of recognition, of how groups are seen and thereby see themselves, is also present at the outset in the work on Algeria discussed above. It is on this basis need for recognition that Bourdieu discusses the importance of symbolic capital: 'One of the most unequal of all distributions, and probably, in any case, the most cruel, is the distribution of symbolic capital, that is of social importance and of reasons for living' (2000: 241). It is here that the state, rather than the economy, takes a central position in his understanding of society. Drawing on Durkheim's notion of the state as a 'social brain' that regulates society's collective conscience, Bourdieu argues that it is the state which is the central bank for symbolic capital. The state is also the site par excellence of social struggle, not so much between the dominated and dominant class, but within the dominant class to shape the 'field of power' (1998 [1996], 2014). In addition, to possessing a monopoly on physical and symbolic violence, the state plays a central role in setting the the exchange rate between the various forms of capital that exist in the social world (Loyal, 2017). The state has the authority and legitimacy to perform three major functions. Firstly, for Bourdieu, it performs a 'diagnostic function', it designates what a thing or person is in a manner that needs to be universally accepted. 'It is an almost divine discourse, which assigns to every one an identity.' Secondly, it furnishes an 'administrative discourse', which determines how people should act or what they should do. Finally it provides 'authorised accounts', for example through police reports stating what a person has done and is. In all of these it sets up a 'legitimate point of view' which is taken up in society as common sense (Bourdieu, 1990: 136).

Contemporary Relevance and Applications

Bourdieu's influence on sociology has been steadily growing, especially since his concepts were explicitly developed to facilitate empirical work.

LANGUAGE, SYMBOLIC POWER AND ACADEMIA

Bourdieu's theory of language offers a critical counterpoint to the linguistic theories of Saussure and Chomsky. In these, the social character of language is considered abstractly, as the foundation of more general theories of the constitution of social life. To Bourdieu, however, the social character of language is substantively important: relations of power in societies fundamentally shape language and linguistic practices. From this perspective, every linguistic interaction is marked by a social structure, which it essentially reproduces, and language is a medium through which interests are pursued. Following his programme of reflexive sociology, Bourdieu applies this theory to academia, presenting it as a field structured by competitive struggles over cultural resources. Academic interaction is shaped by strategies for the accumulation of reputation, with speakers deploying linguistic capital in pursuit of symbolic profit, usually at the expense of others. One example is the common practice of labelling – 'Marxist', 'functionalist', etc. – which Bourdieu describes as the scholarly equivalent of insult and an act of social positioning.

Given the breadth of Bourdieu's influence it is only possible to focus on a few areas in which his work has been taken up and applied. The first has been analyses of education and social reproduction which influenced generations of scholars in the field. His arguments concerning the reproduction of class, culture and knowledge within a context of societies defined ostensibly in terms of meritocracy and social mobility have strongly shaped the sociology of education

(Loyal, 2019). Numerous studies in the sociology of education support his view that schooling and culture play a central role in maintaining social reproduction and inequality. His recognition of the educational field as hierarchical, and in contestation, and the role of teachers in using classifications have become central to the field (see Reay et al., 2005; Reay et al., 2010; English and Bolton, 2016).

Secondly, Bourdieu's work has been hugely influential in conceptualising social class in contemporary sociology. His focus on class as a form of 'group making' has had a considerable influence on sociological discussions of class. In this work, class is not simply seen in terms of occupation but economic, cultural and social capital; that is, it is analysed in terms of how economic processes mix with symbolic and cultural processes concerning identity to constitute a multidimensional phenomenon (Skeggs, 1997; Savage et al., 2013). The third major area in which Bourdieu's work has been employed is in the area of criminology, urbanisation and poverty. Drawing on Bourdieu's discussion of neoliberalism the shift in balance from the left to the right hand of the state, Loïc Wacquant has focused his work on understanding the socio-political processes underpinning urban inequalities in advanced, and increasingly polarised, capitalist societies. In *Urban Outcasts* (2008) Wacquant undertakes a comparative analysis of the differential trajectory of the American black ghetto and the French *banlieues*. His analysis conjoins the analysis of class fragmentation in the city, deindustrialisation, stigmatised neighbourhoods and the emergence of a precariat, with an analysis of ethnic divisions and social classifications. Increased marginalisation and inequality have ensued in contemporary societies not because of the emergence of an underclass, but rather because of the retrenchment of the post-war social-cum-welfare state. This has led to his examination of immigration, crime and increasingly punitive penal policy in modern American society (2009). Growing incarceration rates, especially for Black Americans, not only express a societal reaction to dealing with the averse socio-effects of neoliberalism in terms of creating poverty and crime, but serves historically as one of a number of 'peculiar institutions' that confine, define and control African-Americans following on from chattel slavery, Jim Crow legislation and the ghetto (Wacquant, 2000). Like Bourdieu, a central preoccupation of Wacquant's work is to transcend disciplinary divisions and to question what he terms 'folk' or everyday conceptual understandings which are subsequently employed as analytical tools in media reporting and unreflexive sociological and social policy analysis. This includes concepts such as 'race', 'ghetto', 'underclass', 'problem-districts' and 'no-go areas' (1997, 2008, 2015). As well as dissecting and reconfiguring social processes entailing race, ethnicity, class and the state, Wacquant has also re-emphasised the importance of the body in sociology and the carnal knowledge that pertains to it in his ethnographic study of boxing (Wacquant, 2004: vii). As he notes:

> the fact that the social agent is before anything else a being of flesh, nerves and senses (in the twofold meaning of sensual and signifying),

a 'suffering being'... who partakes of the universe that makes him, and that he in turn contributes to making, with every fibre of his body and heart. Sociology must endeavor to clasp and restitute this carnal dimension of existence, which is particularly salient in the case of the boxer but is in truth shared in various degrees of visibility by all women and men.

Finally, Bourdieu's work has also been extended, albeit critically, in the writings of his former colleague, Luc Boltanski with whom he wrote on the 'Dominant Ideology Thesis' (Bourdieu and Boltanski, 1976; Abercrombie, et al., 1980). Extending his analysis of ideological production in capitalism by drawing on Weber's notion of spirit contained in the *Protestant Ethic* (2001 [1904]), and the work of Albert Hirschman, Boltanski in *The New Spirit of Capitalism* (2005) (written with Eve Chiapello), examines a central and pervasive ideological value underpinning contemporary forms of globalised capitalism in France – the unlimited accumulation of capital as an end in itself – that is, its chrematistic nature. Such a spirit has replaced historically prior forms of capitalist rationalisation and justification centred on investment and risk, whose social carrier was firstly the bourgeois entrepreneur in the second half of the nineteenth century, and who saved to invest; and secondly, a spirit centred on Taylorist hierarchical techniques of production, a division between ownership and management of capital, and rational organisation based on future planning, embodied in the figure of a director of a large bureaucratic corporation, that emerged between 1930 and 1960. However, following May 1968, and as long-standing social and artistic criticisms of capitalism coalesced – the former stemming from the labour movement and calling for a refusal against egoism and suffering, the latter artistic strand rooted in values concerning inauthenticity and liberation, a new 'third' spirit emerged during the early 1970s. The initial response of capitalist firms to May 1968 was to increase rights and wages. However, gradually and over time, the social critique waned while the artistic critique centred on challenging bureaucracy, hierarchy and bourgeois discipline in the name of fluidity, self-development and autonomy, remained prevalent. Firms responded to these libertarian demands by reorganizing their production process and recalibrating it according to values based on flexibility, non-hierarchy, creativity, fluidity and knowledgeability. That is, by incorporating and co-opting what were initially inimical values into the post-Fordist production process. In modern forms of 'connexionist' or 'network' capitalism these values have now shifted as watchwords of the French left of the late 1960s to become defining slogans of business elites, including Bill Gates. This shift is vividly illustrated, the authors argue, in contemporary management texts and literature which foreground the unavoidability of economic change and international competition and advocate teamwork and cooperation through networks. The idealised figure of the new spirit is the 'network extender'. Such texts also recognise that employment security and long-terms fixed labour contracts are a thing of the past.

Criticisms

One of the major criticisms that Bourdieu has faced is that his conceptual schema is deterministic (Jenkins, 1992; Alexander, 1995). However, his indebtedness to phenomenology proves this assertion needs to be qualified. Bodily subjectivity and motor skills, as Merleau-Ponty (1962: 109) argues, have the 'power to reckon with the possible'; for Bourdieu they allow us to move beyond actual situations and improvise into future situations. Individuals are creative actors to the extent that they apply their acquired habitus, as embodied representations and practices, in new contexts and situations within determinate and shifting social contexts. However, there is another sense in which Bourdieu's work does detract from the role of conscious agency in human life, and therefore of the actor as an active agent, demonstrating a certain antinomy in his work. For Bourdieu the imprints on the body remind us that we need to treat the body and the principles and cosmology it embodies as beyond conscious manipulation. As *doxa*, the categories of dominant groups or the state remain unconscious, hidden, inscribed in mental structures and in objects in the social world, on the 'other side of discourse'. It is extremely difficult, therefore, for individuals to stand outside of the thinking of dominant groups and the state, which appears to be pervasive, ubiquitous and omnipotent. In his writings on the state, the latter is often compared to God. This, however, raises issues tied to resistance or political opposition that challenge state power and thinking. The top-down view of the imposition of state categories and their acceptance not only overstates the power of state thinking as recognised by some critics (Swartz, 2013: 146; Loyal, 2017), but also seems to exaggerate the naturalising function of *doxa*. Here the overall moral and ideological consensus characterising the social world is overstated as it was also in his discussion of the operation of a dominant ideology in French society (Bourdieu and Boltanski, 1976; Abercrombie et al., 1980). Individuals may be critical and sceptical of beliefs, yet nevertheless continue to follow them, perhaps for pragmatic reasons or out of fear.

Bourdieu has also been criticised for having an overly strategic conception of agents. Although he distinguishes his approach from the strategic choices that underlie all actions in rational choice theory, Bourdieu's view that agents semi-consciously pursue strategies in all the fields (a view akin to Goffman, whom he admired) to increase their material and symbolic profits detracts from the view that actors may also act solely on a moral or normative basis on what they believe is right or wrong (Sayer, 2005).

Conclusion

Bourdieu is arguably one of the most important sociologists to write in the twentieth century and whose work continues to shape sociology in the twenty-first century. Although his language can be daunting, his work, nevertheless, repays careful reading. In his sociology he has aimed to transcend a number of dualisms that have stifled the development of the discipline into a rigorous social science: between subjectivism and objectivism, micro and macro, constructivism and realism, instrumentalism and autonomous analysis. His work is successful in terms of transcending some of these dichotomies but in other cases he shifts between the two poles of the binary; that is, there exist unresolved antinomies in his work. Nevertheless, his sociological theory has proved eminently useful for carrying out empirical work. In many ways he can be seen as the heir to the republican-inspired social science legacy of his countryman, Émile Durkheim, while adding a significant class and power aspect to the latter's work.

References

Abercrombie, H., Hill, S. and Turner, B. S. (1980) *The Dominant Ideology Thesis*. London: George & Allen Unwin.
Alexander, J. (1995) The Reality of Reduction: The Failed Synthesis of Pierre Bourdieu. In: *Fin de Siècle Social Theory: Relativism, Reduction, and the Problem of Reason*. London: Verso, pp. 128–217.
Anderson, P. (2009) *The New Old World*. London: Verso.
Bennett, T., Savage, M., Silva, E., Warde, A., Gayo-Cal, M. and Wright, D. (2009) *Culture, Class, Distinction*. London: Routledge.
Boltanski, L. and Chiapello, L. (2005) *The New Spirit of Capitalism*. London: Verso.
Bourdieu, P. (1961 [1958]) *The Algerians*. Boston, MA: Beacon Press.
Bourdieu, P. (1977) *Outline of a Theory of Practice*. Cambridge: Cambridge University Press.
Bourdieu, P. (1984 [1979]) *Distinction: A Social Critique of the Judgement of Taste*. London: Routledge.
Bourdieu, P. (1988 [1984]) *Homo Academicus*. Cambridge: Polity.
Bourdieu, P. (1986) The Forms of Capital. In: J. G. Richardson (ed.) *Handbook for Theory and Research for the Sociology of Education*. New York: Greenwood Press, pp. 241–58.
Bourdieu, P. (1987) What Makes a Social Class? On the Theoretical and Practical Existence of Groups. *Berkeley Journal of Sociology*, 32, pp. 1–17.
Bourdieu, P. (1990) *In Other Words: Essays Towards a Reflexive Sociology*. Cambridge: Polity.
Bourdieu, P. (1992 [1990]) *The Logic of Practice*. Cambridge: Polity.
Bourdieu, P. (1992) *Language and Symbolic Power*. Cambridge: Polity.
Bourdieu, P. (1993) Rethinking the State: On the Genesis and Structure of the Bureaucratic Field. *Sociological Theory*, 12(1), pp. 1–19.
Bourdieu, P. (1998 [1996]) *The State Nobility: Elite Schools in the Field of Power*. Cambridge: Polity.
Bourdieu, P. (2000) *Pascalian Meditations*. Cambridge: Polity.
Bourdieu, P. (2008) *Sketch for a Self-Analysis*. Chicago, IL: University of Chicago Press.
Bourdieu, P. (2013) *Algerian Sketches*. Cambridge: Polity Press.
Bourdieu, P. (2014) *On the State: Lectures at the Collège de France, 1989–1992*. Cambridge: Polity.

Bourdieu, P. and Abdelmalek Sayek, A. (1964) *Le Déracinement: La crise de l'agriculture traditionanelle en Algeria*. Paris: Éditions de Minuit.

Bourdieu, P. and Boltanski, L. (1976) La Production de l'Ideologie Dominante. *Actes de la Recherché en Sciences Social*, 3(3), pp. 4–73.

Bourdieu, P. and Passeron, J.-C. (1979 [1964]) *The Inheritors: French Students and Their Relation to Culture*. Chicago, IL: University of Chicago Press.

Bourdieu, P. and Passeron, J.-C. (1990) *Reproduction in Education, Society and Culture*, 2nd edition. London: Sage.

Bourdieu, P. and Wacquant, L. (1992) *An Invitation to Reflexive Sociology*. Cambridge: Polity.

Bourdieu, P., Darbel, A., Rivet, J. P. and Seibel, C. (1963) *Travail et Travailleurs en Algérie*. Paris: Mouton.

Bourdieu, P., Chamboredon, J.-C. and Passeron, J.-C. (1991) *The Craft of Sociology: Epistemological Preliminaries*. Berlin: De Gruyter.

Bourdieu, P., Passeron, J.-C., Saint Martin, M. de, Baudelot, C. and Vicent, G. (1996) *Academic Discourse: Linguistic Misunderstanding and Professional Power*. Cambridge: Polity.

Clarke, S. (1970) *The Foundations of Structuralism: A Critique of Lévi-Strauss and the Structuralist Movement*. Brighton: Harvester.

Descombes, V. (1980) *Modern French Philosophy*. Cambridge: Cambridge University Press.

Durkheim, E. and Mauss, M. (2009) *Primitive Classification*. London: Cohen & West.

English, F. W. and Bolton, C. L. (2016) *Bourdieu for Educators: Policy & Practice*. London: Sage.

Forbes, J. and Hewlett, N. (1994) *Contemporary France: Essays and Texts on Politics, Economics and Society*. Harlow: Longman.

Husserl, E. (1973) *Experience and Judgement*. London: Routledge and Kegan Paul.

Jenkins, R. (1992) *Pierre Bourdieu*. New York: Routledge.

Kojève, A. (1980) *Introduction to the Reading of Hegel: Lectures on the Phenomenology of Spirit*. R. Queneau, assembled. A. Bloom (ed.), J. H. Nichols, trans. Ithaca, NY: Cornell University Press.

Lane, J. (2000) *Pierre Bourdieu: A Critical Introduction*. London: Routledge.

Lane, J. F. (2006) *Bourdieu's Politics, Problems and Possibilities*. London: Routledge.

Lenoir, R. (2006) Scientific Habitus: Pierre Bourdieu and the Collective Intellectual. *Theory Culture & Society*, 23(6), pp. 25–43.

Le Seuer, J. (1998) *Uncivil War: Intellectuals and Identity Politics During the Decolonisation of Algeria*. Lincoln, NB: University of Nebraska Press.

Lévi-Strauss, C. (1949) *The Elementary Structures of Kinship*. Boston, MA: Beacon Press.

Lévi-Strauss, C. (2012 [1955]) *Tristes Tropiques*. London: Penguin.

Loyal, (2017) *Bourdieu's Theory of the State: A Critical Introduction*. New York: Palgrave.

Loyal, S. (2019) Bourdieu and Collins on the Reproduction of Elites. *Thesis Eleven*, 154(1), pp. 80–96.

Merleau-Ponty, M. (1962) *The Phenomenology of Perception*. London: Routledge & Kegan Paul.

Mooney, T. (forthcoming). *On the Phenomenology of Perception*. Unpublished manuscript.

Moran, D. (2005). *Edmund Husserl*. Cambridge: Polity.

Reay, D., Crozier, G. and Clayton, J. (2010) 'Fitting in' or 'Standing out': Working-Class Students in UK Higher Education. *British Educational Research Journal*, 36(1), pp. 107–24.

Reay, D., David, M. E. and Ball, S. J. (2005) *Degrees of Choice: Class, Race, Gender and Higher Education*. Stoke-on-Trent: Trentham Books.

Savage, M., Devine, F., Cunningham, N., Taylor, M., Li, Y., Hjellbrekke, J., Le Roux, B., Friedman, S. and Miles, A. (2013) A New Model of Social Class? Findings from the BBC's Great British Class Survey Experiment. *Sociology*, 47(2), pp. 219–50.

Sayer, A. (2005) *The Moral Significance of Class*. Cambridge: Cambridge University Press.

Skeggs, B. (1997) *Formations of Class & Gender: Becoming Respectable*. London: Sage.

Swartz, D. (2013) *Symbolic Power, Politics and Intellectuals: The Political Sociology of Pierre Bourdieu*. Chicago, IL: University of Chicago Press.

Wacquant. L. (1997) For An Analytic of Racial Domination. *Political Power and Social Theory*, 11, pp. 221–34.

Wacquant, (2000) The New Peculiar Institution: On the Prison as Surrogate Ghetto. *Theoretical Criminology*, 4(3), pp. 377–89.

Wacquant, L. (2004) *Body and Soul: Notebooks of an Apprentice Boxer*. Oxford: Oxford University Press

Wacquant, L. (2008) *Urban Outcasts: A Comparative Sociology of Advanced Marginality*. Cambridge: Polity.

Wacquant, L. (2009) *Punishing the Poor: The Neoliberal Government of Social Insecurity*. Durham, NC: Duke University Press.

Wacquant, L. (2015) Revisiting Territories of Relegation: Class, Ethnicity, and the State in the Making of Advanced Marginality. *Urban Studies*, 53(6), pp. 1077–88.

Weber, M. (2001 [1904]) *The Protestant Ethic and the Spirit of Capitalism*. London: Taylor & Francis.

Yacine, T. (2013) Introduction. In: P. Bourdieu, *Algerian Sketches*. Cambridge: Polity, pp. 1–12

Yair, G. (2009) *Pierre Bourdieu: The Last Musketeer of the French Revolution*. Plymouth: Lexington Books.

Zolberg, V. L. (1990) *Constructing a Sociology of the Arts*. Cambridge: Cambridge University Press.

Giddens

Anthony Giddens was perhaps, until recently, the UK's leading sociologist, renowned especially for his theories of structuration and late modernity, and his championing of 'Third Way' politics. In a broad-ranging sociological vision Giddens attempted to rework the classical and modern sociological tradition through a synthesis of their most powerful theoretical arguments. His early writings focus on critically outlining and interpreting the work of Marx, Weber and Durkheim. This is followed by the development of his own theory of structuration, which attempts to straddle what he designates as a dualism between sociological approaches that focus on agency and those that confine their analysis to social structure. In parallel with this theory he developed a rigorous critique of functionalism and historical materialism within a novel historical sociological approach. This work was followed by another shift in which he attempted to outline and understand modernity, modern identity and globalisation. In his later writings Giddens has focused on the development of a 'Third Way' politics and, more recently, a social policy which takes account of the importance of environmental issues.

Life and Intellectual Context

Giddens was born in Edmonton, London, on 18 January 1938, into a lower-middle-class family. His father worked as a clerk for London Transport. After going to Minchenden School in North London, a grammar school, Giddens attended the University of Hull where he graduated with first-class honours in 1959 in sociology and psychology. He then studied for a Master's degree in sociology at the London School of Economics where he completed a thesis entitled 'Sport and Society in Contemporary England'. In 1961 he became a lecturer in the Department of Sociology at Leicester University, where he taught for the next eight years. At the time the department in Leicester was considered to be one of the foremost sociology departments in the UK and included Ilya Neustadt, Norbert Elias and Percy Cohen as part of the faculty.

During a period of sabbatical leave Giddens held a one-year position at Simon Fraser University between 1966 and 1967, at a time of radical student protest.

This year was followed by a short period at the University of California, Los Angeles, where he encountered an even more flourishing hippy and anti-war movement, as well as the American left student counter-culture. In 1969 Giddens took up a university lectureship at Cambridge becoming a fellow at King's College. Two years later he published his first major work, *Capitalism and Modern Social Theory* (1971a), a critical outline and interpretation of the work of Marx, Weber and Durkheim which garnered critical praise. This was followed two years later by his book *The Class Structure of Advanced Societies* (1973) in which he attempted to develop a theory of class drawing on both Marx's and Weber's analyses. These works, largely aimed at exposition of other writers' ideas and critical commentary, were followed by his first major work on structuration theory, *The New Rules of Sociological Method* (1976). This first volume was followed by a second volume, *Central Problems in Social Theory* (1979), elaborating on his initial arguments. As part of his ongoing critical engagement with the arguments of Marx and Weber and the development of his own unique historical sociology, Giddens published the first of two volumes of *A Contemporary Critique of Historical Materialism* (1981). In addition to a collection of his critical essays and commentaries, *Profiles and Critiques in Social Theory* (1982), he published his third and most comprehensive volume on structuration theory, *The Constitution of Society* in 1984. In the next year, together with John Thompson and David Held, he formed Polity Press, a publishing house geared towards publishing work in the philosophical and social sciences. He also released his second volume of *A Contemporary Critique of Historical Materialism*, namely *The Nation-State and Violence*, in 1985.

In addition to developing a new faculty at Cambridge, the Social and Political Sciences, of which he became dean, he became a full professor at Cambridge. In 1988, Giddens toured the United States and gave lectures at Stanford University, later published as the *Consequences of Modernity* (1990), indicating a new phase in his work. A major introductory textbook on sociology, *Sociology* (1989a), was quickly followed by a book on identity in the modern world, *Modernity and Self-Identity* (1991) and also *The Transformation of Intimacy* (1992). These books, dwelling on an individual's personal life and emotions in modernity and their connection with global processes, partly reflected Giddens' own three-year experience undergoing therapy beginning in 1989 (Bryant and Jary, 1991: 674). During the mid-1990s Giddens became increasingly interested in British politics, publishing a sociological–ideological manifesto, *Beyond Left and Right* (1994), which proposed a mid-way ideological path between conservatism and Marxism. In 1997, he left his professorship in Cambridge to become director of the London School of Economics, a position he retained until 2003. There he continued his engagement with politics in *The Third Way* (1998) and *Runaway World* (1999), initially given as the BBC Reith lectures.

His growing status as the most visible intellectual proponent of 'Third Way' politics drew him into the inner circle of the British Prime Minister at the time,

Tony Blair, who dubbed his own 1998 political manifesto 'The Third Way'. It also became an influential ideological position for the German SDP under Schroder and the US Democratic Party led by Bill Clinton. Subsequent works aimed at shaping contemporary politics included *Where Now for New Labour?* (2002), *The Progressive Manifesto* (2003) and, following Blair's replacement by Gordon Brown in 2007, *Over to you Mr Brown* (2007a) and *Europe in the Global Age* (2007b). In 2004 Giddens was given a life peerage in the House of Lords as Lord Giddens of Southgate. He also visited Libya in 2006 and 2007 to engage in talks with Muammar Gaddafi, trips organised by a US lobbing group, Monitor Group, which sought to improve Gaddafi's international image while Giddens argued that he had sought to foster a market-based democracy in the country. His most recent works and articles have focused on the pressing issues facing the environment and include *The Politics of Climate Change* (2009).

Sociology and the Enlightenment

The *longue durée* of ideas which are rooted in the Enlightenment provides an overwhelmingly important intellectual context for Giddens' own project. The ideas of the Enlightenment not only shaped the latter's writings but also expressed the contours of emerging political ideologies in the shape of liberalism, conservatism and socialism. However, these thinkers and Enlightenment thought in general were interpreted by Giddens against the backdrop of developments in post-war sociology in the UK and United States. In the latter, within a context of growing political radicalism during the late 1960s, such a frontal assault on the Parsonian orthodoxy had come earlier, both from the radical left and from the liberal centre. Liberal reworkings of functionalist theories had been initiated by Robert Merton and subsequently pressed further theoretically by writers from the symbolic interactionist tradition inspired by Schutz and, more radically, by Garfinkel in his theory of ethnomethodology (Merton, 1949; Berger and Luckmann, 1966; Garfinkel, 1967). However, for sheer oppositional force and virulent theoretical and political criticism, the work of two American left-wing radicals, C. Wright Mills (1959) and Alvin Gouldner (1971), stood out above others. Similarly, in the UK, the most vociferous criticisms of Parsons' work came from 'conflict theorists' – most notably those advanced by Rex (1961), Dahrendorf (1958) and Lockwood (1956). Two major critical themes ultimately emerged from this motley group of theoretical standpoints, both of which reflected the political context of rising social conflict, the eruption of student radicalism and a concomitant re-emergence of Marxism. Ethnomethodological and symbolic interactionist critiques focused on the knowledgeability and reflexivity of actors. By contrast, more overt conflict theorists, and political critics on the left, emphasised questions of power, conflict and interest.

It is in relation to these writings, which reasserted both the importance of the individual and of power as domination, within a context of growing student radicalism, that Giddens initiated his own criticisms of Parsons' work. His first attack on Parsons constitutes one of Giddens's earliest papers (1968) and derived largely from a 'conflict' theory perspective (Parsons, 1967). His next theoretical challenge was in a series of essays (1970, 1971b, 1971c, 1972) and in his first major book, *Capitalism and Modern Social Theory* (1971a). Although not referring to Parsons directly, this book clearly invokes the Parsonian trinity. However, Giddens' reworking of the canon replaces Pareto with Marx and questions Parsons' voluntarist framework. He also rejects the latter's narrow interpretation of Durkheim and Weber. Rather than converging upon the idea of an implicit Hobbesian 'problem of order', Marx, Weber and Durkheim were instead all concerned with the profound rupture between capitalism and earlier feudal or traditional social forms:

> it is a basic contention of this book that the overwhelming interest of each of these authors was the delineation of the characteristic structure of modern 'capitalism' as contrasted with prior forms of society. (1971a: xvi)

Historical, Social and Political Context

In addition to the Enlightenment and its reaction, the broad sociological and intellectual legacy which Giddens confronts, it is also important to examine the more immediate political context which shaped Giddens' political worldview. The end of the Second World War saw the Attlee Labour government pursuing a social democratic policy based on the existence of a mixed economy and the development of a welfare state. A National Health System was introduced by Bevan in 1946, while 20% of industries, including coal, water, the railways, civil aviation and electricity, were all brought under public ownership. Despite a huge state debt carried over from the war, full employment, child allowances, investment in public housing and in education including grammar schools all contributed towards a higher standard of living. The three successive Conservative governments from 1951 to 1964 remained committed to a centrist consensus, retaining adherence to Keynesian interventionism and therefore failing to herald any profound socio-economic changes. The country remained a global economic power with major companies in oil, tobacco, finance and shipping. Such was the national mood, sense of optimism and prosperity that in 1959 Harold MacMillan declared that: 'You've never had it so good.' During this period, following state patronage of the arts, various artistic media flourished as new literature, films depicting working-class life through social realism, and plays by individuals from a working-class background, including Harold Pinter and John Osborn, began to appear from the mid-1950s.

The Continuance of Class Inequality

However, the overall economic growth and consumption during the 1960s masked the continuing existence of stark class divisions and emerging social tensions. As Marr ironically notes, even in 1963:

there were still nearly a quarter of a million people in 'domestic service' – maids, housekeepers, valets – and more than six hundred full-time butlers. Britain was still graced with thirty-one Dukes, thirty-eight Marquesses and a mere 204 Earls. (2007: 117)

Britain was also a former major empire in terminal decline, gradually losing its power-prestige, as more colonies acquired independence. Equally, the post-war boom of the 1950s and the late 1960s was marked economically and politically by a rise in financial crises, inflation, industrial disputes, student radicalism and the emergence of youth cultures, including popular music, in bands such as the Beatles, Kinks and the Rolling Stones, defining a distinctive British sound. With the passing of the 1944 Education Act, a tripartite system of education was introduced in the UK. Based on the belief that intelligence was inherited, it distinguished and filtered students into grammar, technical and secondary modern schools. Those considered most academically capable were channelled into grammar schools, whilst the remainder – those predominantly from working-class backgrounds – were shunted into vocationally oriented technical and secondary modern schools. Nevertheless, with continuing investment in education, increasing numbers of universities became established after 1963 and older universities expanded, allowing some children from working-class backgrounds often schooled in grammar schools, to enter into third-level education for the first time. This included their entry into the newly established university discipline of sociology. It was this new generation of both working-class and middle-class students who constituted the main support for protest groups such as CND (Campaign for Nuclear Disarmament), and later protests against the war in Vietnam, as well as challenging a burgeoning British consumerism and conformism. Although on the left, when compared with the collectivist sentiments of the older left working class, these new student radicals differed in their focus on the individual and their self-liberation from harmful social norms and inequality.

After the boom of the early 1960s, economic decline slowly came to characterise the UK, as trade and production fell, and inflation rose. This intensified in the early 1970s, under the Conservative Heath government, which held power between 1970 and 1974. This was a period of profound international economic instability, partly caused by the oil crisis of the early 1970s. The latter resulted in a quadrupling of the price of oil from the Middle East and the emergence of 'stagflation' in the UK – a neologism coined to refer to the combination of economic stagnation and inflation. The result was increasing labour militancy and strike action.

The Rise of Thatcherism and the End of Labour

The Callaghan government (1974–8) attempted to mollify some of this industrial discontent through the creation of a 'social contract' with the unions, but a wave of strikes in the late 1970s and continuing economic decline saw Margaret Thatcher become Prime Minister in 1979. Thatcher ushered a wholly new ideology combining the policies of tradition deriving from an old-fashioned conservatism, with neoliberal economic policies. The Thatcherite revolution was sweeping, including a foregrounding of market forces in preference to state regulation, and the implementation of a monetarist economic policy designed to reduce the money supply and inflation. The Thatcherite period, which lasted for 13 years, gradually, but unrelentingly, chipped away at various state interventionist policy practices, established since the Second World War through the privatisation of state industries and huge reductions in welfare and social spending, a policy agenda bolstered by victory in the Falklands War in 1981, and in the miners' strike of 1984.

Thatcher's fall in 1990, following growing tensions within her own party and an intransigent attempt to introduce a poll tax, saw her replaced by John Major, who shifted the Conservatives slightly to the centre, but under whose premiership social and class disparities in health, education, wealth and life chances continued. The move to the centre also took place on the left, as Labour abandoned many of its traditional policies under the leadership of Neil Kinnock and John Smith. Following the latter's death in 1992, his replacement, Tony Blair, a 42-year-old graduate from Oxford, spoke of the emergence of a 'New Labour' which encapsulated policies ordinarily associated with the Conservative Party, including sympathy to business interests, privatisation, patriotism, anti-unionism, tackling crime and generally appealing to middle-class groups residing in middle England (O'Morgan, 2000: 103). On the platform of third-way politics, Blair became Prime Minister in 1997, pursuing a centre-right agenda which included the invasion of Iraq in 2003, and remained in power until 2007, when he was replaced as leader of the Labour Party by Gordon Brown.

In terms of the history of university institutions, from its inception in the 1920s onwards, sociology in the UK retained at its foundation a strong liberal viewpoint. As Turner (1992) argues, many British intellectuals saw their role as educative and opinion forming. Hence, the influential sociological writings of Leonard Hobhouse, Morris Ginsberg, T. H. Marshall and Percy Cohen contained a strong impulse towards political liberalism which was expressed in their emphasis on individual and ethical responsibility and their strong aversion to evolutionary and structural models of social change (Studholme, 1997). Nevertheless, following the Second World War, British sociology like British society, was formatively shaped by the contextual dynamics of Cold War politics. This was especially the case during the late 1970s and 1980s when an academic divide opened up between sociology and Marxism which confronted and challenged a number of sociologists, including Giddens, who initially attempted to transcend it by finding a middle position.

It was in relation to the latter as well as the actually existing politically opposed co-ordinates of state socialism and industrial capitalism that Giddens developed his ambivalent political ideology. More precisely, Giddens' position as a social theorist reflected the standpoint of a Western left–liberal intellectual, isolated from any working-class practice or party. As an intellectual, he confronted the ideal of a socialism which had degenerated into a bureaucratic and repressive state practice, yet which represented the only significant buffer against, on the one hand, an inegalitarian capitalism, and a morally redundant modern capitalism, on the other. It was in relation to this ambivalent social and political situation that Giddens attempted to criticise simultaneously the alienation and inequality engendered by modern capitalism and the bureaucracy and repressive 'unfreedom' which characterised actually existing state socialism. This was in terms of a synthesis of aspects of the political ideologies of liberalism and socialism: a political standpoint that may be characterised as 'libertarian socialism'. However, as Kilminster (1991) rightly argues, rather than giving both of these values of freedom and equality equal weight within his worldview, Giddens prioritised the concept of freedom, particularly in relation to the individual agent.

Moreover, the political dualism which underlay Giddens' theoretical sociological work neither remained static nor characterised the totality of his writings. Rather, since the dualism itself was an historical expression of the bipolar socio-political relations between capitalism and state socialism, it followed that, when this context disappeared, as it did with the fall of the socialist states following the 1989 revolutions, so too did the corresponding political dualism which underpins Giddens' socio-political worldview. As a result of the demise of state socialism, his subsequent work on modernity and politics tends to focus even more strongly upon the liberal dimension of his original libertarian socialist political dualism. This direction is revealed in his accentuated emphasis on the idea of freedom so central to liberalism with its correlates of individual spontaneity and choice, in opposition to the socialist principle of equality and social regulation expressed most overtly in his political work from the mid-1990s on the 'Third Way', which served as both a grounding for and a rationalisation of Tony Blair's post-Thatcherite, New Labour politics.

Arguments and Ideas

Giddens' intellectual career is best understood in terms of four overlapping periods, each marked by a distinctive set of theoretical concerns. His early work, in 1970–5, focused on the exposition of the classical tradition of European sociology, and he was influential in establishing the canonical trilogy of Marx, Weber and Durkheim as the basis of social theory. Subsequently, until 1989, he focused on the possibility of transcending a series of perceived dualisms within social theory, most significantly that between what he referred to as agency and structure. The resulting theory of structuration led to an attempted rewriting and re-periodising of human history. The third phase of his career, covering 1990–3, developed these theoretical and temporal insights into a more substantive analysis of the contours of modernity and the contemporary stage of what he referred to as 'late modernity'. This prepared the way for the most recent phase in his work, in which he moved from sociology to more directly political–theoretical concerns. Giddens' presentation of the 'Third Way' can be seen as an application of his earlier theoretical work on 'dualisms': an attempt to transcend the dichotomy between left- and right-wing political ideologies.

As we noted above, Giddens' first major book, *Capitalism and Modern Social Theory* (1971a), is also implicitly conceived as a challenge to Parsons' work. This book, as well as defining or setting the scene for the whole of his subsequent *oeuvre*, combines acute scholarship with a systematic attempt to place each of these thinkers in the social and political context within which they wrote. For Giddens, Marx, Durkheim and Weber sought to synthesise liberalism and revolutionary or radical forms of thought in different ways.

The Theory of Structuration

Rather than through a sensitive exegesis of past thinkers, Giddens' most significant contribution to social theory is often seen in terms of his theory of structuration. In three major works, *The New Rules of Sociological Method* (1976), *Central Problems in Social Theory* (1979) and *The Constitution of Society* (1984), as well as in numerous articles, Giddens developed his theory of structuration. This was an attempt to overcome the division between sociological approaches that either emphasised the creative agency of actors or those that emphasised structural constraints or what he terms 'the agency-structure dualism'.

The former, agency perspectives, focused on self-conscious actors – their intentionality, subjectivity, knowledgeability, as well as their ability to construct, create or make the social world they found themselves in. They also tended to discuss micro relations centred on individuals or small-scale groupings. Advocates of such a position included phenomenology, ethnomethodology, symbolic interactionism and rational choice theory. In diametric contrast, structural theories placed more emphasis on objective structural factors, the social determination of the self, and the invisible forces and emergent dynamics that shaped the actions, perceptions and 'second nature' of individuals. These perspectives also tended to focus on larger scale macro or societal dynamics and they included functionalism, structuralism and the many varieties of Marxism:

> If interpretive sociologies are founded, as it were, upon the imperialism of the subject, functionalism and structuralism propose the imperialism of the object. One of my principal ambitions in the formulation of structuration theory is to put an end to each of these empire-building endeavours. (Giddens, 1984: 2)

For Giddens, the agency–structure dualism that informs these two traditions runs through a series of related perspectival and methodological tensions that plague the discipline and which are connected with, but irreducible to, it. These include: individual versus society, micro versus macro, and subjective versus objective frameworks.

In his theory of structuration, Giddens argues that the agency–structure dualism can be overcome only by synthesising insights from this otherwise flawed medley of perspectives. Most significantly, this involves a reformulation of the term 'structure'. For Giddens, prior theoretical applications of the term 'structure' – most significantly those found in functionalism and Marxism – tended to define structure as causally efficacious, patterned social relationships that are not only external to human agency, but also constraining upon it.

However, Giddens discerns a very different understanding of the term 'structure' in Lévi-Strauss's structuralism. Structure here refers to abstract models in the form of binary oppositions and dual relations, existing in and through human beings and that do not exist in time and space but as relations of presence and absence. Utilising this latter approach, Giddens offers his own novel definition of structure. Structures, like languages, are 'virtual' since they exist 'outside of time and space'; are 'subjectless'; and are, for the most part, unintentionally reproduced in practices. By identifying structure with language, Giddens hopes to effect a dynamic juxtaposition between the speech or action implemented by an agent, and the structure that forms the condition of possibility for generating that speech and action. This reconceptualisation entails two changes. Firstly, there is what Giddens refers to as a 'duality of structure': structure is no longer understood as simply constraining, but also as enabling. Structure not only limits speech (or more generally action) through the rules of 'syntax', but also makes possible the generation of speech (or action). Hence if we continue this analogy, although individuals are bound by the rules of language they are nevertheless still free to say a massive variety of things about their social and natural world without being constrained. Secondly, structure is both the medium and the outcome of action. The 'instantiation' of structure in individual action recursively draws upon and reproduces structure in a manner akin to a speech–act drawing upon and reproducing the totality of our language. Every act of social production is therefore simultaneously an act of reproduction. Hence, for example, when individuals draw on the rules of language to say something, they unintentionally reproduce the whole system of language by doing so – language is both the medium and outcome of our speech.

Social Structures as Rules and Resources

More specifically, Giddens sees structures as composed of rules and resources:

> By the term 'structure' I do not refer, as is conventional in functionalism, to the descriptive analysis of the relations of interaction which 'compose' organisations or collectivities, but to systems of generative rules and resources. (1976: 127)

Giddens claims that his analysis of rule following can 'generally [be] treated in the manner of Wittgenstein's analysis of rule following'. To know a rule, 'as Wittgenstein says, is to know "how to go on", to know how to play according to the rule' (Giddens, 1976: 67). By allowing individuals to 'go on', rules imply 'methodological procedures' of social interaction. Thus, rules in social life are 'techniques or generalisable procedures' understood for the most part on a 'tacit' unformulated basis, which can be applied in the enactment and the reproduction of social practices. The types of rules which are of most significance for social theory are those which concern institutions; that is, practices which are most deeply 'sedimented in time-space'. Rules may be explicit or tacit, intensive or shallow, formal or informal, strongly or weakly sanctioned, but should generally be understood, in Wittgenstein's sense, as practical forms of knowledge that 'allow us to go on' in novel circumstances. Resources are 'authoritative' capabilities that generate command over persons or 'allocative' capabilities that generate command over objects or other material phenomena.

Giddens then connects rules with practices, so that rules generate – or are the medium of the production and reproduction of – practices. For Giddens then, structure and agency form two sides of the same coin and are connected through social practices – the things that humans do in their lives. They are inseparable dimensions of the flow of activities in which individuals participate during the course of their day-to-day lives.

Social Systems

Giddens also introduces a cluster of related concepts, the most important of which is the social system. This is expected to do 'much of the work that "structure" is ordinarily called upon to perform' (Giddens, 1984: 18). 'Social system' designates what functionalists and Marxists had formerly referred to as patterned social relations. In contrast to structures, social systems have a 'real' existence in time–space and are empirically manifest in 'the situated activities of human agents'. Social systems are constituted by social practices.

Structure and system relate to each other through social practices. Social systems involve regularised relations of interdependence between individuals and groups that typically can be best analysed as *recurrent social practices*. Social systems are systems of interaction; as such they involve the situated activities of human subjects.

Structuration thereby refers to the dynamic process whereby structures come into being and are reproduced recursively through social practices via the duality of structure. Structures are subject-less memory traces, which possess a 'virtual' existence consisting of rules and resources which 'bind' time–space. Social systems, on the other hand, manifest themselves empirically as regularised patterns of interaction constituting the effects of these generative rules and resources.

The Actor as Agent

In addition to rethinking the concept of structure, Giddens also reconceptualises the concept of the actor and agency. In his stratification model of action, he draws upon and modifies the Freudian notion of the actor to argues that an agent's consciousness has three aspects: a discursive consciousness, a practical consciousness and an unconsciousness (see Figure 1). Loosely corresponding to

Figure 1   Levels of consciousness in Giddens

Discursive consciousness	Practical consciousness	Unconsciousness
Reflexive monitoring	Rationalisation	Motivation

this three-fold division of the consciousness, he refers to reflexive monitoring, rationalisation and the deep motivations for action. Practical consciousness and its rationalisation as the tacit or 'mutual' knowledge that provides agents with the ability to 'go on' in relation to rule-bound social life are most significant for understanding social life.

Although always free to choose, agents follow routines in social life and hence follow predictable patterns of action in order to avoid experiencing what he calls 'ontological insecurity', which involves a disruption to a 'basic security system' internalised during childhood. Moreover, drawing on Merton's classic essay on the unintended effects of purposive action, Giddens argues that an individual's intentional acts often produce unintended consequences. These unintended consequences then become the future unacknowledged conditions that structure the subsequent action of the agent.

A second aspect of Giddens' theory of the actor connects agency to power, arguing that an agent ceases to be such if he or she loses the ability to 'act otherwise'. However, given that there exists a 'dialectic of control' built into the very nature of agency and involving the interplay of autonomy and dependence, a total loss of agency is rare.

Structuration as a Hermeneutical Theory

Giddens characterises structuration theory as a 'hermeneutically informed social theory', and there is little doubt that he wishes consciously to incorporate a sharp distinction between the natural sciences and the social sciences within his framework:

> The social sciences, unlike natural science, are inevitably involved in a 'subject–subject' relation with what they are about. The theories and findings of the natural sciences are separate from the universe of objects and events which they concern. This ensures that the relation between scientific knowledge and the object world remains a 'technological' one, in which accumulated knowledge is 'applied' to an independently constituted set of phenomena. But in the social sciences the situation is different... The implications of this are very considerable and bear upon how we should assess the achievements of the social sciences as well as their practical impact upon the social world. (1984: 348)

In his view, there is not only a 'logical tie' between the concepts of lay members of society and the social scientific community, as philosophers such as Peter Winch argue, but also a two-way relationship in virtue of which the concepts of the social scientist can be appropriated by lay actors themselves and subsequently reapplied as part of their discourse. The theories and the findings of the social sciences necessarily filter into lay discourse and become part of that discourse, thereby altering it irrevocably. Giddens refers to this process as 'the double hermeneutic'. The implication of this position is that consciousness, or, more precisely, reflexive self-consciousness, is an irreducible ontological form which separates the social sciences from the natural sciences by promoting a two-way 'dialogical' relationship between subject and subject rather than a unidirectional 'technological' relation between a subject and an independently existing object.

For Giddens, a number of significant consequences follow from the double hermeneutic. Firstly, the possibility of establishing universal laws within the social sciences becomes problematic. Secondly, the political and practical consequences of the double hermeneutic are that sociology, as an academic discipline, necessarily and unavoidably has to adopt a critical outlook. This transmutation of sociology into critical theory is not an option, but an obligation.

Such a critical standpoint can be adopted, according to Giddens, if a distinction is made between 'mutual knowledge', which is found at the level of practical consciousness and conceived as 'respect for the authenticity of belief', and 'common sense'. For Giddens, such a distinction can be effected by means of an analytical operation, which involves relabelling 'mutual knowledge' as 'common sense', and by examining the latter in terms of its logical rigour and empirical belief claims, in light of the findings of the social sciences. Giddens adds that the discovery of inadequately grounded or false beliefs (logically) necessitates a transformation in action related to those beliefs.

Historical Sociology

In parallel with the development of the theory of structuration, Giddens produced his own historical sociology as a 'positive critique' of Marx's historical materialism, which he considered as economically reductionist and methodologically suspect. In *A Contemporary Critique of Historical Materialism* (1981), he repeats a number of criticisms he has made throughout his work against Marxism. These include the recognition that: (1) there is a need for a distinction between capitalism and industrialism; (2) political factors have played a far more significant role in the latter-day development of advanced societies than Marx had envisaged; (3) the pre-eminence of 'traditional' elements in the capitalist societies is tied to the rise of nationalism; (4) the study of the nation-state within its international context is crucial; (5) there is a need for a move away from evolutionary and endogenous models of social change; and (6) Marxism fails to recognise the influence of military factors in social change. He then elaborates a non-functionalist, non-evolutionary, non-teleological, multidimensional and historically contingent view of social change.

Giddens' broad historical schema incorporates a tripartite societal typology that distinguishes tribal class-divided societies from class societies. These societies are defined according to their level of social and system integration and time–space distanciation. Social integration refers to 'systemness' in circumstances of 'co-presence' or 'face-to-face' interaction, and not only emphasises the spatial significance of presence but also attempts to convey the importance of the 'positioning' of the body within social space. By contrast, *system integration* refers to the reciprocity which exists between actors or collectivities across extended time–space or in relation to absent others outside of the conditions of co-presence. This involves a process of 'time–space distanciation': the 'stretching' of social systems across time and space. In *The Nation-State and Violence* (1985) he develops and modified this framework, exploring the complex symbiotic codevelopment of capitalism, industrialism and the nation-state. For Giddens these three spheres provide the basis for the four irreducible, though connected, 'institutional clusterings' that characterise modern society: capitalistic enterprise, industrial production, heightened surveillance and centralised control of the means of violence. This characterisation of modernity is developed further in the third phase of his work.

Modernity and its Consequences

In *The Consequences of Modernity* (1990) Giddens argues that the critical feature of the dynamic social formation that began to develop in Europe from about the seventeenth century was its sharp, qualitative discontinuity from the previous, traditional social order. This break involved a profound transformation that is both global and personal. Underlying modernity are three sources of dynamism: distanciation, disembedding and reflexivity. The 'separation and recombination of time and space' facilitate and promote an increased 'zoning' of social life. Everyday encounters and interactions become less tied to fixed locales and less dependent on the co-presence of the individuals involved. This, in turn, facilitates the development of modern rationalised organisations, and permits the emergence of a radical historicity in which the past can be appropriated with the aim of shaping the future. More importantly, it facilitates the 'dis-embedding' of social systems. Disembedding refers to the 'lifting out' of social relations from their local contexts of interaction, which permits their restructuring across larger spans of time–space. Modernity is inherently globalising, so that time–space distanciation links the local with the global through disembedding, although there may also be processes of 'reembedding' in which disembedded social relations are again pinned down. The two major types of disembedding mechanism are 'symbolic tokens' and 'expert systems'. Symbolic tokens are media such as money that can be exchanged, regardless of who uses them, while expert systems are systems of technical accomplishment and professional expertise such as those of doctors, lawyers, architects and scientists.

Fundamental to both mechanisms, as well as to the reflexivity of modernity more generally, is the concept of trust. A sense of trust in processes, people and things is a crucial factor in maintaining a sense of ontological security in the modern world, since its absence results in existential angst or dread. By contrast with pre-modern societies, where trust and risk were anchored in the local circumstances of place, rooted in nature and characterised by hazards from the physical world or violence in social life, modernity offers a new 'risk profile' characterised by 'manufactured risk'. Here the pervasiveness of socially organised knowledge in the form of abstract systems means that risk becomes the defining parameter of modern culture and life, even replacing the preoccupation with wealth. Giddens' analysis of modernity leads to the conclusion that in place of the two classic sociological accounts of the experience of modernity – Marx's theory of alienation and Weber's 'iron cage' of bureaucracy – the discipline would be better served by his own image of modernity as a careering juggernaut.

Although in structuration theory reflexivity is a fundamental feature of social action, it takes on a special meaning in Giddens's theory of modernity. Under emerging conditions of 'wholesale reflexivity' everything (including both individuals and institutions) becomes open to reflection and self-monitoring, including reflexivity itself. Social practices are continually examined and re-examined in the light of incoming information and processes of self-evaluation.

This leads Giddens to consider the transformation of the intimate and personal features of day-to-day existence in modernity, especially in his books *Modernity and Self-Identity* (1991) and *The Transformation of Intimacy* (1992). Increasingly, the pressures of work and domestic life push individuals towards the continual reconstruction of self-identities as part of a reflexive project. In this increasingly unavoidable autobiographical project, individual choices are made in the context of an array of trajectories and options engendered by abstract systems. Modernity involves both a transformation of lifestyle and a 'transformation of intimacy' in which personal and erotic ties are formed as 'pure relationships'. According to Giddens, 'pure relationships' involve 'commitment' and demands for intimacy, such that trust develops through mutual disclosure alone, rather than (as in more traditional societies) through criteria – such as kinship ties, social duty or traditional obligations – that exist outside of the relationship itself.

Developing a Third Way in Politics

Building on this theory of modernity, Giddens sets out a general political programme. In *Beyond Left and Right* (1994) and *The Third Way* (1998) he considers how radical politics might be rethought, both theoretically and in practice, in the context of a changing modern world. What he refers to as 'Third Way' politics involves a re-evaluation of socialism, social democracy and conservatism in the light of the altered social conditions of modernity that ultimately render them inoperable. He argues that the collapse of communism has made the distinction between the political 'Left' and 'Right' superfluous. Consequently, the idea of a fixed left/right binary for Giddens needs to be supplanted by the notion of a radical centre or 'active middle' embodying a 'utopian realist' position.

The fostering of an active civil society becomes a central focus for third-way politics. This involves the state and civil society acting in partnership with one another to provide material and social support for local groups to engage in 'generative politics' orientated towards empowerment. Echoing Beck's (1992) discussion of the importance of 'subpolitics' in an era of risk society, Giddens argues that increasing individualisation and reflexivity have led to new forms of democratisation or 'dialogic democracy'. Rather than referring to the extension of social and civil rights, dialogic democracy points towards a 'deliberative democracy' where forms of social interchange, social solidarity and cultural cosmopolitanism can be established. Widening democracy also requires a decentralisation of the state, or what he calls 'double democratization', and a move away from the paternalism of the welfare state.

Emancipatory politics must now be supplemented with a 'life politics' that breaks out of the restrictive cast of class politics. Concerning rich and poor groups alike, this life politics addresses universal issues, less driven by the polarities of social class; that is, issues pertaining to lifestyle, leisure, consumption and identity.

These public policy arguments are further developed in *Europe in the Global Age* (2007b) in which he argues that European societies must rethink their welfare state model in the light of globalisation, and that they must transform them in terms of addressing people's changing lifestyles. Two further books develop and extend these arguments. In *Over to You, Mr Brown* (2007a), while reviewing the successes and failures of the New Labour government between 1997 and 2007, he argues that overall the legacy of the party has been positive though new ideas and a new policy outlook are needed in the future. These include a more market- and business-friendly outlook and a commitment for Labour not to put up taxes. Although societies need to be more egalitarian this has to be done in tandem with maintaining economic dynamism and creating jobs. Here he advocates institutionalising a policy of 'flexicurity' (flexibility plus security) in the labour market.

In *The Politics of Climate Change* (2009), Giddens discusses the political implications and policy parameters pertaining to climate change and energy security, introducing what he rather immodestly calls 'Giddens's Paradox' into the climate debate. This states that since the dangers posed by global warming are not tangible or visible in day-to-day life people will generally remain passive in relation to climate change. However, waiting until they become visible and acute will be too late. At the same time as rejecting green and conservationist arguments based on the precautionary principle of not interfering with nature, Giddens posits a positive view of risk, seen as opportunity rather than danger, as the basis for a model of a low-carbon future. This in turn would be based on a politics of convergence in which the left and right on the political spectrum, as well as rich and poor countries, would come together and co-operate on forging long-term climate policies and sharing the fruits of technological advances. Such long-term planning policy, though requiring state regulation and intervention, would not be dependent upon a top-down state but rather the aforementioned ensuring state.

Contemporary Relevance and Applications

Theoretically Giddens' work has been most vociferously championed by Christopher Bryant and David Jary (1991), Ira Cohen (1989) and Rob Stones (1991). Giddens' theory has been extensively criticised for its lack of empirical applicability (Gregson, 1989; Loyal, 2003). Giddens himself did not seem to be too concerned with its lack of use, arguing that it was merely a 'sensitizing device' to understand empirical processes (Giddens, 1989b). Nevertheless, there have been those who do see it as having some utility (Bryant and Jary, 1991; Stones, 1991). And it has been used as a framework to understand a range of substantive processes. Burman (1988) has used structuration as a basis for understanding unemployment, and Connell (1998) for examining gender and power, while Dandeker draws on his historical sociology to examine processes of bureaucracy, war and surveillance.

In his book *Surveillance, Power and Modernity: Bureaucracy and Discipline from 1700 to the Present Day* (1989) Dandeker draws on Weber, Foucault and Giddens to examine the historical development of bureaucracy and surveillance with regard to the organisational supervision and administration of people. For Dandeker, domination through knowledge is a central feature of modern organisations including the state. Although connected with business and capital, the nation-state and technological developments, bureaucracy nevertheless remains irreducible to these processes. The growth of expertise in bureaucracies has facilitated greater surveillance as demonstrated in military, business and police bureaucracies. Moreover, as citizens demand greater and more equal rights and entitlements, so an increasingly intricate and complex bureaucracy expands. The burgeoning of surveillance, by contrast, has often been rooted in war and military needs.

Giddens' work has been particularly popular in management and organisational studies. Spybey (1984) has used it to examine traditional and professional frames of meaning in management while Roberts and Scapens (1985) have employed it to understand accounting practices in their organisational context. Equally Macintosh and Scapens (1990) have used it to examine the theory of management and accounting while Whittington (1992) has examined management practices through a structuration perspective.

THE JUGGERNAUT OF MODERNITY

While Giddens's description of the advanced stage of late modernity as a juggernaut presents an engaging thesis, it raises important questions for his theoretical and political programmes. The juggernaut is characterised as a runaway world driven by powerful forces, careening through time and space. Though the growth of expert systems enables the possibility of progress, their dominance threatens catastrophe. As a result, there is great uncertainty regarding the future of modernity, with huge risks attached. Furthermore, humanity can exercise only limited control; the juggernaut effectively crushes resistance, enforcing insecurity as a feature of everyday life. While this idea of an oppressive structure operating above the heads of actors is not without validity, overstating the case robs agency of its role in social life and disillusions any programme for progressive politics. Yet, Giddens still advocates a radical politics of utopian realism and remains the architect of structuration theory. How do we reconcile the juggernaut thesis with Giddens's greater *oeuvre*?

Criticisms

Giddens has been heavily criticised for his eclecticism, inconsistency and the lack of empirical utility of his theoretical input. The theory of structuration has for the most part been of little use in substantive sociological case studies or fieldwork, and it does not even appear in his own later policy-oriented studies and arguments. More specifically, he has been criticised for placing an excessive emphasis on individual agency, especially in his theory of structuration. It has also been noted that Giddens' politics evidences a strong liberal idealism, which underpinned his theory of structuration and historical sociology as a worldview. Loyal (2002) argues that although Giddens attempts to move beyond certain traditional dualistic approaches by recognising, for example, that 'agents' only become 'agents' in and through 'social structures', one consequence of his worldview is a residual commitment to a form of epistemological individualism. Despite repeated reference to the importance of social practices, this unnecessary individualism effectively reproduces conceptual binaries relating to structure and agency as well as a number of other dualisms including space and time, micro and macro, and the subjective and objective throughout his work.

Other critics have focused on Giddens' redefinition of social structure as rules and resources. By emending the definition of structure from its previous designation as patterned social relations to the concept of generative rules and resources, many critics have focused precisely on the resulting absence of the concept of causality from his characterisation of social relations. Clegg (1989), Callinicos (1989), Porpora (1989), Layder (1981), Archer (1982) and Thompson (1989) all regard Giddens' theory of structuration as seriously flawed because of its failure to accord any causal value to patterned social relationships. Porpora encapsulates this apprehension:

> Although rules and relationships go together, they are different. The question is which has analytical priority, rules or relationships. Giddens gives analytical priority to rules and in fact denies that the relationships of a social system have any causal properties independent of the rule-following activities of human actors... I will argue that relationships do have such independent causal properties and, moreover, that such relationships, once established, are analytically prior to the subsequent rule-following behaviour of actors. (1989: 206)

The critics, therefore, share the belief that rules and resources provide an inadequate basis for the conceptualisation of 'structure', and argue that a conventional conceptualisation as social relations should be maintained. As Clegg argues: 'notions of structural shaping, selectivity and constraint end up being too facile' (1989: 144). The concept of rules and resources reduces the differential capacities of agents and the unequal power characteristic of social life to effects of instantiation. This is not only too voluntaristic but also excessively idealistic or subjectivistic (Callinicos, 1989; Clegg,1989; Porpora, 1989; Thompson, 1989). Giddens' account of structure fails to acknowledge the prior differential distribution of varying forms of constraint within a given system or collectivity. Instead, power and differential structuring capacity are conceived of as an effect of social practices rather than as shaping those social practices in the first place.

It has also been argued that his more recent political and policy discussions, rather than renewing social democracy as claimed, reflect the influence of a post-Thatcherite neoliberal consensus, often entailing anodyne commentaries on how common goals can be pursued by divergently positioned social actors (Loyal, 2002). These claims are most evident in the sweeping prescriptions of the putative 'Third Way', which, because based ultimately on a liberal doctrine, lead him to ignore the entrenched and unequal distribution of power, and the embedded nature of conflict and social interests – including ethnonational conflicts, struggles over money, private property and wealth – that exist at both the national and global level in the contemporary world.

Conclusion

Giddens has often provided commendable commentaries on many sociological debates as well as offering unique insights into the nature of the social world. And it is probably here that his strength as a sociologist lies. It can be argued that Norbert Elias and Pierre Bourdieu provide more fruitful approaches for transcending the various sociological dualisms that Giddens was concerned with. Their work is also more amenable to and intertwined with empirical and substantive research, while his political sociology lacks a cohesive theory of power and has been overtaken by political events in the real world, effectively rendering it increasingly obsolete.

References

Archer, M. (1982) Morphogenesis versus Structuration: On Combining Structure and Action. *British Journal of Sociology*, 33(4), pp. 455–83.
Beck, U. (1992) *Risk Society*. London: Sage.
Berger, P. L. and Luckmann, T. (1966) *The Social Construction of Reality: A Treatise in the Sociology of Knowledge*. Garden City, NY: Doubleday.
Bryant, C. and Jary, D. (1991) *Giddens' Theory of Structuration: A Critical Appreciation*. London: Routledge.
Burman, P. (1988) *Killing Time, Losing Ground: Experiences of the Unemployed*. Toronto: Wall and Thompson.
Callinicos, A. (1989) Anthony Giddens – A Contemporary Critique. In: A. Callinicos (ed.) *Marxist Theory*. Oxford: Oxford University Press, pp. 105–47.
Clegg, S. (1989) *Frameworks of Power*. London: Sage.
Cohen, I. (1989) *Structuration Theory: Anthony Giddens and the Constitution of Social Life*. London: Macmillan.

Connell, R. (1998) *Gender and Power*. Cambridge: Polity
Dahrendorf, R. (1958) Toward a Theory of Social Conflict. *Journal of Conflict Resolution*, 2(2), pp. 170–83.
Dandeker, C. (1989) *Surveillance, Power and Modernity*. Cambridge: Polity.
Garfinkel, H. (1967) *Studies in Ethnomethodology*. Englewood Cliffs, NJ: Prentice Hall.
Giddens, A. (1968) 'Power' in the Recent Writings of Talcott Parsons. *Sociology*, 2(3), pp. 257–72.
Giddens, A. (1970) Marx, Weber and the Development of Capitalism. *Sociology*, 4, pp. 289–310.
Giddens, A. (1971a) *Capitalism and Modern Social Theory: An Analysis of the Writings of Marx, Durkheim and Weber*. Cambridge: Cambridge University Press.
Giddens, A. (1971b) Durkheim's Political Sociology. *Sociological Review*, 19, pp. 477–519.
Giddens, A. (1971c) The 'Individual' in the Writings of Émile Durkheim. *Archives Europeans de Sociologie*, 12, pp. 210–28.
Giddens, A. (1972) Four Myths in the History of Social Thought. *Economy and Society*, 1, pp. 357–85.
Giddens, A. (1973) *The Class Structure of Advanced Societies*. London: Hutchinson.
Giddens, A. (1976) *The New Rules of Sociological Method*. London: Macmillan.
Giddens, A. (1979) *Central Problems in Social Theory: Action, Structure, and Contradiction in Social Analysis*. London: Macmillan.
Giddens, A. (1981) *A Contemporary Critique of Historical Materialism*. London: Macmillan.
Giddens, A. (1982) *Profiles and Critiques in Social Theory*. London: Macmillan.
Giddens, A. (1984) *The Constitution of Society*. Cambridge: Polity.
Giddens, A. (1985) *The Nation-State and Violence*. Cambridge: Polity.
Giddens, A. (1989a) *Sociology*. Cambridge: Polity.
Giddens, A. (1989b) A Reply to My Critics. In: D. Held and J. B. Thompson (eds) *Social Theory of Modern Societies: Anthony Giddens and His Critics*. Cambridge: Cambridge University Press, pp. 249–301.
Giddens, A. (1990) *The Consequences of Modernity*. Cambridge: Polity.
Giddens, A. (1991) *Modernity and Self-Identity*. Cambridge: Polity.
Giddens, A. (1992) *The Transformation of Intimacy: Sexuality, Love and Eroticism*. Cambridge: Polity.
Giddens, A. (1994) *Beyond Left and Right*. Cambridge: Polity.
Giddens, A. (1998) *The Third Way: The Renewal of Social Democracy*. Cambridge: Polity.
Giddens, A. (1999) *Runaway World*. London: Profile Publishers.
Giddens, A. (2002) *Where Now for New Labour?* Cambridge: Polity.
Giddens, A. (2003) *The Progressive Manifesto: New Ideas for the Centre-Left*. Cambridge: Polity.
Giddens, A. (2007a) *Over to You, Mr Brown*. Cambridge: Polity.

Giddens, A. (2007b) *Europe in the Global Age*. Cambridge: Polity.
Giddens, A. (2009) *The Politics of Climate Change*. Cambridge: Polity.
Gouldner, A. W. (1971) *The Coming Crisis of Western Sociology*. New York: Basic Books.
Gregson, N. (1989) On the (Ir)relevance of Structuration Theory to Empirical Research. In: D. Held and J. B. Thompson (eds) *Social Theory of Modern Societies: Anthony Giddens and His Critics*. Cambridge: Cambridge University Press, pp. 235–48.
Kilminster, R. (1991) Structuration as a World-view. In: C. Bryant and D. Jary (eds) *Giddens' Theory of Structuration: A Critical Appreciation*. London: Routledge.
Layder, D. (1981) *Structure, Interaction and Social Theory*. London: Routledge & Kegan Paul.
Lockwood, D. (1956) Some Remarks on 'The Social System'. *British Journal of Sociology*, 7(2), pp. 134–46.
Loyal, S. (2002) *The Sociology of Anthony Giddens*. London: Pluto Press.
Macintosh, N. B. and Scapens, R. W. (1990) Structuration Theory in Management Accounting. *Accounting, Organizations and Society*, 15(5), pp. 455–77.
Marr, A. (2007) *A History of Modern Britain*. London: Macmillan.
Merton, R. K. (1949) *Social Theory and Social Structure*. New York: Free Press.
Mills, C. W. (1959) *The Sociological Imagination*. New York: Oxford University Press.
O'Morgan, K. (2000) *Twentieth-Century Britain: A Very Short Introduction*. Oxford: Oxford University Press.
Parsons, T. (1967) *Sociological Theory and Modern Society*. New York: Free Press.
Porpora, D. V. (1989) Four Concepts of Social Structure. *Journal for the Study of Social Behaviour*, 19, pp. 195–212.
Rex, J. (1961) *Key Problems of Sociological Theory*. London: Routledge & Kegan Paul.
Roberts, J. and Scapens, R. (1985) Accounting Systems and Systems of Accountability: Understanding Accounting Practices in Their Organizational Contexts. *Accounting, Organizations and Society*, 10(4), pp. 443–56.
Shilling, C. (1992) Reconceptualizing Structure and Agency in the Sociology of Education: Structuration Theory and Schooling. *British Journal of Sociology of Education*, 13, pp. 69–87.
Spybey, T. (1984) Traditional and Professional Frames of Meaning in Management. *Sociology*, 18(4), pp. 550–62.
Stones, R. (1991) Strategic Context Analysis: A New Research Strategy for Structuration Theory. *Sociology*, 25(4), pp. 673–95.

Studholme, M. (1997) From Leonard Hobhouse to Tony Blair: A Sociological Connection? *Sociology*, 31(3), pp. 531-47.

Thompson, J. (1989) The Theory of Structuration. In: D. Held and J. Thompson (eds) *Social Theory of Modern Societies: Anthony Giddens and His Critics*. Cambridge: Cambridge University Press, pp. 56-76.

Turner, B. (1992) Ideology and Utopia in the Formation of an Intelligentsia: Reflections on the English Cultural Conduit. *Theory, Culture & Society*, 9, pp. 183-210.

Whittington, R. (1992) Putting Giddens into Action: Social Systems and Managerial Agency. *Journal of Management Studies*, 29(6), pp. 693-712.

Habermas

Introduction

Jürgen Habermas is widely regarded as the leading social and political theorist and philosopher in the world today, developing a highly original social theory that regards knowledge as a key means of achieving social freedom and human emancipation. Often seen as part of the second generation of Frankfurt School theorists, he was a former assistant of Adorno, though his more positive outlook differs markedly from the entrenched pessimism of the latter, partly since it was written and formulated in a later socio-political conjuncture – the 'thirty glorious years' from the 1940s to the 1970s. Though marked by ruptures and developments, Habermas's work focuses on the importance of emancipation and the development of a public sphere and institutions ensuring uncoerced egalitarian forms of democratic discussion. In addition to philosophy and social theory, he has increasingly taken a role as a public intellectual on many issues, initially with regard to the peace movement, and the consolidation of post-war democratic institutions in Germany, but more recently the development of the European Union and the development of a world society.

Life and Intellectual Context

Habermas was born on 18 June 1929 in Dusseldorf, on the Rhine, though he grew up in Gummersbach near Cologne. The second of three children, he was raised in a prosperous bourgeois household. His father, Ernst Habermas, was executive director of the Cologne Chamber of Industry and Commerce and sympathetic to National Socialism, though this contrasted with his mother, a sensitive intellectual who remained aloof from politics (Moses, 2008: 108). Jürgen was born with a severe cleft palate making speech and oral communication difficult. In addition, in a context where an ideal type of biological German was supposed to exist it constituted a major social stigma affecting Habermas.

Habermas was part of a whole generation of Germans in the Hitler Youth – sometimes referred to as the 'Flakhelfer generation' – which included Niklas Luhmann, Ralf Dahrendorf, Hans Magnus Enzenberger, Wolfgang Mommsen and Gunter Grass, who experienced their childhood, puberty and adolescence under the Nazi state (Brunkhorst and Müller-Doohm, 2017: 1). He became a member of the Hitler Youth, serving as a field-nurse. Fleeing to the countryside rather than fighting as part of the last defence as the end of the war approached, he experienced the war's conclusion with great relief. He was to be deeply affected after the war, especially by the revelations concerning Nazi actions that emerged with the Nuremberg trials:

> At the age of 15 or 16, we sat before the radio and experienced what was being discussed before the Nuremberg tribunal; when others, instead of being struck silent by the ghastliness, began to dispute the justice of the trial, procedural questions, and questions of jurisdiction, there was that first rupture, which still gapes. Certainly, it is only because I was still sensitive and easily offended that I did not close myself to the fact of collectively realized inhumanity in the same measure as my elders. (Habermas, 1983: 41)

The Flakhelfer Generation

In the words of Karl-Otto Apel, a soldier in the war who later became a close friend and colleague, following the war, the '*Flakhelfer* generation' learnt that 'everything was false'. After studying at the George August University in Göttingen in 1949 and then in Zurich, Habermas gained his doctorate, entitled 'The Absolute and History: On the Schism in Schelling's Thought', in 1954 from the faculty of philosophy in Bonn. It was here that he met Karl-Otto Apel, who was 7 years his senior. Following a stint as an independent journalist publishing articles on politics and culture in various periodicals and newspapers, such as *Handelsblaatt*, *Frankfurter Allgemeine Zeitung* and the renowned journal *Merkur*, Habermas moved to Frankfurt to the newly re-established Institute for Social Research where he became an assistant to Theodore Adorno. Under its Director, Horkheimer, he began his *Habilitationschrift*, though because of political and academic differences, he finished it under the supervision of the Marxist political scientist and jurist, Wolfgang Abendroth. This was later published in 1962 and in 1989, in English, as *The Structural Transformation of the Public Sphere*.

Habermas then took up a post as *Privatedozent* in Marburg before accepting a position in philosophy at the University of Heidelberg. In 1961, he took part in the Positivist Dispute, arguing that a hermeneutical science of meaning had to replace 'the hypothetical-deductive connection of propositions'. In 1964 Habermas moved back to Frankfurt to take up a chair in philosophy and sociology, replacing Max Horkheimer, and giving his inaugural lecture on 'Knowledge and Interest'. As well as publishing *On the Logic of the Social Sciences*

(1967) he also produced two major collections of essays, *Theory and Practice* (1963) and *Technology and Science as Ideology* (1968). In contrast to Adorno and Horkheimer, Habermas was initially supportive of the student revolts of 1968, especially their critique of the emergency laws, the SPD–CDU coalition and university reforms. However, he soon denounced them for undertaking 'action for action's sake'. They in turn, challenged him for being a conservative intellectual retreating into theory. In 1971 Habermas took up another newly created position as Director of the Max Planck Institute for the Study of the Conditions of Life in the Scientific-Technical World in Starnberg in Bavaria.

While based there, in addition to *Legitimation Crisis* (1973) he published what is regarded as his major work, *The Theory of Communicative Action* (1984 [1981]), before returning in 1982 to take up a chair and directorship at the Institute for Social Research in Frankfurt. He remained there until he retired in 1994. Here he published a number of books, including *Moral Consciousness and Communicative Action* (1983), *Postmetaphysical Thinking* (1988), *Justification and Application* (1991) and *Between Facts and Norms* (1992). Moreover, following retirement his output remained prodigious: *The Inclusion of the Other* (1996), *The Postnational Constellation* (1998), *Religion and Rationality* (1998), *The Future of Human Nature* (2003), *Between Naturalism and Religion: Philosophical Essays* (2005), *Europe: The Faltering Project* (2009) and *The Crisis of the European Union* (2012). At the age of 90 he continues to publish to this day. He has recently published a massive two-volume work on the history of philosophy (Habermas, 2019).

Habermas's work is not of one piece and undergoes significant development and shifts of focus, as is indicated by the enormous range of intellectual sources he draws upon. In addition to Marxist social theory and the Weberian emphasis on the development of instrumental rationalisation, the Lukácsian discussion of reification and the Freudian discussion of repression, all of which were evident in the work of the Frankfurt School, other influences on his thinking include: German idealist thought from Kant to Hegel; German hermeneutics from Dilthey to Gadamer; the Anglo-American pragmatism of Charles Pierce, George Herbert Mead and John Dewey; the systems theory of Parsons and Luhmann; the speech-act theory of Wittgenstein, Austin and Searle; and the phenomenology of Husserl, Heidegger and Schutz. Although Habermas was deeply influenced by the Frankfurt thinkers Adorno, Horkheimer and Marcuse, his work remained critical of their later intellectual position as too philosophical and not political enough. He was also much more sympathetic to the work of Kant, who remains a massive presence in his thought, especially the latter's political philosophy and ethics as well as the more liberal and social democratic ideas of the pragmatists and functionalists.

Historical, Social and Political Context

The end of the Second World War had huge socio-political and national implications for Germany. Immediately after the war, the world began to be carved up between a communist East and a capitalist West, represented by the two huge power blocs, the USSR and United States, respectively. West Prussia was given to Poland, while Alsace-Lorraine was taken over by France. Moreover, the whole country became divided into two. In a land which was a latecomer to unification in 1871 and in a sense remained divided into federal states, this had profound socio-political implications. As well as social and political collapse, Germany faced huge financial ruin after the war. Yet, it emerged rapidly as a leading industrial power, fuelled by the Marshall Plan, the cancellation of state debt and the ordo-liberalism of Erhard. The economic miracle (*Wirtschaftswunder*), continued into the 1970s.

In the Federal Republic, the new German Chancellor, Konrad Adenauer (1876–1967), looked firmly towards the West (*Westintegration*), taking an uncompromising anti-communist stance and even admitting ex-Nazis into his Cabinet. Born in 1929, the year of the beginning of the Great Depression, Habermas was part of the 'skeptical generation' (Schelsky, 1961) *flakhelfergeneration* or '45ers' (Spectre, 2010: 5) born between the late 1920s and early 1930s who experienced the end of the war and the beginning of liberal democracy. As Habermas admitted: 'What really determined my political life was 1945' (Dews, 1986: 73). His work from the 1950s to the end of the century reflects Germany's post-war transition from National Socialism to a liberal democratic model of the state and political culture, based on the rule of law, rather than personal authoritarian politics. As he noted: 'The unreserved opening of the Federal Republic to the political culture of the West is the great intellectual achievement of the post-War period, of which my generation in particular can be proud' (cited in Spectre, 2010: 2). It was this newly established state that sought to protect the private sphere from state violation, serving as a spiritual anchor for democracy and the German Federal Republic.

Post-war Germany and its Pre-war Continuities

However, this 'opening' towards liberal democratic values and institutions was by no means straightforward. After the Third Reich disintegrated, the newly established German state nevertheless preserved many Nazi aspects, partly because of the efforts of right-wing, Conservative, German jurists. Ex-Nazis gained prominent posts in the 'new' state, scuppering any chances of a redemptive break with the past. These positions included academics who influenced Habermas's thought, such as Heidegger, and his first teacher in Bonn, Oskar Becker. Habermas viewed the 1950s as a time of conservative restoration, especially in the spheres of state and university. The shift from the Nazi authoritarianism of the 1930s, to the Christian democracy of the 1950s, was characterised by a lack of reflection or discussion on the crimes perpetrated by German fascism. Instead, for the most part these violations remained ignored or simply left to stand in silence. For example, when Martin Heidegger republished his book, *An Introduction to Metaphysics* in 1953 (2014 [1953]), he failed to renounce his pre-war affiliation with the Nazis. In reaction Habermas published 'Thinking with Heidegger against Heidegger: On the Publication of his Lectures of 1935'. He also highlighted the appeal of far-right thinkers such as Carl Schmitt, another apologist for the Third Reich. The failure of de-Nazification, and the continuation of irrationalist, anti-modernist, anti-Enlightenment, pre-war attitudes led to a heated discussion by historians about memory and politics – to which Habermas contributed in the mid-1990s. As Müller-Doohm notes: 'How can totalitarian worldviews and forms of rules be prevented? ... this question forms the core of Jürgen Habermas's overall social and theoretical project, as well as his commitments as an intellectual' (2016: 347). Habermas, like Adorno, believed that Germany had not confronted its own immediate Nazi past as a post-totalitarian, post-genocidal country both in recognising its atrocities and their motivation, and making a moral break with them.

There were, however, also significant ruptures with the Nazi past. The new German Federal Republic was a parliamentary democracy bereft of a military, and eschewing the death penalty. In a developing Cold War consensus, the FDR, however, became both virulently anti-communist and, after US prompting, began to remilitarise once again joining NATO in 1954. In 1957, NATO decided to equip European member-states with nuclear weapons. Many Germans were opposed, but Adenauer nevertheless introduced them into West Germany, leading the CDU into an expanding ideal of military securitisation. In reaction to its electoral defeat around the same time, the SPD, at a conference in Bad Godesburg in 1959, began a rightward shift transforming itself from its origins as a party of the workers, to a party of the people: in essence, socialist transformation was now an ethical choice rather than immanent in history. The Godesburg platform was opposed by Habermas, together with his supervisor Abendroth, who was more sympathetic to the idea of a social market economy.

The 1960s were an equally turbulent period in world history. The decade included, *inter alia*, the Cuban Missile Crisis, an escalating US invasion of Vietnam (supported by the FDR), increasing CIA activities in South America, the assassination of Martin Luther King, as well as John F. Kennedy, the emergence of a radical civil rights movement in the United States, the development of anti-colonial movements, the Six-Day War in the Middle East and a military coup in Greece. In August 1961, the government of the German Democratic Republic (government of East Germany) began to build a wall to prevent dissidents and refugees escaping to the West – an *Ostflucht* of about 200,000 a year. In response, a coalition government led again by Adenauer was re-elected. Habermas, however, lamented the lack of party diversity in Germany and talked of the establishment of a 'Chancellor Democracy'. Moreover, during the 1960s, he saw himself as a committed pacifist, and integrally involved with the German peace movement.

Habermas also slowly began to emerge as a leading public intellectual, later the foremost intellectual in Germany. He published on a number of causes and events including the democratisation of the universities, the German constitution, the Cuban Missile Crisis of October 1962 and the Spiegel affair in which the editors of the *Spiegel* magazine were arrested for revealing state secrets about NATO. Following the death of a student protestor, Benno Ohnesorg, at the hands of the police, Habermas became alarmed at the disintegration of democratic processes, supporting instead a transformation of capitalist structures along more socialist and welfare lines. However, he later criticised the actions of the leaders of the student movement, including Rudi Dutschke, for their excessively voluntaristic, and pre-emptive acts of violence. According to Habermas, they acted for the sake of action, constituting a form of 'left-wing fascism'.

Rather than abating with the end of the 1960s, a section of radical left-wing politics continued into the 1970s, including using increasing acts of violence, for example, the Baader-Meinhoff faction. The German state responded to what it perceived as terrorist incidents including the assassinations of leading industrial and political figures, by increasing its repressive actions. Germany also experienced an ideological and political shift to the right during this decade, expressed in the rise of Helmut Kohl to power from 1969 to 1982, and the ousting of the social-liberal coalition. Habermas, however, continuing a stance he'd adopted since the 1960s, sought a political position mid-way between the Social and Christian Democrats, and the ultra-leftism of student radicals. By contrast to their political positions, he advocated a policy of radical reform and of increasing democracy within the context of constitutional democracy. Although he drew on Marx's ideas, especially in his earlier work, and is associated with the Frankfurt School, he also remained highly critical of Marxism, and his political worldview may instead be seen as that of a republican or radical social democrat, greatly sympathising with the work of Kant, and especially the latter's writings on cosmopolitan peace and the liberal-democratic socialism of the pragmatic philosophers. His position has become increasingly more liberal over the years.

According to Habermas, modern Western capitalist states were ridden not only by exploitation, but also by a Weberian instrumental rationality leading to bureaucratic domination. In such a context, he has sought to revivify the more substantive aspects of rationality that remained latent in the West, envisaging an ideal or utopian West of the future. His works have attempted to reinvigorate liberal constitutionalism and active democracy through the development of a communicative rationality.

Ideas and Arguments
The Public Sphere

Habermas's work is not of one piece, and has undergone several revisions, especially in the face of ongoing criticism. Nevertheless, certain dominant and recurring motifs run throughout his work, which are evident even from his earliest major works, especially *The Structural Transformation of the Public Sphere* (1989 [1962]). This work, in developing his *habilitation* thesis, supervised and influenced by the Marxist Wolfgang Abendroth, engages with the media-dominated, conformist, depoliticisation of society in the 1950s. The book attempts to examine the historical development and disappearance between the eighteenth and twentieth centuries of what he terms a bourgeois, liberal 'public sphere'. In the midst of feudal social and political remnants, such a sphere contained free and open discussion and debate between cultured individuals who considered themselves social equals. In these discussions, reason, through the force of a better argument, held sway.

The public sphere was engendered by specific social and economic conditions, principally the development of capitalism, and enshrined in the emergence of a bourgeois constitutional state. Habermas's notion of a public sphere does not refer to a physical space or place, which is how it is rendered by the problematic English translation of the German word *Öffentlicheit*, but to an abstract idea of 'public-ness' or publicity' which contrasted with a private sphere. This binary was first fully employed in ancient Greek thinking where a distinction was made between the public sphere of the *polis* – where political discussion and collective action took place – and the private sphere of the household, or *Oikos*, limited to production and consumption. The modern distinction, however, entails the displacement of an extremely hierarchical form of 'representative publicity' in which the monarch was the sole public figure, characteristic of the Middle Ages. In a social world bereft of public or private institutions, public referred to a social status in which power represented itself. Under the impetus of major social and economic developments, including the rise of capitalism, commerce, trade and print media, a new bourgeoisie emerged which challenged this heretofore unquestioned domination of the ruling state and monarchy. Spurred by print media including newspapers – which initially reported commercial interests, but later became a voice for questioning political rule and legitimate government – a bourgeois reading public began to discuss issues of power and domination in emerging coffee houses and salons. This took place initially in the UK, but later spread in the nineteenth century to various European capitals:

> The principle of publicity, which initially, on the basis of a public constituted by cultivated, reasoning private persons, capable of enjoying art, asserted, in the medium of the bourgeois press, an unambiguously critical function vis-à-vis the secretiveness which was the praxis of the absolutist state. (Habermas, 1988: 4)

Such a form of rational critical debate became a feature of a civil society, which, as Hegel noted, demarcated a sphere of capitalist economic competition and family life. Civil society became slowly separated from the state and began to hold the latter accountable.

The initial uncoerced, rational and free discussions within the public sphere, however, began to decline under the very market forces which had engendered them. Over time, and especially during the twentieth century, the boundary between state and society blurred. The public sphere became replaced by a leisure and culture industry with commercial and advertising interests guiding and manipulating discussion and debate. Public opinion was now manufactured, and criticism and rational debate became less common. Such a process indicated the re-emergence of earlier forms of unequal, exclusionary discussion in which politicians now represented themselves to voters in a manner akin to monarchs before their subjects. This process constituted a 'refeudalisation' of the public sphere. As Habermas noted:

> the ever more densely strung communications network of the electronic mass media today is organised in such a manner that it controls the loyalty of the depoliticised population, rather than serving to make the social and state controls in turn subject to a decentralised and uninhibited discursive formation of the public will, channelled in such a way as to be of consequence – and this in spite of the technical potential for liberation which this technology represents. (1988: 4)

According to Habermas, the re-emergence of deliberative, open, democratic public spaces and institutions was crucial, not only in the political sphere of parties and government, but also throughout all organisations in civil society. This also required a politically engaged public.

Marxism and Capitalist Development

Although drawing on the work of Marx and therefore sometimes regarded as a Marxist, Habermas remained critical of Marx. In his early essays, 'Dialectics and Rationalisation' (1954) and 'Perspectives on Marx' (1954), for example, he questioned Marx's focus on the forces and relations of production and their role in engendering social emancipation. In *Communication and the Evolution of Society* (1979) and his paper 'Towards the Reconstruction of Historical Materialism' (1975), Habermas also argued that Marx failed to develop a coherent and rigorous moral standpoint as the basis of his critique of capitalism, especially as his work was increasingly interpreted within a positivistic framework. Marxism had become too rigid, reductionist and one-sided in its materialist preoccupation with the economy and for its neglect of politics and culture. Marx's preoccupation with the concept of social labour in which humans transformed their material environment through instrumental reason ignored the importance of cultural factors, including morality, norms and values, and especially the role of language. *Pace* Marx, human reproduction involved not only social labour but also a kinship structure, culture and, most importantly, language and communication. Moral regulation had shaped society and underpinned its transformation, including economic development:

> The development of these normative structures is the pace-maker of social evolution, for new organizational principles of social organization mean new forms of social integration; and the latter, in turn make

> it possible to implement available productive forces, or to generate new ones, as well as making possible a heightening of social complexity. (Habermas, 1979: 120)

For Habermas capitalism must be understood in terms of evolutionary development. Although societies evolve, this is not as Marxists believe through the mechanisms of social conflict, political struggle and social movements but through moral–practical knowledge:

> the species not only learns technical knowledge relevant for the development of the productive forces, but also the decisive dimension of moral-practical knowledge which can be embodied into structures of interaction. The rules of communicative action do not automatically follow changes in the field of instrumental and strategic action; they develop rather by virtue of their own dynamics. (Habermas, 1975: 294)

Legitimation Crisis

Habermas extended his ideas of examining the relationships between culture, politics and economics in his work *Legitimation Crisis* (1976 [1973]), which drew heavily on the systems theory of Parsons and Luhmann. According to Habermas, Marx's theory was deficient with respect to understanding contemporary societies. In late capitalism, the economy had become controlled through state intervention, and wealth and prosperity normalised. In a situation where economic resources were partially redistributed, albeit following social struggles, the working class had become de-radicalised. Instead, various social movements tied to peace, gay rights, ecology and women's rights began to emerge, indicating that the central locus of conflict in modern societies was no longer found in the sphere of labour, but rather in the political and cultural domains. With the displacement of economic crises through state intervention, 'motivation' and 'rationality crises' arose challenging the social order. Moreover, an interventionist state became subject to contradictory pressures of serving the interests of property owners and capital in relation to growth, while also sustaining broad electoral support and legitimacy from the masses. Welfare and social spending programmes that aimed to accrue legitimacy resulted in heavy borrowing, inflation, and a loss of profits for capital and private property, resulting in economic crises – a form of 'rationality crisis'. In such a context, there emerged a technocratic ideology in which politics had become reframed as a relation between active experts who made decisions, and a passive electorate, who putatively benefited from them. However, economic crises in system integration, and rationality crises in social and system integration, also resulted in a 'motivational crises' in social integration, and the sphere of culture. Individuals increasingly felt unable to participate in the political sphere and decision making, but also religiously informed historical ideals and values tied to work, career and family became challenged by secular structural trends tied to the economy, bureaucracy and the rise of radical extra-parliamentary social movements.

Knowledge and Interests

In *Knowledge and Human Interests* (1972), Habermas attempted to ground epistemology in social theory by developing a 'programme for a theory of science ... a theory which is intended to be capable of grasping systematically the constitutive conditions of science and those of its application' (1972: 7). As Habermas notes in the preface, the notion of reflection is central:

> I am undertaking a historically oriented attempt to reconstruct the prehistory of modern positivism with the intention of analyzing the connections between knowledge and human interests. In following the process of the dissolution of epistemology, which has left the philosophy of science in its place, one makes one's way over abandoned stages of reflection. Re-treading this path from a perspective that looks back toward the point of departure may help to recover the forgotten experience of reflection. That we disavow reflection is positivism. (1972: vii)

Behind the multiplicity of human desires and interests that exist within modern societies, Habermas discerns the existence of three primary interests and correlative theories that have characterised the development of humans, and that have been necessary for their existential reproduction. These three theories entail three corresponding 'cognitive interests'.

Rather than the ability to transform nature and the environment through the use of tools as distinctive of humans as compared with animals, it is the human's ability to use language and communicate with one another. Nevertheless, both capacities allow humans to develop different corresponding forms of knowledge. The ability to labour provides the basis for the development of technical knowledge and a cognitive interest in developing knowledge to control and to shape nature instrumentally. Such an interest is reflected in the development of the 'empirico-analytic sciences' or positivism, and expressed through the burgeoning of instrumental reason. This technical interest puts knowledge into practice through what he designates as the 'media of work'. However, *pace* Adorno and Horkheimer, the development of such technical knowledge is not singularly problematical but, in fact, necessary for human beings to bring the external forces of nature under control. The problem of modern societies concerns the *predominance* of this type of knowledge over others. Science has become reduced to a positivistic understanding based on the idea of disinterested contemplation, and the belief that there exists an ordered world independent of the knowing subject.

By contrast, language, which also alters the environment, is correlated with the 'practical interest' of understanding. This understanding engenders the 'hermeneutical sciences' – the social sciences and humanities which attempt to understand and interpret human interactions and how individuals understand one another, as well as the ends and aims of social actions and social organisations. Practical interests develop through the 'media of interaction'. In contexts of uneven power and domination, however, communication becomes distorted and manipulated, so that people systematically misunderstand and do harm to one another. As a result, the technical and practical interests in turn, give rise to an 'emancipatory interest' geared towards the removal of domination in society and nature, and distorted forms of communication. The emancipatory interest uses 'the media of power' and generates a form of critical theory. Here the paradigm is not only Marxism, which indicates the social constraints that exist in the human environment, but, more importantly, psychoanalysis, which makes unconscious factors (internal constraints) guiding behaviour, conscious, and lays them before the demands of an expanded, as opposed to instrumental, reason. By clearing away structural obstacles and unjust distorting rules in communication and interaction, critical theory fosters the development of universal forms of consensual decision making in which all individuals can equally and democratically participate. If positivism is geared to a human interest in control, and hermeneutics towards understanding, then critical theory aims to develop autonomous self-directing human actors; that is, actors free from constraint and the obstacles in the way of their freedom.

The Theory of Communicative Action

Following substantial criticism of Habermas's position concerning the ambiguous correlation between reflection and emancipation, he modified his views on knowledge and human interests. He now made a distinction between 'rational reconstruction', which reflects on the conditions and possibilities of action, and 'self-criticism', which focuses on examining socially created constraints. The former became the basis for his next major work on communicative rationality and discourse ethics, *The Theory of Communicative Action (TCA)* (1984, 1987a). Published in two volumes and arguably his magnum opus, the *TCA* draws upon and criticises a range of philosophical and sociological approaches, including functionalism, phenomenology, linguistic and pragmatist theories, and theories of rationality, by attempting a synthesis of their positive insights. Habermas questions the earlier critical theories of the Frankfurt School not only for their entrenched pessimism concerning the unrelenting expansion of instrumental rationality, but also for their belief that a utopian society was one free of constraints. Instead, he posits a world of mutual, intersubjective understanding, based on reason – or what he refers to as the force of the better argument. A domineering instrumental and technological rationality can be exorcised through a countervailing communicative rationality.

As part of the work on developing a comprehensive analysis of communicative rationality, Habermas attempts to move away from a Cartesian philosophy of consciousness to one focusing instead on language and dialogue, shifting attention from the relation between the subject and the world, to one grounded in the intersubjectivity of communication. Drawing heavily on the speech act theory of John Austin and John Searle, he argues that language and communication constitute a central component of all human action and provide the basis for a richer conception of rationality: a procedural conception of communicative rationality which dwells on the procedures by which knowledge can be acquired. Developing an approach that he dubs 'Universal Pragmatics', he aims to demonstrate the universal norms or 'validity claims' that are necessarily invoked for rational speech to take place. Connected to this he develops a theory of communicative competence which forms the basis for a discourse ethics. According to Habermas, communicative competence is akin to Noam Chomsky's belief that humans, at a young age, share an innate capacity for acquiring grammar. In addition, he argues, the work of the developmental psychologist Lawrence Kohlberg suggests that the moral development of the child can be seen as taking place in three stages: a pre-conventional stage in which children understand actions and their consequences, but for the most part retain an egoistic view of the world; a conventional stage, where they conform to moral norms through obedience based on authority; and a post-conventional stage, where the child becomes an adult and justifies his or her actions through a rational framework without leaning on blind authority. According to Habermas, the child attains linguistic competence in the conventional stage.

The key concern of universal pragmatics is the analysis of meaningful speech or speech acts. Speech acts, as John Austin (1975 [1962]) recognises, contain both locutionary force – they are propositional, referring to some external state of affairs or human action – and illocutionary force, entailing something being done by the utterance. This results in perlocutionary force, an effect produced in the listener. According to Habermas, all competent speakers and listeners must be able to present speech acts with locutionary and illocutionary aspects, as well as being able to distinguish between these. For the hearers to understand and to accept the speech act they must judge some level of sincerity on the part of the speaker – these are pragmatic universals. Agreement in communication requires four validity claims to be met: what is said must be intelligible; that it is true; that it is morally right or appropriate; and that it is sincere.

All human communication presupposes the inherent existence of these various 'validity claims' about what is true and false about the nature of the world, what rules are correct and incorrect, and which actions correspond to them. It is only on the basis of consensus on these positions that everyday human action and interaction are possible. Although these four validity claims are not always met in reality, they nevertheless constitute claims that can be appealed to as implicit in all rational dialogue. They form counterfactual ideals with which to measure actual communication practices – an ideal speech situation. In hierarchical power contexts, consensus regarding validity claims can become distorted and 'manipulated' by powerful 'systematically distorted' communication. Nevertheless, by drawing on a theory of 'Universal Pragmatics', critical theorists can uncover the universal norms and uncoerced validity claims that should be invoked for speech and understanding to take place, based on reason or the force of the better argument. As Seidman notes:

> Habermas took this argument for the foundations of critical theory one step further. At the core of the hope for a rational consensus is a social ideal that is implicit and that Habermas explicitly invoked as justifying the moral standpoint of critical theory. The logic of rational consensus or a consensus shaped by the force of the reasons advanced is unthinkable without assuming a social condition in which discourse is open to all individuals who are not constrained by lack of resources or fear of repercussions in contesting validity claims and therefore power hierarchies ... Rational consensus presupposes what Habermas called an 'ideal speech situation,' a social condition in which the parties to public discourse are in a situation of equality and autonomy. (2012: 124)

[Republished with permission of John Wiley and Sons from *Contested Knowledge Sociological Theory in the Age of Postmodernism*, Seidman, 2012. Reproduced with permission of the Licensor through PLSclear]

The ideal speech situation is therefore not an empirical phenomenon, but a 'transcendental assumption' that within all individual speech acts there exist equal partners, although this is not always realised. Ideal speech situations possess four characteristics that construct validity claims: mutual understanding between participants; equal opportunity to participate; recognition of the force of the better argument; and freedom to radicalise every argument in an unconstrained manner. Habermas's standpoint has affinities with Kant's regulative idea of a kingdom of ends in which people act only according to the moral law in which every individual is an end in themselves. Truth is effectively consensual – only the best argument succeeds. It is a consensus based on generalisable interests in which all can participate equally.

In *The Theory of Communicative Action*, Habermas also expands his earlier discussion on the contradiction between capitalism and democracy in which two 'opposed principles of societal integration compete for primacy' (1987a: 345). The 'steering media' of money and power, impersonal orders representing 'the imperatives of autonomous subsystems' (1987a: 354) begin to 'colonise' the diverse and complex communicative practices and consensual democratic values found in the 'life-world'. That is to say, markets and administrative systems distort and displace the social solidarity inherent in the life-world. The life-world is itself composed of shared traditions, cultures and values geared to motivating individuals, and creates social identities, communal solidarities and institutional stability. By contrast, the social system refers to the domain responsible for co-ordinating resources and controlling the social and natural environment. Colonisation, in Habermas's understanding, no longer refers to the appropriation of distant lands but to processes internal to nation-states as the life-world becomes expropriated by market, administrative and legal system imperatives, and increasingly reified. Only political resistance, increased democratisation and the mobilisation of communicative power within an expanded public sphere in civil society can serve as a bulwark against such proliferating colonisation.

Later Writings

In Habermas's later work he continues to focus on issues concerning globalisation, law, democratisation and the importance of communicative reason. In his *Philosophical Discourse of Modernity* (1987b) he defends the Enlightenment tradition not only against Adorno and Horkheimer but also against several post-modernist thinkers, including Foucault and Lyotard. Given his focus on communicative rationality as an expression of modernity, and as something which is internal to interpersonal interactions, Habermas believes that this offers an alternative to instrumental notions of rationality.

In his *The Future of Human Nature* (2003), and constituting a further shift in his work, Habermas states his qualified opposition to genomic manipulation. Genomes may be manipulated in order to repair and restore them but not to enhance or expand them. For Habermas (2003: 29), zygotes (fertilised human egg cells), embryos and genomes possess 'the dignity of human life', and they should not be manipulated for instrumental reasons through genetic engineering serving consumerist needs found in the marketplace. This view of genetic manipulation should form the basis of a broad society-wide consensus (Barnes and Dupre, 2009: 23–42).

In other more political forms of sociology, Habermas argues that in modern societies nation-states are becoming less relevant. As Keucheyan (2014: 121–22) notes, developments in weaponry have made military conscription less urgent, while nuclear weapons have rendered wars less likely because of the possibility of mutually assured destruction. Furthermore, increasing migration, travel and the growth of international media have engendered a form of cultural relativism and cosmopolitanism. Finally, the social and human sciences have become insulated from the state through incremental professionalisation, further severing the link between historians and nationally focused research and becomes displaced by the subsequent development of national narratives that filter into schooling and education. Taken together, with increasing economic globalisation, these processes mean that nationalism has lost its urgency and the emergence of a 'post-national identity'. In *The Postnational Constellation* (2001 [1998]), Habermas extends this examination of the role of traditional nation-states in a global era. More specifically, he analyses democracy, legitimacy, identity, culture and human rights, in the context of global inequality and unequal capitalist forms of resource distribution. An increasingly deregulated global economy, he argues, cannot be controlled successfully by inwardly focused nation-states but instead, only by democratic supranational or post-national structures or constellations based on a post-national cosmopolitanism. A united, cohesive and progressive thinking Europe Union underpinned by a European public sphere concerned with distributive justice, is necessary to face the negative effects ensuing from globalisation. Such a post-national cosmopolitan order, as well as transcending national identity, should focus on human rights that bypass those restricted rights given to citizens by inviolable sovereign national states. Such an order, with the UN serving as a partial model, would, therefore, contain a cosmopolitan law, overriding traditional international law, and conferring justiciable, universal rights on individuals.

In an essay written with Derrida (Habermas and Derrida, 2005) he resumes his arguments concerning the creation of a 'core Europe', a post-national democracy defined by a secular, multilateral, Enlightenment-oriented, social democratic base. These are further elaborated in *The Divided West* (2006), *Europe: The Faltering Project* (2009) and in *The Crisis of the European Union* (2012). The latter book examines the role Europe will play in shaping the globe in the twenty-first century, especially in a context in which the peoples of Europe have adopted an increasingly democratic role in shaping Europe's policies, as well as discussing the hurdles preventing a reinvigorated European public sphere fostering communication and dialogue.

Contemporary Relevance and Applications

In developing his work through dialogue with other approaches Habermas has participated in a number of significant debates both with philosophers and sociologists, including Hans-Georg Gadamer and Niklas Luhmann.

HABERMAS AND MARXISM

Habermas's relationship to Marxism is complex and disputed by critics. Initially, Habermas elaborated a programme of social theory intended to extend that of Marx. With his reconstructive approach – breaking a theory apart and reconfiguring it to better achieve its aims – Habermas revisited Marx's central concepts, drawing insights from across the social sciences. The category of labour was displaced by that of interaction, historical materialism was realigned to focus on the moral evolution of social structures, which in turn were transposed from the moral development of individuals, and social evolution was linked to communicative learning processes. The theory of false-consciousness was superseded by a theory of systematically distorted communication, and the theory of crisis was realigned to consider legitimation and meaning deficits. This reconstruction phase ended with *The Theory of Communicative Action*, however, which Habermas considered a full replacement for Marx's social theory. Claiming some valid function for the capitalist economy, critics argued that this work stepped outside Marxism altogether, despite Habermas insisting the contrary.

In his debate with Hans-Georg Gadamer, Habermas was perceived by Gadamer as attempting to provide an overly 'objectivist' account of social processes that escapes from prejudiced forms of understanding. This, for Gadamer, was impossible since all understanding takes place through a 'fusion of horizons' presupposing background traditions. However, for Habermas an interpretive, *Verstehen*-based, hermeneutical understanding of the social world was necessary to criticise positivism, and to provide a methodological grounding for the human sciences. But such an understanding also needed to be underpinned by a materialist critique of power and exploitation. Gadamer, he argued, remained too wedded to the importance of tradition and authority in his theory.

By contrast, in his exchange with Luhmann, the central question that both thinkers address was whether social processes could be understood in terms of social systems – as organised patterns of behaviour. It also focused on the ethical question of what the implications of systems theory were for understanding modern society and for understanding humans as freely acting beings (Bausch, 1997). Although Habermas accepted a great many of the premises inherent in systems theory, he remained critical of it. For Habermas, social action requires consensual decision making, while for Luhmann, in complex, pluralistic societies such consensus was impossible and societies instead required the regulation of impersonal systems.

Habermas has exercised a considerable impact on the development of the social sciences through his philosophical social theory, and on German political life more generally, through his role as the country's foremost public intellectual. His influence on the English-speaking academic world grew from the early 1980s not only in sociology but also in moral philosophy, legal theory and international relations. His ideas and arguments have also been widely supported and diffused, especially through his students, who include Axel Honneth, Seyla Benhabib, Hans Joas and Thomas McCarthy, but also others including Nancy Fraser.

Benhabib, a political philosopher, draws on both Habermas and Kant in exploring the development of an institutional, cosmopolitan standpoint. Examining the development of the relationship between a plurality of interacting cultures and democracy, she interrogates how it is possible to reconcile certain universalistic principles centred on human rights, including autonomy and freedom, with particular concrete identities derived from members of communities distinguished by language, by ethnicity or by religion. In an increasingly globalised society, Benhabib sees the gradual emergence of a global civil society that can legitimise the existence of cosmopolitan norms through a process of 'democratic iteration'.

Although Benhabib focuses on women, gender plays a more significant role in the work of Nancy Fraser. In *Justice Interruptus,* Fraser recognises that Habermas's notion of the public sphere remains 'an indispensable resource' (1997: 69), especially in its examination of the limits of democracy and political practice in late capitalism. However, she argues, Habermas's notion remains wedded to a model of an idealised bourgeois public which is both patriarchal and normatively inadequate to meet the needs of a critical theory for today. Fraser attempts to build a post-bourgeois model of the public sphere by addressing this exclusion of gender and other public spheres which stand in contestation with dominant publics, which she designates as subaltern counter-publics:

> I contend that, in stratified societies, arrangements that accommodate contestation among a plurality of competing publics better promote the ideal of participatory parity than does a single, comprehensive, overarching public… I propose to call these subaltern counterpublics in order to signal that they are parallel discursive arenas where members of subordinated social groups invent and circulate counter discourses, which in turn permit them to formulate oppositional interpretations of their identities, interests, and needs. (1997: 81)

> [Republished with permission of Routledge from *Justice Interruptus: Critical Reflections on the 'Postsocialist' Condition*, N. Fraser, 1997. Permission conveyed through Copyright Clearance Center, Inc]

Fraser has extended her work by focusing on the intersection of economic inequalities and culture and discourse, or what she terms redistribution and recognition, especially in a context where the disjointed struggles of emancipatory groups, and especially between those focusing on economic distribution, and those centring on identity, were becoming increasingly prevalent. According to Fraser a politics of recognition and a politics of distribution are two analytically distinct but empirically connected forms of struggle in post-Fordist late capitalism. Although sometimes at variance, both need to be incorporated into a broader 'perspectival dualist framework' of social justice. In modern democratic societies, where the parity of participation is central, different forms of life need to be respected and individuals need to be sufficiently materially well-off to engage in politics and have their voices heard.

Such a standpoint has led Fraser into a major debate with Axel Honneth, a former student of Habermas, and another leading 'third-wave' critical theorist. In his book *The Struggle for Recognition* (1995) Honneth, like Habermas, foregrounds social interactions and communication. His work indicates a shift away from material production and the redistribution of wealth, and instead, drawing on the work of both Hegel and Mead, focuses more exclusively on the centrality of mutual recognition. Recognition is crucial for the development and maintenance of a person's social identity for ratifying their moral expectations. The major institutions in modern life – the family, law and the market – engender three specific forms of recognition: love, respect and esteem. This, for Honneth, provides the basis for a normative model. Human emancipation and flourishing depend on a well-developed 'ethical life', or *Sittlichkeit* in Hegel's terms, which emerges following a struggle for recognition. Humans are moral beings geared towards self-realisation, and this is only possible on the basis of recognition by others. Only mutual recognition provides the self-esteem, self-confidence and self-respect needed to become an autonomous person. Honneth also acknowledges increasing commodification, reification and inequality in contemporary societies and the impact this has on individual's sense of recognition.

Honneth's work has also influenced another wave of critical theory as developed by his student, Harmuth Rosa. In his book *Social Acceleration* (2013) he argues that the increasing speed of life in all society's disparate social spheres is central to understanding the process of modernity and modern life. Rosa examines how such processes of accelerated time lead to social suffering, and alienated and damaged lives, and attempts to suggest a diagnostic remedy in the spirit of critical theory.

Criticisms

Habermas's work has been heavily criticised by both Marxists and mainstream sociologists. Held (1982: 250) has argued that critical theory is 'especially prone to hostile and inadequate polemic'. According to Held this is because critical theorists antagonise established orthodoxies by criticising and drawing upon a wide range of disparate schools, recasting the terms of sociological enquiry, yet simultaneously fail to 'specify "what is to be done"'. Nevertheless, in light of many criticisms, Habermas has subsequently modified his positions. Marxist critics such as Perry Anderson (1983) have argued that his work contains underlying unresolved tensions. This is indicated in his shift from discussing the importance of social interaction to a stronger focus on communication:

> the notion of social interaction – vague enough in all conscience, but generally denoting the realm of cultural and political forms in their widest sense, as opposed to the economy – tended increasingly to give way to that of communication, as if the two were simply equivalent, the latter being more precise. But, of course, there are many forms of social interaction that are not, except in a purely abusive or metaphoric sense, communication: war, one of the most salient practices in human history, is the most obvious example, while the associated labour of material production is itself social interaction of the most basic kind. (1983: 60–1)

Communication in turn has increasingly become displaced by language, as if both were also interchangeable therefore ignoring non-linguistic forms of communication. Moreover, language which was initially deemed on an equal par with labour has eventually come to take precedence over it, as what constitutes humans as humans. For Anderson, the shift from seeing language as the medium of social life to seeing it as the foundation and paradigm of social life overrates the role of language and produces an angelic view of language creating a, 'curious innocence in Habermas's vision' in which conflict and contradiction become effaced (Anderson, 1983: 66). As well as seeing Habermas's work as too preoccupied by philosophical issues and excessively idealist (Therborn, 1977), Marxists have also questioned his engagement with Marx. As Outhwaite notes:

> it is clear that Habermas's engagement with specific elements of Marxism has never been as thorough as his alternative 'reconstructions'. More importantly, he has so far had rather little to say about production and class relations even in advanced capitalist societies, let alone the rest of the world, or even about human interaction with nature. (1994: 152)

Habermas's theory of the public sphere, written before the emergence of the internet, but still acknowledged as a significant contribution to sociological understanding, has also been criticised for ignoring how both women and the working classes were debarred from entering fully into the bourgeois public sphere. The development of the public sphere, as Fraser (1997) noted above, presupposed the shunting of women into a private sphere.

Habermas's discussion of knowledge and human interests has also been questioned. Although his recognition that knowledge and interests are integrally connected is taken as given, his understanding of scientific knowledge entails disastrous misconceptions. Rather than three different kinds of knowledge, with three correlative interests, Barnes has stated that: 'it could be argued that all knowledge, "scientific", "hermeneutic" or otherwise, is primarily produced and evaluated in terms of an interest in prediction and control' (1979: 15).

Habermas's theory of communicative reason has also been criticised. While open debate may lead to better mutual understanding, it does not necessarily lead to consensus. The belief that individuals will succumb to 'the force of a better argument' presupposes individuals agreeing on what constitutes a better argument, especially across different cultures. Moreover, Barnes's questions Habermas's standing as a critical analyst of modern society given his belief in the intrinsic evolutionary value of differentiated systems of purposive rational action. Such a view not only questions Marx's theory of alienation, but also the idea that meaningful work could ever be part of a future good society. In effect Habermas's position is that of an apologist for capitalism:

> Even though he goes onto recognize that instrumental rationality is liable to get out of hand, and that certain forms of unfortunate reification are endemic under capitalism, his work still amounts to an unequivocal statement of the (rational) superiority of modern capitalist societies and their unique position at the end of the line of progressive change. (Barnes, 1995: 123)

Conclusion

Habermas has remained committed to Horkheimer's earlier discussion of critical theory as a critique of the social sciences geared towards human emancipation. And although he recognises the problematic and dominating consequences of the Enlightenment project, as they did, he nevertheless remains a champion of its positive aspects. He also shared the earlier theorists' view that capitalism had fundamentally changed since Marx's day: modern late capitalism is a form of monopoly capitalism rationalised and expressed through a positivist social science. Like them, he saw positivism as a technocratic ideology but one which, he argued, needed to be replaced by a 'reconstructive science' facilitating the development of greater democracy. Given his attempt at such a wide-ranging theoretical synthesis, centred on communicative rationality, it was inevitable that certain problems would surface in his work. Resolving these by modifying his theory on an continuing basis by shifting gradually more rightwards, has been a central ongoing concern, but has in turn engendered futher difficulties in his work.

References

Anderson, P. (1983) *In the Tracks of Historical Materialism*. London: Verso.

Austin, J. (1975 [1962]) *How to Do Things With Words*. Cambridge MA: Harvard University Press.

Bausch, K. C. (1997) The Habermas/Luhmann Debate and Subsequent Habermasian Perspectives on Systems Theory. *Systems Research & Behavioral Science*, 14, pp. 315-30.

Barnes, B. (1979) *Interests and the Growth of Knowledge*. London: Routledge and Kegan Paul.

Barnes, B. (1995) *The Elements of Social Theory*. London: UCL Press.

Barnes, B. and Dupre, J. (2009) *Genomes and What to Do With Them*. Chicago, IL: University of Chicago Press.

Brunkhorst, H. and Müller-Doohm, S. (2017) Intellectual Biography. In: H. Brunkhorst, R. Kreide and C. Lafont (eds) *The Habermas Handbook*. New York: Columbia University Press, pp. 1-26.

Dews, P. (1986) *Autonomy and Solidarity: Interviews with Jürgen Habermas*. London: Verso.

Fraser, N. (1997) *Justice Interruptus: Critical Reflections on the 'Postsocialist' Condition*. London: Routledge.

Habermas, J. (1973 [1963]) *Theory and Practice*. J. Viertel, trans. Boston, MA: Beacon Press.

Habermas, J. (1988 [1967]) *On the Logic of the Social Sciences*. S. Weber Nicholsen and J. A. Stark, trans. Cambridge, MA: MIT Press.

Habermas, J. (1968) Technology and Science as 'Ideology'. In: J. Habermas (1970) *Toward a Rational Society: Student Protest, Science and Politics*. J. J. Shapiro, trans. Boston, MA: Beacon Press, pp. 81-122.

Habermas, J. (1972) *Knowledge and Human Interests*. J. J. Shapiro, trans. Boston, MA: Beacon Press.

Habermas, J. (1976 [1973]) *Legitimation Crisis*. T. McCarthy, trans. Boston, MA: Beacon Press.

Habermas, J. (1975) Towards a Reconstruction of Historical Materialism. *Theory and Society*, 2(3), pp. 287–300.

Habermas, J. (1979) *Communication and the Evolution of Society*. T. McCarthy, trans. Boston, MA: Beacon Press.

Habermas, J. (1983) The German Idealism of the Jewish Philosophers. In: J. Habermas, *Philosophical-Political Profiles*. F. G. Lawrence, trans. Cambridge, MA: MIT Press, pp. 21–44.

Habermas, J. (1990 [1983]) *Moral Consciousness and Communicative Action*. C. Lenhardt and S. Weber Nicholsen, trans. Cambridge, MA: MIT Press.

Habermas, J. (1984) *The Theory of Communicative Action, Vol. 1: Reason and the Rationalization of Society*. T. McCarthy, trans. Cambridge: Polity Press.

Habermas, J. (1987a) *The Theory of Communicative Action, Vol. 2: Lifeworld and System: A Critique of Functionalist Reason*. T. McCarthy, trans. Cambridge: Polity Press.

Habermas, J. (1987b) *The Philosophical Discourse of Modernity: Twelve Lectures*. F. Lawrence, trans. Cambridge: Polity Press.

Habermas, J. (1992 [1988]) *Postmetaphysical Thinking: Philosophical Essays*. W. M. Hohengarten, trans. Cambridge: Polity Press.

Habermas, J. (1989) *The Structural Transformation of the Public Sphere: An Inquiry into a Category of Bourgeois Society*. T. Burger and F. Lawrence, trans. Cambridge, MA: MIT Press.

Habermas, J. (1994 [1991]) *Justification and Application: Remarks on Discourse Ethics*. C. Cronin, trans. Cambridge, MA: MIT Press.

Habermas, J. (1996 [1992]) *Between Facts and Norms: Contributions to a Discourse Theory of Law and Democracy*. W. Rehg, trans. Cambridge: Polity Press.

Habermas, J. (1998 [1996]) *The Inclusion of the Other: Studies in Political Theory*. C. Cronin, trans. Cambridge, MA: MIT Press.

Habermas, J. (2001 [1998]) *The Postnational Constellation: Political Essays*. M. Pensky (ed. and trans.). Cambridge, MA: MIT Press.

Habermas, J. (2002 [1998]) *Religion and Rationality: Essays on Reason, God, and Modernity*. E. Mendieta (ed.) Cambridge: Polity Press.

Habermas, J. (2003) *The Future of Human Nature*. Cambridge: Polity Press.

Habermas, J. (2008 [2005]) *Between Naturalism and Religion: Philosophical Essays*. C. Cronin, trans. Cambridge: Polity Press.

Habermas, J. (2006) *The Divided West*. C. Cronin, trans. Cambridge: Polity Press.

Habermas, J. (2009) *Europe: The Faltering Project*. Cambridge: Polity Press.

Habermas, J. (2012) *The Crisis of the European Union: A Response*. C. Cronin, trans. Cambridge: Polity Press.

Habermas, J. (2019) *Auch Eine Geschichte Der Philosophie*. Two Volumes, Frankfurt am Main: Suhrkamp.

Habermas, J. and Derrida, J. (2005) February 15, or, What Binds Europeans Together: Plea for a Common Foreign Policy, Beginning in Core Europe.

In: D. Levy, M. Pensky and J. Torpey (eds) *Old Europe, New Europe, Core Europe: Transatlantic Relations After the Iraq War.* London: Verso, pp. 3–13.
Heidegger, M. (2014 [1953]) *An Introduction to Metaphysics.* Yale, CT: Yale University Press.
Held, D. (1982) *An Introduction to Critical Theory: Horkheimer to Habermas.* Los Angeles, CA: University of California Press.
Honneth, A. (1996) *The Struggle for Recognition: The Moral Grammar of Social Conflicts.* J. Anderson, trans. Cambridge, MA: MIT Press.
Keucheyan, R. (2014) *The Left Hemisphere: Mapping Critical Theory Today.* London: Verso.
Moses, A. D. (2008) *German Intellectuals and the Nazi Past.* Cambridge: Cambridge University Press.
Müller-Doohm, S. (2016) *Habermas: A Biography.* Cambridge: Polity Press.
Outhwaite, W. (1994) *Habermas: A Critical Introduction.* Cambridge: Polity Press.
Rosa, H. (2013) *Social Acceleration: A New Theory of Modernity.* New York: Columbia University Press.
Schelsky, H. (1961) *Der Mensch in der wissenschaftlichen Zivilisation.* Cologne: Westdeutscher Verlag.
Siedman, S. (2012) *Contested Knowledge: Social Theory for Today.* Oxford: Wiley-Blackwell.
Specter, M. G. (2010) *Habermas: An Intellectual Biography.* Cambridge: Cambridge University Press.
Therborn, G. (1977) The Frankfurt School. In: New Left Review (ed.). *Western Marxism: A Critical Reader.* London: New Left Books, pp. 83–139.

16

Luhmann

Introduction

When Niklas Luhmann died in 1998 he was already regarded as the towering figure of German sociology. Many obituaries described him as the most significant sociologist since Max Weber. Even those who were not particularly sympathetic to his project considered him to be, together with Habermas, the most influential German social theorist. Moreover, his intellectual impact was already recognised beyond sociology in such diverse areas as cybernetics, administrative science, law and the arts. Luhmann was extolled for developing a highly original and uniquely consistent theory of social systems. Although he was initially deeply influenced by the work of Talcott Parsons, Luhmann devised a novel model of understanding the social world that does not resemble much of the latter's framework. Luhmann was also a highly prolific scholar producing no less than 40 books and over 250 articles. Nevertheless, despite this enormous influence within German academia during his lifetime, Luhmann was largely unknown in the English-speaking world. It is only recently that, with new translations of his key works, he has become known throughout the world.

In this chapter we analyse his key concepts and ideas by situating their development within the broader social, political, intellectual and biographical contexts. We also briefly explore the contemporary applications of his theoretical framework as well as the major criticisms of his system theory.

Life and Intellectual Context

Luhmann was born in the North German town of Lüneburg in 1927. He grew up in an upper-middle-class Lutheran, but secular, family: his paternal grandfather was a senator in Lüneburg, his father, Wilhelm, owned a brewery and malthouse, whereas his mother's family were Swiss hoteliers. Since much of his family on his mother's (Dora Gurtner's) side were living in Switzerland, young Niklas would spend his summer holidays there. His family was not sympathetic to Nazi rule and the young Luhmann remained quite distant from Nazi ideology. However, because of the plethora of military defeats on the Eastern front, the German military widened its conscription base to involve old men and young teenagers. Hence, in 1943, 15-year-old Luhmann was conscripted into the Luftwaffe as an auxiliary to man anti-aircraft guns and was sent to South Germany where he served for two years.

At the end of war, he was captured by US troops and taken as a prisoner of war in a labour camp near Marseille, until September 1945, when he was released. He found this experience traumatic as he was often beaten up and his possessions were stolen from him. Since the war interrupted his secondary school education, he was required to take an equivalency exam that would allow him to study law at the University of Freiburg. Upon graduation he became a civil servant and after quick promotion was an adviser in the Lower Saxony Ministry of Culture in Hannover from 1955 to 1962. During this period, he read extensively both legal and sociological literature. His first academic publications were in journals of administration.

The American Influence

In 1960 Luhmann married Ursula von Walter. During this period, he also received a scholarship to spend a year at Harvard's Littauer Center for Public Administration (1960–1). This scholarship constituted a pivotal moment in Luhmann's career as he had the opportunity to attend Talcott Parsons' lectures and quickly realised that it was sociology that interested him much more than the law.

The time spent in American academia was crucial for Luhmann's decision to leave the German civil service and embark upon an academic career. In 1962 he was appointed a research consultant at the University for Public Administration at Speyer (near Mannheim), and also published his first sociological contributions including an influential article 'Function and Causality'. In 1964 he completed his first book, *Functions and Consequences of Formal Organisations*, which clearly reflected the strong influence of Parsons. The book was well received, and consequently Luhmann gained strong support from, at that time, the leading conservative German sociologist, Helmut Schelsky (1912–84). Schelsky's influence was crucial initially in securing a teaching and research position for Luhmann at the University of Münster in 1965, and then, also in helping him attain a professorial post at the newly established University of Bielefeld. Nevertheless, to qualify for this appointment he had to complete not only his PhD, but also his *Habilitation* (a post-doctoral qualification), which he managed to attain within a single year, in 1966 (Joas and Knöbl, 2009: 250). This was possible through the retroactive acceptance of his two previously published books.

Before the new Bielefeld University was opened in 1968, Luhmann also taught at the University of Frankfurt (where he briefly occupied Theodor Adorno's former chair). He remained at Bielefeld University until his retirement in 1993.

His wife died young in 1977, and he was the sole carer for their three children. Luhmann was a visiting professor at several universities in the world, including the New School of Social Research in New York, and Chicago and Northwestern Universities in the United States. In 1988, Luhmann received the prestigious Hegel Prize from the City of Stuttgart. He was an extremely prolific author, publishing no less than 40 books and over 250 articles. He died in 1998 after a brief, but severe, illness.

As Stichweh (2015: 382) points out, the young Luhmann enjoyed reading literary classics such as Fyodor Dostoevsky, Thomas Mann, Jean Paul, Friedrich Hölderlin and Albert Camus. He was also fond of phenomenological philosophy where Edmund Husserl (1859–1938) was a particularly strong influence throughout much of his academic career. In Stichweh's view Husserl's philosophy underpins some of Luhmann's key ideas including a strict separation between consciousness and communication, which Luhmann formulates as the division between psychic systems and social systems. Furthermore, Husserl's emphasis on the centrality of meaning is also present in Luhmann's work. They both share the view that meaning is a mode of selectivity 'which builds complexity by remembering even those possibilities that were not chosen' (Stichweh, 2015: 383). By appropriating and then reformulating these ideas Luhmann was able to develop a theory that shifts the focus from intentionality and intersubjectivity, that are now associated solely with psychic systems, towards social systems which for Luhmann represent the dominant mode of social life.

The Legacy of Parsons

However, it was the work of Talcott Parsons (1902–1979) that left the strongest imprint on Luhmann's work. The year spent at Harvard attending Parsons' lectures shaped Luhmann's intellectual worldview. Initially, he was attracted to Parsonian structural functionalism as it helped him understand and explain the dynamics of complex social organisations that were part of Luhmann's own world: the civil service, educational systems, the state apparatus and even the military organisation that he was part of early in his life. His first book *Functions and Consequences of Formal Organisation* (1964) was a study of social organisations which was deeply influenced by Parsonian theory and also highly critical of the existing approaches in the sociology of organisations.

Although the influence of Parsons was present in most of his publications, Luhmann was far from being a mere interpreter of Parsons. On the contrary, his other early books such as *Fundamental Rights as an Institution: A Contribution to Political Sociology* (1965) and *The Goal Concept and System Rationality: On the Function of Goals in Social Systems* (1968) had already demonstrated the gradual development of a novel sociological approach. As Joas and Knöbl (2009: 252) emphasise, Luhmann was never an orthodox follower of Parsons. Instead, he used some of Parsons' concepts and reformulated them in such a way that they would be unrecognisable to any Parsonian scholar.

For example, he borrowed Parsons' notion of a social system, but this concept attains a very different meaning in Luhmann's theory. Unlike Parsons, who focuses on the functional roles of specific structures, Luhmann is much more interested in the process of structure formation: while Parsons centres on the question of functionality of a particular unit within the system (i.e. family or neighbourhood within larger society), Luhmann analyses how systems emerge and develop (i.e. how the family system transpires and operates). In this sense, Luhmann switches from Parsonian structural functionalism towards a functional–structural theory: whereas the former prioritises 'the concept of structure over the concept of function' the latter places 'the concept of function before that of structure', which allows the researcher 'to scrutinise the purpose of system formation itself'. In this way 'a functional-structural theory can probe the function of system structures, without having to make a comprehensive system structure the point of reference for any investigation' (Luhmann, 1970: 114).

Luhmann was also interested in intellectual developments outside of social science and the law. He had an encyclopaedic knowledge of different academic fields including cybernetics, biology and cognitive psychology. In his later years he was particularly influenced by the pioneers of artificial intelligence studies, namely the cognitive psychologist Herbert Simon, cybernetic scholar W. Ross Ashby, and biologists Karl Ludwig von Bertalanffy and Humberto Maturana among others.

Luhmann was driven to natural scientists and their concepts in part because he understood sociology to be, like them, a non-normative discipline capable of establishing universal generalisations. He appropriated and then substantially reformulated many existing concepts and idioms from science and philosophy. For example, he made extensive use of Donald Campbell's notion of 'variation, selection and retention', Henri Altan's 'order from noise', Franz Heider's 'medium and form', Reinhart Koselleck's 'historical semantics' and, most of all, Humberto Maturana's 'autopoiesis'. He also utilised and significantly changed established sociological concepts such as Robert Merton's 'functional equivalents', Erving Goffman's 'interaction order' and Gregory Bateson's 'difference that makes a difference'.

In this process of conceptual reformulation, as Stichweh (2015: 383) indicates, Luhmann challenged established views and the dominant ways of theorising. He preferred to utilise research models that developed outside of sociology and, when engaging with sociological approaches, the tendency was to identify less known and often forgotten authors over established authorities. For example, in one of his influential works (Luhmann, 1981) he identifies the little-known French Enlightenment stoic philosopher Luc de Clapiers, Marquis de Vauvenargues, as the ultimate authority on the relationship between time and action.

Niklas Luhmann lived a rather conventional academic life where constant reading and writing were occasionally interrupted with travels and a few non-academic pursuits. Unlike Habermas, who from early on acquired an aura of being a public intellectual, Luhmann was wary of public engagement and avoided exposure in the mass media. He did not like mass media, would advise students against spending time reading newspapers and did not even own a television set. In many respects Luhmann was a very traditional intellectual who did not engage much with the wider world and who devoted most of his time to developing a complex and highly abstract sociological analytical apparatus. The strong commitment to this lifelong ambition was already clear when he was appointed to a chair in the University of Bielefeld: when filling in the administrative form on his current research project in 1968 he entered: '"theory of society"; length: 30 years; costs: none' (Joas and Knöbl, 2009: 251).

Historical, Social and Political Context

The Post-war Period

Following the Second World War, German academia, just as much of German society, was defined by the long-term processes of coming to terms with the (recent) past, a phenomenon with a specific name in German: *Vergangenheitsbewältigung*. Some intellectuals, such as Martin Heidegger, Carl Schmitt or Ernst Bergmann, were held responsible for their direct involvement with the Nazi movement, while many others were condemned for their passiveness towards the Nazi authorities or for their indirect support of Nazi ideology. In this context many German social scientists working from the 1950s, 60s, 70s to the 1980s were eager to distance themselves from this legacy and also reflect critically on the past. For example, Jürgen Habermas was an early influential voice in condemning the Nazi atrocities and their authoritarian state. He also articulated an alternative intellectual tradition which is deeply rooted in the classical Enlightenment project and which speaks for the liberal-democratic idea of a new Germany. Niklas Luhmann was part of the same generation of intellectuals that grew up during and after the war. He too was directly affected by this legacy and the war experience shaped his intellectual development.

However, his response to this legacy was different from that of Habermas and others in the sense that he consciously avoided engagement in social and political debates. One of the reasons for this decision was Luhmann's view that sociologists as social scientists could maintain their analytical objectivity only by keeping away from ideological conflicts and everyday politics. For this reason, Luhmann remained detached from the German public sphere and rarely if ever engaged in current debates on social or political issues. Nevertheless, many contemporary commentators on Luhmann argue that he was very interested in political developments as well as in dealing with the legacy of war (Philippopoulos-Mihalopoulos, 2010; Stichweh 2015). In fact, it seems that Luhmann's initial decision to study law was driven by this war legacy – to comprehend the disintegration of the rule of law in the Nazi period. Similarly, pursuing a career in public administration, and then academia, could also be interpreted as an attempt to understand, and then perhaps contribute to, the dynamics of social order.

However, for Luhmann, intervening in everyday political debates was likely to generate moralising debates that simply could not capture and deal with the inherent complexity of social systems. For example, his attitude to the 1968 student movements differed profoundly from that of Habermas and other leftist German intellectuals. Unlike the left-leaning sociologists who were initially supportive of this social movement, Luhmann did not approve of student actions. Nevertheless, he also showed no interest in joining the conservative intellectuals who resisted the student sit-ins, demonstrations and occupations of campuses such as the Free University of Berlin. For Luhmann the student-led social movements represented an attempt to moralise complex social issues which, in his understanding, could not be addressed by revolutionary means. In his view, the intellectual foundations of these movements, including Marxism, critical theory and Maoism, were incapable of tackling the long-term and highly complex behaviour of social systems in an advanced society. The moralist arguments advanced by the various social movements were perceived by Luhmann as ultimately self-serving and as such a highly destructive force that undermines the many advancements made in the post-war social order.

New Germany

Hence, Luhmann's focus was never on social conflicts, or the role that agency plays in galvanising social change. Instead, he was much more interested in how social systems emerge, develop and expand. In this context, post-WWI Germany was a perfect social laboratory of ever-expanding complexities. The aftermath of the war brought about a complete devastation of German society, but its social order was reconstituted relatively quickly. Throughout the 1950s and 1960s West Germany experienced a period of unprecedented economic growth, often referred to as *Wirtschaftswunder* ('economic miracle'), that in the 1950s stood at a staggering 8% and in the 1960s still at 4.6% (Braun, 1990).

Furthermore, despite enormous war-time destruction, involving many of its main cities, industries, communication and transport networks, West Germany was swiftly rebuilt and within two to three decades it boasted one of the strongest economies in the world. The new state was also characterised by a great degree of stability and social cohesion as its economic development relied extensively on negotiated agreements between the state authorities, private businesses and trade unions. By implementing a particular version of Keynesian economics that offered relative security of employment, rising salaries, secure pensions and other extensive welfare provisions, German society experienced decades of economic prosperity and social stability. In this environment many German citizens also attained a degree of social mobility that many of their predecessors could only dream of.

This unparalleled social and economic development was also achieved with the help of immigrants from Turkey, Italy, Greece, Portugal, Yugoslavia and other less developed countries. Throughout the 1960s the German government signed bilateral recruitment agreements that allowed for a substantial increase in immigrant labour to Germany under the temporary residence *Gastarbeiter* programme. Since the *Gastarbeiter* programmes tended to bring in mostly lower skilled or unskilled, and hence poorly paid, labourers, many German citizens also benefited from this arrangement as they further improved their social mobility. This almost uninterrupted period of economic success and social development provided an impetus for the proliferation of educational institutions, industrial enterprises, the continuous expansion of the state apparatus, the development of the cultural and artistic sectors, and so on. In other words, German society was at the forefront of ever-increasing social complexity. Thus, it is no accident that Luhmann's system theory transpired in this historical environment. His focus on the dynamics of complex social systems mirrors the historical trajectory of post-war German society. Although his sociological theory is universalist and as such is devised to explain the transformation of 'physic systems' and 'social systems' throughout the entire world, regardless of individual specificities, there is no doubt that this theory is strongly rooted in a particular place and a specific moment in time, namely the second half of twentieth-century West Germany.

In addition to this broader social and historical context, the development of Luhmann's key ideas owes a great deal to the vibrant intellectual environment in post-war Germany. Luhmann articulated many of his central concepts in a dialogue with his contemporaries, German sociologists, philosophers and legal scholars. Most of all it was the decades of debates with Habermas that proved crucial in refining Luhmann's system theory. The defining point of this debate was *Theory of Society or Social Technology – What Does System Research Do? (Theorie der Gesellschaft oder Socialtechnologie – Was leistet die Systemforschung?)*, a 1971 book jointly authored by Habermas and Luhmann. The book focuses on the viability of the Enlightenment project in the era of advanced modernity. More specifically the two authors tackle the question of whether the notion of rationally directed human emancipation is still meaningful in a highly complex, contemporary world. Their answers differ profoundly: while Habermas insists that the guiding principles of Enlightenment philosophy still stand, and that high modernity is fully compatible with emancipatory politics (via communicative action), Luhmann argues that such a project is not meaningful in the world of complex social systems. In contrast to Habermas's idea that the contemporary world requires a more reflexive and reconstructed theory of emancipation in order to address the key ethical concerns, Luhmann contends that such a theory cannot deal with the pervasive dominance of systems in modernity. Hence, while Habermas insists that emancipation is possible by countering the processes where, to use his terminology, the system (institutional authority) attempts to colonise 'the life-world' (social interactions), Luhmann is highly sceptical about this claim. Instead, Luhmann argues that there is no escape from the dynamics of systemic organisation and that moral questions cannot impinge on the explanatory logic of system theory.

Arguments and Ideas

Despite the fact that his approach gradually developed in a very different direction from the models devised by Talcott Parsons, Luhmann shared the same ambition as his teacher: to build a universal theory of society. This gargantuan project of grand theory building aimed at formulating an explanatory model that could elucidate any aspect of social relations. Since Luhmann understands sociology in a positivist sense, as a science that can clearly differentiate between the facts and values, he is adamant that one can create a theoretical framework that can eliminate all normative premises and explain the dynamics of the social world as it is. Hence, his general theory of social systems is conceptualised as the universal theory of social order. Nevertheless, this explanatory universalism differs from conventional positivist accounts focused on identifying fixed casual chains. Instead, he was adamant that 'in complex systems of action it is extremely difficult to identify clear cut causes and effects, making predictions and prognoses almost impossible' (Joas and Knöbl, 2009: 255).

Social Systems

In contrast to Parsons and much of the sociological theory before him, Luhmann finds no value in individualist concepts such as 'agency', 'motivation', 'person', 'action', 'means' and so on. Instead of seeing society as being composed of interrelating individuals, Luhmann's starting point is the view that the complex social orders operate through the interaction of systems with their environment. He understands a system as an entity defined by a boundary that separates it from its environment. In this view, a world is composed of numerous systems that vary in size, complexity and durability and can range from an organic cell to the army unit, the private corporation, the state apparatus or the entire world society.

For Luhmann, every system has distinct features that are continuously shaped and reproduced through communication within the system and between systems. This communication is built around activities considered to be meaningful in the sense that they perform specific functions that stem from their structure. As Bausch (2015: 391) emphasises, the concept of 'meaning' plays an important role in Luhmann's theory. Because systems overproduce communication and other entities, it is paramount to reduce this surplus. Hence meaning is the way of dealing with surpluses; it is 'a selection that simplifies experience and maintains the complexity of the world. It simplifies experience by selecting the objects of experience and action.' In other words, for Luhmann, social systems are not composed of individuals but of communications: the physical bodies and minds of human beings are part of the environment of specific social systems, but what really matters are their communicative acts which are part of social systems (i.e. voting behaviour, initiating rituals, socialising, taking part in sporting competitions, etc.). The identity of a particular system is underpinned by its structural properties which help differentiate that system from its environment. The systems operate in such a way that they reduce incessant complexities by focusing on specific functions (i.e. specialisation). The life of a particular system depends on the ability to maintain its identity and once this fails, the system dissolves, becoming part of the environment.

Luhmann differentiates between social and non-social systems. In this understanding, social systems are defined by production, reproduction and processing of meanings, which is not the case with most other non-social systems ranging from machines to psychochemical systems and biological systems. However, Luhmann identifies psychic systems as the only non-social system that involves meaningful activities. Hence, much of his analytical focus is on these two entities: social systems and psychic systems. These two systems are interdependent through shared meanings and language as well as by constituting the only environment for each other. Drawing on Husserl's approach, Luhmann identifies thoughts as the elementary units of a psychic system. Since thoughts are usually linked to each other in the sense that a present thought might be a reflection of a previous thought, or a springboard for a future thought, Luhmann conceptualises psychic systems as systems of consciousness. The equivalent elementary units of a social system are communications.

He argues that 'social systems only consist of communications and there is no communication outside of social systems' (Stichweh, 2015: 385). Although human beings are bound through communications and communicative action is central to sociability, for Luhmann they are not part of the social system: 'it is not people who communicate but communication itself' (Joas and Knöbl, 2009: 275). Societies, being the most extensive form of social system, are defined by an incessant flow of communication and they can exist only as long as there is communication. The communication is further dissected into three interdependent components: information, utterance and understanding. Following Bateson (1972), Luhmann conceptualises information as 'a difference that makes a difference'. In other words, information is something that is generated through comparison with another entity. In order for this information to become part of the communication process it is necessary that it is uttered. The utterance is a process that can be intentional or unintentional. However, utterance by itself does not constitute communication, as this can only occur through the presence of another system, capable of understanding the information uttered. Hence it is only when all three components are present – information, utterance and understanding – that communication can transpire.

Nevertheless, the mere presence of these components does not by itself lead to communication within or between social systems. Moreover, having these three mechanisms in place does not explain how and why social systems interact with each other. One of the central questions for system theory from Parsons to Luhmann is: How do social systems communicate and operate without blocking each other? In more general sociological terms this question can be reformulated as: What makes social order possible?

Luhmann's (1995) book *Social Systems* was written as an attempt to provide a viable solution to this problem, often referred to as 'the double contingency'. Luhmann formulates this double contingency in the following way: 'Action cannot take place if alter makes his action dependent on how ego acts and ego wants to connect his actions to alter's' (1995: 103). Unlike Parsons who focuses on social action and as such cannot resolve this paradox, Luhmann insists that the solution lies in shifting one's attention towards what he calls the autopoietic properties of social systems. By utilising the biological concept of autopoiesis, developed by Maturana (1975) and Varela (1979), Luhmann sees systems as having the propensity to self-reproduce. In his view both social and psychic systems are operationally closed in the sense that they utilise resources from their environment, but such resources are not part of the system itself: 'Autopoiesis means that everything that functions as a unity in a system – element, operation, structure, boundary – is due to the production process of the system itself' (Stichweh, 2015: 386).

In addition to having this capacity for constant self-reproduction these systems also continuously interact with their environment, which allows them to incorporate different elements from that environment as well as to release other elements that the system no longer requires. Hence, the system's autopoietic properties provide for the durability of a particular system while the periodic incorporation of new elements contributes to the system's development and expansion. Luhmann defines these elements of social system as 'events', entities that generally possess a short life ('a temporal atom'). Their key feature is to keep the system operational by replacing old elements and then allowing for situation where they too are replaced by new events. This highly dynamic quality of social systems is rooted, according to Luhmann, in systems' operational capacity to choose a particular option among various possibilities. These choices are based on observations – operational acts centred on differences. In this sense he links the operation of autopoiesis, which involves processing and filtering of information acquired from the system's environment, to a computer program: they are both based on a series of logical distinctions.

Drawing on Bateson, Luhmann sees social systems as being constantly involved not only in observation, but also in self-observation. This auto-referential propensity largely has a binary structure in the sense that the system can select or reject a particular choice and that the choices made determine whether the system eventually expands or disintegrates. This brings us back to the centrality of meaning in communication within and between systems. For Luhmann communication is autopoietic, indicating that communicative actions generate more communication or the end of communication as such. In this context, the systems choose meanings which ultimately shape their direction. However, as Luhmann emphasises, there is no meaningless communication as all choices result in the creation of particular meanings because selecting a particular element while rejecting another as meaningless is a process that creates meanings as such. In his own words: 'Meaning is an un-negateble category, a category devoid of difference [whose negation as] meaningless is ... possible only in the domain of signs and resides in a confusion of signs' (Luhmann, 1995: 62).

Theory of Society

Luhmann's general theory of social systems also underpins his more specific theory of society. The starting point of his analysis is the rejection of what he calls a humanistic tradition in sociology, which in his view wrongly overemphasises the role agency plays in social processes. For Luhmann, human beings are not part of society or even any social system. Instead, it is their communications that sustain social systems and thus society. Furthermore, humans are constituted by society in the sense that society is the environment of human beings while they themselves are the environment of society. To understand fully how they shape each other in Luhmann's theory of society one has to unpack the three principal levels of system formation: interaction, organisation and society.

Drawing on Goffman's model of the interaction order, Luhmann conceptualises interaction systems as everyday encounters involving face-to-face physical contact as well as the reciprocity of perception. Although these encounters fill much of human everyday life, they are usually repetitive, temporary and limited. In contrast, organisations are much more durable forms of systems. They entail a formalised structure including regulated conditions of membership and a formalised set of rules and regulations that govern the actions of that specific organisation. For Luhmann, an organisation is an autopoietic system that is operationally closed. This involves restrictive decision-making processes that are closed off to non-members. Above organisations stands the final level of the organisational system – society. In Luhmann's model, society is the most encompassing form of social system that incorporates all organisations and all interactions. This also means that society has only non-social environments (i.e. biological systems, machines, etc.). For Luhmann, society is composed of specific social systems including the economy, politics, science, law, art, religion and love. In his theory, he posits that in the modern world we have moved towards the social reality where there is only one societal system – World Society.

These three levels of system formation are an integral part of Luhmann's general theoretical model that contains three more specific theories of systems: the theory of differentiation, the theory of evolution and the theory of communication.

Differentiation

The theory of differentiation is developed in order to explain how systems manage the ever-increasing complexities of modern social orders. Talcott Parsons, who was the original creator of this theory, was interested in how social systems deal with the increased complexities by creating subsystems to navigate the difference between the system and the environment. In Parsons's AGIL model (see Chapter 1) subsystems operate according to a logic of their own and as such are located in what he called 'the pattern maintenance of each system'. This means that individual subsystems would pursue the process of differentiation, but through constant communication with other subsystems they were likely to foster social change geared towards reaching an equilibrium.

Luhmann agrees that differentiation is a crucial process in the operation of social systems, but he also argues that Parsons' AGIL schema cannot capture the variability of differentiation processes. Hence, Luhmann understands differentiation as a process of system formation that materialises in four different ways: segmentary differentiation, stratification, centre/periphery differentiation and functional differentiation (Luhmann, 2013 [1997]).

Drawing on Durkheim's theory of division of labour, Luhmann identifies segmentary differentiation as the processes through which parts of the system are divided along the axis of their near identical qualities, such as the same internal structure, the same social role or status or the same function they perform. For example, fast food outlets operate according to the logic of segmentary differentiation in the sense that every restaurant is organised in a very similar way where the employees can be easily moved from one outlet to another because they all perform the same role – produce and serve nearly identical food.

In contrast to segmentary differentiation, stratification or hierarchical differentiation is the process that divides social orders into hierarchically organised systems where every stratum fulfils a particular function in the system. For example, the fast food chain entails the presence of top leadership (CEOs), state and regional managers as well as ordinary employees. This process is defined by ranked inequalities and as such has dominated much of human historical experience. Unlike segmentary differentiation where inequality might be persistent but is not functional to the operation of the social system, in hierarchical differentiation status ranking is crucial for the functioning of the system as such. For example, the very existence of imperial orders was dependent on each stratum performing its specific role.

The third type of differentiation is the centre/periphery model. This type of differentiation often links stratification and segmentation in the sense that is often hierarchical, but also allows for the segmented substitution of different parts. A typical example of this situation is the urban vs. rural divide where the large cities often maintain economic and status dominance over the countryside, even though they remain dependent on the resources generated in the countryside. The segmented nature of this relationship is visible in the fact that individual cities or rural areas are often replaceable by other such urban or rural congregations.

The final and most significant type for Luhmann is functional differentiation, which he sees as being dominant in the contemporary world. In Luhmann's view, this is the most complex form of differentiation as it is composed of different systems covering politics, economics, law, religion, science and so on. Although they might possess hierarchical attributes, such systems are seen by Luhmann as being too complex, too variable and too interdependent to maintain simple hierarchical social relationships. In contrast to the segmentary or centre/periphery models, functional differentiation involves indispensable functional systems – self-substitutive orders that cannot be replaced by other systems. However, this systemic interdependence is based on the autonomy of subsystems. For example, the fast food chain operates through the combination of interdependence and independence of its subsystems – the meat and vegetable delivery systems, the transport networks, the employees, the infrastructure of individual outlets, the financial systems, and so on. Each of these subsystems is fully autonomous in its operations yet they all form part of the large system and if one of these subsystems, such as the transport network or the vegetable and meat delivery system, stops functioning, the entire system is likely to stop functioning too.

Evolution

Since the Parsonian version of structural functionalism has traditionally been criticised for its inability to explain long-term social change, Luhmann's theory of society attempts to address this problem by utilising the key tenets of evolutionary theory. Hence, Luhmann replaces Parsonian concepts such as modernisation or development with the Darwinian language of variation, selection and retention. More specifically, he borrows from Donald T. Campbell's neo-Darwinian evolutionary model to make the case that contingency plays an important role in the formation of social structures. Furthermore, Luhmann was convinced that the key evolutionary mechanisms including variation, selection and retention are highly useful conceptual tools that can shed some light on the long-term transformation of social systems. Hence, he identifies the variation mechanism as present in communicative situations in the sense that saying yes or no to a particular choice is likely to shape the direction of the system transformation on the macro level. The selection mechanism also contributes to system dynamics, as it is premised on the presence of binary codes in the communication media and this helps sort new meanings that arise from the processes of negotiation. Finally, the retention mechanism helps the stabilisation of selected meaning complexes. This is linked with differentiation of the systems and their material complexity where new systems emerge, and new meanings are created. In this context, the process of stabilisation of selected meanings contributes towards identifying the location of possible points of change or repudiation in the new system. For Luhmann, these three evolutionary mechanisms are deeply linked as they help maintain system operation over long periods of time: variation allows for contingency; selection helps with the choice of implausible meaning demands; and retention is crucial in reorganising the material dimensions of systems undergoing differentiation.

Communication

In Luhmann's theoretical framework the theories of differentiation and evolution play significant roles in explaining the social change and variability of systems. Nevertheless, the principal bedrock of this theory is communication. In order to explain how human beings negotiate different opinions and interests, Luhmann introduces the theory of the symbolically generalised media of communication. The focus of this theory is on language as this medium adequately expresses differences in viewpoints and interests. Here again, Luhmann's model differs substantially from Parsons': while for Parsons a language and other forms of exchange media serve a mediating role between systems, for Luhmann communication media are integral to the internal operation of systems. In other words, symbolically generalised communication media address problems that emerge within the system around the situations where there is a demand for additional means to deal with improbable demands. For example, Luhmann identifies love, power and money as typical examples of the symbolically generalised media of communication. In his analysis love is understood to be a communicative phenomenon characterised by the complete realignment of actions between people who experience the world in a similar way and this realignment of one person fosters the realignment of another person. In a similar way, power is conceptualised as a functional product of communicative relationships where one is motivated by the principle of attempting to avoid the possible negative sanctions of power holders. Money too is defined as a symbolically generalised media of communication where material transactions are rooted in the system-wide shared perceptions that the possession of money not only provides one with the freedom to purchase particular items, but also signifies that money can be exchanged for any other goods. In this sense money is a form of economic communication. For Luhmann, most forms of human activity involve the symbolically generalised media of communication, most of which are framed around binary code structures that underpin media exchange, such as true/false, lawful/unlawful, beautiful/ugly and so on.

Contemporary Relevance and Applications

Luhmann's system theory is characterised by an interesting paradox. On the on hand the theory is generally regarded as exceptionally abstract and highly saturated with what many regard to be almost incomprehensible concepts (Mingers, 2002; Mathur, 2005). Even Luhmann recognised this by stating that his theory is 'labyrinth like' and as such is highly demanding on the reader. Yet, this theory has had profound influence throughout the world – from Germany to Japan to Brazil and further afield.

THE LUHMANN–HABERMAS DEBATE

Though engaging with each other directly only through their joint publication in 1971, the Luhmann and Habermas's debate actually continued indirectly up until Luhmann's death in 1998. The points of contestation were both theoretical and normative. Theoretically, Habermas problematised Luhmann's assertion that systems theory could capture all of society, claiming some processes can only be perceived from the perspective of social actors. Normatively, Habermas worried about the political consequences of applying Luhmann's theory to public administration, given its neglect for actors and their moral and ethical claims. While fundamentally important, an exclusive focus on these points of contestation overlooks the extent to which the debate shaped later developments. Luhmann's Social Systems and Habermas's Theory of Communicative Action – both towering contributions to late twentieth-century social theory – are largely the product of this continued engagement with the other on the part of two highly original and innovative theorists.

Moreover, Luhmann's work has been operationalised and applied in a variety of areas – administrative systems, organisational studies, translation scholarship, law and governance, religious studies, education, cultural analyses, cybernetics and so on (Philippopoulos-Mihalopoulos, 2010). Although, since the 1980s, his work was already well known and highly influential in the German-speaking world, it was only after his death in 1998 that Luhmann was identified as a world-leading social theorist whose contributions have shaped current debates in different parts of the world. For example, his concepts have been successfully utilised in management and organisation studies where Seidl and Becker (2006) and Nassehi (2005) have analysed organisations as systems involved in continuous construction and reconstruction through distinctions and decisions. Similarly Wolf and her collaborators (2010) have focused on the role system communication plays in the creation of new knowledge and the acquisition of such knowledge between different systems. Baralou et al. (2012) have also applied Luhmann's ideas to organisational studies, arguing that organisations are first and foremost social systems that are coupled with psychic systems. In contrast to dominant agency-driven perspectives, such as the rational choice or interactionist models of organisational behaviours, Baralou and her collaborators insist that it is organisations, not individuals, that determine the course of social change: 'organisations use the construct of "membership" for including psychic systems, i.e. in firm the employees as communication addresses ... employees intentionally decide to become members of organisations or to quit membership, however during the time of their membership, they comply with the rules of the organisation' (Baralou et al. 2012: 296). In this view, organisations are dynamic systems where the members of the organisation communicate by selecting a limited amount of relevant information. Hence, an organisation is conceptualised as a self-sustaining system that provides information with reduced complexity. All organisations are dependent on the use of relevant data which match the system's needs and expectations, and the use of which is bound to make a difference between the situation that existed before that information was gathered and used. In the context of educational organisations such as schools or universities, organisational functionality depends on students' acquisition of skills and knowledge through the different phases. Hence, it is paramount for a fifth-grade student already to possess the requisite knowledge generated in the third and fourth grades so that he or she can progress further. Similarly, a business organisation depends on acquiring reliable information that would make it operational – access to stock market listings matters much more than information on the weather report.

Since Luhmann considered his theory to be universal and as such applicable to any social phenomenon, researchers have recently started deploying his models not only to conventional macro-level issues such as organisational systems or the law, but also to micro-level interactions involving personalised and intimate relationships between individuals. For example, his work on love has influenced several recent works, all of which attempt to move away from the traditional agency-centred accounts of intimacy towards the systemic study of face-to-face close interactions. Starting from Luhmann's idea that love is a form of communication where the participants share a specific code, Seebach (2017) explores how intimacy operates in the contemporary world. He follows Luhmann's idea that passionate and intimate love is something historically associated with relationships taking place outside of marriage. It is only in modernity, when social conditions dramatically change, that intimacy becomes the cornerstone of a loving relationship in one's household. For Luhmann this transition from contract-based marriage relationships towards personalised intimate relationships is a product of a system-based cultural transformation.

Furthermore, although romantic love often involves two individuals, this in itself does not imply that love as such can be reduced to its interpersonal dimension. Instead, in the Luhmannian tradition love is understood as something that belongs to the social sphere. It is a 'generalised symbolic medium of communication' that operates in the intimate context where it generates a semantic field that makes close personalised communication possible. In this way, love adds to the formation of a durable autopoietic system that is shaped around the envisaged shared future of those involved in this intimate relationship. This strong shared experiential bond also reduces system complexity and contributes towards the creation of conditions for the perpetuation of that system.

Drawing on Luhmann and Simmel, Seebach (2017: 42) argues that intimate relationships can be conceptualised as micro-level social systems of interpersonal interpenetration which allow us to engage in the process of communicative openness with a special other. In this context deep intimacy is premised on the existence of a special language which is unique to those involved in a loving relationship. This 'lovers' discourse' often constitutes a couple's shared narrative that comprises unique memories, stories, problems and other shared moments from their past. Just like Luhmann, Seebach argues that love is not a feeling but a code of communication that creates a context for the development of emotions and experiences filled with meanings. However, Seebach (2017: 2) is closer to Simmel in his understanding of love as a 'new second order form', that is 'a moral centre of the late modern society'. As such, love is seen to be a 'scattered and fragmented' entity that lacks a fixed centre, but it appears in various combinations and differentiations.

Despite its abstractness Luhmann's work on love has also been applied outside of sociology. For example, German artist Jorinde Voigt has produced a series of drawings (21 in total) exhibited in several galleries and all inspired by Luhmann's book *Love as Passion: Codification of Intimacy* (1982). In these paintings she utilises Luhmann's ideas to relate the experience of art to that of love – as a medium of communication (Shilling-Janoff, 2014).

Criticisms

Luhmann's system theory has been criticised on several grounds: its inflexible functionalism underpinned by strong teleological accounts; its rampant epistemological anti-humanism; its neglect of agency, political power and social inequalities; its formalist structure and the use of impenetrable language; its pronounced methodological problems and its positivist ambitions; as well as its conservative and depoliticised character, among others.

There is no doubt that Luhmann's theory is deeply rooted in some key functionalist premises. Although his functional structuralism is much more reflexive and dynamic than Parsonian structural functionalism, Luhmann's model of society is still shackled by its overemphasis on stability and continuity over discontinuity and transformation. In other words, this theory tells us a great deal about the operations and functions of specific parts of the system, but it does not tell us much about the process of social change. Hence Luhmann is good at explaining how large-scale bureaucratic apparatuses or private corporations work but cannot explain properly why and how wars and revolutions happen. Furthermore, system theory is conceived as a universalist model capable of explaining any social phenomenon. However, the explanations it offers have a strong teleological quality in the sense that explanations are built around existing categories and as such are rather circular: a particular phenomenon is interpreted by invoking the effects that are attributed to that phenomenon. Hence, in Luhmann's work the operations of a particular system are explained by referring to the activities of another system.

System theory is also explicit in its rejection of the human subject. As many critics have emphasised, this is a theory that leaves no room for people. In Luhmann's theory human beings are not independent actors that compose social order; instead they are not even part of society but only of its environment. In his view humans are not persons as such, they only have the potential to become persons: we are all born with the capacity to become persons, but this can happen only through the interaction with others. Although Luhmann defends his epistemological anti-humanism through this sharp distinction between humans and persons, his theory still remains deeply reductionist and as such incapable of fully explaining the role that agency plays in social action. System theory's vision of the social world resembles that of the cybernetic species of Borg from the *Star Trek* series where there is no room for individuality or free will and where the system (i.e. Borg) assimilates everything and everyone. This certainly is not what the human world looks like.

Luhmann's model has also been criticised for its pronounced lack of engagement with the questions of political power and social inequalities. His overreliance on biological concepts such as autopoiesis or segmentation leads to the conclusion that societies resemble nature in the sense that they too have organic qualities. However, these simple analogies do not provide for good sociological models as the social world is very different from the world of nature. Although animals too are involved in hierarchical orders these biologically established hierarchies are highly distinct from the much more dynamic and situational stratification patterns of the human world. By deploying concepts such as 'hierarchical differentiation' to all social systems Luhmann cannot distinguish clearly what is distinct about the social hierarchies among humans. Moreover, this concept is very descriptive as it just traces the direction of a particular social phenomenon rather that attempting to explain how inequalities and asymmetrical power relations emerge, develop and change over long periods of time.

System theory has often been characterised as a rigid formalist model built around incomprehensible technical language that does not help us much in making sense of everyday social reality. Dirk Kaesler (1984) is particularly harsh in his criticism, accusing Luhmann of deploying formal and empty categories which present trivial facts in an obscure discourse and as such do not contribute much to our understanding of the social world. Luhmann's standard defence was that he intentionally created this abstract maze to prevent others from simplifying and misinterpreting his arguments. Nevertheless this ad hoc pragmatic justification does not seem to be particularly convincing as the sociological analysis should be as accessible as possible without the need to hide behind highly effusive and impenetrable language.

The unusually abstract components of Luhmann's theory have also proved difficult for the operationalisation and use of this theory in concrete empirical contexts. This is important as system theory is conceived in a strong positivist sense, as the most general and universal theory of society. Luhmann was adamant that his theory is capable of explaining all aspects of social phenomena. Leaving to one side this Promethean ambition where there is no room for falsification (hence tautology), the key issue for any such generalisable model is the capacity for testing that rigorously follows the established methodological requirements such as validity, reliability and replicability. Although system theory has found application in different, mostly macro contexts, most of these applications have been questioned in terms of whether they fulfil the conventional methodological requirements. Hence rather than undergoing rigorous empirical scrutiny most applications of Luhmann's theory remain on the metaphorical and anecdotal level.

Finally, although Luhmann made a lot of effort to stay away from the political and social debates of his time and perceived sociology as a value-free discipline that should stay away from moral prescriptions, his theory has often been criticised as rather conservative. For one thing, the central preoccupation of system theory is conservation – the ability of self-referential systems to maintain their self-referential capacity. Hence, the theory focuses on stability, consensus and continuity. For another thing, despite its nominal commitment towards political neutrality, the long-term implications of this position are inevitably political as its focus on conservation and stability leave no room for tackling the informal power dynamics, the less visible social sources that sustain the status quo relations or the dominance of privilege among some social groups at the expense of others. Even though Luhmann distanced himself from all politics his theoretical model reflected the dominant social and political perspectives of his time. This is particularly visible in his concept of world society where he reproduces the key tenets of the progressivist paradigm of the ever-expanding unification of the globe and leaves no room for the role that nationalism plays in social life (Malešević, 2019).

Conclusion

Niklas Luhmann was an original and syncretic social thinker who took social system theory in a new and highly creative direction. Building on Parsons' functionalist legacy he fashioned a unique explanatory framework that borrowed innovatively from cybernetics, biology, legal studies, psychology, logic, phenomenological philosophy and even medieval scholasticism. In this process he created a highly elaborate and complex model composed of idiosyncratic concepts that are largely coherent, comprehensive and mutually interdependent, but also very difficult to comprehend for outsiders. In some respects, Luhmann has created a discursive world of his own that makes much sense to those who are sympathetic to system theory and in particular to this type of social analysis. However, the presence of this convoluted and jargon-laden language that underpins much of Luhmann's work has also had rather mixed or negative impacts on those who stand outside of this intellectual tradition. Despite this mixed legacy, Luhmann's theoretical framework is still largely regarded as one of the few fully articulated, universalistic, sociological paradigms capable of dealing with the changing dynamics of the twenty-first century.

References

Bateson, G. (1972) *Steps to an Ecology of Mind*. Chicago, IL: University of Chicago Press.

Bausch, K. C. (2015) Luhmann's *Social Systems*: Meaning, Autopoiesis, and Interpenetration. *International Encyclopedia of the Social & Behavioral Sciences*, 2nd edition, Vol. 14, pp. 390–5.

Baralou, E., Wolf, P. and Meissner, J.O. (2012) Bright, Excellent, Ignored: The Contribution of Luhmann's System Theory and Its Problem of Non-Connectivity to Academic Management Research. *Historical Social Research/Historische Sozialforschung*, 37 (4): 289–308.

Braun, H. J. (1990) *The German Economy in the Twentieth Century: The German Reich and the Federal Republic*. New York: Routledge.

Habermas, J. and Luhmann, N. (1971) *Theorie der Gesellschaft oder Sozialtechnologie: Was leistet die Systemforschung?* Frankfurt: Suhrkamp.

Joas, H. and Knöbl, W. (2009) *Social Theory: Twenty Introductory Lectures*. A. Skinner, trans. Cambridge: Cambridge University Press.

Kaesler, D. (1984) Soziologie: 'Flug über den Wolken' [online]. Available at: https://www.spiegel.de/spiegel/print/d-13511556.html (accessed 31 January 2020).

Luhmann, N. (1964) *Funktionen und Folgen formaler Organisationen*. Berlin: Duncker & Humbolt.

Luhmann, N. (1965) *Grundrechte als Institution: Ein Beitrag zur politischen Soziologie*. Berlin: Duncker & Humbolt.

Luhmann, N. (1970) *Soziologische Aufklärung 1: Aufsätze zur Theorie sozialer Systeme*. Cologne, Opladen: Westdeutscher Verlag.

Luhmann N. (1981) *Soziologische Aufklärung 3: Soziales System, Gesellschaft, Organisation*. Cologne, Opladen: Westdeutscher Verlag.

Luhmann, N. (1986 [1982]) *Love as Passion: The Codification of Intimacy*. Cambridge, MA: Harvard University Press.

Luhmann, N. (1995) *Social Systems*. J. Bednarz, Jr and D. Baecker, trans. Stanford, CA: Stanford University Press.

Luhmann, N. (2013 [1997]) *Theory of Society*. Stanford, CA: Stanford University Press.

Malešević, S. (2019) *Grounded Nationalisms: A Sociological Analysis*. Cambridge: Cambridge University Press.

Mathur, P. (2005) Neither Cited nor Foundational: Niklas Luhmann's *Ecological Communication*: A Critical Exegesis and Some Theoretical Suggestions for the Future of a Field. *Communication Review*, 8, pp. 329-62.

Maturana, H. (1975) The organization of the living, a theory of the living organization. *International Journal of Man Machine Studies*, 7, pp. 313-32.

Mingers, J. (2002) Can Social Systems Be Autopoietic? Assessing Luhmann's Social Theory. *Sociological Review*, 50(2), pp. 278-99.

Nassehi, A. (2005) Organizations as Decision Machines: Niklas Luhmann's Theory of Organized Social Systems. *Sociological Review*, 53(1), pp. 178-91.

Philippopoulos-Mihalopoulos, A. (2010) *Niklas Luhmann; Law, Justice, Society*. London: Routledge.

Schilling-Janoff, A. (2004) *Jorinde Voigt – Codification of Intimacy: Works on Nikolas Luhmann*. The Brooklyn Rail. Available at: https://brooklynrail.org/2014/06/artseen/jorinde-voigt (accessed 3 July 2020).

Seebach, S. (2017) *Love and Society: Special Social Forms and the Master Emotion*. London: Routledge.

Seidl, D. and Becker, K. H. (2006) Organizations as Distinction Generating and Processing Systems: Niklas Luhmann's Contribution to Organization Studies. *Organization*, 13(1), pp. 9-35.

Stichweh, R. (2015) Luhmann, Niklas (1927-98). *International Encyclopedia of the Social & Behavioral Sciences*, 2nd edition, Vol. 14, pp. 382-9.

Varela, F. (1979) *Principles of Biological Autonomy*. New York: Elsevier-North Holland.

Wolf, P., Meissner, J. O., Nolan, T. et al. (2010) Methods for Qualitative Management Research in the Context of Social Systems Thinking. *Historical Social Research/Historische Sozialforschung*, 36(1).

Gellner and Mann

Introduction

Although the classics of sociology such as Weber, Marx and Durkheim all valued long-term historical analyses, much of sociology after the Second World War has become distinctly ahistorical. Hence, instead of linking contemporary social changes to *longue durée* trends the tendency is to search for the immediate causes and, for the most part, non-historical explanations of social phenomena. From rational choice theory, symbolic interactionism to systems theory or structuralism the focus seems to be almost exclusively on the trans-historical variables. In direct contrast to these dominant paradigms, historical sociologists aim to provide a historically contextualised interpretations of social change. Following in the footsteps of the classics of sociology they combine social theory with a nuanced historical analysis. Hence, unlike historians, who focus only on the particular, and conventional social scientists, who zoom in only on the universal, historical sociologists look for the universal through the particular and vice versa. Ernest Gellner and Michael Mann are the leading historical sociologists who have developed original theories of social change. Although their approaches differ substantially, they both aim to provide a *longue durée* type of social analysis aiming to explain contemporary developments through the prism of long-term historical patterns.

In this chapter we explore their key concepts and theories by zooming in on several themes that dominate their work. Furthermore, we look at their biographical and intellectual background as well as the broader historical, social and political context under which these ideas transpired. Finally, we briefly analyse current applications and the principal criticisms of these approaches.

Life and Intellectual Context

Ernest Gellner

Gellner was born in Paris in 1925 but grew up in Prague in a family of secular, lower-middle-class, German-speaking Czech Jews. Although young Ernest's childhood was characterised by economic hardship as his family struggled during the economic crisis of the 1930s, the Gellners were well educated and invested substantially in their children's education. Hence Ernest was enrolled into the Prague English grammar school where he was an excellent student. This early regular exposure to three language communities (English, German and Czech) contributed substantially to his lifelong focus on understanding different cultural universes.

The rise of the National Socialists in neighbouring Germany had an instant effect on the young and fragile Czechoslovakia. This multi-ethnic country had a large German minority that not only inhabited most of its main cities, but was also a major population of the country's western region – the Sudetenland. Under sustained Nazi propaganda many Sudeten Germans supported unification of their region with Germany. Following the British and French governments' politics of appeasement at Munich in 1938 the Sudetenland was annexed by Nazi Germany. In this new context of ever-increasing anti-Semitism and attacks on Jewish properties in the soon to be established German-controlled protectorate of Bohemia and Moravia (1939) the Gellners decided to emigrate. Since Rudolf's sister lived in London the family moved to England, thus escaping the Holocaust.

Initially the family had a difficult immigrant life and struggled financially. Hence young Ernest could not continue his studies without a scholarship. However, he was successful in the Oxford entrance exams and received a full scholarship to study philosophy, economics and politics at Balliol College, Oxford. Over time his family became much more prosperous as his father established a very successful, plastic-making business in London.

Despite his genuine interest in philosophy Ernest disliked the epistemological idealism of the Wittgenstein-influenced philosophy of language that dominated Oxford in the 1940s. In this context he focused more on the social sciences. Gellner interrupted his studies in 1944 to volunteer to fight in the military operations to liberate Czechoslovakia. As a soldier of the 1st Czechoslovak Armoured Brigade he took part in the siege of Dunkirk and also participated in the parade of the liberators in 1945, in Prague. As soon as the war was over he returned to Oxford and graduated with first-class honours in 1947. He was planning to return to Prague but as it became clear that post-war Czechoslovakia would be a Soviet satellite state he decided to take up a lecturing post at the University of Edinburgh. In 1949, he moved to the London School of Economics where he was appointed a lecturer in the Department of Sociology and where he remained for the next 35 years.

In 1959 Gellner published his first book, *Words and Things*, a fierce attack on the linguistic philosophy of his Oxford teachers. The book sparked a controversy and a debate on the pages of the leading British newspaper at that time, *The Times*, which helped the still youthful Gellner to become a household name in the UK.

During this period, he was involved in a handful of prolonged fieldwork trips to Morocco where he studied the kinship structures of the Berbers.

This fieldwork was also important as the analysis of the data constituted the backbone of his PhD thesis, which was completed in 1961 and later published in a revised form as a book, *Saints of the Atlas* (1969). In 1962 Gellner was appointed a professor of philosophy 'with special reference to sociology' that reflected well his wide interests. He moved from the LSE to Cambridge in 1984, where he was appointed William Wyse Professor of Anthropology at King's College. He retired in 1993 and accepted the invitation to take up a Directorship of the Centre for the Study of Nationalism at the newly established Central European University in Prague. Gellner died in Prague on 5 November 1995.

Michael Mann

Mann was born in 1942 in Manchester in a lower-middle-class family. His father was a salesman for an asbestos company. He went to Manchester Grammar School where he was better at arts than sciences. Mann was initially strongly influenced by his father who was a supporter of the Liberal Party. Mann's father was a primary influence and he suggested that Michael enrol as a law student at Oxford. However, as he was much more interested in history he decided to switch courses after the first semester. At Oxford he initially joined the Liberal club, but as his political views developed, he soon transferred to the Labour club. At Oxford he was taught by a leading philosopher, Isiah Berlin, and the prominent British historian, David Fieldhouse. After graduation he stayed at Oxford for another year and completed a diploma in public administration. Completing this programme was instrumental in Mann's attaining his first academic job as a researcher on a project funded by the General Food Corporation. In this project, he interviewed hundreds of factory workers and this experience influenced his newly discovered fascination with sociology. Consequently, he completed a diploma in sociology and registered as a PhD student at Cambridge but switched later to Oxford, where he was supervised by the prominent British sociologist John Goldthorpe. After completion of his thesis Mann worked at Oxford for several years and in 1970 moved to the University of Essex where he was employed as a lecturer until 1977. At Essex he had the opportunity to work with another leading British sociologist, David Lockwood. During this period, he was politically active within the Labour Party in Colchester where he also wrote a Fabian pamphlet focusing on reconciling the left- and right-wing segments of the party. In 1977, Mann was appointed Reader in Research Methods at the London School of Economics. There he teamed up with Ernest Gellner and John A. Hall and together they ran the highly successful 'The Patterns of History' seminar, which attracted well-known speakers. The first volume of his four-volume *The Sources of Social Power* was published in 1986. In 1987 Mann left for the United States where he was appointed professor of sociology at UCLA and where he taught until retirement in 2016. Mann was elected a fellow of the British and American Academies in 2015.

Historical, Social and Political Context
The Cold War Context

The wider context of the Cold War served as a decisive factor in the intellectual development of both Gellner and Mann. The legacy of war has played an important role in the development of both thinkers. While Gellner was deeply influenced by the economic and ideological changes brought by the twentieth-century tectonic transformations, Mann's work was primarily shaped around the key political and military factors that underpinned these large-scale transformations. Nevertheless, unlike much of the mid- and late twentieth-century mainstream sociology, which focused on establishing trans-historical generalisations about the social order, Gellner and Mann shared a commitment towards developing historically sensitive theories of social change. In contrast to conventional sociological models that tend to delineate sharply between the traditional and modern world and then focus almost exclusively on modernity, Gellner and Mann shifted their attention towards the past in order to understand the historically variable patterns of social change.

Hence rather than taking the post-war environment as the pinnacle of social development Mann and Gellner emphasised the incidental character as well as the structural fragility of this historical period. Unlike much contemporary sociology that seems to be centred on what is historically a very short period of time, both Mann and Gellner studied social transformations over the course of the entire history of the human race. For Gellner, the pathways towards the twentieth century were shaped by the structural changes in the economic sphere, while for Mann it was the broader geopolitical environment together with the different trajectories of state formation and warfare that played a pivotal role in the transformation of social orders. These analytical differences stem in part from different biographical and social environments that the two scholars experienced.

Gellner's Central European background reflected the complex social realities of the early twentieth century. He was deeply influenced by the history of the post-Habsburg world where ideological conflicts were particularly pronounced and visible. On the one hand this was the world that experienced often violent shifts from multi-ethnic and heterogeneous empires towards homogenising ethnic nation-states. This was also the world that was gradually transitioning from a highly stratified and hierarchical model of economic and political organisation based on inherited status orders, towards politically more egalitarian type of polity. Hence, in this environment ideological conflicts played an important and highly visible role. On the other hand, Central Europe was a site of tremendous social and economic change with a gradual shift from agrarian rural economies, towards developing industrialised cities. The Prague of Gellner's youth was at the forefront of these changes. Following the military defeat and the collapse of Austria–Hungary in 1918, Czechoslovakia emerged as a new independent state. Although the new polity was conceived as a national state of Czechs and Slovaks the country retained large

German-, Hungarian- and Polish-speaking minorities, most of whom were not enthusiastic about living in the new Czechoslovak state. In this context the large German population (3.5 million out of 14 million Czechoslovak citizens) was considered by some a serious threat to the new state. Although Czechoslovakia was a stable parliamentary democracy (from 1918 to 1938) it remained beset by competing and hostile ethno-nationalisms. Furthermore, the new state was equally plagued by economic disparities.

In contrast to Bohemia (including Prague), which was a highly industrialised and developed region, the rest of the country was dominated by small, mostly impoverished, agricultural dwellings. The western part of the country, Bohemia and the Sudetenland, inherited over 70% of all the Austro-Hungarian industrial outlets, which meant that these regions were among the most industrialised parts of the world. For example, in 1938 Czechoslovakia was ranked 10th in the world for industrial production (Berend, 1998). However, much of industrial ownership was in the hands of the German-speaking industrialists and bankers who had an ambiguous relationship with the new Czechoslovak state. At the same time the eastern parts including Slovakia and Ruthenia had almost no industry at all. These regional and economic disparities, coupled with the ethnic divides, contributed towards the inherent instability of the new polity. Furthermore, with the rise of Nazis in Germany and the expansion of authoritarianism throughout the region, the geopolitical situation changed substantially, making the already fragile Czechoslovak state even more precarious. The British and French governments' policies of appeasement opened the door for the gradual disintegration of the new state. Although Czechoslovakia remained the only Central European democracy in the 1930s, that did not prevent the Western powers from trading in its independence for a short period of peace with Nazi Germany.

Hence, by 1938, the Sudetenland was annexed by Germany while the rest of the country was divided into the puppet state of Slovakia and the German-ruled protectorate of Bohemia and Moravia. These highly turbulent social and historical conditions had a profound influence on Gellner and shaped his sociological interests in nationalism, industrialisation and social change. Nevertheless, since Gellner's intellectual development also took place in post-war England his theoretical contributions also reflected this changed environment. Hence, the relative economic prosperity of the late 1950s to the early 1970s, characterised by the rise of the welfare state and a degree of cross-class consensus at home, together with the policies of decolonialisation abroad, contributed towards the widely shared understanding that modern industrial social order engenders stability.

The Geopolitical Tensions

Although Mann was also influenced by many of these historical events and processes his focus was less on stability and consensus and much more on the social conflicts that underpin these long-term social changes. As Mann was younger than Gellner his intellectual development took place in a world that was already moving from relative stability and continuous economic growth towards more stagnant economic outputs and ever-pronounced social and political clashes. In this environment, Mann shifted his gaze towards the broader international context, trying to understand the changing world by zooming in on the roles that geopolitics, state formation and capitalism play in the transformation of social relations. The 1970s and 1980s were characterised by deep economic and political crises, including the oil shocks of 1973 and the intensified arms race between NATO and the Warsaw Pact countries. The direct outcome of this ever-increasing arms race was Soviet and US involvement in the proliferation of proxy wars throughout Africa, Asia and Latin America.

These global events had profound local consequences as many mid-sized and small countries experienced sudden and sharp economic downturns as well as intense political pressures to get involved in the arms race. Radicalisation of Cold War rhetoric followed by deployment of new missile systems in the UK and the rest of NATO-dominated Europe, provoked the rise of anti-war and other movements which challenged the new Conservative governments of the UK, the United States and Germany, as much as NATO itself. All these structural changes affected Mann's understanding of the world. The ever-present threat of nuclear Armageddon, the deeply hostile class polarisation and the British government's direct involvement in proxy wars abroad all shaped Mann's sociological horizons. To explain this shift from the relative global economic and political stability of the 1950s and 1960s towards the much more turbulent 1970s and 1980s, Mann became preoccupied with the long-term historical transformations and the role that state, war and geopolitics play in this process.

Arguments and Ideas

Both Gellner and Mann share the Enlightenment-inspired understanding of social change that differentiates between the traditional and modern forms of social order. One of their shared central analytical concerns is the question: What historical conditions made modernity possible? However, unlike much contemporary social thought which is more focused on the character of the modern world itself, both Gellner and Mann shift their attention towards the pre-modern world in order to explain how and why modernity transpired in the first place. Rather than taking the classical Enlightenment narrative of social progress for granted they see the transition from the traditional to *the* modern social orders as historically astounding and almost improbable.

In contrast to the teleological evolutionary accounts of social change that present history as a relatively fixed ladder that humans climb as they inevitably advance, Gellner and Mann see the transition to modernity as historically contingent, and in many ways a miraculous process. In fact they were both principal contributors to the famous debate on the 'European miracle' (1988) where they argued that the structural breakthrough to modernity was a product of several unlikely events and processes that only crystallised in Western Europe in the early eighteenth century. Nevertheless, to frame this astounding social transformation as a miracle does not imply that Europeans were predisposed for this breakthrough. Instead, as Gellner (1989: 1) makes clear: 'The phrase should not be read as – the *European* miracle. It must be read – the European *miracle*. We know not what we do, and we do not know what hit us. We cannot take credit for it.' Furthermore both Gellner and Mann emphasise the inherent fragility of the modern social condition: there is nothing that is inevitable here – the historical conditions that gave birth to modern life can and do change so everything can unravel in the same way it was built up. Although Gellner and Mann share this general diagnosis of modernity's birth they offer two rather different explanations of how the modern world came into being.

Ernest Gellner and the Industrial World

Gellner's historical sociology is framed around three ideal types of social order: the world of foragers, the agrarian civilisations and the industrial world. These models of social organisation differ profoundly in terms of their economic, political and cultural structure. However, for Gellner it is the economic conditions that underpin the social dynamics of the these three structures. Hence, he argues that the dominant type of economic organisation shapes the character of that social order: hunting and gathering determines the life of foragers, the cultivation of arable land shapes the agrarian world, and the reliance on science and technology underpins the industrial universe. In his view the transition from one to another form of social order is historically extremely difficult and thus rare. The Neolithic revolution was an exceptional event as it allowed a shift from foraging to farming in some parts of the world. However, an even more unprecedented event was the transition from 'Agraria' to 'Industria'.

To account for this social change Gellner introduces his 'Big Ditch' argument. The two models of social order stand on opposite sides of a big ditch. Agraria is characterised by the Malthusian world of a stagnant economy centred on the production and storage of food where there is 'a ceiling on possible production, though not on population growth' (Gellner, 1997: 17). In contrast, Industria is a vibrant world underpinned by continuous economic growth, the use of scientific discoveries, innovation, division of labour and pervasive social mobility. These differing economic foundations generate incompatible social orders: in the stringently hierarchical agrarian universe, honour trumps labour and individuals 'starve according to rank', whereas industrial society is built around the principles that value labour, meritocracy and social dynamism. While Agraria is rooted in predation, where small sections of nobility dominate vast peasant populations, Industria privileges production and allows the rulers to dominate through the appropriation of wealth, rather than through the use of violence.

Since the use of science and technology aids economic growth, this generates what Gellner cynically calls 'an expanding bribery fund' which helps translate potentially violent conflicts into the consumerist chase for status. The two ideal types also differ in cultural terms. Agraria is composed of a culturally stratified universe: the transnational aristocratic elite immersed in a 'high' literate culture amid an ocean of illiterate, vernacular, 'low' cultures of peasantry. In this world culture does not unify the social order; instead culture is used to reinforce the difference between the aristocrats and the rest of society. Moreover the 'low' unstandardised cultures of the peasantry have little or no connection between each other as the inhabitants of distant villages do not interact with each other. In contrast Industria entails a substantial degree of social cohesion: the work in a factory requires the existence of a mutually comprehensible communication and sharing and understanding of specific meanings. In this dynamic environment of increased geographical and social mobility, a context-free form of literacy becomes the norm. For Gellner, the cultural shift from the highly hierarchical, agrarian cultural organisation towards the relative cultural unity of the Industrial Age is largely grounded in the changed economic structure: as the character of production changes so do the values that underpin that society.

Nationalism

Although Gellner (1964) utilises the classical sociological distinction between the traditional and modern world, he is highly sceptical of the view shared by some sociological classics that modernity is inversely proportional to cultural difference. In contrast to Marx, for whom nationhood was largely a relic of past eras, and as such an obstacle to modernisation, for Gellner nationhood is the bedrock of modernity. His pioneering theory of nation formation equally questioned the nationalist narratives which see nations as timeless, natural and normal forms of group identity, as well as the Enlightenment-influenced perspectives that posit nationalism as a pathological obstacle to social development.

Instead, for Gellner, nationalism is a historically contingent but sociologically necessary ingredient of modernisation. To understand fully how nationalism becomes the central glue of modern polities one has to move away from the present centric views that often project national categories deep into the past. As Gellner shows, for much of our history human beings have lived in and identified with much smaller entities (clans, kinship networks, city-states, villages, etc.) or were part of the much larger world (i.e. monotheistic religious systems, empires, etc.). It is only in the last 250 years or so that nationhood has gradually become the dominant form of group identity. To explain the rise of nationhood Gellner invokes his ideal types: nationalism underpins the historical transition from Agraria to Industria. In his view, there is no room for national identifications in the agrarian world: since in this world culture primarily serves to underpin the structural differences between various social strata, collective identification follows a transnational pattern. The dominant aristocratic elites do not identify in any way with their 'own' peasantry but exclusively with other aristocrats, many of whom live outside of their polity. In this context, specific cultural practices are devised to differentiate the aristocracy from the commoners (i.e. from different ways of speaking, dressing and entertaining to marrying exclusively within their stratum – the aristocratic endogamy).

The shift from agrarian to industrial production changes these cultural practices as the new economic and political organisation of society presupposes greater social mobility that ultimately fosters greater cultural uniformity. With the dramatic changes in the dominant character of economic production many individuals move from the countryside to urban areas in search of work. However, to operate fully in this new working environment they require certain semantic skills including unhampered communication. Hence, to accommodate this large-scale social change the industrial state generates society-wide and state-supervised educational systems that teach these skills through a standardised linguistic medium. While the original rationale of state-level educational and linguistic standardisation resides in the changed character of economic production, its long-term consequences are cultural and political – the forging of common cross-class nationhood. For Gellner nationalism is not a psychological phenomenon but something that emerges as a structural consequence. The strong sense of attachment to one's nation is for the most part a product of organisational transformation, whereby in modern polities an overwhelming majority of young citizens are required to undergo secondary socialisation through nation-centric education and other institutions. In Gellner's memorable phrase: 'it is nationalism which engenders nations, and not the other way around' (1983: 55). That is:

> nationalism is about entry to, participation in, identification with, a literate high culture which is co-extensive with an entire political unit and its total populations, and which must be of this kind if it is to be compatible with the kind of division of labour, the type or mode of production, on which this society is based. (1983: 95)

Civil Society

In contrast to the dominant perspectives that often reduce civil society to the presence of non-governmental institutions and other organisations capable of counterbalancing the power of the state, Gellner offers a more nuanced understanding of civil society. In his view, civil society presupposes the existence of individual autonomy. Although pre-modern social orders such as clans or tribes were often autonomous from the state they could not be characterised as representing civil society because they put firm constraints on one's personal liberty. In Gellner's (1994) jovial phrase, this was the world where one could occasionally escape the tyranny of the monarchs but only by experiencing 'the tyranny of the cousins'.

Hence, the emergence of civil society entails the transformation of social relations: a shift from fixed social status towards more contractual arrangements where human beings become 'modular' creatures who, like modular furniture, are flexible and can assume different social and professional roles. For Gellner, modularity is the prerequisite of civil society and it is only in modernity that one can truly develop such attributes. Whereas in the traditional world one's social status was assigned at birth and then reinforced through ritual and coercion, in modern industrial societies social relations involve substantially more flexibility and as such are also much more instrumentally framed. Gellner captures this well in his statement that in a modern world one can become a member of a political party 'without slaughtering a sheep' and one can also leave that party 'without incurring the death penalty for apostasy' (Gellner, 1994: 103).

Another important feature of civil society involves a clear separation between economic and political power. For Gellner civil society cannot operate properly in the environments where political institutions direct and control the economic sphere, as was the case with Soviet-type polities, because this regularly impedes economic growth and innovation, leading towards a coercive type of state power. The same logic applies to situations where the economy dominates politics, as in the case of neoliberal orthodoxy. This model weakens political power and makes both the state and the non-state associations dependent on the economic power of private corporate monopolies. Ideological monopolies also stifle the development of civil society. In situations where the entire social order is sacralised, as in the case of theocracies or other ideology-centred authoritarian societies, there is no ideology-free space for the emergence of civil society. In Gellner's (1994: 137) view, civil society entails 'an amoral order', which means that individuals cannot be compelled to be a part of the uniform moral universe.

Islamic Worlds

Gellner's analytical interests stretched wide, including the study of kinship systems, the philosophy of history, psychoanalysis, ideologies, analytical philosophy, post-modernism, social theory, state socialist systems, intellectuals and social anthropology, among others. However, one of his central preoccupations was the historical sociology of the Islamic world. Two of his early books, *Muslim Society* (1981) and *Saints of the Atlas* (1969), were focused on the role Islam plays in the process of modernisation. Drawing on Ibn Khaldun's theory of cyclical nature of social orders in North Africa, Gellner argues that although the Islamic world might be in part resistant to secularisation this does not mean that it is hostile to modernisation. On the contrary, he insists that since Islamic societies are in possession of an authentic scriptural 'high culture', including the rich literary tradition built around Hadith and the Qur'an, there is space for the emergence of 'Protestant'-style modernisation movements within Islam.

For Gellner, the scriptural 'high culture' of Islam has the potential to galvanise modernisation and mobilise public support around issues of cultural authenticity and traditional symbols in the same way that nationalism has done in Europe and other parts of the world. In this way, Gellner challenged the conventional perceptions of a 'backward' Islamic world, arguing that Islam is the most modern of the monotheistic religions. This strong association with modernity stems in part from its puritan character: there is a degree of 'generic Protestantism' in Islam, which, as Hall (2010) puts it, postulates 'a rigid and austere deity [who] had no cognitive favourites', thus allowing for a relatively smooth transition from the agrarian to the industrial world. Hence the rise of radical Islamism does not necessarily lead to retreat into the past as these same semantic tools could just as successfully be deployed to modernise one's social order.

Michael Mann and the Power Networks

Mann's historical sociology exhibits a degree of affinity with Gellner's approach. Mann also emphasises the centrality of the *longue durée* type of historical analysis without which one cannot fully understand the character of the modern world. He also emphasises the role that economic and ideological factors have played in the transformation of the social world over the course of human history. In this context he explores the impact that civil society, citizenship and nationalism have had in this historical process. However, his approach differs from Gellner's in several important ways. For one thing, in contrast to Gellner's economics-centred account of social change, Mann articulates a multifactored theory of history that identifies four distinct sources of social power: economic, political, ideological and military. For another thing, unlike Gellner who is for the most part a sociologist of consensus, Mann offers a much more conflict-centred theory of social relations, where war and other forms of organised violence are perceived to be crucial mechanisms of social change throughout history. Finally, Mann departs from Gellner in his abandonment of the idea of society as a key sociological category.

Social Power

The first volume of Mann's magnum opus *The Sources of Social Power* (1986: 1) opens with a sharp attack on the traditional, mostly functionalist, understandings of social order. In direct contrast to Parsons and other system theorists, Mann argues that societies are not systems but the conglomerates of 'multiple overlapping and intersecting socio-spatial networks of power'. Rather than treating societies as unified wholes, he argues, it is paramount to recognise that their composition is variable, dynamic and uneven in the sense that the networks of power have different spatial researches and extents. For example, big private corporations such as Google or Microsoft might have extremely wide economic powers but their political and ideological influence is much smaller and their military power is almost non-existent. Even the most powerful state such as the United States is characterised by an uneven and differential spatial power reach. This polity possesses a vast and wide, although not total, military might. The US state also has enormous influence in the economic sphere, but this capacity is weaker as it remains tied to the wider networks of capitalist markets. Some entities such as the Catholic Church have substantial ideological power while their political, economic and military powers have a much smaller reach and influence.

Hence, in Mann's theory power is conceptualised as a multifaceted phenomenon that appears in a variety of guises. He first differentiates between distributive and collective power, where the former stands for dominance of one over another ('power over'), whereas the latter involves joint social action that results in greater strength over nature or the third parties ('power through'). Furthermore, he distinguishes between extensive and intensive forms of power as well as between authoritative and diffused power models. All of these taxonomies are used to show that the power networks are extremely dynamic and as such their exact configurations and influence can only be detected through careful historical–sociological analysis. In the four volumes of his *Sources of Social Power* Mann provides many examples to illustrate this variability of different power structures. Hence the strength of military power can be gauged in different ways: while the modern US or French Army command structure is characterised by authoritative and intensive power as their HQs maintain stringent control over their troops, traditional imperial military organisations such as those of ancient China or the Roman Empire had authoritative and extensive power in the sense that they loosely controlled remote territorial possessions. The same applies to economic power: twenty-first-century market exchange stands for diffused and extensive power because it is composed of numerous ancillary interactions over global space, whereas nineteenth-century-type general strikes such as the 1877 St. Louis General Strike or the 1892 New Orleans General Strike were characterised by diffused but intensive power because they involved a strong sense of solidarity that was not clustered in the same (factory) space. Mann deploys this conceptual apparatus in his analysis of power structures over the course of human history.

He identifies the emergence of state power as the crucial mechanism for expanding organisational dominance over large numbers of individuals. The pristine states of the ancient Middle East developed in response to the need to protect the agricultural surplus. In this context, military and political powers were the leading edge of state expansion and centralisation. Mann refers to this process as social caging as the states gradually attained capacity to 'cage' individuals within the confines of specific territories ruled by the centralised political authorities. The shift from hunter gathering towards a sedentary lifestyle, was in part premised on the state's ability to provide a degree of security and relative prosperity in exchange for obedience to its authority. For Mann, war and the preparations for war played a highly significant role in this process of social caging because, through the intensification of warfare, the states that survived were able to enhance their organisational capacities. War experience was also decisive for the rise of science and technology since the investments in military technologies often lead towards new inventions and have contributed to the increase of social power.

The State

Mann sees state power as playing a vital role in the transformation of social relations over the course of human history. Internally the increase in the organisational capacity of states has shaped the social development of different parts of the world. To account for these long-lasting social changes Mann differentiates between the despotic and the infrastructural capacities of states. Despotic power stands for the repressive capacities of the state. This is a power that the state rulers can deploy without any negotiation with their civil societies:

> the Chinese Emperor, as the 'Son of Heaven', 'owned' the whole of China and could do as he wished with any individual or group within his domain. The Roman Emperor, only a minor god, acquired powers which were also in principle unlimited outside of the restricted area of affairs nominally controlled by the Senate. (Mann 1984: 193)

In contrast, infrastructural power stands for the capacity of the state to penetrate civil society and 'to implement logistically its political decisions throughout the realm'. The rising infrastructural capacity of states is dependent on the existence of effective transport and communication networks, standardised weights and measures, the presence of singular currency in use to successfully facilitate the exchange of goods and services, the increased levels of literacy among the population and the ability to regularly provide centrally run services that rely on the complex division of labour. Mann argues that modernity has historically been characterised by the gradual expansion of the infrastructural powers of the state at the expense of their despotic capacities. In this context liberal democracies are characterised by very high infrastructural powers and quite low despotic powers. However, not all types of polities have followed this trend. For example, both the Soviet Union and Nazi Germany, just as contemporary China or North Korea, have developed as states with high despotic and infrastructural capacities.

In addition to these internal characteristics, the state's external position was also instrumental in shaping the social order and the relationships between individuals inhabiting that social order. In contrast to much mainstream sociology, which almost exclusively focuses on the internal features of societies, and largely ignores the social impact of inter-state dynamics, Mann attributes a central role to geopolitics in the transformation of social relations. Hence in Mann's view one cannot fully capture the long-term social dynamics of class, ethnicity, gender and other social divisions without a historical exploration of inter-state relations. He identifies the geopolitical competition between states, involving ideological, economic, political and military conflicts, as the driving force of social change.

Hence, in contrast to Marxist-inspired analyses which interpret class conflicts through the prism of economic inequalities and profit maximisation, Mann adds to this the changing geopolitical conditions and the autonomous logic of state power, both of which have historically generated different patterns of social stratification in the world. For example, he criticises T. H. Marshall's highly influential theory of citizenship as lacking a wider geopolitical understanding of social change. Rather than assuming that all modern states have followed similar citizenship regimes, Mann shows how different modes of class politics and nation-building have stimulated the development of very different citizenship policies. For example, the early emergence of economic liberalism in the United States and UK (together with the wide middle-class participation in the American Revolution and UK parliamentary politics, respectively) fostered the development of a constitutional type of citizenship. In contrast, authoritarian states with a large agrarian base such as Germany, Russia or Austria–Hungary have experienced much more protracted and violent conflicts over the extension of civil, political and social rights. Nevertheless, in all of these cases citizenship developed as a mechanism of social control by the state and military elites. By gradually and unevenly extending some citizenship rights to various classes the state rulers were able to pacify their domestic politics in order to pursue their geopolitical goals. Furthermore, the successes in the geopolitical arena have all fed back into class politics as rising nationalism soothed and even stifled class conflicts (Mann, 1993, 1988).

Contemporary Relevance and Applications

Both Gellner and Mann emphasise the significance of long-term historical analysis. In contrast to much mainstream contemporary sociological thought, which seems to be focused more on the short-term trends, Mann and Gellner offer a *longue durée* type of analysis which often proves superior in tracking down the complexity of long-term social change. The relevance of this type of historical sociology is well illustrated by its capacity to identify and then explain patterns of social development that the short-term analyses often cannot detect.

SOCIAL THEORY, HISTORY AND MODERNITY

It took until the post-war era before the social theories of Marx, Durkheim and Weber became regarded as the classical canon of sociology. In that time, however, universities had become more formalised and vocational, leading to a somewhat fragmented interpretation of their main contributions. While the synchronic, universal and trans-historical aspect of classical theory was largely championed, the diachronic, particular and historical aspect was sidelined. From this perspective, the historical sociology of Gellner and Mann is a welcome counterpoint. The largely unrecognised problem for contemporary social theory, however, remains that faced by the classics in their own day: how to combine both aspects in an analysis that captures and characterises the main direction of social change in the present. This is especially important at the contemporary conjuncture, where the future of modernity is fraught with acute uncertainty.

For example, until quite recently much social science scholarship was dominated by the analytical positions that conceptualised globalisation as a profoundly novel and almost teleological phenomenon. The assumption, most forcefully advanced by Ulrich Beck (2000), was that in a new globalised world there is no room for the 'old' national categories. For Beck (2007: 1; 2000: 85): 'the cosmopolitan project' has replaced the 'nation-state project' and 'anyone who adheres to the old national dogmatism (to the fetish of sovereignty …) will be skipped over, rolled over and won't even be in position to complain about it'. Nevertheless, these highly popular and influential short-term diagnoses articulated only a decade ago did not age well. The world-wide rise of nationalist and populist movements from the United States, India, China, the UK and Israel to Russia and further afield testifies that such ahistorical accounts have proved inadequate.

In contrast to these popular but present-centric diagnoses, Mann and Gellner offered a historically more grounded analysis which tended to situate globalisation within wider historical trends. Hence, when most social scientists subscribed to the view that globalisation was bound to decrease the influence of nation-states and nationalisms, both Gellner and Mann showed convincingly why this could not be the case. Instead of perceiving globalisation as a historically unique phenomenon that pits states against markets, this scholarship demonstrated successfully that such trends have existed before, and that rather than being adversaries, markets cannot expand for long without state support. Hence Mann's analyses, in particular, were highly instrumental in charting the historical moments when the political and military powers coalesced with the economic and ideological powers to initiate a new wave of globalisation. In this context, as Mann (2013, 1997) shows, this current wave of globalisation is very similar to the one that occurred at the end of the nineteenth and in the early twentieth century when the British Empire fostered economic liberalisation and the increased mobility of people. Although the new technologies have facilitated more mobility and trade, the contemporary patterns of economic liberalisation are not substantially different from those taking place at the end of the nineteenth century.

These *longue durée* analyses are also valuable in tracking the historical dynamics of ideological change. Gellner's work on Islam and nationalism has been useful in helping us understand current developments. The same applies to Mann's contributions on ideological power and nationalism in particular. In contrast to Beck or Giddens, who tend to see nationalism and religious revivals as ideological discourses bound to be weakened by the onset of globalisation, both Gellner and Mann show otherwise. Whereas Mann ties nationalism to state power, for Gellner nationalism and economic prosperity are two central pillars of political legitimacy in the modern world. Thus, they both see strong national identifications as being fully compatible with globalisation. For Mann, the strength of nationalism stems in part from its organisational might, so as the infrastructural capacities of states increase one is likely to see more, not less, nationalism. Gellner argues that economic prosperity often stifles excessive nationalist outbursts. However, since modern social orders justify their existence in national (and economic) terms it is difficult to see how nationalism could disappear in a world still dominated by nation-states.

Furthermore, as Gellner identifies, nationalism is a social phenomenon that underpins the transition from the agrarian to industrial modes of production. As this transition intensifies throughout the world, one is to expect the proliferation of nationalism as well. The focus here is on the gradual shift from the agrarian world, where culture is used to reinforce the difference between the elite and the rest, towards the modern industrial universe, where shared culture becomes a source of cross-class social cohesion. In this context nationalism becomes a dominant social glue that helps justify the existing social order and, in this way, holds the class and other intra-group conflicts in check. For Gellner, modernisation is defined not only by urbanisation, industrialisation or secularisation, but also by a cultural transformation involving a process whereby 'low' vernacular cultures become 'high' cultures that underpin the apparatuses of nation-building. A similar ideological change takes place throughout the world.

However, in different cultural traditions religious doctrines might perform an almost identical role to that of nationalism. For Gellner, the distinction between the scriptural ('high') and popular ('low') Islam allows for the emergence of various ideological movements that utilise Islamic cultural and religious tropes to mobilise large groups of people in order to build new social orders. Although some of these groups invoke purist religious markers and seem to be advocating a return to the past, in reality they perform a similar role to nationalist ideologues who embrace a discourse of authenticity and 'back to the roots' mantra. Nevertheless, as Gellner shows, one should not read too much into these claims as both nationalists and Islamists inevitably, and often unwillingly, contribute towards the modernisation of social order. Even the most radical groups which nominally completely reject modernity tend to embrace its structural and organisational logic – from science and technology to the division of labour, modern armaments, medicine, mass media and so on. In this way even ISIS and the Taliban were not immune to these fruits of modernisation.

Criticisms

Since both Gellner and Mann subscribe to the view that the modern social order has its roots in Europe and that European developments were decisive for the transformation of the entire world, they have regularly been criticised as offering Eurocentric interpretations of social change (Blaut, 2000). Some of these criticisms are very harsh and perhaps empirically unjustified. For example, Blaut (2000: xi) describes both Mann and Gellner as 'Eurocentric' scholars whose theories exhibit a propensity towards what he calls 'Eurocentric diffusionism', which stands for 'the fundamental assumption that progress is somehow permanent and natural in the European part of the world but not elsewhere, and progress elsewhere is mainly the result of the diffusion of innovative ideas and products from Europe and Europeans'. Nevertheless, if one reads their works carefully it is clear that both Gellner and Mann recognise that modernity had many roots and what happened in Europe was nothing more than a historical contingency. Similarly, Mann is clear that throughout much of history Europe was not the centre of social development – it was only since the seventeenth century that this continent became more influential in world affairs. Furthermore, Mann (2007) also emphasises the dark side of European expansion and writes about European involvement in both 'production and predation'.

A more subtle critique of the historical sociology of Gellner and Mann comes from scholars who focus on the timing and the structural reasons behind nineteenth- and twentieth-century Europe's dominance. Hence a number of influential historians such as Hobson (2004), Darwin (2008), Goldstone (2002) and Pomeranz (2000) argue that the European economic, political and military developments were very slow to materialise and, rather than originating in the early modern period, can be traced only to the nineteenth century. For these scholars the rise of Western Europe had less to do with cognitive revolution and Enlightenment ideas and much more with the relatively unique geographical and historical conditions, including the abundance of cheap coal reserves in the UK (which stimulated the Industrial Revolution) and the mass acquisition of resources from the colonies. Whereas Mann and Gellner emphasise the internal causes of the European breakthrough, Darwin, Hobson and Pomeranz insist on the external reasons behind this dominance, where imperial colonial expansion plays a central part.

Gellner's approach has also been criticised for its economic determinism, functionalist reasoning and the neglect of violence. Hall (2010) and O'Leary (1998) argue that Gellner's theory of nationalism is reductionist in the sense that it leaves no room for power politics while overemphasising economics. For one thing the theory cannot explain properly why the transition from Agraria to Industria resulted in the creation of so many nation-states rather than only one or just a handful. For another thing, Gellner does not explain why some cultural movements transform into political-nationalist organisations that advocate independence, while others remain cultural-nationalist only. Laitin (1998) questions Gellner's functionalism, pointing out that his argument is circular – nationalism and the structural transitions within Islam are explained on the basis of the consequences they generate. While nationalism and scriptural Islam might be functional to the operation of modern social orders, they cannot be the causes of such an order because they appear after the change has already taken place.

Furthermore, Gellner's overly structuralist approach leaves no space for the individual or collective agents. Although the earlier articulation of his theory of nationalism (1964) did focus on specific social groups (i.e. intellectuals, peasantry, workers, etc.) the later versions of his theory tend to ignore agency and overemphasise the structural factors. As a twentieth-century scholar who attributed great explanatory potency to industrialisation, Gellner was not sensitive towards the ecological consequences of unrestrained economic growth. Finally, Gellner's Enlightenment-inspired theory of modernity offers a highly optimistic take on social development. Although he recognises that the story of human development is not linear, involving various historical ups and downs, his approach still ignores the central role that violence has played in this process. In particular, for Gellner violence belongs to Agraria while Industria is conceptualised as a world that does not require violence. However, the historical record indicates that more people were slaughtered in the industrial era than ever before in human history (Malešević, 2017, 2010).

Unlike Gellner, Mann is aware that war and violence were crucial mechanisms of social change in history. However, many of the criticisms of his position focus on Mann's overemphasis of these factors. For one thing, Mann's four-partite model of power has been challenged by several Weberian scholars, including Hall, Poggi and Schroeder, who argue that military power is rarely if ever an independent entity, but something tied to political power. As political power largely stems from one's access to coercive means of control it is difficult to disentangle political from military power. Since much of this power stems from one's position within the state apparatus, such a distinction is often superfluous.

Mann's approach has also been criticised for its downplaying of ideological power. While he recognises that at some historical junctures ideology was a driving force of social change, he is adamant that ideological power cannot operate without organisation and for that reason the political, economic and military powers have often been more significant in history. This view has been questioned by Gorski (2006), who insists that religion and modern ideological discourses have regularly been decisive in the transformation of specific social orders. Schroeder (2013) has challenged Mann's neglect of science and technology in his typology of social power, arguing that techno-science is an autonomous source of power which has only increased with the expansion of modernity. Others have also criticised Mann's state-centric and overly structuralist understanding of social relations. For example, Kiser (2006) and Malešević (2017) put the spotlight on Mann's neglect of the micro-level mechanisms that generate and sustain social relations, including power dynamics. Although his recent studies on the perpetuators and the core constituencies of the various genocides have remedied this problem to some extent, much of his focus remains firmly on the structural contexts of power.

Conclusion

Peter Burke (2005: 3) once described the relationship between social theory and history as a 'dialogue of the deaf'. His point was that although both sociologists and historians study societies, they focus on different issues, use different concepts and in this way tend not to understand each other. Whereas sociologists are generalists who look for the universal aspects of social change, historians are particularists who emphasise the unique qualities of historical events. In this context historical sociology attempts to bridge this gap. Both Mann and Gellner offer analyses that bring together historical evidence and social theory. Although they have developed very different approaches, both of these scholars emphasise that centrality of long-term historical analysis for understanding different social processes. Nevertheless, they also show that simple historical narratives without in-depth social theorising cannot tell us much either. Hence historical sociology is a promising a way out of this 'dialogue of the deaf'. In this chapter we analysed the key contributions made by historical sociologists and also identified some pitfalls of these approaches.

References

Beck, U. (2000) *What is Globalization?* Cambridge: Polity.
Beck, U. (2007) The Cosmopolitan Condition: Why Methodological Nationalism Fails. *Theory, Culture & Society*, 24(7-8), pp. 286-90.
Berend, I. T. (1998) *Decades of Crisis: Central and Eastern Europe Before World War II*. Berkeley, CA: University of California Press.
Blaut, J. M. (2000) *Eight Eurocentric Historians*. New York: Guilford Press.
Burke, P. (2005) *History and Social Theory*. Cambridge: Polity.
Darwin, J. (2008) *After Tamarlane: The Global History of Empire since 1405*. New York: Bloomsbury.
Gellner, E. (1959) *Words and Things, A Critical Account of Linguistic Philosophy and a Study in Ideology*. London: Gollancz.
Gellner, E. (1964) *Thought and Change*. London: Weidenfeld & Nicolson.
Gellner, E. (1969) *Saints of the Atlas*. London: Weidenfeld & Nicolson.
Gellner, E. (1981) *Muslim Society*. Cambridge: Cambridge University Press.
Gellner, E. (1983) *Nations and Nationalism*. Oxford: Blackwell.
Gellner, E. (1989) Introduction. In: J. Baechler, J. A. Hall and M. Mann (eds) *Europe and the Rise of Capitalism*. Oxford: Blackwell, pp. 1-5.
Gellner, E. (1994) *Conditions of Libert: Civil Society and Its Rivals*. London: Hamish Hamilton.
Gellner, E. (1997) *Nationalism*. London: Phoenix.
Goldstone, J. (2002) Efflorescences and Economic Growth in World History: Rethinking the Rise of the West and the British Industrial Revolution. *Journal of World History*, 13, pp. 323-89.
Gorski, P. (2006) Mann's Theory of Ideological Power: Sources, Applications and Elaborations. In: J. A. Hall and R. Schroeder (eds) *An Anatomy of Power: The Social Theory of Michael Mann*. Cambridge: Cambridge University Press, pp. 101-34.
Hall, J. A. (2010) *Ernest Gellner: An Intellectual Biography*. London: Verso.
Hobson, J. (2004) *The Eastern Origins of Western Civilisation*. Cambridge: Cambridge University Press.
Kiser, E. (2006) Mann's Microfoundations: Addressing Neo-Weberian Dilemmas. In: J. A. Hall and R. Schroeder (eds) *An Anatomy of Power: The Social Theory of Michael Mann*. Cambridge: Cambridge University Press, pp. 56-70.

Laitin, D. (1998) Nationalism and Language: A Post-Soviet Perspective. In: J. Hall (ed.) *The State of the Nation*. Cambridge: Cambridge University Press, pp. 135-57.

Malešević, S. (2010) *The Sociology of War and Violence*. Cambridge: Cambridge University Press.

Malešević, S. (2017) *The Rise of Organised Brutality: A Historical Sociology of Violence*. Cambridge: Cambridge University Press.

Mann, M. (1984) The Autonomous Power of the State: Its Origins, Mechanisms, and Results. *Archives européennes de sociologie*, 25, pp. 185-213.

Mann, M. (1986) *The Sources of Social Power: A History of Power from the Beginning to AD 1760*. Cambridge: Cambridge University Press.

Mann, M. (1988) *States, War and Capitalism: Studies in Political Sociology*. Oxford: Blackwell.

Mann, M. (1993) *The Sources of Social Power: The Rise of Classes and Nation-states, 1760-1914*. Cambridge: Cambridge University Press.

Mann, M. (1997) Has Globalization Ended the Rise and Rise of the Nation-state? *Review of International Political Economy*, 4(3), pp. 472-96.

Mann, M. (2007) Production and Predation in European Imperialism. In: S. Malešević and M. Haugaard (eds) *Ernest Gellner and Contemporary Social Thought*. Cambridge: Cambridge University Press, pp. 50-74.

Mann, M. (2013) *The Sources of Social Power: Globalizations, 1945-2011*. Cambridge: Cambridge University Press.

O'Leary, A. (1998) Ernest Gellner's Diagnoses of Nationalism: A Critical Overview, or, What is Living and What is Dead in Ernest Gellner's Philosophy of Nationalism. In: J. Hall (ed.) *The State of The Nation*. Cambridge: Cambridge University Press, pp. 40-90.

Pomeranz, K. (2000) *The Great Divergence: China, Europe, and the Making of the Modern World Economy*. Princeton, NJ: Princeton University Press.

Schroeder, R. (2013) *An Age of Limits: Social Theory for the 21st Century*. Basingstoke: Palgrave Macmillan.

Collins

Introduction

Despite being one of the most original and highly prolific authors, Randall Collins has not received the level of academic recognition that Habermas, Foucault or Bourdieu enjoy, within or outside of sociology. Collins has made enormous contributions to sociological theory, political and historical sociology, the sociology of education and intellectuals, and the study of social stratification, emotions, power, violence and state formation among various areas. His concepts, ideas and theories are widely read, cited and applied across a range of disciplines and his work has been translated into numerous languages. However, Collins is yet to be acknowledged as a great sociological theorist. One of the reasons for this relative neglect is the fact that he produces work that does not follow any academic trends and fashions. Although he generally engages in current debates on the state of sociological research and thought, much of his work is situated largely outside the dominant theoretical paradigms. Another reason for his omission is that his sociology does not fit easily into the existing sociological approaches. Although he was initially regarded as a neo-Weberian scholar his work has been influenced as much by Marx, Durkheim, Goffman and a plethora of other classical and contemporary scholars. In particular, his propensity to generate unusual and original syntheses and reinterpretations of the classics has made it difficult for commentators to precisely label and box his work.

This chapter introduces Collins' central ideas, concepts and theories. We chart the key moments from his biography and look at the broader intellectual and political context that have shaped his work. As in previous chapters we then address the contemporary applications of Collins' work as well as the existing critiques of his contributions.

Life and Intellectual Context

Randall Collins was born in 1941 in Knoxville, Tennessee, but spent much of his childhood in Europe where his family was stationed after the war. Both his grandfather and his father were employed by the US military. His German-born grandfather was a non-commissioned officer in the US Army for 30 years while his father, a professor of German and a low-ranking diplomat, worked for US Army Intelligence and the State Department and in this capacity was sent to Berlin in 1946 and then to Moscow from 1949 to 1951 (Iranzo, 2015: 211). Once he reached his teenage years Collins was sent to a boarding school in New England where he personally encountered the hierarchies of status and class. Although he grew up in an upper-middle-class family his boarding school was dominated by the upper-class students who were all part of the same social networks from which he was largely excluded.

The Harvard and Berkeley Years

Collins completed his undergraduate studies at Harvard in 1963, where he was taught by Talcott Parsons and George Homans. Initially Collins studied engineering, mathematics and literature but soon switched to a social relations degree which incorporated sociology, anthropology and social psychology. Soon after he moved to Stanford University where he enrolled as an MA student in psychology and had the opportunity to attend Leon Festinger's courses. He graduated in 1964. Dissatisfied with the overly experimental and cognitivist character of psychology at Stanford, Collins moved to Berkeley to study sociology and where he received his MA in 1965 and PhD in 1969. At the end of the 1960s, and in the early 1970s, Berkeley was the centre of intellectual and political movements and its sociology department was the centre of academic excellence. Here Collins had the opportunity to work with Reinhard Bendix, Erving Goffman, Herbert Blumer, Joseph Ben-David, Martin Lipset and Leo Lowenthal among others.

At Berkeley Collins was active in academic and political circles. He soon became an assistant to a leading sociologist of science and education, Joseph Ben-David, and had the opportunity to work on the larger project on the origins of experimental psychology, focusing on the network analysis of nineteenth-century German intellectuals. He also started a collaboration with a prominent US-based German Weberian scholar, Reinhard Bendix, who introduced Collins to comparative historical sociology. Bendix was a strong early influence in two ways: he introduced Collins to Weber as a political sociologist (as opposed to the dominant Parsonian, cultural interpretations of Weberian intellectual heritage), and he also provided an opportunity for Collins to be involved in several research projects on the state and society.

Collins' early publications, including his highly influential *Conflict Sociology* (1975), were all shaped by this intellectual debt to Bendix. Other important early influences were Blumer and Goffman. As a student Collins was impressed by Goffman's ideas and was regularly at his crowded lectures. However, he found Goffman difficult on a personal level and gradually their relationship become strained. In contrast, Blumer was more approachable and supportive of graduate students. Collins was impressed by his commitment to symbolic interactionism in theory and practice. For example, even though Blumer was not a highly political person he encouraged his students to make links between sociological theory (and particular interactionist connects) with their own everyday reality (Iranzo, 2015: 212).

However, unlike Blumer or Goffman, who preferred to stay away from politics, Collins was always interested in current political developments. Since Berkeley was also the hub of student political activity, Collins soon joined the anti-war and the free speech movements. He was a regular participant in student demonstrations, and the non-violent sit-ins focusing on the Vietnam War and anti-racial discrimination protests. During this period Collins was sympathetic to radical socialist ideas and was also interested in alternative lifestyles. At some point he joined a hippy commune, studied Buddhism with Tibetan and Japanese monks, went to group therapies and embraced other aspects of the hippy lifestyle. As an anti-war activist he was also briefly arrested in 1964.

New Sociological Thinking

After completing his PhD in 1969 Collins was appointed assistant professor at the University of California, San Diego, where he had the opportunity to work with Alvin Gouldner, who was a visiting professor at San Diego at that time. During this period Collins was involved in setting up what would later become two leading social theory journals – *Theory and Society* and *Sociological Theory*. While at San Diego he also published three path-breaking books (*The Discovery of Society*, 1972, with M. Makowsky; *Conflict Sociology*, 1975; and *The Credential Society*, 1979) and many influential academic articles, all of which made him a recognisable name among American sociologists. In 1977 Collins left San Diego and decided to become a professional writer. Hence in 1979 he published a detective novel *The Case of the Philosophers' Ring*. He returned to academia in 1978 by accepting a professorship at the University of Virginia where he worked until 1982. From 1982 to 1985 he took another break from academia and focused largely on writing. Although he was nominally a visiting professor at several universities (UCLA, Chicago, University of California, Riverside, and Southern California) most of his time was spent on writing. During this period, he published several books including *Sociology since Mid-Century* (1981a), *Sociological Insight* (1982), *Sociology of Marriage and Family* (1985a), *Three Sociological Traditions* (1985b) and *Max Weber: A Skeleton Key* (1985c). In 1985 he was appointed professor at the University of California, Riverside, where he stayed until 1997. In 1986 and 1988 he published another two influential books, *Weberian Sociological Theory* and *Theoretical Sociology*, respectively. In 1997 he moved to the University of Pennsylvania where he was appointed the Dorothy Swaine Thomas Professor of Sociology and where he is now emeritus professor. At Pennsylvania Collins continued his highly prolific career, publishing some of his most influential books including the monumental *The Sociology of Philosophies* (1998) focusing on the analysis of the most influential philosophical networks throughout the world over the course of human history. This book was a culmination of 30 years of painstaking research. Another important publication was *Macro-History* (1999), which was followed by the path-breaking *Interaction Ritual Chains* (2004) and *Violence: A Micro Sociological Theory* (2008). More recently he has published co-authored books on the future of capitalism (*Does Capitalism Have a Future?*, 2013, with Wallerstein et al.) and on the sociology of emotional energy of charismatic leaders (*Napoleon Never Slept*, 2015, with McConnell). Collins was elected president of the American Sociological Association between 2011 and 2012.

Historical, Social and Political Context

American Sociology

Although the early American sociologists such as Robert Park, W. E. B. Du Bois, Lester Ward and Albion Small were deeply influenced by European intellectual traditions, much of American sociology remained disconnected from the sociological developments taking place elsewhere. Instead, the focus was on trying to understand and explain social change by emphasising the unique features of American society. It is only with the arrival of European political émigrés and Jewish intellectuals fleeing the Nazis in the late 1930s and early 1940s, that American sociology became more open to an international outlook. However, despite these important European influences much of American sociology remained quite insular and was characterised by a strong propensity towards methodological nationalism well into the 1960s. This tendency was most pronounced in applied and quantitative research but was equally present among scholars such as Talcott Parsons, who studied in Europe and whose theories were shaped by strong European theoretical influences. Although Parsons was a generalist who aimed to develop a grand sociological theory that would be applicable across different social contexts, there is no doubt that his models were geared towards, and reflected fully, the social realities of the 1940s, 1950s and early 1960s in the United States (Black, 2012).

With the gradual expansion, and later almost complete dominance, of quantitative-oriented studies the overwhelming majority of American sociologists avoided comparative sociological analyses and became preoccupied with the study of domestic social issues ranging from race and ethnicity to social stratification, religion or education. In this methodologically nationalist environment, sociologists were for the most part unwilling to look at the wider social, historical and geographical contexts to understand the long-term dynamics of global (and thus also national) social changes. More specifically, sociologists were not so keen to study the impact of war and the geopolitical changes or the shifting dynamics of state power and prestige. Similarly, there were no systematic attempts to explore the relationships between micro-level conflicts and the broader macro-level violent clashes. In many respects, American sociologists were inward looking and paid little attention to the role that Cold War politics or decolonisation struggles played in shaping the environment after the Second World War. Although American sociology was rich and versatile in terms of having a wide and diverse range of sociological approaches, most of them were focused on 'internal' social issues that were analysed through the prism of the non-comparative and the non-historical categories of analysis.

The fact that Randall Collins grew up in post-war Germany and Russia and witnessed the legacies of war as well as the post-war diplomatic wranglings of the Great Powers made him more sensitive towards these wider geopolitical, military and ideological factors. In addition, his direct student involvement in the anti-war protests at Berkeley contributed further to his understanding of the wider geographical, political and historical context of social change. In contrast to the Parsonian and other mainstream sociological traditions that were focused on the internal sources of social change, Collins was adamant that one should also study the external contexts and find out how the largely macrostructural forces shape micro-sociological processes and vice versa. Hence the rise in the 1960s of different social movements (civil rights, race consciousness, gender equality, anti-war, hippy and many other groups) was to be interpreted by looking not only at the changed class or stratification patterns or the value changes within American society, but also at the geopolitical transformations and the US involvement in various wars abroad.

Vietnam War

Although the enormous casualties of the Korean War (1950–3) had already had some impact on social relations in the United States as it established the structural foundations of the Cold War ideologies and reinforced the political and economic role of the military within American society, it was the experience of the Vietnam War (1955–75) that completely reshaped the character of the American polity. As the French Empire gradually crumbled and its defeated military withdrew from the former colonial possession of French Indo-China, the US government brought in military advisers in the 1950s, who by the early 1960s were replaced by regular military troops. By 1961 the troop levels tripled and a year later they tripled again. From the mid-1960s the United States deployed regular combat units that were involved in a highly destructive war which at one point engulfed the neighbouring states of Laos and Cambodia.

In 1968, the Viet Cong launched the Tet Offensive, which initially failed in defeating the South Vietnamese government but was highly successful in changing the public perception of the war in the United States. Since US mass media had almost unrestricted access to the frontline, they were able to report on the enormous human carnage of this war. The horrifying images of killed and mutilated civilians, such as those from the My Lai massacre where in 1968 up to 500 hundred unarmed civilians were killed by Company C of the US 23rd Infantry Division, were instantly beamed to the American public. The consequence of this public visibility of war horrors coupled with ever-increasing casualty rates among, mostly very young, US soldiers led to a substantial shift in public opinion.

Hence by the end of the 1960s and in the early 1970s the Vietnam War was extremely unpopular, provoking a large-scale resistance including draft dodging, anti-war protests, and even violent actions against the military and government officials. Although many sociologists were generally sympathetic towards these developments, for the most part they lacked the theoretical tools to explain these social changes. The dominant sociological perspectives of this period, structural functionalism and neo-Marxism, proved inadequate in fully capturing the direction of these social developments. The Parsonian-style functionalists focused on the stability and attainment of social equilibrium and as such had no proper answers to the questions about the origins and social dynamics of conflicts that engulfed American society. Although the neo-Marxists were better at pointing to the centrality of struggle in social relations, their overemphasis on class and economics proved insufficient for understanding and explaining the roots of the civil rights movements, the middle-class resistance or the role geopolitics played in galvanising domestic uprisings.

For Collins, who wanted to comprehend what was happening in the world of the 1960s and 1970s, these established approaches seemed inadequate. For example, as an active participant in the civil rights movements the young Collins realised that such groups were formed often around non-instrumental motives where strong emotional attachments generated new social dynamics. At Berkeley he shared the emotional experience of other participants who protested against the Vietnam War, racism, patriarchy, capitalism and imperialism:

> there was the real sense that the world is horrible. On the other hand, the movement had so much élan, so much collective effervescence, that it really had a feeling of 'this is tremendous energy' and a sense that we were doing something important – and kind of happiness. And I had the feeling, like a lot of other people at that time, that this was the first time in my life I had ever done anything worthwhile. Everything before that was sort of this period of routine. (Maclean and Yocom, 2000: 3)

In this context he could see the sheer interdependence of the macro and micro realities: the geopolitical conflicts and wars fought far away had a direct impact on the mobilisation of social action at home and this mobilisation in turn changed the existing social order, which ultimately transformed the geopolitical realities as well.

Hence, there is no doubt that wider historical and political contexts have deeply influenced Collins' sociology. He soon realised that the US experience was not unique, and that these macro–micro links shaped much human collective existence. Thus, to capture fully the patterns of social change it is paramount to think historically and comparatively. In this sense Collins revisited and re-interpreted the classics of social thought, namely Weber, Marx, Durkheim and Simmel, all of whom were historical sociologists who developed their generalised theories of social change through comparative analyses.

By following in the footsteps of the classical comparative historical sociologists Collins was able historically to trace long-term social change and on the basis of this even identify some future trends. Since Collins perceives sociology as a cumulative social science that possesses a predictive capacity, he made several long-term predictions. For example, he was almost unique among the social scientists who successfully forecast the demise of the Soviet Union in the 1970s (Collins, 1978, 1982). This prediction was rooted in his geopolitical theory that emphasised the historical transformation of the Russian state as a peripheral empire to the Soviet Union, and as an overstretched state unable to protect its extensive borders, thus experiencing gradual decline. More recently, Collins (2013) has deployed this historically grounded analytical framework to make a prediction about the decline of capitalism. Focusing on the ever-increasing technological advancements in industry, including the greater reliance on robotics and automation, he argues that capitalist enterprises will not require much human labour in the near future. This environment is likely to generate a dramatic increase in unemployment leading to a situation where the majority of the population will have no resources to purchase products and services, thus ultimately triggering the collapse of capitalist economies.

Arguments and Ideas

Early in his career, Collins was regularly characterised as a neo-Weberian scholar who emphasised the macro-political aspects of the Weberian intellectual heritage. His first publications, including the highly influential *Conflict Sociology* (1975) and *The Credential Society* (1979), as well as his later books such as *Max Weber: A Skeleton Key* (1985c), *Weberian Sociological Theory* (1986) and *Macro-History: Essays in the Sociology of the Long Run* (1999), all bear the strong hallmark of a distinct version of a neo-Weberian conflict approach. However, Collins was never a purist representative of a particular sociological tradition. Instead, many of his early publications indicate that his approach was grounded not only in a unique interpretation of Weber but also by borrowing analytically from other classics including Durkheim, Goffman, Marx, Simmel, Mead, Blumer and many others.

For example, one of his early path-breaking articles, 'The Micro-Foundations of Macro-Sociology' (1981b), was almost completely focused on the everyday rituals and other micro-interactionist underpinnings of social order. In this article, just as in many of his later contributions, Mead, Blumer, Goffman and Durkheim play as an important intellectual inspiration as does Weber. Hence Collins' theoretical opus was always richer and wider than the conventional labels would allow. Furthermore, for much of his career Collins was dedicated to reconciling the macro and the micro levels of sociological analysis. Nevertheless, in contrast to the overly syncretic attempts of Anthony Giddens or Margaret Archer, who aimed theoretically to surpass the agency vs. structure dichotomy, Collins was more interested in the empirical and analytical interdependency of the micro and macro worlds. Hence, while he recognises that these are two different levels of analysis, what is sociologically relevant is to find out empirically how and when they interact or shape each other. Although he is adamant that theory is central for understanding and explaining the dynamics of the social world, he also remains committed to developing theoretical models that are grounded in empirical realities and can be deployed analytically to illuminate such realities.

Conflict Theory

One of Collins' earliest books, *Conflict Sociology* (1975), displays many of the attributes that have characterised his entire life's work. This work navigates between the Scylla and Charybdis of positivist empiricism and relativist interpretivism that have dominated much of the social sciences, including sociology. While rejecting positivism as being inept at capturing the reflexivity and complexity of social relations, Collins also makes a strong case against anything-goes interpretivism, arguing that sociology is in fact a cumulative discipline capable of generating reliable findings. While sociology lacks a cognitive consensus and the rapid discovery model that underpins the natural sciences it is quite efficient in explaining social processes through the use of empirically gathered evidence. For Collins, the very fact that the leading sociological theories might interpret the same evidence in a very different way says more about the lack of cognitive consensus, often grounded in ideological disputes, than about the quality of research that has been undertaken.

Thus, *Conflict Sociology* was written as an attempt to integrate and synthesise the compatible elements of what are usually regarded as incompatible sociological approaches: Weberian, Marxist, Durkheimian and Goffmanian analytical traditions. By zooming in on the results of empirical research in state formation, social stratification, market evolution and everyday interactions, among others, Collins aims to show that the cumulative knowledge of sociology can help us explain a wide range of social situations. In this context, he develops a conflict-oriented approach that incorporates some tenets of the Marxist theory of class struggle but also offers a much wider understanding of social conflict. In a similar vein he integrates some key propositions of Durkheimian/Goffmanian theory, yet these ideas are now linked to wider social processes. For example, in contrast to conventional views, which see Marx, Weber, Durkheim and Goffman as providing a mutually incompatible explanation, Collins finds a great deal of similarity between them. Not only do Marx and Weber both offer a conflict-centred theory of stratification, but their main ideas are also consistent with those of Goffman and Durkheim. Although Collins emphasises the significance of Weber's original understanding of conflict, he links this to the contributions of Goffman and Durkheim:

> Durkheim and Goffman are to be seen as amplifying our knowledge of the mechanisms of emotional production, but within the framework of Weber's conflict theory. For Weber retains a crucial emphasis:

> The creation of emotional solidarity does not supplant conflict but is one of the main weapons used in conflict. Emotional rituals can be used for domination within a group or organization; they are a vehicle by which alliances are formed in the struggle against other groups; and they can be used to impose a hierarchy of status prestige in which some groups dominate others by providing an ideal to emulate under inferior conditions. (1975: 56–61)

This focus on synthesis, albeit on Weberian terms, is also present in his later works on nation-states, geopolitics, violence and war. In all of these studies he sees conflict as a defining feature of social life. Hence, his *Weberian Sociological Theory* (1986), *Macro-History* (1999) and many journal articles develop a macro-level, conflict-centred analysis of social relations. The starting point of this approach is that human beings are sociable and conflict-prone creatures who strive to maximise their status position. However, as humans are generally averse to violence the overt forms of conflict require an organisationally generated mobilisation of individuals. In the modern world the pre-eminent organisational power is the nation-state. For Collins nation-states are defined not only by their legitimate monopoly on the use of violence over a particular territory, but also by incessant status struggle.

He sees nation-states as organisations involved in the geopolitical struggle over prestige, power and resources. More specifically he argues that nation-states rely on nationalism as a principal source of legitimacy: the presence of real or fictitious external threats tends to increase social cohesion and thus help mobilise public support for the state's rulers. The symbolic or material victories in the international arena tend to enhance the prestige of individual nation-states and this is also often perceived as an increase in the prestige of populations inhabiting such states. As Collins puts it: this resembles football fandom as loyalty is boosted by victories: 'A victorious state experiences the greatest nationalism ... [while] a long string of defeats saps national loyalty' (1986: 155). The geopolitical position of nation-states is also determined by the size and location of their territory. Collins distinguishes between the heartland and marchland territorial organisations whereby the former tends to possess certain advantages in material resources (larger population size, wider tax base and greater natural resources) while the latter are more capable of defending their borders and preserving their geopolitical autonomy. Hence prolonged wars tend to affect adversely the heartland states as they tend to over-expand militarily (having to maintain large military forces far from the capitals) and politically (incorporating culturally too diverse populations).

More recently, Collins has shifted his attention towards the micro-level dimensions of conflict. In particular, in his book *Violence: A Micro-Sociological Theory* (2008) he explores how human beings engage in and disengage from violent conflicts. Drawing on a variety of empirical sources including videos, photography and eyewitness testimony, Collins argues that most people are averse to the use of violence in face-to-face interactions and are also incompetent in violent encounters. Since violence breaches the everyday routine and collectively entertains ritual co-operation, most individuals avoid face-to-face violent encounters, and when trapped in such situations they tend to be paralysed by confrontational tension and fear. For Collins (2013: 33), this pattern characterises all face-to-face violence: 'where human confrontation raises emotional stress to such a level that fighters become clumsy and are paralysed or wildly incompetent in using their weapons. In combat of all kinds, the height of courage is usually just to keep oneself from running away.' Hence, in contrast to the popular media representations of violence as being ubiquitous and easy to do, most instances of violent conflict entail prolonged organisational work involving the development of techniques for training human beings to be efficient fighters. However, even after centuries of such organisationally imposed training practices most violent acts including homicides or war-related killings are undertaken by a 'violent few' who are capable of transcending the confrontational tension/fear dynamics.

The Sociology of Educational and Intellectual Networks

Another important topic that features prominently in Collins' research opus is the social production of knowledge. His 1979 book *The Credential Society: A Historical Sociology of Education and Stratification* offered a path-breaking analysis of educational credentials in the contemporary world. In contrast to the popular perceptions that see education as a highly successful mechanism for social mobility, Collins demonstrates convincingly that in fact the educational attainment rarely if ever can dramatically transform the patterns of social stratification. Collins also challenges the conventional functionalist accounts that link social development and technological advancements to the continuous expansion of education that generates a highly skilled workforce needed to fulfil new job requirements. However, using a variety of empirical evidence Collins shows that there is a very weak link between one's formal educational credentials and the actual job skill requirements.

Rather than focusing primarily on the development of requisite cognitive and instrumental skills, the educational systems are generally centred on inculcating the conventional values of propriety and sociability (Collins, 1979: 19). Instead of providing expertise, the public school system is first and foremost a mechanism of secondary socialisation focused on teaching and promoting the middle-class values centred on individual achievement and competition. In an argument reminiscent of Bourdieu's theory of social reproduction, which was developed around the same time, Collins argues that the US public educational systems reproduce middle-class cultural values and, in this way, preserve the existing political, cultural and economic monopolies of the Anglo-Protestant elites. In the US context, this monopoly is preserved through the existence of prestigious schools and colleges where the children of the elite are selectively separated and trained to maintain the existing power positions. For Collins, a key feature of the modern educational system is the formal credentials which allow movement towards the next level of education or to better employment prospects. In other words, the possession of requisite skills matters less than formal diplomas and degrees: 'the rise of a competitive system for producing abstract cultural currency in the form of educational credentials has been the major new force shaping stratification in twentieth-century America' (1979: 94). Hence the students become preoccupied with attaining formal qualifications rather than mastering the requisite skills. For Collins the educational credentials have become 'artificial goods' required for obtaining respectable occupational positions.

Furthermore, his study has demonstrated that the continuous expansion of educational systems and the dramatic increase in the number of people with college degrees have not substantially changed the levels of inequality. Instead the extensive expansion of educational institutions and students accepted at third-level colleges has stimulated an inflation of 'credentialism'. For Collins, this concept stands for the never-ending pursuit of the more advanced degrees rooted in a misguided expectation that such degrees will lead towards better-paid and more respected jobs that bring about higher social status. Nevertheless, this continuous chase for more and better degrees coupled with the ever-increasing proliferation of educational systems ultimately generates a credential inflation of individuals with high degrees who often end up disappointed as their expectations could not be met.

While Collins' early work was more focused on the institutions and the mass production and use of knowledge, his later publications tackle the elite level as well. More specifically he analyses how intellectuals generate new knowledge and how some theories and approaches attain public visibility and influence while others remain marginal. In his magnus opus *The Sociology of Philosophies: A Global Theory of Intellectual Change* (1998), based on over 30 years of research, Collins explores the rise, expansion and decline of various intellectual networks throughout the course of human history. He compares and contrasts the dominant philosophical traditions of thought in ancient Greece, China, India, Japan, medieval Christendom, the Islamic and Jewish cultural worlds as well as the leading philosophical schools of modern Europe. In this study he debunks the popular idea of an individual genius by demonstrating how much of knowledge production emerges as a collective enterprise of relatively small networks of well-connected thinkers. This massive, macro-historical analysis traces the long-term patterns of intellectual change by zooming in on the social processes that make the particular intellectual positions dominant.

Collins argues that there is a limit on how many different philosophical schools could develop and sustain their ideas in the existing intellectual attention space. By comparing different historical and geographical contexts, Collins concludes that regardless of the diverse structural environments and the ideas they articulate, the history of intellectual networks follows a similar pattern: only a small number of philosophical positions have managed to establish themselves as viable in the public eye – mostly no more than six at the same time. For Collins intellectual development entails the presence of organisationally and ideologically well-established schools of thought that often depend on inter-generational chains and are regularly engaged in competition with other such schools. Hence, creativity involves more than new ideas, it requires internal and external dynamics – the continuous vigorous disagreements within a particular school of thought as well as the external shocks and ideational attacks. In this context, intellectual creativity is dependent on the internalised conversations with the leading contemporary thinkers as well as with the most influential historical figures that have shaped the legacies of distinct philosophical traditions.

However, Collins does not treat these intellectual networks as homogeneous or egalitarian communes of scholars. Instead, he emphasises that most such networks are internally stratified and shaped around different levels of solidarity, and these factors often influence the internal dynamics of these networks. He shows how the personal ties within schools (i.e. master and disciples) and between different schools impact on the wider intellectual change, but he also stresses that much of intellectual development entails inter- and intra-organisational links between different networks. When such organisational vessels are well embedded within the wider networks one can witness the proliferation of creativity, as was the case in ancient Greece and China as well the Islamic world between the eighth and thirteenth century. In all of these cases, new ideas and practices emerged in the context of organisational interaction and dialogue between very different schools of thought. In his view, the creative developments entail the existence of many organisational networks involved in protracted conflicts of ideas centred around a small number of prominent and interlinked schools of thought capable of attracting wider attention. In contrast, intellectual stagnation tends to be defined by a pronounced lack of dialogue and interaction between the networks or when networks become too decentralised.

Interaction Ritual Chains

Despite traditionally being characterised as a new-Weberian sociologist, Collins owes just as much to Durkheim and Goffman. This is most apparent in his micro-sociological studies, most of which centre on the ritualistic, routinised and emotional underpinnings of social life. This line of analysis was already present in his early works including *Conflict Sociology* (1975) but has become much more visible in his recent publications, such as *Interactional Ritual Chains* (2004), *Violence: A Micro-Sociological Theory* (2008) and *Napoleon Never Slept: How Great Leaders Leverage Social Energy* (2015, with McConnell). In these three books Collins articulates a micro-sociological approach which posits emotions and what he calls 'interaction ritual chains' as the driving force of the micro-social life. For Collins human beings differ in terms of their emotional energy. By this term he means 'the amount of emotional power that flows through one's action' (1988: 362). The emotional energy is not fixed nor confined to a specific emotion. Rather it represents a continuum that ranges from very high levels of enthusiasm, confidence and determination to achieve a particular goal to very low feelings of apathy, depression, lack of confidence or self-doubt. In Collins' view, high-energy individuals feel 'pumped up, bodily and mentally' and they are as a rule forward moving and proactive (Collins and McConnell, 1915).

However, Collins attempts to avoid a form of psychological determinism by focusing instead on how individual emotional energy translates into collective action and also how collective behaviour helps generate and sustain high levels of emotional energy. In this context, he introduces the concept of 'interaction ritual chains', which stands for the social mechanism through which people create shared symbols of group membership that enhance one's emotional energy. In other words, for Collins successful social action entails the presence of symbolically charged interaction rituals that help generate and sustain group solidarity. Drawing on Schegeloff and Sacks' micro-interactional analysis of conversations, as well as on Turner and Barbalet's sociology of emotions, Collins posits interaction rituals as the driving force of collective action. In his view, interaction ritual is a causal mechanism that helps explain the variations in group behaviour. It is often reflected in, and thus can be measured through, the level of collective attachments to group symbols and through the degree of inter-group solidarity. For Collins, a high intensity of interaction rituals can be observed in the focused attention of group members, regularly characterised by shared bodily rhythms as well as by their co-ordinated emotional action. Linking Durkheim and Goffman, Collins argues that interaction ritual chains can generate high emotional energy that periodically is transformed into collective effervescence – the state when members of a group simultaneously communicate, share the same thoughts and participate in the same action.

However, unlike Durkheim who sees collective effervescence as a durable macro phenomenon, Collins is adamant that such shared and intense feelings of group belonging are temporary phenomena, mostly confined to small groups. In contrast to Durkheim, who writes about relatively stable and fixed collective personalities, Collins shifts attention towards social situations where reflexive individuals become caught in interaction ritual networks. In other words, Collins analyses social action as a dynamic process whereby individuals flow from situation to situation and are drawn towards interactions that are likely to generate greater payoff in terms of their emotional energy. Hence, interaction rituals operate in market-like environments where individuals tend to compete over participation in the best rituals their cultural capital could give them access to. In his own words:

> what allows an IR [Interaction Ritual] to be constructed is assembling human bodies in face-to-face interaction. Further ingredients are the rapid back-and-forth of micro-behaviors (voice tones and rhythms,

bodily movements); focusing attention on the same thing and thereby recognizing mutual intersubjectivity; feeling the same emotion or mood. When these ingredients reach a sufficiently high level, they intensify through a system of feedbacks: emotions grow stronger; bodily gestures and voice patterns become closely coordinated, down to the level of micro-fractions of a second. A successful IR builds up to a condition of high entrainment in a shared rhythm that Durkheim called collective effervescence. At high levels, this is what humans experience as the most powerful force in their lives; it constitutes the great moments and shapes their most deeply held views and values. Thus, human action is oriented around the attractiveness of different situations of social interaction: we are motivated towards those that are more successful IRs, and away from those that are mediocre or failed IRs. (2011: 25 January)

Collins applies these ideas to a variety of social situations including the evolution of love and sex, smoking rituals, the changing patterns of social stratification and to the modern Western elite ritualism of power and deference, among many others.

Contemporary Relevance and Applications

Collins is a highly prolific and creative author who has generated a plethora of new concepts, ideas and theories, many of which have been applied to different areas of social life. For example, his work on credential society has been widely used to assess the role credentialism plays in different spheres of society, including race relations in the labour market (Gaddis, 2015), higher education in Korea (Jung, 1985), and the patterns of stratification in Japan (Ishida and Slater, 2009) among others. More recently scholars have deployed Collins' theory of interactional ritual chains to explain the role religious institutions play in the contemporary world.

For example, Wellman et al. (2014) utilise Collins' work to assess sociologically the character of the megachurch phenomenon that has spread throughout American society. After selecting a representative sample of 12 such church congregations (out of 1,250 known megachurches in the United States) they conducted a survey and organised focus groups to find out more about the social dynamics of megachurch congregations. Their study challenges the conventional interpretations that see megachurches as entities unable to generate genuine feelings of belonging. Drawing on Collins' theory, they demonstrate convincingly that rather than standing for the insincere form of religiosity centred on public entertainment, megachurches in fact foster intense feelings of group identity. As Wellman et al. argue, the megachurches are successful interaction ritual venues where individuals experience strong emotional bonds, a heightened sense of spirituality and shared feelings of morality, all of which contribute toward fostering the increased emotional energy of churchgoers.

COLLINS AND THE 1968 GENERATION

The context of Collins' intellectual development is paradigmatic of a great sea change that took place in American sociology after 1968, whereby the coming of age of 'Generation X' ruptured what had been previously taken for granted. Parsons's structural functionalism lost its near-hegemonic hold on the discipline, giving way to a plurality of micro and meso perspectives, of which the symbolic interactionism of Goffman and Blumer is usually the most noted. The focus on consensus was replaced by conflict, and the concern with stasis was replaced by radical social change in the historical context of an American society that suddenly seemed altogether different in light of an explosion of new social movements. From this perspective, Collins' oeuvre is a profound intellectual encapsulation of much broader historical and intellectual tendencies that shaped his biography.

Collins' work on violence has also been an inspiration for many scholars. For example, both Nicole Rafter and Stefan Klusemann have recently used Collins' concepts to explain the dynamics of genocide. For Rafter (2016) the notions of 'turning point' and 'hot and cold violence' help us explain how potentially violent situations can turn into actual violence and also how the individuals involved in genocides operate within a particular emotional group space. Similarly, Klusemann deploys Collins' concepts of forward panic and the emotional dominance in violent situations.

For Collins, a turning point is a condition when the feelings of tension/fear are abruptly resolved through redirection or the reorganisation of emotions of all involved in the interactional process – the antagonists, the audience and bystanders. Rafter works with this concept to explore how the genocidal processes unfold. She identifies the key turning points in several genocides. In the case of the Herrero and Nama genocide that took place between 1904 and 1907 the turning point was German General von Throta's signing of the order to exterminate these populations (which resulted in up to 100,000 deaths, two-thirds of the Herrero population). In the 1915 genocide of Armenians the turning point was 24 April when the Turkish military started attacking Armenian civilians. In the Rwandan case the turning point was the shooting down of President Habyarimana's aircraft in April 1994. All of these situations involved what Collins refers to as the reorganisation of emotions as an interactional process involving those present.

As Rafter (2016) points out, these turning points were decisive in reframing victims as enemies and the perpetuators as righteous avengers. These situations transformed individual perceptions of reality, generated new emotional dynamics and contributed substantially towards the forging of new identities. Thus, these moments of strong emotional change create conditions for violence as the feelings of tension and fear are often violently resolved by attacking weak adversaries who cannot defend themselves. These turning points stimulate violent outbursts as the perpetrators are involved in an emotionally charged and communally shared sense of righteousness. Rafter identifies this pattern of behaviour among the genocide perpetrators in 1915 Turkey, 1904–7 Namibia and 1966–90 Guatemala, all of whom shared similar emotional dynamics. Rafter also uses Collins' distinction between hot and cold violence, demonstrating how the transition from potential to actual violent escalation is regularly mediated by a shared emotional change. For example, the Rwandan genocide generated a strong sense of camaraderie among those directly involved in mass killings:

> Suddenly Hutus of every kind were patriotic brothers without any partisan discord... We forgot all quarrels and who had fallen out with whom in the past ... we had work to do and we were doing our best ... we were no longer in our each-to-his-own mood. We were doing a job to order. We were lining up behind everyone's enthusiasm. We gathered into teams on the soccer field and went out hunting as kindred spirits. (Rafter, 2016: 101)

Stefan Klusemann (2010) also draws on Collins' theory of violence although his focus is more on the relationship between emotional and physical dominance in violent conflicts. By analysing the dynamics of mass killings in the 1995 Srebrenica massacres Klusemann shows how the Bosnian Serb military established not only physical but also emotional dominance over the Bosnian Muslim population, which was then slaughtered en masse. The mass killings followed the gradual build up of emotional dominance:

> we saw an emotional flow over time with a build-up phase and a situational trigger when the peace-keeping commander showed himself paralyzed in the face of an implicit threat to kill both UN troops and refugees, and the defeated Muslims themselves turned passive. It was at this moment that the local commander gave the order for the massacre. Locally given orders to kill, where they occur, are themselves the result of micro interactions and their emotional outcomes. (Klusemann, 2010: 289)

In this case, just as in other instances of mass murder as discussed by Rafter, the perpetrators were engaging in what Collins calls a 'forward panic'. This concept stands for a process through which the fear and tension that follow violent situations are abruptly released, leading towards unprecedented acts of violent behaviour. Hence in Srebrenica, just as in Rwanda or in Namibia, the perpetrators 'resolved' their emotional tension by entering an 'emotional tunnel of violent attack', taking a 'moral holiday' and engaging in exceptional acts of cruelty (Collins, 2008: 85–7).

Criticisms

Collins' intellectual opus is vast and rather bold in its attempt to produce generalised sociological theories that on the one hand successfully link the macro and micro worlds and on the other hand provide a strong empirical grounding for the key theoretical tenets. This highly ambitious undertaking has inevitably encountered criticisms from different quarters.[1] For example, some critics have questioned Collins' attempt to bring together very different sociological traditions of research. In particular his earlier, more politically materialist, neo-Weberian approach has recently been amalgamated with the more culturalist turn heavily influenced by Durkheim and Goffman's work on interaction, emotions and rituals.

Thus Patrick Baehr (1999) finds this attempt at explanatory synthesis problematic: 'A sociological interpretation is only as powerful and illuminating as the categories it employs; Collins' derive from a mélange of theories of conflict, of interaction ritual, of exchange and of social networks... But his categories run out of steam when they are turned on the social psychology of intellectuals.'

For Baehr, Collins' theoretical apparatus does not explain successfully how the inner process of intellectual life operates. While Baehr zooms in on the lack of psychological and micro-sociological depth in Collins' approach, Gilbert (2016) questions Collins' macro sociology. Gilbert argues that Collin's overemphasis on face-to-face emotional interaction cannot fully capture the long-term historical dynamics of emotional change. For Gillbert, Collins makes a similar mistake to Talcott Parsons in reducing the emotional dynamics to the micro-level interaction. This contrasts with Elias's analysis, which explores emotional mechanics through long-term civilising processes.

Collins' early, more Weberian, work on conflict, status and prestige has been periodically criticised by neo-Marxist and other neo-functionalist perspectives. However, it is his recent studies on intellectuals, interactional ritual chains and violence that have received much more critical attention.

Although there is a near-unanimous agreement among sociologists that *The Sociology of Philosophies* is a monumental piece of work, some scholars have been critical of different aspects of this study. For example, Steve Fuller (2000) argues that Collins' book sticks too closely to the philosophers' own understanding of the history of philosophy. Hence, Collins is seen to be guilty of not exposing fully the reflexive implications of philosophers' own belief systems that underpin their distinct approaches. Fuller believes that *The Sociology of Philosophies* privileges epistemology and metaphysics over value theory as the principal forces driving the history of philosophy and as such cannot adequately capture the political consequences of philosophical thinking.

Baehr (1999) and Misztal and Freundlieb (2003) focus more on Collins' lack of engagement with individual intellectuals and the inner dynamics of creativity. Hence Misztal and Freundlieb describe Collins' argument as 'historically determinist' while Baehr claims that Collins overemphasises the role networks play in this process and underestimates the individual motivation of philosophers. In his own words:

> But what, then, has happened to the 'inner processes of intellectual life' now that creativity has been subsumed under attention seeking,

> the emulation of heroes, and the brute realities of success and reputation?... Did Boris Pasternak write *Dr. Zhivago* to seek access to the 'attention space?' Obviously, there would have been no point in writing the book without the hope that it would one day be read. But why did Pasternak hope for that eventuality? ... the motives of intellectuals are complex, and success, or the expectation of it, is not their only *sine qua non*. Nor is the source of intellectual 'exultation' reducible to 'ideas that feel successful'. The sense that ideas are apposite or beautiful is also a powerful source of exhilaration. (Baehr, 1999: 2)

Collins' work on interaction ritual chains has also experienced some criticism. In particular several commentators find his concept of emotional energy too metaphorical or underdeveloped. When describing intense emotional energy Collins resorts to rather colloquial words such as 'feeling pumped up ... confident and proactive, forward moving' (Collins and McConnell, 2015) which are not easy to operationalise or measure. Boyns and Luery see Collins' key concept as being too vague and disconnected from the concrete emotions:

> While Collins clearly conceptualizes what he means by emotional energy, it remains ambiguous how emotional energy might be operationally defined or empirically measured. It is also uncertain how emotional energy can be linked to concrete, primary emotions—like fear, anger, sadness, or happiness—or to secondary elaborations of primary emotions—like pride, shame, love, and embarrassment. (2015: 149)

Furthermore, they argue that Collins uses this concept in a rather asymmetrical sense: instead of exploring the variety of emotional states his focus is almost exclusively on the positive side of emotional energy. In contrast Boyns and Luery (2015: 149) point towards the 'dark side' of interaction ritual chains when emotional energy is driven by negative emotions such as enmity, irritation, frustration, anger, shame, hatred or rage, among others. They conclude that since Collins' theory is focused almost solely upon positive emotions: 'it hasn't reached its full expression in articulating the ritual dynamics of the dark side of emotional experiences' (2015: 149).

Other critics have raised issues about Collins' theory of violence. Both Kalyvas (2011) and Wieviorka (2014) question his overemphasis on the micro-interactional side of violent encounters. Kalyvas insists that Collins' work does not engage with the meso level of analysis and as such over-aggregates the concept of violence, while Wieviorka believes that Collins' approach too closely resembles that of symbolic interactionism, and as such, cannot adequately address the issue of subjectivation in violence. In his critical review, Armstrong (2008) also questions Collins' lack of engagement with the neurophysiological aspects of emotions or the fact that the majority of violent acts are committed by young men. Furthermore, Armstrong argues that Collins relies too much on the abstract concepts that have rather transcendental quality, such as solidarity and the confrontational tension/fear, while the idea and practice of violence changes through time, hence requiring to be historically situated. Armstrong (2008: 984) also feels that the following sociological questions have not be addressed by Collins:

> how does Collins' theorizing bear on the literature in gender studies that situates rape within broad, patriarchal power structures? What are the practical considerations of Collins' assertion that acting like a victim helps to intensify violent situations?... What are the ontological foundations that allow for a mechanical separation of micro situational and macro historical factors?'

Conclusion

Collins' work is characterised by its depth, variability, creative synthesis and novelty of highly applicable concepts and theories. Although many of his concepts, such as 'credential society', 'emotional energy', 'the micro foundations of macro sociology', 'forward panic' and 'interaction ritual chains', have found use and application throughout the social sciences and humanities, Collins has yet to be recognised as a sociologist of similar stature to Bourdieu or Habermas. In this chapter we explored his main contributions and the broader social, political and historical contexts that influenced his life's work. We have also briefly analysed the recent applications and some criticisms of his theories. Despite these critiques there is no doubt that Randall Collins has made marked and long-lasting contribution to sociological theory.

Note

1 See the special issue of *Thesis Eleven* dedicated to critical assessments of Collins' entire intellectual opus (Malešević and Loyal, 2019).

References

Armstrong, P. (2008) Book Review: Violence: A Micro-Sociological Theory by Randall Collins. *Canadian Journal of Sociology*, 33(4), pp. 982–5.
Baehr, P. (1999) Review of 'The Sociology of Philosophies'. *Canadian Journal of Sociology*. Available at: https://sites.ualberta.ca/~cjscopy/reviews/socofphil.html
Black, M. (2012) *The Social Theories of Talcott Parsons*. New York: Prentice Hall.
Boyns, D. and Luery, S. (2015) Negative Emotional Energy: A Theory of the 'Dark-Side' of Interaction Ritual Chains. *Social Sciences*, 4(1), pp. 148–70.
Byungjoo, J. (1985) *A Study of the Korean Higher Education Expansion: A Status Competition Theory*. Seoul: Chungang University Press.

Collins, R. (1978) *The Case of the Philosophers' Ring*. Brighton: Harvester Press.

Collins, R. (1975) *Conflict Sociology: Toward an Explanatory Science*. New York: Academic Press.

Collins, R. (1978) Prediction in Macrosociology: The Case of the Soviet Collapse. *American Journal of Sociology*, 100(6), pp. 1552–93.

Collins, R. (1979) *The Credential Society: An Historical Sociology of Education and Stratification*. New York: Academic Press.

Collins, R. (1981a) *Sociology Since Mid-Century: Essays in Theory Cumulation*. New York: Academic Press.

Collins, R. (1981b) The Micro-foundations of Macro-sociology. *American Journal of Sociology*, 86, pp. 984–1014.

Collins, R. (1982) *Sociological Insight: An Introduction to Non-Obvious Sociology*. New York: Oxford University Press.

Collins, R. (1985a) *Sociology of Marriage and Family: Gender, Love and Property*. Chicago, IL: Nelson-Hall.

Collins, R. (1985b) *Three Sociological Traditions*. Oxford: Oxford University Press.

Collins, R. (1985c) *Max Weber: A Skeleton Key*. London: Sage.

Collins, R. (1986) *Weberian Sociological Theory*. Cambridge: Cambridge University Press.

Collins, R. (1988) *Theoretical Sociology*. London: Harcourt Brace Jovanovich.

Collins, R. (1998) *The Sociology of Philosophies: A Global Theory of Intellectual Change*. Cambridge, MA: Harvard University Press.

Collins, R. (1999) *Macro-History: Essays in Sociology of the Long Run*. Stanford, CA: Stanford University Press.

Collins, R. (2004) *Interaction Ritual Chains*. Princeton, NJ: Princeton University Press.

Collins, R. (2008) *Violence: A Micro-Sociological Theory*. Princeton, NJ: Princeton University Press.

Collins, R. (2011) Interaction Rituals and the New Electronic Media. *The Sociological Eye: Writings by the Sociologist Randall Collins* [blog]. 25 January. Available at: http://sociological-eye.blogspot.com/2011/01/interaction-rituals-and-new-electronic.html (accessed 14 May 2019).

Collins, R. (2013) Does Nationalist Sentiment Increase Fighting Efficacy? A Skeptical View from the Sociology of Violence. In: J. A. Hall and S. Malešević (eds) *Nationalism and War*. Cambridge: Cambridge University Press, pp. 31–43.

Collins, R. and McConnell, M. (2015) *Napoleon Never Slept: How Great Leaders Leverage Social Energy* [e-book]. San Diego: Maren Ink.

Collins, R. and Makovsky, M. (1972) *The Discovery of Society*. New York: Random House.

Fuller, S. (2000) In Search of an Alternative Sociology of Philosophy: Reinstating the Primacy of Value Theory in Light of Randall Collins's 'Reflexivity and Embeddedness in the History of Ethical Philosophies'. *Philosophy of the Social Sciences*, 30(2), pp. 246–56.

Gaddis, S. M. (2015) Discrimination in the Credential Society: An Audit Study of Race and College Selectivity in the Labor Market. *Social Forces*, 93(4), pp. 1451-79.

Gilbert, T. K. (2016) Elias and the Sociology of Ideas: A Critique of Randall Collins's Microsociology of Intellectual Change. *Human Figurations*, 5(1), pp. 1-5.

Iranzo, J. M. (2015) Collins, Randall (1941-). *International Encyclopedia of the Social & Behavioral Sciences*, 2nd edition, Vol. 4. New York: Elsevier, pp. 211-17.

Ishida, H. and Slater, D. (2009) *Social Class in Contemporary Japan: Structures, Sorting and Strategies*. London: Routledge.

Kalyvas, S. (2011) Comment on Randall Collins: Linking the Micro and the Macro in the Study of Violence. *Sociologica*, 2, pp. 1-4.

Klusemann, S. (2010) Micro-situational Antecedents of Violent Atrocity. *Sociological Forum*, 25(2), pp. 272-95.

Maclean, A. and Yocom, J. (2000) Interview with Randall Collins [online]. Available at: https://www.ssc.wisc.edu/theoryatmadison/papers/ivwCollins.pdf (accessed 14 May 2019).

Malešević, S. and Loyal, S. (2019) Introduction to Special Issue: The Sociology of Randall Collins. *Thesis Eleven*, 154(1), pp. 3-10.

Misztal, B. and Freundlieb, D. (2003) The Curious Historical Determinism of Randall Collins. *European Journal of Sociology*, 44(2), pp. 247-69.

Rafter, N. (2016) *The Crime of All Crimes: Toward a Criminology of Genocide*. New York: New York University Press.

Wallerstein, I., Collins, R., Mann, M., Derluguian, G. and Calhoun, C. (2013) *Does Capitalism Have a Future?* Oxford: Oxford University Press.

Wellman, J. K., Corcoran, K. E. and Stockly-Meyerdirk, K. (2014) 'God is like a drug ...': Explaining Interaction Ritual Chains in American Megachurches. *Sociological Forum*, 29(3), pp. 650-72.

Wieviorka, M. (2014) The Sociological Analysis of Violence: New Perspectives. *Sociological Review*, 62(2), pp. 50-64.

De Beauvoir, Oakley and Smith

Introduction

Since its foundation as an independent academic discipline sociology has been dominated by men. The long-term legacy of the patriarchal social order that directed much of human history was also reflected within sociological theory where there were very few women's voices. Furthermore, this implicit or explicit silencing of women meant that mainstream sociologists have tended to neglect or ignore topics that underpin gender divisions within the social order. Hence even gender-sensitive scholars have largely reproduced the norms and assumptions that upheld the male-centred social order as a norm. Although some early female scholars such as Christine de Pizan, Margaret Cavendish and Mary Wollstonecraft have challenged these male-centric views, it is only in the twentieth century that one encounters fully developed, feminist, sociological perspectives. In this chapter we present the contributions of the three, now classical, feminist authors who have articulated original approaches that have influenced sociological thought – Simone de Beauvoir, Ann Oakley and Dorothy Smith. The chapter briefly explores the biographical and intellectual trajectory of these three scholars and then looks at the wider social and political contexts that have shaped their worldviews. We then explore their key theoretical contributions, provide a brief look at the contemporary relevance of their work and also identify some critiques of the feminist tradition of research within sociology.

Life and Intellectual Context

Simone Lucie Ernestine Marie Bertrand de Beauvoir

De Beauvoir was born in Paris in 1908. She grew up in a middle-class family that experienced a degree of downward mobility as it lost much of its wealth after the First World War. Her mother came from a very wealthy and highly conservative family of bankers, while her father was a civil servant with a strong interest in the arts, literature and acting. De Beauvoir attended a private convent school, the Institut Adeline Désir. Although as a child she was a devoted Catholic, by the age of 14 she had abandoned her old belief system and became an atheist. Simone's father was an important early influence as he encouraged her intellectual curiosity and also provided young Simone with the key works of world literature. De Beauvoir was a diligent and bright student who in 1925, at age 17, passed all her baccalauréat exams in mathematics and philosophy. In the same year she enrolled to study mathematics at the Institut Catholique and literature and languages at the Institut Sainte-Marie.

In 1926, she passed her exams for the Certificate of Higher Studies in French literature and Latin and soon embarked on studying philosophy at the Sorbonne. Between 1927 and 1928 she passed the exams in all of her subjects (including sociology) and wrote a graduate thesis on Leibniz under the supervision of a leading philosopher, Léon Brunschvicg. She was also required to complete teaching practice at the local lycée, which she undertook, together with her fellow students and later leading thinkers – Claude Lévi-Strauss and Maurice Merleau-Ponty. In 1929, de Beauvoir took second place in the highly prestigious and very competitive philosophy agrégation exam at École Normale Supérieure. Even though she was not a registered student Simone attended the classes and took exams where she beat all the other students who took the extensive preparatory tutorials and only lost to Jean-Paul Sartre who was retaking the same exam. At 21 years of age, de Beauvoir was the youngest student ever to pass this exam and was also the youngest philosophy teacher in France at that time. During this period, she met Sartre and they developed a lifelong intellectual and romantic relationship that only ended with his death in 1980. Their, at that time highly unusual, open relationship had a detrimental impact on de Beauvoir's career.

The deeply patriarchal attitudes of the interwar France affected de Beauvoir's reputation and her intellectual development, and she was periodically reprimanded for her feminism, pacifism and liberal attitudes towards sexuality. In the 1930s and 1940s, she worked as a teacher in several lycées in France. During and after the war she published several highly influential works which made de Beauvoir a household name in France and later throughout the world. In the 1970s she became very active in the women's liberation movement in France, pushing for the legalisation of abortion and other causes. Simone de Beauvoir died from pneumonia in 1986.

Ann Rosamund Oakley

Oakley (née Titmuss) was born in London in 1944 into an academic household. Her father was a professor of social policy at the London School of Economics, whose work influenced substantially the British government's welfare state policies. Her mother was a social worker. Oakley was educated at

Haberdashers' Aske's School for Girls. This period was important as the young Oakley became politically radicalised in this environment and had also experienced a nervous breakdown. In 1962, she was enrolled for a degree in philosophy, politics and economics at Somerville College, Oxford. She also took a sociology course in 1964, which was a newly offered subject in Oxford. After graduating from Oxford in 1965, Oakley focused on writing novels, short stories and scripts for children's television programmes. Soon after she returned to full-time studies at Bedford College, University of London, where she gained a PhD with a thesis on women's attitudes to housework, in 1969. The research collected for the thesis was later used for writing three highly influential academic books on the sociology of housework, all published in the early 1970s.

By this time Oakley had also become active in the British feminist movement, advocating liberation and the emancipation of women. In the 1970s she was employed as a researcher at Bedford College, where she published another two important books on the transition to motherhood. In addition to her academic work, Oakley continued to write fiction and poetry. Although she wrote several novels over the years it was only in 1988 that one of them was published and achieved a great deal of success – *The Men's Room* (1988). This work was also made into a BBC television film series. Throughout the 1990s she published six other novels. In 1985, she was appointed deputy director of the Thomas Coram Research Unit at the Institute of Education, University of London. In 1990, Oakley established and headed the new research unit at the Institute focusing on health, education and welfare (SSRU). In 2011 she received a Lifetime Achievement Award from the British Sociological Association.

Dorothy E. Smith

Smith (née Place) was born in Northallerton, England, in 1926. She grew up in a middle-class family. Her education was interrupted by war as she had to take a variety of paid work during and after the war. She soon settled into the role of a clerical assistant for a publishing house in London. Nevertheless, Smith was eager to continue her education and finally was accepted in her 20s as an undergraduate student at the London School of Economics (LSE), where she attained a bachelor's degree in sociology and social anthropology, in 1955. At the LSE she had the opportunity to work with several young lecturers who would later shape British sociology, including David Lockwood, Ralph Dahrendorf and Norman Birnbaum, among others. She decided to continue her studies in the United States and enrolled in the PhD sociology programme at the University of California, Berkeley.

At Berkeley, she was introduced to diverse sociological traditions of thought but was influenced particularly by phenomenology and symbolic interactionism. She was highly impressed by Tamotsu Shibutani's course on interactionism where she learned much about George Herbert Mead's approach that fostered her later interest in Merleau-Ponty's phenomenology. Between 1964 and 1966, she worked as a lecturer at the University of California,

Berkeley, where she also became involved with the women's liberation movement and organised seminars for graduate students where they could share their experiences about gender inequalities in academia. In the late 1960s she lectured briefly at the University of Essex in England and in 1967 accepted a teaching post at the University of British Columbia (UBC) in Vancouver where she soon established a Women's Studies Programme. At UBC she also created an activist women's action group that was focused on improving the status of women. In 1977 Smith moved to Toronto where she was a professor of sociology at the Ontario Institute for Studies in Education. After her retirement she remained an adjunct professor at the University of Victoria.

Historical, Social and Political Context

Although the leading French socialist intellectual, Charles Fourier, coined the term 'feminism' France was not at the forefront of women's rights until well into the mid-twentieth century. In fact, women did not have the right to vote in France until 1944, and the dominance of conservative forces in the post-war period prevented any serious discussions about women's rights. It was the UK, United States and Australia where the first fully fledged feminist movements developed and made a visible impact on social and political life. These movements, often referred as the first wave of feminism, started in the mid-nineteenth century and were mostly centred on promoting gender equality in legal terms with a focus on property rights, marriage, parenting and equal contract rights. The first tangible success of the movement in the UK was the Custody of Infants Act (1839), which for the first time provided that women had the right of custody of their children.

By the end of the nineteenth century the movement was also effective in fostering change in terms of property rights and in 1870 the British parliament approved the Married Women's Property Act. While the patriarchal regimes accepted some, mostly economic, gender reforms, there was much more resistance to political reform. Hence, at the turn of the century the focus shifted towards electoral rights where the Suffragettes and their sympathisers advocated full rights for women to vote and to stand for political office in the UK and its colonies. This movement also developed and spread in North America and later also affected many other countries in Europe, Asia and South America. The Suffragettes were often arrested and regularly exposed to hostile media attacks. However, the leading names of the movements, such as Emmeline Pankhurst in England and Lucretia Mott in the United States, were influential in changing public opinion and have substantially contributed to electoral change. Thus, after the First World War, the UK enacted the Representation of the People Act (1918), which granted the vote to property-owning women over the age of 30 and by 1928, all women over 21 were granted the same right. In the United States the universal suffrage movement achieved its principal goal with the enactment of the nineteenth amendment to the US constitution (1919) that granted the right to vote to women in all states.

The Feminist Waves

Although there were significant feminist voices throughout the early twentieth century it was really in the 1960s that feminist movements became better organised and more vocal. Feminist ideas were largely stifled in the conservative environments of the 1930s in Europe and United States, while the onset of the Second World War contributed to the spread of masculinist militarism and traditional views of gender roles. Although the shortage of labour during the war forced the governments of many Western states to open the labour force to women, at the end of the war governments were eager to establish the pre-war status quo. Nevertheless, despite the intense societal pressure to return to the traditional gender roles the war experience of working women generated a structural change that could not be easily undone. Hence, these tensions came to the fore with the second wave of feminist movements in the 1960s.

Unlike the first wave of feminism, which was preoccupied with a small number of economic and political issues, the 1960s movement focused on a much wider agenda including the economic, political and cultural inequalities of women. The second wave of feminism attempted to emancipate women through activities centred on demonstrating how one's personal experiences are in fact profoundly political because they are structured by the deeply ingrained patriarchal order. To capture this rather hidden form of domination, Carol Hanisch, a feminist author, coined the phrase 'The Personal is Political', which became a popular motto not just for the feminists but also for a variety of counter-cultural movements in the 1960s and early 1970s. In the United States, the feminist movement advocated unconstrained access to the labour force and equal pay for women, and campaigned for the end of gender discrimination in different social spheres.

The publication of Betty Friedan's book *The Feminine Mystique* (1963) had a significant influence on the rise of support for feminist ideas in the United States. In her highly popular book that sold over a million copies, Friedan reflected the widespread discontent and unhappiness that many American women felt as they were stifled by patriarchal gender roles. Her book drew on interviews with well-off suburban housewives who had families but who felt constrained by their mother–wife–homemaker roles. Frieden also dissected how the education system, advertising and women's magazines reproduce the ideals of womanhood that centre on the domestic sphere only, while the public sphere was almost exclusively reserved for men. Frieden was also actively involved in organising demonstrations and public events to voice the frustration with the existing patriarchal order. Hence in 1966 she became the founder and first president of the National Organization for Women (NOW) and was also involved in organising a national strike for women's equality in 1970 that attracted over 50,000 participants.

Women in Europe

The second wave of feminism started later in Europe where some states did not fully implement the demands advocated by the late nineteenth- and early twenty-first-century feminist movements. For example, women in Switzerland did not have the right to vote until 1971 and in some cantons not until 1990. In the Netherlands, France and Ireland married women were not allowed to work until 1957, 1965 and 1973, respectively. In this context Simone de Beauvoir's ideas and particularly her highly influential book *The Second Sex* (1949) contributed substantially to the development of the second wave of feminism in France. Unlike the United States where feminist movements were often aligned either with individualist liberalism or minority rights campaigns, in France feminism was often linked with the more radical left-wing movements. Hence de Beauvoir's blend of existentialist Marxism with feminist ideas found a strong appeal among the political left but was mostly resisted or rejected by other political groups.

France in the 1960s was an unusual case where women had substantial political rights but a highly unequal social status and economic position. The feminist movement only gained in significance with the May 1968 society-wide demonstrations, strikes and civil unrest. In this environment the feminist groups established the Women's Liberation Movement, which focused on the rights to contraception and abortion as well as the bodily and legal autonomy of women. Although the 1967 Neuwirth Law legalised the use of birth control in France the subsequent conservative governments blocked the application of this law until the mid-1970s when Simone Veil became a minister of health and in this capacity made access to contraception easier. In 1975, under organised pressure from various groups including the women's rights organisations, Veil successfully pushed through the legislation that legalised abortion in France despite the stern resistance by her own conservative party MPs. The early writings of de Beauvoir influenced not only gender rights activists but also a new wave of feminist authors who developed the concept of *écriture feminine* ('feminine writing'), which successfully challenged the patriarchal establishment.

The second wave of feminism was also slow to take root in the UK. The post-war emphasis on recovery and the image of the traditional family as a nucleus of the developing states prevented growth of feminist movements until the 1960s and 1970s. Although trade unions and the Labour Party supported some measures that would foster a degree of women's equality, there was little enthusiasm to overhaul the entire social system in order to make it gender equitable. However, the women's liberation movement and other pressure groups of the 1960s managed to influence a change of legislation in several areas, including the introduction of the contraceptive pill on the National Health Service in 1961, for married women, and in 1967, for all women, and the Abortion Act of 1967, which legalised abortions in England, Scotland and Wales.

One of the defining moments of the women's movement in this period was the 1968 Dagenham Ford factory strike for equal pay when sewing machinists led by Rose Boland, Vera Sime and others organised industrial action to protest against the policy where women workers were paid 15% less than men for the same type of labour. The relative success of this strike contributed to the foundation of the National Joint Action Campaign Committee for Women's Equal Rights, which organised demonstrations in London in 1969 and, together with the Ford factory strikers, pushed the British government to pass the Equal Pay Act in 1970. In 1975, parliament also passed the Sex Discrimination Act that outlawed discrimination on the grounds of one's gender or marital status. This changing social environment impacted greatly on the intellectual development of Ann Oakley and Dorothy E. Smith, both of whom grew up and received their undergraduate education in the UK.

Arguments and Ideas

Simone de Beauvoir was not a sociologist in the formal sense and much of her work was transdisciplinary and eclectic. She was also a committed activist who was eager to combine her scholarly work with novels and other writings to impart a particular vision of social change rooted in Marxist and feminist-imbued existentialist philosophy. De Beauvoir was influenced by the diverse social and political thought stretching from Descartes, Kant, Hegel and Marx to Husserl, Heidegger and Bergson. Nevertheless, this heterogeneous intellectual background was fruitfully developed to articulate an original account that focuses on the key sociological and philosophical question of how human beings can live together so that they can experience their freedom without diminishing the freedom of others. De Beauvoir made substantial contributions to sociological thought in three areas: gender and feminism, cultural studies and ethics.

The Second Sex

De Beauvoir's 1949 magnum opus *The Second Sex* is her most influential book. This was a pioneering and revolutionary work that offered one of the first systematic feminist analyses of gender relations. The main argument of this two-volume study is that for much of history women have been oppressed by men through the process of 'Othering'. Drawing on Hegel and Sartre, de Beauvoir articulates an existentialist argument centred on the idea that the self requires otherness to define itself as a subject. In this context women have historically been defined as the Other of men and by men who appropriated the position of the Self. In her own words:

> humanity is male and man defines woman not in herself but as relative to him; she is not regarded as an autonomous being ... she is defined and differentiated with reference to man and not he with reference to her; she is the incidental, the inessential, as opposed to the essential. He is the Subject, he is the Absolute – she is the Other. (de Beauvoir 1965: 8)

Utilising her existentialist concepts, de Beauvoir argues that all human existence involves uncertain interaction between immanence and transcendence.

However, what other existential thinkers neglect is that historically men have been associated with transcendence and intellectual creation, while women were confined to a repetitive and fallow life of persistent immanence. *The Second Sex* explores the myths that sustain the unequal position of the two sexes. She acknowledges that physiology impacts on different gender experiences with women being uniquely associated with menstruation, pregnancy or lactation that men lack. Nevertheless, biological givens do not determine social relations as different social orders establish their own regimes of gender relations which can and do change through time. Hence, for de Beauvoir, gender has less to do with essences and much more to do with social existences. As she puts it starkly: 'One is not born, but rather becomes, a woman. No biological, physical, or economic destiny defines the figure that the human female takes on in society; it is civilisation as a whole that elaborates this intermediary product between the male and the eunuch that is called feminine' (de Beauvoir, 1965: 267). She challenges the established views of women as being born 'feminine', arguing that such perceptions are created through socialisation where women are required to renounce their authentic subjectivities and accept passive roles of feminine objects.

In contrast, men are expected to embrace the role of active and transcendent members of society. In this context women are shackled by the myth of 'eternal feminine' form which they cannot escape. This myth assigns to women collectivist roles such as the mother, the daughter, the wife, the virgin, the motherland or the mother nature through which one's individuality is denied. Men are expected to have individual subjectivities while women are associated with the collectivist roles they perform. Thus, through the myth of the 'eternal feminine', women are expected to conform and aspire to achieving impossibly high expectations set by society – being a caring mother who sacrifices for her children while simultaneously performing the role of loyal wife and the bearer of the family morality. De Beauvoir analyses a variety of documentary evidence to show how gender inequalities and asymmetrical power relationships develop and are sustained by social structures. She explores the role of family, educational systems, the state, media and civil society in reproducing these unequal power relationships. However, as an existentialist she sees all human beings as capable of realising their ontological freedom, which means that patriarchal domination is not inevitable but can be abolished through the full emancipation of women.

De Beauvoir wrote several highly successful novels including *L'Invitée* (She Came to Stay) (1943), *Le Sang des Autres* (The Blood of Others) (1945), *Tous les Hommes sont Mortels* (All Men are Mortal) (1946) and *Les Mandarins* (The Mandarins) (1954), which won the highly regarded Prix Goncourt award. In She Came to Stay, de Beauvoir offers a fictionalised account of a complex romantic and personal relationship between her, Sartre and the Kosakiewicz sisters in the 1930s. This study, highly unusually for its time, explores the ideas of free love, sexual jealousies and the existential battles for selfhood. In this book de Beauvoir explores the fragility of intimate relationships, showing how love entails continuous commitment and choice. This existential angst underpins all her other novels including The Mandarins, where the focus is on the responsibility of intellectuals towards their own societies. The book explores the tensions that arise between the personal and political allegiances of intellectuals and how they navigate the ever-changing geopolitical and ideological environments of Europe in the 1950s. Much of de Beauvoir's fiction is profoundly sociological and philosophical in the sense that her narratives address the existential and contextual questions of social life, individual mortality, the role of intellectuals, morality and social responsibility.

The Sociology of Ageing

The same topics are also addressed in her more academic contributions. One of her most sociological works, *La Vieillesse (The Coming of Age)* (1972), explores the social and cultural context of ageing. The book centres on the fear of ageing as a sociological phenomenon. De Beauvoir provides a historical analysis of how old age is perceived differently across time and space and how the perceptions of one's age is often determined by class, gender, professional status or ethnic background. For example, she demonstrates how wealthy professional men are often seen by society as being younger than their poor working-class female counterparts. This social portrayal of ageing is then contrasted with the views of the senior citizens themselves, trying to understand how they perceive the world around them and how they relate to their own ageing bodies. De Beauvoir also explores the social stigma and the dehumanisation processes that are often associated with old age, including the idea that the elderly are expected to become socially invisible so as not to remined the younger members of society that ageing and death are inevitable.

De Beauvoir's most influential philosophical studies, such as *Pyrrhus et Cinéas* (1944) and *The Ethics of Ambiguity* (1947), address the key theme of existentialism – the question of how human beings can realise their full freedom in a world that is characterised by absurdness and meaninglessness. In *Pyrrhus et Cinéas* de Beauvoir explores the meaning of human action. She argues that the presence of the other is a precondition for one's freedom – one cannot be fully free without other human beings. This topic is further explored in *The Ethics of Ambiguity* where she emphasises that human existence is contingent and precarious and that our presence in this world is not a necessity. This existential context creates a situation where there is no pre-existing standards of value and no established or fixed human essences. Hence such an environment might generate a nihilist view of the world, but it can also be liberating in the sense that human beings can realise their freedom.

The Sociology of Family

Ann Oakley has made substantial contributions in three areas of sociological research: (1) the sociology of family; (2) gender and sexuality; and (3) childbirth and motherhood. The *Sociology of Housework* (1974a) and the *Housewife* (1974b) were pioneering studies that explored until then a completely neglected area – the experience of living and working as a homemaker. The two books reconceptualised and reframed the traditional understanding of housework. For centuries housework was invisible, marginalised and tightly associated only with the woman's role within the marriage. What Oakley's books did is to explore and reconfigure housework as a specific mode of labour. Hence Oakley measured the degree of job satisfaction in the same way other employment is assessed and found that most homemakers were highly dissatisfied with the monotonous and fragmented nature of domestic work.

Furthermore, her studies indicated that most homemakers work long hours, experience loneliness and feel alienated by the low social status associated with being 'just a housewife'. Her research points out that most housewives value the autonomy of housework. However, the autonomy of the homemaker is in fact limited to the daily routines as most women remained economically and socially dependent on their spouses and had no autonomy in decisions outside of the household domain. Oakley also found that the homemaker role was emotionally draining for most women and this unacknowledged form of labour reflected how deeply patriarchy has been ingrained in the framing of what constitutes legitimate employment and work. The two books opened an ongoing debate on the masculinism of sociology as a discipline which until this period did not regard housework and the social realities of homemakers as relevant areas of study. By giving voice to the marginalised and powerless, yet very large, sector of the population Oakley changed the direction and content of debate on gender dynamics within households.

These early studies on housework prompted Oakley to dig deeper and explore the wider issues concerning the social and historical dynamics of patriarchy. She had already discussed this problem in her first book *Sex, Gender and Society* (1972), where she pioneered the now well-established distinction between sex and gender, where the former is associated with the biological features that distinguish men and women and the latter associated with the culturally specific framing of masculinity and femininity. In her later publications on this topic she acknowledged that her original formulation was not sensitive enough to issues of biological complexities where the sexual differences are not binary but allow for a variety of forms. However, she remains adamant that this distinction is sociologically valuable as it allows researchers to differentiate between the cultural and biological sources of power inequalities. Oakley has written many articles and monographs focusing on gender, sexuality and female body including *Subject Women* (1982), *Taking It Like a Woman* (1984), *Gender on Planet Earth* (2002), *Fracture: Adventures of a Broken Body* (2007) and most recently *Women, Peace and Welfare* (2018). Much of her work combines personal narratives, including her own experiences, sociological analysis and feminist activism. For example, *Subject Women* and *Taking It Like a Woman* both focus on female experiences within a patriarchal world: while the former book centres on women's rights the latter deals with the middle-class conformism that constrains female liberation.

Motherhood

Another prominent theme in Oakley's sociological research is motherhood. In several of her books and articles she analyses how the birth of children transforms women's bodies, minds and their social roles. The still-dominant patriarchal order ties women's identities to their family-grounded roles, which leave no room for the individual subjectivities of women. Hence in the family context daughters are expected to become mothers and grandmothers, and if they do not aspire towards these roles they are shamed by the wider society. As Oakley states:

> Male-dominated culture has designated as female all labours of emotional connectedness... The principal mode of developing this sensitivity in women is the gender-differentiated nuclear family. Women mother. Daughters are transformed into mothers. An autonomous sense of self ... does not need to develop. Women's sense of identity is thus dangerously bound up from early childhood with the identities of others. (1984: 201)

However, Oakley does not see motherhood as an obstacle for women's liberation.

On the contrary, she argues that motherhood is a question of individual choice and those who opt to have children often find themselves developing new subjectivities: 'Motherhood is a handicap but also a strength; a trial and an error; an achievement and a prize' (Oakley, 1979: 308). In her recent publications Oakley zooms in on female bodies as they are affected by childbirth and ageing. She argues that new technologies and new, consumer-centred practices aim to change the relationship between culture and nature where the focus shifts towards controlling and commodifying female bodies. For example, the increasing popularity of plastic surgery, weight-loss programmes, rejuvenation treatments and many other practices have not helped liberate women from traditional roles but have in fact only commodified their bodies. In this youth- and physical-beauty-centred environment childbirth and ageing are perceived as obstacles to be overcome or made invisible. In *Fracture: Adventures of a Broken Body* (2007) Oakley explores how, as they age, female bodies become either confined to one's household where they are made invisible or the subject of 'institutionalised concern from many experts'. Old women are not expected to be seen or heard while the objectification of their bodies shifts from the sexual to the medical gaze. In Oakley's own words: 'We regularly receive "invitations" to have our breasts squeezed between the blades of mammography machines, our uterine cervices scraped, and the state of our bones quantified... The main function of medical screening isn't to prevent disease, but to change identities – to produce patients' (2007: 101).

The Feminist Standpoint Theory

While de Beauvoir and Oakley provided the foundations for the sociologically informed feminist understandings of social reality, Dorothy E. Smith was among the first sociologists to develop a distinct feminist sociological theory. Drawing creatively on phenomenology, symbolic interactionism and Marxism, Smith articulated what is now established as feminist standpoint theory. This approach was originally developed in her highly influential *The Everyday World as Problematic: A Feminist Sociology* (1987) and was then refined and expanded in other books including *Writing the Social: Critique, Theory and Investigations* (1999) and *Institutional Ethnography: A Sociology for People* (2005).

In these books, Smith argues that despite its nominal commitment to objectivity and rational explanation, mainstream sociology remains wedded to the male-centric understanding of social reality. Smith's starting position is the apparent disconnect that most female sociologists experience between their professional and personal lives – the two irreconcilable subjectivities – the home vs. the university. In her own words:

> My experience was of contradictory modes of working existence: on the one hand was the work of the home and of being a mother; on the other hand the work of the academy, preparing for classes, teaching, faculty meetings, writing papers, and so on. I could not see my work at home in relation to the sociology I taught, in part, of course, because that sociology had almost nothing to say about it. (Smith, 2005: 11).

To explain this structural and experiential disconnect, Smith (1990) utilises phenomenological and Marxist conceptual tools. More specifically, she argues that all knowledge is socially created and socially constructed and is also shaped by the wider structural contexts. Hence the existing social hierarchies create knowledge that is structurally and conceptually asymmetrical – the dominant groups not only receive much more attention, but also shape the categories of analysis. The existing power relations determine which social issues are deemed to be relevant and worthy for research and which issues are marginalised or ignored. Smith combines Marxist ideas of structural dominance and hegemonic representation with the phenomenological emphasis on the fluidity of knowledge construction.

In this context Smith criticises conventional sociology for explicitly or implicitly reproducing the existing male-centric understanding of social reality. To counter this problem, she advocates standpoint theory, which recognises the structural and ideational biases that are inherent in all social practices including one's attempts at an objective analysis of social reality. She argues that all knowledge originates from a particular standpoint and any claims to unbiased universalism tend to hide particularistic biases. However, Smith's point is not that human beings are inherently biased but that the larger economic and political structures produce power asymmetries that generate structural biases. Thus, Smith aims to articulate a sociological approach which focuses on women's standpoint. This means developing concepts, theoretical frameworks and methodologies that take into account often ignored female social experiences, including sexual reproduction, childbearing and rearing, household life, and so on. Women's standpoint theory allows one to question and analyse the existing social institutions and social arrangements by focusing on the distinct perceptions and experiences of women.

Relations of Ruling

In *The Everyday World as Problematic* (1987) Smith introduces the concept of 'relations of ruling'. This idea, derived from the Marxist tradition, aims to capture the social relations that develop in the context of a capitalist and patriarchal order. She defines relations of ruling as 'a complex of organised practices, including government, law, business and financial management, professional organisation, and educational institutions, as well as the discourses in texts that interpenetrate the multiple sites of power' (Smith, 1987: 3). The focus here is on how the existing power dynamics objectify established patriarchal and class relations and reproduce them as normal and natural modes of the social order. In this type of environment women and other marginalised populations do not have equal representation and cannot formulate the dominant discourses, yet they are required to master the existing norms and practices and are also expected to support the existing structures through their housekeeping, maternal and familial roles.

Another crucial concept in Smith's opus is the idea of 'bifurcation of consciousness'. By this she means that human beings see the world in two different ways – through our own experience and through the conceptual categories that we learn. In other words, there are two distinct modes of understanding – one originating in one's body and the space this body occupies and one that originates outside of one's own physical and spatial experience. This distinction allows Smith to explore the way gender relations operate in everyday life. She argues that the bifurcation of consciousness involves two divergent modes of being a woman: one associated with their physical givens (i.e. childbearing, menstrual cycles, etc.) that have socially been tied to their expected 'domestic' roles (i.e. motherhood, housekeeping, etc.); and the other involving their wider social activities. For Smith, unlike men who historically dominated this wider social realm and as such did not have to differentiate between the physical and the social spheres, women had to navigate the two modes of being in order to assert themselves as able and skilled individuals within the wider world. She insists that this dichotomy is also visible within sociology as the discipline reflects the male-dominated categories of analysis and has little understanding of the experiences of ordinary female subjects.

Hence to take into account this 'bifurcation of consciousness' it is necessary to devise different research methods within social science. Smith argues that the conventional research techniques are inadequate as they operate on the traditional, male-centred parameters of the social and as such cannot identify the dynamics of the local and the particular that shape the female experience. In this context she developed the method of institutional ethnography. This method is in part derived from Alfred Schütz's distinction between *mitwelt*, which stands for one's social and cultural environment, and *umwelt*, which refers to one's physical experience. Smith (1987: 83) argues that *umwelt*, which involves intimate, face-to-face relations and one's bodily practice, is more 'central in women's lives'.

Thus, to explore adequately this *umwelt* experience it is necessary to deploy a methodology which is capable of tapping into this less visible realm.

For Smith institutional ethnography can do this because it focuses on how social relations shape the everyday lives of individuals. More to the point, this method aims to map the way how wider social relations frame individuals' activities within specific institutions. The institutional ethnography, as Smith (2004: 5) explains in an interview:

> takes the social activities of the institution as a starting point and hooking on to activities and relations both horizontal and vertical it is never confined to the very institution under investigation. Hereby the connections between the local and extra-local are made, making the workings of society visible.

This method zooms in on the ways that the local realm is institutionally related to the extra-local and the trans-local. In the institutional ethnography the researcher is not concerned with testing a particular hypothesis but approaches the research process as a form of discovery. By drawing on ethnomethodological tradition the idea is to find out 'how our everyday worlds are put together in relations that are not wholly discoverable within the everyday world' (Smith, 1987: 47).

Contemporary Relevance and Applications

The rise of feminist sociology had a significant influence within academia and even more within the wider public sphere. Feminist scholarship has successfully challenged and continues to challenge the patriarchal structures of most societies in the world. While early feminist activism was focused on addressing rampant legal inequalities facing women, the second and the third waves of feminist movements have focused their attention on the less visible forms of gender discrimination – from unequal employment opportunities to equal pay, reproductive rights, dress codes, sexuality, family, domestic violence and rape.

FEMINISMS

Feminist theory may be described most broadly as a general set of ideas about social life extrapolated from a woman-centred perspective and oriented by the normative principle of equality. Though encompassed under this umbrella, feminist theory is far from a homogeneous block, however. This label includes cultural feminism, intersectionality theory, liberal feminism, post-modern feminism, psychoanalytic feminism, radical feminism and socialist feminism, among others. Each approach gives contrasting emphasis to certain aspects of women's experiences as well as providing distinct critical explanations. These are based variously on gender inequality, gender difference, gender oppression, greater structural oppression or the cultural construction of gender itself. Rather than a single feminism, it is perhaps more accurate today to speak of feminisms.

In this context de Beauvoir, Oakley and Smith provided the conceptual and analytical tools to explore and identify the social structure of patriarchy. Moreover, Oakley also generated a number of empirical studies that offer credible evidence on gender-based discrimination and inequalities which underpin many modern societies. In some respects, Beauvoir, Oakley and Smith were the leading intellectual contributors which spurred, but also provided, sound sociological backing for the claims expressed in the second wave of feminism. However, their ideas have also influenced the development of alternative feminist voices that continue to shape the current debates. Hence some contemporary sociologists have focused on bringing feminist ideas and psychoanalysis together.

For example, Nancy Chodorow in *The Reproduction of Mothering* (1978) argues that the social construction of gender differences can be traced back to the Oedipal complex identified by Sigmund Freud and Karen Horney. Chodorow explains that all children develop their egos in relation to the dominating figure of the mother. However, while male children tend to imitate their fathers and as such attain early independence, female children develop split loyalties and as such their ego development is thwarted and delayed. Chodorow argues that in this early stage boys are more likely to experience love as a dyadic relationship while girls tend to develop triadic libidinal relationships where one's ego is split between love for both parents. According to Chodorow these different relationships influence the social construction of gender roles where women are often degraded in society and expected when married to focus on children and have less interest in their sexuality.

Other contemporary scholars such as Nancy Fraser have brought together feminism and Frankfurt School sociology. Hence in her influential book *Fortunes of Feminism: From State-Managed Capitalism to Neoliberal Crisis* (2013) Fraser distinguishes between two forms of justice: (1) justice of recognition with emphasis on the equal representation of all groups within a society; and (2) distributive justice where the focus is more on equity in the resource distribution within a society. Fraser argues that the second wave of feminism together with other movements in the 1960s and early 1970s have overemphasised group recognition of equality, and that identity politics often refocuses attention from the structural causes of all inequalities (including gender discrimination).

Other contemporary feminist scholars such as Donna Haraway and Gayatri Spivak have also questioned the conventional narratives that underpin the second wave of feminist thinking. Drawing on the post-structuralist approaches they offer a radical critique of gender, insisting that all gender categories are arbitrary and malleable. Thus Haraway (1990: 149) argues that: 'there is nothing about female that naturally binds women together into a unified category. There is not even such a state as "being" female, itself a highly complex category constructed in contested sexual scientific discourses and other social practices.' Her key contribution, 'A Cyborg Manifesto' (1985), makes a radical case against the conventional concepts of sex and gender. Haraway argues that the second wave of feminism overemphasises gender identities as a source of political action. Instead, she advocates coalitions based not on identity but on 'affinity'; that is, bringing together 'oppositional consciousness' that is rooted in 'otherness, difference and specificity' (1985: 149–81). Her concept of cyborg is a metaphor for a being that transcends the established liberal and humanist visions of subjectivity. It is a representation that envisages a genderless, raceless, classless and non-violent world that embodies collective rather than individual consciousness.

For Haraway the cyborg image is an attempt to go beyond established dualisms such as mind vs. body or men vs. women. In her *Simians, Cyborgs and Women* (1991) she elaborates that the cyborg metaphor is proposed with an aim of overcoming inherent contradictions in feminist theory by connecting and accepting differences in a similar way that a cyborg represents a conjoining of a human and a machine. Drawing on post-structuralist ideas Haraway challenges not only the notion of gender identity but also the idea that science can generate objective knowledge. In her 1990 book *Primate Visions: Gender, Race and Nature in the World of Modern Science* she argues that primatologists claim objectivity, yet their work tends to reproduce masculinist stereotypes about 'aggressive alpha males' and 'receptive females'. She insists that science is far from being immune to ideological representations that underpin one's everyday life. Hence the established findings of primatologists require deconstruction of their narratives and Haraway shows how some feminist primatologists successfully question these established narratives.

Gayatri Spivak was also influenced by post-structuralist and deconstructivist thought. Her publications are compatible with Haraway's criticisms of science and gender essentialisms. Nevertheless, her work also focuses on feminist ideas and practice outside the West. Thus, in her most influential work 'Can the Subaltern Speak?' (1988) she explores the historical marginalisation of those who live on the periphery of the imperial and post-imperial world where they have little possibility of being heard. By subaltern she means those populations that are outside of the hegemonic power structures that rule colonies. Exploring the Eurocentric representations of widow sacrifice (sati) in India she argues that: 'in the context of colonial production, the subaltern has no history and cannot speak, the subaltern as female is even more deeply in shadow' (1988: 287). For Spivak, the Eurocentric representations of intellectuals constitute the subaltern Other of Europe as voiceless and anonymous:

> For the 'figure' of woman, the relationship between woman and silence can be plotted by women themselves; race and class differences are subsumed under that charge. Subaltern historiography must confront the impossibility of such gestures. The narrow epistemic violence of imperialism gives us an imperfect allegory of the general violence that is the possibility of an episteme. (1988: 28)

The highly influential works of Chodorow, Fraser, Haraway and Spivak, among others, have influenced the contemporary feminist debates and have facilitated the transition from the second to the third wave of feminism.

Criticisms

The classical feminist sociology associated with the contributions of de Beauvoir, Oakley, Smith and others has been challenged within sociology, within feminism and also outside these two intellectual traditions. Thus, some sociologists find feminist interpretations as lacking in objectivity: the argument is that these interpretations are driven by normative rather than explanatory concerns. In this context some scholars question the conventional feminist accounts that reject objectivity and see all knowledge as relative and situational. For example, Buber-Agassi (1995) argues that this attitude to research can lead to a radical relativism and irrationalism and as such would undermine empirical studies that provide sound evidence of women's inequality within society. She insists that some feminist accounts do not distinguish clearly between the established facts and fictional narratives and as such foster irrationalism:

> [there is] the absence of the formulation of any hypothesis to be tested, or even of an initial problem. They appear to be opposed to 'objectivism', meaning by this term not only researchers' traditional claim to scientific objectivity, but also the striving for maximal objectivity, and even the very fact that the researcher views the researched as an 'object' of research. (Buber-Agassi, 1995: 153)

This type of criticism targets especially the works of de Beauvoir and Smith. While de Beauvoir is accused of failing to differentiate clearly between fiction and social reality, Smith's standpoint feminism is critiqued for its essentialist character. Hence, as de Beauvoir's work combines literary and academic contributions some social scientists argue that such an approach is too vague and lacking in methodological rigour to yield generalisable findings. Smith's position is challenged on the grounds that it reproduces the essentialist discourses that already underpin patriarchal relationships. By insisting that there is a relatively uniform and unique 'women's experience' that creates a distinct form of knowledge she leaves little room for the diversity of individual experiences. Moreover, such a distinction reintroduces the essentialist and quasi-biological differentiation between the sexes through the back door. If all women are assumed to share similar perceptions of reality (i.e. the women's standpoint), then this also wrongly assumes that men are incapable of developing feminist subjectivities.

Whereas the sociological criticisms have focused on the explanatory deficiencies of feminist approaches, contemporary feminist writers have challenged the classics as being insufficiently feminist. In other words, while some social scientists dislike the normative and activist commitments that underpin the work of de Beauvoir, Oakley and Smith, the third and fourth waves of feminist scholars believe that the classics do not go far enough in their activism and social prescription.

The third wave of feminist movements, which developed in the 1990s and 2000s, directed their attention towards the multiple sources of structural inequality in the world. In this context Kimberlé Crenshaw (1989) coined the term 'intersectionality', which stands for the complex and manifold sources of discrimination. Her point was that in everyday life women suffer 'layers of oppression' involving gender, race, ethnicity, class and status. Starting from her own experience Crenshaw (with Cho and McCall, 2013) argues that traditional feminist accounts tended to focus on middle-class women and as such left no room for the intersectional discrimination experienced by working-class women of colour. In her view the structural inequalities that face minority women who come from impoverished backgrounds are very different and they cannot be adequately understood solely through the prism of gender, race or class, but through all of them (and others) simultaneously as they often reinforce each other. For example, Oakley's research focus on the white middle-class British housekeepers who live in relatively affluent areas of London cannot relate much to the Afro-Caribbean women who live on the poorer estates of Birmingham.

The ongoing fourth wave of feminism, which started in the 2010s, has pushed some of these issues and concerns further. The rise of new technology, and social media in particular, has made feminist issues much more visible to a global audience. By directly sharing their everyday experiences of sexual harassment and violence women activists have galvanised wide networks of social media users who are now able to organise quickly various feminist campaigns. Hence this new wave of feminist groups utilises networking technology (blogging, Facebook, Twitter, Instagram, YouTube, etc.) to question the patriarchal dominance and less visible everyday misogynist behaviour. It also criticises the traditional feminist scholarship seeing it as incapable of addressing contemporary concerns ranging from campus sexual assaults, cyberbullying and cyber-shaming of women to everyday sexism, domestic rape and the issues concerning complex sexual identities (homosexual, transgender, bisexual, etc.). The most influential movements associated with the fourth wave of feminism are #MeToo and the 2017 and 2018 worldwide Women's Marches.

Finally, feminist sociology has also experienced criticism outside of the discipline and feminist movements. Some critics have questioned the increasingly radical misandrist (anti-men) discourses of some feminist groups. So Christina Hoff Sommers (2013) sees some contemporary cultural productions such as novels, plays, films and TV shows as being hostile to men by dehumanising them and portraying them as sadists, child abusers, rapists and oppressive brutes while most men do not belong in any of these categories. They argue that some forms of feminism have become ideologically too rigid to accommodate men who are willing to challenge the patriarchy. Others have criticised what they see to be too vague and commercialised displays of contemporary feminist discourse.

Thus Jessa Crispin (2017) argues that the genuine concerns about gender inequalities have been colonised and banalised by the capitalist enterprises that 'fight to allow women to participate equally in the oppression of the powerless and the poor'. Crispin believes that key feminist ideas have been manipulated by groups and individuals who use this label to discredit others and narcissistically claim the moral upper hand through the narratives of perpetual victimhood and righteous action: 'I define myself as feminist and so everything I do is a feminist act'. Crispin critiques this type of 'spoil yourself stupid' feminism that has proliferated in women's magazines where gender empowerment has become nothing more than a form of personalised gain.

Conclusion

The main, and lasting, legacy of the classical feminist sociological tradition is its undermining of the dominant male-centric understanding of the social world. De Beauvoir, Oakley and Smith have created a body of work that has substantially influenced how sociologists look at the societies they study. While before the mid-twentieth century scholars mostly ignored the gender divisions and the analysis of structural inequalities based on one's sex, today most sociologists have become aware of these issues. However, this is not to say that the patriarchal norms have disappeared or that all sociologists now produce gender-sensitive scholarship. While classical feminists have shaped current debates within social science, the feminist perspectives are still far from being integrated within the mainstream of sociological thought. Despite some significant changes that have taken place recently, sociology is still dominated by men and the male-centric categories of analysis. However, the different waves of feminism continue to influence sociology, and the ever-growing number of gender-sensitive sociologists also continue to influence the new waves of feminism.

References

Beauvoir, S. de (1943) *L'Invitée*. Paris: Gallimard.
Beauvoir, S. de (1944) *Pyrrhus et Cinéas*. Paris: Gallimard.
Beauvoir, S. de (1945) *Le Sang des Autres*. Paris: Gallimard.
Beauvoir, S. de (1946) *Tous les hommes sont mortels*. Paris: Gallimard.
Beauvoir, S. de (1947) *Pour une morale de l'ambiguïté*. New York: Citadel Press.
Beauvoir, S. de (1949) *Le Deuxième Sexe*. Paris: Gallimard.
Beauvoir, S. de (1965) *The Second Sex*. New York: Bantam Books.
Beauvoir, S. de (1972) *The Coming of Age*. London: Weidenfeld and Nicolson.
Buber-Agassi, J. (1995) Epistemological and Methodological Concerns of Feminist Social Scientists. In: I. Jarvi and N. Laor (eds) *Critical Rationalism, the Social Sciences and the Humanities*. New York: Springer, pp. 153-65.
Cho, S., Crenshaw, K. W. and McCall, L. (2013) Toward a Field of Intersectionality Studies: Theory, Applications, and Praxis. *Signs*, 38(4), pp. 785-810.
Chodorow, N. (1978) *The Reproduction of Mothering: Psychoanalysis and the Sociology of Gender*. Berkeley, CA: University of California Press.

Crenshaw, K. (1989) Demarginalizing the Intersection of Race and Sex: A Black Feminist Critique of Antidiscrimination Doctrine, Feminist Theory and Antiracist Politics. *University of Chicago Legal Forum*, 1(8), pp. 139-67.
Crispin, J. (2017) *Why I Am Not a Feminist*. London: Melville House.
Fraser, N. (2013) *Fortunes of Feminism: From State-Managed Capitalism to Neoliberal Crisis*. Brooklyn, NY: Verso.
Friedan, B. (1963) *The Feminine Mystique*. New York: W.W. Norton.
Haraway, D. J. (1991 [1985]) A Cyborg Manifesto: Science, Technology, and Socialist-Feminism in the Late Twentieth Century'. In: D. J. Haraway *Simians, Cyborgs and Women: The Reinvention of Nature*. New York: Routledge, pp. 149-81.
Haraway, D. J. (1990) *Primate Visions: Gender, Race, and Nature in the World of Modern Science*. London: Routledge.
Hoff Sommers, A. (2013) *Freedom Feminism: Its Surprising History and Why It Matters Today*. Washington, DC: AEI Press
Oakley, A. (1972) *Sex, Gender and Society*. London: Maurice Temple Smith.
Oakley, A. (1974a) *The Sociology of Housework*. Oxford: Basil Blackwell.
Oakley, A. (1974b) *Housewife*. Harmondsworth: Penguin.
Oakley, A. (1979) *Becoming a Mother*. Oxford: Martin Robinson.
Oakley, A. (1982) *Subject Women*. London: Fontana.
Oakley, A. (1984) *Taking It Like a Woman*. London: Flamingo.
Oakley, A. (1988) *The Men's Room*. London: Virago Press.
Oakley, A. (2002) *Gender on Planet Earth*. New York: The New Press.
Oakley, A. (2007) *Fracture: Adventures of a Broken Body*. Bristol: Policy Press.
Oakley, A. (2018) *Women, Peace and Welfare: A Suppressed History of Social Reform, 1880-1920*. Bristol: Bristol University Press.
Smith, D. E. (1987) *The Everyday World as Problematic: A Feminist Sociology*. Boston, MA: Northeastern University Press.
Smith, D. E. (1990) *The Conceptual Practices of Power: A Feminist Sociology of Knowledge*. Toronto: University of Toronto Press.
Smith, D. E. (1999) *Writing the Social: Critique, Theory and Investigations*. Toronto: University of Toronto Press.
Smith, D.E. (2004) Institutional Ethnography – Towards a Productive Sociology (An Interview). *Sosiologisk Tidskrift*, 12(2), pp. 1-8.
Smith, D. E. (2005) *Institutional Ethnography: A Sociology for People*. Oxford: AltaMira.
Spivak, G. C. (1988) Can the Subaltern Speak? In: C. Nelson and L. Grossberg (eds) *Marxism and the Interpretation of Culture*. London: Macmillan Education.

Latour, Hochschild and Hill Collins

Introduction

Contemporary sociology is very rich in new perspectives and modes of analysis. There are hundreds of different and versatile subfields of sociological research and thousands of creative individual sociologists working on topics as diverse as artificial intelligence, consumerism, spirituality, war, food, celebrity, sexuality, poverty, climate change social media and new technologies, among many others. Although classical sociologists were also interested in different topics it is really with the rise of social movements in the late 1960s and early 1970s that sociologists have dramatically expanded their research gaze. In this chapter we zoom in on the three key thematic areas that became highly influential over the past four decades – the sociology of science, the sociology of emotions and the intersectional perspectives within sociology. These distinct analytical areas opened the door for the rise of many new perspectives that dominate contemporary sociological thought. The chapter explores the contributions of three scholars who made these 'new directions' possible – Bruno Latour, Arlie Hochschild and Patricia Hill Collins. As in previous chapters we look briefly at the biographical, historical and social contexts and then analyse the main concepts and theories developed by these sociologists. The last two sections zoom in on the contemporary relevance and criticisms of these three scholars.

Life and Intellectual Context

Bruno Latour

Latour was born in 1947 in Beaune, Burgundy, France. He grew up in an affluent Catholic family of wine growers. He completed his first degree in Dijon where he studied theology and philosophy. As Latour (2013) later recalls, in his early youth until the age of 28 he was 'a militant Catholic'. These early interests pushed him further towards theology and the work of the Catholic writer Charles Péguy. In the early 1970s he commenced his PhD project at the University of Tours where he graduated in 1975, with a dissertation on Péguy. His PhD project was centred on the possibility of communication between different worldviews and as such was also highly influenced by the leading French philosopher, Michel Serres. Serres developed a philosophy of science that rejects a singular metalanguage and promotes the notion that one needs to translate constantly between different knowledge domains.

During this period, Latour was required to undertake compulsory military service but in lieu of this he opted to teach in West Africa where he was appointed lecturer at the University of Abidjan. The two years spent in the Ivory Coast had a profound impact on the young Latour as he encountered the legacies of colonial order for the first time and also 'discovered all at once, the most predatory forms of capitalism' (Latour, 2013). While in the Ivory Coast he also undertook fieldwork on colonialism, race and industrial relations with the support of anthropologist Marc Auge. Upon completion of his PhD, Latour accepted an invitation from Roger Guillemin, the neuroscientist who won a Nobel Prize in medicine in 1977, to move to California where he commenced, together with Steve Woolgar, his ethnographic study of the laboratory and scientists working at the Salk Institute of Biology in San Diego. This ethnographic work would later result in one of Latour's most influential books, *Laboratory Life: The Social Construction of Scientific Facts*, co-authored with Woolgar in 1979. From 1977 to 1981, Latour was an assistant professor at the Conservatoire National des Arts et Métiers, while between 1982 and 2006 he was professor at the Centre de sociologie de l'Innovation at the École nationale supérieure des mines in Paris. In 2006 he was appointed to the first Gabriel Tarde Chair at the Sciences Po in Paris where he stayed until his retirement in 2017. At Sciences Po he established the médialab that utilises social theory to understand the dynamics of digital media. In 2013, Latour was awarded the Holborg Prize, often referred to as the Nobel Prize for social science and humanities.

Arlie Russell Hochschild

Hochschild was born in 1940 in Boston, Massachusetts. Her father was a diplomat who held ambassadorial posts in Israel, New Zealand, Ghana and Tunisia. Hence much of her early childhood took place abroad where she and her mother were inadvertently immersed in the world of high diplomacy and international relations. This experience of living in different countries had a profound impact on the young Hochschild as she became aware of different cultural traditions and different ways in which human beings express their emotions. Hochschild completed her undergraduate studies at Swarthmore College, Pennsylvania, in 1962. During this period, she met a writer and journalist,

Adam Hochschild, who became her lifelong partner. They were also both active participants in the 1960s civil rights movements on US university campuses.

In 1965, Hochschild attained a Master's degree in sociology at the University of California, Berkeley, where she also completed her PhD studies and graduated in 1969. Upon graduation she was appointed assistant professor at the University of California, Santa Cruz, where she worked for two years. In 1971 she was appointed as assistant professor at UC Berkeley but found it difficult to balance a young family, a full-time academic career, political activism and teaching. So Hochschild led a group of feminists who demanded the establishment of part-time tenure track positions, which at that time did not exist. After some resistance this pressure group was successful and such positions were introduced first at Berkeley, and then in other US universities. She remained at Berkeley until her retirement in 2016. Hochschild is the recipient of many awards and honorary degrees including the Ulysses Medal from University College, Dublin (2015).

Patricia Hill Collins

Hill Collins was born in 1948 in Philadelphia, Pennsylvania. Her parents met in Washington, DC, where both moved during the war in search of work. Her father was a war veteran and a factory worker, and her mother was a secretary. In the 1950s her family moved to North Philadelphia, where they lived in a working-class area. In Philadelphia, Patricia attended primary and secondary schools where most students came from a white middle-class background. She was a good student but regularly experienced everyday racism, which affected her personality. As she writes later remembering these early years:

> Beginning in adolescence, I was increasingly the 'first', 'one of the few', or the 'only' African American and/or woman and/or working-class person in my schools, communities, and work settings. I saw nothing wrong with being who I was, but apparently many others did. My world grew larger, but I felt I was growing smaller. I tried to disappear into myself in order to deflect the painful, daily assaults designed to teach me that being an African American, working-class woman made me lesser than those who were not. (Collins, 1990: xi)

Collins received a scholarship and pursued her undergraduate studies at Brandeis University, Massachusetts, where she graduated in 1969 with a major in sociology. She soon decided to become a teacher and enrolled in a Master's degree in teaching at Harvard University where she graduated in 1970. From 1970 to 1976, she was employed as a teacher at the St. Joseph Community School in Roxbury, Boston. During this period, she was involved with several educational initiatives to improve the inner city schooling system. Between 1976 and 1980, she was the director of the African American Centre at Tufts University. Soon after she returned to her studies and completed a PhD in sociology at Brandeis University in 1984. While still working on her doctorate Collins started teaching at the University of Cincinnati where she was appointed assistant professor in 1982. In 1996, she was appointed Charles Phelps Taft Distinguished Professor of Sociology. In 2005, she became Wilson Elkins Professor of Sociology at the University of Maryland. In 2009, she was the first African American woman to be elected president of the American Sociological Association. Her work received numerous awards including the William E. B. Du Bois Career of Distinguished Scholarship Award (2017), the Joseph B. and Toby Gittler Prize (2013), the Morris Rosenberg Award (2009) and the C. Wright Mills Award (1991) among many others.

Historical, Social and Political Context
Science and Technology in Modern World

The Enlightenment heritage has played a crucial role in establishing science as the principal authority in the modern world. While before the modern era religious teachings and interpretations were understood to be the only legitimate framework for understanding the world, this is no longer the case. In fact, over the past two centuries science has largely replaced religion (and magic) as the dominant, and in many contexts even hegemonic, mode of explanation. Hence when somebody requires a hip replacement operation the tendency is to seek help from the medical professional, a surgeon, rather than to look for the shaman or magician who could cast a spell on the evil spirts causing the hip weakness. Similarly, if a farmer requires water to grow crops, he or she is less likely to opt for help from protracted prayer or a ritualistic rain dance and more likely to use established irrigation methods or to plan farming following the weather forecasts.

The success of science is in part rooted in its ability to deliver tangible, and often quick, results – from more efficient technology to cheaper, more reliable and more effective solutions for a variety of everyday problems. Thus, for much of the nineteenth and early twentieth centuries science and scientists have become the dominant and almost unquestioned epistemic authorities. While scientific methods have always been contested and challenged by alternative worldviews, many of these perspectives largely remained on the academic margins until the second half of the twentieth century. It is only with the profound social, political and economic crises of the late 1960s and early 1970s that some scholars articulated serious doubts about the role of science in social life. The 1968 student revolts together with the wider civil rights movements in the United States and Europe started to question the status quo and, in this process, also opened the debate about the centrality of science and technology in the reproduction of existing power structures. While previously science was understood to be a most reliable vehicle of progress, in the aftermath of the 1960s movements science and technology became perceived as the instruments of power. Critics have challenged what they identified to be the guiding belief system among many ruling groups in the world – scientism. This notion stands for the ideology that espouses the idea that science can successfully proscribe normative values and as such its principles can be applied to all spheres of human life. Scientism is also rooted in the positivist idea that all knowledge can be reduced to testable propositions which can be measured and falsified. The 1968 rebels opposed this ideology, which they associated with the ruling technocrats, who tended to deploy science and technology as a means of social control. By depicting all social problems through the prism of technological and scientific solutions, it was alleged that the rulers had successfully depoliticised and atomised the public sphere. The critics zoomed in on the processes through which politics has become hijacked by science and technology and how any criticism of the existing social orders (both in the capitalist West and the communist East) has often been delegitimised through the discourse of science.

For example, critiquing existing gender or class inequalities has often been dismissed as an irrational attack on progress, which, with the help of science and new technologies, was bound to bring about continuous growth and economic prosperity for all. Nevertheless, civil society groups representing ethnic minorities, women, low-paid labourers, sexual minorities and many other excluded groups tended to perceive scientists and technologists as accomplices in government policies aimed at reinforcing the status quo. The key point is that these highly skilled professionals work with and are funded by the establishment and as such they are inevitably focused on finding solutions only to the problems identified as such by those in power.

One example of this is the military industry, which relies expensively on new scientific and technological inventions. In fact the majority of new technologies and novel products and services that we all now rely on – from fast food, penicillin, computers, television to the internet and nuclear power – have been pioneered in the military sector and have only later found their application among civilians (Giddens, 1986; Malešević, 2017). Hence most countries prioritise the use of science and technology for military (and policing) purposes while often cutting budgets for health, education and welfare. This predominance of military power and its interdependence on the government and business were already identified by several public intellectuals including sociologist C. Wright Mills (1956), who wrote about the dominance of the 'military–industrial complex' in the United States. However, it was the tangible experience of protracted and devastating wars in Algeria and Vietnam that galvanised popular opposition to the use of science and technology as vehicles of control and destruction.

In the French context the 1968 student uprising represented the culmination of popular discontent that intensified with the French government's involvement in the colonial wars of the 1950s and 1960s. The First Indo-China War (or the French War in Vietnam), which ended in 1954 with French defeat and retreat from its former colony, resulted in substantial human losses on both sides (*c*. 800,000). The legacy of this war polarised French society and the national humiliation caused by the unexpected defeat contributed to a political stubbornness that characterised the behaviour of the French political elites who felt determined to avoid a similar fate in Algeria.

However, the Algerian War (1954–62) was another disaster where, after six years of vicious fighting and enormous losses, the French government retreated, and Algeria became an independent state. These two long wars had a very negative impact on society and also affected the French economy. As the state prioritised military and police spending it could not accommodate workers, students and other groups. Hence in May 1968 this general dissatisfaction escalated with massive demonstrations and general strikes throughout the country involving over 11 million workers. The protesters stood against the imperial wars, the social inequalities produced by capitalism, and also challenged the established institutions including the way science and technology had been used to prop up the status quo. The 1968 movement also voiced discontent over gender and ethnic discrimination and gave rise to new social movements.

The Civil Rights Movements

The US-based civil rights movements articulated similar ideas. They too opposed the imperial projects and overseas wars, focused on class, race, ethnic and gender inequalities and were often led by students. They also challenged the established institutions and the status quo and attacked the 'military–industrial complex', which was particularly singled out for its responsibility for the Vietnam War. This protracted and highly destructive war triggered active resistance and with the Tet Offensive in 1968 it generated a wide movement against the war. The civil rights movement started in the South where the asymmetries of power were most pronounced. During the late 1960s and early 1970s many African Americans joined the inner city riots, demanding an end to racial segregation, including the integrated education system, and an end to racist courts and the wider exclusionist policies. The various civil right groups also demanded full citizenship rights, decent housing, better employment prospects, increased federal works programmes and the enactment of meaningful civil rights protections.

With the establishment of Black Power and the more radical Black Panther organisation, civil rights protests escalated resulting in several violent episodes involving human casualties. The assassination in 1968 of Martin Luther King, Jr, the leader of the peaceful civil rights protests, spurned larger protests throughout the United States, involving more than 100 cities. The struggle for the political rights of African Americans developed into a wider social movement that opposed the military draft and sending of young men to Vietnam, demanded greater social rights and anti-poverty programmes, and advocated substantive liberalisation in the public sphere, including more free speech and free assembly. The movement also became associated with the specific youth counter-culture that despised the establishment and the conventional and conformist lifestyle of their parents. In this context, the late 1960s and early 1970s gave birth to the hippy culture which promoted peace, anti-violence, free love, environmentalism, spiritualism, yoga, the occult, experimenting with recreational drugs, and hostility towards science and technology. The movement also affirmed the free expression of emotions and attacked rationalism that had been associated with the controlling and exploitative industrial society. Self-interested competitive individualism was perceived as the principal evil of the modern social order and the movement aimed to replace it with an egalitarian, collectivist ethos which privileged shared emotional experiences over rationalist culture. There was pronounced hostility towards middle-class values and ambitions such as holding a permanent and well-paid 9-to-5 job and living in a comfortable house in suburbia. In contrast, the movement advocated alternative lifestyles with communal living and sharing of resources and relationships. The 1960s counter-culture was also eager to address the rights of many marginalised and excluded groups including women, gays, the handicapped and children, among others. Although the movement lost much of its wide support by the late 1970s, it left a strong legacy that spawned later waves of civil right campaigns involving a variety of social issues – from feminism, environmentalism and anti-militarism to the rights of ethnic and racial minorities.

Arguments and Ideas
The Social Construction of Knowledge

Bruno Latour's early work was deeply influenced by the legacy of the social and political changes that took place in the late 1960s and early 1970s. His first book, co-authored with Steve Woolgar, *Laboratory Life: The Social Construction of Scientific Facts* (1979), challenged the well-entrenched idea that science progresses through a chain of successful experiments. Instead this study, based on the year-long ethnography of the Salk Institute's neuro-endocrinological laboratory, demonstrated that experimental work depends heavily on the subjective decisions made by the scientists and the wider consensus culture that underpins scientific process. In other words, Latour and Woolgar argue that most experiments tend to generate inconclusive data which is open to and requires researchers' interpretation. In this process the scientists do not produce unbiased truths but in fact create knowledge by privileging some experimental data while ignoring the information that does not fit the established scientific conventions.

Hence in line with Thomas Kuhn's (1962) *The Structure of Scientific Revolutions*, they insist that scientific progress is not a linear and objective 'development by accumulation' but is in fact a socially constructed enterprise that involves negotiations, interpretations and reformulations by the scientists themselves and the wider scientific community. This empirically rich study came to the conclusion that despite the popular perception of science as a cumulative process that generates uncontested and testable knowledge, scientific activity is also dependent on, and reproduced through, shared cultural practices and norms. This highly successful publication was followed by two of Latour's books, both of which focus on the sociology of science and technology.

In *Science in Action: How to Follow Scientists and Engineers Through Society* (1987), Latour argues that scientific discoveries are often presented as sudden and almost magical events while in fact they are highly contingent long-term processes that involve the work of many individuals and group alliances. Hence, to understand fully how science and technology operate it is paramount to explore it 'in action'; that is, its process of creation and establishment. In this context, the book explores the institutional context of science, the means through which inventions are accepted by the scientific community, the role of the scientific literature and the activities of laboratories. For Latour science and technology (or 'technoscience' as he calls it) develop through networks of connected individuals, things and processes. He sees technoscience as a relation of power between 'actants' (agents) who operate through established networks of alliances that involve not only scientists, technocrats and wider societies, but also the machines and scientific instruments that scientists create and use. This book also further develops Latour's actor–network theory, which became a very influential research tool over the two following decades.

His 1988 book, translated as *The Pasteurization of France*, analyses the career of Louis Pasteur as a symbol of the relationships between science, technology, power and social change. With his discovery of microbes Pasteur became an instant celebrity in France and his image was used to establish a popular idea of a scientific genius and every town in France had a street named after him. However, as Latour shows, Pasteur's discovery depended less on his innate genius or his brilliant experimental work and much more on the social context and historical contingencies that made his discoveries acceptable to other scientists and French society at large.

To succeed Pasteur had to build alliances with the medical hygienists who were generally in conflict with the clinical physicians, farmers who were terrified by the sudden anthrax outbreak in France and were willing to lend their chicken farms for experimentation, and politicians eager to support the new health policies in order to generate tangible results at home and in the colonies of France. Hence, profound social change such as the introduction of compulsory vaccination could never take place through scientific inventions alone. Instead, such transformation entails the confluence of different factors and different social interests. The book charts how Pasteur was able to attain the support of different groups, including politicians, industrialists, scientists and farmers, to enact a profound social change.

Latour's interest in the sociology of knowledge and science led him to question some well-established ideas in academia. For example, in his highly influential *We Have Never Been Modern* (1993 [1991]) he offers a sharp critique of the modernity vs. post-modernity debate within the social sciences and humanities. Unlike post-modernists, who tend to challenge the universalism and rationalism of the Western European 'grand narratives' and look 'beyond modernity', and modernists, who cherish the heritage of Enlightenment, Latour insists that our world has not yet attained the state of modernity. He zooms in on the central distinction between nature and society and argues that in the pre-modern world there is no clear differentiation between the two realms. While modernist projects aimed to establish a firm distinction by privileging society over nature, this attempt never succeeded, which is evident in the rise of post-modern and anti-modern movements that aim to reintegrate nature and society. Latour points to a variety of issues – from global warming to pandemics and the new biotechnological developments – all of which mix science, politics and popular culture with conspiracy theories and anti-science discourses. He insists that this in itself indicates that the conventional thinking that separates science from nature is highly problematic as such a dichotomy is empirically unsustainable. Instead, Latour proposes new thinking, which he calls a 'Parliament of Things', which would treat social and natural phenomena as well as the discourses about these phenomena as part of the same process.

In his more recent books, such as *Reassembling the Social* (2005), *On the Modern Cult of the Factish Gods* (2009), *Facing Gaia: Eight Lectures on the New Climatic Regime* (2017) and *Down to Earth: Politics in the New Climatic Regime* (2018), Latour explores several contemporary processes including the continuous dominance of science and technology and the upcoming environmental disaster. He argues that the 'ecological mutation' that we experience today is linked with globalisation-induced economic deregulation and the corresponding unprecedented global inequalities. In Latour's view, as the global elites accept that ecological disaster is inevitable, they focus on their own survival and start abandoning the idea of a shared world. In this context Latour proposes rethinking of the notion of belonging to a specific territory.

Emotional Labour

Just as with Latour, Hochschild's work originated in the context of social unrest in the 1960s and early 1970s. However, while Latour centred on demystifying science and technology as the foundational basis of the modern world, Hochschild focused on untangling and questioning another pillar of modernity – rationality. Hence in contrast to much of social and political thought, which since the Enlightenment has privileged reason and rationality as the dominant explanatory frames, Hochschild identifies emotions as the primary generators of social action. However, unlike the conventional approaches, which see only the biological underpinning of emotions, she emphasises the social aspects of emotional experiences. While all human beings possess the same emotional repertoire, it is the different social and cultural contexts that shape these emotional states.

For example, in different societies some emotions are downplayed while others are overemphasised – in more traditional, collectivist, social contexts shame is the dominant negative social emotion, while in other, more individualist, societies guilt dominates over shame. Similarly, some languages do not differentiate between several emotional states while others possess a complex range of words to distinguish between several emotions. For example, in several south Slav languages being happy and being lucky are described with the same word (*sretna*) while other languages offer a variety of words for these two experiences. Hochschild (2003) also mentions that in the Tahitian language sadness, grief, envy and depression are all referred to as being 'sick'. All these examples illustrate how emotions are shaped by specific cultural contexts.

While some classical sociologists, such as Durkheim and Goffman among others, singled out emotions as playing significant roles in social interactions, they remained wedded to a static, instinctual concept of emotionality. Hochschild challenges these views, arguing that the emotions do not simply happen but entail a great deal of work: 'simply having personality does not make one a diplomat, any more than having muscles makes one an athlete' (1983: x). In both of these cases one encounters 'a sense of the active emotional labour'. In her ground-breaking early book *The Managed Heart: Commercialization of Human Feeling* (1983) she introduces a number of new concepts to explain how central emotions are for social interaction. One of her key ideas is the notion of emotional labour, which stands for the process through which individuals self-regulate their emotions in public. This activity regularly involves distinct facial and bodily displays that convey a particular emotional reaction. Hochschild expands Goffman's concept of impression management, where the focus is on self-presentation in order to influence others, towards emotional control centred on fulfilling the expectations of others. In other words, emotional labour involves managing feelings to achieve the requirements of one's job or family.

For example, department store employees are expected to regulate their emotional reactions during their interactions with customers, their superiors as well as with co-employees. Hence, instead of acting out their emotions the employees are involved in a complex process of decision making and assessing how to react in different situations and with different individuals, regardless of their own emotional preferences. This process also involves the suppression of one's affects and acting out according to the expectations of others. Hochschild differentiates between three main emotion regulation strategies: (1) cognitive emotional work, where an individual aims to change a particular ideas and images with the hope of changing the feelings associated with such ideas and images (i.e. remembering a happy moment from one's childhood and thinking about that moment to overcome a present state of sadness); (2) bodily emotional work, where an individual aims to change a particular physical state in order to generate a different emotional experience (i.e. undertaking physical exercises to overcome fear and anxiety); and (3) expressive emotional work, which is reflected in one's change in expressive gesticulations in order to change how one feels (i.e. overcoming anger through intentional laughter). Hochschild argues that emotional labour is more associated with the public sphere where individuals are required to behave in emotionally conformist ways, while the private sphere of family, home and friendships involves emotional work which is less formalised.

Nevertheless, the ever-increasing commodification of work impacts on one's emotional experiences in the public and private spheres, and as individuals became estranged from their own feelings at work this often has a negative reflection in the private sphere too. This topic is addressed in three of her books: *The Second Shift: Working Families and the Revolution at Home* (1989), *The Time Bind: When Work Becomes Home and Home Becomes Work* (1997) and *The Commercialization of Intimate Life: Notes from Home and Work* (2003). In the latter two books Hochschild analysed the experiences of working parents employed in a successful private company and found how their public and private lives gradually became entangled. This situation created emotional contradictions where most of the employees emphasised how central the families are for their lives, yet they felt that their workplace provided them with more emotional support than their own homes. Hochschild situates these contradictions within the context of highly competitive neoliberal economies which put pressure on individuals to succeed at work and at home.

In her more recent publications Hochschild explores the changing features of intimacy and the relationships between emotions and politics. In *The Outsourced Self: Intimate Life in Market Times* (2012) she analyses how the emotional lives of individuals have become marketised as they outsource their intimacy through paid-up internet dating, commercial surrogacy, 'rent a friend' services and expensive long-distance care for elderly parents. This ever-increasing individualisation associated with what she calls 'the emotional terms of engagement' affects political life too. Thus, in her 2016 book *Strangers in Their Own Land: Anger and Mourning on the American Right*, Hochschild shows how emotions influence political choices. Drawing on five years of ethnographic research among the deeply conservative voters in Louisiana, she found that their political preferences were less influenced by self-interest and much more by, what Hochschild terms, 'deep stories'. The deep stories are shared narratives that underpin key features of one's everyday life. Hence her respondents were willing to accept new information about the world and the moral precepts only if those fit with the already established deep story narratives. The knowledge that Louisiana was one of the poorest, least educated and most environmentally degraded US states had no impact on the popular support for regulating polluting industries or for investing in public education. Thus, rather than being driven by narrow economic rationality, political choices remain rooted in deep story emotional attachments.

Intersectionality

Patricia Hill Collins' work is also shaped by civil rights movements in the 1960s and early 1970s. While Latour and Hochschild challenged the hegemony of rationality and science, Hill Collins zoomed in on the institutional origins and structural reproduction of group-based domination. More specifically, in her path-breaking first book *Black Feminist Thought: Knowledge, Consciousness, and the Politics of Empowerment* (1990), Hill Collins develops a theory of intersectionality that identifies different but interdependent forms of oppression. Unlike traditional Marxists or feminists who would identify class or gender as the primary source of discrimination, Hill Collins expands on Kimberlé Crenshaw's notion of intersectionality and argues that racial, sexual, class-based and gender-based domination are intersecting and mutually interdependent power structures. Not only is one oppressed as a woman, an ethnic or sexual minority or a poor person, but also these categories tend simultaneously to overlap as they reflect the power realities of the existing world.

The book's key argument is that since oppression operates at various levels (i.e. politics, economics, ideology, etc.) it cannot be addressed on one level only. For example, focusing exclusively on economic inequalities and class hierarchies does not allow one to identify the sources of racism and sexism.

Her analysis centres on the historical experience of African American women to show how they remain invisible in the public sphere and how their voices had no place in the conventional narratives of the past. Bringing together literary figures and academic scholarship, including the work of Audre Lorde, Alice Walker and Angela Davis among others, Hill Collins sees the historical trajectory of African American women as the quintessential example of intersectional oppression involving race, gender, sexuality and class. Nevertheless, precisely because these women share this oppressive past (and present) their voices could give better insight on how power structures operate. In other words, this relatively unique historical experience opens the analytical window for understanding how intersectional domination affects other groups of individuals. Hill Collins' pioneering book also articulates a distinct version of the standpoint theory.

However, unlike Dorothy Smith and Sandra Harding, who focus almost exclusively on the gender standpoint dimension, Hill Collins brings together gender, race and class to develop a form of the standpoint theory that views the social world through the prism of African American women. In this approach knowledge is firmly associated with one's social position. Hence, Hill Collins rejects the view of social science as an objective enterprise, arguing that the disadvantaged groups attain unique access to knowledge that the more privileged groups lack. In this context she identifies African American women as having a unique vantage point that is shaped by the historical legacies of multiple forms of oppression: racism that denied them political and civil rights; class exploitation that deprived them of the fruits of their labour; and patriarchal ideological control that reduced their role to the domestic sphere of homecare and childrearing. Being an underprivileged group in terms of race, gender and class African American women have developed a distinct understanding of social reality which they can share with others to understand and transform the social world in which we all live.

This standpoint approach is developed further in her second book, *Fighting Words: Black Women and the Search for Justice* (1998), which explores how African American women experienced and dealt with 'internal' oppression; that is, with the asymmetrical power relations and exploitation that occurred within 'Black communities'. She defines African American women as 'outsiders within' who confront two layers of injustice – one from the dominant white hegemonic mainstream society that all minority groups experience and the other stemming from the gender hierarchies that exist within African American communities. The book zooms in on many issues that affect black women including mothering, economic deprivation, the entrenchment of white supremacy, the rise of Afrocentrism and the ever-increasing 're-segregation of American society by race and class'. She also makes an important theoretical point in the context of how the conventional approaches distinguish between theory and thinking. Hill Collins offers a critique of conventional understandings that are inclined to differentiate between perspectives that support the status quo and refer to them as 'theories' while perspectives that challenge the injustice are usually called 'thoughts'. In her own words: 'It is not that elites produce theory while everyone else produces mere thought. Rather, elites possess the power to legitimate the knowledge that they define as theory as being universal, normative, and ideal' (Hill Collins, 1998: xiii).

While sexuality was discussed in her first two books it is in her 2004 book, *Black Sexual Politics: African Americans, Gender, and the New Racism*, that this becomes a central topic. This book applies her intersectional theory to the complex experiences of the African American population. She argues that heterosexism and racism tend to operate together as they establish normative parameters around what constitute the ideals of femininity and masculinity. While the old racism was defined by slavery and Jim Crow laws, contemporary new racism is much more subtle because it is reproduced through mainstream education and the mass media and is also internalised by many African Americans and other minorities. One of the key features of this new racism is its reproduction of the values that glorify heterosexual models of beauty and material success while expressing stern hostility towards homosexuality and other non-heterosexual experiences. Hill Collins points out that African American LGBT individuals tend to be invisible in the public eye and that most churches that have black congregations show animosity towards sexual minorities. She insists that resistance to racial and gender oppression cannot transpire at the expense of LGBT individuals and other minorities.

In her more recent publications such as *From Black Power to Hip Hop: Racism, Nationalism, and Feminism* (2006) and *Another Kind of Public Education: Race, Schools, the Media, and Democratic Possibilities* (2009), Hill Collins provides a focused analysis of everyday experiences of racism, sexism and class-based discrimination in American society. She also zooms in on the relationship between black nationalism and feminism in hip-hop culture, arguing that despite some structural changes that have taken place after the 1960s civil rights movements, racism remains entrenched in the public educational system, mass media, popular music and other spheres of everyday life.

Contemporary Relevance and Applications

Since its institutional establishment as an academic discipline in the late nineteenth century sociology has been inspired by Enlightenment ideals, including its commitment to identifying the most rational and most efficient analytical tools that would help with understanding and explaining how the social world works. In this context sociology was envisaged as a science capable of distinguishing clearly between facts and values and between truth and non-truth. Mainstream sociology prioritised reason and logic over emotions on the assumption that most human actions can ultimately be explained through the rational traits of human conduct. This positivist paradigm left no space for particularisms of any kind and professed the idea that science (including social science) exists only in the context of verifiable truths and as such is blind to all value orientations.

However, this Enlightenment ideal of social science as the value-neutral project was largely shattered by the social and political crises of the late 1960s and early 1970s. The new scholarship challenged this well-established paradigm, arguing that the commitment to reason and value-free science does not shield one from implicit biases, veiled political preferences or indiscernible economic predilections that might underpin one's research. The new scholars pointed out that the nominal neutrality of science often hides its central role in perpetuating the status quo and thus maintaining the asymmetrical power relations where men dominate women and majorities dominate ethnic minorities. This critical scholarship, later fully articulated by such sociologists as Latour, Hochschild and Hill Collins, has influenced contemporary debates on the impartiality and value of science (including social science) in everyday life.

SOCIOLOGY, PUBLIC ISSUES AND MODERN SOCIETY

The new directions in social theory lead us to consider the relationship between sociology and public discourses in the twenty-first century. On this, public sociology has been distinguished from professional sociology. Public sociology advocates using disciplinary expertise to engage with issues of public concern in a style accessible to non-academic audiences. While distinctive, this concept obscures the extent to which sociology is always already intrinsically linked to public issues, however – a point made clear in C. Wright Mills' concept of the sociological imagination. Considering modern society as characterised by communicative awareness of its own self-creation and structured by ideas attempting to guide this self-creation, sociology is an integral part of this. Sociology produces knowledge that reflects on, clarifies, and criticises insights derived from society. As such, sociology is a specialised reflexive discourse that articulates the self-description, self-analysis and self-critique of modernity. From this perspective, the intellectual development of sociology is inherently bound up with the historical development of society itself.

The fierce criticisms of science gave birth to the anti-foundationalist perspectives which, following Feyerabend (1987, 1975), argue that knowledge is not a product of consistent and cumulative activity where scientists simply discover and test new ideas and gradually move forward, bringing about scientific progress in a linear fashion. Instead they point out that new scientific breakthroughs have regularly been contested and even discouraged by the academic establishment. As Feyerabend points out, the discoveries of both Copernicus and Galileo were not products of cumulative science but in fact went against the existing parameters of knowledge:

> The church at the time of Galileo was much more faithful to reason than Galileo himself, and also took into consideration the ethical and social consequences of Galileo's doctrine. Its verdict against Galileo was rational and just, and revisionism can be legitimized solely for motives of political opportunism. (1975: 206)

Influential anti-foundationalists such as Jacques Derrida, Michel Foucault, Jean Baudrillard and Jean-Francois Lyotard argue that science should not have a privileged status but requires the same treatment as other meta-narratives – to be scrutinised, contested and deconstructed. For anti-foundationalists, all belief systems and truth claims have a degree of legitimacy, and since human relations are highly dynamic and malleable, different cultural worlds are bound to articulate different and mutually incommensurable discourses of truth.

In this context, Latour's research on how scientists work has influenced current debates on the hegemonic role of scientists in the modern world but has also inadvertently contributed to recent debates about the declining influence of science and knowledge in the post-truth era. In the world of 'alternative facts' Latour's ideas about the social construction of factual knowledge have been appropriated by anti-science movements including climate change deniers, religious fundamentalists and other such groups. To counter this very recent trend Latour (2017) has defended science, arguing that such a defence requires a different strategy:

> We will have to regain some of the authority of science. That is the complete opposite from where we started doing science studies. Now, scientists have to win back respect. But the solution is the same: You need to present science as science in action. I agree that's risky, because we make the uncertainties and controversies explicit. (2017: 1)

By challenging science, scholars have also questioned the centrality of reason and rationality in understanding the social world. Hence Hochschild's pioneering contributions inaugurated the new area of study – the sociology of emotions. The sociologists of emotion such as Jonathan H. Turner, Thomas Scheff, Randall Collins and Jack Barbalet among others emphasise how central emotions are for understanding social relations. These researchers demonstrate how emotions are embedded in everyday interactions of human beings and how they can be instrumentalised by political leaders, private corporations, and friends and family members. Drawing on Durkheim, Goffman and Hochschild, scholars explore how individuals regulate their feelings to conform with the dominant norms or specific situational contexts. Emotions also underpin many ritualistic events and are central to establishing and maintaining social networks. While Scheff (2006) identifies shame and rage as key emotions that cause social conflicts, Hill Collins focuses on the role of interaction ritual chains, which can be interrupted by fear and emotional tension.

However, the most vocal criticisms of the rationalist and positivist paradigms of social science have been voiced by the standpoint approaches that challenge the idea of scientific objectivity and value neutrality. Drawing on Dorothy Smith and Hill Collins among others, the standpoint theorists argue that power is rooted in one's individual knowledge and experience, and consequently one's view of the world is shaped by one's class, gender, ethnicity, race, sexuality and other social categories. While they see all group identities as socially constructed, the standpoint theorists such as Nancy Hartsock, Donna Haraway, Sandra Harding, Tina Campt or Alison Wylie insist that one cannot transcend one's standpoint and pretend that one is speaking from some universal and neutral vantage point.

Instead they argue that all knowledge claims are deeply rooted in one's specific social conditions. Hence while a scientist can aspire to offer value-neutral analyses of social reality, one's gender, ethnicity, class or sexual orientation will inevitably shape one's view of the world. Standpoint theory has influenced recent public debates on 'white privilege' in the United States and the UK, where the female, ethnic and sexual minority academics and students have challenged what they see to be a hegemony of the white male worldview which has defined the parameters of what constitutes recognised knowledge and scholarship. The standpoint perspective has also played a significant role in the rise of international social movements such as Black Lives Matter (BLM) that campaign against institutionalised racism and violence against minority populations in the United States. This movement highlights police brutality, racial profiling and the failings of the criminal justice systems in the United States.

Criticisms

The new directions in sociological theory that centre on the critique of positivism, scientism, instrumental rationalism and 'white privilege' have reinvigorated social thought. Hence, a number of sociologists, including Latour, Hochschild and Hill Collins, have articulated their ideas in the public arena and have given numerous interviews and commentaries in the mass media. This form of public sociology has galvanised interest in these topics beyond the narrow confines of academia. In some respects, as sociologists tackle the everyday social and political issues, they have received a degree of public attention not seen since the late 1960s and early 1970s. However, this rising visibility of 'new directions' critical scholarship has also generated criticism from various quarters. Thus, Latour's work has been characterised as problematic in the sense that it encourages relativism, irrationalism and mysticism. For example, scientists Gross and Levitt (1994) argue that Latour's critique of scientific enterprise jeopardises trust in science and in this way opens the door for the proliferation of superstitious and irrational views. They insist that Latour relativises science, turning it into an arbitrary and ritualistic set of practices while the scientific process involves rigorous testing, scrupulous decision making, creativity, skill and knowledge. In a similar vein the philosopher John Searle (2009) describes Latour as an 'extreme social constructivist' whose analyses undermine rational thinking. For example, Searle finds many of Latour's claims nebulous, including his view that the Egyptian pharaoh Ramses II could not have died from tuberculosis, as such a characterisation of the disease did not exist until Koch's discovery, in 1882.

While Latour's work has been criticised for its relativist and anti-scientific implications, Hochschild has been critiqued for the lack of conceptual clarity. Hence Bolton (2005) argues that the concept of 'emotional labour' is flawed in the sense that it misinterprets the dynamics of labour power. Bolton (2005) finds this concept too wide to capture the complexity of social experiences that take place in organisational settings. She insists that Hochschild conflates the physical labour process with the emotional labour of public sector workers. In this context she 'tends to use the terms "public" and "commercial" interchangeably, [thus] creating an oversimplified dichotomy' (Bolton, 2005: 60). In other words, Hochschild makes no differentiation between commercial service emotional work and the emotional labour that stems from 'professional norms of conduct, or emotion work during normal social interaction in the workplace' (Bolton, 2005: 60). Following Marx, Hochschild sees the two forms of labour as generating worker's alienation from their labour as they are separated from control and ownership of their labour. However, Bolton emphasises the difference between the two forms of labour: 'unlike the factory worker, they [public workers] own the means of production and, therefore, the capacity to present a "sincere" or "cynical" performance lies within the emotional labourer' (2005: 61). Other scholars have criticised different aspects of Hochschild's theory of emotion management. Hence Addison (2017) argues that Hochschild's distinction between the 'real' and 'false' self is unsustainable as all expressions of selfhood are real in some sense. Following Goffman, Addison insists that 'all of our performances are real in the sense that they simply take place – there is no unchanging core that is the "real" self, only an ongoing and increasing personal portfolio of roles' (2017: 10). Theodosius (2006) has also criticised Hochschild's overemphasis on the structural determinants of emotion management, arguing that workers often manage to resist managerial control of their emotions and maintain a substantial degree of emotional autonomy in the workplace.

Hill Collins' work has also received critical scrutiny. Some scholars have questioned her assumption that oppressed minority groups are by themselves an agent of social change. As Ramirez (2016: 1) points out in his critique of *Black Feminist Thought*, one's gender, ethnicity or sexuality does not constitute a political programme as such but requires intense and organised social action. While Hill Collins believes that 'creation of a critical mass of African-American women' within academia would create a tipping point for social change, Ramirez is highly sceptical of such a position. In his own words:

> The presence of a collection of bodies does not necessarily imply the collection of a uniform ideology and platform. This is a major problem when any attempt to change, the kind for which Collins calls—which maps onto the position of black female feminists, though it can be

applied more generally to the intersections that contaminate all oppressed bodies—is met with resistance from within in the sense that no cohesion remains intact in a structure of bodies without an ideological architecture. (Ramirez, 2016: 1)

Other theorists have focused on the logical pitfalls of intersectionality and standpoint theory. For example, Reilly-Cooper (2013) argues that intersectionality homogenises the complexity of human experiences and simply assumes that one's oppression is bound to generate a uniform understanding of social reality. However, this line of reasoning cannot account for the situations where the same experience of oppression is interpreted very differently by different individuals, with some acknowledging and resisting their subjugated position and others interpreting the same situation as a normal and natural state of affairs. This line of criticism is developed further by Brubaker (2004, 2015, 2016), who perceives both intersectionality and standpoint theory as reinforcing 'groupism' within social science. By groupism Brubaker means 'the tendency to take discrete, sharply differentiated, internally homogenous and externally bounded groups as basic constituents of social life, chief protagonists of social conflict and fundamental units of social analysis' (2004: 164). In this sense both intersectionality and standpoint theory are prone to reification of group membership, which leaves no room for individual diversities and the dynamic complexity of social action.

Since the new directions in sociological theory often blend social analysis with political activism, they are much more visible in the public arena. However, this openness to the wider world has also generated substantial criticism as some scholars believe that being an activist and a social scientist are mutually exclusive endeavours. The argument is that, unlike activists who are focused on marshalling simple slogans and mobilising a large number of people around the black and white 'lowest common denominators', sociologists tackle complex, contradictory and dynamic realities of the ever-changing social world.

Conclusion

The social movements of the 1960s and early 1970s gave birth to many novel ideas and have played a crucial part in the development of sociology as a versatile academic discipline. This period created opportunities to ask new questions and to challenge the existing paradigms and the established social order. Hence scholars such as Bruno Latour, Arlie Hochschild and Patricia Hill Collins, among many others, opened new avenues of research and set the foundations for new directions in sociology. They questioned the conventional understandings of science, rationality and established power relations by developing new interpretative horizons and novel concepts and theories including actor–network theory, the emotional labour approach and intersectionality. These new research directions have further generated a variety of subdisciplines and thematic fields within sociology and have inaugurated novel theoretical perspectives that define contemporary sociological thought.

References

Addison, M. (2017) Overcoming Arlie Hochschild's Concepts of the 'Real' and 'False' Self by Drawing on Pierre Bourdieu's Concept of Habitus. *Emotion, Space and Society*, 23 (1), pp. 9–15.

Bolton, S. (2005) *Emotion Management in the Workplace*. Basingstoke: Palgrave Macmilan.

Brubaker, R. (2004) *Ethnicity without Groups*. Cambridge, MA: Harvard University Press.

Brubaker, R. (2015) *Grounds for Difference*. Cambridge, MA: Harvard University Press.

Brubaker, R. (2016) *Trans: Gender and Race in an Age of Unsettled Identities*. Princeton, NJ: Princeton University Press.

Collins, P. H. (1990) *Black Feminist Thought: Knowledge, Consciousness, and the Politics of Empowerment*. London: Unwin Hyman.

Collins, P. H. (1998) *Fighting Words: Black Women and the Search for Justice*. Minneapolis, MN: University of Minnesota Press.

Collins, P. H. (2004) *Black Sexual Politics: African Americans, Gender and the New Racism*. London: Routledge.

Collins, P. H. (2006) *From Black Power to Hip Hop: Racism, Nationalism, and Feminism*. Philadelphia, PA: Temple University Press.

Collins, P. H. (2009) *Another Kind of Public Education: Race, the Media, Schools, and Democratic Possibilities*. Boston, MA: Beacon Press.

Feyerabend, P. (1975) *Against Method: Outline of an Anarchistic Theory of Knowledge*. London: New Left Books.

Feyerabend, P. (1987) *Farewell to Reason*. London: Verso.

Giddens, A. (1986) *The Nation-State and Violence*. Cambridge: Polity.

Gross, P. R. and Levitt, N. (1994) *Higher Superstition: The Academic Left and its Quarrels with Science*. Baltimore, MD: Johns Hopkins University Press.

Hochschild, A. R. (1983) *The Managed Heart: Commercialization of Human Feeling*. Berkeley, CA: University of California Press.

Hochschild, A. R. (1989) *The Second Shift: Working Families and the Revolution at Home*. New York: Viking.

Hochschild, A. R. (1997) *The Time Bind: When Work Becomes Home and Home Becomes Work*. New York: Metropolitan Books.

Hochschild, A. R. (2003) *The Commercialization of Intimate Life: Notes from Home and Work*. Berkeley, CA: University of California Press.

Hochschild, A. R. (2012) *The Outsourced Self: Intimate Life in Market Times*. New York: Metropolitan Books.

Hochschild, A. R. (2016) *Strangers in Their Own Land: Anger and Mourning on the American Right*. New York: The New Press.

Kuhn, T. S. (1962) *The Structure of Scientific Revolutions*. Chicago, CA: University of Chicago Press.

Latour, B. (1987) *Science in Action: How to Follow Scientists and Engineers Through Society*. Cambridge, MA: Harvard University Press.

Latour, B. (1988 [1984]) *The Pasteurization of France*. A. Sheridan and J. Law, trans. Cambridge, MA: Harvard University Press.
Latour, B. (1993 [1991]) *We Have Never Been Modern*. Hemel Hempstead: Harvester Wheatsheaf.
Latour, B. (2005) *Reassembling the Social: An Introduction to Actor-Network Theory*. Oxford: Oxford University Press.
Latour, B. (2009) *On the Modern Cult of the Factish Gods*. Durham, NC: Duke University Press.
Latour, B. (2013) *An Inquiry into Modes of Existence: An Anthropology of the Moderns*. C. Porter, trans. Cambridge, MA: Harvard University Press.
Latour, B. (2017) *Facing Gaia: Eight Lectures on the New Climatic Regime*. Oxford: Polity.
Latour, B. (2018) *Down to Earth: Politics in the New Climatic Regime*. Cambridge: Polity.
Latour, B. and Woolgar, S. (1979) *Laboratory Life: The Social Construction of Scientific Facts*. London: Sage.
Malešević, S. (2017) The Organization of Military Violence in the 21st Century. *Organization*, 24(4), pp. 456–74.
Mills, C. W. (2000 [1956]) *The Power Elite*. New edition. New York: Oxford University Press.
Ramirez, M. (2016) *Black Feminist Thought And The Pitfalls Of A Critical Mass*. Public Seminar. Available at: https://publicseminar.org/ (accessed 8 July 2020).
Reilly-Cooper, R. (2013) Intersectionality and Identity Politics. *Rebecca Reilly-Cooper*, 15 April [blog]. Available at: https://rebeccarc.com/2013/04/15/intersectionality-and-identity-politics/ (accessed 20 June 2019).
Scheff, T. (2006) Aggression, Hypermasculine Emotions and Relations: The Silence/Violence Pattern. *Irish Journal of Sociology*, 15(1), pp. 24–39.
Searle, J. R. (2009) Why Should You Believe It? *New York Review of Books*, 24 September [online]. Available at: https://www.nybooks.com/articles/2009/09/24/why-should-you-believe-it/ (accessed 20 June 2019).
Theodosius, C. (2006) Recovering Emotion from Emotion Management. *Sociology*, 40(5), pp. 893–910.

INDEX

Abendroth, Wolfgang 315, 318, 319
abortion rights 401
actor–network theory 423
Adams, John 187
Adams, John Quincy 187
Addison, M. 432
Adenauer, Konrad 171, 317
*ad-hoc*ing 68, 69
Adorno, Gertrud 167
Adorno, Theodore 143, 144, 158, 159,
    160–1, 165–84, 314, 315, 316,
    318, 327
  Adorno–Benjamin debate 179–80
  against systems and systemic
    thinking 174–6
  contemporary relevance and
    applications 181–3
  criticisms 183–4
  culture industry 170, 177–9, 182,
    183–4
  Dialectic of Enlightenment 166,
    170, 174, 176–7, 178, 181
  historical, social and political
    context 168–72
  ideas and arguments 172–81
  life and intellectual context 165–8
  Negative Dialectics 167, 169, 176,
    181, 183
  negative dialectics and identity
    thinking 172–3, 183
  studies in fascism, prejudice, and
    authoritarian personality 180–1
Adorno della Piana, Maria Calvelli 165
Ady, Endre 103
African Americans 25, 26, 56, 418, 421
  ghettos 287
  over-incarceration 160, 287
  racism/heterosexism intersection
    428
  women 160, 427–8, 432–3
  women's and intersectionality 427
  women's standpoint 427–8
  see also civil rights movement;
    racism

agency and agents
  actors as agents 302–3
  Althusser's denigration 140
  Bourdieu's antinomy 289
  Lukács' emphasis on 98, 111, 118
  neglect in system theory 352
agency–structure dichotomy 31, 299,
    300, 309, 381
AGIL schema 20–1, 346–7
aging 404, 406
Agnes (intersexed person) 69
Agnew, Robert 28–9
Albert, Hans 183
aleatory materialism 135–6
Alexander, Jeffrey 27–8, 29, 48
Algeria 268, 269, 275, 276, 281, 285
Algerian War of Independence
    (1954–62) 124, 125, 189, 210,
    231, 269, 274, 420, 421
alienation 98, 108, 117, 127, 139
Althusser, Charles-Joseph 120
Althusser, Louis 94, 120–41, 160–1,
    228, 230, 231
  aleatory materialism 135–6
  anti-humanism 128–9
  contemporary relevance and
    applications 136–8
  criticisms 138–40
  For Marx 120, 121, 127–8, 138–9
  historical, social and political
    context 123–7
  ideas and arguments 127–36
  ideology and ideological state
    apparatuses 133–5, 138, 140
  life and intellectual context 120–3
  murder of Hélène Rytmann 122,
    136
  overdetermination 131–3
  Reading Capital 120, 122, 129
  theory of knowledge 130–1,
    139–40
  the two Marxisms 127–8
Althusser, Lucienne Marthe (née Berger)
    120

American Sociological Association 15, 35, 57, 187, 188, 204
analytical realism 18
analytical sociology 199, 202
Anderson, Perry 92–3, 95, 100, 136, 160, 183, 257, 331
anomie
   and the danger of authoritarianism 17
   and normlessness 26
anthropology 207, 220, 275
anti-communism 17, 150–1, 232, 318
anti-foundationalism 429–30
anti-humanism 128–9, 138, 232, 346, 352
anti-positivism 57, 137
anti-psychiatry movement 37
anti-Semitism 180, 181, 248–9, 250, 357
Apel, Karl-Otto 144, 315
Archer, Margaret 381
aristocracy
   differentiation from commoners 363
   England 92–3
Aristotle 2, 134, 145, 278
Armenian genocide (1915) 389, 390
arms race 212, 361
Armstrong, P. 392–3
Aron, Raymond 189, 269
Arrighi, Giovanni 92
asylums 44–6
Attlee, Clement 296
Auge, Marc 417
Auriol, Vincent 124
Auschwitz 169, 180
Austin, John 36, 270, 324, 325
Austria, annexation (1938) 56
Austria–Hungary 55, 57–8, 102–3, 250, 368
authoritarian populism 95
autopoiesis 339, 345
axiological rationality 198–9

Bachelard, Gaston 121, 123, 127
Bacon, Francis 2
Baehr, Patrick 391–2
Balibar, Etienne 122, 129
Banton, Michael 201
Baralou, E. 350
Barber, M. D. 55, 58–9
Barnes, B. 51, 332

Barthes, Roland 206, 212
   arguments and ideas 215–17
   contemporary influence and applications 221
   criticism 222–3
   'The Death of an Author' 217, 221
   Elements of Semiology 216
   The Fashion System 216
   historical, social and political context 209–12
   life and intellectual context 207–8
   Mythologies 208, 215–16, 221
   post-structuralism and text 216–17
   signs and images 215–16
Bateson, Gregory 36, 48, 57, 339, 344, 345
Bauman, Z. 59–60, 72
Bausch, K. C. 343
Béarn peasantry 276–7
Beck, Ulrich 369
Becker, K. H. 350
Becker, Oskar 317
Becket, Samuel 178
behavioural organism 20
behaviourism 193
Bell, Daniel 151
Ben-David, Joseph 376
Bendix, Reinhard 376
Benhabib, Seyla 329
Benjamin, Walter 166, 167, 176, 182
   Adorno–Benjamin debate 179–80
Bentham, Jeremy 204, 239
Benton, T. 132–3
Berg, Alban 166
Berger, Peter 70–1, 113
Bergmann, Ernst 340
Berkeley, University of California 34–5, 38, 208–9, 229, 376, 377, 380, 398–9, 418
Berlin, Isiah 358
Berlin Wall 171, 318
Berman, Marshall 38–9
Bernstein, Eduard 104, 168
Bevan, Aneurin 296
Bhaskar, Roy 137–8
binary oppositions 214, 222, 301
Binswanger, Ludwig 228, 230
bio-power 240–1
Birdwhistell, Ray 34, 36
Bismarck, Otto von 250

Black Lives Matter (BLM) 221, 431
Black Panthers 151, 160, 421
Blacks
    youth as 'folk devils' 94
    see also African Americans
Blair, Tony 294–5, 298, 299
Blau, Peter 200
Blaut, J. M. 370
Bloch, Ernst 99, 166, 167, 168, 182, 183
Blumer, Herbert 34, 35, 376–7, 389
bodily propriety 256
body/ies
    anatomy-politics of 240–1
    beyond conscious manipulation 289
    female 405, 406
    gender and stylisation 218
    and 'habitus' 279
    importance in sociology 287
    inscribed by power 237–40
    as means of understanding the world 271
    as objects of 'positive knowledge' 234
Bolshevik Party 117
Bolshevik Revolution *see* Russian Revolution
Boltanski, Luc 288
Bolton, S. 432
Bordiga, Amadeo 77
Bordo, S. 223
Bottomore, T. 171
Bouchet, D. 222
Boudon, Raymond 186, 196, 204
    contemporary relevance and applications 201–2
    criticisms 202–3
    historical, social and political context 191–2
    life and intellectual context 188–9
    rational choice theory 198–9
Bourdieu, Pierre 1, 48, 72, 136, 197, 310, 268–89, 310, 384
    Algeria 276
    arguments and ideas 275–85
    Béarn peasantry studies 276–7
    centrality of recognition and misrecognition 285
    contemporary relevance and applications 286–8
    criticisms 289
    cultural, social and symbolic capital 280–2
    Distinction 272, 282–3
    education and social reproduction 277–8, 287
    habitus 278–9
    historical, social and political context 271–5
    life and intellectual context 268–71
    Outline of A Theory of Practice 269, 275, 281–2
    reflexivity 283
    social fields 280
    the state 285–6, 289
    symbolic power 284
bourgeoisie 253, 256
    Gramsci's view 81, 82, 84, 90
    Hobsbawm's view of Italian 79
    Lukács' view 103, 107, 110, 111
    in one-dimensional society 157
    the reading public 320
    thought-style 115
Bourguiba, Habib 232
boxing 287
Boyns, D. 392
breaching experiments 67–8
Brecht, Bertolt 166, 167
Bretton Woods Accord (1971) 190
Britain *see* UK
Brown, Gordon 295, 298
Brubaker, R. 9, 433
Brym, R. 30
Buber-Agassi, J. 412
bureaucracy 306, 308
Burke, Peter 372
Burman, P. 308
Burns, Tom 38
Butler, Judith Pamela 138, 212
    Bodies That Matter 218–19
    contemporary influence and applications 221–2
    criticisms 223–4
    Excitable Speech 219
    Frames of War 219–20
    Gender Trouble 217, 218
    historical, social and political context 212
    life and intellectual context 208–9
    performing gender 217–19
    Precarious Life 219

California 61–2, 170
Callaghan, James 297
Callinicos, A. 139–40
Cambodia 38
Campbell, Donald T. 348
Camus, Albert 210, 274, 338
Canguilhelm, Georges 229, 230, 269, 284
capital *see* cultural capital; economic capital; social capital; symbolic capital
capitalism 95, 241, 305, 408, 421
   alternative possibilities 155–6
   change since Marx 333
   contradictions of 80–1, 105, 157, 179, 182
   decline predicted 381
   dominant structures of 132
   and educational ideological state apparatus 133–4
   in England 92–3
   and fascism 147, 180–1
   vs. feudalism 8, 254, 296
   Habermas and 319, 320, 321, 322, 326, 329, 333
   ideological value underpinning 288
   inherent untruth 145–6
   in Italy 79, 80–1
   late 182, 323, 329, 330, 333
   monopoly 153, 156, 170, 175, 333
   'network' 288
   and the Protestant ethic 13
   and reification 107–8, 109
   and separation of producers from one another 102
   'state' 170, 180
   and state socialism 298–9
   and stolen freedom 127
   and surplus repression 154
   as totalising phenomenon 110
   in US 151, 170
   welfare 25
Carter, Jimmy 38
Castoriadis, C. 222
Castro, J. E. 262
Catholic Church 80, 90–1, 366
Catholicism 121, 123
causality 3
Cavour (Camillo Benson, Count of) 79, 80

censorship, of speech 219
centre/periphery differentiation 347
CERPA 189
Chaplin, Charlie 166
Chicago School 36, 190, 203
Chicago University 34, 35, 38, 188, 191, 203
China 367
   Communist Revolution 123, 150
   Cultural Revolution 124, 223
   Great Leap Forward 123
   Sino-Soviet split 123–4
Chirac, Jacques 274
Chodorow, Nancy 410
Chomsky, Noah 324
   Foucault–Chomsky debate 242
Church/state separation 3
citizenship, inter-state differences 367–8
civil rights movement 29, 37, 151, 160, 318, 380, 418, 419, 421–2
civil society
   development of idea 5
   East vs. West 86
   Gellner's view 364–5
   global 329
   Gramsci's conception of state and 86–7
   and the public sphere 320–1
   and Third Way politics 306–7
civilisation/s
   'clash of' 276, 277
   Elias' account of development 252, 254–8, 264
class
   contemporary conceptualisation 298
   education and reproduction of 277–8
   'fraudulent' status symbols 40
   and hegemony 82–3
   and intersectionality 50, 426–7
   and taste 282–3
class conflict 37, 90–1, 195, 367–8
class consciousness 110–12, 113, 116, 117–18
class inequality 272, 420
   UK 296–7
Classical Sociological Theory (Loyal and Malešević) 1, 2, 8
Clayman, S. E. 72
Clegg, S. 309

climate change 307
Clinton, Bill 295
cognitive rationality 199
Cohen, Herman 101
Cold War 16–17, 36, 61, 123, 124, 125, 147, 151, 157, 171, 273, 298, 318, 359–60, 361, 379
Coleman, James Seymour 186, 203, 204
    contemporary relevance and applications 201–2
    Foundations of Social Theory 197–8
    historical, social and political context 189–91
    life and intellectual context 187–8
    rational choice theory 196–8
    reports on education 188, 203–4
'collective representations' 43
collective traumas 28
Collins, Randall 36, 37–8, 48, 375–93, 430
    arguments and ideas 381–8
    Conflict Sociology 376, 377, 381, 382–3, 386
    conflict theory 382–4, 388–9, 392–3
    contemporary relevance and applications 388–90
    The Credential Society 377, 381, 384–5
    criticisms 390–3
    historical, social and political context 378–81
    interaction ritual chains 386–8, 392, 431
    life and intellectual context 375–8
    and the 1968 generation 389
    sociology of education and intellectual networks 384–6, 391–2
    The Sociology of Philosophies 377–8, 385–6, 391–2
colonialism 80, 210, 215–16, 243, 254–5
Comintern (Communist International) 77, 80–1, 169
commodity fetishism 101–2, 109, 117, 175
commodity form 107, 108
common sense
    and hegemony 90, 94
    as mutual knowledge 304
    understanding of the world 62, 63, 65, 66, 68, 73
    see also doxa
communication
    Habermas and 321, 324–6, 331
    Luhmann and 345, 348–9, 351
communicative action theory 324–6
communicative competence 324–5
communicative rationality 324, 327, 333
communism
    collapse of French 124
    as scientific ideal 23
    US/Western fear of 16–17, 36, 150–1, 157
Communist Party 160
    as 'modern prince' 90
    and proletarian consciousness 111–12
Communist Party of China 123
Communist Party of France (PCF) 86, 120, 121, 122, 123, 124, 125–6, 127, 132, 140, 209, 210, 231, 272, 273, 274
Communist Party in Germany (KPD) 81, 169, 171
Communist Party of the Soviet Union (CPSU) 120, 125
Comte, Auguste 7
Condorcet, Nicolas de 3, 6
confidence tricksters 40–1
conflict theory 295–6, 382–4
Connell, R. 308
consciousness
    bifurcation of 408
    class 110–12, 113, 116, 117
    intellectual shaping of 90
    and phenomenology 59–60, 270
    reification of 109
    three aspects of 302–3
conservatism 295, 297, 306, 353
    cultural 167
    dominance in US, 1950s 16, 17
    Mannheim's analysis 113–15
Conservative governments, UK 296, 297–8, 361
'constellations' 176
consumerism and consumption 16, 157, 170, 178

contraception rights 401
'convergence thesis' 18
conversation analysis 71–2
counter-culture 37, 151–2, 160, 294, 421–2
Courreges, Pierre 121
court nobility 253–4, 255, 258
Craib, I. 184
Cremshaw, Kimberlé 413, 426
Crispin, Jessica 413–14
critical realism 137–8
critical sociology 174, 304
critical theory 143–6, 168, 330, 332–3
    and emancipatory interest 324
    origins 144–5
    and traditional theory 145–6
    see also Frankfurt School
Croce, Benedetto 78, 81, 82
Cuban Missile Crisis 318
Cuban Revolution (1959) 150
Cuff, E. C. 73
cultural capital 277–8, 280–1, 285
cultural diversity 214–15, 222
Cultural Revolution, China 124, 223
cultural studies 93–5, 221
culture
    Adorno and 177–80, 182, 183–4
    Agraria and Industria 362–3, 363–4, 370
    Gramsci and 87, 91, 95
    Kultur vs 'civilisation' 255
    Levi-Strauss and 213, 214–15
    Marcuse and 157, 162
    marginalised in utilitarian tradition 203
    media appropriation 157
    and social action 13, 18, 20
    strong cultural programme 28, 29
    in Western Marxism 92
culture industry 144, 170, 177–9
    today 182
Custody of Infants Act (1839), UK 399
cyborg concept 411
Czechoslovakia 357, 359–60
    communist takeover (1948) 150

Dagenham Ford factory strikes (1968) 401–2
Damiens, Robert, execution 237
Dandeker, C. 308
Davis, Angela 160

de Beauvoir, Simone Lucie Ernestine Marie Bertrand de 207, 210, 396, 414
    arguments and ideas 402–4
    The Coming of Age 404
    contemporary relevance and applications 410–11
    criticisms 412–14
    and existentialism 404
    historical, social and political context 400–1
    life and intellectual context 396–7
    The Mandarins 403–4
    The Second Sex 401, 402–3
    She Came to Stay 403
de Clapiers, Luc 339
de Gaulle, Charles 125, 209, 210, 211, 231, 272
de Saussure, Ferdinand 210, 214
deconstructionist turn 221
Defert, Daniel 229
democracy 329
    bourgeois 138, 152–3
    vs. capitalism 326
    dialogic 306–7
    Habermas and 319, 327, 333
    Schutz's view 59
    see also social democracy; liberal democracy/ies
Democratic Party, US 295
Derrida, Jacques 95, 135, 136, 181, 221, 328, 430
Descartes, René 145, 253
determinism 30, 92, 123, 215, 289, 371
    economic 371
    mechanical 79, 80
deviance
    Agnew's expanded strain theory 28–9
    Merton's strain theory 26, 30, 31
Dex, S. 202
dialectic
    Adorno's negative 172–3, 176, 183
    critical theory 146
    Engels 106
    of Enlightenment 176–7
    Goldmann 116
    Hegel 101, 106, 131, 146
    Lukács 101, 107–8
    Marx 70, 105–6, 131–2
dialectical materialism 126, 128, 130, 131, 150

dialogic democracy 306–7
differentiation 346–8
Dilthey, Wilhelm 101, 146, 148
disciplinary gaze 238–9
discourse
    Foucault's account 234, 235–6, 245
    Orientalism as 242–3
distributive justice 194
division of labour 108, 347, 367
    and reification 106–7
documentary method of interpretation 68
Douglas, J. D. 68
doxa 270, 275, 281, 285, 289
Dumezil, George 229, 230
Dunning, Eric 250
Durkheim 1, 8, 17, 24, 35, 70, 72, 213, 215, 216, 231, 250, 356, 368, 425, 430
    Bourdieu and 269, 271, 275, 278, 281, 285, 290
    Collins and 375, 380, 381, 382, 386, 387, 388, 391
    Giddens and 293, 294, 296, 299, 300
    Goffman and 34, 36, 41, 43, 51
    Parsons and 18, 21, 65
    and social facts 66, 122, 271
    and structuralism 220
Dutschke, Rudi 319

Ebert, Friedrich 149
economic capital 290
economic power 367
economy of practices 281–2
education
    and class inequality, UK 297
    credentialism 384–5, 388
    and nationhood 364
    and social reproduction 277–8, 286–7
    US policy 188, 203–4
Eisenhower, Dwight D. 151
Eisler, Hans 166
Elias, Hermann 248, 249
Elias, Norbert 48, 248–65, 293, 310, 391
    arguments and ideas 253–61
    contemporary relevance and applications 261–4
    The Court Society 249, 253–4
    criticisms 264–5
    The Established and the Outsiders 250, 258–9
    figurational (process) sociology 253
    The Germans 251, 261
    historical, social and political context 250–3
    involvement and detachment 260–1
    life and intellectual context 248–50
    On the Process of Civilisation (*The Civilizing Process*) 249, 250, 251, 252–3, 254–8, 259, 262, 264, 265
    and Parsons 262
    Quest for Excitement 250, 261, 264
    state formation 255–7
    state as a monopolisation of violence and taxation 258
    What is Sociology? 260
Elias, Sophie 248, 249
Elliott, G. 126, 139
Elster, Jon 201
Emerson, Richard 200–1
emotional energy 386–7, 392
emotional labour 424–6, 432
emotions
    and politics 426
    regulation strategies 425
    romantic glorification 6
    and social action 49, 424–5
    sociology of 430–1
empathy 5, 60
empiricism 93, 128, 130, 161, 193, 270, 382
    as Enlightenment principle 3
Encyclopédie (Diderot and d'Alembert) 4
Engels, Friedrich 77, 98, 99, 106, 126, 132
England 92–3, 187, 192, 219, 255, 360
Enlightenment 115, 144, 167, 209, 246, 295, 327, 333, 342, 419
    dialectic of 176–7
    key principles 3
    and sociology 1–2, 3–6, 295–6, 428–9
environmental disaster 423
epistemes 244–5
Equal Pay Act (1970), UK 402
Erasmus 256
Eros 154–5

essentialism 412
established-outsider relationships 258–9
'ethico-political history' 78
'ethnic revival', US 30
ethnology 207
ethnomethodology 54, 56, 61–2, 64–9, 73–4, 221, 295, 300
   coining of term 57
   contemporary relevance and applications 71–2
   criticisms 72–3
Eurocentrism 30, 222, 223, 246, 370–1, 411
Eurocommunism 94, 122
Europe Union 328
European Community 273
European miracle 361–2, 370–1
evolutionary theory
   of social change 8, 17, 21–2, 348
   of system differentiation 30
Ewan, Stuart 182
'existential determination' 113
existentialism 210, 230, 402, 404
extermination camps 169

F-scale personality test 181
face (positive social value) 41–2
Falklands War (1981) 298
family and family life 86, 244
   patriarchal 29
   sociology of 404–5
fascism 77, 81, 84, 144, 149, 176, 177–8
   Adorno's studies 180–1
   in Italy 77, 81
   Marcuse's understanding 147, 152–3
   rise of 168–9
fashion 216
fear of death 64
Federal Republic of Germany
   see West Germany
feminism 222, 242, 396–414, 418
   and black nationalism 428
   Butler's criticism 218
   feminisms 409
   first wave 399
   fourth wave 413–14
   second wave 400–2, 409, 410
   'spoil yourself stupid' 413–14
   third wave 409, 411, 412–13
feminist standpoint theory 406–7, 412
Ferguson, Adam 4–5

Festinger, Leon 376
feudalism
   vs. capitalism 8, 254, 296
   dominant structures 132
   religious Ideological State Apparatus 133
   southern Italy 79
Feuerbach, Ludwig 121, 127, 169
Feyerabend, P. 429–30
Fieldhouse, David 358
figurational (process) sociology 248, 252–3, 260
Fine, G. 40
fire, and civilisation 263
First Indo-China War (1946–54) 124, 210, 231, 420
First World War 55, 80, 98, 99, 103, 146, 149, 161, 249, 250
flat earth theory 199
focus group method 15, 27, 31
force/consent balance 83–4, 95
Fordism 81, 150
forward panic 389, 390
Foucault 37, 48, 95, 123, 136, 181, 206, 212, 215, 218, 227–46, 269, 327, 430
   The Archaeology of Knowledge 229, 235–6
   The Birth of the Clinic 229, 234
   contemporary relevance and applications 242–4
   criticisms 244–6
   Discipline and Punish 230, 232, 237–9, 246
   from discourse to power 236–7
   Foucault–Chomsky debate 242
   governmentality 240–1
   the great confinement 233–4
   historical, social and political context 231–2
   The History of Sexuality 230, 239–40, 245
   ideas and arguments 233–41
   life and intellectual context 227–31
   Madness and Civilization 227, 228, 229, 233–4, 244
   The Order of Things 229, 235
Foucet, Christian 232
Fowler, B. 116
frame and framing 48
   gender 47

France
    feminism and women's rights 399, 401
    Fifth Republic 210, 274
    Fourth Republic 209–10
    German occupation 124, 188, 208, 228
    long durée of political instability 273–4
    post-war 124–5, 209–10
    socio-economic problems, 1970–90s 272–3
    student uprisings 211–12, 273, 420–1
    Third Republic 271–2
    utilitarianism in 191–2
    use of 'civilisation' 255
    Vichy regime 209, 228, 273
    see also Communist Party of France
Franco, Francisco 169
Frankfurt School 92, 143, 162, 165, 180, 208, 249, 314, 316, 319, 324, 410
    and reification 112–13
    see also critical theory
Franz Joseph I 103
Fraser, Nancy 223–4, 232, 329–30, 410
freedom
    concept and object 173
    vs. equality 299
    and escape from totality 175
Freikorps, Germany 251
French Communist Party
    see Communist Party of France
French Enlightenment 3–4
French Revolution 115, 153, 234, 254
Freud, Sigmund 19, 127–8, 148, 167, 177, 250, 252, 410
    Marcuse's use 154–6, 161
Freundlieb, B. 391
Friedan, Betty 400
Front Nationale 274
Fuller, Steve 391
functional analysis 25
functional differentiation 347
functional structuralism 339, 352
functionalism 59, 197, 300, 371
    see also structural functionalism

Gadamer, Hans-Georg 329
Gaddafi, Muammar 295
Galbraith, John Kenneth 151
Galileo 430

game models 260
Gamson, W. A. 38
Garaudy, Roger 125
Garfinkel, Abraham 56
Garfinkel, Arlene (née Steinback) 57
Garfinkel, Harold 36, 50, 51, 54, 69, 74, 221, 295
    contemporary relevance and applications 71–2
    criticisms 72–3
    ethnomethodology 64–9
    historical, social and political context 61–2
    life and intellectual context 56–7
    Studies in Ethnomethodology 67–9
Garibaldi 79, 80
Gastarbeiter programme 341–2
Gates, Bill 288
Gellner, Ernest 72, 223, 356, 358, 372–3
    Agraria and Industria 362–3, 370, 372
    arguments and ideas 361–6
    civil society 364–5
    contemporary relevance and applications 368–70
    criticisms 370–2
    historical, social and political context 359–60
    Islamic worlds 365–6, 369, 370, 371
    life and intellectual context 356–8
    nationalism 363–4, 371
gender
    arbitrariness 410–11
    Barthes and 223
    distinction from sex and sex category 50, 218, 405
    framing of 47
    and intersectionality 50, 426–7
    as performance 49–50, 69, 223–4
    and the public sphere 329
gender equality 379, 399
gender inequality 409, 420
gender relations 402–3, 408
gender roles, and social stability 29
gender studies 263
genetic manipulation 327
'genetic structuralism' 116
genocide 389–90
geopolitics 360–1, 367–8, 380
Geras, N. 140
German Democratic Republic (GDR) 318, 171

German Enlightenment (*Aufklärung*) 5
German Revolution (1919) 149, 161, 168
Germany 144, 368
   East/West division 171, 316–17
   Flakhelfer generation 315–16, 317
   Kultur concept 255
   national habitus 261
   Nazi 14, 149, 169, 181, 209, 251, 315, 357, 360, 367
   Nuremburg Laws (1935) 149
   post-war 171–2, 251–2, 317–19, 340–1
   pre-First World War 250–1
   Weimar period 150, 151, 168, 251
   see also Communist Party in Germany (KPD); German Democratic Republic (GDR); West Germany
Gerritsen, J. W. 263
Giddens, Anthony 48, 162, 222, 249–50, 293–310, 369, 381
   actor as agent 302–3
   arguments and ideas 299–307
   Capitalism and Modern Social Theory 294, 296, 299–300
   The Consequences of Modernity 294, 305–6
   contemporary relevance and applications 307–8
   criticisms 309–10
   developing a Third Way in politics 294–5, 306–7, 310
   historical, social and political context 296–9
   historical sociology 304–5
   life and intellectual context 293–6
   social structures as rules and resources 301–2, 309–10
   social systems 302
   structuration theory 300–1, 302, 309
   structuration as a hermeneutical theory 303–4
gift exchange 281
Gilbert, T. K. 391
Gilroy, P. 95–6
Giscard d'Estaing, Valéry 273
global inequality 423
globalisation 191, 307, 368–9
Goethe, Johann Wolfgang von 6
Goffman, Angelica Schuler (née Choate) 34, 35
Goffman, Ann (née Auerbach) 33

Goffman, Erving 33–51, 289, 376, 382, 386, 387, 389, 391, 425
   Asylums 34, 35, 37, 39, 44–6
   contemporary relevance and applications 48–50
   'On Cooling the Mark Out' 34–5, 40–1
   criticisms 50–1
   'On Face Work' 41–2
   early writings 40
   Forms of Talk 35, 48
   Frame Analysis 35, 48
   front and backstage 43–4
   Gender Advertisements 35, 47
   historical, social and political context 36–9
   ideas and arguments 39–48
   life and intellectual context 33–6
   political ambivalence 38–9
   The Presentation of Self in Everyday Life 34, 40, 42–4
   Stigma 35, 37, 38, 46–7
Goffman, Gillian (née Sankoff) 35
Goffman, Max 33
Goldmann, Lucien 116
Goldthorpe, John 196, 249, 358
Gorksi, P. 372
Goudsblom, Johan 263
Gouldner, Alvin 29, 39, 50–1, 61, 72–3, 295, 377
governmentality 241
   of the soul 243–4
Gramsci, Antonio 76–96, 100, 133, 160–1
   arguments and ideas 81–92
   criticisms 95–6
   force and consent 83–4, 95
   hegemony 76, 82–3
   historical, social and political context 79–81
   ideology, intellectuals and culture 89–92
   influence and application 92–5
   life and intellectual context 76–8
   the organic and the conjunctural 85–6
   Prison Notebooks 76, 77–8, 81–2, 95
   state and civil society 86–9, 95
   strategies for gaining power in the East and West 86
Gramsci, Francesco 76, 77
Gramsci, Guiseppina (née Marcias) 76
Gramsci, Julia (née Schuct) 77

grand theory 18, 29, 61, 343, 378
   Merton's view 24–5
Great Depression 149, 187, 317
Great Refusal 158, 159
Gross, P. R. 431
Group Analytical School of Psycho-
   therapy 249
'groupism' 9, 433
Grunberg, Carlo 166
Guha, Ranajit 92
Guillemin, Roger 417

Habermas, Ernst 314
Habermas, Jürgen 72, 73, 159, 182–3, 222, 223, 232, 314–32, 340
   and capitalist development 321
   contemporary relevance and applications 328–31
   criticisms 331–2
   historical, social and political context 316–19
   ideas and arguments 319–28
   Knowledge and Human Interests 323–4, 332
   later writings 327
   Legitimation Crisis 316, 322
   life and intellectual context 314–16
   Luhmann-Habermas debate 342, 349
   and Marxism 319, 321, 322, 323, 328, 331–2
   the public sphere 319–21, 329, 332
   The Theory of Communicative Action 316, 324–6, 328, 331, 349
habituation 71
habitus
   Bourdieu 278–9
   Elias 254
   Husserl 271
Hall, John A. 358, 365, 371
Hall, Stuart 94–5, 136, 221
Hanisch, Carol 400
Haraway, Donna 410–11
Harvard 13–14, 35, 187, 338, 376, 418
   Department of Social Relations 14, 57
Hayek, Friedrich 58, 116
Heath, Edward 297
Hechter, Michael 192, 201
Hedström, Peter 202

Hegel, Georg Wilhelm Friedrich 86, 145, 167, 173, 230, 250, 270, 330
   Althusser and 121, 126, 128, 131, 139, 141
   dialectic 101, 131, 146
   Lukács and 98, 99, 100, 101, 105, 116
   Marcuse and 146, 147, 148, 153
   Marx and 98, 128, 139, 153
hegemony 76, 81–2, 92
   and common sense 90
   post-structuralist deconstruction 93
Heidegger, Martin 1, 113, 135, 146, 148, 230, 231, 232, 270, 271, 317, 340
Held, David 183, 294, 331
Henderson, Lawrence Joseph 14, 187, 193
Herder, Johann Gottfried 6
Heritage, J. 67–8
heterosexism 428
hierarchical differentiation (stratification) 347, 352–3
Hill Collins, Patricia 416, 433
   Black Feminist Thought 426–7, 432–3
   Black Sexual Politics 428
   contemporary relevance and application 431
   criticisms 432–3
   Fighting Words 427–8
   historical, social and political context 421–2
   intersectionality 426–8
   life and intellectual context 418–19
Hindess, Barry 73, 137, 202
hippy culture 294, 377, 421–2
Hirst, Paul 137
'historic bloc' 84, 94, 96
historical materialism 127, 128, 130, 140, 304
historical sociology 356, 359, 361–74, 375, 376, 380–1
   contemporary relevance and applications 368–70
   criticisms 370–2
   Gellner 361–6
   Giddens 304–5
   Mann 366–9
historicism 128–9

Hitler, Adolf 147, 149, 166, 169, 249, 251, 261
Hitler Youth 315
Hobbes, Thomas 2–3, 4, 135
Hobsbawm, E. J. 79, 83, 95, 264–5
Hochschild, Adam 417–18
Hochschild, Arlie Russell 416, 431, 433
   contemporary relevance and applications 430–1
   criticisms 432
   emotional labour 424–6
   historical, social and political context 421–2
   life and intellectual context 417–18
   The Managed Heart 425
   The Outsourced Self 426
   Strangers in Their Own Land 426
Hoff Summer, Christina 413
Holocaust 169, 180, 209, 357
Homans, George Casper 186, 200, 204, 376
   contemporary relevance and applications 200–1
   criticisms 202–3
   English Villagers of the Thirteenth Century 187, 192
   historical, social and political context 189–91
   The Human Group 192–3
   life and intellectual context 186–7
   Social Behaviour 193
   social exchange theory 192–5
Homer 82
homosexuality 17, 428
Honigswald, Richard 249
Honneth, Axel 112, 159, 330–1
Hopi Native Americans 21
Hórthy, Miklos 104
Horkheimer, Max 144, 145, 146, 158, 160–1, 165, 166, 180, 315, 316, 327, 332–3
   Dialectic of Enlightenment 166, 174, 176–7, 178, 181
Horney, Karen 410
House Committee on Un-American Activities 17, 150
housework 404–5
Hughes, J. 263
Huizinga, J. 264
Hume, David 4–5
Hungarian Communist Party 99, 105
Hungarian (Aster) Revolution (1918) 99, 103–4, 161
Hungarian uprising (1956) 100, 231
Hungary 102–3
   Soviet invasion (1956) 210
Husserl, Edmund 55–6, 57, 59–61, 73, 166, 230, 269, 270–1, 338
Hyppolite, Jean 228, 229, 230

Ibn Khaldun 2, 365
ideal speech situation 325–6
idealism 96, 126, 130, 140
   epistemological 29, 72, 222, 357
   German 145, 177, 208
   historical 78
   liberal 309
identity thinking 172–3, 176
ideological power 366, 369, 372
ideology
   Althusser's theory 122, 133–5, 138, 140
   as form of manipulation 216
   Gramsci and 90, 91
   Mannheim's conception 113, 114
Ikegami, E. 262
immigration 341–2
imperialism 125, 243, 264
incest taboo 212–13
individualism 138, 191, 196, 309, 422
   methodological 186, 189, 192, 193, 194, 198, 199
   moral 51
Industrial Revolution 92–3
industrial society 8, 158, 421–2
   and domination 155–6
   Gellner and the industrial world 362–6
   one-dimensionality 156–7
industrialism 305
Institute for Social Research 143–4, 146–7, 166, 167, 315, 316
institutional ethnography 408–9
institutionalisation 71
instrumental rationality 155, 157, 162, 170, 172–3, 177, 198, 319, 324, 324, 327, 332
intellectuals
   Collins' networks 385–6, 391–2
   Gramsci's conception 89–91, 95–6
   societal responsibilities 403–4
intentionality 59, 270, 271

Index

interaction ritual chains 386–8, 392, 431
interpretive sociology 60–1, 64
interpretivism 382
intersectionality 50, 413, 426–8, 433
intersubjectivity 60, 64, 73
intimacy, outsourcing of 426
Iraq invasion (2003) 298
Islam, and modernisation 365–6, 370, 371
Israel 209
Italian Communist Party (PCI) 77
Italian Socialist Party (PSI) 77, 79
Italy
    and the First World War 80
    and the Russian Revolution 80–1
    unification 79–80

Jakobson, Roman 211
Jameson, Frederick 182
Japan 223, 262
    cultural history 217
Jay, Martin 162, 167, 180, 183
Jefferson, Gail 71–2
Jefferson, Tony 94
Jeffries, S. 160
Jessop, B. 138
Jews 14, 24, 33, 55, 56, 99, 143, 146, 165, 180, 207, 208, 231, 248–9
    deprived of German citizenship 149
    emancipation, Hungary 103–4
    'Final Solution' 169
    Jewish thought 167
    Kristallnacht pogrom 251
    stripped of French citizenship 207
    as unassailable Other 181
    White Terror, Hungary 104
    see also anti-Semitism; Holocaust
Johnson, Lyndon B. 37, 151
Jones, S. 87, 91, 96
Junker class 250

Kaesler, Dirk 353
Kalyvas, S. 392
Kant, Immanuel 5, 6, 51, 109, 176, 316, 319, 326, 329
Károlyi, Mihály 103
Kautsky, Karl 78, 104, 161
Kellner, Douglas 149–50, 158–9, 182
Kennedy, John F. 37, 318
Keucheyan, R. 327
Keynesian economics 190, 191, 203, 272, 296, 341

Khomeini, Ayatollah Ruhollah 230
Khrushchev's speech and Report on Stalin 125, 231
Kierkegaard, Søren 101, 166
Kilminster, R. 100, 299
King, Martin Luther 151, 318, 421
Kinnock, Neil 298
kinship structures 212–13, 222
Kiser, E. 372
Kluseman, Stefan 390
knowledge
    Althusser's theory of 130–1, 139–40
    codes of (*epistemes*) 235–6, 244–5, 275
    Elias' sociological theory of 260–1
    human beings as objects of 234, 235
    and human interests 323–4, 332
    as instrument of domination 167, 172–3, 176–7
    and power 236, 237, 246
    as social construction 407, 422–4, 430
    and standpoint theory 427, 431
Kohl, Helmut 319
Kohlberg, Lawrence 324–5
Kojève, Alexander 230, 270
Kolakowski, L. 98, 167, 183
Korean War (1950–3) 17, 150, 379
Korbut, Andrei 71–2
Korsch, Karl 92, 148, 160–1, 167
Kracauer, Siegfried 166
Kristeva, Julia 221
Kuhn, Thomas 422
Kumar, K. 114
Kun, Béla 99, 104

labour (worker's) movement 79, 80, 81, 140, 232, 288
Labour governments, UK 296, 307
Labour Party, UK 298, 358, 401
    see also New Labour
Lacan, Jacques 123, 127, 215, 228, 230
Laclau, Ernesto 93
Laitin, D. 371
Lane, J. 270–1
language
    Bourdieu's theory 285, 286
    and emotions 424
    Habermas' conception 321, 323–4, 324, 332
    identified with structure 301
    Luhmann's conception 348–9

as 'organ of thought' 6
structure of, and knowledge 235
symbolic power, academia and 286
see also communication
Last National Bank collapse 24
latent vs. manifest functions 25
Latour, Bruno 416, 433
   contemporary relevance and applications 430
   criticisms 431–2
   historical, social and political context 419–21
   Laboratory Life 417, 422
   life and intellectual context 416–17
   The Pasteurization of France 423
   Science in Action 422–3
   the social contrition of knowledge 422–4, 430, 431–2
   We Have Never Been Modern 423–4
Lazarsfeld, Paul 57, 166, 188, 189
Le Pen, Jean-Marie 274
Leach, Edmund 220
legitimation crisis 322
Leicester University 293
Lenin, Vladimir 78, 79, 81, 88, 98, 100, 104, 105, 112, 122, 161, 168, 250
Lévi-Strauss, Claude 122, 212, 230, 231, 301, 397
   arguments and ideas 212–15
   contemporary relevance and application 220
   criticisms 222
   Elementary Structures of Kinship 212–13, 271
   historical, social and political context 209–12
   life and intellectual context 206–7
   Mythologiques 213–14
   La Pensée Sauvage 214–15
Levitt, N. 431
Lewis, Helen 49
Leys, S. 223
LGBT individuals, African American 428
liberal democracy/ies 171, 176, 243, 367
   in Germany 317, 340
   and totalitarianism 152–3, 162, 180
liberalism 115, 295, 298, 299, 300
   economic 368
   and fascism 147, 152, 183
Lie, J. 30

Liebknecht, Karl 103, 149, 168, 251
life-world/s 59, 60, 63, 64, 73, 270, 326, 342
linguistics 211, 214, 215
Lipset, Seymour 151
Locke, John 2–3, 6
Lockwood, David 295, 358
logical positivism 58
Lois XIV 253
love 349, 350–1
Lowie, Robert 207
Lowinger, Joseph 99
Loyal, S. 309
Luckmann, T. 70–1
Ludendroff, Erich 250–1
Luery, S. 391
Luhmann, Niklas 27, 29, 322, 336–54
   arguments and ideas 343–9
   communication 348–9
   contemporary relevance and applications 349–51
   criticisms 351–3
   differentiation 346–8
   evolution 348
   historical, social and political context 340–2
   life and intellectual context 336–40
   Luhmann-Habermas debate 329, 342, 349
   and Parsons 337–9, 343, 346–7, 348, 354
   social systems 342, 343–5
   Social Systems 344–5, 349
   theory of society 346–9
Luhmann, Wilhelm 336
Lukács, Georg 92, 98–118, 146, 160–1, 167–8, 172, 174
   class consciousness 110–12
   contemporary applications and influence 112–16
   criticisms 116–17
   historical, social and political context 102–5
   History and Class Consciousness (HCC) 98, 100, 101, 102, 105–6, 109–10, 116
   ideas and arguments 105–12
   life and intellectual context 99–102
   the proletariat as the subject-object identical 110
   reification 98, 101, 102, 107–9, 112, 167–8

Lukes, S. 245
Luxemburg, Rosa 103, 104, 105, 112, 149, 168, 251
Lyotard, Jean-Francois 327, 430

Machiavelli, Niccolò 2, 78, 81, 83, 122, 135
Macintosh, N. B. 308
Macintyre, Alistair 51, 161
MacMillan, Harold 296
macro–micro connections 39, 72–3, 379, 380, 381–2
madness
  and the great confinement 233–4, 244
  social construction of 233
Major, John 298
Malcom X 151
Malešević, S. 372
manifest vs latent functions 25
Mann, Michael 356, 372–3
  arguments and ideas 361–2, 366–9
  contemporary relevance and applications 368–9
  criticisms 370–1, 372
  historical, social and political context 359, 360–1
  life and intellectual context 358
  power networks 366–9
  social power 366–7, 372
  The Sources of Social Power 358, 366, 367
  the state 366–8
Mann, Thomas 166, 252
manners, transformation of 255–7
manners books 255–6, 263
Mannheim, Karl 13, 99, 113–15, 249
Mao Zedong 123, 124, 150, 223
Marburg School 101
March Action (1921), Germany 81
Marcuse, Carl 146
Marcuse, Erica (née Sherover) 147
Marcuse, Herbert 143–63, 165, 180, 316
  arguments and ideas 152–8
  contemporary relevance and applications 158–60
  criticisms 160–2
  Eros and Civilisation 147, 148, 154–6, 161–2
  fascism and totalitarianism 152–3
  Freud and Marx 154–6

Hegel and Marx 153
historical, social and political context 149–52
life and intellectual context 146–8
and the New Left 159
One-Dimensional Man 147, 156–8
Reason and Revolution 147, 152, 153
Marcuse, Inge (née Neumann) 147
Marcuse, Sophie 146, 147
market
  and neo-classical economics 190–1
  and reification 108
Marr, A. 296–7
Marshall, T. H. 367
Marshall Plan 150, 209
Marx, Karl 1, 72, 77, 78, 86, 99, 100, 101, 121, 143, 146, 167, 168, 258, 261, 269, 294, 299, 300, 363, 368, 380, 382, 432
  and agency 98, 118, 140
  and alienation 98, 116–17, 127
  base-superstructure model 84, 87, 124, 126, 144, 167
  break between early and late works 127–8, 131
  Capital 98, 101, 106, 122, 130, 139
  capital as social relation 106
  capitalism/feudalism distinction 8, 254, 296
  and commodity fetishism 101–2, 117, 175
  dialectic 70, 105–6, 131–2
  and Freud 154–6, 161
  and Hegel 98, 128, 139, 153
  and objectification 117
  and the proletarian point of view 117
  and the role of practice 130
Marxism 82, 138, 250, 295, 324, 401, 408
  Adorno and 167, 170, 171, 175
  Althusser 120–41
  analytical 136–7, 201
  and anti-capitalism 25
  Barthes and 216, 223
  and critical theory 144–5, 150
  Foucault and 229, 231, 232, 245
  and the Frankfurt School 144
  Giddens' criticisms 300, 304

Gramsci 76–96
  Habermas and 319, 321, 322, 324, 328, 331–2
  Lukács 98–118
  Mannheim's attack 116
  Marcuse and 143, 146, 148, 151, 153, 159, 161
  orthodox (crude, reductive, vulgar) interpretations 78, 92, 98, 106, 124, 126, 132–3, 144, 170
  post-Marxist challenges 211
  resurgence 231, 295
  revisionist interpretations 105, 106
  split with sociology 298
  and structuralism 210
  and totality 101, 108
  Western 92, 125–6, 160–1, 167, 175
Masters of Sociological Thought (Coser) 1
Matthew effect 23–4
Mauss, Marcel 213, 281
May 1968 125, 126–7, 211, 232, 273, 288, 401, 421
Maynard, D. W. 72
McCarthyism 17, 150–1
Mead, George Herbert 35, 44, 330, 398
meaning, centrality of 338, 343, 345
medical 'gaze' 234
megachurches 388
Mennell, S. 66, 73, 252–3, 262–3
Merleau-Ponty, Maurice 113, 125, 269, 270, 271, 277, 289, 397, 398
Merton, Aaron 14
Merton, Robert 12, 31, 189, 295–6, 303, 339
  arguments and ideas 22–7
  contemporary relevance and applications 27, 28–9
  criticisms 30–1
  functional analysis 25
  historical, social and political context 15–17
  life and intellectual context 14–15
  methodological techniques 27, 31
  middle-range theories 24–5, 31
  Science, Technology & Society in Seventeenth Century England 14, 23
  'The Self-fulfilling Prophecy' 24
  sociology of science 23–4, 28

theory of deviance 26–7, 30, 31
Mészáros, István 104, 113
methodological individualism 186, 189, 192, 193, 194, 198, 199
micro-macro connections 39, 72–3, 379, 380, 381–2
Middle Ages 7, 233, 241, 256, 257, 320
middle class 39, 58, 255, 258, 261, 272, 278, 298, 368, 384, 405, 413, 422
  rise in US 15–16
middle-range theories 24–5, 31
militant society 8
military–industrial complex 420, 421
military power 366, 372, 420
Milliband, Ralph 138
Mills, C. Wright 29, 34, 295, 420, 429
Mind Circle, Vienna 58
miner's strike (1984) 298 cg
minorities
  'tokenism' 9
  under-representation amongst sociologists 8–9
Mises Circle, Vienna 55, 58
Misztal, B. 391
Mitterrand, François 192, 211, 273, 274
modernity 7, 327, 331, 342
  and emancipatory politics 342
  Gellner's theory of 362–6, 369–70, 370–1
  Giddens' analysis 299, 305–6
  and intimacy 351
  juggernaut of 308
  Mann's theory of 366–9, 369, 372
  social theory, history and 368
  as unattained state 423–4
  West/Europe as cradle 22, 361–2, 370–1
Mollet, Guy 125
Moore, Wilbert E. 57
money, as symbolically generated media of communication 349
Montesquieu 3–4
motherhood 405–6
Mouffe, Chantal 93
Muslims 273, 390
Mussolini, Benito 77, 81, 169
My Ly massacre (1968) 379
mythemes 214
myths
  Barthes on 215–16
  Lévi-Strauss on 213–14

Index

Nairn, Tom 92
Namaste, V. 224
Nassehi, A. 350
Nasser, Gamal 125
nation states
    capitalism, industrialism and 305
    and conflict 383
    increasing irrelevance 327
    as pre-eminent organisational power 383
National Centre for Scientific Research 189
National People's Party (DNVP), Germany 251
nationalism
    and globalisation 369
    Gramsci's conception 84, 95
    methodological, US 378
    and modernisation 363–4, 370, 371
    'post-national identity' 327
    and state legitimacy 383
native American myths 213–14
NATO 171, 318, 361
Natorp, Paul 101
natural vs. philosophical attitude 60, 63
nature
    domination of 173, 177
    as poor analogy for human society 352
    separation from society 423
Nazi Germany 14, 149, 169, 181, 209, 251, 315, 357, 360, 367
Nazis and Nazism 100, 144, 146, 148, 152, 166, 169, 171, 183, 188, 249, 264, 273, 317, 337, 340, 378
Needham, Rodney 220
neo-classical economics 190–1, 192, 203
neo-Kantianism 100–1, 107
neoliberalism 191, 192, 203, 212, 274–5, 287, 310, 365
neo-Marxism 201, 380, 391
Neuwith Law (1967), France 401
New Labour, UK 298, 299, 307
New Left 92, 94, 136
    and Marcuse 147, 159
New School of Social Research, New York 56, 207, 338
Nietzsche, Friedrich 167, 172, 177, 231, 232
Nisbet, R. A. 6
Nixon, Richard 38, 152

November Revolution (1918), Germany 103
NPD, Germany 171
nuclear weapons 318, 327, 361
Nuremberg trials 315
Nussbaum, M. 223

Oakley, Anne Rosamund 396, 414
    arguments and ideas 404–6
    contemporary relevance and applications 410–11
    criticisms 412–14
    Fracture 406
    historical, social and political context 401–2
    life and intellectual context 397–8
    the sociology of family 404–5
    motherhood 405–6
objectification 71, 117
objectivism vs. subjectivism 72, 278
O' Connor, B. 161–2, 175
Oedipal complex 410
Ohnesorg, Benno 319
oil crises, 1970s 190, 211, 212, 272, 361
O'Leary, A. 371
Oppenheimer, Robert 17
Ordino Nuvo, L' 77
organic and conjectural movements 85–6
organisations
    Baralou's conception 350
    and 'generalised reinforcements' 195
    Luhmann's conception 346
organisations studies 263, 350
Orientalism 242–3
Others and Othering 243, 402, 411
Outhwaite, W. 332
overdetermination 131–3

Panopticon 239
Parekh, B. 117
Pareto Circle 187
Parkinson, G. H. R. 101, 117–18
Parks, Rosa 56, 151
Parsons, Talcott 12, 14, 25, 31, 34, 35, 39, 57, 61, 65, 200, 279, 322, 348, 376, 378, 391
    arguments and ideas 18–22
    contemporary relevance and applications 27–8
    criticisms 29–30, 295–6, 299

and Elias 262
evolutionary theory 21–2
historical, social and political context 15–17
life and intellectual context 12–14
and Luhmann 338–9, 343, 346–7, 348, 354
renewal of 27
Schutz-Parsons correspondence 56, 70
social systems 19–21, 65
The Structure of Social Action 18–19
Pascal, Blaise 116, 134–5
Pasteur, Louis 423
patriarchy 29, 218, 396, 400, 405–6, 408, 410, 413, 427
patriotism 84
pattern variable 20
Payne, G. C. F. 73
Péguy, Charles 417
performance principle 154–5
personality systems 19–20
Pétain, Philippe 228, 273
phenomenological *epoche* 60, 62, 63, 270
phenomenology 54, 57, 61, 122, 143, 208, 300, 337, 406
   Bourdieu and 72, 269–70, 278, 289
   contemporary relevance and applications 68–71
   criticisms 72–3
   Foucault and 230
   Heidegger 148, 230, 271
   Husserl 59–61, 73, 230, 269, 270–1, 338
   influence 73–4
   and Marxism 148
   Merleau-Ponty 269, 271, 398
   Schutz 54, 62–4, 69–71, 72–3
Picasso, Pablo 167, 178
Pinel, Philllipe 233
Plekanov, Dimitri 82, 98, 104
Podemos, Spain 94
politics
   and emotions 426
   Goffman's ambivalence 38–9
   Marxist theory 83
   'Third-Way' 293, 294–5, 299, 306–7
Pollack, Frederick 143, 166, 170

Pompidou, Georges 273
Popper, Karl 167
Porpora, D. V. 309
positivism 7, 29, 59–60, 73, 78, 106, 107, 144, 145, 151, 161, 173, 174, 177, 222, 270, 271, 323, 324, 329, 333, 343, 382, 429, 431
   see also anti-positivism
Positivist Dispute 167, 184, 315
positivist epistemology 193
post-colonial studies 92, 222, 242
post-Marxism 27, 93, 137, 211
post-modernism 12, 27, 211, 224, 423
post-structuralism 93, 206, 209, 211–12, 215, 216–20, 410
   arguments and ideas 216–20
   contemporary influence and applications 221–2, 224
   criticisms 223–4
Poulantzas, Nicos 138
power
   and agency 303
   and established–outsider relationship 259
   as functional product of communicative relationships 349
   Foucault's account 236–9, 245
   Mann's power networks 366–9
   and mismatch of individual rewards 195
   separation of economic and political in civil society 365
   see also symbolic power
power–dependence theory 200–1
Prague School 211
praxis (practice) 106, 112, 116, 130, 244–5
prisons and imprisonment 232
   of African and Native Americans 160, 287
   Davis' view 160
   Foucault's analysis 238–9
process sociology *see* figurational sociology
Project Camelot 188
proletariat 92–3, 104
   Gramsci's view 79, 80, 84, 90
   Lukács' view 105, 106, 110, 111–12, 114, 117
   Marx' view 127, 144, 153, 170
   as subject–object identical 110, 117

Protestant ethic, and capitalism 13
Protestants
   objection to Dual Alliance 250
   Pietism, and rise of science 23, 30
psychic systems 345, 350
psychoanalysis 324, 410
psychology
   and management of subjectivity 243–4
   sociology as derivate of 195
public sociology 429, 431
public sphere 319–21, 329, 332
punishment, and control 237–8
Puritanism, and rise of science 23, 30
Pussy Riot 221–2
Putnam, Robert D. 197

race and ethnicity
   and educational inequality 203
   and intersectionality 50, 413, 426–7
   and rational choice theory 201–2
   and urban inequalities 286–7
Racine, Jean 116
racism 24, 96, 418, 427, 428, 431
Radcliffe-Brown, A. 17, 34, 36
Radomysler, Asik 249
Rafter, Nicole 389
Ramirez, M. 432
rational choice theory (RCT) 138, 186, 192, 195–9, 289, 300
   contemporary relevance and applications 199, 201–2
   criticisms 202–4
rationality and rationalism
   Althusser's strong form 139
   attacked by hippy movement 421–2
   centrality challenged 424, 430
   and critical theory 145
   as Enlightenment principle 3, 5, 115
   practical 66
   stretched in utilitarian tradition 202
   see also axiological rationality; cognitive rationality; communicative rationality; instrumental rationality; technical rationality
Reagan, Ronald 38, 191, 192, 212
reality principle 154

reason
   centrality in Hegel 153
   and madness 233
   see also rationality and rationalism
recognition
   and misrecognition 285
   and redistribution 330
reflexivity 283
   'wholesale' 306
Reich, Wilhelm 147
reification
   Adorno and 167–8, 174, 183
   and the Frankfurt School 112
   Lukács' theory of 98, 102, 106–8
   spread of 109
Reilly-Cooper, R. 433
'relationism' 114
relations of ruling 408
relativism 73, 129, 246, 412, 431
relativist epistemology 223
religion 213, 372, 419
   relationship with science 23
repression 148, 154–5, 158, 161–2, 256
Repressive State Apparatuses (RSAs) 133
Resch, R. P. 137
Revolutionary Socialist Students, Budapest 99
Rickert, Heinrich 101
Ringer, Fritz 162
risk, pervasiveness 305–6
Risorgimento 79, 84
Roberts, J. 308
Robins, J. 184
Rockmore, T. 105
Rogers, Mary 38, 51
romanticism 6, 115
Rosa, Hartmut 144, 331
Rose, Gillian 117, 172, 173
Rose, Nikolas 243–4
Rousseau, Jean-Jacques 4, 51, 135
Roussel, Raymond 229
Royal Society 23
Russia 86, 124, 168, 250, 368
   see also Soviet Union
Russian (Bolshevik) Revolution (1917) 80–1, 92, 98, 99, 103, 104–5, 117, 149, 161, 168, 169, 250
Rwandan genocide 389, 390
Ryazanov, David 100
Ryle, Gilbert 166
Rytmann, Hélène murder 122, 136

Sacks, Harvey 71–2
Said, Edward 242–3
Saint-Simon, Henri de 6–7
Sartre, Jean-Paul 36, 125, 160–1, 207, 210, 230, 231, 232, 244–5, 270, 274, 397, 402, 403
Scapens, R. 308
Scheff, Thomas 49, 430–1
Schegloff, Emanuel 71–2
Scheler, Max 1, 55
Schelling, Thomas 35, 36
Schelsy, Helmut 337
Schiller, Friedrich 6
Schmitt, Carl 318, 340
Schoenberg, Arnold 166, 167, 178
Schroder, Gerhard 295
Schroeder, R. 372
Schumpeter, Joseph 13
Schütz, Alfred 36, 54, 74, 295, 408
   contemporary relevance and applications 69–71
   criticisms 72–3
   historical, social and political context 57–61
   life and intellectual context 54–6
   phenomenology 62–4
   The Phenomenology of the Social World 55, 60, 62, 70
   Schutz-Parsons correspondence 56, 70
Schutz, Ilse (née Heim) 55
Schutz, Johanna (née Fialla) 54, 55
Schutz, Otto 54, 55
science and technology
   anti-foundationalist attacks 429–30
   and axiological rationality 198–9
   CUDOS ideals 23
   decisive for war 366
   decrease of trust in 28
   and domination of man by man 155–6
   and domination of nature 158, 176–7
   as Enlightenment principle 3
   Habermas' theory of 323
   and ideological representations 411
   and knowledge for control 177
   Merton's sociology of 23–4
   in the modern world 419–21
   Pietism and Puritanism and rise of 23, 30
   post-structuralist hostility 223
   rooted in the everyday world 59
   and social change 7, 423
   and the social construction of knowledge 422–3, 431–2
   social science distinguished 303–4
   sociology as 'queen of sciences' 7
   as source of power 372
   value-neutrality challenged 429
   winning, constructing and confirming 284
scientism 418–20
Scotson, John 250, 258
Scottish Enlightenment 4–5
Searle, J. R. 324, 431–2
Second International 77, 78, 79, 80–1, 104, 105, 126, 170
Second Viennese School 166
Second World War 14, 15, 16, 56–7, 61, 121, 124, 149–50, 169, 187, 207, 208, 209, 337, 357, 400
Seebach, S. 341
segmentary differentiation 347
Seidle, D. 350
Seidman, S. 326
self
   Goffman's exploration 36, 40–8, 51
   'real' and 'false' 432
   and otherness 402
   'therapeutic culture of' 244
self-control 253, 257, 263
self-defeating prophecies 25
self-expression, US discourse of 37–8
self-fulfilling prophecies 24
self-identity 306
self-interest 2, 5, 40, 102, 110, 190, 193, 196–7, 200, 202, 204
self-presentation 42–4, 425
   online 49
self-realisation 151, 152, 161, 330
semiology 216
Serge, Victor 100
Serres, Michel 417
sexism 427, 428
sexual harassment 413

Index

sexuality
    and African Americans 428
    Foucault's history of 239–40
Shalin, D. 33
shame and embarrassment 49, 256
Shetland Isles 34, 42
Shilling, C. 308
signs
    and meaninglessness 345
    and reproduction of social order 215–16
    signifier and signified 211
Simmel, Georg 8, 36, 99, 101, 351, 380
Simon, Roger 95
singularity theory 220
Skinner, B. F. 193
Small, Albion 35, 36, 378
Smart, B. 239
Smith, A. 59
Smith, Adam 4–5, 108
Smith, Dorothy E. 396, 414
    arguments and ideas 406–9
    contemporary relevance and applications 410–11
    criticisms 412–14
    The Everyday World as Problematic 407, 408
    feminist standpoint theory 406–7, 412
    historical, social and political context 401–2
    life and intellectual context 398–9
    relations of ruling 408–9
Smith, John 298
Smith, Philip 28
social action
    and consensus 329
    and culture 18, 20
    and emotions 49, 424–5
    and individual will 27–8
    and interaction rituals 387–8
    Parson's voluntaristic theory 18–19, 20
    and reflexivity 306
    role of agency 352
    symbolic nature 213
    unintended consequences 25, 73
    utilitarian models 193, 196, 197, 201
social capital
    Bourdieu 280–1
    Coleman 197–8

social change
    Comte's historical phases 7
    and evolutionary theory 8, 17, 21–2, 348
    and historical sociology 304–5, 356, 359, 361–74
    Parsons' modernisation theory 30
    science, technology and 7, 423
    US sociology and 378–9
social constructionism 70–1
social contract theory 2–3
social democracy 81, 95, 252–3, 296, 306, 310
Social Democratic Party, Germany (SPD) 98, 104, 149, 168, 250, 251, 295, 318
social exchange theory 186, 192–5
    contemporary relevance and applications 199, 200–1
    criticisms 202–4
social facts
    Adorno's conception 271
    Durkheim's conception 65, 66, 122, 271
    Garfinkel's conception 65–7, 68
social fields 280
social functions and dysfunctions 25
Social Gospel movement 13
social interaction/s
    centrality of emotions 425
    Goffman and 39–40, 42, 47, 48
    Habermas' shift to communication 331
    and long-term benefits 200
    utilitarian views of 193, 195, 200
social media 49, 413
social mobility 15–16, 286, 341, 342, 362
    Industria, 363, 364
social movements 61, 322, 379, 416, 421–2, 431, 433
    France 211, 269
    Germany 341
    US 212, 389
    see also civil rights movement; student movements
social power 366–7
social stratification 367, 384, 388
    and perceptual differentiation 195
social structure/s
    anti-humanism and 129
    and gender inequalities 403

and habitus 257, 279
and individual actions 195, 196
individual adaptation to 51
vs. natural structures 137
reproduction of 66, 286
as rules and resources 301–2, 309–10
social system
   Habermas' contrast with life-world 326
   Parsons conception 20, 65
social systems
   Giddens 302
   Luhmann 343–5, 329, 339
   Parsons 19–21
socialisation 83, 88, 403
   habitus contrasted 279
   primary 18, 21, 29, 71
   secondary 18, 71, 364, 384
socialism 77, 83, 93, 104, 105, 115, 124, 135, 250, 275, 295
   European split 168
   failure and defeat 149, 161, 168–9
   'libertarian' 299
   Soviet 159
   see also state socialism
Socialist Party (PS), France 273
society/ies
   Luhmann's theory of 346–9
   and persons 137–8
   as socio-spatial power networks 366
sociology
   American 295, 378–9, 389
   centrality of individual behavior 197
   closeness to economics and psychology 193, 195
   and the Enlightenment 1–2, 3–6, 295–6, 428–9
   establishment at Harvard 13–14
   institutional growth 15
   liberal viewpoint, UK 298
   and logical deduction 200
   male domination 8–9, 396, 407, 408, 414
   need for reflexivity in 'doing' 68–9
   nominal creation 6–7
   peculiarity of neo-utilitarian 200
   pre-Enlightenment roots 2–3
   predictive capacity 381
   public issues, modern society and 429
   as 'queen of sciences' 7
   as study of meaningful action 18
   and universal theories 24–5
   see also analytical sociology; critical sociology; figurational (process) sociology; historical sociology; interpretive sociology; public sociology
sociology of aging 404
sociology of education 286
   educational and intellectual networks 384–6
sociology of family 404–5
sociology of knowledge 1, 70–1, 113
sociology of science 14, 23–4
sociology of sport 261, 263–4
Solzhenitsyn, A. 232, 274
Sombart, Werner 33
Sorel, George 99
Sorokin, Pitirim 14
South West (Heidelberg) School 101
Soviet Union (USSR) 125, 170, 317, 367
   Cold War 16–17, 123
   demise 381
   invasion of Hungary (1956) 125, 210
   Marxist-Leninism 150
   Sino-Soviet split 123–4
   Stalinism 149, 161
   state socialism 144
   see also Communist Party of the Soviet Union
Sparticist League 149
speech acts 325
Spencer, Herbert 8
Spiegel Affair, Germany 171, 318–19
Spinoza, Baruch 123, 127
Spivak, Gayatri 411
sport, sociology of 261, 263–4
Spybey, T. 308
Sraffa, Pierro 78
Srebrenica massacre (1995) 390
Stalin, Joseph 126, 132, 149, 169, 231
Stalinism 120, 124, 126, 140, 149, 176, 210, 262, 274
standpoint theory
   African American women 427–8
   feminist 431, 433

state/s
- Bourdieu's account 285–6, 289
- co-development with capitalism and industrialism 305
- despotic vs. infrastructural capacities 367
- Elias on formation of 257–8
- emergence as form of social contract 2–3
- Gramsci's conception of civil society and 86–7, 95
- and hate speech 219
- Ideological State Apparatus (ISA) 133–4
- investment in arms race 157
- 'left hand'/'right' hand conflict 275
- legitimation crisis 322
- as a monopolisation of violence and taxes 258
- Repressive State Apparatus (RSA) 133
- separation from Church 3
- as a social relation 138
- see also nation states

state capitalism 170, 180
State of Nature 2–3, 4
state socialism 144, 165, 175
- vs. capitalism 298–9
- demise 299

state power 366–8
Stauth, G. 262
Stichweh, R. 338, 339
stigma 46–7
structural functionalism 12, 16, 17–27, 31, 200, 338, 339, 380, 389
- contemporary relevance and applications 27–9
- criticisms 29–30

structural inequality 9, 410, 412–13
structural linguistics 214
structuralism 122–3, 128, 206, 209, 210–11, 224, 230–1, 234, 269, 271, 300, 301
- arguments and ideas 212–16
- contemporary relevance and applications 220–1
- criticisms 222–3
- what's structural about 220

structuration theory 300–1, 302, 308, 309
- as a hermeneutical theory 303–4

structure–agency dichotomy 31, 299, 300, 301, 309
student protests 124, 294
- Berkeley 377, 379, 380
- France 125, 126–7, 211–12, 273, 420–1
- Germany 167, 171, 316–17, 318, 341

Stuermann, Eduard 166
subaltern groups 82, 84, 92, 330, 411
subject, and ideology 135
subject–object relationship 172, 176
subjectivism-objectivism opposition 72, 278
subjectivity, management of 243–4
Sudetenland annexation (1938) 357, 360
'Suez crisis' 125
Suffragettes 399
suicide, coroner's interpretations 68
Sunday Circle 99, 113
surveillance 239, 305, 308
symbolic capital 280–1, 284, 285
symbolic interactionism 35–6, 295, 297, 300, 389, 392, 398, 406
symbolic power 284, 286
symbols and symbolism 213
systems theory
- Adorno's criticism 174–6
- Habermas and 329
- Luhmann 29, 322, 329, 342, 343–354
- Parsons 18–22, 322, 328

Szabo, Ervin 99
Sztompka, Piotr 28

talk, forms of 48
Tannhaüser 256
taste 282–3
Taylorism 81, 108, 288
technical rationality 156, 157–8
teilaktion 105
Teller, Wilhelm Abraham 5, 6
temporality 270, 281
Tet Offensive (1968) 379, 421
texts
- intertextuality 221
- post-structural analysis 216–17

Thalia 99
Thanatos 155
Thatcher, Margaret 94, 191, 192, 297–8

Thatcherism 94, 297–8
Theodosius, C. 432
theory/thinking differentiation 427–8
Third International 100, 116, 126, 170
'Third Way' politics 294–5, 299, 306–7, 310
Thompson, E. P. 138, 140
Thompson, John 294, 309
Togliatti, Palmiro 77
Tolokonnikova, Nadya 222
Tönnies, Ferdinand 8
total institutions 44–5
totalitarianism 152–3, 232
totality
    Adorno and 174–5, 183
    Lukács and 98, 107–8, 174
trade unions 16, 80, 191, 273, 297, 401
traditional theory 145
'transfer of control' 196–7
Transformational Model of Social Activity 137–8
Treitschke, Heinrich von 250
Truman, Harry S. 150, 151
trust 305
Turner, B. 298

UN 328
unconscious 148, 156, 201, 256, 271
unintended consequences 25, 73, 303
United Kingdom (UK)/Britain 136, 320, 361
    class inequality 296–7
    criticism of Parsons 295
    feminism 399, 401–2
    rise of Thatcherism and end of Labour 297–8
    socio-political context, post-war 296
    'white privilege' 431
    women's suffrage 399
United States 184, 317, 368
    bourgeois welfare state order 39
    capitalism 151, 170
    civilising process 262–3
    Cold War ideology 16–17
    consumerism 16, 151
    counter-culture 37, 151–2, 160, 294, 421–2
    criticisms of Parsons 295
    discourse of self-expression and freedom, 1960s 37–8, 151
    economic growth, post-war 15–16, 36–7, 151
    education policy 188, 203–4
    educational credentialism 384–5
    feminism 399, 400
    industrialisation 150–2
    megachurches 388
    Marcuse's analysis 162
    Office for Strategic Services (OSS) 147
    post-structuralism 212
    power reach 366
    rise of the middle classes 15–16
    'second red scare' 16–17, 150–1
    social division and protest, 1960s 37, 151–2
    social problems, 1970s and 1980s 212
    sociology 378–9, 389
    socio-political shift, 1970s 38
    State Department 147
    sources of economic rise and decline 189–91
    vulnerability and violence 219
    'white privilege' 431
    women's suffrage 399
    youth cultures 37, 62, 151
    see also Vietnam War
universalism 342, 343, 352, 407
    as Enlightenment principle 3
    as scientific ideal 23
University of California, Los Angeles (UCLA) 57, 166, 294, 358
urban inequalities 286–7
utilitarian analytic tradition 188, 204
    arguments and ideas 192–9
    contemporary relevance and applications 199–202
    criticisms 202–4
    historical, social and political context 189–92
    peculiarity of neo-utilitarian sociology 200
utilitarianism, in France 191–2
utopia 114, 160, 168, 183

Veil, Simone 401
Versailles Treaty (1919) 168, 251
Verstehen 61, 63, 328
Vienna 99–100
Vienna Circle 55, 58, 161

Viennese Enlightenment 57–9
Vietnam War 29, 38, 151, 171, 297, 318, 377, 379–81, 420, 421
violence
    Collins' theory of 383–4, 389–90, 392–3
    Elias' view of modern decrease 256–7, 264–5
    industrial era 372
    state monopoly on 258
    see also conflict theory
Voigt, Jorinde 351
Volkov, V. 262
Voltaire 3
von Walter, Ursula 337, 338

Wacquant, Loic 286–7
Walesa, Lech 230
war
    mass media depiction 219–20
    and social caging 366
    'war of manoeuver' 86
    'war of position' 81, 86
Warner, Lloyd 34
Weber, Alfred 13, 249
Weber, Marianne 13, 249
Weber, Max 23, 67, 70, 87, 170, 198, 261, 288, 294, 296, 306, 308, 336, 368, 380
    Bourdieu and 269, 282, 284
    Collins and 376, 381, 382–3
    Elias and 250, 253–4, 258, 262
    Giddens and 293, 294, 296, 299, 300
    Lukács and 99, 101, 102, 108, 109
    Parsons and 13, 18, 262
    Schutz and 55, 58, 60–1, 64
Weil, Felix 144
Weimar Republic 113
welfare state 39, 94, 272, 296, 307, 360
    and warfare state 157
Wellman, J. K. 388
Wellmer, Albrecht 182
West, Candace 49–50
West Germany (Federal Republic of Germany) 167, 171, 317, 318, 240–1
    new Germany 341–2
White Terror, Hungary 104

Whitfield, S. 162
Whittington, R. 308
Wiesengrund, Oskar 165
Wieviorka, M. 392
Wilhelm II 168, 250
Williams, Raymond 92
Willow Run community, Detroit 15–16
Windleband, Wilhelm 101
Wittgenstein, Ludwig 36, 57, 214, 301, 302, 357
Wolf, P. J. O. 350
Wolff, Christian 5, 6
Wollstonecraft, Mary 6
women
    African American, and intersectionality 160, 427, 432–3
    and the Enlightenment 6
    in Europe 400–2
    feminist perspectives 218, 402–14
    and kinship theory 212–13, 222
    and the labour market, France 272
    and the private sphere 332
    silencing in sociology 396
women's liberation movement 397, 399, 401
Woolgar, Steve 417, 422
workers movement see labour movement
working class 81, 258, 268–9, 274, 297, 322, 413
    capitalist incorporation 161, 171–2
    economic improvement under capitalism 170
    educational disadvantage 277, 278
    in Hungary 103
    impotence 149
    Marxist views on 81, 82, 83, 86, 93, 232
    in one-dimensional society 157
    organic intellectuals 91
    support for fascism 169
    student radicals 297
    youth subculture 94
working parents 425–6
world society 346, 353
worldview (*Weltanschaung*) 113
Wouters, C. 263
Wrong, Dennis 34

Yale University 208
Young, K. 262
Young Hegelians 127
youth cultures 37, 62, 94, 151, 297, 421

Zimmerman, Don 49–50
Zinoviev, Grigory 100
Žižek, Slavoj 182, 183
Zuckerman, Harriet 23